SOURCE MATERIALS
AND THE
INTERPRETATION OF MUSIC

SOURCE MATERIALS
AND THE
INTERPRETATION OF MUSIC

A Memorial Volume to Thurston Dart

Edited by Ian Bent

STAINER & BELL : LONDON

© 1981 Stainer and Bell Ltd.
on behalf of the editor and contributors.

Printed and bound in Great Britain by The Camelot Press, Southampton

Set in Garamond

ISBN 0 85249 511 0

Source materials and the interpretation of music.
   1. Music – History and criticism – Sources –
   Case studies
   I. Dart, Thurston   II. Bent, Ian
   780'.01   ML3797

Contents

Contributors 9
Preface 11
Abbreviations 15
Robert Thurston Dart *Allen Percival* 21

PART I   THE STUDY OF MANUSCRIPT AND PRINTED SOURCES

1   The Manuscript Presentation and Notation of Adam de la
    Halle's Courtly Chansons *John Stevens* 29
2   Rota versatilis—Towards a reconstruction *Margaret Bent* 65
3   Robertus de Anglia and the Oporto Song Collection
    David Fallows 99
4   Petrucci at Fossombrone: Some New Editions and Cancels
    Stanley Boorman 129
5   Music Manuscripts of John Browne (1608–91) and from
    Stanford Hall, Leicestershire *Nigel Fortune* 155
6   Gregorio Piva and Steffani's Principal Copyist *Colin Timms* 169
7   'Tang Music' and its Fate in Japan *Laurence Picken* 191

PART II   INTERPRETATION AND PERFORMANCE

8   English Music for the Scottish Progress of 1617 *Philip Brett* 209
9   English Keyboard Fingering in the 16th and early 17th
    Centuries *Peter Le Huray* 227
10 The Musical Aims of J. S. Bach's 'Clavierübung III'
    Peter Williams 259
11 The 'Erotokritos': Variation in a Cretan Folksong
    Lucy Durán 279

PART III   THE USE OF ARCHIVES

12   Archival Material relating to Music in England, 1660–1720
                                                Margaret Laurie   303
13   Musical Information in the Archives of the Church of
       S. Maria Maggiore, Bergamo, 1649–1720   *Robin Bowman*   323
14   Music and British Travellers Abroad, 1600–1730
                                              Michael Tilmouth   357
15   Music in Auctions: Dissemination as a Factor of Taste
                                                  Lenore Coral   383
16   Daniel Defoe's Plan for an Academy of Music at Christ's
       Hospital, with some Notes on his Attitude to Music
                                                 Brian Trowell   403

PART IV

Robert Thurston Dart: Bibliography of Publications
                  Davitt Moroney and William Oxenbury
       Abbreviations   431
       Editions of Music   433
       Revisions of Other Editors' Editions   437
       Gramophone Records   438
       Broadcast Talks   441
       Periodical Articles   443
       Reviews   447
       Other Writings   450

       Index   455

List of Plates

Chapter 2

I   Voices II and IV of *Rota versatilis* from *GB-Lbm* Add. 24198   69

II   Voices II and IV of *Rota versatilis* from *GB-Ob* Bodley 652   72

III Voice IV of *Rota versatilis* and ?I of *Rex sanctorum angelorum* from *GB-Ob* Bodley 652   73

IV Fragments of *Rota versatilis* from *GB-Lbm* Add. 40011B binding strips   75

Chapter 4

V   Examples of the letter V2 as evidence for dating Fossombrone editions of *Corona I*   137

VI   Examples of the letter B6 as evidence for dating Fossombrone editions of *Corona I*   139

VII Examples of the letter A11 as evidence for dating Fossombrone editions of *Corona I*   141

Chapter 5

VIII Order of the House of Lords in John Browne's hand, 1641   156

IX   The cantus part of a pavan signed J.B., from *GB-Och* Mus. 473   159

Chapter 6

Xa   The application of Gregorio Piva for the post of music librarian at Bonn   174

Xb   The opening of Scene I, *Il Tassilone*   175

Xc   The hand of 'scribe A'—the most important copyist of Steffani's music   175

Chapter 8

XI   Print of the City and Castle of Edinburgh by Morris and Hogg, *c* 1765   224

Chapter 9
  XII   Table of ornaments by Edward Bevin from *GB-Lbm* Add.
      31403   253

Chapter 11
  III   Cretan blanket showing Erotokritos and Aretousa and also
      Prince George and the Royal Family   283
  XIV   Cretan *lyra* accompanied by *daouli*   289

Contributors

IAN BENT, Professor of Music, University of Nottingham

MARGARET BENT, Professor of Music, Princeton University

STANLEY BOORMAN, Acting Director of the Center for Early Music, New York University

ROBIN BOWMAN, Lecturer in Music, University of Southampton

PHILIP BRETT, Professor of Music, University of California at Berkeley

LENORE CORAL, Librarian, Mills Music Library, University of Wisconsin at Madison

LUCY DURÁN, Assistant Director, British Institute of Recorded Sound, London

DAVID FALLOWS, Senior Lecturer in Music, University of Manchester

NIGEL FORTUNE, Reader in Music, University of Birmingham

MARGARET LAURIE, Music Librarian, University of Reading

PETER LE HURAY, Fellow of St Catharine's College, Cambridge

DAVITT MORONEY, House Editor, Editions de l'Oiseau-Lyre, Monaco

WILLIAM OXENBURY, Secretary, Musica Britannica Trust

ALLEN PERCIVAL, Former Principal, Guildhall School of Music and Drama, London

LAURENCE PICKEN, Fellow of Jesus College, Cambridge

JOHN STEVENS, Professor of Medieval and Renaissance English, University of Cambridge

MICHAEL TILMOUTH, Tovey Professor of Music, University of Edinburgh

COLIN TIMMS, Lecturer in Music, University of Birmingham

BRIAN TROWELL, King Edward Professor of Music, University of London

PETER WILLIAMS, Director, Russell Collection of Harpsichords and Clavichords, University of Edinburgh

Preface

This volume is much more than a collection of essays. It is a set of case-studies built round a central theme. It does indeed present the findings of recent research in musical scholarship, and thus will be read with interest by musicologists and by performers. But it has more to offer than this. It will open up to the historically-minded undergraduate or postgraduate the world of the musical source. We should reject the idea that such writing is the preserve of the 'researcher'. Margaret Bent's manuscript jigsaw puzzle, for instance, in Part I, or Philip Brett's deep-analysis of a consort song in Part II, or Robin Bowman's picture of music in Bergamo in Part III, specialist though they are, all bring to life vividly the music of the time that they describe: the 14th century, with an elaborate play on words and ideas between *rota, rondellus, rotulus* and the wheel to which St Katherine of Alexandria was bound; the 16th century, with a display of how the English Chapel Royal and its music could be used as an instrument of state policy; and the 17th century, with social status and conditions of work revealed through pay-rolls and inventories.

From its inception, the volume has been conceived and planned as a unity. Each contributor takes an aspect of source-study. In so doing, he or she illuminates some part of music history—but more particularly *demonstrates a method of working*. In this way, the volume has become a case-book of musical research. It could serve usefully as an adjunct to a seminar or lecture course on research method in music.

It exemplifies most of the main areas of investigation. Thus notation is treated by John Stevens, for monophonic music, and by Margaret Bent and David Fallows, for polyphony. The latter two relate notational phenomena to their contemporary music theory; all three also offer studies in manuscript structure and interrelationship between sources. Such inter-relationships are cast into sharp relief by Laurence Picken, who studies a similar interrelationship, but for Chinese and Japanese sources. His study seeks to restore a Chinese repertory through the surviving Japanese sources, by relating the latter to what is known of instrumental techniques, and then stripping away the layers of ornamentation which have accrued. His study takes the volume to its earliest point in musical history: the 9th century. Handwriting and scribal identification is exemplified by Colin Timms and by Nigel Fortune, who deals also with provenance and ownership. Bibliographical method for early printed material is demonstrated by Stanley Boorman, who discusses the distribution of capital letters and their gradual decay, the use of paper and watermarks, printing and publishing practices.

Still very much concerned with notational reading and with interrelationship between sources, is Peter Le Huray's study in Part II. This compares English seventeenth-century keyboard fingerings with contemporary Italian and German systems. But this study moves into the realm of interpretation by investigating ways in which fingerings may indicate phrasing, articulation and ornamentation patterns. Philip Brett's analysis of music diplomacy has already been cited above. Peter Williams looks at the styles and techniques present in J. S. Bach's *Clavierübung III*, and seeks to uncover Bach's reasons for assembling such a collection of pieces. The final step is taken by Lucy Durán. She investigates a melodic tradition whose source is living performance: a tradition without native notational form. She bases her investigation on the fruits of her field trips to Crete; and her interpretative study is an examination of the variants that she recorded there, brought into conjunction with other strands of evidence.

Part III presents non-musical source materials which provide valuable information for musicians. In moving out of the directly musical realm, it seemed right to include at the head of this Part a rather more didactic essay. Thus Margaret Laurie, taking English materials, describes each of the main types of archival documentation and demonstrates what kind of evidence may be drawn from it. Her contribution is paralleled by that of Robin Bowman, who takes approximately the same period of time and draws evidence from Italian archives. Lenore Coral draws attention to a less obvious source of information: the auction catalogue. She shows how the historian may trace the provenance of a source by its means, or discover the contents of private collections and thus—with due caution—assess taste in domestic music-making and concert performance. Michael Tilmouth and Brian Trowell both draw largely on published materials: the former using diaries, memoirs and itineraries to adduce evidence about the encounters which English travellers abroad had with music; the latter, stretching the concept of archival materials to its extreme, using the pamphlets and books of one writer—Daniel Defoe—to build up a broad social picture and to uncover a remarkable educational venture.

The volume was conceived and planned in this way, as has been said, from the beginning. Each contributor undertook to provide a study within the pre-determined scheme. From that point on, however, authors worked independently, without knowledge of each others' contributions. The result is partway between an integrated book and a random collection of essays: it is a set of case-studies with the structure of a book. This gives it unity of purpose while allowing diversity of style and approach.

The contributors to the volume, and the editor himself, form an association with Thurston Dart throughout the full span of his teaching career. Two of them, William Oxenbury and Laurence Picken, were long-standing friends and associates. The remainder represent three generations of his students. From the time of Dart's appointment at Cambridge in 1947, to the early 1950s—a period vividly described in the verbal portrait of Dart which follows this Preface—come Allen Percival and John Stevens. From the main line of his doctoral students at Cambridge during the decade 1954-64 come nine contributors, the senior among them Nigel Fortune, Peter Le Huray, Michael Tilmouth and Brian Trowell, and the younger Margaret Bent, Philip Brett, Margaret Laurie, Peter Williams and myself. The third generation of students dates from Dart's time at the University of London King's College. Three of them, Lenore Coral, David Fallows and Colin Timms, did their first degrees elsewhere and came to King's for Dart's new M.Mus. course. The others, Stanley Boorman, Robin Bowman, Lucy Durán and Davitt Moroney, were undergraduates on Dart's radical B.Mus. course and proceeded to postgraduate study. The present positions of all these contributors can be seen above in the list of Contributors.

As might be expected, the subject matter of the case-studies in this volume reflects to a considerable extent the fields of interest of Dart himself. More particularly, so too do the types of enquiry. For Dart loved notational problems, the tracing of provenance, the identification of scribal hands. He was fascinated by the technical processes of printing, and the details of house-practice among printers and publishers. (His own corrections of proofs, with their exceptionally detailed instructions to the printer, exhibited this, as did all his dealings with Musica Britannica and with Stainer & Bell Ltd.) He was absorbed by politics and economics, and constantly probed the implications of both for any music under discussion. He sometimes said that if he had not been a musician or a statistician he would have been a politician. He had a healthy mistrust of theorists (as he did also of watermarks), and brought their statements into a very careful balance with the evidence of musical sources.

The Bibliography of Publications by Dart which concludes this volume is an immediate witness to the man's energy, fecundity and sheer range of vision. It does not fully represent his main interests, however. There is, for example, very little to reveal his research into the sources of Couperin's keyboard music, or into the life and music of John Fludd (Lloyd), both of which preoccupied him deeply. For him, publications were 'chips off the block' of research, rather than the goal of research; thus, much that he discovered was shared with others in conversation rather than passed to posterity in print.

Manuscripts (at least those in European and North American libraries) have been designated in this volume by the internationally accepted system of *sigla* of the *International Inventory of Musical Sources (RISM)*. These are in some cases admittedly more cumbersome than the *sigla* for individual manuscripts devised by scholars working in specific areas. However, they are free of ambiguity: they avoid the multiplicity of existing systems, and the duplication of *sigla* from area to area which has hitherto arisen. However, in acknowledgement of one or two particularly well-established *sigla* systems, notably that for troubadour and trouvère manuscripts, the *RISM siglum* for a source has been followed by the old *siglum* in parentheses. The *RISM sigla* used in this volume are listed among the Abbreviations, on pp. 15–19. Each *siglum*, in its full form, comprises a designation for the country of present location, followed by a hyphen, followed by designation of town or city, and then by designation of library, followed by shelf-mark of the manuscript itself. Designations for country and town are in capital letters, that for library is in lower-case letters.

In fairness to the authors of this volume, it should be said that most of them wrote their contributions as long ago as 1975. They have made every effort to keep their material up to date during the extended period of the volume's production, but they should not be blamed if an item of very recent bibliography has been omitted. In the very nature of scholarly publication, the scholar's opinions will often have advanced by the time that publication sees the light of day; and this is no less the case with the present publication than with others.

Finally, thanks are due to David Baker for preparation of the Index to the volume, and my wife, Caroline, for help in the reading of proofs.

Ian Bent
January 1980

Abbreviations

A	Arras, Bibliothèque municipale, 657 (formerly 139) (*Chansonnier d'Arras*)
a	Rome, Biblioteca Apostolica Vaticana, Reg.lat.1490 (*Chansonnier du Vatican*)
AcM	*Acta musicologica*
AMw	*Archiv für Musikwissenschaft*
arr.	arranged by
A-Wn	Austria: Österreichische Nationalbibliothek, Vienna
B	Breve (brevis)
b.(bb.)	bar(s)
BAMw	Beihefte zum Archiv für Musikwissenschaft
BerK	Berlin, Staatsbibliothek, 78 C 28
BWV	Bach-Werke-Verzeichnis
c	*circa*
CG	Rome, Biblioteca Apostolica Vaticana, C.G.XIII.27
CH-Zz	Switzerland: Zentralbibliothek, Zurich
CMM	Corpus mensurabilis musicae
CNRS	Centre National de la Recherche Scientifique, Paris
c.o.p.	*cum opposita proprietate*
CS	E. de Coussemaker: *Scriptorum de musica medii aevi novam seriam a Gerbertina alteram* (Paris, 1864–9)
CSM	Corpus scriptorum de musica
D-B	Germany: Staatsbibliothek, Berlin (West)
D-Bds	Germany: Deutsche Staatsbibliothek, Berlin (East)
D-DÜha	Germany: Hauptstaatsarchiv, Düsseldorf
DK-Kk	Denmark: Det kongelige Bibliotek, Copenhagen
D-LEm	Germany: Musikbibliothek der Stadt Leipzig
D-Mbs	Germany: Bayerische Staatsbibliothek, Munich

D-MÜs	Germany: Santini-Bibliothek, Münster
DTB	Denkmäler der Tonkunst in Bayern
D-W	Germany: Herzog-August-Bibliothek, Wolfenbüttel
E-BUlh	Spain: Monasterio de Las Huelgas, Burgos
ed. (eds)	edited by; editor(s)
E-E	Spain: Real Monasterio de El Escorial
EECM	Early English Church Music
E-Mn	Spain: Biblioteca nacional, Madrid
EMS	Early Music Series
E-Sc	Spain: Archivo capitular de la Catedral, Seville
f.(ff.)	folio(s)
facs.	facsimile (edition)
F-AS	France: Bibliothèque municipale, Arras
F-Dm	France: Bibliothèque municipale, Dijon
F-Pc	France: Bibliothèque nationale (ancien fonds du Conservatoire national de musique), Paris
F-Pn	France: Bibliothèque nationale, Paris
GB-Bu	Great Britain: University Library, Birmingham
GB-Cfm	Great Britain: Fitzwilliam Museum, Cambridge
GB-Cgc	Great Britain: Gonville and Caius College, Cambridge
GB-Cjc	Great Britain: Jesus College, Cambridge
GB-Ckc	Great Britain: Rowe Music Library, King's College, Cambridge
GB-Ctc	Great Britain: Trinity College Library, Cambridge
GB-Cu	Great Britain: University Library, Cambridge
GB-CW	Great Britain: Chatsworth House
GB-DRc	Great Britain: Cathedral Library, Durham
GB-En	Great Britain: National Library of Scotland, Edinburgh
GB-Lbm	Great Britain: British Museum (and Library), London
GB-Lcm	Great Britain: Royal College of Music, London
GB-Lgc	Great Britain: Gresham College (Guildhall Library), London
GB-Mp	Great Britain: Central Public Library (Henry Watson Music Library), Manchester
GB-Ob	Great Britain: Bodleian Library, Oxford
GB-Occ	Great Britain: Corpus Christi College Library, Oxford
GB-Och	Great Britain: Christ Church College Library, Oxford
GB-Onc	Great Britain: New College Library, Oxford

GB-Owc	Great Britain: Worcester College Library, Oxford
GSJ	*The Galpin Society Journal*
HMC	Royal Commission on Historical Manuscripts, Report
I-Ac	Italy: Biblioteca communale, Assisi
I-Bc	Italy: Civico Museo Bibliografico-Musicale, Bologna
I-BGc	Italy: Biblioteca civica 'Angelo Mai', Bergamo
I-Bu	Italy: Biblioteca universitaria, Bologna
I-Fc	Italy: Biblioteca del Conservatorio di Musica 'L.Cherubini', Florence
I-Fn	Italy: Biblioteca nazionale centrale, Florence
I-Fr	Italy: Biblioteca Riccardiana, Florence
I-Mb	Italy: Biblioteca nazionale Braidense, Milan
I-Mc	Italy: Biblioteca del Conservatorio 'Giuseppe Verdi', Milan
I-MC	Italy: Biblioteca dell' Abbazia, Monte Cassino
I-MOe	Italy: Biblioteca Estense, Modena
IMSCR	*International Musicological Society Congress Report*
I-PAVu	Italy: Biblioteca universitaria, Pavia
I-PEc	Italy: Biblioteca communale Augusta, Perugia
I-Rc	Italy: Biblioteca Casanatense, Rome
I-Rvat	Italy: Biblioteca Apostolica Vaticana, Rome
I-TRmn	Italy: Museo Provinciale d'Arte, Trento
I-VEaf	Italy: Biblioteca dell'Accademia filarmonica, Verona
I-Vnm	Italy: Biblioteca nazionale Marciana, Venice
JAMS	*Journal of the American Musicological Society*
L	Long(a)
L	*The Listener*
LoF	British Museum, Add.40011 ('Fountains Fragment')
LSJ	*The Lute Society Journal*
M	*Music*
MB	Musica Britannica
MD	*Musica Disciplina*
MGG	*Die Musik in Geschichte und Gegenwart* (Kassel, 1949–)
ML	*Music & Letters*
MR	*Music Review*
MT	*The Musical Times*
NOHM	The New Oxford History of Music (London, 1954–)

O	Paris, Bibliothèque nationale, fonds fr.846 (formerly 7222 ³; Cangé 66) (*Chansonnier Cangé*)
Ob	Oxford, Bodleian Library, Canonici misc.213
P	Paris, Bibliothèque nationale, fonds fr.847 (formerly 7222 ⁴; Cangé 65)
Pn	Bibliothèque nationale, Paris
P-Pm	Portugal: Biblioteca Pública Municipal, Porto
PRMA	*Proceedings of the Royal Musical Association*
PS	Purcell Society Edition
R	Reprint
r	*recto*
RBM	*Revue Belge de musicologie*
ReM	*Revue musicale*
rev.	revised by; revised edition
RISM	*Répertoire international des sources musicales* (Kassel and Munich-Duisberg, 1960–)
RMA	Royal Musical Association
RMARC	*R.M.A. Research Chronicle*
RMI	*Rivista musicale italiana*
RN	*Renaissance News*
Rvat	Biblioteca Apostolica Vaticana, Rome
ser.	series
SRPN	*Society of Recorder Players Newsletter*
TCBS	*Transactions of the Cambridge Bibliographical Society*
trans.	translated by; translator
transcr.	transcribed by; transcriber
U.	University
US-CA	United States: Harvard University Music Library, Cambridge, Mass.
US-Cn	United States: Newberry Library, Chicago
US-NH	United States: Yale University, Library of the School of Music, New Haven, Conn.
US-NYp	United States: New York Public Library at Lincoln Centre
US-PRu	United States: Princeton University Library
US-R	United States: Sibley Music Library, University of Rochester
US-U	United States: Music Library, University of Illinois at Urbana

US-Wc	United States: Music Division, Library of Congress, Washington, D.C.
v	*verso*
VMw	*Vierteljahrsschrift für Musikwissenschaft*
vol. (vols)	volume(s)
W(x)	Paris, Bibliothèque nationale, fonds fr.25566, main manuscript (first section)

Pitch nomenclature uses the Helmholtz system in italic letters, *C-B, c-b, c´-b´, c´´-b´´, c´´´-b´´´* etc, where *c´* is middle C. Capital letters in Roman type refer to pitch class; thus 'A' refers to the note A at any register.

Robert Thurston Dart

Allen Percival

Bob, as all his friends and most of his acquaintances called him, was born in Kingston, Surrey, on 3 September 1921. His father was a schoolmaster; his mother, though she came from Devon, had Belgian and Russian antecedents which often came to his mind. At Hampton Grammar School, he sang in the choir at Hampton Court which gave him the clear consonants of a chorister carried into a way of speaking that, even in the Devonshire accent he would occasionally use in fun, was always carefully articulated, mannered, not precious. A large and ungainly figure, unsuited to sport of any kind, might have embarrassed him at school but he always spoke of Hampton warmly and was almost childishly pleased when he was asked to return as a governor. (Characteristically he proposed student representation on the Governing Body long before it came into fashion.) A year at the Royal College of Music in London left him with a permanent debt, freely acknowledged, to Arnold Goldsborough as a harpsichordist. Amongst the fellow-students he was later most to enjoy working with were Hugh Bean and Neville Marriner.

In 1939, the family moved to Kingswear on the river Dart in Devon and sent him to the 'local' university, Exeter, where he took a mathematics degree awarded by London University. Mathematics always influenced his methodical approach to everything in life and could also provide some of the more quirky beliefs that he later held, such as maintaining that the Fibonnacci theory of numbers could show everyone what size future orchestras should be. In the Royal Air Force, he was a statistician, operational researcher and self-styled 'boffin'. On the few occasions after the war when he could be persuaded to go to anything formal where 'medals were worn' a keen observer could have seen the 'Mention in Dispatches' pinned discreetly in place.

Immediately after he left the RAF, he resumed the Belgian connection as a family guest of the distinguished musicologist, Charles van den Borren. Living and studying there for a year brought fluent French (still with the ever-careful declamation), some Flemish which later led to learning Dutch and a conviction, for Dart, that 'abroad' meant the Low Countries. Ever after, apart from unavoidable professional visits, he would go for choice only to Antwerp, Liège, Brussels, Amsterdam, Scheveningen or The Hague. The one exception—a 'convalescent' trip to Taormina in 1959—merely increased his conviction.

The choice was logical, not only because his chosen musical instrument owed much of its history to the area. The main subject of his musical research, John Bull, had left his secrets there. And where better to indulge his other musical passion, the collection of musical instruments, than Holland with its far-seeing students of Indonesian and oriental musical cultures? Perhaps the only other place to which he might have been tempted had he lived would have been China (for he had already started to teach himself Chinese). Although he enjoyed his short sabbaticals in Harvard and Seattle and once almost gave in to pressing invitations to Australia, he hated travel and particularly travelling alone. He was content that his international reputation should rest on his writing and recording.

After the van den Borrens, he made his home with the Moules at Royston, near Cambridge. Henry Moule was a lecturer in music at Cambridge, a more enlightened pedant than many undergraduates ever discovered, and a historian whose musical subject was Thomas Morley. There, Bob served as research assistant and began, with Moule's approval, to communicate some of their results to the outside world. The first Dart paper to the Royal Musical Association, on Morley's Consort Lessons, coincided with his first appointment, as Assistant Music Lecturer to the Cambridge faculty.

There were about six of us at the first lecture. We had never heard anything like it (except for traces of Moule vocabulary): clear blackboard technique, a structured pattern, formal rhetoric, questions posed and answered, impeccable keyboard illustrations and a stop-watch timing at 55 minutes. After a week or two, the lecture was inevitably followed by beer and sandwiches at the 'Eagle'. Two Magdalene undergraduates were particularly fired by his passion for 'Early Music' (then little performed) and he freely gave them supervision in elementary paleography: one became the brilliant scholar who contributes chapter 1; the other—the writer—became a happy general practitioner of music, and a lifelong friend.

By the time I returned to Cambridge as his first research assistant, in 1950, Bob Dart was already in demand both as harpsichordist and lecturer. He played regularly with the Boyd Neel Orchestra, made many recordings for his beloved patrons Dr Geoffrey Hanson and his wife, Louise Dyer, on the Oiseau-Lyre label in France, specially looked forward to the Handel opera performances under Anthony Lewis at the Barber Institute in Birmingham, and seemed to need a season ticket to the BBC. What we called 'bobs-doggying' (for he enjoyed word-twisting) was for me pleasure and instruction, whether simply checking, making initial transcriptions— always meticulously acknowledged in his editions—or proofing final versions. We lodged in an immensely musical Cambridge house with the Vlastos, and for relaxation we all sang madrigals and attempted viol consorts (which became a lot better after I had left). In the old University Music School, late at night, we would improvise for hours on two pianos. His ear, whether for continuo realisation or jazz improvisation, was immensely cultivated. This was not a question of perfect pitch but an instinctive feeling for harmonic progression in any style: at those two pianos he would call out 'Richard Strauss' or 'Clementi' and I would try through imitation to match him. He never called 'Bach', who was too sacred. Seriously, we played a vast amount of the piano duet repertory, and 'lightheartedly' (with as much rehearsal as the 'Ring', for Bob never did anything unprepared in public) contributed to University Music Club Saturday concerts.

The years between 1952 and 1962 were Bob Dart's happiest. First a member of Caius, then Selwyn and finally a Fellow of Jesus (with rooms of his own for the first time in his life), his workload—a word he would have loathed—was, added to his teaching and playing, phenomenal. For Stainer & Bell (of which he was a director and ultimately Chairman) he revised, with successive assistants, the Fellowes editions of madrigals, lutesongs and Byrd; began the series of 'English Keyboard Music' and 'Invitation to Madrigals'; and as Secretary to the Musica Britannica Committee, of which his friend Anthony Lewis was (and is) General Editor, he saw through some 30 volumes. For Hutchinson, he wrote his only published book, *The Interpretation of Music* (1954).

He was as careful with the written word as with speech. The etymology of words fascinated him and he believed in economy with directness. This may have alarmed some of his scholarly colleagues more used to 'one should consider' than 'you should consider', but it certainly made for lively reading even in his most deeply perceptive moments. As a critic—no holds barred—of a newly finished manuscript he could suggest more cutting than the best sub-editor: 'Write active not passive', 'another abstraction', 'who needs to know?', 'who cares?'—this last probably about a pet discovery which you found interesting but which, often rightly, he judged was not of much interest to anyone else. His cavalier way with such a manuscript was sometimes resented and, of course, he was not always right, but if you finally said 'That's staying in' he respected you even if he left it with 'Ho-hum' or 'Ah, well'!

The thoughts behind all his own writing were subjected to his personal creed. Did he believe that, by making the thought public, we would understand the music more and so perform it with fresh ears? He treated most of his interests as cases to investigate and gathered evidence from any available source. Notation, printing, provenance and the composer's society all had to be studied but the final 'solution' always depended on the way the music sounded to him. As the Great Detective he believed in following hunches. Some of his case solutions could be and have been queried, since they were hard to accept both for scholars and performers. Hornplayers howled at being deprived of the B minor Mass 'Quoniam' and Brandenburg One by his theories on the 'Corno da Caccia', which gave their parts to trumpets. But few solutions have been proved absolutely false and he maintained that, as mathematical 'proof' required initial assumptions, he was prepared to make an assumption if he 'felt the pricking in the thumbs'.

When he was challenged, he could be haughty: '. . . it's all there. Look at the music'. 'Read the books' was the dusty answer to many who asked to be taught to play the harpsichord. Although he never actually said 'Elementary, my dear x' to anyone who finally came round to agreeing with his solution, it would not have been hard to imagine. And he needed a Watson, as all his research assistants found, as well as those with whom he shared house or stayed frequently.

He believed that to know how to study history, allied to performance, would teach the whole of music to undergraduates. As early as the discussions on reshaping the Cambridge Music Tripos in the 1950s, relations between Dart and 'those composers and organists' became strained. Even those of us who believed that practical harmony and counterpoint coupled with analysis was a necessary prop were on the other side. The remodelled syllabuses did not go far enough for him by any means. As long as he had his stable of postgraduate researchers from his own college and from other universities (particularly Birmingham), however, the hurt did not seem too deep. In any case, from 1955 to 1959 he was too busy with the fortunes of the Philomusica of London.

The Boyd Neel Orchestra, in which he had played since 1948, had lost its eponymous founder to Toronto and some of its stalwarts—Granville Jones, Neville Marriner, Cecil Aronowitz and Bernard Richards among them—felt, with Dart, that there could be a more specialized chamber orchestra in London. The broader repertory favoured by Boyd Neel was against this and the breakaway became inevitable. The name of the new orchestra was in some sense disproportionately important to him, but nevertheless in keeping with his 'pricking thumbs' theory we had to keep on and on until it was found. By a thumb it failed to become the 'Phoenix' orchestra; the two thumbs made it 'Philomusica'. To run the orchestra, he chose W. J. ('Bill') Oxenbury. For four years what the natural conceit of the best chamber music players in London called 'the band' did wonderful work for the 17th- and 18th-century repertory. Recordings for Oiseau-Lyre and the BBC may give today's listeners a bouquet of their flavour but, as with all good dishes, only those who tested the chef's original really know the thrill of discovery. With all respect to the skill of those players (who *hated* Corelli bows to begin with), Thurston Dart was the chef.

Such happy bands—and they *were* happy for a while, with a full order-book and a Festival Hall following for the '5.55' concerts that was remarkable for the time—cannot last for long in London, where the pressures on the best players in the end become intolerable. The pressure on Dart in his life as performer, don and musicologist led not to a spec-tacular farewell but to a disillusionment. In 1959 he resigned and with little regret returned to musicology and turned, perhaps for the first time, to a genuine interest in musical education.

A genuine interest, contrasted with the all-embracing interest in every waking moment, meant that Bob went back to sources. He visited infant schools (interested in movement and music), teacher-training colleges, comprehensives and polytechnics. He talked to inspectors, music advisers, ex-students and students about what they thought they were doing. All this should have been crowned in 1962 by his election to the Chair of Music in Cambridge—truly unsought and apprehensively accepted.

But his attitude to his colleagues (particularly the composers and organists) and his educational mission in a still 'non-vocational' educa-tional institution made it impossible for him to remain *primus inter pares* as the Cambridge structure requires. Not for nothing was he an admirer of Charles de Gaulle. Despite the assertions of the opposition, he was not unbalanced but equally he was an insupportable Professor at the time. He needed a faculty of his own and after considerable heartsearching he accepted the invitation to become King Edward Professor of Music in the University of London. He was to start the first internal music faculty at King's College with the possibility of building a postgraduate musical research centre such as he had always sought.

None could have supported Professor Dart more than his Principal at King's, Sir John Hackett, and his administrator, Bill Oxenbury. Yet lack of finance and Bob's unwillingness—indeed inability—to compromise in accepted university political terms prevented the full development they sought. His zeal for reforming musical education grew to the detriment of his own research: he had ceased to regard himself as a performer. The long study of John Bull remained unfinished. 'I've got it all wrong' was all he said. So many times we had heard him say of other performers and editors, 'he's just got it wrong'.

Sick with cancer, his moods became more unpredictable and his gifts remained available only to a chosen few. His mind remained inquisitively active until the end, which came whilst he was in the middle of recording with Neville Marriner the new thoughts they had discussed—as in earlier days—on the Brandenburg Concertos. The recording was planned to herald a return to performing. Without being a devout Christian, he believed firmly in the words of 'Nunc Dimittis'. He departed in peace in the early hours of 6 March 1971 and his ashes, by his wish, are in his family's grave in Torquay.

It is for scholars and listeners to judge Dart's editions, writing and recordings. As a harpsichordist, his virtuosity was hard-earned. He could not stand over-registration and had a suitable contempt for 'manual-jumpers'. His playing could sound aggressive, and he certainly looked it, with his jaw stuck out, appearing to see the instrument as his enemy. Yet he loved the instrument Tom Goff made for him and was always loyal to the 'jamboree' when, from the days of Boris Ord onwards, the annual concert of Bach concertos for two, three and four harpsichords (all Goff) became a South Bank Pilgrimage. Boris Ord he revered; others 'got it wrong'.

I think it true to say that Bob performed for the music and not for himself or his audience. He was not without conceit—more than once we accused him of imagining he had a Divine Right—and he had a flaring temper, but his rational outlook always brought him back from the brink. Emotional, he hated casual physical contact. His appetite for everything— food, learning, affection—was large. He seldom showed deep affection and he scarcely disguised dislike, but his warm generosity extended to acquaintances in all corners of his life.

Whatever my wife and I knew of Bob—whom we loved—there will be those who knew a different person and who, as they read, will fill out his life with their own memories. For those who never knew him, this tribute attempts to picture a human being behind the musician, Thurston Dart.

Part I

THE STUDY OF MANUSCRIPT AND PRINTED SOURCES

1

The Manuscript Presentation and Notation of Adam de la Halle's Courtly Chansons

John Stevens

Amongst the many things for which Thurston Dart's pupils have cause to be grateful, and not only his pupils but English musical scholarship in general, his passion for sound editing ranks high. Anyone who had the privilege of working with him on the preparation of a volume in the Musica Britannica series remembers with gratitude the exhausting meticulousness of his standards, his ingenious delight in the apt symbol, and, perhaps above all, his insistence that a good edition can serve the purposes of both scholars and practical musicians. He never, so far as I know, turned his mind to the problems of early monophonic songs. I am sure that, if he had, there would have been many opportunities for him to murmur, 'Occam's razor, Occam's razor, my dear sir—*entia non sunt multiplicanda*!'.

The task of an editor is not always regarded as a 'critical-aesthetic' one. We are perhaps still too much in the grip of a pseudo-scientific, materialistic approach, with all its implications of fully definable problems with mechanical solutions. But the meaningful presentation of an old object to a modern reader, or performer, must involve not only rendering its bare structure into comprehensible modern symbols but also conveying, as best possible, its life—to use a vague term. This 'life' is a complex affair and has largely to be grasped through our sense of historical context on the one hand and our awareness on the other of the inadequacies of modern (as of ancient) musical notation to convey the nuances of living music. Editing is a sort of translation. No one is now so naive as to believe that a run-of-the-mill translation—or even an inspired one, for that matter—can fully represent the original. Yet the idea dies hard that the development of musical notation has been all gain and no loss—gain in clarity and definition, without loss of subtlety and essential suggestion. However, an editor has one great advantage over a translator: he not only may but has a duty to describe the object he is trying to present, in such a way that its complexities are apparent and the manner in which an edition must falsify them is clear for all to see.

Adam de la Halle must count among the most interesting and many-sided 'makers' of the 13th century. And, if the testimony of the extant manuscripts can be relied upon, he was admired no less for his skill as a trouvère in the high courtly fashion than for his plays and his polyphonic music (16 rondeaux and five motets). His monophonic songs fall into two categories: *chansons courtoises* and *jeux-partis*. Here I shall concern myself mainly with the former.

As a result of Adam's general reputation his literary texts have been several times edited, and his musical works twice in their entirety. The most recent literary edition of the courtly chansons is by John H. Marshall, *The Chansons of Adam de la Halle* (Manchester, 1971), which I have used extensively. Marshall has provided critical apparatus (of variant readings), notes and glossary, as well as a general introduction, metrical analysis, rhyme-chart and other helpful aids to study.

It cannot be said that the music has yet fared so well. The pioneering edition of Edmond de Coussemaker (1872) is marred by inaccuracies and has long been out of date. The publication in 1967 of *The Lyric Works of Adam de la Halle*, ed. Nigel Wilkins, CMM, xliv, was all the more welcome. The process of using it has, however, prompted certain reflections on the editing of early monophonic song and suggested to my mind some ways in which it could have fulfilled its purpose better.

The prime requirements for an edition of Adam de la Halle's chansons are: (1) a description of the manuscript sources and the different ways Adam's songs are presented in them; (2) a statement of the reasons for the choice of a basic text, with consideration of the degree to which variants from it are significant and of the best method of incorporating or recording them; (3) an exposition of the variety of notations used by the original scribes and of the problems of interpretation which they pose. The enterprise is, in my judgment, not an easy one; and perhaps the greatest service an editor can do is to avoid the temptation of an easy and specious conclusiveness. I shall attempt in the following pages to assemble some of the information an edition should provide under heads (1) and (3).

Musical texts for the chansons of Adam de la Halle are found in ten Old French chansonniers. They are, with their customary *sigla* (standard since Raynaud's *Bibliographie*) and titles, as follows[1]:

Arras, Bibliothèque municipale, 657 (formerly 139) (*A*) (*Chansonnier d'Arras*)

Paris, Bibliothèque nationale, fonds fr.846 (formerly 7222[3]; Cangé 66) (*O*) (*Chansonnier Cangé*)

Paris, Bibliothèque nationale, fonds fr.847 (formerly 7222[4]; Cangé 65) (*P*)

Paris, Bibliothèque nationale, fonds fr.1109 (formerly 7363), ff.311-25 (*Q*)
Paris, Bibliothèque nationale, fonds fr.1591 (formerly 7613) (*R*)
Paris, Bibliothèque nationale, fonds fr.12615 (formerly suppl. fr.184) (*T*)
(*Chansonnier de Noailles*)
Paris, Bibliothèque nationale, fonds fr.24406 (formerly La Vallière 59) (*V*)
Paris, Bibliothèque nationale, fonds fr.25566 (formerly La Vallière 31), first
section [*Wx*]
Paris, Bibliothèque nationale, fonds fr.25566, main manuscript (*W*)
('Complete Works')
Rome, Vatican City, Biblioteca Apostolica Vaticana, Reg.lat.1490 (*a*)
(*Chansonnier du Vatican*)

All 36 chansons are listed in Raynaud's *Bibliographie*, with their sources. This information is repeated in the CMM edition (where unfortunately a completely different and apparently private set of manuscript sigla is used) and in Marshall. Music survives for 35 chansons. Only no. 33, *De tant con plus aproisme mon pais*, lacks a melody: in *W*, f.22*v*, the ten staves ruled for music were never filled; in *T*, f.231*v*, the song is written as if it were a continuation of the preceding one (though with a marginal mark to indicate the fact)—no staves were ruled, but it is in a section of the manuscript where the staves have in any case been left void.

The ten chansonniers are briefly described by Jeanroy;[2] but only one, *Pn* 846 (*O*: the *Chansonnier Cangé*), has been fully treated from the musical point of view, by Beck in his facsimile edition of 1927. I omit it from the following discussion. The contents of the manuscripts are listed in Raynaud (1884), i. They are not described by Marshall or by Wilkins.

All the manuscripts containing Adam's songs with music have their individual characteristics: some are comprehensive trouvère chansonniers, others are manuscripts of miscellaneous courtly character but with a chanson section; most contain only monophonic music, a few—*Pn* 25566 (*W*), *Pn* 12615 (*T*), *Pn* 846 (*O*)—polyphonic motets and/or rondeaux. But in their presentation of the songs themselves they all share certain basic characteristics.

The chansons are normally, though not invariably, presented in double columns. An ornamental initial marks the beginning of each song; the first verse is written out in full with its music, subsequent verses follow arranged as prose with a dot 'above the line' indicating the line-divisions. The later verses have each their own small ornamented letter and are aligned to the left-hand margin. An unfailing characteristic is the careful alignment of musical and verbal text; the words seem almost invariably to have been written first; the notes have then been added above the syllables to which they refer, either as single notes, or as ligatures, or exceptionally as visual groups. (For the special procedures of *Pn* 1591 (*R*), see below.) A four-line red staff is usual (five- or three-line staves also occur) with C- or F-clef.

The symbols used are those of square neumatic notation. They are analogous to, and clearly derive in their essentials from, plainsong notation; moreover, they are the notational symbols of early polyphonic music also. These three broadly distinguishable systems use the same symbols, as different languages may all be written in Roman letters, but it is obvious do not use them in the same way. This would scarcely be worth saying, were it not for the persisting tendency to deny the secular monophonic notations a *notational* validity of their own. The long-standing tradition of interpretation in accordance with the principles of 'modal rhythm' is of its very nature external. Whether applied rigidly, as in some transcriptions, or flexibly and musically, as by Wilkins in the CMM edition of Adam, it remains external—a way of deciding what the notation 'means' by a kind of *ex cathedra* pronouncement derived from the poetic metre. This method of interpretation has done scholarship a disservice by distracting attention from the notation itself, which is long overdue for a thorough-going and searching analysis such as Gregorian scholars have devoted to the paleography of the chant.[3] It may well seem that the supreme remoteness has been achieved in the CMM edition itself, which contains neither a description of the notations used (the plural is necessary, as I hope to show), nor an explanation of the rhythmical interpretation adopted; nor indeed does it even distinguish *plica* notes from ordinary notes—a distinction which has remained for most 20th-century editors the one necessary concession to notational peculiarity.

By concentrating on notational peculiarity and diversity, I hope in the course of this paper to help restore a sense of the genuine validity of the various notations used by the scribes of Adam de la Halle's chansons. The notational styles are not simply crude and needlessly elaborate ways of indicating pitches by copyists who failed meantime to give any precise indication of their rhythmic intentions. The styles have themselves perhaps a meaning—shadowy and elusive in many respects, but not to be disregarded on that account. The elusive nature of the notations is, of course, related to the elusive and variable nature of the melodies themselves; the two cannot be separated. Hendrik van der Werf and other scholars have done much in recent years to awaken us to the real problems posed by the existence of troubadour and trouvère melodies in many divergent versions.[4] The most likely explanation for these divergencies, some slight, some substantial, is that the melodies were transmitted in both written and oral forms. It is futile, and indeed anachronistic, to look for one 'authentic' version of a medieval song:[5]

> . . . there were, in principle, three opportunities for variations to occur: variations made by the participants in the oral tradition, outright errors made by the scribes in the process of notating and copying the melodies and, finally, the possibility that the scribes made some variations and perhaps some deliberate changes of their own.

It is this third possibility, especially, which should make us attentive to scribal habits of notation. The corpus of Adam de la Halle's courtly chansons is, in fact, a comparatively compact and closed one, as we shall see; and the amount of melodic variation in the simplest and most obvious sense is rather smaller than in the repertory as a whole. Despite this there is wide divergence of notational practice—so wide, it seems, as to make it most likely that in many instances the act of copying (or notating from memory?) was no simple mechanical act with a single 'correct' answer but an art which remained flexible, individual and creative, to match these same qualities in the singer's and composer's art. In order to give the reader some idea of these qualities, we turn now to the individual chansonniers.

F-AS 657 (A) (Chansonnier d'Arras)

This has been thoroughly described by Alfred Jeanroy, editor of the facsimile edition.[6] It consists, in fact, of three separate manuscripts. arbitrarily bound up together because of their similarity in size and style of handwriting. (Jeanroy(1918), Introduction, p.5). The second of these is dated c1300 and runs from f.129 to f.160. It is itself a hotch-potch: between two series of chansons, both of which are truncated, are inserted two complete gatherings of *jeux-partis* in a different hand (for the words, at least). The chanson series is itself wrongly ordered, according to Jeanroy, and the incomplete gathering, ff.129–135, which contains Adam's chansons, was originally the third and not the first of the gatherings. The argument is based on the close analogies between the arrangement of songs in this fragment and that of *Rvat* 1490 (*a*). What we have, then, are fragments of a chansonnier which once included a 'run' of chansons by Adam beginning with songs 1, 2, 4, 3, 5, 32. The initial sequence is very close to that of *Rvat* 1490 (*a*) and suggests that the scribe may have embarked on a substantial section of songs by Adam. An elaborate illumination over the rubric 'Adans li bocus fist ces kancons' shows the poet seated at a writing desk, scraper in one hand and pen in the other.

Notation (Chart I)

This, like other chansonniers, has its notational individuality. The music hand seems to have been quick and fluid. The scribe's style is considerably less formal than that of the scribe of *Pn* 25566 (*W*) for instance: he has a slightly offhand manner of writing the *podatus* and the *torculus*, for example.[7] His vocabulary of symbols is, considering only six songs by Adam are involved, quite rich, especially in compound *plicas*.[8] There is only one double *plica* form (i.e. doubled at pitch without ligature) (Chart I: 2a). He also has a wide variety of *conjunctura* and *climacus* forms; they appear as usual to be interchangeable (see Chart I: 4a-h). On the other hand he is sparing of other *plica* forms. He has the expected single *plicas* (2a,b), with more or less equal tails; the down-*plicas* are usually long and slim and have slightly rounded heads. The later mensural forms of *plica* (*brevis* with left-hand tail; *longa* with right-hand) do not often occur (1c,d). Forms of the ligature *cum opposita proprietate* (*c.o.p.*) are found (5a,b; but b is dubious) as part of a larger melisma, and singly (5c) with very short left-hand stroke; the general significance of *c.o.p.* forms will be referred to later.

I-Rvat 1490 (a) (Chansonnier du Vatican)

This is a parchment chansonnier of 181 folios dating from the early 14th century (?late 13th, Schwan). There are many mutilations. The basic arrangement is by genres: *cancons* (ff.5–109, preceded by manuscript index); *pastoureles*; *motet et rondel*; *chancons de Nostre dame*; *partures*. Within the chanson section, which comes first as in *Pn* 25566 (*W*), songs are arranged by author, pride of place being given, as customary, to Thibaut, *le roi de Nauare*. Adam de la Halle's songs originally began on f.46, but the leaf has been removed. *D'amourous cuer* (song 1) has been entirely lost (see manuscript index) and stanzas 1–4 (with the music) of *Li jolis maus* (song 2). There then follow in unbroken sequence songs 4, 3, 5, 32, 22, 17, 15, 26, 27, 9, 18, 19, 30, 20, 21, 24, 7, 16 (see Marshall, p.17). The remaining song by Adam, *Glorieuse virge Marie* (song 36) finds its place on f.126 amongst the songs to the Virgin.

One most unusual feature of the Adam sequence is that it concludes with a one-voice *rondeau*, beginning *Dame or sui trais* (Boogaard, *rondeau* 75).[9] The melody is the middle voice of Adam's three-voiced *rondeau* (CMM, no.7, p.54) written in the same non-mensural notation as the courtly chansons which precede it. Such confusion of genres is quite unusual. The compilers of the trouvère chansonniers were as a rule perfectly conscious of the different requirements of the two genres and of the notational styles generally appropriate to each. A *rondeau* is a less aristocratic creation than a chanson; it is associated with the huge *refrain* repertory of 'courtly-popular' song-tags and it is, characteristically, measured. After this *rondeau* there is a *lacuna* in the source, but the manuscript index makes it clear that there were no further songs by Adam de la Halle; those of Gaidifer d'Avion follow.

The presentation is the standard one, with two columns to a page. Each song has a large and hefty initial letter, totally without tracery; the small initials for subsequent verses have delicate flourishes. If the last stave is not taken up completely with the music of verse 1 the scribe fills it with ornamental patterns.

Notation (Chart II)

The music hand is not a very precise one by the standards of the best chansonniers but it is less cursive, less on-flowing than that of *AS* 657 (A). The scribe shares *AS* 657's tendency to lighten the upper note of the *podatus*. Considering that 18 chansons are involved, his repertory seems more restricted than that of *AS* 657's scribe. As Chart II shows, he has every standard form of *climacus* and *conjunctura* and uses them. He is slightly less inventive with compound *plicas* (though example 3f is odd in the extreme) but he has four forms of the double *plica* as against *AS* 657's one. He does not in the Adam songs use the single *plica* form with double down-tails, though his rare, curved single down-*plica* with left-hand tail verges towards it. His single *plica* with right-hand up-tail is common. There are no *c.o.p.* ligatures in these chansons. Longs and breves are undifferentiated except for last-note longs (12a).

The *rondeaux* in this manuscript are not by Adam de la Halle, except for the one already mentioned, classified as a chanson. They are ten in number (Boogaard, nos.84–93), monophonic, and all by Guillaume d'Amiens. Their notational style is sometimes simpler than that of the chansons but not essentially different. The notation is simpler when the melodies are simpler. No distinction is made between longs and breves. However, the *porrectus* has the third note turned inwards (8b) perhaps to indicate its lengthening.

It is only in the polyphonic motets that the scribe begins to use, though not consistently, the clear mensural forms which he had at his command—

longs and breves, semibreves in groups, *c.o.p.* ligatures (see, for example, f.114*v*) etc.

F-Pn 25566, Main Section (*W*)

This manuscript is justly famous for containing the 'complete works' of Adam de la Halle. It has formed the basis, presumably for this reason, of the musical editions of Coussemaker and Wilkins—a necessary basis for the polyphonic compositions, less necessary though still one obvious choice (Marshall uses *Pn* 847 (*P*)) for the chansons and *jeux-partis*.

The manuscript consists, as has been observed, of two completely different and originally separate entities. Between f.1*v* (with its rubric 'Chi commencent les canchons maistre adan de la hale') and f.10, where the chansons referred to actually begin, there has been inserted at some time or other one eight-folio gathering of smaller size, evidently from another chansonnier now lost. I shall refer to it as *Wx* and describe it separately.[10]

Short descriptions of *Pn* 25566 (*W*) occur in Coussemaker, Schwan, Raynaud (with list of contents), Jeanroy and Reaney. (It is not described by the CMM editor, although he uses it to almost entire exclusion of other sources.) It is a parchment manuscript of the late 13th century (Adam's play *Robin et Marion* is usually dated 1283) and contains a continuous sequence, after the chansons: f.23*v les partures* (i.e. *jeux-partis*); f.32*v li rondel adan*; f.34*v li motet adan*; f.37 *li ius du pelerin*; f.39 *li gieus de robin et de marion cadans fist*; f.48*v Li ius adan* (i.e *Feuillée*); f.59*v* the epic *du roi de sezile*; f.65 *li ver damours*; f.66*v li congies adan*. The rest of the manuscript (283 folios in all) is taken up with other authors and works such as the Bestiary (splendidly illuminated) of Richart de Furnival, Bodel's *St Nicholas* and the *Renart nouvel*, one of the principal sources of *refrains*.

The manuscript was thoroughly planned from the beginning. The sequence of Adam's works runs across the gatherings (ff.10–17*v*; 18–25*v*; 26–33*v*; 34–41*v*; 42–49*v*; 50–57*v*; 58–65*v*; 66–73*v* etc.); each gathering is complete and is both numbered, in Roman, and cued, for the binder. There are no mutilations or *lacunae*.

The chanson section, characteristically taking first place because of its courtly significance, is headed by a fine miniature, roughly 75 x 75 mm. In a house-frame (?) two men occupy a bench; the right-hand one, with legs crossed, holds up a paper on which the words 'Damoureus coer uel cant [finger obscures] auoir aid [finger] e' are just visible (= song 1). To the right is an audience of seven persons, two (?) of them women. No instruments are shown. The *jeux-partis* are introduced with a slightly smaller illumination; the *rondeaux* and *motets* have none. The chansons are presented in the standard format, two columns to a page.

Perhaps the most unusual feature of this collection of Adam's music and poems is the way in which each of the two monophonic sections, chansons and *jeux-partis*, is concluded with a Latin song. This is odd in itself. That it should be the same Latin song in each case (ff.23*v*, 32), almost identical in notation, is even odder. The text is as follows:

> Adest dies hec tertia
> passi redemptoris,
> qua surrexit caro pia.
> et si uobis oris
> non sufficit testimonium,
> ecce locus, sudarium,
> lapis signum, foris.
> hic sepultus et occultus
> erat fons dulcoris
> alleluya.

It appears to be a rhymed trope to the alleluia, but I have not yet been able to trace it. Many hymns and sequences begin 'Adest dies' but continue differently. For the melody not printed in CMM edition, see ex.1.

Notation (Chart VIII)

The music hand is the most elegant of all the 'Adam' hands, neat and formal, with precisely square note heads and finely drawn strokes. The scribe is thoroughly professional. Clarity rather than inventiveness seems to characterise the notational procedures of this music-scribe. His range of symbols is not as wide as some. His complete avoidance of the double *plica* except in one instance (Chart VIII: 2a) is noteworthy. He uses all his forms of the single-note *plica* frequently. His assortment of compound *plicas* is less impressive than it looks at first sight, since four of the more ambitious *ligaturae plicatae* occur in the Latin song *Adest dies*. Those that remain are common and straightforward enough with the exception of 3m which combines a single up-*plica* with a following *conjunctura* to make a five-note melisma.

'Longs' and 'breves' are undifferentiated in this section of the manuscript, though occasionally the first or the highest note in a phrase appears to have a purposefully elongated tail, as well as the final. However, the essentially unmeasured character of the notation is un-

Ex. 1 *Adest dies*

mistakeably clear as soon as we come to compare it with the clearly measured polyphony or with the monophonic *refrains* of the *Renart nouvel* later in the manuscript. All the music is apparently in the same hand. This invites comment. It is tempting to assume that we are dealing with a music scribe who has himself thoroughly mastered the metrical intricacies of Franconian notation and has consciously and deliberately chosen to use a different notation to transcribe courtly chansons. This could be the case; the scribe is, as I have said, fully professional and therefore unlikely to have been a merely mechanical copyist. On the other hand, he *is* a copyist and could simply have been faithfully reproducing from different exemplars. The most that can be safely argued is, I think, that the person(s) responsible for the compilation of this unique collection of Adam's compositions saw nothing in the least incongruous, and may have seen something positively apt, in retaining the traditional chanson notation in close juxtaposition to 'modern' mensural styles. If the scribe exercised initiative at all, his familiarity with the *contemporary* mensural system may explain his somewhat austere use of the vocabulary of conventional monophonic symbols, and his introduction of four forms of the ligature *c.o.p.* (see 9a-d). In the *rondeaux*, too, he frequently employs the form of the *conjunctura* which looks like three descending semibreves; it is interesting that, unlike some chansonnier scribes (*F-AS* 657 (*A*), *I-Rvat* 1490 (*a*), *F-Pn* 847 (*P*), *Pn* 1591 (*R*), *Pn* 12615 (*T*) etc), he does not introduce it here in copying the chansons.

One chanson in *Pn* 25566 (*W*) calls for particular comment—no.20 *Amours m'ont si doucement*. It is notated almost entirely in longs (the length and uniformity of the tails leaves the matter in no doubt). Those notes which are not longs are *ternariae* in the unusual form (4j), not found elsewhere in the chansons; this form of the *climacus* occurs 16 times in eight phrases. Two notes remain—an up-*plica*, common enough; and an oblique *clivis* (7b) peculiar to this chanson. Why this unusual notation? It is hard to say; the only other source, *Pn* 847 (*P*), presents it in conventional guise. The song, however, is an unusual one. Dr Marshall describes it as 'a *chanson de femme*, distinctly more popular in tone and simpler in versification than the courtly *chanson*' (p.126). The distinction applies also to the musical form ($ABB^1C + D$ repeated) which is not that of the courtly chanson.

It might seem as if the notation, by deliberate choice, of this piece in apparently equal note values tells against the hypothesis that in general syllabic equivalence (iso-syllabism) should be the guiding principle of rhythmical interpretation. The argument has some weight. Such insistence on what one would suppose taken for granted seems to undermine the general idea. But the notation of this song suggests a rhythm in fact much more rigid and inflexible than might be appropriate in a high-courtly chanson. This may well be its very purpose.

F-Pn 25566, First Section [Wx]

There is little that can or need be said further about this fragment of a chansonnier, in general terms. Whether it is part of a manuscript devoted to Adam de la Halle or part of a general trouvère chansonnier, there is no means of telling. The eight leaves (of the early 14th century?) contain, in conventional chansonnier presentation, the same 14 songs as open the chanson section of the main manuscript, and in the same order. This is, of course, a significant parallel and, taken with *Pn* 847 (*P*), testifies to some kind of stable and coherent written tradition embracing these manuscripts. All the more surprising then to find that *Wx* and *W* have little in common notationally, within the broad tradition of non-mensural monophonic notation.

Notation (Chart IX)

The music hand of *Wx* is quite presentable but does not bear comparison for elegance or economy with that of *W*. The scribe's writing is clear but there is perhaps an element of the haphazard in the way he forms his symbols. His nine or ten varieties of double *plica* (which the *W* scribe, we recall, did not use) cannot all be the result of deliberate choice or of a desperate search for the definitive nuance (Chart IX: 2a-h). On the other hand he is not careless, and if he makes an error he corrects it (see, e.g., song 13). Again unlike the *W* scribe, he revels in esoteric varieties of compound *plica* (3f-k) and has an unusual number of symbols in which a *plica* or double *plica* replaces the first note of a *conjunctura* (e.g. 3k, which occurs more than once). He occasionally uses a *c.o.p.* ligature, most often in the form 9b (a *ternaria*).

Such differences in notational style, however close the melodies of the two manuscripts appear in a modern transcription, surely indicate a complete lack of immediate rapport between *W* and *Wx* in the copying stage.

F-Pn 847 (P)

This is an important source for Adam de la Halle studies. It is essentially a chansonnier (unlike *Pn* 25566 (*W*)); the only extraneous work which it contains, the *Roman du Vergier et de l'arbre d'amour*, comes immediately before the Adam de la Halle songs. Jeanroy (p.8) and Schwan (p.87) describe it, however, as composite—not originally planned to include what it now contains. Whether it is, in fact, two separate manuscripts (Schwan) or three (Jeanroy), one thing is agreed: the 'Adam de la Halle chansonnier' is a separate entity. The main manuscript(s) is a member of the group *NKXP*; none of these chansonniers contains songs by Adam. His compositions occupy two complete gatherings (ff.211–218*v*; 219–226*v*); to these are added two pages, 227–228*v*, the last song being a *jeu-parti*, *Assenes chi grievilier jugement*, the only one included. After the verses of the *jeu-parti* (f.228*v*, col.2) two red staves, which never had music on them, are harshly erased and *fin* is written (perhaps by a later hand). It is unusual for a single *jeu-parti* to be appended to a chanson section.

The manuscript contains 33 chansons in the order 1–14, 16–24, 26–32, 34–6 (Marshall, p.16). Marshall uses it as his base text and describes it linguistically as containing a mixture of Francien and Picard forms.

The chansons are presented in two columns to the page in the usual manner.

Notation (Chart III)

There is a close melodic correspondence between *Pn* 847 (*P*)and 25566 [*Wx*] (closer than with the main *W*). This is paralleled by certain features of the notation. The hand is clear and not unattractive but again will not stand up to comparison with that of *W*. In its wealth of *plica* symbols, this scribe rivals the scribe of *Wx*. Admittedly we have the evidence of 33 songs as against 14 from *Wx*. Both manuscripts contain between 25 and 30 identifiable types of single, double and compound *plica*. *Pn* 847 (*P*) slightly fewer than *Wx*. But the *P*-scribe makes up for it in variety of *conjunctura* and *climacus* forms. Like *Wx*, *Pn* 847 (*P*) has several ingenious combinations of *plica* and *conjunctura* (cf Chart III: 3k with IX: 3k, 30). It looks sometimes as if these scribes act on the principle that a *plica* or *plica* stroke may be inserted anywhere into a ligature. And there are certainly grounds for thinking that, at least in *P*, some *plicas* were added later, in a lighter browner ink.

One may have the same reservations about *Pn* 847 (*P*) as about *Wx*. The scribe's apparent inventiveness may be the result of graphic uncertainty as much as of melodic subtlety. Nevertheless, both manuscripts testify, I suggest, to the existence of a notational code especially suited to the needs of a melodic musical tradition—a code more diverse, more flexible and more susceptible perhaps to personal manipulation than the necessarily more formal and rigid mensural notations of the same period. This great notational diversity acts in the interests of suggestiveness rather than of prescription, and we have been perhaps wrong in searching so diligently over the years for a key which would unlock the code with the same mechanical ease and precision with which one might unlock a door.

The manuscript's other notational characteristics can be speedily dealt with. Both the instances I have noted of *c.o.p.* ligatures are in different ways dubious (8a-b). Longs and breves are undifferentiated. A tail of the same length as the head is deep is the norm.

F-Pn 12615 (T) (Chansonnier de Noailles)

This large vellum manuscript of 233 folios contains 481 songs, 358 of them with their music. The main manuscript is dated *c*1300 (Jeanroy, Reaney) and contains not only chansons and *jeux-partis* but *lais* (two being Provençal). The last 50 folios of the manuscript are later and contain, *inter alia*, 87 motets (listed Reaney, *RISM*, B/IV/1, pp.381-93) and poems about Arras, the chansons of Jean de Renti (see Raynaud, 1955, p.27) and the chansons of Adam de la Halle. Some blank pages have been used for 15th-century poems.

Once again, we discover Adam's chansons as a separate entity, not integral to the main chansonnier. It is interesting, incidentally, that a collector who had already added a huge group of French motets to his chansonnier thought it worthwhile adding, further, the courtly monody of a distinguished trouvère. The main chansonnier is not without its puzzles. Although the gatherings follow regularly and are cued in sequence, there are two series of gathering numbers which are as they stand incompatible with each other (gathering 'I' runs ff.23-30v; but ff.71-78v are marked, very lightly, 'XI'). However, the non-relatedness of the gatherings which contain 'the Adam chansonnier' to the rest of the manuscript is quite clear. A complete gathering, unheralded by cue or number-sequence, runs ff.224-230v (*sic*: f.226 is doubled through mis-foliation). This is cued to three further leaves, ff.231, 232, 233 (now gummed together, though there is sewing in the fold of 231v-232). The sequence begins formally with rubric Les chancons adans li bocus and a most beautifully floriated initial 'O' (in red) and ends appropriately with Adam's chanson to the Virgin (song 36) *Glorieuse virge marie*. The second half of f.233 and the whole of f.233v is blank; the sequence was evidently complete. In another sense, unfortunately, it is incomplete: up to f.226*v music is supplied (12 songs); void staves follow to f.230v; thereafter spaces for staves are unruled. The section was designed to contain in all 33 songs. Throughout the manuscript the songs are written in long lines across the large page in an impressive and handsome style.

Notation (Chart VI)

The notational style of *Pn* 12615 (*T*) is the most economical of all, using only about 30 symbols, as contrasted to approximately 55 in *Pn* 1591 (*R*), 50 in *Pn* 25566 [*Wx*], and over 40 in *W* itself. The style is thoroughly professional and rivals that of *W* in its neatness and elegance.

It is in his limited employment of compound *plicas* that the scribe most clearly shows his restraint. With one thoroughly traditional exception (3a: *clivis* + down-*plica*), all his compound *plicas* consist simply in the addition of an up- or down-stroke to a standard ligature. For his single-note *plicas*, although he has not entirely abandoned the older type of double-tailed *plica* (1b and 1f) he makes great use of the 'Franconian' type consisting of a single stroke up or down from the note head (1a, c). He has, similarly, simplified the double *plica*, instead of abolishing it as the scribe of *Pn* 25566 (*W*) has in effect done; the doubling of the note clearly has significance for him, but the graphic forms are much less fussy than in other manuscripts. He also, rather unusually, has a *pressus* figure without *plica* (7b). His various *conjunctura* forms, varying only the first note (4d, f, g) appear to be used without essential distinction. Ligatures *c.o.p.* do not form part of his vocabulary.

There is not in *Pn* 12615 (*T*), as in *Pn* 25566 (*W*), the same clear contrast between a mensural polyphonic and a non-mensural monophonic notation, a contrast which in any case is most meaningful when a single scribe compiled both sections. The motets of *Pn* 25566 (*W*) are, in fact, notoriously difficult to transcribe.

F-Pn 1591 (R)

This manuscript is the oddest of all: it is a vellum manuscript of the early 14th century containing music for 235 songs. It is briefly described by Raynaud, Jeanroy, Schwan; and in great detail by Johann Schubert (1963).[11] Schwan had argued that it consists of three manuscripts; it seems truer to say that it consists of two, very similar, bound up as one. That there is a major break in the manuscript after f.36*v* is certain: the page is blank; and halfway down the recto is written 'Explicit carmina' (ff.33–36*v* is a gathering of 4). On f.37 the chansonnier starts again, as it were, with a decorated capital 'F' (for *Fine amours*). It is nicely executed in blue, red and gold, in the same style as the capital 'S' on f.1 (perhaps the owner had ordered a further instalment from the same scriptorium?). The gatherings then follow regularly, usually with cues (occasionally themselves built into little decorated edifices—e.g. f.121*v*). Schwan argues that the third manuscript begins on f.62, at which point the sequence of anonymous songs begins; but, as he observes, there is no physical discontinuity (f.62 is in the middle of a gathering, 61–67*v* (*sic*: f.64 is doubled)) and the same copyist continues through. (Schwan can only mean that the copyist switched from one source to another.) Schubert distinguishes five sections in the manuscript, and concludes that it was made up from a number of separate 'repertories' with further additions.

Something has gone wrong, it is clear, with the incorporation of the Adam de la Halle chansons. Gathering ff.154–161*v* is cued with 'gñt deduit a' but f.162 begins with a different Adam song *Tant me plest vivre* (song 15). *Grant deduit* (the only *unicum* for Adam in *Pn* 1591 (*R*)) had, in fact, already been copied earlier; it was the first complete song of a gathering, ff.98–105*v*, unattributed, and *not* starting at the head of the page. The *later* gathering (ff.162–169*v*) is in fact entirely devoted to Adam de la Halle. There follows a 'non-Adam' gathering (ff.170–177*v*) which is cued to a gathering of only two leaves, mid-sewn, which contains the last two Adam songs of the manuscript. The source ends on f.184*v*, after a gathering of five leaves (1 + 4) with the rubric 'Explicit les chansons au roy de nauare. Et as autre princes'.

The manuscript, then, is by and large a single homogeneous whole without great variation in style of layout, handwriting, or, it may be added, notation. It may not originally have been designed as a whole but it forms one. And among the elements which went to its creation was a collection (or two or more, since two songs appear twice in varied versions) of the chansons of Adam de la Halle.[12]

However, the oddity of *Pn* 1591 (*R*) does not consist in the way it was put together but in the character of its melodies and of the style in which they are notated. The verbal texts are not noticeably 'incorrect' or 'unreliable': the variants, for Adam de la Halle's songs at least, are of a kind that can be recorded. The musical and notational variants, by contrast, are extreme; and only a complete transcription could do justice (if that is what they deserve) to their weird eccentricity. See, for example, *R*'s version of song 3, *Je nai autre retenance*, on the Comparative Notational Chart (Chart X, below).

The songs are neatly written in long lines across the page (cf *Pn* 12615 (*T*)) not in double columns. Unfortunately, the vellum has become deeply discoloured in many places (illegible yellow, and legible white, pages alternating with the smooth and rough sides of the skin). Notes show through so strongly in some places that even with the original manuscript in one's hands it is not always easy to make out what has been written.

There are several paradoxes in *Pn* 1591 (*R*). One, already mentioned, is the contrast between the conventional reliability of the verbal text and the occasional non-conformist, quite unpredictable, melodic variations. Another is between the evident neatness of the musical text and the sometimes apparently haphazard notational procedures. A thorough analysis of the musical variations, indeed deviations, of *Pn* 1591 (*R*) has been undertaken by Schubert. My immediate concern is with the idiosyncratic notation.

Notation (Chart V)

The scribe of *Pn* 1591 (*R*) uses a very large number of symbols (between 50 and 60) but he never seems to be sure which one to choose on any particular occasion and tends to write them in a way which blurs their traditional shapes and, presumably therefore, their significance. His range of *conjunctura* and *climacus* forms is bewildering. And, with his fondness for the oblique forms of ligatures, he devises more different kinds of *clivis* than all other chansonnier scribes put together. 'Modern' features of his style include the frequent use of *c.o.p.* ligatures (9a-f) and various single-note forms (see 12a-d). It is often difficult to tell what these latter are. They sometimes look like *conjuncturae* which have fallen apart (4n shows how this can begin to happen); sometimes like badly written breves, i.e. rhomboid shapes in the so-called 'English' style, approximating to clumsy 'semibreves'. The apparent isolated minim must surely be an error (12a), but the tail is definitely there. A negative sign of his 'modernity' is, I should say, his extremely sparing use of *plicas* except the single-note kind and in these he prefers the later variety (cf *Pn* 12615 (*T*) with single tail (1b, e, f)).

But 'modernity' is hardly the right term. A truly modern notational style for monophonic music in the 14th century is illustrated by the songs of Jehan de l'Escurel at the beginning of the *Roman de Fauvel* manuscript (*Pn* fr.146) with mensural ligatures and *plicas*, groups of three and four semibreves, and abundant use of *c.o.p.* in two-note ligatures (*binariae*). What we have in *Pn* 1591 (*R*), I believe, is evidence of a disintegration of the old unmeasured monophonic notation. At this date (14th century) the scribe had all the notational apparatus, and the models, to notate the chansons metrically if he had wished to. But he wished to do something different and perhaps more old-fashioned. The real puzzle is to decide how a copyist could have got so out of touch with the essential tradition *musically* whilst presumably having access to a number of poetically reliable chansonniers.[13] Admittedly not all his sources may have had music:[14] he writes a whole *jeux-partis* section (ff.16–26*v*) simply as a literary text (cf *Pn* 1109 (*Q*)). But he, or his customer, was sufficiently interested in melodies to copy out two of Adam's songs twice (songs 14 and 16): the melodies are in essence the same each time (cf, however, the two versions of 16: phrases 4–5 are considerably divergent).

However, what is odder than anything in *Pn* 1591 (*R*) is the self-evidently weak grasp that the scribe has on the central tenet of the whole troubadour-trouvère tradition—the perfect numerical matching of note groups to syllables. This concept is basic: whatever else they may be, the melodies of the trouvères (and Adam de la Halle is no exception) are a *syllabic* music. The scribe of *Pn* 1591 (*R*) has let his notation disintegrate to the extent that he, and we, can no longer be sure that the number of musical, i.e. notational, symbols will precisely equal the number of syllables. As a consequence, he has to resort to a device, almost unknown to and certainly un-needed by, the scribes of other manuscripts: he marks off, though not with entire consistency, single words or word groups with upright strokes in the musical stave itself, in order to clarify his intentions. In fact, many ambiguities remain.

The manuscript remains a puzzle. If the scribe was a mere copyist, surely he could have transcribed more accurately, or found better sources, than he has done? If he was a musical innovator on his own account, what precisely was he hoping to achieve?

F-Pn 1109 (Q)

This, a vellum manuscript of 329 folios of the early 14th century, is an important source for Adam de la Halle. It contains 23 chansons, all except the first three with music, and 20 *jeux-partis* (one not by Adam) for which music was never envisaged (they are written as prose). *Pn* 1109 (*Q*) differs from other manuscripts in being essentially a literary collection: it starts with Brunetto Latini's *Li Livres dou Tresor*, and the last work before the chansons is *Les enseignemens des philosophes*. It is a fat book, neatly written throughout in two columns to a page, with ornamented letters (blue and red alternating with red and black). Various hands have contributed, all formal and much of a size; the general impression is of homogeneity.

The gatherings immediately before the chansons are regular and cued. But there is no cue from f.310*v*, which is a blank, to the 'chansonnier' (the only musical item in the manuscript). The chansons and *jeux-partis* occupy two gatherings which were clearly planned as a unit (a 'cue' on f.318*v* leads to f.319). The chansons are headed 'Chi comencent les canchons dadan'. The text hand in this section is different from earlier hands; but there is the same layout, margins, page-size, flourished letters and small red and blue capitals as throughout. This section is, then, all of a piece with the rest of the manuscript, even though perhaps added as an afterthought. There is a further small gathering (ff.327–329) containing a Dance of Death poem, before the manuscript ends.

Pn 1109 (*Q*) is the only manuscript to present both chansons-written-as-poems and chansons-with-music. The latter are, however, presented in a fully professional manner and laid out in the traditional manner already described, two columns to a page.

Notation (Chart IV)

The music hand is neat, attractive and competent. The scribe makes use of a wide variety of symbols (between 45 and 50), writes them all efficiently and understands their function (4j, 7c, 5a are among his few eccentricities). There is some apparent variation of notational style from song to song which suggests that he may have been making use of different sources. His version of song 6, *Helas, il n'est mais nus ki n'aint* is thick with old-style *plicas* (2d), whilst in *Au repairier* (song 14) he introduces two symbols—a double *plica* and a *pressus*-like figure (2b, 11b)—which he has not previously used and does not, as far as I have observed, repeat.

As one might expect at this date, his style incorporates various 'modern' features. He has some neat single-stroke *plicas*, both single (1b) and compound (3a, b). Generally speaking, though, his range of both single and compound *plicas* is narrow. On the other hand, he has a far wider variety of *c.o.p.* ligatures than any other scribe—nine in all, including two *binariae* (5d, j). In some chansons he uses a *c.o.p.* ligature ascending, where other scribes use a *scandicus* in one form or another; *Pn* 1109 (*Q*) shares this characteristic with *AS* 657 (*A*). It is difficult to say whether such ligatures have mensural connotations or not; in Franconian terms, the result would be to shorten the two first notes (two semibreves), thereby throwing the melodic weight on to the third note (practically all *c.o.p.* ligatures in these chansonniers are *ternariae*). At least one should be on one's guard against assuming that *no* ligatures in monophonic notation can have a mensural meaning.

One unique feature of *Pn* 1109 (*Q*) is the scribe's presentation of the single note. It is his invariable practice to write all such notes as clear 'longs'. There is no suggestion of larger 'metrical' patterns consisting of long and short notes.

F-Pn 24406 (*V*)

This is a vellum manuscript, written in part at the end of the 13th century and in part at the beginning of the 14th. It contains two sections of chansons, ff.1–119 and ff.148–158, with literary matter in between. Only the first section need concern us and that not for long: it is related to group *KNX* by the order of chansons, some 300, which are grouped according to composer but without actual attribution. Between f.95*v* and f.119 are seven chansons of Adam de la Halle interspersed haphazardly with others. That ff.1–119 are a planned sequence is suggested by the survival of very lightly written, early, binding letters and numbers (often the first four leaves are signed, e.g. *pi, pij, piij, piiij*). These gatherings start with 'e'; another sequence runs [i] to [xiv] with some numbers missing or clipped off. Each of these sequences ends at f.112*v* leaving one irregular '7' gathering (sewn 4 + 3), ff.113–119*v*, containing three of the Adam songs. The manuscript provides useful corroboration that Adam de la Halle's courtly chansons were not always put into a separate category from those of other composers.

Notation (Chart VII)

No very firm generalisations can be made on the basis of the seven Adam songs alone. The notation tends to align itself with *Pn* 1591 (*R*), rather than with other manuscripts, in a preference for single *plicas* and in the use of *c.o.p.* ligatures. Breves are occasionally written as rhombs, in the 'English' fashion. The *conjunctura* without a tailed head note is very common (4a).

★   ★   ★

This cursory examination of the main individual manuscripts containing the chansons of Adam de la Halle has, I hope, drawn attention to the existence of a genuinely diversified notational tradition for monophonic song. In the brief space that remains we shall consider a single chanson in all its versions. What, if anything, can be learnt about the meaning of the different styles of notation, or about the nature of the music they exist to convey, by the comparison of one melody with another from the nota-tional standpoint? The chansons of Adam are, in fact, a particularly suitable field in which to examine the question, for the reason that the ten chansonniers (*Pn* 1591 (*R*) sometimes excepted) present an unusually coherent and stable tradition in which, it is reasonable to assume, oral transmission, with its tendency to wider variation, played little part. If one wishes to compare notational styles, it is easier done when the basic melodic outline remains fairly constant. This the 'Adam' chansonniers provide. At the same time, notational and melodic concerns cannot be kept separate. It is essentially the nuances of a melodic style which we are trying to recapture. And on occasion it may be necessary to trespass outside the notational area.

One preliminary caution is perhaps not superfluous. The object of the exercise in hand is not to establish what Adam de la Halle originally wrote. Not that this would be a pointless exercise, though I am convinced it would be an unsuccessful one. (In passing, it may be questioned whether the unargued assumption of Coussemaker and Wilkins, that *Pn* 25566 (*W*) always contains the 'best' text of Adam's melodies, is always true.) The present object is to define a style, not to reconstitute a text. The scribes may not all of them all the time have been trying to notate precisely the same melody; but assuredly they are trying to convey a single style. They belong, with various degrees of centrality, to the same tradition.

As our main example we may take song 3, *Je n'ai autre retenanche* (see Chart X, Comparative Notational Chart). The nine surviving versions of the melody present the most striking skeletal similarity—that is to say, generally speaking notes of the same pitch are ranged over the same syllables in every manuscript. (Even the scribe of *Pn* 1591 (*R*) has made a tolerable shot at reproducing the standard melody. However, since there are substantial variants in phrases 3 and 6, his version will not be taken consistently into account.) There is one marked variation from the norm, in *AS* 657 (*A*): the variation appears to begin with a pitch error (mistaken clef) at 6.7; phrase 7 has at least the expected cadence, but after that the melody develops quite differently. *I-Rvat* 1490 (*a*) is aberrant and incorrect (the terms seem justified) in phrase 6; the copyist seems to have repeated part of phrase 5 (3–4) and then got into difficulties, ending with eight units for a 7-syllable line. In phrase 6 (evidently an unstable point) the reading of *Pn* 25566 (*W*) differs from all other manuscripts; there may be a pitch error, 6.1–2.[15]

The notation of the melodies, however, presents the kind of diversity which we should by now expect. The most stable elements in phrase 1, for example are symbols 3 and 5, the only single notes; but the 'long' of one manuscript is contradicted by the 'breve' of another. The two *conjuncturae* (1.3, 8) are melodically identical in all sources but are recorded in a wide variety of *conjunctura* and *climacus* figures, with preference for the former. One should hesitate before calling every notational symbol in this group an 'equivalent' to all the others. The term I prefer and shall use is 'correspondence'. However, it does appear likely that, with the possible exception of the *plica* figures at 1.2 in *Pn* 847 (*P*) and 25566 [*Wx*], these ways of notating the 'descending three' are identical in meaning and distinct only graphically. Whether the *scandicus* of 1.6 comes into the same category is hard to say; it could be that the *c.o.p.* forms in *AS* 657 (*A*) and *Pn* 1109 (*Q*) indicate a rhythmic nuance. *I-Rvat* 1490 (*a*), also, has an unusual symbol at this point.

'Equivalence' should certainly not be assumed with regard to the *plicas* at 1.1 and 1.7. These 'corresponding' double and single *plicas* (not to mention the compound *plica* of *a*) may well represent slightly different renderings of the two-note descent, or at least be different 'ways of putting it'. These correspondences do not in themselves tell us anything definite about the nature of the *plica*, though the prevalence of the double *plica* in some sources strongly suggests that a lengthening, or weighting, of the main note was an essential part of it. What the comparative notational chart does, however, make absolutely clear is that a descending *plica* is something quite different not only in theory but in practice from a descending two-note ligature (or *clivis*). The correspondences in this and in other chansons are decisive. A *plica* often 'corresponds' to a single note; it very rarely 'corresponds' to a ligature. The agreed *podatus* symbols at 1.4, 3.4, 2.6, 4.6 etc. are instructive. The symbol at 7.6 varies between *climacus* and *clivis*; but a *plica* is inadmissible, it seems. The situation as regards the compound *plica* at 11.3 is similar: a two-note ligature simple may correspond to the *ligature plicata* (see *a*), but in no source is the third note an ordinary note.

Examples could be multiplied. But the evidence is clear. The *conjunctura* is not treated as a special sign; the *plica* almost invariably is. For this reason, if for no other, it is particularly unfortunate that the most recent edition of Adam's chansons should completely ignore the existence of the *plica* and treat it as an ordinary note in ligature. There is, of course, a further reason why the *plica* should always be clearly indicated in modern transcription, and that is because it involves a note of indeterminate pitch. In Adam de la Halle the problem is generally of fairly easy solution, since, as song 3 shows, *plicas* are most often attached to notes conjunct to each other or at the interval of a 3rd—though in the first instance the editor has to decide whether to take the *plica*-note *below* the next main note (e.g. A *F* G) or to give it an anticipatory function (A *G* G).

Monsignor Anglès in a special study of the meaning of the *plica* in medieval music came to the conclusion that 'der rhythmische Wert der Plika, so wie sie die spanischen Kopisten verwenden, ist der einer gewöhnlicher Note schlechthin mit demselben rhythmischen Wert wie die Hauptnote, von der sie abhängt'.[16] In the case of the 'Adam' chansonniers, admittedly a very much smaller corpus of melodies, exactly the opposite appears to be the case—it does not have a 'normal' value. And the suggestion which Anglès makes about the Las Huelgas Codex (*E-BUlh*), that the scribes adopted the *plica* as a purely scribal convenience, certainly does not apply to these French chansons. Probably a clear distinction needs to be made, in discussing this, between *plica* usage in monophonic and in polyphonic sources.

There are, I am conscious, several aspects of manuscript presentation which I have not touched on at all and for which no space is available—in particular the problems of transposed melodies and of manuscript accidentals, neither of which are quite so transparently 'non-problems' as one might deduce from the latest edition.

However, the foregoing descriptions and analyses do, I hope, give an increased depth to the study of Adam de la Halle's chansons. The discussion has centred on two questions: (1) the relationship of his chansons, as physical objects in a manuscript, to the other material of the manuscript; and (2) the notational presentation of the chansons by the different scribes. Findings in relation to the first question chiefly confirm and amplify those of Schwan (1886) who first described the comparatively circumscribed and self-contained group of 'Adam' chansonniers.[17] Their isolation and general close agreement emphasise the sense which contemporaries must have had of Adam de la Halle as a special figure amongst the trouvères; they also testify in their number and general fineness to the high estimation in which, around the turn of the 13th century and into the 14th, the elaborate and sophisticated art of courtly monophony was still held. That the group is comparatively self-contained, should make us cautious in generalising too freely about trouvère song on their sole basis—though it is fairly evident that Adam's chansons were not felt by his contemporaries to be a new departure in any important sense. That the group is also comparatively late, as it seems, gives it again a special, but not a less important, significance.

The second question, concerning manuscript notations, opens up issues which have neither in relation to Adam de la Halle, nor more generally, been much treated. My main concern has been to suggest that the notation itself has a validity and a significance beyond the simple provision of note pitches and note groups. It is, of course, easier to assert the notion of inherent notational validity than to define wherein the validity lies. However, the following tentative observations may be made.

The first and simplest observation is that, in these sources at least, the *plica* is in no sense an optional extra or an alternative method of writing a note which might just as well have been written in ligature. It is what the theorists say it is, a special kind of note, and the one which by many scribes is the most diversely used of all. It belongs to the analysis of melodic style rather than of notation to observe that melodically the *plica* has a 'concording' or 'harmonizing' function; it glides over gaps. But the extensive use of double and compound *plicas* may lend some support to the view that the notation itself suggests a type of *repercussio*, whether *gutturis* or of some other organ.

Secondly, the notations seen in their manuscript and general historical context give apparently clear indication that the scribes were positively *avoiding* clear mensural patterns and metrical schemes composed of long and short notes measured in strict proportion. Some of the 'Adam' chansonniers are palpably late in the tradition; many of the scribes are evidently acquainted with some form of mensural notation. One's sense of a consciously adopted notational style receives the strongest confirmation from the 'Complete Works' chansonnier: *Pn* 25566 (*W*) juxtaposes, in a carefully planned, homogeneous collection, non-mensural courtly chansons with mensurally notated *monophonic* music (the *refrains* of *Robin et Marion* and of *Renart nouvel*), to say nothing of the polyphonic pieces. This is not to say that the chanson notation totally excludes symbols which may in some contexts have a rhythmic, or even a durational, suggestiveness—some 'longs' and 'breves', ligatures *c.o.p.*, double *plicas*, a few extensive ligatures forming melismas to a single syllable. But the main contrast is clear.

Thirdly, the theory, the hypothesis, that courtly monody rests essentially on *number*, syllable-and-note-group-counting, gets the strongest visual support from the manuscript presentation of the chansons. Every source (except *Pn* 1591 (*R*) in the scribe's more aberrant moments) exercises a care so precise and so successful that it has scarcely been necessary to mention it in the above discussion. What we see before us is a visually striking, unwaveringly *unitary*, syllable-by-syllable presentation of the melody. That this suggests roughly equal units more strongly than any precisely metrical or patterned combination and supports 'iso-syllabism' rather than 'modal rhythm' is, I think, temptingly obvious. Temptingly, because we must not expect too much from notation; there are too many 'lost traditions' for that. And in the end we may have in certain matters to rely on our sense of style to interpret the notation as much as we rely on the notation to 'give' us the style.[18] But visual evidence *is* evidence. Notation is not simply an intellectual code.

Finally, there is one general observation about the musical style of Adam's chansons to which, as I see it, a detailed study of the notation does inevitably lead. From a close examination of the notational practices of the different scribes (and they *are* all different) there emerges a positive picture of diversity, versatility and inventiveness, carried sometimes to the point of eccentricity. It is by no means unusual for a single scribe to employ 40 or 50 distinguishable symbols; a modern editor will use perhaps a dozen. This versatility, which it is difficult, if not impossible, to convey in a modern edition, conveys more vividly than anything else the sense of a melodic style *très nuancée*, flexible, elusive, not easy to pin down in a precisely conceived scheme of consistent note values. It is through the original notation that we can glimpse the nature of the difficulty, the size of the gap between written record and living performance. It is, I believe, naive and unhistorical to assume that there is here simply either an abstruse puzzle of which the solution has eluded us, or on the other hand mere 'primitive' notational inadequacy. In this respect at least—'le style, c'est la notation'.

NOTATIONAL CHARTS

In the following charts precise graphic reproduction has not been aimed at; there is, of course, much variety of penmanship in the manuscripts. By 'double' *plica* is meant a *plica* sign in which two notes are written at the same pitch. By 'compound' *plica* is meant a note-group or ligature to which a *plica*-sign is attached. A question mark means that there is doubt what the scribe intended or what the symbol means. Square brackets enclose a symbol which is referred to in the text but which does not occur in Adam de la Halle's chansons.

In Chart X, each 'bar' represents a phrase of the song. References to it in the text in the form '6.1–2' mean 'phrase 6, note-groups (= syllables) 1–2'.

Chart I

		a	b	c	d	e	f	g	h	j	k
1	Plica single										
2	double										
3	compound										? 4e
4	Conjunctura & climacus										
5	Ligature c.o.p.										
6	Scandicus										
7	Podatus										
8	Clivis										
9	Torculus										
10	Porrectus										
11	Other forms										

Chart II

		a	b	c	d	e	f	g	h	j	k
1	Plica single										
2	double										
3	compound										
4	Conjunctura & climacus										
5	Scandicus										
6	Podatus		?10a								
7	Clivis										
8	Porrectus										
9	Torculus										
10	Ligature c.o.p										
11	Other forms										

Chart III

		a	b	c	d	e	f	g	h	j	k	l	m	n
1	Plica single													
2	double				?									
3	compound			?	ꞈ=4c					?+k				
4	Conjunctura & climacus													
5	Scandicus													
6	Podatus													
7	Clivis													
8	Ligature c.o.p.		?											
9	Torculus													
10	Porrectus													
11	Other forms													

Chart IV

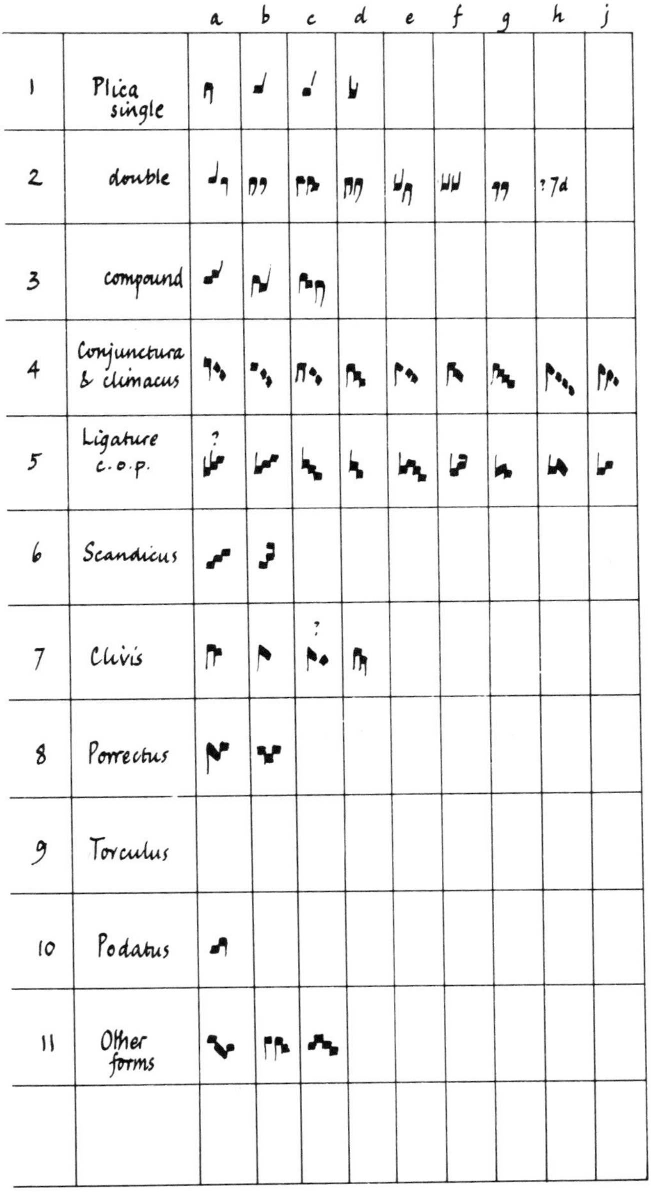
a b c d e f g h j
1 Plica single
2 double
3 compound
4 Conjunctura & climacus
5 Ligature c.o.p.
6 Scandicus
7 Clivis
8 Porrectus
9 Torculus
10 Podatus
11 Other forms

Chart V

		a	b	c	d	e	f	g	h	j	k	l	m	n	o	p
1	Plica single															
2	double	none														
3	compound		? 6c													
4	Conjunctura & climacus															
5	Scandicus			?												
6	Podatus			?												
7	Clivis						?									
8	'Long' & 'Breve'	12 d														
9	Ligature c.o.p.															
10	Torculus															
11	Porrectus															
12	other forms	?	? 4b													

Chart VI

		a	b	c	d	e	f	g	h
1	Plica single	♩	♫	♩	♫ (?)	♩ (?)	♭		
2	double	♫♫	♫♫	♫♫	♫♩	♫♫			
3	compound	♫♫	♩♩	♫♩	♫♫ (?)	♫			
4	Conjunctura & Climacus	♫♩	♩••	♩••	♩•••	♩••	♩••	♩••	♩•••
5	Scandicus	♩							
6	Podatus	♩	♩						
7	Clivis	♩	♩						
8	'long' & 'breve'								
9	Ligature c. o. p								
10	Torculus								
11	Porrectus	♩	♩						
12	Other forms	♫							

Chart VII

		a	b	c	d	e	f	g	h
1	Plica single								
2	double								
3	compound								
4	Conjunctura & climacus								
5	Scandicus								
6	Podatus								
7	Clivis								
8	Ligature c.o.p.								
9	Torculus								
10	Porrectus								
11	other forms								
12	'Long' & 'breve'								

Chart VIII

		a	b	c	d	e	f	g	h	j	k	l	m	n	o
1	Plica single														
2	double														
3	compound														9c
4	Conjunctura & climacus		cancelled				cancelled			Song 20					
5	Scandicus														
6	Podatus														
7	Clivis														
8	'Long' & 'Breve'	all thro' 20													
9	Ligature c.o.p.														
10	Torculus														
11	Porrectus														
12	Other forms														

Chart IX

		a	b	c	d	e	f	g	h	j	k	l	m	n	o
1	Plica single				?	?									
2	double														
3	compound					cancelled						?			? ?=4k
4	Conjunctura & climacus									?					
5	Scandicus														
6	Podatus														
7	Clivis														
8	'Long' & 'Breve'														
9	Ligature c.o.p.														
10	Torculus														
11	Porrectus														
12	Other forms														

NOTES TO CHAPTER 1

1.   G. Raynaud: *Bibliographie des altfranzösischen Liedes*, rev. and enlarged H. Spanke (Leiden, 1955), which is a revision of vol.ii of G. Raynaud: *Bibliographie des chansonniers français des XIIIe et XIVe siècles* (Paris, 1884). I have given a separate *siglum, Wx,* to the short, incomplete chansonnier which is bound in with *W*.

2.   A. Jeanroy: *Bibliographie sommaire des chansonniers français du moyen âge (manuscrits et editions)* (Paris, 1918/R1965).

3.   Since this paragraph was written, the monumental study by B. Stäblein, *Schriftbild der einstimmigen Musik*, Musikgeschichte in Bildern, iii/4 (Leipzig, 1975), has become available. Since the book covers all monophonic notations, liturgical as well as secular, only a small amount of space could be spared for trouvère notations, but the context provided is invaluable.

4.   H. van der Werf: *The Chansons of the Troubadours and Trouvères: a Study of the Melodies and their Relation to the Poems* (Utrecht, 1972), see especially chap.2, 'Written and oral traditions'. It is one of the gaps in van der Werf's most useful study that he does not discuss the individual notations so as to bring out their relevance to this issue. On oral and written traditions more generally, see W. Wiora, *The Four Ages of Music* (New York, 1965). The discussion by Patricia Carpenter, Leo Treitler and others about 'the musical object', in *Current Musicology*, v (1967), 49–115, vi (1968), 85–126, bears interestingly on the theoretical and aesthetic problem.

5.   Van der Werf, p.29.

6.   A. Jeanroy: *Le chansonnier d'Arras: reproduction en phototypie* (Paris, 1925). The chansonniers used for the present article are described in varying degrees of detail by Jeanroy (1918) (see F. Gennrich's review in *Zeitschrift für romanische Philologie*, xli (1921), 294–346); Raynaud (1884); Raynaud (1955); E. Schwan: *Die altfranzösischen Liederhandschriften* (Berlin, 1886); G. Reaney in *RISM*, B/IV/1 (1966) (manuscripts containing polyphony only). I have not thought it necessary to give precise references to these standard works for each chansonnier.

7.   Throughout the article I use a mixed terminology. The compound ligatures are referred to by their more precise plainsong names: *podatus, climacus,* etc. But I refer to 'long' and 'breve' rather than to *virga* and *punctum*, and to *plica* rather than to 'liquescent'.

8.   For simplicity's sake I speak throughout as if the particular scribe were personally responsible for individualities in the notation, e.g. 'he has simplified the double *plica* . . .'. This may, of course, be strictly true in the literal sense; it is more likely that the scribe has been copying a manuscript, or following a tradition of notating, in which double *plicas* are simplified as described. The main argument is not affected: at some time or other the diverse notational symbols must have been invented by someone.

9.   N. H. J. van den Boogaard: *Rondeaux et Refrains, du xiie. siècle au début du xive.* (Paris, 1969).

10.   The CMM editor in his 'Table of Manuscript Sources' helps to perpetuate the misleading assumption that the two chansonniers are integrally connected. The distinction between them is not mentioned.

11.   J. Schubert: *Die Handschrift Paris BN fr 1591: Kritische Untersuchung* (Frankfurt am Main, 1963). His valuable detailed description of the manuscript from many points of view appears to rest on the assumption of a literary, written, and not of a mixed written and oral tradition. His primary interest is in the analysis of repertory, based on musical as well as literary evidence; the manuscript was put together from numerous repertories, he concludes, with miscellaneous additions. Studies of similar depth and detail are needed for all the chansonniers.

12.   Schubert believes (see p.183) that the scribe of *Pn* 1591 (*R*) was in fact making his collection of Adam's chansons from miscellaneous sources which formed the basis of *Pn* 25566 (*W*) and *Pn* 1591 (*P*).

13.   Schubert (p.179) suggests that the 'reliable' MSS from which the verbal texts were taken may in some cases have ceased to be available at the stage of music-copying.

14.   *GB-Ob* Douce 308 (*I*) is one of several examples of 'literary' chansonniers for which music was never intended.

15.   The variations and errors described above are not noted in the CMM edition.

16.   H. Anglès: 'Die Bedeutung der Plika in der mittelalterlichen Musik', *Festschrift Karl Gustav Fellerer zum 60. Geburtstag* (Regensburg, 1962), 28–39.

17.   Schwan, 223–6. The discussion is very brief and concentrates on the order of the chansons within the manuscripts.

18.   In a paper, ' "La grande chanson courtoise": the Songs of Adam de la Halle', *PRMA*, ci (1974–5), 11–30, I have attempted to set out some of the evidence on which an 'aesthetic' of the courtly style might be based.

2

Rota versatilis—towards a reconstruction

Margaret Bent

The legend of St Katherine of Alexandria relates how the saint escaped unharmed from the wheel to which she was bound, while the wheel itself was fragmented and caused fatal injury to onlookers. The turning wheel of fate has wrought more orthodox damage on the composition which forms the subject of this paper, one of the most interesting and ambitious of English compositions of the period c1300 and of all medieval musical offerings to this saint. Thus, the musical substance has survived its ordeals less well than she did hers. The following study of it is offered here in gratitude for the life of Bob Dart by one whose debt to him is complex and abiding, and who sorely misses the pleasure of sharing with him musical jigsaws such as the present, which was among the last pieces of work that she discussed with him.

The temptation to present the material in the order of discovery is strong, but clarity will be better served by a brief description of the partially-reconstructed composition. It is not a *rota*, as the incipit might lead one to hope or expect (the first three sections begin with the words 'Rota', 'Orbis' and 'Rota'), but a large-scale, five-section rondellus for two voices accompanied by a supporting pair of apparently freely-composed tenors. It survives in two distinct versions in four different sources, all fragmentary, and the problems of determining its authentic form and rhythmic details arise from two particular considerations, both also with 'round' elements: these are the format of the sources, one of which was probably a *rotulus* (i.e. a roll of parchment), and the notation, particularly the interpretation of the *signa rotunda*. In the full (and probably original) form, the two lower parts (III and IV in the transcription at the end of this study) state and repeat their material in each of the five sections. Occupying as they do ranges about a 5th apart, they do not employ voice-exchange for the repeats. The upper parts (I and II) do exchange material, together with text or wordless melisma, for each repeat. (The repeats are not written out in the transcription.) Each voice therefore sings text and melisma alternately, and in opposite phase to the other. Each of the five sections has a different and self-consistent syllable count and rhyme scheme. This is paralleled by a different and consistent rhythmical treatment in the music of each section, using changes of rhythmic mode and a steady progress from the use of duplex longs in the first section to groups of two or three semibreves in the last. Firm criteria for the interpretation of these semibreve groups are lacking: this problem will be discussed further below.

The five sections will henceforth be referred to by their opening words: 'Rota versatilis', 'Orbis dominatio', 'Rota Katerine', 'Katerina spe' and 'Virgo perduxerat'. An edition of the piece is supplied at the end of the chapter, and this is preceded by the full text with translation and commentary by Roger Bowers.

The manuscript *GB-Lbm* Royal 12 C VI is a collection of musical and miscellaneous treatises from the Benedictine Abbey of Bury St Edmunds, written in various hands of the 13th and 14th centuries, and including the only surviving medieval copy of the 13th-century treatise of Anonymous IV.[1] A 15th-century list of contents includes nearly half the surviving treatises in the volume (more, if 'tractus (*sic*) de musica' embraces more than one of the musical items), and names a few others which do not correspond with the present contents. One of these was entitled *Modus componendi rotam versatilem*, and its loss is especially regrettable in that it deprives us of the opportunity to set what may have been a unique testimony to compositional procedure beside the composition of this name, itself with many unique features, which now survives in three incomplete sources and is quoted in a fourth. It might in addition have cast light on the problems raised by these sources, of which some description now follows.

Two of them were known to Bukofzer and Handschin,[2] though it appears from their comments that neither scholar progressed very far with a transcription. Handschin reports of the piece that 'two voices of it are preserved in B.M. Add.24198 and (as Bukofzer adds) fragments of a third voice in B.M. Add.40011B'. The entry in *RISM*, B/IV/1 for the former manuscript lightly camouflages the title as *Rosa versaulis*, under which misreading the concordance in *Ob* 652 is also reported.

GB-Lbm Add.24198

This is an early 14th-century Augustinian missal from St Thomas', Dublin, preserving contemporary copies of motets (I shall use the term here loosely to include conductus and rondellus compositions) on its three flyleaves, which are evidently from a substantial collection arranged in alphabetical order, as was observed by Levy.[3] It may be in place to give here an inventory and amplification of the evidence for alphabetical organization (which is used also in another manuscript from St Thomas', Dublin, a set of sequences in the Dublin Troper, *GB-Cu* Add.710):

Folio	Music	Heading
132r	*Rota versatilis*, voices II and IV (concordances discussed below)	blue 'VI'
132v (below)	*Rosa mundi*, voice I only *Regis aula*, voice I only (II and T in *US-PRu*)	red 'R'
133r	*Surgere jam est hora*, voices II? and T	blue 'VIII'
133v-1r (below)	*Trinitatem veneremur/Trinitas et deitas/Trinitatis vox* [Tenor] *Te domina regina/Te domina Maria* [Tenor]	133v: red 'T' 1r: blue 'I'(?) erased, red 'II' replacing it.
1v	*Triumphat hodie*/[Tenors] *Trop est fol*/[*Si que la nuit*] (I and III only in *GB-Onc:* the highly profane French song is evidently divided between the supporting voices in the musical alternation: A B A B A	red 'T'

A B A B A
ending with textless melisma incorporating A, varied)

F.132 is here placed before f.133 because of the alphabetical pattern established by the originally adjacent ff.133–1. The present foliation preserves the correct status of rectos and versos.

In the headings, the placing of red letters on each verso draws attention to the alphabetical arrangement. The blue Roman numerals must apply to each folio or motet in a separate sequence for each letter of the alphabet and not to the entire collection, the 'VIII' on 133r immediately preceding the 'I' (or 'II') on 1r. The folio facing f.132v would therefore have carried a blue 'VIII' unless, as did f.1r, it needed correction. There must therefore have been at least eight motets commencing with 'R', eight with 'S' and at least two with 'T'. This suggests a collection, even if not with eight for each letter of the alphabet, probably of 100 compositions or more.

The two compositions on ff.133v-1r are complete. A third, *Triumphat hodie*, acquires its complementary tenor part from *GB-Onc* 362, though layout of the two incomplete sources does raise the question as to whether another upper voice might also be lacking. *Regis aula* has some additional matter in *US-PRu* Garrett 119, and the partial reconstruction of *Rota versatilis* is the subject of the present discussion.

The voice of *Rota versatilis* (Plate I) that I have called II is an upper part with melismatic passages (provided with rubricated textual cues) alternating with (black-) texted portions. Contrary to the expectations stated at the beginning of this article, the alternating sections do not coincide; neither can their music be superimposed. This is true of the first four sections. The fifth, however, has a normal rondellus double statement: this section, 'Virgo perduxerat', begins without further text, following with a fully texted part with different music. These two voices can be successfully superimposed. The tenor correspondingly has a single statement for each of the first four sections and a written-out repeat for the fifth. The missing facing page presumably contained the other two voices, I and III, in a similar version. Fig. 1 shows the contents of this version as it

Fig. 1 *Lbm* Add. 24198   ⌇⌇⌇ text   ——— no text

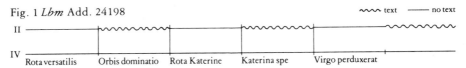

II ——————————
IV ——————————
  Rota versatilis   Orbis dominatio   Rota Katerine   Katerina spe   Virgo perduxerat

has survived here: it appears to be an abbreviated one dispensing with all rondellus repeats except the last. Assuming the presence of the missing page, a complete rondellus performance would oblige the singers of the upper voices to read their music in the order of the numbers below (T = text, M = melisma):

	Verso		*Recto*
1M	'Rota versatilis' text	1T	'Rota versatilis' melisma
2M	'Orbis dominatio' melisma	2T	'Orbis dominatio' text
3T	'Rota Katerine' text	3M	'Rota Katerine' melisma
4M	'Katerina spe' melisma	4T	'Katerina spe' text
5T	'Virgo perduxerat' text	5M	'Virgo perduxerat' melisma
5M	'Virgo perduxerat' melisma	5T	'Virgo perduxerat' text

I: 1T, 1M, 2T, 2M, 3T, 3M, 4T, 4M, 5T, 5M
II: 1M, 1T, 2M, 2T, 3M, 3T, 4M, 4T, 5M, 5T

It is not easy to understand why the material for the final section, 'Virgo perduxerat', should be thus duplicated if the facility for switching pages in the above manner were expected for the other sections. It is this consideration which leads me to think that this copy was made for shortened

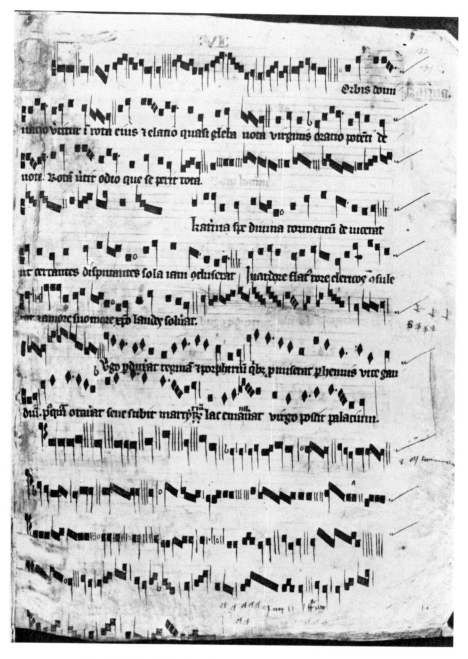

Plate I *GB-Lbm* Add. 24198, f.132*r*: voices II and IV of *Rota versatilis*.

performance, although full rondellus is not precluded. A closely analogous situation exists in another extended rondellus, *Hostis Herodes impie* in *GB-Ob* Hatton 81, whose form and layout correspond to the first four double sections of *Rota versatilis* in fig.1. (There is no fifth section and no musical duplication.) It may be more than coincidental that this formal problem affects two of the longest surviving rondellus compositions. The apparently shortened form adopted in both cases may be due to the practical expedient of accommodating the entire composition on a single opening of the manuscript (the other, fully notated, Hatton rondelli are discussed below), or it may reflect contemporary judgment that full performance was in some cases too long. The existence of other provisions for *Rota*, now to be discussed, offers some support for this view.

GB-Ob Bodley 652

This is a manuscript of miscellaneous contents having two musical endpapers: each present bifolium was a single leaf, folded and stitched along the spine of the book. Each was originally pasted to the cover boards of a late medieval binding preceding the present post-medieval one. The front bifolium is now numbered i-ii, and the back pair 69–70. The contents are as follows:

Folio	Music
69r–70v	*Rota versatilis* (end of II, start of IV)
ir–iiv	The rest of IV
(below)	*Rex sanctorum angelorum* (?I only)
iv–iir	*Regina celestium* (II and T)
	—upside down
(below)	*Salve sancta virgula/Salve sancta parens* (?I and T)
	—also upside down
70r–69v	. . . *rogativam potuit* . . . *naturalibus* (end of ?I only)
(below)	*Benedicamus domino* (I and first half of II)

Despite the presence of incipits with 'R' and 'S', there is no evidence of alphabetical arrangement for this source.

Assuming that the two sides of *Rota versatilis* (see Plates II–III) were the same way up, the music on the verso of the second (i.e. on iv–iir) is upside down in relation to the other three sides. This reinforces certain problems about the format of this source to which I shall return after other questions about the rondellus have been aired.

Ff.ir–iiv (Plate III) contain, as stated, most of the upper voice and one stave of voice IV, the same voices as those preserved in *Lbm* 24198, but differ from them in presenting a full rondellus version. Each tenor statement, for each of the five sections, is written out twice in identical form. Voice II survives only imperfectly, complete from near the end of the second section, giving first a melismatic and then a texted passage for each section. Successive performance of the two passages in each section is clearly envisaged, as it equally clearly was not for *Lbm* 24198: the missing voice I, which would have duplicated this music in alternating phase, can be supplied by superimposition for *Rota Katerine* and *Katerina spe* (see fig.2).

Fig. 2 *Ob* 652

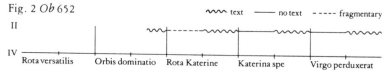

None of the other music in this fragment is known from any other sources and only the fragmentary triplum . . . *rogativam potuit* . . . is notationally akin to our rondellus, using groups of two or three semibreves marked off by dots.

GB-Lbm Add.40011B (*LoF*)

Of similar date, but a source to which this piece was a later addition, is the set of parchment strips mounted in this source together with the more famous paper leaves a century younger in date known as 'the' Fountains fragment. The strips served as spine reinforcements to the same 15th-century Fountains memoranda book for which the later paper leaves provided cover padding. Both sets are described in the introduction to a forthcoming facsimile of all three Fountains fragments to be published by the Boethius Press. The fragments of an upper voice of *Rota versatilis* on strips 6*v* and 7*v* (Plate IV, upper pair; noted by Bukofzer[4]) appear at first sight to complement that in *Lbm* 24198 (they are shown in Fig.3). A short

Fig. 3 *Lbm* 40011B

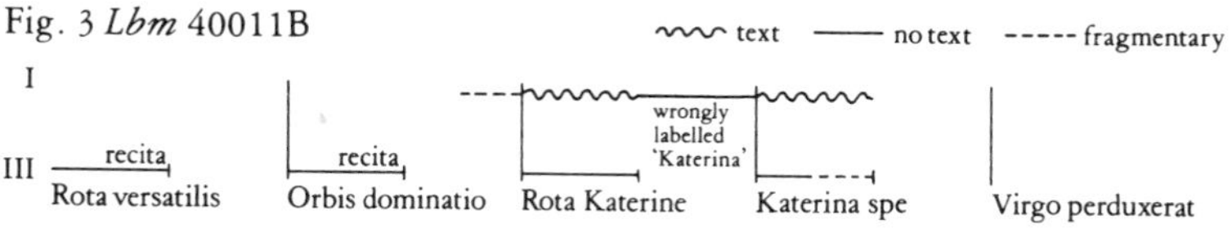

and fragmentary textless portion appears to fit with the end of the texted 'Orbis dominatio' of *Lbm* 24198, and it is followed by a texted section, 'Rota Katerine' (identical with the same passage in *Ob* 652) which

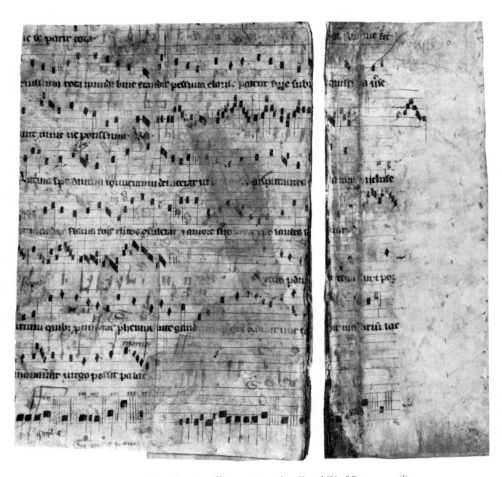

Plate II *GB-Ob* Bodley 652, ff.69r—70v: voices II and IV of *Rota versatilis*.

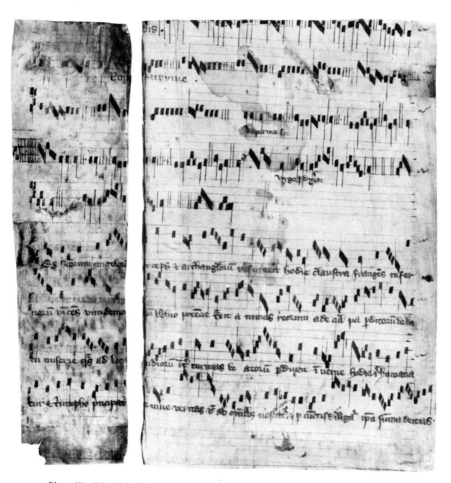

Plate III *GB-Ob* Bodley 652, ff.ir—iiv: voice IV of *Rota versatilis* and ?1 of
Rex sanctorum angelorum.

complements the melisma over that cue in *Lbm* 24198 (imperfectly preserved in *Ob* 652). The next section, labelled 'Katerina' but otherwise textless, is identical with the 'Rota Katerine' melisma in *Lbm* 24198 and *Ob* 652: it does not fit with the other music for 'Katerina spe', and the only possible inference is that the wrong text cue has been given— 'Katerina' should read 'Rota Katerine'. This 'error' may be significant for the original form of the piece and will be taken up later. The last section preserved on these fragments is musically identical with the texted 'Katerina spe' of the other two sources, though any text has now been cut away. This voice is clearly in opposite phase to voice II in *Ob* 652 (and as preserved in shortened form in *Lbm* 24198). Since it gives texted followed by melismatic portions for each tenor section, it corresponds to voice I of a rondellus: voice II, when written in full as in *Ob* 652, gives melismatic followed by texted portions. This confirms that two separately written top voices, re-ordering the same musical material, did exist for this piece, in addition to the short version preserved in *Lbm* 24198.

The Fountains fragment makes yet a further important and hitherto unrecognised contribution to this reconstruction. It preserves, on strips 4*v*-5*v* (Plate IV, lower pair), the upper tenor part (III) from the beginning to the end of the section 'Katerina spe', though completely devoid of any textual clues. This fits perfectly with voice IV as preserved in *Lbm* 24198.[5] The wrongly-labelled 'Katerina' melisma in voice I has no corresponding section in voice III: for the four sections for which the lower voice survives, wholly or partially, only one statement is provided for each. This version was, however, a full-length one (not truncated) as confirmed musically by voice I and in voice III by the word *recita* placed at the end of each of the first two sections to indicate repetition. (It is missing for the third statement, and thereafter the manuscript is cut away.) Lines have been drawn to indicate the precise point from which the repeat is effective.

This word *recita* is used elsewhere: on fragment 8 before the incipits 'Formosa' and 'Christiana'. The word is twice used in *GB-DRc* C.I.20, in both cases for pieces (not rondelli) with concordances. *Barrabas dimittitur* has the tenor *Babilonis flumina* stated once, embodying three isorhythmic taleae. Three-and-one-third statements of this tenor are required for the motet. The incomplete concordance in *Ob* E.Mus.7 has no indication of the repeat, apparently, while *DRc* has *recita*. *Orto sole serene* requires four statements of its tenor, marked *recita*: in *GB-Cgc* 543/512 the tenor is written out in full. *Recita* is also used in *Ob* Hatton 81 for the tenor parts of two fully-notated rondelli, *A solis ortus cardine* and *Ovet mundus*. In the latter, which survives complete, Harrison comments that 'each of the

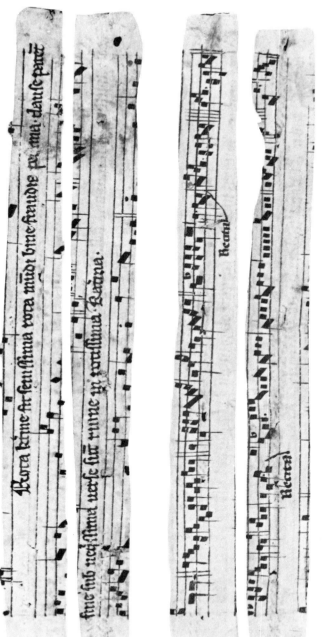

Plate IV *GB-Lbm* Add.40011B, binding strips, ff.6v/7v (upper) and ff.4v/5v (lower): fragments of *Rota versatilis*.

two verses of the poem is repeated with interchange of the two upper parts and simple repeat, marked *recita* in the manuscript, of the two lower parts, which are wordless'." He did not actually point out that the former piece, although lacking its facing verso page, permits reconstruction of the rondellus between the upper voices by virtue of being written out in full. It now lacks only the upper of the two tenor parts (corresponding to the 'quatruplex' of *Ovet mundus*).

Moreover, this 'new' rondellus bears very striking resemblances to *Ovet mundus*. In addition to being its structural twin, notated in the same manner, the part ranges are identical, they share tenor contour, melodic motifs and second-mode rhythms, and both are concerned with Christmas and have affinities of text. Further examination of the use of plainsong paraphrase (noted by Harrison) may indicate whether the two rondelli in fact form a single composition, or whether they are related constituents of a Christmas/Epiphany cycle which could also include *Hostis Herodes*—the three pieces are on three consecutive openings. If *Ovet mundus* does turn out to be simply the latter half, or final section, of a longer rondellus, the arguments below based on the otherwise evident English preference for accommodating a whole composition on a single opening would lose weight, especially in view of the presence of the economically notated *Hostis Herodes* in the same source. The words 'Hostis Herodes' begin the second 'half' of an alphabetical hymn by Sedulius of which *A solis ortus* is the opening. The Hatton texts do not maintain identity with the hymn. The two compositions, moreover, are separated by *Ovet mundus* and are differently notated, which leaves little room for postulating a closer link between them.

All uses of *recita* have in common that the tenor has to be repeated in order to fit the upper voices as written in that source. It is not used in any case where the upper voices are presented in curtailed form, and where repetition, if envisaged at all, is practically laborious and in no sense mandatory.

Lbm Add.4909 (= Partial Copy of *Lbm* Cotton Tiberius B IX)

A final source contributes another tiny but important fragment of music. It is a music example in the treatise of Robertus de Handlo, whose *explicit* carries the date 1326. This seems a plausible date and can be accepted provisionally as a *terminus non post quem* for this composition. The significance of even an approximate date for a single piece within a repertory virtually devoid of such clues need not be spelt out. The example comprises the opening of the missing top voice, adding two words to those used as identifying incipits in the other sources. The passage is misprinted by Coussemaker without its caption. The medieval source, *Lbm* Cotton Tiberius B IX, was burned in the Cotton fire of 1731, removing all trace of Handlo's treatise.[x] We have it only in the early 18th-century transcript, *Lbm* Add.4909, ff.1–11, made for Pepusch—an improvement on Coussemaker's version, although still apparently corrupt (see fig.4).

Fig. 4

Assuming a missing duplex long rest at the beginning, two errors then have to be assumed in order to achieve a satisfactory fit with the other parts. The last three single breves, g', f', e', make rhythmic sense as they stand: but they fit better if the second is assumed to be a long (ex.1*a*). The other problem is the first ligature. If the opening is transcribed as in ex. 1*b*, it disturbs the first-mode pattern that is otherwise used exclusively in this section, and requires the only use of an altered breve. The last note of the ligature is slightly detached: my inclination is to assume that this note was long, either as a separate stemmed note or as the final of a ligature with its head reverted (ex.1*c*). There are, of course, other less credible possibilities.

Ex. 1

In Dittmer's translation of this theorist, this is one of the places where he substitutes 'comparable [examples] which better illustrate the text'. He appears not to have consulted the manuscript source.[9]

The paragraph preceding this music example states that longs may be mixed with breves or with major or minor semibreves, but not with minims or *minorate*. Breves may be mixed with duplex longs, with semibreves and oblique figures, thus:—and here follows the example. (The problem seems to be that the example relates to the earlier sentence but not to the latter. The reader might perhaps have been expected to know that duplex longs occur in the lower voices at this point. I cannot recall any other case from this period of a melodic example in a treatise standing also for its accompanying polyphonic voices.) The next clause permits the imperfection of a duplex long by a breve, which is called for in all other surviving voices of this section.

Fig. 5 shows how the various surviving portions of the rondellus fit together, and hence how much can be reconstructed by the superimposition of complementary material.

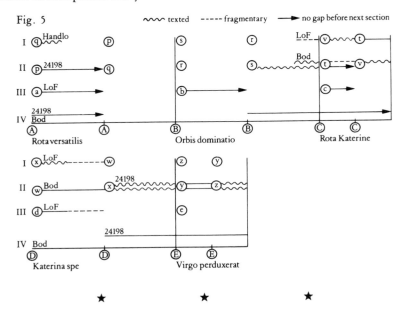

Fig. 5

The notation is for the most part orthodox post-Franconian, while retaining many graphic features of modal arrangement in its *sine littera* writing. The *similis ante similem* rule, whereby a note may not be imperfected if it is followed by another of the same denomination, is strictly observed between breves and longs, and there are no irregular ligatures, except possibly in the Handlo excerpt. The interpretation is self-evident, with a few exceptions. The first of these concerns the probably corrupt transmission of the opening, discussed above. The second relates to the evaluation of semibreve groups of two or three, one of the main areas of ambiguity in this period of English music. The third involves the use of a special sign, the *parvulus circulus* or *signum rotundum*.

Various English sources, both theoretical and practical, use a small circle from *c*1300, most commonly to clarify values smaller than a minor (i.e. unaltered) semibreve. *Rota versatilis* does not divide the breve beyond three, and this interpretation of the sign cannot therefore apply. It also seems unlikely that the circle implies changes to *tempus perfectum* from *tempus imperfectum*: Hanboys describes this as modern usage later in the century, and, in addition, the affected passages in *Rota versatilis* are concerned little or not at all with semibreves. It makes no sense to treat the passages in this way. (The unique usage of small circles in the Roberts-bridge manuscript (*Lbm* Add.28550) also throws no light on the interpretation of those in the present composition.)

Three distinct uses of the circle are evident in the sources of *Rota*:

(1) This can be eliminated from further discussion at once. The small circle with oblique stroke through it in *Ob* 652 is used simply to identify and place portions omitted by the scribe. One passage in voice II and one in voice IV was omitted, both in the section 'Katerina spe' (though not simultaneously), and both are readily explicable cases of haplography. The significant feature is that the same omission is made (and signalled to a single insertion) in both statements of the tenor of this section, indicating that it was very probably copied from a version in which the tenor repetition was not written out, and in which this error also occurred (*pace RISM*, B/IV/2, these are not mensuration signs).

(2) In voice II in *Lbm* 24198, a circle is placed at the end of a first-mode passage before a change to second mode, and also at three similar points of change in voice IV, one of which coincides with the start of a new section, 'Orbis dominatio'. The same function is served in *Lbm* 40011B by placing a dot over the first note of the second mode passages (bb.58, 61 and 63 in the transcription). (In *Lbm* Add.38651F, there is a circle at the beginning of a second-mode piece requiring section repetition, 'Astrorum aliitudinem'.)

(3) Some circles are placed in the two lower voices to mark off the major sections of the piece. *Ob* 652, which has tenor repetitions written out in full, has none. *Lbm* 40011B requires repetition: where legible, the repetition is indicated by the word *recita* and a small circle (possibly as a later addition) over the first note of each tenor section. The circle here possibly functions as a sign indicating the first note of the repeat: there is no sign over the first note, for the point of return is obvious. (Hanboys, in describing the use of the circle for *tempus perfectum*, states that it may be

placed before the passage or above the first and beneath the last affected notes.) Similar usage occurs in *Ob* Hatton 81, where a single circle, or three in vertical alignment, mark off the main tenor sections in the rondellus *Hostis Herodes*, discussed above. In no case where tenor repetition is required to fit the upper voices as written is a circle deemed sufficient to indicate the repeat. The tenor is either written in full (as in the Bodley version of *Rota* and its final section in *Lbm* 24198) or marked *recita* (as in the Fountains version of *Rota*, although circles are also present, and in the two fully notated rondelli in Hatton). Circles do not therefore seem to demand repetition, though on the present limited evidence they appear to mark off sections to which repetition would be applied in the case of full rondellus performance in incompletely notated pieces.

There are no grounds, as indeed Handschin suspected, for designating *Rota versatilis* a rota in any sense other than that of its rondellus structure. The incipit designates nothing of greater musical excitement than the wheel on which the saint was tortured, though the analogy was unquestionably deliberate, as was probably the circular course described through various levels of notation and structure. Rondellus is here applied only to the upper voices, as was normal. It is conceivable, however, that a version which alternated the lower parts, despite their disparate ranges, might have been contrived, on the lines of the version of *Thomas gemma / Thomas caesus* in GB-Ob lat.lit. d. 20. This is one of the very few other compositions to show some reworking between sections: not only are the lower parts rearranged, but the notation of *Ob* 652 is in paired semibreves (to be read trochaically) while GB-Cgc 543/512 and US-PRu Garrett 119 present versions notated in longs and breves.[10]

Because rondellus, unlike canonic rota, could be applied as an afterthought to pieces composed without it, it is possible that some potential rondelli remain undetected, particularly if singers of the time were undaunted by the practical problems of rotating between two parts.

The contents of the three main sources have been described, but some problems of format need further discussion before their relationship and function become clear, and before turning to the second of the three problems mentioned above, that of semibreve interpretation.

Lbm 24198 contained, presumably, voices I and II on a missing verso preceding the surviving recto with voices II and IV (f.132*r*). The entire piece in this shortened version was thus probably accommodated on a single opening (see above). It is possible that this spatial consideration was the reason for presenting the short version: there would not have been room, with this scribe and in this format, to present a full version on one opening. It is just possible that the final section, 'Virgo perduxerat', was given in full because there was, after all, room for it, but this is more likely to have been for reasons of musical balance. However, performance of the complete rondellus from this copy would have required the singers undertaking a part-exchange, rotating between right and left pages for each change of section. A simpler, though equally economical arrangement could have been devised had it been required in this source: repetitions of the tenors present no problems and the points are indeed indicated by the 'o' signs probably retained from the exemplar.

Lbm 40011B on the other hand, provides for full rondellus performance, on the musical evidence both of what is preserved of voice I and of the *recita* indications in voice III. The smaller script makes it possible for this source to have contained the whole piece on a single opening. The music on the other sides of these strips does not, indeed, belong to *Rota versatilis*. While some decisive identifications might yet disprove that all four strips are from the same folio, evidence of parchment and format suggests that this was the most likely arrangement. The error mentioned above, the incorrect labelling of the 'Rota Katerine' melisma in voice I with the incipit of the next section, 'Katerina', might be a simple slip, or it might indicate that this copy was expanded by the scribe from a compact version, perhaps like that of *Lbm* 24198. Although a later addition to this manuscript (without red colour), this has many signs of being the earliest version of *Rota versatilis*, and it may in fact have been expanded from a source that was close to the composer, who would not have needed to notate the rondellus *ad longum*.

Ob 652 is the source with the most problematical format. As it survives voices II and IV are presented in full on the same opening, followed by the start of a different composition. Presumably, voices I and III were presented similarly, which would produce a format without precedent in a polyphonic manuscript of this period. The possibility of this being a partbook giving only voices II and IV is not strong, for the other music preserved is evidently for two or three voices. Even if, as an alternative solution, voice I was required to derive his part from the written voice II (in which case, a more logical arrangement would be the inverse one), III required separate notation: there is not likely to have been sufficient space for it to precede II, which is in itself a most unconvincing arrangement.

These leaves are almost certainly membranes from a roll, and not leaves from a book. F.70 has two rows of stitching holes along its vertical edge. Some have pulled through altogether, and the direction of pull of one set generally suggests zig-zag stitching to a horizontally adjacent membrane.

(While I know of no other surviving fragments from a roll with evidence of horizontal rather than vertical format, there are, of course, pictures which suggest the use in performance of horizontal rolls or strips.)

Ff.69r-70v were thus to the left of and adjacent to ir-iiv. The wide lower margin of ff.69r-70v suggests that it was the bottom of the membrane: some three-and-a-half staves at the top of the surviving eight-and-a-half would accommodate the beginning of voice II of *Rota versatilis*. Ff.ir-iiv are from the top of the next membrane, since the tenor part is continuous. If about three more staves are assumed to be lost from the foot of this membrane, there would have been room for the tenor of the lower piece, *Rex sanctorum*. (This was to have been copied, for a C4 clef was entered, though without any music.) The verso of the first membrane (now ff.69v-70r) also lacks one or more staves at the head, for the first surviving word is not the first of the piece. If the musical and textual refrain 'Ergo tenere . . .' was appended to sections of similar length, some three more staves at the head would be sufficient. The verso of the second (now ff.iv-iir) has the music upside down in relation to its recto. Fortunately there is no need to seek any continuity between this and the other verso, for the lower piece is possibly complete. For the upper piece, *Regina celestium*, the texted voice starts on the top surviving line (although the music is cut off); a minimum of four more staves above could have carried a texted triplum. Thus it seems possible that voices I and III of *Rota versatilis* could have been contained on membranes to the left of the present ff.69r-70v, in which case the whole composition could have been spread out and performed without page turns or other practical problems. It is possible that the compositions now upside down in relation to each other existed as separate membranes and were joined together, creating this anomaly, when *Rota versatilis* was copied on their backs. No practical problem arises from such reversal in the case of a roll.

It is difficult to place these three versions in a chronological order, particularly since each of them shows some sign of having been copied from an exemplar which preserved a different version from itself. The copy in *Lbm* 24198 is probably the latest, on both formal and paleographical grounds.

The authorship remains, as for almost all English compositions of this period, obscure. The case for regarding Handlo as the author because he uses it to exemplify one of his rules is no stronger than other suggestions of authorship which have been put forward in the case of other theorists. The notation employs no devices peculiar to any of Handlo's cited authors, and it would be rash to see too much significance in its adherence to Handlo's own tenets. However, the treatise *Modus componendi rotam versatilem* was in a Royal manuscript of Bury provenance, which also contained the treatise of Anonymous IV. This treatise, in turn, was also in a manuscript which contained the only known copy of Handlo's treatise, *Lbm* Cotton Tiberius B IX, also from Bury (see footnotes 2 and 9). Since there is no evidence that the other musical sources share the provenances of the manuscripts for which they provided binding material, this is as far as we can press the question of provenance at the present.

★   ★   ★

The sectional nature of this piece with its changing combinations of note values and modal patterns is almost as unusual as the phenomenon of a treatise apparently devoted to the process of composition of a single piece. The details of the modal and notational arrangement of each section are given in the Commentary below, from which can be seen the extent to which the various sections present a compendium of different aspects of notation. The impression gains ground that *Rota versatilis* was a demonstration piece or a didactic essay: this invites attempts to match it with theoretical systems, particularly those of Handlo—for it is used as an example in his treatise. I have already said that any correspondence with Handlo's notation does not provide a strong argument for association, but it is worth noting that sections of the rondellus do correspond in some measure to the *mores mediocris* and *lascivus* attributed by Handlo to Petrus le Viser. [11] There are at least two objections to invoking this passage of the treatise: first, it is not clear how relevant Viser is to the rest of Handlo's argument. Only once again does he allude to these categories (in maxima 9 of the 13th rubric, to the *mos lascivus*), and nowhere else does he reconcile Viser's *dicta* with his own, particularly in the two areas which might bear most strongly upon *Rota versatilis*, namely the discussion of note combinations in which the incipit of *Rota* is cited, and in his exclusion elsewhere in the treatise of any provisions for binary mensuration of the breve. Further, Viser's *mores* are neither comprehensive enough to provide a system to which all eventualities can be referred, nor, in their rigid provisions, apparently built on anything more than an arbitrary basis—witness the statement that if paired breves are equal, then paired semibreves are not, and vice versa. In view of the inconsistencies between

Viser and the mainstream of English theory of this period as transmitted by Handlo, it seems unwise to subject the evaluation of semibreves in *Rota versatilis* to extraneous arbitration. Application of Viser's *mores* would lead to equal semibreves in the sections 'Orbis dominatio' and 'Virgo perduxerat'. The latter section, above all, is the one that seems to call for a triple subdivision of the breve, however, both on internal evidence and by parallels with other pieces. I have chosen to reject the *dicta* of Viser, and have rendered all semibreve pairs unevenly in the transcription.[12] Fuller details are given in the Musical Commentary.

Rhythmic features have been discussed here in some detail, because of the very unusual changes of pattern and the ambiguities of detailed interpretation. Harmonically, the piece is characteristically English in its use of full sonorities. Although main beats usually have a vertical 5th or octave, the placing of harmonic and melodic 3rds is such as to exploit their colour to the maximum. The low range of voice IV, notated in the F4 clef and descending to $B\flat$, and the participation of all four parts for much of the composition (insofar as it survives) both assist the sonorous effect. Above all, the music is melody dominated: whether the tune is in I or II is of course irrelevant, but it articulates its text rhythmically, and moves by step or by 3rd (excepting solely the 4th in b.56). The other parts are rhythmically and melodically subsidiary, and their main function is to harmonize the principal voice. There are some slight signs to suggest that the melodic material itself is also organised to show an inventory of processes, or at least a progression through the work. For each of the four sections where the texted part has survived, the cadence centres for the ends of phrases follow a simple pattern of repetition, moving away and (like the wheel) returning to pitch: 'Orbis dominatio', c', c', d', c'; 'Rota Katerine', c', c', b', c'; 'Katerina spe', e', c', e', c'; 'Virgo perduxerat', c', c', f', c'. The pattern of repetition of melodic cells characteristic of the second and third sections also becomes more adventurous as the later sections are composed. There is a similar regular irregularity in the musical counterparts to the four (strictly equal) text lines for each verse. The text lines themselves show a pleasing pattern of rotation which is certainly deliberate:

Section	Syllables per line
'Rota versatilis'	6 + 6 = 12
'Orbis dominatio'	7 + 6 = 13
'Rota Katerine'	6 + 5 = 11
'Katerina spe'	8 + 7 = 15
'Virgo perduxerat'	6 + 8 = 14

While the distribution of syllables for the first section can not be determined the others do show a similar pattern in their musical settings: in 'Orbis dominatio', each line of text is set to eight longs, though the duplex long rest is omitted at the end of the third line. In 'Rota katerine', the third phrase again has a depleted rest, here of a breve instead of an imperfect long: the second phrase is extended to one beat longer by not having any syllable set solely to a semibreve. The fourth section marks out the third phrase again, by making it the only one without a change of rhythmic mode. In the last, it is reasonably the last phrase that is distinctive, with a different rhythmic pattern from the other three. It is of the same length as they are, for the last note is a duplex long, making seven longs in that phrase in the final statement, corresponding with the others' six longs plus one rest.

The detailed structure has been discussed at some length, for it shows the extent to which this might be seen as a didactic piece, or at least as a display of different possibilities: what has not yet been remarked is the underlying musical structure. The spiral nature of the text patterns has already been mentioned and this is matched by the musical shape. Discounting any further refinements that might yet emerge from the discovery of a complete first section or of firm evidence on semibreve interpretation, the presence of some proportional balance is undeniable. A tabulation of the lengths of the five sections will make this immediately clear:

'Rota versatilis'	27 duplex longs = 54 longs = 162 breves	162
'Orbis dominatio'	38 longs = 114 breves	
'Rota Katerine'	27 imperfect longs = 54 breves	168
'Katerina spe'	40 longs = 120 breves	
'Virgo perduxerat'	27 imperfect longs = 54 breves	174

The two layers of balance are obvious; on the one hand, the symmetrical increase in length that parallels the steady exploration of different rhythmic modes and text patterns in each section: and on the other, the form that produces repeated sections of 27 longs (in the last case discounting the duplex long which ends the second statement).

These additions to the rondellus repertory as discussed by Harrison[13] do amplify our picture of what might be seen as the classic stage of this genre, where the incidental, short-term or overlapping rondellus of some 13th-century examples gives way to interchange between long, self-contained sections. These 14th-century specimens bear a similar relationship to their predecessors as do the formally standardised 15th-century isorhythmic motets to theirs. The danger of ossification is present in both cases. Shortened performances of the longer rondellus compositions may have been provided for in much the same way and for similar reasons as undermined the full performances of *formes fixes* in the late 15th century. At any rate, *Rota versatilis*, probably written before 1326, seems to stand at the peak and at the final stages of this genre: while there may be later examples, no more ambitious ones have survived.

THE TEXT

The following edition and translation of the text of *Rota versatilis* has been provided by Dr Roger Bowers, who responded to my request for help over the text in characteristically generous fashion. My discussion, above, has not been rewritten in the light of his contribution, which he undertook after mine had been sent to press.

Text

1   Rota versatilis   rubens versucia
     [—
     —
     —   ]

5   Orbis dominacio   vertitur in rota
     eius et elatio   quasi gleba vota
     virginis oratio   potenti devota
     rotam vertit odio   que se perit tota.

     Rota katerine   fit sevissima
10   rota mundi bine   fraudis pessima
     clause patent fine   sub nequissima
     verse sunt ruine   vi potissima.

     Katerina spe divina   tormentum devicerat
     ut certantes disputantes   sola iam concluserat
15   In ardore flatus rore   clericos consulerat
     et amore suo more   christo laudes solverat.

     Virgo perduxerat   reginam et porphirium
     quibus promiserat   perhennis vite gaudium
     postquam oraverat   seve subit martyrium
20   lac emanaverat   virgo poscit palacium.

Translation

1–4   The revolving wheel, reddening with wiliness, ...

5–8   The lordship of the world is being turned on a wheel, and its final
disposal is just as a votive clod of earth.
The holy prayer of the virgin turns [her] wheel with powerful
malevolence, and it disintegrates totally.

9–12   The wheel of Katherine is made most cruel, a most evil wheel of a
world of twofold deceit.
Enclosed [organs] lie open under a most vile death; 'the ruins have
been overturned' with most remarkable force.

13–16   [Fortified] by divine hope, Katherine had vanquished her torture, just
as—alone—she had already confounded the disputants
contending [against her].
In the burning heat the breeze had comforted the clerks with dew, and,
in its fashion, had rendered praises to Christ with love.

17–20   The virgin had converted the queen and Porphyrium, to whom she had
promised the joy of eternal life.
After she had prayed, she undergoes savage martyrdom. Milk [had]
flowed forth. The virgin demands [admission to] the palace [of
heaven].

Sources

1   Handlo

5–8   *Lbm* 24198. Last three words of line 8 visible on *Ob* 652: [*qu*]*e separit
tota.*

9–12   *Lbm* 40011B. Also *Ob* 652 (defective): line 12 *ve* for *vi.*

13–16   *Lbm* 24198. Also *Ob* 652 (defective).

17–20   *Lbm* 24198. Also *Ob* 652 (defective): line 19 *martirium* for *martyrium*;
line 20 *possit* for *poscit.*

Observations

8   Read *separat* for *se perit* (*Lbm* 24198), *separit* (*Ob* 652).

14   Read *confuserat* (non-classical form of *confuderat*) for *concluserat.*

15   *consulerat* appears to be a contracted form of *consolaverat.*

Commentary

The events surrounding the interrogation and martyrdom of St Katherine of
Alexandria were readily available to medieval versifiers, most conveniently in the
widely-known 'Golden Legend'—the *Legenda Sanctorum* compiled by Jacopo de
Voragine, Archbishop of Genoa (*b* 1228/30; *d* 1298). Latin text ed. T. Graesse,

Jacobi a Voragine Legenda Aurea (Leipzig, 2/1850), 789–97; modern English trans. in G. Ryan and H. Ripperger: *The Golden Legend of Jacobus de Voragine* (New York, 1941), 708–16; fuller details of the narrative features of the poem may be sought in these sources.

Little can be done with the single surviving line of stanza 1, and the translation presented here offers no more than a whimsical attempt to reproduce the alliteration which characterises the original Latin.

The text of stanzas 2–5 appears to be a compilation; stanzas 4–5 are of a character quite different from 2–3, and it seems improbable that all could derive from a single original poem. 4–5 consist of straightforward narrative doggerel of the usual sort; but 2–3 are much more rewarding, being epigrammatic and characterised by puns and oblique references and allusions, in pursuit of obscure but perceptive lines of thought. For instance, although the focus of the thought throughout stanza 2 is evidently Katherine's wheel, the direct allusion in lines 5–6 appears to be to a different wheel, the Wheel of Fortune, and to its associated idea of the transience and illusory nature of earthly authority. Lines 7–8 then proceed to draw a parallel between the futility of trust in the Wheel of Fortune, which will raise expectations but produce only disappointment, and the futility of preparing the wheel for Katherine, which, in response to her prayer, disintegrated and collapsed to nothing before it could be put to use.

Line 11 appears to refer to Katherine's eventual martyrdom by decapitation; the 'twofold deceit' of the previous line presumably represents the fact that the cruel world proceeded to the injustice of this second means of execution undeterred by the failure of the first.

Line 12 has a significance beyond its literal meaning. The text makes sense only if it be understood to incorporate an allusion to the rather improbable etymology of the name Katherine proffered by Jacopo de Voragine in the 'Golden Legend'. His suggestion was that 'Katherine' derived from Greek *Kata* (total) and Latin *ruina* (ruin); Katherine, that is, spelled total ruin for the devil and all his works. This proposed etymology appears to be the idea lying behind the phrase *verse sunt ruine*.

Now while the 'Golden Legend' is known to have been largely compiled from pre-existing hagiographies, the bizarre etymologies of saints' names which characterise it are considered to be among the recurring mannerisms that were contributed by Jacopo de Voragine himself. So the poem from which stanzas 2 and 3 were taken certainly seems to have drawn its phraseology at least indirectly from the 'Golden Legend' itself, and must therefore postdate its promulgation. The 'Golden Legend' was compiled over some period between *c*1250 and 1292, and it seems unlikely that it can have become at all well known in England much before *c*1300. Meanwhile, the first line of *Rota versatilis* occurs in Handlo's treatise, one manuscript copy of which was dated 1326. Very tentatively, therefore, the compilation of the text of *Rota versatilis*, and the composition of its music, may be attributed to the first quarter of the 14th century.

MUSICAL COMMENTARY

This aims to point out the interesting features of the piece, rather than merely to show precisely which notes of the transcription have a specific degree of negative or positive support from the various sources.

I and II refer to the voices as presented in this transcription, in which the repeats are not written out: in a full rondellus performance, voice I would always sing the texted portions first. T = a texted section; M = melisma.

'Rota versatilis'

I (T)   Incipit survives only as an example in Handlo's treatise (see above).

II (M)   *Lbm* 24198

III   *Lbm* 40011B, written once. *Recita* written before the end of the section, so that the never-entered text incipit for the next section would be aligned with its music. A line indicates the point of repetition after b.27.

IV   *Lbm* 24198 written once: *Ob* 652, twice, with first two clefs and most of the second statement lacking. Bb.26–7 in ligature, *Ob* 652.

The lower three voices are notated exclusively in duplex longs, longs (perfect and imperfect) and breves. Alteration of breves is specifically precluded by dots whenever three breves occur between two longs. This accords with Viser's *mos lascivus*, which would require semibreve pairs to be read minor-major. The duplex long is sometimes imperfected by a breve or a breve rest, as allowed by Handlo in the next music example following the incipit of *Rota versatilis*.

All long rests cover three spaces and are written in pairs for duplex longs. Some, in this section of *Lbm* 40011B and in later sections in *Lbm* 24198, appear to occupy three-and-a-half spaces. This is not consistent enough to be purposeful (cf Robert de Brunham's perfect rests cited in Hanboys' treatise, *CS*,i, 447).

'Orbis dominatio'

I (M)   *Lbm* 40011B, last few notes preserved, but lengths, rests and therefore placing are uncertain. Present in *Ob* 652, but bottom stave line only visible.

II (T)   *Lbm* 24198. *Ob* 652 preserves the last three words and the bottom stave line—followed by the untexted section = I. Most semibreves are written separately even though not syllabic.

III   *Lbm* 40011B, written once. *Recita* with indicating line at the end.

IV   *Lbm* 24198, written once. *Ob* 652, twice; top of the upper stave cut away; b.37 written as two longs, second in ligature, both statements, *Ob* 652.

This section adopts second-mode patterns in contrast to the first-mode rhythms of the preceding. Altered breves are required before longs and long rests, and dots leave no room for ambiguity. *Mos lascivus* would preclude altered breves and could no longer apply. *Mos mediocris* fits this situation but, unlike the other *mores*, requires pairs of semibreves to be read equally.

Use of 'o':

II *Lbm* 24198, before first note.

III *Lbm* 40011B: above first note (?later addition)

IV *Lbm* 24198: before first note, after rest

'Rota Katerine'

I (T)   *Ob* 652. *Lbm* 40011B, lower one or two stave lines only; b.55, ?only one long rest, *Lbm* 40011B.

II (M)   *Lbm* 24198. *Lbm* 40011B, wrongly labelled 'Katerina': some lacunae. *Ob* 652: fragmentary.

III   *Lbm* 40011B, written once: no *recita*; b.47, dot after last note.

IV   *Lbm* 24198, written once. *Ob* 652, twice; 53.3 *c*, *Lbm* 24198.

All longs are imperfect, no breves are altered. These two facts would suggest *mos mediocris* and *mos lascivus* respectively. If evaluated as the former, semibreve pairs would be equal, unequal if the latter. Viser's system appears not to cater for this case.

All rests cover a single space and do not resolve the basic value of the long. The grouping of these rests in twos or threes varies, apparently arbitrarily, between *Lbm* 24198 and *Ob* 652—e.g. in bar 49, 2 x 3 and 3 x 2 respectively. In II, there are dots in *Lbm* 40011B (where visible) between groups of three semibreves.

Use of 'o':

III *Lbm* 40011B, above first note (?later addition)

IV *Lbm* 24198, before first note

'Katerina spe'

I (M)   *Ob* 652

II (T)   *Lbm* 24198. *Ob* 652. *Lbm* 40011B incomplete.

III   *Lbm* 40011B, opening only. Dot after b.57. From b.60, top one or two staves only survive, with a few notes and rests.

IV   *Lbm* 24198, written once. *Ob* 652, twice. Omission of IV, bb.70–74 (both statements) and II, bb.60–61, I signalled by ø in *Ob* 652.

This section alternates phrases in first and second mode, except for the third line of verse. Perfect longs and altered breves are required. Semibreve pairs occur only in first-mode phrases. Rests are carefully grouped L + B or B + L. Alternation of the *mores lascivus* and *mediocris* would be required.

Use of 'o':

II *Lbm* 24198, before bb.58, 63, 73. Returns to the first mode shown by rest groupings—b.70, rests L B o B L.

Ob 652 places dots above the ends of first-mode passages where visible.

Lbm 40011B places dots above first notes of both first- and second-mode sections, where visible (bb.58, 61, 63).

IV   *Lbm* 24198, at beginning, and before bb.58, 63.

'Virgo perduxerat'

I (M-T) *Lbm* 24198. *Ob* 652.

II (T-M) *Lbm* 24198. *Ob* 652; b.78, 3 semibreves *Lbm* 24198, 2 semibreves, *e'*, *f'* *Ob* 652.

IV   *Lbm* 24198, written twice. *Ob* 652, twice. b.83, first statement, *f*, *c* included in preceding ligature. Second statement, *f* replaced by 3 semibreves *f*, *e*, *d*, *Lbm* 24198. In *Ob* 652 both statements as the first of *Lbm* 24198. Final statement, both sources have final maxima instead of long as in first statement.

No perfect longs or altered breves are called for or even possible. Semibreves are present in quantity but are clearly marked by dots into groups of two or three. All pairs unless plicated or in ligature have two syllables, while all groups of three have only one syllable. *Mos mediocris* would produce equal semibreves when paired, three being unequal. However, English tradition strongly suggests triple subdivision of the breve. Harmonic considerations and musical evidence from other compositions suggest that, contrary to most official statements, pairs should be trochaic. Long rests cover two spaces in both sources.

Use of 'o':

IV   *Lbm* 24198, preceding first statement.

ROTA VERSATILIS

For full rondellus performance, repeat each section exchanging upper parts.

Ro - ta ver - sa - ti - - lis____ ru - bens ver -

- su - ci - a.

Or – bis do – mi – – na – ti – o

ver – ti – tur in ro – – ta   E – ius et e – – la – ti – o   qua – si gle – ba

vo - ta. Vir - gi - nis o - ra - ti - o po - ten - ti de - vo - ta

Ro - tam ver - tit___ o - di - o que se pe - rit to - ta.

Ro - ta Ka - te - ri - ne fit se - vis - si - ma Ro - ta mun - di bi -

ne frau - dis___ pes - si - ma   Clau - se pa-tent fi - ne   sub ne - quis - si -

Bod:

- ma   Ver - se sunt ru - i - ne vi po-tis - si - ma

Ka - te - ri - na spe di - vi - na   tor - men - tum de - vi - ce - rat

Virgo perduxerat reginam et porphirium

solverat

Quibus promiserat perhennis vite gaudium   Postquam oraverat se-

Bod:

-ve subit martyrium   Lac emanaverat virgo poscit palacium.

NOTES TO CHAPTER 2

1. The only other known copy perished in the Cotton fire of 1731. For an exemplary description of Royal 12 C VI, see F. Reckow: *Der Musiktraktat des Anonymus 4*, i, BAMw, iv (1967), 1–7.

2. J. Handschin: 'The Sumer Canon and its Background', *MD*, iii (1949), 83. Handschin at this point raises the question whether the word *Rota* in the title may designate the rondellus form of the piece. It is clearly not a perpetual, or even a non-perpetual, canon. See also M. F. Bukofzer: *Studies in Medieval and Renaissance Music* (London, 1951), 87, and *'Sumer is icumen in': a Revision*, University of California Publications in Music, ii/2 (1947), 97.

3. K. Levy: 'New material on the Early Motet in England', *JAMS*, iv (1951), 222.

4. See note 2.

5. Also noticed by Ernest Sanders, to whom I am grateful for a friendly exchange of ideas by letter on this piece. Two articles by Prof. Sanders mentioning this piece appeared after the present article was completed: 'The Medieval Motet', in *Gattungen der Musik in Einzeldarstellungen: Gedenkschrift Leo Schrade*, ed. W. Arlt and others (Bern and Munich, 1973), 564f; 'England: from the Beginnings to c.1540', in *Music from the Middle Ages to the Renaissance*, ed. F. W. Sternfeld (New York, 1973), 289.

6. F.Ll. Harrison, in NOHM, iii, 90.

7. *CS*, i, p.391a, second example.

8. Reckow (1967), 7–14.

9. *Roberto de Handlo,* trans. and ed. L. Dittmer, Musical Theorists in Translation, ii (New York, 1959).

10. See my article: 'A Preliminary Assessment of the Independence of English trecento Notations', *L'ars nova italiana del trecento IV: Certaldo 1975*, 65–82. I suggest there that the notation in longs and breves is not necessarily more primitive than that in semibreve pairs. Apart from being more explicit at that level it accommodates the ornamental cadence patterns of the Princeton version, whose further subdivision could not have been notated with any precision had those breves been semibreves already.

11. *CS*,i, 388. See also E. Sanders: 'Duple Rhythm and Alternate Third Mode in the 13th Century', *JAMS*, xv (1962), 250–7 for a translation and interpretation. *Mos longus* is not relevant here for it divides the breves into groups of more than three.

12. Some of the arguments for trochaic versus iambic interpretation of semibreve pairs are set out in the article cited in note 10.

13. *NOHM*, iii, chap.3, and 'Ars Nova in England: a New Source', *MD*, xxi (1967), 67–85. I am reluctant to adopt his term 'rondellus-conductus' for pieces whose only claim to the latter term is the absence of an identified *cantus prius factus.*

3

Robertus de Anglia and the Oporto Song Collection

David Fallows

It now seems that English music was influential on the continent for a relatively short period, between about 1420 and a little after 1440, years that represent the only time in history when anybody outside England has taken more than a passing interest in English composers or their work. English music was acknowledged by continental writers as an influence; and works by Dunstable, Leonel Power and other less prolific English composers occupied large sections, even specifically English fascicles, in the manuscripts now at Aosta, Bologna, Trent and Modena. That reputation was to remain for a few more years. Music of clearly English origin appears in the later Trent codices; and a few English musicians have been found on the continent, their nationality evidently a recommendation of high artistic standards. Their position may have seemed uncomfortable, with no particular figurehead after Dunstable's death and with the widespread feeling echoed by Tinctoris that Dunstable had no worthy successors. To their credit, many of them made no attempt to imitate Dunstable; but their work is nonetheless sometimes distinctively English, as this chapter aims to show.

Small though it is, the collection of 19 songs at the end of the manuscript Oporto, Biblioteca pública municipal 714, deserves notice as the last continental source with a substantial proportion of English music. It was probably prepared in Ferrara: only in the 18th century did it come to Portugal. English ascriptions for seven of the songs, the repeated use of the suffix 'de Anglia' and the evidence that pride of place was given to a certain 'Ro. de Anglia' suggest that the compiler had some special interest in the secular music of English composers. They also make the manuscript an important document for any student of the subject today.

The English Composers

John Bedyngham (*d* 1459 or 1460), one of the three English composers

named, is a relatively well-known figure. Of the three songs ascribed to
him here, two appear in over a dozen sources each, so it is no surprise to
find his work in a collection with an English bias.

Two pieces ascribed to 'Galfridus de Anglia' present a different case.
Their texts indicate that Galfridus may have lived at Ferrara in the 1440s;
but nothing else is known of the composer. Geoffrey and Wilfred, the
English equivalents of the Latin Galfridus, do not appear among the
known names of English musicians in the 15th century; and the 'Frater G.
de Anglia' who finished copying the treatise of Anonymous VI (*CS*, iii,
403: *US-Cn* 54.1, f.6*v*) at Pavia in October 1391 is surely far too early—
perhaps he was the composer Gervays. The suggested identification of
Galfridus with Walter Frye is contradicted by the unprepossessing quality
of the music; and in any case the very clarity and confidence of the Oporto
scribe make it unlikely that he wrote Galfridus when he meant Gualterus.
By contrast with the three Bedyngham songs, these pieces seem slight
indeed. They are the only ones in the manuscript in a mere two parts, and
it is perhaps easy to dismiss them too readily on that count; but one is
bound to wonder whether anything apart from the nationality of their
composer earned them their place in the collection.

The two Italian songs of 'Ro. de Anglia', on the other hand, are the first
and last pieces in the collection and were evidently important to the
compiler. They are also the two longest and the only ones in which all
three voices are texted throughout. They invite more attention on each of
those counts as well as because it has too often been suggested that their
composer was Robert Morton.[1]

Morton was employed at the Burgundian ducal chapel from 1457 to
1476. Nothing else is known of his career, but several factors seem to
support the theory that these two songs are his. First, he was English, and
his works appear in practically all surviving secular song manuscripts from
the second half of the 15th century. Second, the Oporto collection contains a song—also with Italian text—by Gilles Joye, a colleague of Morton
at the Burgundian chapel. Third, four songs ascribed to Morton do have fragments of Italian text, while an international profile is given to his work by one
song with a German text and another with an entirely convincing Spanish
text. Two more Italian songs by Morton could be a distinct possibility.

I have recently argued elsewhere that several of the songs ascribed to
Morton are not his and that only the eight works with unassailable French
texts really belong to him;[2] but there is quite enough stylistic unity even
among all the 12 songs ascribed to Morton for the two 'Ro. de Anglia'
pieces in Oporto to stand out as being entirely different. Morton's songs—

always ascribed simply to 'Morton': his first name is known only from documents—are very much in the northern French tradition of his time, whatever the language of their texts. His lines are strongly melodic, with the discantus in particular carefully moulded and shaped, almost to excess. The two main sections have a strict balance, that of the classic French song tradition inherited from Binchois and Dufay. As concerns contrapuntal technique, Morton always maintains a firm control of the relation between discantus and tenor: these two voices together form a coherent whole, and the contratenor stays in most cases carefully below the tenor line, in accordance with the new trend of the years when Morton was at the Burgundian court. This is all worlds away from Ro. de Anglia's O *fallaze e ria Fortuna* (see ex.2, p.117) with its homophonic declamations, its strongly irregular rhythms, its elaborate cadential melismas and intertwining voice parts. Further evidence is needed before the two Oporto pieces can be attributed to Morton with any real conviction. The ascriptions say merely that they were written by a man named Robertus who came from England.

The stylistic features just identified in O *fallaze* actually recall the songs of Robert Fayrfax rather than those of Robert Morton. This is not to suggest for a moment that they could be by Fayrfax, whose career as a composer probably did not begin before 1490; but the affinity is more in that direction. The real point here, however, is that Robertus was a common name among English musicians of the mid-15th century. A limited search reveals, besides Morton and Fayrfax, Robert David, Robert Derby, Robert Jones, Robert Mychelson, Robert Wydow and John Robert.[3] Almost all are conceivable candidates for the authorship of the 'Ro. de Anglia' music; and then again, the number of English composers whose names are not known must be considerable.

But there is one man who demands closer attention. In September 1460 'Dominus Robertus de Anglia' came to Ferrara Cathedral on the invitation of the cantor to instruct the clerics in singing.[4] He was still there on 5 September 1461 and perhaps remained until 1467 when he took up an appointment nearby at Bologna. On 1 April 1467 the chapter of San Petronio, Bologna, enrolled 'Dominum Robertum de Anglia' as *magister cantus*, with the condition that he sing in the choir on all festal days.[5] His regular monthly payments are recorded throughout the years from April 1467 until September 1474 when he left to return to England.

This Robertus had been in Italy and probably Ferrara even before his appointment at Ferrara Cathedral. A notarial record of 19 August 1454 includes him as a witness of property dealings concerned with the Abbey of Santa Maria di Pomposa, near the Adriatic coast due east of Ferrara. The document refers to him as follows:[6]

> Venerabili viro domino Roberto cantore filio honorabilis viri Petri Suchar de Anglia, ad presens habitatore cum prefato Reverendissimo domino Commendatorio.

The said 'commendator' with whom Robertus was living was a member of the Este family: born about 1430, Rinaldo Maria d'Este was one of the many illegitimate children of the Marchese Niccolo III, and as a result of his illegitimacy could almost certainly not hold major orders, so he was probably resident not at Pomposa but at the court in Ferrara. Unfortunately the name 'Suchar' cannot convincingly be connected with any known English name of the time, so it must be considered an Italian approximation for someone who was otherwise apparently known as 'Robertus de Anglia'. For what it is worth, a cleric called 'Robertus Fulsham' joined the London Guild of Parish Clerks in the year ending Ascension Day 1475, six months after our Robertus left for England: if any evidence could be brought to justify the distant but just feasible corruption of Fulsham to Suchar then we could say also, on the basis of the Leet book of the Guild,[7] that Robertus died in the year ending Ascension Day 1480. But without any further corroboration both the names Suchar and Fulsham must remain approximations, and it would be far more prudent for the time being to retain the form of his name by which he was known, and evidently preferred to be known, in Italy: Robertus de Anglia.

In any case his name was clearly not Morton. And since Morton's presence at the Burgundian court during precisely these years is equally fully documented it is certain that at least two of the many English musicians called Robert held positions in fine European choirs at the time: there is no reason to think that the composer of the Oporto songs was Morton. Perhaps it is worth adding a brief note here on yet another English Robertus—or possibly three of them—in major continental choirs slightly later in the century. According to Haberl, 'Robertus Anglicus' was at the choir of St Peter's, Rome, in 1485; and a 'Ro. de Anglia' was in the Papal private chapel (Cappella Sistina) in 1492. Either might be identical with 'Rob. de Lignoquercu' (? Oakwood) who sang in the Cappella Sistina from November 1479 to September 1483 and again in 1493; and it is just possible that they are to be identified with 'Ro. Bonetti' who sang in the Cappella Sistina from 1484 to 1491. There seems to be no other singer named Robert in the published lists of the chapel. In 1499 the *cantor* 'messer Roberto Inglese' joined the singers at the Ferrarese court.[8]

Returning to the Robertus documented at Ferrara Cathedral and at San Petronio, Bologna, there is evidence that he did compose songs. The Bolognese poet Cesare Nappi, born around 1440, published his poem *Iti caldi suspir'e mente afflitta* with an annotation to the effect that Master Robert the Englishman had set the poem to music (*super qua est cantus magistri Roberti Anglia*). Cesare Nappi included annotations about the music to several of his poems—a most unusual procedure, suggesting that he was particularly interested in music and that he probably knew (or at least knew of) the most important musicians in his home town of Bologna. And if he had been able to name any prominent musicians at all he would surely have known the name of the man who held the most prestigious musical post in the city during the years between Nappi's mid-twenties and his mid-thirties: our Robertus de Anglia. So if his 'Magister Robertus Anglia' was not the *magister cantus* of that name Nappi would certainly have qualified his statement. In the absence of any such qualification it seems more than probable that Robertus the choirmaster set that song. The music is lost, but Nappi's testimony suggests that here is another English song composer who might lay claim to the Robertus music in Oporto.[9]

An English musician called Robertus is also mentioned in Ramos de Pareia's *Musica practica*, published at Bologna in 1482 but written, according to Spataro, ten years earlier, that is, during the final years of Robertus's tenure at San Petronio.[10] Ramos is merciless about Robertus:[11]

> But Master Robert the Englishman, ignoring the geometrical propriety of note-values, said the opposite, which is: when no mensuration sign is to be found, he considered the time to be perfect. He was thus saying that almost all compositions without mensuration signs are badly composed. For he, ignorant of learning, put art before nature whereas the opposite is clearly the case, that art imitates nature as far as it can.

Robertus, then, had opinions about mensuration, including the view that if there was no mensuration sign the music should be assumed to be in perfect time. He may even have written a treatise defending his position.

But the final clue linking the Robertus mentioned by Ramos with the composer of the two Robertus songs in the Oporto collection has apparently gone unnoticed and lies within the manuscript itself: the notation of the 19 songs in the Oporto manuscript precisely follows the law laid down by Robertus, as quoted by Ramos. The pieces in imperfect time all have mensuration signs in not just one voice but all, with the sole exception of the contratenor in Dufay's *Adieu m'amour* where its omission is evidently an oversight. Twelve of the 19 pieces are in perfect time; and the only trace of a mensuration sign among them is a very small one entered in the margin by the discantus of Dufay's *Entre les plus plaines*, where it would have been covered by the illuminated letter that was never added. But this was not intended for the reader. It was probably a reminder for the scribe, since Dufay's piece treats perfect time in an unusually free manner: the whole first section of the song is syncopated, and not until the arrival of the second full cadence (at b.11 in Besseler's edition) does the syncopation resolve itself. A scribe could easily be misled by this, and it is understandable that he should have written that mensuration sign in the margin for his own reference.

What is perhaps even more surprising is that among continental sources of the 15th century the Oporto manuscript appears to be unique in this respect. Something similar happens in the first layer of one insular manuscript of English carols and liturgical music, *GB-Lbm* Egerton 3307: a clear dividing point in that manuscript occurs before f.49 where a new gathering begins a section of carols that leads almost to the end of the volume and includes many pieces in imperfect time without mensuration signs; but in the section before f.49 the only exceptions to the rule described by Ramos are a superfluous   in all three voices on f.48 and a   omitted from all three voices on f.42. Nevertheless I have not encountered any other 15th-century source that even approaches such a systematic treatment of mensuration signs, let alone a treatment that follows these principles. I take this to support my previous suggestion that the compilation of the song collection at Oporto shows strong English influence; and given the placing of the Robertus songs at the beginning and end of the collection, it seems that the compilation of the manuscript must be very closely connected with Robertus or his circle.

So, quite apart from any stylistic considerations, the Robertus who composed the songs is not Robert Morton. He is almost certainly the Robertus mentioned by Ramos, who must also be the one who was choir-master at San Petronio when Ramos was writing his treatise in the same city (and at the same time as Robert Morton was at the Burgundian court)—and he was presumably also the composer of music to Cesare Nappi's poem. Whether he was himself the compiler or merely a strong influence on whoever assembled the manuscript requires a much closer examination of the document itself.

The Manuscript

Though the manuscript has been discussed several times,[12] it has never been described in any detail. The song collection is preceded by two theoretical treatises which have hitherto eluded identification; but in view of the manuscript's probable Ferrarese origin, they are easily located. Both are distillations from the extensive *Declaratio musice discipline* of Ugolino of Orvieto who spent the last 30 years of his life at Ferrara Cathedral: the first is an explanation of solmisation and the modes taken from Book I of Ugolino's treatise;[13] the second is the extremely common *Libellus cantus mensurabilis* of Johannes de Muris with explanatory glosses taken from Book III of Ugolino, itself a farsed version of the *Libellus*.[14]

The entire manuscript is written in a single hand with uniform style. The scribe was an accomplished copyist, both of text and of music, who was fluent in Latin but slightly less so in Italian and French. An apparent slight difference in the hand for the song collection is partly explained by his hesitancy with the French and Italian texts, but more as an inevitable consequence of the change from the continuous flow of copying a treatise to the more interrupted work of adding text to music, particularly when— as in this case—special care is taken with the details of the underlay.[15] From the microfilm it may look as though the hands change; but careful examination of the manuscript itself convinced me that everything was written by a single scribe.

Physical format: 83 parchment leaves (including two paste-downs), approx. 20 x 14 cm, with a writing area approx. 14 x 8 cm; theoretical texts (ff.01–50*v*) written on a uniform 27-line page, point-ruled; music (ff.51*v*–79) written on a uniform six-stave page; staves ruled by hand, not by rastrum, for they vary from 11 to 14 mm deep; wooden binding boards covered with tooled leather, apparently original; two metal clasps survive on back cover, though both are missing from the front.

Foliation: pencil: x^1–1, '01', 1–48, [49 omitted], 50 [in black ink], 51–79, 80 [in black ink]; the two ink foliations probably added earlier, for if the pencil foliation had begun with the first surviving text page (f.'01') instead of the second it would not have had to skip the number 49. Two original numberings are visible: each gathering is numbered at the bottom right of its last verso, thus showing that no gathering has been lost, unless at the very end; and the sheets of the first half of each gathering were apparently numbered 1–4 at the bottom right of the recto, though most of these numbers have now been cut off.

Collation: (a) [x]^2: endpapers, ruled with six black staves; first leaf pasted to binding board. (b) 1^9 (first leaf missing), 2^{10}, 3^6 (but textually complete): first treatise. (c) 4^{10}, 5^{10}, 6^{10}: second treatise, but ending in the middle of gathering 6 on f.50*v*. (d) 6^{10} (beginning in the middle), 7^8, 8^8, 9^8: song collection, ruled with six red staves. (e) [y]^2: endpapers, ruled with six black staves; second leaf pasted to binding board. The third gathering, concluding the first treatise, is complete in spite of having only six leaves: the numbers '1', '2' and '3' at the bottom right recto of ff.19, 20 and 21 suggest that the copyist was aware of the irregularity, for though similar numbers are found elsewhere in the manuscript they are much smaller and mostly cut off in binding.

Provenance: probably prepared at Ferrara, after 1460, but possibly at Bologna in 1467, as argued later in this chapter. Evidently still in Italy in the early 18th century according to the annotation in the back cover (f.81): 'Paoli 250 lire in Venezia a di 3 Xbre [i.e. December] 1712'. Soon after that it came to Portugal, for it is included as no.86 in the catalogue of books at the monastery of Santa Cruz, Coimbra, made by D. Pedro da Encarnação and finished in 1771.[16] An inscription on the first leaf reads: 'Pertenie ao cantor mór [i.e. choirmaster] de Santa Cruz'. This was probably D. Pedro da Encarnação himself (1729–1808), who in 1748, at the age of 19, was made librarian of Santa Cruz and was shortly afterwards promoted from 2nd cantor to choirmaster.[17] An inscription on f.'01' enables a fairly precise dating for its acquisition at Oporto since it is signed by Diogo de Goes Lara de Andrade, librarian of the Biblioteca pública municipal from its foundation in July 1833 until October 1836. During those three years the library acquired from Santa Cruz practically all of its present collection of early manuscripts, largely through the efforts of the sub-librarian, the distinguished historian Alexandre Herculano.[18] The bookplate inside the front cover, 'Biblioteca portuense', is from the 20th century.

The structure of the manuscript shows that the second treatise and the song collection must always have been together, for the end of the one and the beginning of the other are within the same gathering. And although it is possible that the first treatise was a slightly later addition, the sequential numbering of each of the nine gatherings in what appears to be the original hand shows that at the time of binding the manuscript was almost exactly as it is today.

From the collation it is equally clear that the first leaf of the volume is missing. On its verso was a Guidonian hand, as implied by the references on f.'01' and f.1 to a diagram: 'Sunt enim in hac figura seu manu hic figurata tres proprietates'. On its recto there must have been a most elaborate initial: the small opening initial on the first surviving page is the same size as the other internal initials in that treatise (ff.9*v*, 12*v* and 21) and the following one (ff.26, 27, 38, 39*v*, 42*v*, 44*v*, 46, 47*v*, 48, 48*v*) but far smaller than the one that opens the second treatise (f.25) which is now the largest in the manuscript—though it would be reasonable to suppose that the scribe expected the illumination at the beginning of the song section (f.51*v*) to be larger than it is, for he wrote the ascription 'Ro. de Anglia' on the right-hand page of the opening, not as elsewhere on the left.

A further irregularity suggests that the manuscript was finished in a hurry: whereas the first 14 songs each begin with an illuminated initial, the final gathering contains no illuminations; moreover, while red ink is used freely throughout the manuscript for staves and to indicate sub-heads, special annotations, part names, etc, the gold stops after f.50*v* and blue is used no more after f.55*v*. If the manuscript was being prepared against a deadline, for a particular occasion, it is possible that at the last moment there was no time to have the final gathering illuminated because the volume had to be sent to the binder. Perhaps the compiler hoped to have the illuminations completed at some later date, after the presentation.

The collation endorses this conclusion. The third gathering has only six leaves, whereas the other text gatherings have ten leaves each. This smaller gathering brings us to the end of the first treatise, after which the second treatise begins a new gathering. Since the manuscript structure is otherwise regular, it would seem that the volume was originally intended to begin with the second treatise and that plans changed at some point in the copying process. Perhaps the actual occasion for the dedication did not appear until things were well under way. A manuscript had to be prepared at short notice. How could it be finished in time? By taking an almost complete manuscript and completing it. A new treatise added on the front would also permit the inclusion of a dedication page appropriate to the occasion.

Another manuscript written by the same scribe adds weight to this theory and confirms what internal examination has already told us about the missing leaf. *D-B* Mus. ms. theor. 1599 contains the same distillation from Ugolino that constitutes the first treatise in Oporto: the first leaf has on its recto the opening of the treatise with a fine illuminated initial and a coat of arms; on the verso is a Guidonian hand.[19] This manuscript has the same size of leaf and of writing area as the Oporto manuscript but with 31 lines to a page rather than 27, and with more words to the line, so that the treatise takes up only 22 folios as against the 25 in Oporto. The Berlin manuscript is less pretentious in other ways: it is on paper rather than parchment and is less elaborately illuminated; but it is unmistakably the work of the same scribe and illuminator. So it would be reasonable to conclude that the Oporto scribe had the material for the first treatise close at hand if he suddenly needed to make the addition suggested above.

Moreover the presence of a mere four internal illuminations in the first treatise of Oporto as against ten in the second also points to some haste in preparing the first.

Without the lost dedication page of Oporto there is little hope of guessing the occasion or the intent of its compilation. It might, for instance, have been an attempt by Robertus to curry favour with a potential patron. But if that had been the case, one of the treatises would surely leave some hint of Robertus's participation or at least contain a reference to the eccentricity in mensural preferences that made Robertus such an object of scorn for Ramos. There is no sign of this.

Nor indeed is there evidence that the treatises have any bearing on the 19 songs that follow. The first treatise discusses monophonic music while the practical collection is entirely polyphonic (and recent scholarship has shown that the theory of the modes was not applied to polyphonic music before Tinctoris except in one isolated case[20]); the subsequent treatise on mensuration concerns topics which were no longer applicable at the time of the 19 songs, whose mensurations are vastly more simple, in principle, than those described by Johannes de Muris or even by Ugolino's exegetical comments on Johannes. Moreover all of the music mentioned in the theoretical section is sacred: there is no reference to secular music. So while it may seem visually as though the 19 songs do represent a collection exemplifying the precepts put forward in the two treatises, nothing supports such a view.[21] It is more as though the short theoretical preface such as appears in the contemporary Dijon and Colombina chansonniers (F-Dm 517 and E-Sc 5-I-43) is now expanded to exceed the length of the actual song collection as a result of a change of plan during preparation. The apparent symmetry of the song collection itself is not further reflected in the structure of the volume as a whole. And the gathering structure, which has already shown that the first treatise may have been an afterthought, shows a further discrepancy: the theoretical collection is in ten-leaf gatherings, whereas the song collection is in eight-leaf gatherings except for its first section, which occupies the last half of the final theory gathering. The important role of Robertus in the compilation of the song collection does not necessarily apply also to the earlier parts of the volume.

Dating

But the importance of some of the music it contains demands an attempt to establish the date of compilation as accurately as possible. This discussion of the volume's physical make-up and of the English composers represented has overlooked the composer with the greatest number of pieces, Dufay. He is represented by eight of his finest and latest songs, four of them otherwise unknown. I am not inclined to think that such a large proportion of songs by Dufay tells us very much about the nature of the manuscript: after all, Dufay was the supreme master of his day and the inclusion of his works merely testifies to some degree of musical discrimination on the part of the compiler. But the presence of these works makes the manuscript important for Dufay studies; and even more so because it seems hitherto to have been dated at least ten years too early.

All the descriptions known to me date the source before 1450.[22] The fullest statement is that of Pirrotta (1970)—the first writer to draw attention to the Ferrarese connections in the manuscript—who identified the texts of the two songs by Galfridus de Anglia among the works of the little-known Ferrarese poet Girolamo Nigrisoli. He added that Professor Gianfranco Folena of Padua had spontaneously suggested a possible Ferrarese origin for the dialect betrayed by the orthography of the six Italian pieces. Also, the style of the illuminations seemed to fit the hypothesis that the source was copied in or around Ferrara. Since the two texts set by Galfridus included references to the princess Isotta d'Este, the whole story seemed to tie together and suggest that the manuscript was written at Ferrara, possibly at the time of her first wedding in 1444, which is mentioned by implication in one of the texts and more specifically in the longer poem from which both are taken.[23] Pirrotta continued:[24]

> Even so, we cannot date the manuscript any later than 1450, because of its black and red notation, and because Leonello d'Este died in that year, and we shall see that his interest in polyphony does not seem to have been shared by his successor Borso. Nor is it possible to assume that the poem of such an obscure poet as Nigrisoli might have travelled far from Ferrara, to places where nobody could have cared for Isotta's name, which is preserved . . . in the first of Galfridus' settings.

Pirrotta's suggestion of Ferrarese origin is now strongly endorsed by the documents telling of Robertus's presence in Ferrara and by the discovery that the theoretical material is all distilled from Ugolino, who spent the last 30 years of his life there. But several qualifications of the arguments concerning the date may now be proposed.

First, if the compiler was specifically interested in the work of English composers he might well have included pieces honouring a princess for whose name he did not care. Second, whatever the state of music at the Ferrarese court under Borso d'Este (and subsequent research tends to modify Pirrotta's opinion[25]), there is now unambiguous evidence that Robertus was still at Ferrara in the 1460s.

Third, the use of black and red notation is no evidence as to date. It is true that black notation became less common on the continent after the first decade of the 15th century—in fact it became very rare—but it did not entirely disappear. Shortly after 1458 Johannes Gallicus (Legrense) included an example in black notation in his treatise *De ritu canendi*,[26] though admittedly as a retrospective example. Also (though it is not susceptible to a secure dating in the second half of the century) the main manuscript of Ugolino's *Declaratio* (*I-Rc* 2151) includes three pieces by Ugolino in full black and red mensural notation.[27]

More important: English manuscripts habitually used the full black notation well into the 16th century. If the Oporto manuscript was a collection with a marked English bias displaying in addition the notational eccentricities of Robertus de Anglia, it seems less strange that its notation should be so strikingly similar to that of the Fayrfax manuscript (*GB-Lbm* Add. 5465), copied in England around 1500.[28] The note heads in the Fayrfax manuscript are more tear-shaped and the text hand is more English in its style, but there are remarkable similarities in the clefs, the details of the notational practice and the use of rubrication. The only detail found in Oporto but not in the later manuscript is the unusual treatment of mensuration signs that is so characteristic of Robertus. Only the singular dearth of English song manuscripts from the 15th century makes the most closely comparable manuscript one written as late as 1500. While not suggesting that the Oporto manuscript can be that late, nor that it could conceivably have been copied anywhere but in the Ferrara area and for an Italian recipient, I should point out that if it is seen in the context of English song, which it so heavily represents, there is nothing in its notation to preclude its dating from long after 1450.

There is one document that may seem to fix the date of the Oporto manuscript once and for all. Rinaldo Maria d'Este has already been mentioned as the employer of Robertus de Anglia in 1454. On 19 October 1453 Rinaldo paid for the illumination of a book of music theory:

> Mastro Gulielmo de Magri, laminadore [receives 5 lire] per sua mercegna et spexa de avere aminiato uno libro . . . de ragione de canto et un altro, nominado Tibulo.

The same 'libro de ragione de canto' is mentioned again in a payment record of 25 May 1454.[29]

But it would be rash to assume that this manuscript was the one now at

Oporto. There is no reason to suppose that the 1453 manuscript survives at all; moreover Rinaldo Maria, if he ordered one manuscript of music theory, probably ordered several in the course of his life: plainly he was interested in music otherwise he would not have employed Robertus. There is also the more complicated matter, to be discussed presently, of the repertory and concordances for the Oporto manuscript clearly pointing to a later date.

Yet the most important consideration here is that Gulielmo Magri is the painter much better known as Guglielmo Giraldi, considered by many to be the founder of the Ferrarese school of illumination in the later 15th century. Giraldi's most famous works date from the 1460s and 1470s, and it was on the basis of those that the art historian Hermann Julius Hermann first attempted to outline his career and importance. He first appears in the Este accounts as an illuminator in 1445, so he was already a mature and experienced painter by 1453; but only one work from before the 1460s is signed by him, a manuscript of Aulus Gellius dated 1448, now in the Biblioteca Ambrosiana at Milan. Its two main illuminations are of a grandeur quite different from the less pretentious Oporto and Berlin manuscripts, but the smaller initials show some distant similarity in the 'white-vine' patterns (*bianchi girari*) that were so characteristic of Italian illumination throughout the Middle Ages.[30]

Oporto, like the Ambrosiana Gellius of Giraldi, has a colouring scheme with letters in gold of a quality that still startles the eye: a deep blue fills the outer border and the remainder of each illumination is red, blue and green with a light yellow-brown wash in some of the floral patterns. I am grateful to my colleague Dr J. J. G. Alexander for the observation that the 1448 Gellius is more plastic, more aware of space and its potential than are any of the illuminated letters in Oporto or the single one at the beginning of Berlin. This opinion must, of course, await a fuller study of Giraldi's earlier years and a wider selection of comparative material, but it seems most unlikely that the illuminations in Oporto can be the work of an artist of Giraldi's status.

The only possibility here would be that the missing first leaf of Oporto was much more elaborate than the one in Berlin and that it indeed contained an illumination by the premier Ferrarese illuminator of the time. Yet against that possibility we must put the evidence offered earlier that the first fascicle was itself an afterthought—and certainly not a matter for the eight months' work implied by the documents of 1453–4.

Ultimately, however, we must return to the repertory of the Oporto manuscript, a body of music which repeatedly suggests that it was compiled in the 1460s, not in 1453 when Giraldi illuminated a manuscript of music theory for Rinaldo Maria d'Este.

Nothing in the Oporto collection appears in any of the early 15th-century song collections, neither the enormous Bodleian manuscript (*GB-Ob* can. misc. 213), which was finished in the late 1430s, nor the first Escorial chansonnier (*E-E* V.III.24), perhaps a few years later, nor Trent 87 (*I-TRmn* 87) dating from the 1440s; and between them these manuscripts contain practically all that survives of the French song tradition from the early 15th century. By far the earliest concordant manuscript, and the only one firmly before 1450, is the small Vatican chansonnier (*I-Rvat* Urb. lat.1411) dating from about 1440: it shares only one piece with Oporto, *O rosa bella*, one of the most widely distributed of all 15th-century songs and therefore the one whose sources would be expected to spread widest chronologically. And whereas Oporto has this single concordance from the first half of the century, it has several concordances with manuscripts from the very end of the century (*I-Fr* 2356, *I-Rvat* C.G.XIII.27) and even from the beginning of the next (*DK-Kk* 1848), while none of the manuscripts known to date from before 1450 is represented so late except for certain liturgical settings that recur heavily revised and augmented in the choir-books of the Vatican, of Milan Cathedral and of Segovia Cathedral.

This indication that the Oporto collection dates from well into the second half of the century is endorsed by the dates of those manuscripts containing the largest number of concordances. The only manuscripts sharing six pieces with Oporto are the second Escorial chansonnier (*E-E* IV.a.24), from the 1460s, and the Berlin Kupferstichkabinett manuscript (78 C 28) reliably dated 1465–6; the latter contains only 45 (or perhaps 44) songs, so the inclusion of so many in common with Oporto is evidence of similarity of taste, and since taste changes relatively quickly it is at least an indication of similarity of date. Three manuscripts share five songs with Oporto and all of them date from the 1470s and later.

A different kind of approach is to consider the dates of manuscripts which are the sole additional source for a song in Oporto. These are the Cordiforme chansonnier of Jean de Montchenu (*F-Pn* Rothschild 2973), reliably dated 1470–77, that at Montecassino (*I-MC* 871), cautiously dated around 1480, the Florence manuscript 178 (*I-Fn* Magl.XIX,178), convincingly dated in the late 1470s, the second Escorial chansonnier, probably from around 1470, and the Berlin Kupferstichkabinett manuscript of 1465–6. Some of these dates are based on a series of hypotheses—like the widely accepted dating *c*1440 for Oporto—but most are founded on securely datable pieces and are therefore more likely to be too early than too late. But the tremendous weight of evidence from the concordances makes it seem obstinacy to persist in dating Oporto around 1440 merely because of its black notation and at the best perverse to date it 1453 merely because we know that a manuscript of music theory was prepared in that year. In terms of its repertory it belongs firmly in the 1460s.

It may be possible, in terms of notation and concordances, to date the Oporto manuscript more closely still. Very much in the spirit of hypothesis, I would like to suggest 1467 as a possible date of compilation and Bologna as the place.[31] Only 40 kilometres from Ferrara, Bologna could display the traits of dialect detected by Professor Folena. Since Robertus had been in Ferrara he could have brought with him the songs by Galfridus; and if the initials are specifically Ferrarese in style, the volume could well have been sent this short distance for illumination. The attraction of the Bologna hypothesis is of course partly that this is the town where Ramos and Cesare Nappi lived; and it is the town in which Robertus occupied an important position. But the real reason for wishing to date the manuscript in 1467 stems from the group of five Dufay songs at the end of the collection.

Dufay seems to have returned to Cambrai in 1458 and to have remained there until his death 16 years later; but of course new music could still be sent south, and the evidence of his letter of 1456 to Giovanni and Piero de' Medici[32] is that he remained eager to circulate his work even after he had become an established international figure. Two documents from 1467 show this process in action. In 1467 Gille Arpin arrived at the court of Savoy with music from Dufay;[33] and on 1 May of the same year Antonio Squarcialupi wrote from Florence to Dufay acknowledging the receipt of letters brought by colleagues from the choir of Cambrai Cathedral.[34] Might these both refer to the same delegation which, on its way, could also have stopped at Bologna, where Dufay had lived for some years? It is possible, even likely.

If the last five Dufay songs came to Robertus from Arpin in 1467, this would explain why the final gathering was not illuminated. It was the last part of the volume to be planned: it was copied at the last moment, and one of Robertus's own songs was tacked on to the end to give the collection some sense and symmetry. All but one of the new Dufay songs is unique to the Oporto manuscript, so it is difficult to evaluate their readings; but they seem to be excellent in the music though extremely poor in the text. It is as though the scribe had no understanding of the French language and merely aped the letter-forms as best he could. The consistency of the incompetence in French texts throughout the manuscript strongly suggests that the failure was in the copyist, not in the exemplar. He could well have been working from a copy that came straight from the composer.

But that cannot be considered more than a hypothesis. The firm conclusions drawn from this study of the manuscript are (1) that it was a presentation copy for a particular occasion, (2) that there is no particular connection between the song collection and the preceding theoretical works even though they were together at the time of presentation and the writing is uniform throughout, (3) that it must date from no earlier than 1460, (4) that Robertus de Anglia the choirmaster, songwriter and theorist was a focal figure in the compilation and notational style of the song collection and (5) that the compiler had a special interest in English music and composers.

The English Music

Following almost inevitably from this is the conclusion that the three ascriptions to Bedyngham must be considered definitive even though all three are contradicted elsewhere. Somebody who was so obviously interested in the work of English composers (and who could even spell Bedyngham's name correctly) may be taken as a far better authority than the compiler of one of the larger mixed manuscripts to whom the name 'Dunstable' was a synonym for 'English'. *Durer ne puis* and *Mon seul plaisir* have already appeared as 'doubtful works' in the standard editions of Dunstable and Dufay respectively; the question of *O rosa bella* is more difficult, and Dunstable scholarship still inclines to regard it as his, but here again the authority of the Oporto manuscript must be considered overwhelming.

On the other hand, none of the four unascribed songs is likely to be by an English composer: two are ascribed elsewhere, one to Johannes Legrant and the other to Dufay. When Besseler suggested that *Le serviteur hault guerdonné* was by Morton in spite of an ascription elsewhere to Dufay, he was working from the incorrect assumption that Robertus de Anglia was identifiable with Robert Morton. He observed that *Le serviteur* is unlike Dufay's mature style and appears in sources as late as the 16th century; and he concluded that since Morton remained well-known into the 16th century there could be no doubt that one of the four anonymous pieces in Oporto, *Le serviteur*, was by him.[35] It is a pity that Besseler gave no further reasons for this identification, for it is quite possible that the finest connoisseur of 15th-century musical style noticed something about *Le serviteur* that recalled characteristics of Morton's music, though I can find none. And it is a pity that no further evidence appears to support his conjecture, for *Le serviteur* is one of the finest songs of its time and its attribution to an English composer would substantially alter the picture of English influence on the continent after the death of Dunstable. But there is no apparent trace of English style in this or in any other of the unascribed pieces in Oporto.

But the core of seven pieces ascribed specifically to English composers yields the most tantalising clues that they may all have originated with English texts. Bedyngham's *Mon seul plaisir* contains several features suggesting that it began life as a setting of the English version of that poem, found in the British Library manuscript of the 'English Poems of Charles of Orleans' (*GB-Lbm* Harl.682) as *Mi verry joy*; and the suggestion has been advanced that his *O rosa bella* originally had English text. These suggestions are based on formal considerations and on musico-poetic characteristics which are not otherwise explicable.[36] But the songs of Galfridus and Robertus present a different kind of clue to their English origin.

That the songs of Galfridus present the nearest continental equivalent to a group of songs in the only surviving collection of English song from the middle of the 15th century (*GB-Ob* Ashmole 191) can be seen from a comparison of the opening of one of his pieces (ex.1a) with that of *Alas, departyng is ground of woo* (ex.1b). The Oxford manuscript has normally been dated some time in the 1440s, and Pirrotta's findings about the Galfridus texts, dating them *c*1444, lend support to this hypothesis. The similarity of the two pieces consists not only in their tonality, their ambitus and their melodic shapes, but also in their phrase lengths and even overall length (78 semibreves in *Io zemo* and 73 semibreves in *Alas, departyng*). Seen in this context Galfridus's songs begin to take on a little more meaning, perhaps not as works of great intrinsic value but as two more pieces that can help rebuild the lost picture of what was happening in English polyphonic song during those middle years of the 15th century from which so few sources survive. And having seen the similarity of the Galfridus songs to those in the Oxford manuscript, one is struck even more forcibly by the substantial stylistic difference between them and the rest of the continental repertory among which they appear.

But perhaps the most fascinating is the evidence of musical palimpsest in Robertus de Anglia's *O fallaze e ria Fortuna*. The first section of the music is repeated, with *aperto* and *chiuso* endings, and is followed by a longer second half. This is characteristic of the ballade, a form which in

Ex. 1a

Ex. 1b

the later 15th century was a particular favourite of English composers and only rarely employed by their continental contemporaries. But the text contains no suggestion of ballade form: it is constructed in four quatrains. The first quatrain is underlaid to the first section of the music, and the second is underlaid to its repeat; the other two take the rest of the music. The first two quatrains have different rhyme schemes; but it is most unusual in the song style of the 15th century for lines with different rhyme schemes to be underlaid to the same music. Further observation suggests that the music may originally have been written not for this Italian text but for an English ballade.

The details of the text underlaid in the manuscript are unusually clear throughout the song: they flout all the conventions of Italian scansion. The second eight-syllable line, for instance, is expanded to ten syllables: elisions are not taken, or to put it more correctly, there are two cases of hiatus. This expansion continues throughout the song consistently enough for it to be clear that the scribe, at least, was quite confident of his correctness.

Moreover all attempts to re-underlay the text on more traditional and rational lines fail completely. There seems no musical or practical way of underlaying the text which differs significantly from that presented in the manuscript and in ex.2. The reason is not far to seek: the music perfectly fits a ten-syllable line, moving syllabically except where there are flourishes, resolutions of suspensions or closing melismas (bb.10–14).

Ex. 2

While it is not always possible to discern the composer's intentions, it does seem that the music is considerably better suited to a line of ten syllables than to one of eight. Ten-syllable lines predominate in English verse of the 15th century. To suggest that the original text was an English ballade or rhyme-royal stanza with a ten-syllable line would explain some of the idiosyncrasies of *O fallaze e ria Fortuna*. The Italian text would have been added as well as possible to make the piece acceptable in circles where English was not understood.

This again suggests for the song a musical context that makes more sense. Among the handful of English songs surviving from the years 1450–80 there are several whose stylistic characteristics are similar to those of *O fallaze*. Ex.3 comes from the Ritson manuscript (*GB-Lbm* Add. 5665), a confusing assembly of independent musical documents including a group of eight songs probably from the 1470s.[37]

Ex. 3

The homophonic movement of the first bars is similar, with its free declamatory accentuation, while the subsequent melisma has much of the open ebullience that appears in bb. 10–14 of *O fallaze* and was to become a major feature in the songs of Fayrfax and his contemporaries:

Ex. 4

Such a conclusion about the song that opens the Oporto collection would not be possible if the underlay were less clearly written. If the song had been preserved anonymously in a less careful manuscript, or in one less closely connected with its composer, it might have been difficult to identify the English characteristics. But once seen in this light, the song manifests a decidedly English style, and adds perhaps one more piece to that scanty collection of surviving English secular music from the years that led up to the astonishing song tradition of the Fayrfax manuscript.

Besseler once remarked that although there is a clear English style in

15th-century sacred music, no such characteristics appear in the secular song repertory.[38] I would like to suggest that we have some in these pieces. And here too is surely the essential difference between Robert Morton and his namesake in Bologna. Morton wedded himself entirely to the Burgundian song style and left no apparent clues or fingerprints on his work to reveal his nationality.[39] The choirmaster at Bologna preferred the sobriquet 'de Anglia', thereby perhaps capitalising on being the compatriot of Dunstable and Leonel Power. So we can imagine why he incurred the displeasure of Ramos, a Spaniard who was also living as an alien in the city of Bologna. Robertus, as choirmaster at San Petronio, must have represented the establishment to Ramos, the man who spent ten years lecturing in Bologna, waiting for the university chair which never came to him. Robertus had the mark of success. Perhaps he also gave preferential treatment to the slender abilities of his countryman Galfridus. In any case he seems to have played on the fact of being English—so much so that we shall probably never know his real surname.[40]

INVENTORY OF SONG COLLECTION

The columns are as follows: (a) serial number for the purposes of this list; (b) modern pencil foliation; (c) text incipit (Discantus); (d) ascription, with ascriptions from other sources in square brackets; (e) mensuration signs; (f) number of voices; (g) form (Ba = ballata; Berg = bergerette; R4^{10} = rondeau with a four-line stanza and a ten-syllable line); (h) other sources, text sources given only selectively. @ = ascribed; (i) selected editions.

(a)	(b)	(c)	(d)	(e)	(f)	(g)	(h)	(i)
1	ff.51v–54	O fallaze e ria Fortuna	Ro. de Anglia	C C C	3	—	—	G&R
2	ff.54v–56	O rosa bella (text attrib. Leonardo Giustiniani)	Joh Bedyngham [or Dunstable]	C C C	3	Ba	RU 'Domstaple' BerK Col Cord EscB MC Pav Pix Tr89 90 93 Wolf Intab: Bux	MB, viii
3	ff.56v–57	Che faro io dolorosa (text: Girolamo Nigrisoli)	Galfridus de Anglia	C C	2	—	—	G&R
4	ff.57v–58	Io zemo suspiro (text: Girolamo Nigrisoli)	Galfridus de Anglia	C C	2	—	—	G&R
5	ff.58v–59	Durer ne puis	Bedynghm de Anglia [or Dunstable]	[O] [O] [O]	3	R4^{10}	EscB 'Dunstable'	MB, viii
6	ff.59v–60	Mon seul plaiser (text: Charles d'Orléans)	Idem [or Dufay]	[O] [O] [O]	3	R4^{8}	F176 'Duffay' BerK Col Cop 1848 Cord EscB Lab M9659 Pav Pix RiccII Scbed Wolf Text: Rob	CMM, i/6
7	ff.60v–61	Va t'en mon cuer	Dufay	[O] [O] [O]	3	R5^{8}	BerK Text: Rob	CMM, i/6

(a)	(b)	(c)	(d)	(e)	(f)	(g)	(h)	(i)
8	ff.61v–62	Per le leguarde (reguard)	Idem	[O] [O] [O]	3	R4⁸	BerK Col Cop17 EscB Lab Mel@ M9659 Pav Pix MC@ Tr93 Wolf Intab:Bux Text:Jard	CMM, i/6
9	ff.62v–64	Fortune lasse moy la vie	—	C C C	3	Berg	Pav Trin Wolf Text:Lans	—
10	ff.64v–65	Le servitour mal guerdoné	[Dufay]	[O] [O] [O]	3	R5⁸	MC@ BerK CG Col Dij EscB Cord Pav Per Pix Riccl Tr90 Wolf Intab:Bux Text:Jard Lans Rob	CMM i/6
11	ff. 65v–67	Poy che crudel Fortuna	Joye	[O] [O] [O]	3	?Ba	F176	—
12	ff.67v–69	Helas n'array ie mais mieux	—	[O] [O] [O]	3	Berg	Cord	—
13	ff.69v–70	Las ie ne puis oir novelle	[Jo Legrant]	[O] [O] [O]	3	R4⁸	Tr-90@ BerK EscB Pix	CMM, xi/2
14	ff.70v–72	Adieu m'amour	Dufay	₵ ₵ [₵]	3	R5⁸	MC@ Text:Jard Rob	CMM, i/6
15	ff.72v–73	[Q]u'est devenue leaulté	Dufài	[O] [O] [O]	3	R4⁸	—	CMM, i/6
16	ff.73v–74	[E]ntre les plus plaines	Dufai	o [O] [O]	3	R4⁸	—	CMM, i/6
17	ff.74v–76	[H]elas mon duel	Dufai	C C C	3	Berg	—	CMM, i/6
18	ff.76v–77	[J]e triumphe de Crudel (= En triumphant de Cruel)	Dufay	[O] [O] [O]	3	R5⁸	Text:Rob	EMS, xxiii
19	ff.77v–79	[E]l mal foco arda	Ro. de Anglia	[O] [O] [O]	3	—	—	G&R

Editions

CMM, i/6: *Guillelmi Dufay: Cantiones*, ed. H. Besseler (Rome, 1964)
CMM, xi/2: *Early Fifteenth-century Music*, ed. G. Reaney (1959)
EMS, xxiii: *Guillaume Dufay: Two Songs*, ed. D. Fallows (London, 1975)
G&R: *Galfridus and Robertus de Anglia*, ed. D. Fallows (Newton Abbot, 1976)
MB, viii: *John Dunstable*, ed. M. Bukofzer (London, 1953, rev. 2/1970
     by M. and I. Bent and B. Trowell)

Text Sources Cited

Siglum	Call-number	Pieces in Porto	Date
Jard	Le jardin de plaisance et fleur de rethorique (Paris, 1501)	(2) 8, 10, 14	1501
Lans	GB-Lbm Lansdowne 380	(1) 9, 10	?
Roh	D-B 78 B 17	(4) 6, 7, 10, 14, 18	c1470

Additional Notes on the Songs

1. Perhaps originating with English text, see pp. 116–117. The ascription is exceptionally on the right-hand page.

2. Perhaps originating with English text. For a discussion of the texting see MB, viii (1953, rev. 2/1970), 200; the conclusions are drawn in M. Bent: 'The Transmission of English Music 1300–1500: some Aspects of Repertory and Preparation', *Studien zur Tradition in der Musik: Kurt von Fischer zum 60. Geburtstag* (Munich, 1973), 65. Further on the authorship see my article 'Bedyngham' in *The New Grove*, but note also that the ascription to Dunstable in *RU* is almost entirely erased, as are several other ascriptions in that manuscript. Pirrotta, in 'Ricercare e variazioni . . .' (1972), concludes that the song was most probably by neither Dunstable nor Bedyngham but by another Englishman. Facs. of ff.54v–55 in MB, viii, Pl.4.

3. and 4. Both texts come from a single longer poem by Nigrisoli, see p.109 above.

5. The spelling of 'Bedyngham' almost exactly accords with that in *GB-Lbm* Royal 24.d.2 (the Baldwin Manuscript), whose late date should not be permitted to cast doubt on Bedyngham's authorship for the pieces it ascribes to him.

6. The text in the Charles d'Orléans manuscript begins *Ma seule plaisant doulce joye* but continues exactly as this poem; see also p.115 above.

8. Dufay's most widely distributed song.

10. Besseler rejected the Dufay ascription in *MC* on stylistic grounds. This may be valid, but his hypothetical attribution to Morton is best ignored, see p.114

above. More expansive than some of Dufay's other songs though it is, its quality places it far beyond most of the possible composers, and its range of ideas and invention make one hesitate to attribute it to Busnoys or Hayne.

11. Gilles Joye spent most of his life in the north, see F. Molle: *Identification d'un portrait de Gilles Joye attribué à Memlinc* (Brussels, 1960). Why he should have written a song with an Italian text is a mystery; its style is quite unlike anything in the other four songs ascribed to him.

12. Contains many turns of phrase strongly reminiscent of Dufay's later songs, see esp. i & ii 11/ i 18/ iii 22/ i-iii 25/ i-iii 31-2/ i-iii 34. It is either by Dufay or by someone consciously aping his style.

13. This song is so much later than the other songs ascribed to Jo. Legrant (see CMM, xi/2, 68f) that he may be a different composer entirely.

14. Facs. in *MGG*, iii, col. 898.

16. The very small mensuration sign 'o' is entered in the margin where it would have been covered by the illuminated letter, which was never completed, see p.104 above.

18. Discussed in D. Fallows: 'Two More Dufay Songs Reconstructed', *Early Music*, iii (1975), 358-60, and 'Postscript . . .', *Early Music*, iv (1976), 99.

LIST OF CONCORDANT SONG MANUSCRIPTS

Dates are more fully explained in the references given. Many of the citations are to Allan W. Atlas: *The Capella Giulia Chansonnier* (Brooklyn, 1975), not because the thinking necessarily originates there, but because this is the most comprehensive, responsible and clear recent discussion of the manuscripts at the time of writing. Published studies by Perkins and H. M. Brown are expected in the near future, but should not substantially alter the dates for which Atlas is cited. If there is no convincing recent dating no reference is given: the dating suggested is in many cases further discussed in my dissertation.

Siglum	*Call-number*	*Pieces in* Porto	*Date*
BerK	D-B 78 C 28	(6) 2, 6, 7, 8, 10, 13	1465-6, see Peter Reidemeister: *Die Chanson-Handschrift* (1973)
Bux	D-Mbs Cim 352b	(3) 2, 8, 10	c1465, see B. A. Wallner: DM, 2nd ser., *Hand-schriften-Faksimiles*, 1 (1955) vii
CG	I-Rvat C.G.XIII.27	(1) 10	1492-4, see Atlas

Siglum	Call-number	Pieces in Porto	Date
Col	E-Sc 5-I-43 (parts of which are now in F-Pn n.a.fr.4379, f.1-42)	(4) 2, 6, 8, 10	?1480-90
Cop17	DK-Kk frag.17	(1) 8	c1460, cf Besseler, CMM i/6
Cop1848	DK-Kk Ny kgl.sam.1848 2°	(1) 6	1500-1525, see Glahn in Fund og forskning, v-vi (1958-9), 90-109
Cord	F-Pn Rothschild 2973	(4) 2, 6, 10, 12	1470-77, see Atlas, 240
Dij	F-Dm 517	(1) 10	?1470-80
EscB	E-E IV.a.24	(6) 2, 5, 6, 8, 10, 13	1460s, see Atlas, 242
F176	I-Fn Magl.XIX,176	(2) 6, 11	late 1470s, see Atlas, 246-7
Lab	US-Wc M2.1 L25 Case	(2) 6, 8	?1475-85
MC	I-MC 871	(4) 2, 8, 10, 14	after 1480, see Atlas, 248
Mel	US-NH 91	(1) 8	1470s, before 1476, see Atlas, 249-50
M9659	D-Mbs Mus. Ms. 9659	(2) 6, 8	c1460
Pav	I-PAVu Aldini 362	(5) 2, 6, 8, 9, 10	?1480
Per	I-PEc 431 (G20)	(1) 10	after 1480, see Atlas, 253-4
Pix	F-Pn fr.15,123	(5) 2, 6,8, 10, 13	c1484, see Atlas, 254-5
RiccI	I-Fr 2794	(1) 10	?1480s
RiccII	I-Fr 2356	(1) 6	c1480-85, see Atlas, 256
RU	I-Rvat Urb.lat.1411	(1) 2	c1440
Sched	D-Mbs Cgm 810	(1) 6	1460-67, see Besseler, CMM, i/6
Tr89	I-TRmn 89	(1) 2	?1480, cf Federhofer: 'Trienter Codices', MGG
Tr90	I-TRmn 90	(3) 2, 10, 13	?1470, cf Federhofer, op cit
Tr93	I-TRmd 93	(2) 2, 8	?1470, cf Federhofer, op cit
Trin	GB-Ctc R.2.71	(1) 9	c1480
Wolf	D-W Cod.-Guelf 287 Extrav.	(5) 2, 6, 8, 9, 10	early 1470s

NOTES TO CHAPTER 3

1. Bukofzer in *NOHM*, iii (1960), 133; Besseler in *AcM*, xl (1968), 203; Pirrotta in 'Two Anglo-Italian Pieces in the Manuscript Porto 714', *Speculum Musicae Artis: Festgabe für Heinrich Husmann* (Munich, 1970), 253-61, fn.21. The suggestion seems to originate with the 2nd edition of H. Davey: *History of English Music* (2/1921, R 1969), 56.

2. See my dissertation *Robert Morton's Songs: a Study of Styles in the Mid-fifteenth Century* (U. of California at Berkeley, 1978). Allan Atlas disagrees and explains his viewpoint in the preface to his forthcoming edition of Morton's works (which he kindly sent me in draft and discussed with me).

3. For further documentation see F. Ll. Harrison: 'Register and Index of Musicians', in his *Music in Medieval Britain* (London, 1958, 2/1963), 454-65; H. Baillie: 'Some Biographical Notes on English Church Musicians, Chiefly Working in London (1485-1569)', *RMARC*, ii (1962), 18-57; R. Rastall: 'The Minstrels of the English Royal Households, 25 Edward I-1 Henry VIII: an Inventory', *RMARC*, iv (1964), 1-41.

4. 'Venerabilis vir dominus Robertus quondam Petri de Anglia ['presbiter secularis' *crossed out*] conductus pro Cantore ad docendum Clericos Ferrariae in cantu . . . dixit et confessus fuit quod habet penes se . . . infrascripta bona mobilia, res et libros sibi hodie consignatos per eundem dominum Bartolum [Tarufum] et que tenere et salvare promisit et de eis bonam redere rationem et ea restituere cum opus fuerit . . .'. The entire document was kindly transcribed for me by Dr Adriano Franceschini from Ferrara, Archivio di stato, Notaio Ludovico Miliani, Matricola 100, Pacco 4. I am most grateful to him as well as to Professor Lewis Lockwood who drew my attention to the document and put me in touch with Dr Franceschini.

5. G. Gaspari: 'La musica in S. Petronio', *Atti e memorie della deputazione storica in Romagna*, ix (Bologna, 1870), repr. in *Musica e musicisti a Bologna* (Bologna, 1970), 119-21. The documents he prints are all from the Archivio capitolare at San Petronio, Bologna.

6. The document was discovered by Dr Franceschini and communicated to me by Professor Lockwood—some of whose phrasing I have retained for want of better.

7. *GB-Lgc* 4889, a document that can easily be misunderstood unless the reader has at hand the study by R. H. Adams: *The Parish Clerks of London* (London and Chichester, 1971), 124f. For showing me that the document should be called a Leet book rather than a Bede roll I am grateful to Dr Roger Bowers.

8. F. X. Haberl: 'Die römische "Schola cantorum" und die päpstlichen Kapellsänger bis zur Mitte des 16. Jahrhunderts', *VMw*, iii (1887), 238, 241-6, see also the informative footnote in B. Trowell: 'Faburden and Fauxbourdon', *MD*, xiii (1959), 68. On the Roberto at Ferrara, see L. Lockwood: '"Messer Gossino" and Josquin Desprès', *Studies in Renaissance and Baroque Music in Honor of Arthur Mendel*, ed. R. L. Marshall (Kassel and Hackensack, 1974), 15-24, on p.18.

9. For the poem, see L. Frati, ed.: *Rimatori bolognesi del quattrocento* (Bologna, 1908), 255. Nappi's poems are difficult to date. The dates in the manuscript Frati used (*I-Bu* 52) range from 1478 to 1514; moreover the only poem in Frati's collection which resembles *Iti caldi suspiri* in form is firmly dated 1512, so the aforementioned Robert Bonetti could possibly be the composer. Nevertheless Nappi was almost certainly writing poetry as early as 1460, when he was a student. In the following years he was accepted as a notary and held several posts before receiving his first public appointment in 1470. Frati knew nothing of the choirmaster except Gaspari's information that he was at Bologna from 1467 to 1474; so presumably he found such an early date consistent with his understanding of Nappi's life and poetry, see L. Frati: 'Per la storia della musica in Bologna dal secolo XV al XVI', *RMI*, xxiv (1917), 449–78, esp. p.453.

10. C. Palisca: 'Ramos', *MGG*; see also O. Mischiati: 'Un'inedita testimonianza su Bartolomeo Ramis de Pareia', *FAM*, xiii (1966), 84ff. Although the chair of music at Bologna University was established in 1440 it was apparently not occupied until after Ramos left Bologna; and Spataro, writing to Pietro Aaron in 1532, gave as the reason for Ramos's departure his disappointment at having lectured at the university without receiving the chair.

11. Magister vero Robertus Anglicus proprietatem notularum in geometria ignorans contrarium dicebat, hoc est: quando signum temporis non reperitur, perfectum esse tempus arbitrabatur. Omnes fere cantus signis carentes male compositos esse dicebat. Ipse enim inscius doctrinae artem praeponebat naturae, cuius contrarium manifestum est, quia ars imitatur naturam in quantum potest. See J. Wolf, ed.: *Musica practica Bartolomei Rami de Pareia*, Beihefte der Internationalen Musikgesellschaft, ii (Leipzig, 1901), 88.

12. See particularly G. Moldenhauer: 'Nachweis älterer französischen Handschriften in portugiesischen Bibliotheken', *Archiv für das Studium der neueren Sprachen und Literaturen*, cli (1927), 69–76, on pp.75f; H. Anglès: 'El "Chansonnier français" de la Colombina de Sevilla', *Estudis Universitaris Catalans*, xiv (1929), 227–58, on p.228 (passing mention based on Besseler's photographs at Heidelberg); B. Meier: 'Die Handschrift Porto 714 als Quelle zur Tonartenlehre des 15. Jahrhunderts', *MD*, vii (1953), 175–97; N. Pirrotta: 'Two Anglo-Italian Pieces in the Manuscript Porto 714', *Speculum Musicae Artis: Festgabe für Heinrich Husmann* (Munich, 1970), 253–61; L. Lockwood: 'Dufay and Ferrara', *Dufay Quincentenary Conference*, ed. A. W. Atlas (Brooklyn, 1976), 1–25, on pp.6ff.

13. See A. Seay, ed.: *Ugolino of Orvieto: Declaratio musicae disciplinae*, CSM, vii (1960–62), vol.1, pp.31, 38, 40–43, 103f, 106ff. Precisely the same distillation appears in the Berlin treatise, *D-B* Mus. ms. theor. 1599, discussed later. Several passages are not accounted for in this analysis;but there can be no question of the direct connection. It is of more than passing interest to note that in the document of 26 Sept 1460 (see note 4 above) there is mention of Robertus having had possession of 18 parchment quinterns 'pro cantu' compiled by Ugolino of Orvieto.

14. Seay, CSM, vii/2, pp.54, 58f, 83f, 92f, 140ff, 161–7, 175ff, 184, 187f, 194f, 203ff, 225–36, 265f. On nearly 50 surviving sources for the *Libellus* and the reasons for accepting the ascription to Johannes de Muris, see U. Michels: *Die Musiktraktate des Johannes de Muris*, BAMw, viii (Wiesbaden, 1970), 27–40.

15. A good example is on f.54 where the first note of the tenor has been erased and placed at the end of the preceding line (on f.53*v*). But other examples of obvious care in the underlay can be seen throughout the song section.

16. [Eduardo Augusto Allen on material by Diogo Kopke (*d* 25 Feb 1844)]: *Catalogo da Bibliotheca Publica Municipal do Porto: Indice preparatorio do catalogo dos manuscriptos, 1° fasciculo: Mss. Membranaceos* (Oporto, 1880), 39. On the library of Santa Cruz see Joachim Martins Teixeira de Carvalho: 'A livraria de Santa Cruz de Coimbra', *Boletim bibliográfico da biblioteca da universidade de Coimbra*, i–iii (1914–16); further on its history, see António Cruz: *Santa Cruz de Coimbra na cultura portuguesa da idade media*, i: *Observações sobre o 'scriptorium' e os estudos claustrais* (Oporto, 1964).

17. See António Gomez da Rocha Madahil: *D. Pedro da Encarnação e a livraria de Santa Cruz de Coimbra* (Coimbra, 1937).

18. Eduardo Braga: *Biblioteca portuense 1833–1933* (Oporto, 1933).

19. Facs. of dedication page in J. Smits van Waesberghe: *Musikerziehung: Lehre und Theorie der Musik im Mittelalter*, Musikgeschichte in Bildern, iii/3 (Leipzig, 1969), 185; also, p. 141, facs. of f.1*v*, with the Guidonian hand. Further on the manuscript see *Versteigerung der Musikbibliothek des Herrn Dr. Werner Wolffheim*, ii (Berlin, 1929), 8, and M. Huglo: *Les tonaires: inventaire, analyse, comparaison* (Paris, 1971), 370, 428. It is impossible to be certain about the original collation of the Berlin manuscript as the paper has rotted away: the leaves were remounted in 1963. I could not identify the coat of arms on f.1 with the presumably humanistic name 'Apomoni', though Professor Lockwood points out that a very similar name appears on the title-page of one of the main Ugolino manuscripts, *I-Rvat* Rossi 445 (facs. in CSM, vii, pl.1).

20. See R. L. Crocker: 'A New Source for Medieval Music Theory', *AcM*, xxxix (1967), 161–71, on p.165.

21. Meier (1953) sets out to demonstrate the connection of the musical anthology with the preceding treatises, but after a brief description of the treatises can discuss the songs only in terms of other late 15th-century theoretical works. It would be fair to say that no relevant connection was perceptible to Meier.

22. H. Besseler: *Guillelmi Dufay: Cantiones*, CMM, i/6 (Rome, 1964), xx: Italy, 1440–50. Pirrotta (1970) and 'Ricercare e variazioni su "O rosa bella"', *Studi musicali*, i (1972), 59–77: Ferrara, before 1450. A. W. Atlas: *The Cappella Giulia Chansonnier* (Brooklyn, 1975): 'no later than about the middle of the fifteenth century'. Lockwood (1976): Ferrara, about 1449 or 1450.

23. The slight preference for 1444 rather than the year of Isotta's second marriage, 1446, is expressed not by Pirrotta but by Lockwood (1976): her first husband, Oddantonio de Montefeltro, died two months after the wedding, so the references in the poem to Isotta as a virgin and Ferrara as a widow would have been inappropriate on the occasion of her second marriage.

24. Pirrotta (1970), 256. Despite my disagreement with some of his detailed conclusions my study would have been impossible without Pirrotta's work.

25. L. Lockwood: 'Music at Ferrara in the Period of Ercole I d'Este', *Studi musicali*, i (1972), 101–31, esp. p.105: 'Under Borso the musical forces became somewhat more stabilised and apparently enlarged . . .'.

26. Gallicus: *CS*, iv, 369f. The author states that he began his treatise in the reign of Pope Pius II (1458–64); the surviving sources are *GB-Lbm* Harl.6525 and *Lbm* Add.22315 of which the latter was copied by Burzio and may therefore be later still.

27. See facs. in CSM, vii/1; Seay may be a little early in his estimated dating 'middle 15th cent.', op. cit., 5.

28. Facs. of three openings in MB, xxxvi (1975), xxv–xxvii.

29. H. J. Hermann: 'Zur Geschichte der Miniaturmalerei am Hofe der Este in Ferrara', *Jahrbuch der kunsthistorischen Sammlungen des allerhöchsten Kaiserhauses*, xxi (Vienna, 1900), 117–271, on p.258. Once again I am grateful to Professor Lockwood for pointing me to this reference.

30. P. Liebaert: 'Un'opera sconosciuta di Guglielmo Giraldi', *L'arte*, xiv (1911), 401–6. Further on Giraldi and the style of *bianchi girari* see J. J. G. Alexander: *Italian Renaissance Illuminations* (London, 1977), 12–13, 84–9. I am grateful to Dr Alexander for pointing out an illustration similar to that on f.1 of the Berlin manuscript in Ferrara, Bibl. Ariostea,

Ms. Cl. 1. 147, f.1, published in M. Salmi: *Pittura e miniatura a Ferrara nel primo rinascimento* (Milan, 1961), pl.IX.

31. In a paper presented to the American Musicological Society annual convention at Chicago in Nov 1973 entitled 'John Bedyngham and the Composition of *O rosa bella*' I argued that the available evidence could just as strongly support Bologna as Ferrara, but that was before knowing any of the documents connecting Robertus with Ferrara: my position is now much more tentative though I think the Bologna possibility must be kept firmly open.

32. Facs. in Besseler: 'Dufay', *MGG*; on the evidence for dating it 1456 rather than 1454, see C. Wright: 'Dufay at Cambrai: Discoveries and Revisions', *JAMS*, xxviii (1975), 175–229, on p.190.

33. S. Cordero di Pamparato: 'Guglielmo Dufay alla corte di Savoia', *Santa Cecilia: rivista mensuale di musica sacra e liturgica*, xxvii (1925), no.2, p.19, no.3, p.34: payment of four ducats to 'messire Gille Arpin . . . qui venoit de Picardie et alloit à Rome et appourta de la part de Messire Guillaume du Fays aucunes messes faites en l'art de musique nouvellement'.

34. O. Kade: 'Biographisches zu Antonio Squarcialupi dem Florentiner Organist im XV. Jahrhunderte', *Monatshefte für Musikgeschichte*, xvii (1885), 1–7, 13–19.

35. H. Besseler: 'Falsche Autornamen in den Handschriften Strassburg (Vitry) und Montecassino (Dufay)', *AcM*, xl (1968), 201–3, on p.203.

36. For a fuller discussion see D. Fallows: 'Words and Music in Two English Songs of the Mid-15th Century: Charles d'Orléans and John Lydgate', *Early Music*, v (1977), 38.

37. They are edited by J. Stevens in MB, xxxvi (1975), 2–10.

38. 'Bedingham', *MGG*.

39. Since first preparing this chapter I have suggested a slightly different explanation of the style of Morton's songs, see 'English Song Repertories of the Mid-fifteenth Century', *PRMA*, ciii (1976–7), 61–79, on p.75; but the difference in intention between Robertus and Morton remains.

40. I would like to express my gratitude to Dr Maria Fernanda de Brito and Sr Vale, both of the Biblioteca pública municipal at Oporto, for their help in establishing the history of the manuscript and for generosity with their facilities when I visited the library at a moment of extreme political instability; to Brad Robinson and Dr Rudolf Elvers for help with the related manuscript in Berlin; to Dr Adriano Franceschini and Professor Allan W. Atlas for allowing me to see some of their unpublished work; to Professors Allan W. Atlas, Margaret Bent, Philip Brett, Richard L. Crocker, Philip Gossett, Daniel Heartz and Edward E. Lowinsky for their careful comments on earlier versions of this chapter; and particularly to Professor Lewis Lockwood who offered several important criticisms and kept me continually abreast of his extremely important work in the Ferrara archives.

4

Petrucci at Fossombrone:
Some New Editions and Cancels

Stanley Boorman

The discussion of Petrucci's work that follows is one product of a study that I had the privilege of starting under (or, as he would have preferred, with) Bob Dart, and which has been influenced by his ideas. It shows the effect of one of the sharper weapons in his armoury to which reference has already been made, Occam's razor,[1] with its ruthless cutting away of the unnecessary. Indeed, it is an interesting case of the cleansing influence of the razor in one direction seeming to open up new complications in another.

When Catherine Chapman wrote her study on Antico in 1964, she was able to say that his output exceeded Petrucci's for the second decade of the 16th century, at least in part because of the number of reprints that Antico produced.[2] In suggesting the *Motetti de la Corona* to me as a topic of interest, Dart had no reason to think that such a view would need modification, despite the one re-edition that was already known through the work of Sartori.[3] However, a number of other editions of Fossombrone titles has survived, hidden under colophons carrying the original dates of publication. Some of these have already been discussed elsewhere, and similar evidence has emerged for cancel sheets.[4] We can now see that there were many more editions than we had expected, and that Petrucci was willing to produce cancels for single sheets, sometimes long after the original publication.

The most obvious evidence of variant editions or of cancel sheets is typographical. The distinction between editions is normally simple, for in the re-setting of type, few compositors followed the original placings so precisely that differences cannot be seen on the majority of pages: in addition there are many purely typographical elements that a compositor felt free to change. Distinguishing between cancels and proof-corrections can be harder: in the case of Petrucci, however, it is made much easier by his use of the multiple impression process. A proof-correction is unlikely to involve a re-setting of both music and text on all pages of the sheet, whereas a cancel implies it. In the case of the volumes discussed here, the re-setting of the type shows on even a cursory examination. The different editions of the first book of *Motetti de la Corona* (to be called hereafter '*Corona I*') have different title pages, and the setting of type (both text and music) is different throughout. There are also complete sets of part-books for different editions for two of the three Josquin mass volumes (that is, of the Fossombrone editions in addition to those printed at Venice) as well as for *Corona II*.

There are, in addition, many cases where the variants between copies do not extend through all partbooks. In some cases all the books do not survive anywhere: for example, the edition of *Corona I* surviving in libraries at Bergamo, Leipzig and Venice with a Bassus part in Erwin Jacobi's collection[5] at Zurich, has no extant tenor part. In other cases a copy turns out to be composite: the Bologna copy of *Corona II* is one such, with the Superius and Bassus coming from the two different extant editions.

The range of readings between these various editions is usually very slight, an indication of the care that Petrucci's men took over their work. But, in assessing these variants, it is clearly important to try and date the editions as closely as possible, or at least to give them an order of precedence. The study of watermarks is of course of prime importance in confirming the distinct editions, and, it might be thought, also in grouping the editions, if Petrucci followed any pattern in buying paper. Valuable work has been done on this matter by Jeremy Noble,[6] and I do not intend here to go over the same ground, though I shall have occasion to cite one of his conclusions where I have been unable to consult a copy. However, the evidence of paper patterns, when allied to the dating on typographical grounds that I offer here, shows that for some critical periods Petrucci bought the same type of paper consistently. Without beta-radiographs, and with the small number of surviving copies, it is unlikely that the watermarks themselves will support or contradict a detailed chronology for many of the last prints and reprints.

In a previous study, I used the state of certain types, especially of the capital letters, to determine the order of printing of the various editions of *Corona I*. Here, I propose to return to this technique, in part because it provides an easy demonstration of variant editions, and in part because it assists materially in dating them.

It is important to stress that these capitals, each individually cut, were unique. Petrucci owned individual capitals as any other printer of the period did, and on the same basis as the woodcuts and borders that were to be found in almost all printing houses. Such blocks were designed and cut for the printer, often by distinguished artists of the day.[7] Probably in all cases they could not be preserved as matrices, as were founts of type, for they were not made by this process. Therefore replacement sorts (individual pieces of type) could not be made. This is clearly true of the Petrucci letters, and also of the ornamental blocks that decorate the most lavish of all his prints, the *de recta Paschae . . . .* of Paulus de Middelburgo.[8] The individual letters can be traced through his prints, gradually deteriorating, and there is no case where we have to postulate two letters of the same design. Further, stronger, evidence lies in the placing of these letters through the gatherings that make up the prints. Each gathering of eight leaves (16 pages) was printed on two sheets of paper. One made up folios 1, 2, 7 and 8 of the gathering and the other folios 3–6. Since each sheet was printed on both sides, a gathering contained four formes or arrangements of type on the bed of the press.[9] (Each of these formes was repeated for the second impression (music or type) and for a third in the early Venetian prints; so that something of the complexity of the process can be seen.) In the mass volumes, in particular, it often happens that a given capital occurs more than once in a gathering—for the start of two Kyries, for example. When the two letters appear on different formes, then the same sort can be used, and often is: when however, they lie on the same forme, letters of different design are used, without exception.

The letters to different designs were cut for Petrucci at different times and can be grouped together both by size and design and by when they were first used. Apparently he started with two principal sets (styles 2 and 3 below). Some of the letters in these were used more than others and decayed faster, showing more and more damage until there came a point at which Petrucci seems to have decided to replace them. Since certain letters remained serviceable throughout, he never again had a complete alphabet cut, but was content to acquire only those letters which he needed.

The old letters remained in the shop, however, and could be called into service if the layout of the type required more sorts of one letter than were immediately to hand. In one edition of Josquin's Masses I an early pattern of letter 'S' (S3) is used in the tenor partbook, where the other two currently used sorts are already needed.

I have assigned 'style' numbers to each of the sets of capitals; although in some cases the arrangements of sorts are rather arbitrary, they provide a ready means of distinguishing individual letters:

1. Large format letters, used for the title pages of the volumes of *Odhecaton* and for the early motet anthologies.

2. Basically *c*26–7mm high, these letters appear in *Odhecaton A* or immediately thereafter; the letter V2 is used in the illustrations to this study.

3. Also *c*26–7mm high, and also found in the earliest titles; it appears that Petrucci had two examples of the most popular letters cut at the start; many of these differ from style 2 by having a greater duplication of filigree lines.

4. 18mm high; only the letters A, E, K, P and S survive, being used first in the early mass volumes, for which they were presumably cut.

5. Used for a single 26mm 'S' which only appears in 1502.

6. 26–7mm letters apparently cut over a fairly long period, though probably all by the same man; they show less consistency of style than earlier designs and, in many cases, the internal structure of the letter is rather unbalanced; the earliest appear in the *Misse Brumel* of 1503; the letter B6 is used in this paper.

10. A set of 16mm letters which appear in Petrucci's second complete Fossombrone volume, Josquin's Masses III of 1514.

11. A set of letters of height *c*19–20mm, whose appearance is critical for the dating of some editions; the work of a less skilled hand, they are sometimes related in design to earlier letters.

12. A curious and unattractive set of letters of *c*16mm; many are small versions of earlier letters, not all of style 11; also important for dating.

13. Letters that do not need to fit into the sequence; these include some that are cut inside a square, which were designed for the non-musical volumes, and only appear within the musical ones if necessary; similar letters are frequent in the work of printers from the Marches and particularly from Venice.[10]

The letters of styles 11 and 12 only appear in certain copies of most of the titles where they are used at all. Their appearance coincides with a deterioration in the state of those earlier letters that are retained; thus they provide a guide to grouping some of the editions later in Petrucci's work.

The distribution of some of these letters through the relevant volumes and copies of Petrucci's Fossombrone work is shown on pp. 133–5. Here, the titles are arranged according to the official date of publication, appearing in the colophon. It will immediately be clear that such an arrangement follows no logical pattern, and that the various editions of a title cannot reasonably have been printed in close succession. (I believe the

TABLE 1. DISTRIBUTION OF CAPITAL LETTERS, BY EDITION.

	BOS. II	JOS. III		COR. I			FRO. XI	JOS. II		MOU.	FEVIN		JOS. I			COR. II		COR. III		COR. IV		PISA.
		i	ii	i	ii	iii		i	ii	ii	i	ii	i	ii	iii	i	ii	i	ii	i	ii	
G 2				●	●																	
G 6				●	●	●		●												●		
G 10				●	●	●	●															
G 11																						
H 3	●						●			●				●		●	●	●				
H 10																						
H 11																						
H 12																						
J 10													●		●	●	●●	●		●		
J 11																						
J 12																						
K 2		●						●	●	●	●	●	●	●	●							
K 4		●						●	●	●	●		●	● (○)								
K 6		●						●	●	●			●	●								
K 12																						
L 2	●			●●	●		●	●	●	●	●●											●
L 3																						
L 6																						
L 10																						
L 12																						
M 3				●	●		●									●	●	●		●		
M 11				●																		
N 3	●			● (○)	●●		●									●	●					●
N 10				●																		
N 11				●																		
N 12																						
O 2	●			●●	●		●●									●	●	●		●	●	
O 6				●																		
O 10				●																		
O 11																						

134

	BOS. II	JOS. III i	JOS. III ii	COR. I i	COR. I ii	COR. I iii	FRO. XI	JOS. II i	JOS. II ii	MOU. ii	FEVIN i	FEVIN ii	JOS. I i	JOS. I ii	JOS. I iii	COR. II i	COR. II ii	COR. III i	COR. III ii	COR. IV i	COR. IV ii	PISA.
P 2	••	•••	••				•	•••	•	•	•••	••	••	••	•	•	•	••		•		
P 3		••••	••					•••			••		•••	••	••							
P 4										••	••	••		••	••							
P 11																						
P 12																						•
Q 2	•	•	•	•	•		•			•	•	•				•	•	•		•		
R 3	••						•				•											
R 6																						
R 11							•										•		•			
S 3	••	••	•••	••	••	•	•••	••	•••	•••	••	••	••	••	••••	•	••	•	•			
S 4													•••		•	•						
S 10																						
S 11																			•			•
S 12																						
T 2		•		•	•	•	•	•	•	•	•	•	•		•	•	•	•		••		
T 10																						
T 11																						•
T 12																						
V 2	•			•	•	•	•					•				•	•	•		•		
V 11																	••					

135

possibility, not unknown in the 16th century, of a publisher employing two different printers to run off parallel editions can be discounted in this case, because of the amount of type common to the variant editions.) The titles can be re-arranged so that they are grouped according to which styles of letters were most in use. If this is done few anomalies appear, although it is not possible to go further and arrange the individual editions: the letters most likely to be used in mass volumes are not necessarily needed at all in volumes of motets, and so only a crude arrangement can be made: further, it is one that leaves many details unresolved.

However, the other aspect of these letters, their gradual decay, either through use, or through violent damage, can be much more closely plotted. There are, of course, several factors that weaken such evidence, all concerned with the printing process itself. Thus some of the poor examples of letters in various editions are the products of variations in the process. In some cases the letter has failed to make a fair impression either because of poor inking or because the paper was too dry: for some the letter itself apparently acquired pieces of dirt or felt in corners, probably from the ink-balls, obscuring the state of some of the more fragile filigree; in others, the outer edge of the letter has not taken at all, probably because it was concealed by the edge of the tympan (as for example the letter B6 in *Corona II*, f.A6*v*, Venice copy): and finally some of the possible flaws in letters are obscured by the stave lines over which they are printed. However, once allowance has been made for all these elements, there are several letters which show a clear progress towards uselessness. If this form of evidence could support others for different editions of *Corona I*, it can sometimes also suggest the precise sequence of printing for individual editions. Since relatively few copies have survived for most of Petrucci's titles, it is not possible for us to go further and adduce sequences of printing between individual copies, thence further details of house practice.

An attractive example of the way in which this evidence can be used is shown in Plate V, where six examples of the letter V2 are shown. Plate V(a), from long before Petrucci's return to Fossombrone, shows the letter in almost pristine condition. By the time of the Plate V(b)—the Bossinensis lute volume of 1511 (almost certainly Petrucci's first title after his return)—there is a startling change: the top of the letter has gone completely and a crack has begun to open at the foot. Three years later, in the first edition of *Corona I*[11] now in Bologna (*I-Bc* Q70—Plate V(c)), further cracks are appearing at the top and on the right. The letter is in a similar condition in the second edition (illustrated from the Munich copy—Plate V(d));[12] this is hardly surprising, whenever this second edition

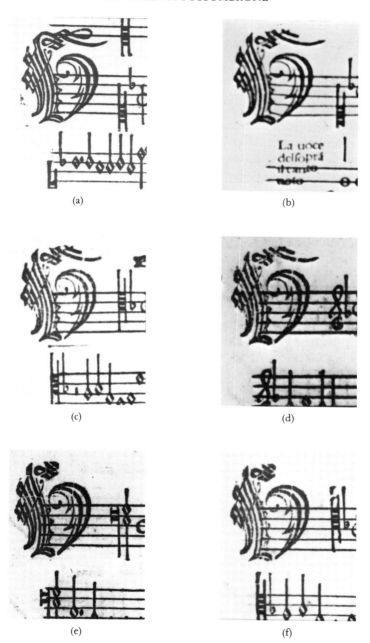

Plate V The letter V2: (a) *Motetti 4* (1505), B6r, *GB-Ob*; (b) Bossinensis II, C3v, *I-Mb*; (c) *Corona I*, H4v, *I-Bc* Q70; (d) *Corona I*, B4v, *D-Mbs*; (e) *Corona IV*, G3v, *CH-Zjacobi*; (f) *Corona I*, H4v, *CH-Zjacobi*.

was printed, for there would be little demand for the letter in volumes of mass music. The last two illustrations (Plate V(e) and (f)) show the only extant edition of *Corona IV*, dated 1519, and the latest known of *Corona I*. In spite of the apparent hairline crack on the left of the *Corona IV* illustration (which may indeed well be a hair), I believe that this shows an earlier state than the other for, in that, additional cracks are appearing at the foot. These pictures also show the dangers implicit in this technique, with, for example, the odd patches of faulty inking in the Bologna (*I-Bc* Q70) copy of *Corona I*. However, they can be used, with similar examples of other letters, to show that the last edition of *Corona I* was not printed until after October 1519 (the date of *Corona IV*), more than five years after the first. We need not be surprised; there was sufficient interest for Giunta to reprint much of Petrucci's material in the next decade.

The second letter illustrated, B6, in Plate VI, helps in similar manner to place the second edition of *Corona I*. Already, by the time of the first edition (Plate VI(a)), this letter is not perfect, though there is little further deterioration before the only extant copy of *Frottole XI* (Plate VI(b)). However, the retention of the base with the marked break-up of the top left place the example from the second edition (Plate VI(c)) before the following examples, a late edition of Josquin Masses III (Plate VI(d)) and the first edition of *Corona II* (Plate VI(e)). I believe that the strange effect on the right of the letter in the Josquin volume is another case of masking paper that masks too efficiently, for in other respects that edition is clearly earlier than the example from *Corona II*.

Similar evidence can be used to sort out the order of the various editions of the Josquin masses. The final results can be seen at the end of this chapter ('Probable Sequence of Printing at Fossombrone'), and they are based in part on a study of the letters A6 and E10.

I have already said that letters of the patterns 11 and 12 are of great value. Table 1 shows that these appear only in certain copies of many titles. In *Corona III* and *IV*, where there are basically only single editions with cancel sheets, letters of these patterns do not appear (except in the cancel to volume 3). At this stage Petrucci is still using many of his Venetian letters supplemented by letters of style 10. We have already seen that the last edition of *Corona I* was printed after *Corona IV*, and it is significant that it is this edition that carries letters of style 11. Indeed, all the editions that use letters of either style 11 or style 12 can be shown to date from after *Corona IV*. The last series of illustrations therefore takes one of these letters, A11 in Plate VII, and uses it to demonstrate the arrangement of these late editions.

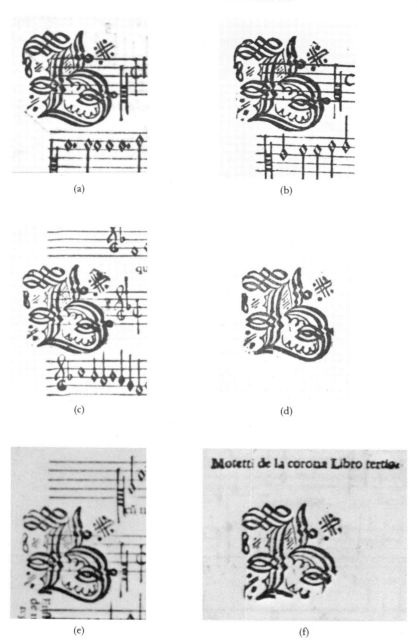

Plate VI The letter B6: (a) *Corona I*, A3*v*, *I-Bc* Q70; (b) *Frottole XI*, A6*v*, *E-S*; (c) *Corona I*, A7*v*, *I-Bc* Q74; (d) Josquin Masses III, F1*r*, *CH-Zjacobi* (e) *Corona II*, A6*v*, *I-Vnm*; (f) *Corona III*, G1*r*, *I-Vnm*.

So far, no account has been taken of the editions of Févin and Mouton, both of which ostensibly lie within the period of the early re-editions of Josquin. The unique surviving partbook of Févin that can be shown (convincingly) to belong to a first edition with 1515 as the date of publication (the Viennese bassus partbook) also uses letters that are in better condition than either the second edition of *Corona I* or the first Fossombrone edition of Josquin I. I have seen no copy of the Mouton masses that could be a first edition, though I understand from Jeremy Noble that the Berlin set of books is one such. All the other copies of Mouton that I have seen, and all the rest of the Févin copies belong to later editions. They all use letters of styles 11 and 12, and can in each case be assigned to a second edition, after the volume of Pisano printed in 1520. The evidence for this is shown in the illustrations: the critical area of the letter is at the foot on both sides. The earliest state is that of the last edition of *Corona I*: this is followed by the last extant edition of Josquin I and then by the Pisano—the 'last printed music edition of Petrucci' as is always assumed. This is then followed by three other complete editions, Févin, Mouton and *Corona II*. The evidence for placing the Févin volume here in the sequence does not, of course, depend on this example, which is a poorly inked specimen, although the intact filigree inside the left base is significant.

Leaving aside the last of these illustrations for the moment, we must for a while turn to the evidence of watermarks, to see how far they support the hypotheses outlined above. The paper evidence advanced by Jeremy Noble[13] is much more extensive than I can offer here. All I wish to do is to draw attention to one or two aspects of the distribution of marks and to add one or two to the many he gives.

It has often been said, and most authoritatively by Stevenson, that printers of this period tended to buy paper separately for each volume.[14] This was in part a result of the high cost of paper, one of the largest elements in the cost of book-production when the output of mills had not caught up with the explosion of printing. (It is for this reason that many printers had contracts requiring their patrons, authors or publishers to supply the paper.) Significantly, the papers in the three non-musical titles of Petrucci do not appear in the musical volumes. A corollary of such practice is the scholarly postulate that the paper variations between different titles need not be significant for chronology. Without beta-radiographs (which cannot be supplied by many of the libraries holding Petrucci volumes), and a study of twin marks, little can be deduced about the patterns of use or chronology from the appearance of related marks in

(a)

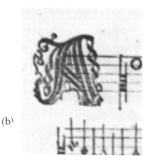

(b)

(c)

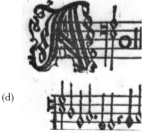

(d)

(e)

(f)

(g)

Plate VII The letter A11: (a) *Corona I*, H2*v*, *CH-Zjacobi*;
(b) Josquin Masses I, A4*v*, *I-BGc* = (c) Pisano Musica, E1*r*, *E-S*;
(d) Févin Masses, H6*r*, *CH-Zjacobi*; (e) Mouton Masses I, H7*v*,
CH-Zjacobi; (f) *Corona II*, H2*r*, *CH-Zjacobi*; (g) *Corona III*,
A4*v*, *I-Vnm*.

different titles. It is interesting that Petrucci does not always follow the pattern, however, of having one paper for a whole volume. While this is fairly frequent during his Venetian days, several of the Fossombronese prints have assortments of papers in them (as shown by Noble). This probably reflects in part the difficult political situation, in which he might have had to accept whatever he could get, and in part Petrucci's own position more as a publisher, perhaps keeping a small stock of paper. One paper, however, dominates all the later editions of the table at the end of this chapter: a crescent mark, resembling Briquet 5203.[15] Petrucci had used it a little in earlier editions, but after the first edition of *Corona II*, it is used consistently. This in itself would be a strong indication that these later editions were indeed printed after 1519. It is a simple mark, tending to keep its shape, and, as normal in an oblong quarto format, it is cut by the upper edge of the page. Therefore it is not of much use in constructing the detailed chronology of these editions, though its concurrency does help (in the way that the free use of papers in other editions sometimes does not) in detecting the presence of cancel sheets.

The cancel implies a resetting of type for a whole sheet or for a pair of leaves, normally after completion of the press-work, and therefore often on a different paper. There is a number of such sheets in the Fossombrone volumes, some obvious, some only evident from detailed typographical or paper study. One of the most clear-cut is the outer sheet of gathering D (-D1, 2, 7, 8) of the London copy of Josquin II. While all the rest of the volume is printed on paper with the crescent mark, this sheet has paper that corresponds to the first edition. Further, the type for the text happens to be distinguishable: between the two printings, Petrucci had changed from a rotonda typeface to a fount of Roman: the odd sheet in the London copy uses the rotonda text type, and the rest is set in Roman. The single sheet can be identified as belonging to the earlier edition by comparison with other copies (listed at the end of this chapter). (There is also an odd sheet, of an older paper, in the Bologna copy of the first Fossombrone edition, at E3, 4, 7, 8. Here, there is no evidence suggesting that the type was set at a different time, and it therefore is probably an old sheet slipped into the pile at press to be used up.) Another London copy, that of Josquin I, has a similar sheet, though this also comes from an earlier edition. These two are not, of course, strictly cancels, for they existed before the rest of the edition. They are more likely to be remnant sheets from the earlier edition incorporated into stock: they do however well illustrate the method used.

In *Corona III* there is a more important variant: the inner sheet of gathering A (ff. 3–6) exists in two different settings of type. The paper here is the standard crescent paper in both settings, and so the evidence of the type is necessary to determine which was first. The table of capital letters shows clearly that the letters used in the London, Bergamo and Venice copies do not match the rest of the volume. Indeed, they are clearly much later; just how much later is of interest. They show a heavy preponderance of letters of styles 11 and 12, most frequently used at the time of the volume of Pisano. These letters are not all susceptible to the form of analysis used above: they are poorly cut, and rarely take the ink evenly: letters of style 12, in particular, seldom make a good impression (technically or visually). However, a pattern of decay in the letter A11 was used above, and the last illustration in this series shows the state of the letter in one of the cancel pages of *Corona III*. It is at least as bad as and possibly worse than the letter as found in the second edition of *Corona II*: other letters in the cancel also suggest that it was printed after that edition, that is, well over a year after the edition it was intended to cancel. Half the extant copies were already sold by the time the cancel was prepared. If the volume had survived in many more copies, the relative number of un-cancelled and cancelled copies might have told us something about the rate at which copies left Petrucci to be sold.

This is one of two cases where there are two extant versions of the same pages, in which one must have been intended to replace the other. (The variant editions listed at the end of this chapter are all complete editions, or complete partbooks; while the readings involved may differ between the editions, the principle by which one assesses them is different. The other variant sheets have been shown to belong to complete editions.) The relationship between a sheet and its cancel (or indeed any replacement) is a complex one. We cannot assume the 'normal' situation, in which an error of major proportions in the original version led to its withdrawal: if this were so, one could assume that the readings of the later version were likely to be preferable, even allowing for the normal ration of new errors. However, replacement sheets may also have been prepared because the original stock ran out (a miscalculation of paper when printing): in this case, we should assume that the type-setter had a copy of the original version beside him and that he followed it closely and at a normal rate of work. Variants, if any, should then be within the normal range of number and type, although the opportunity may have been taken to 'improve' readings. Alternatively, there may have been some minor disaster in the warehouse, in which the remaining stock of a sheet was damaged or destroyed: in such a case, the replacements would have been set up in haste, possibly from the original printer's copy, or from some casual unannotated shop copy. In such a situation, the nature of the readings would be vastly different: layout would probably be different and signs of haste apparent. It is seldom possible to know with certainty why a cancel was prepared, although it is usually possible to tell which version came first. When this can be done, the nature of the variants can lead to a reasoned assessment of their merits.

In the example from *Corona III*, we do know which version was the later, although we do not know whether it was a true cancel or merely a replacement, and, in fact, cannot be sure even after the readings are examined. There are, normally, very few variants of reading between different editions in Petrucci's work, although this sheet carries more than its fair share. On f.A3r, a correct three breves' rest in the first edition appears to be only two in the second. Since, however, there are other places in this sheet where one breve rest is scarcely inked, this may have occurred here. On the same page, towards the end of the work (Josquin's *Preter rerum seriem*) the second edition changes the spelling *misterium* to *mysterium*, conforming with the other voices. The other variants are on f.A6r, in Lebrung's *Recumbentibus undecim*: two adjacent long rests in the Verona (first edition) copy have the top half of the second scratched through. In the second state, they are correctly printed as a long and a breve rest. Finally, at the foot of the same page, the Verona copy has two spelling errors in the repeated word *sequentibus*: first time, the first letter *e* is inverted, while in the second appearance the second *e* is an *a*. Both are correct in the later sheets.

Although the Verona is the earlier state, it seems unlikely that such minor variants would justify replacing a whole sheet, especially since the other case (to be mentioned) involves a half-sheet. Further, there are some indications that ink corrections may have been made in the printing shop before the copies came up for sale. The Florence and Venice copies of *Corona III* and *IV* have the same manuscript emendations, apparently in the same ink and plausibly made by the same hand. The same ink also makes correction to the Florence copy of *Corona I*, corrections that are incorporated in the text as printed in the third edition. These tend to suggest that such corrections may have been made at Fossombrone, corrections that are more important than the changes that appear in the two versions of the sheet of gathering A of *Corona III*. All this argues that the replacement of *Corona III* may be the result of some minor problem in the house, possibly a miscalculation over paper.

The other example has already been discussed by Edgar Sparks, who was primarily concerned with the ascription of one piece appearing on the sheet, the inner of gathering B, *Corona IV*.[16] His conclusions are based on technical matters of layout, not directly related to the priority of the two versions, but lay an unnecessary stress on aesthetic considerations.

The sheet exists in one form in the Venice copy, and another common to all others. Despite the suggestion of Sparks, it is most unlikely that any printer of the period would re-set a page because he was dissatisfied with the appearance of the original. (One of the major changes involves the capital letters used.) Certainly, Petrucci and his type-setters took considerable care over layout, but this was to a large extent a mechanical process, as it probably was for the other stylists among early 16th-century printers. Sparks, in recognising, and deducing from, a consistent pattern in the running heads and captions, is himself aware of the extent to which such matters were routine. Thus any argument postulating that the prime reason for re-setting a page or sheet is to improve mechanical aspects of its appearance (by a different use of capitals) is bound to be weak. It leads to the hypothesis that the Venetian copy is the earlier, despite the fact that (as he notes in a footnote of the 'later' reading in the other copies) 'even in the early 16th century it could hardly have been thought an improvement'. Since this alteration is related to the change in capitals, it cannot be seen, either, as a casual printer's error.

Fortunately, we have no need to postulate the deliberate substitution of an inferior reading: the typographical evidence shows clearly that the Venetian copy incorporates the later version. In the other copies, with the inferior reading, the state of the capitals is commensurate with their condition in other gatherings of the volume, which can be equated with the date in the colophon. Further, it can be shown that the letter O10 on f.B6r is not merely in the same state as in other partbooks, but is also in an earlier state than as it appears in the last edition of *Corona I*. The letter P4 on f.B6v of these copies is in an earlier state than in the late edition of Josquin I, etc. (Any user of the recent facsimile of these volumes of Josquin is liable to be seriously misled.[17] Many pages have been so heavily touched up that they are useless for bibliographical study. Of the appearances of P4, one in each partbook, only one can reasonably be said to have been left alone.)

In the Venice copy of *Corona IV*, the use of the letter O10 in all partbooks except the superius matches its state in the other copies: reasonably so, for these exist in only the one edition. However, the letter as it appears on f.B6r is in a later state, not merely than the other copies, but also than *Corona I*. The 'D' on f.B3v, D13 of my series, is later than its condition in the other copies, and is, so far as I can tell from microfilm, very close to the solitary appearance of this letter in the volume of Pisano. Unfortunately, since so few letters are involved, and since most of them are not printed clearly, we cannot be more precise than to say that the later Venetian sheet was printed after the last edition of Josquin I and almost certainly before the reprint of *Corona II*. That this is a genuine cancel is shown by the nature of the variant readings (discussed by Sparks).

Three other cases of anomalous paper are worth mentioning, although my analyses have so far produced no explanations for them: two are in editions of *Corona I*. The copy of the first edition (*I-Bc* Q70) uses one paper throughout, except for the inner sheet of gathering E. There are also two marks on the outer sheet, suggesting that this may be made up from two half-sheets, one a cancel. The other is in the second edition (*I-Bc* Q74; *I-Fn*; *D-Mbs*), where there is apparently a transition from one paper to another. The Florence bassus is made up of the later paper. However, in the Bologna copy the two gatherings of the later paper are the first of the two partbooks, superius and tenor. This distribution does not suggest any obvious pattern, though there are too few copies to make any valid deductions. All extant copies of the first edition of Josquin Masses III (*A-Wn*, *GB-Lbm*, *I-Bc*, *US-R*) have an anomalous paper for the centre sheet of gathering A. This may be no more than the use of an odd batch of paper, for no other reason can as yet be detected.

There is also the question of the varied papers and typographical practices of the second edition of *Corona I*. Here, two sets of papers, two sets of signatures and of other details, only approximately coincide. Since, however, the type appears to be of the same state, I assume that they are the result of two compositors working at the same time, rather than of two not consecutive operations. All these situations need further research.

However, the application of Occam's razor to the apparently random spread of capitals has, as promised, produced a different type of complexity. The number and range of new editions is startling. None of the secular volumes seems to have gone to a second edition,[18] while the reprinting even of the Févin volume points to a continuing demand for the French repertory. We know already that these books were sold in many places far from Petrucci's home town, and the reprinting of French court music at a time of political strife and confused alignments argues strong support for its popularity. Petrucci's political position during the period was far from secure. Vernarecci[19] has shown that he took a leading role in delegations to the Pope—and this has something to do, I am convinced, with the hiatus in printing in the middle of the decade. It may also have had something to do with the number of editions, for Petrucci must have known that they comprised fewer copies than the market would bear. (The survival of so many hybrid copies is of interest here: it can be shown that the unique copy of *Odhecaton*, first edition (*I-Bc*), is in fact a composite copy with several sheets from the second edition of 1503.) With the cost of paper so high, he would have been unwilling to tie up capital in so easily destroyed a form. It is of interest that he purchased a paper mill after his retirement from printing. In this, as in his frequent reprinting, Petrucci showed a strong business acumen: his equally successful choice of repertory is shown in the many reprints that were undertaken by Giunta and his printers in Rome during the next decade.[20]

Addendum (1978)

Two folios (neither complete) of an otherwise unknown Petrucci print have survived at the Biblioteca Passionei at Fossombrone. These were known to Vernarecci, and are cited as pages from the lost Frottole Book 10 in his *Ottaviano De' Petrucci da Fossombrone . . .* (1882), 271. Jeppesen, in *La Frottola*, iii (1968), 36, refers to the fragment and adds that it seems to be the work of Petrucci. It has now been published in facs. by Giuseppe Ceccarelli and Maurizio Spaccazocchi (*Tre carte musicali a stampa inedite di Ottaviano Petrucci*, Fossombrone, 1976) alongside the leaf of *Motetti de la Corona IV* in the same library.

I am grateful to Monsignor Ceccarelli for allowing me to examine these leaves and also further pages that he has found (on which he intends to publish later: these do not add new editions to our list).

It is immediately apparent that the two folios (originally joined) comprised ff. A3 and A4 of a madrigal print, and that they cannot have been printed as early as 1512. I believe that they were printed by Petrucci, despite certain anomalies. The format is unusual, only five staves per page, and the size of staves is not met with elsewhere in Petrucci's work: however, the same is true for the volume of Pisano's *Musica*, published in 1520. It is perhaps significant that both the Pisano and the present volumes apparently contain a Florentine repertory.

The bibliographical evidence for dating this print is rather limited, not least because the two leaves are not in good condition. However, it appears to have been printed in 1520 or (just possibly) early 1521. It therefore holds a very early place in the history of both the madrigal and Verdelot's music. I suggest it be called [*Musica Libro XII*].

LIST OF COPIES AND EDITIONS

This list does not cite all the extant copies of all titles, but only those that I have
studied in sufficient detail to be able to place in sequence. The Roman numerals
in the second column indicate settings of type, not always complete editions,
sometimes merely cancel sheets for a few leaves.

Bossinensis: *Tenori e contrabassi . . . Libro Secundo* (10 May
1511)
  Sartori 46, *RISM* 1511

Unique copy: *I-Mb* AP.XVI.40

Frottole libro decimo (1512)
  Sartori 47

Not extant

Paulus de Middelburgo: *de
recta Paschae* . . . (8 July
1513)

GB-Lbm 216.d.15; 472.e.8;
696.1.15; *GB-Ob* Rigaud c.14; *US-
CA* Typ.525.13.675F (lacks GG6);
*fNC.P2863.513p (lacks GG6)

Castiglione: *Epistola de vita et
gestis Guidobaldi* . . . (29 July
1513)

GB-Lbm 1199.c.3

Josquin: *Missarum Josquin Liber
Tertius* . . . (1 March 1514)
  Sartori 48, *RISM* J673,
  J674. Note that both the
  copies cited at *RISM* J674 are in
  fact of the present edition
  having had their colophon
  pages exchanged at some
  time for those in Josquin's
  first volume (see below).
  That at *A-Wn* SA.77.C.19
  has now been rebound
  correctly.

(i) *A-Wn* SA.77.C.20 (*S,T,A*); *GB-
     Lbm* K.1.d.9 (*S,T,A,B* except
     D2,7); *I-Bc* Q73 (*S,T,A,B* except
     D2,7); *I- PEc* I.M.1079(1) (*S*, lacks
     B1,10); *US-CA* Mus.786.2.501 (*T*,
     lacks C3,10,12); *US-R* 154579-80
     (*S,B*)

(ii) *A-Wn* SA.77.C.19 (*S,T,A,B*); *CH-
     Zz* (*B*); *GB-Lbm* K.1.d.9(D2,7); *I-
     Ac* (*S,T,A,B*); *I-Bc* Q73 (D2,7); *I-
     BGc* 0.10.84 (*S*); *I-Rvat* Sist 235–8
     (*S,T,A,B*)

Motetti de la Corona Libro Primo
(17 Aug 1514)
  Sartori 49, *RISM* 1514¹. Note
  that the copy cited in *RISM* as at
  A-Wn is of 1526¹ while that at *I-
  Bc* Q74 is incorrectly listed in
  RISM as of 1526¹.

(i)   *I-Bc* Q70 (*S,T,A,B*); *I-PEc*
      I.M.1079(2) (*S*, lacks A1)

(ii) *D-Mbs* 4°.mus.pr.247
      (*S,A*); *I-Bc* Q74 (*S,T*); *I-Fn*
      Landau-Finaly 8 (*B*, lacks
      G3)

(iii) *CH-Zz* (*B*); *D-LEm* (*B*); *I-BGc* (*S*);
      I-Vnm Musica 203–5 (*S,A,B*)

Frottole Libro undecimo (20
  Oct 1514)
    Sartori 50, *RISM* 1514[2]

Unique copy: *E-S* 12–1–28

Josquin: *Missarum Josquin Liber*
  secundus . . . (11 April 1515)
    Sartori 51, *RISM* J671

(i) *A-Wn* SA.77.C.20 (*S*,*T*,*A*); *GB-*
  Lbm K.1.d.10 (D1,2,7,8); *I-Ac*
  (*S*,*T*,*A*,*B*); *I-Bc* Q72 (*S*,*T*,*A*,*B*);
  US-R 154577–8 (*S*,*B*)

(ii) *A-Wn* SA.77.C.19 (*S*,*T*,*B*); *GB-*
  Lbm K.1.d.10 (*S*,*T*.*A*.*B*, except
  D1, 2, 7, 8); *I-BGc* (*S*); *I-Rvat* Sist
  235–8 (*S*,*T*,*A*,*B*)

Mouton: *Missarum Joannis*
  mouton. Liber primus . . . (11 Aug
  1515)
    Sartori 52, *RISM* M 4015

(i) *D-Bds*, not seen

(ii) *A-Wn* SA.77.C.18 (*S*,*T*,*A*); *CH-Zz*
  (*B*); *GB-CW* (A); *GB-Lbm*
  K.1.d.11 (*S*,*T*,*A*,*B*, lacks B8
  blank); *I-BGc* (S); *US-Wc*
  M.1490.M915 (*S*,*T*,*A*,*B*)

Févin: *Misse Antonii de*
  Fevin . . . (22 Oct 1515)
    Sartori 53, *RISM* 1515[1] and F689

(i) *A-Wn* SA.77.C.17 (*B*)

(ii) *A-Wn* SA.77.C.17 (*S*,*T*,*A*); *CH-Zz*
  (*B*); *F-Pc* Res 416 (*S*,*T*,*A*,*B*, lacks
  B8 blank); *GB-CW* (A); *GB-Lbm*
  K.1.d.12 (*S*,*T*,*A*,*B*, lacks B8
  blank); *I-BGc* (*S*)

Missarum decem libri 2 (1515)
    Sartori 54

Probably printed by Petrucci: not
extant

Josquin: *Liber primus Missarum*
  Josquin . . . (29 May 1516)
    Sartori 55, *RISM* J669, J670.
    See the note of Josquin Masses
    III, above.
    For various reasons, the
    arrangement offered here is
    at present conjectural, and
    depends on further personal
    examination of all copies. In
    particular, the order of
    printing (i) and (ii) needs further
    study.

(i) *D-Mbs* 4°. mus.pr.184/1
  (Bl-10, G1, 2, 7, 8, H1–8);
  GB-Lbm K1.d.13 (H1, 2, 7,
  8); *I-Rvat* Sist 235–8 (*B*);
  US-R 154575–6 (B5–6, G1,2,7,8,
  H1,2,7,8)

(ii) *I-Bc* Q71 (*S*,*T*,*A*,*B*); *I-Rvat*
  Sist 235–8 (*S*,*T*,*A*); *US-R* 150820 (*S*)

(iii) *D-Mbs* 4°.mus.pr.184/1 (A1–8,
  G3–6); *US-R* 154575–6 (A1–8,
  B1–4, 7–10, G4–5, H3–6)

(iv) *A-Wn* SA.77.C.19 (*S*,*T*,*A*,*B*); *D-*
  Mbs 4°.mus.pr.184/1 (*T*,*A*); *GB-*
  CW (A); *GB-Lbm* K1.d.13
  (*S*,*T*,*A*,*B*, except H1,2,7,8); *I-Ac*
  (*S*,*T*,*A*,*B*); *I-BGc* (*S*);

Paulus de Middelburgo: *Parabola Christi* . . . (20 Nov 1516)

GB-Lbm 3835.a.17

Motetti de la corona Libro secondo. (17 June 1519)
Sartori 56, *RISM* 1519[1]. The copy cited in *RISM* as at *A-Wn* is of 1526[2].

(i) *D-LEm* (*B*); *D-Mbs* 4°.mus.pr.247/2 (*S,A*); *I-Bc* Q75 (*S*, lacks A2,3); *I-Fn* Landau-Finaly 8 (*B*); *I-Vnm* Musica 203–5 (*S,A,B*)

(ii) *CH-Zz* (*B*); *GB-Lbm* K.1.d.14 (*S,T,A,B*, lacks blank H10); *I-BGc* (*S*); *I-Bc* Q75 (*B*)

Motetti de la corona Libro tertio. (7 Sept 1519)
Sartori 57, *RISM* 1519[2]. The copy cited in *RISM* as at *A-Wn* is of 1526[3]

(i) *CH-Zz* (*B*); *D-LEm* (*B*); *D-Mbs* 4°.mus.pr.247/3(*S,A*, except A3–6); *GB-Lbm* K.1.d.15 (*S,T,A,B*, except A3-6, lacks B9. D6, H10 all blank); *I-Bc* Q76 (*S*); *I-BGc* (*S*, except A3–6); *I-Fn* Landau-Finaly 8 (*B*); *I-Vnm* Musica 203–5 (*S,A,B*, except A3–6); *I-VEaf* (*S,T,A,B*)

(ii) sheet A3–6 for the copies at *D-Mbs, GB-Lbm, I-BGc* and *I-Vnm*

Motetti de la corona Libro quarto. (30 Oct 1519)
Sartori 58, *RISM* 1519[3]. The copy cited in *RISM* as at *A-Wn* is of 1526[4].

(i) *CH-Zz* (*B*); *D-LEm* (*B*); *D-Mbs* 4°.mus.pr.247/4 (*S,A*); *GB-Lbm* K1.d.16 (*S,T,A,B*, lacks F6, H8 both blank); *I-Bc* Q77 (*S,T*); *I-BGc* (*S*); *I-Fn* Landau-Finaly 8 (*B*); *I-Vnm* Musica 203–5 (*S,A,B*, except B3,6)

(ii) *I-Vnm* Musica 203–5 (*B*,3,6)

Pisano: *Musica de meser Bernardo pisano* . . . (23 May 1520)
Sartori 59, *RISM* P 2451.

Unique copy: *E-S* 12–1–31(1) (lacks F5–6)

PROBABLE SEQUENCE OF PRINTING AT FOSSOMBRONE

Sartori	Short title	Date	Edition or copy in my list
46	Bossinensis II	10 May 1511	I-Mb
47	Frottole X	1512	
—	Paulus: de recta Paschae	8 July 1513	all
—	Castiglione: Epistola	29 July 1513	GB-Lbm
48	Josquin Masses III	1 March 1514	(i)
49	Corona I	17 Aug 1514	(i)
50	Frottole XI	20 Oct 1514	E-S
51	Josquin Masses II	11 April 1515	(i)
52	Mouton Masses I	11 Aug 1515	(i)
53	Févin Masses	22 Nov 1515	(i)
55	Josquin Masses I	29 May 1516	(i)
—	Corona I	—	(ii)
—	Josquin Masses III	—	(ii)
—	Paulus: Parabola Christi	29 Nov 1516	GB-Lbm
—	Josquin Masses I	—	(ii)
—	Josquin Masses II	—	(ii)
—	Josquin Masses I	—	(iii)
56	Corona II	17 June 1519	(i)
57	Corona III	7 Nov 1519	(i)
58	Corona IV	31 Oct 1519	(i)
—	Corona I	—	(iii)
—	Josquin Masses I	—	(iv)
59	Pisano Musica	23 May 1520	E-S
—	Févin Masses	—	(ii)
—	Mouton Masses I	—	(ii)
—	Corona II	—	(ii)
—	Corona III	—	(ii)

The cancel sheet for the Venice pages of *Corona IV* cannot be placed in this series: it is roughly contemporary with the Pisano Musica. The information about Sartori 52 was kindly reported to me by Jeremy Noble.

NOTES TO CHAPTER 4

1. Whether this was actually devised by William of Occam is now in doubt. See W. M. Thorburn: 'The Myth of Occam's Razor', *Mind*, xxvii (1918), 349–53, and G. Sarton: *Introduction to the History of Science*, iii *Science and Learning in the Fourteenth Century* (Baltimore, 1947), 552f. The authenticity or otherwise of the statement has nothing to do with its sharpness.

2. C. W. Chapman: *Andrea Antico* (diss., Harvard U., 1964), 1.

3. C. Sartori: *Bibliografia delle opere musicali stampate da Ottaviano Petrucci*, Biblioteca di bibliografia italiana, xviii (Florence, 1948), which has to be used in conjunction with his 'Nuove conclusive aggiunte alla "Bibliografia del Petrucci"', *Collectanea historiae musicae*, i (1953), 175–210. The work concerned is discussed as no.49 of the list of titles.

4. S. H. Boorman: 'Petrucci at Fossombrone: the Motetti de la Corona', *IMSCR, Copenhagen 1972*, i, 295–301; J. Noble: 'Ottaviano Petrucci: his Josquin Editions and Some Others', Festschrift for Myron Gilmore (forthcoming). I am most grateful to Mr Noble for allowing me to consult the manuscript of his article before publication. An example of a cancel is discussed in E. H. Sparks: *The Music of Noel Bauldeweyn* (New York, 1972), 17–23. This discussion does have the merit, rare among evaluations of Petrucci's music, that it shows some awareness of the bibliographical aspects of the work, although, as will appear, the conclusions need revision.

5. I am grateful to the late Professor Jacobi for drawing my attention to his bassus partbook. This contains, bound together, the following titles: *Motetti de la Corona, I-IV*, Misse Févin, Misse Mouton I, Josquin Masses III. Professor Jacobi also kindly arranged for me to receive a microfilm of the whole volume. Since this was written, the collection has been acquired by the Zentralbibliothek, Zürich.

6. See note 4 above. Noble has been able to group various editions together on the strength of the watermarks and of the two text types—rotonda (= black-letter) and Roman—that Petrucci used. Since he has been able to consult copies other than those that I give here, the material in this study needs to be read in conjunction with his.

7. One has only to think of the range of men employed by Feyerabend of Nuremberg, and to remember that both Burgkmair and Dürer worked freely for printers, to realise the individual character and status of this work. It is probable that Francesco Griffo of Bologna did work for Petrucci at some time, perhaps including the set of letters that I have called style 10.

8. This large folio was printed on 8 July 1513. It survives in many copies. Of the four that I have seen, all appear to use the same paper and to come from the same printing.

9. Gatherings consisting of a different number of leaves follow similar patterns: a 12-leaf gathering uses three sheets, one of six leaves a sheet for ff.1,2,5,6 and a half-sheet in the middle. A ten-leaf gathering tends to place the half-sheet at the centre.

10. For examples of these, see H. Brown: *The Venetian Printing Press* (London, 1891) and F. Ongania: *L'Arte della stampa nel rinascimento Italiana* (Venice, 1894; Eng. trans. London, 1895, as *Early Venetian Printing Illustrated*), as well as the many more recent detailed studies.

11. The reasons for believing this to be not merely the earliest extant edition, but in fact the first are given in the paper cited in note 4.

12. For this and other reasons, I suspect that the Munich copy of this edition went through the press early in the run, for this stage of the process.

13. Article cited in note 4.

14. A. Stevenson: *The Problem of the Missale Speciale* (London, 1967) and 'Watermarks are Twins', *Studies in Bibliography*, iv (1951–2), 57–91.

15. C. M. Briquet: *Les filigranes: dictionnaire historique des marques du papier* (Geneva, 1907/R; Leipzig, 2/1923).

16. See note 4. The plates that accompany Sparks' discussion are not adequate for bibliographical study, though they can be used to clarify my discussion of the case.

17. *Missarum Liber Agricole, Ghiselin, de la Rue, Josquin* (Rome, 1973). This facs., like that of the Trent codices also published by Vivarelli e Gulla, is useless for all source studies. In the latter the majority of stave lines that carry music can be shown to have been 'touched up', as superficial comparison with black staves will immediately show, and there are many other places where similar work appears to have been applied to the musical text. This is also true throughout the Petrucci facsimile. In addition, both the copies of the facs. that I have used have an error in the arrangement of the tenor partbook of Josquin Masses III: the folios C5–8 are printed before C1–4. That this is not a binding error is shown by the modern pagination which is consecutive. I have not been able to check the Assisi copy of the original from which the facs. was made, but even if that is similarly bound, as is possible, the facs. should have corrected the arrangement.

18. Although only one copy of each has survived, the bibliographical evidence in each case points to it being of an edition that can be assigned to the date given in the colophon. It is, of course, possible that any or all of these titles may have had later editions. The limited number of surviving copies of all Petrucci's secular titles is worthy of notice.

19. A. Vernarecci: *Fossombrone dai tempo antichissimi* (Fossombrone, 1903/R 1967) and *Ottaviano de' Petrucci da Fossombrone: inventore dei tipi mobili metallici fusi della musica nel secolo XV* (Bologna, 1882, rev.1884).

20. I am grateful to all the libraries that have allowed me to consult their holdings of Petrucci material, either in person or on microfilm. These are the holders of the copies that appear listed at the end of the chapter.

5

Music Manuscripts of John Browne (1608–91) and from Stanford Hall, Leicestershire

Nigel Fortune
in collaboration with Iain Fenlon

This chapter[1] identifies a number of manuscripts of 17th-century English music that were owned, and in part copied, by John Browne, Clerk of the Parliaments, who, as will be seen, was also an amateur musician. It also considers other manuscripts with which he may have had connections: a feature common to most of them and to some of those that he definitely owned is that they were once at Stanford Hall, Stanford-on-Avon, near Rugby. Browne's family had originally come from Bury St Edmunds, Suffolk, but his grandfather and father had prospered as substantial merchants in London during the later 16th century.[2] He was born almost certainly in 1608, read law and became a member of the Middle Temple. He made two good marriages. His first wife, who died in 1634, was Temperance, daughter of Sir Thomas Crewe, Speaker of the House of Commons, through whom he entered Northamptonshire society: he soon owned estates in the county, and he lived on and off for the rest of his life at Eydon, in the south-west corner. His second wife, whom he married in 1636, was Elizabeth, daughter of John Packer, of Groombridge Place, Kent, who had been Clerk of the Privy Council. Browne was appointed Clerk of the Parliaments in March 1638 and first held the post until it was abolished in 1649. Like his second father-in-law he was a Puritan, but apparently not an intransigent one, for he had no difficulty in being reappointed Clerk at the Restoration in 1660, and he held office until his death. He was buried at Eydon on 8 June 1691, aged 83, and his second wife was buried alongside him only five days later.

Browne's ownership of several music manuscripts, mainly of viol music, can be postulated from the appearance in them of his hand, which is readily verifiable from the large number of parliamentary documents that he copied and signed (see Plate VIII). Moreover, it seems that the five extant partbooks of an original set of six, now in the possession of Franklin B. Zimmerman of the University of Pennsylvania, Philadelphia,[3] once belonged to him, since the flyleaves of the cantus, quintus and sextus

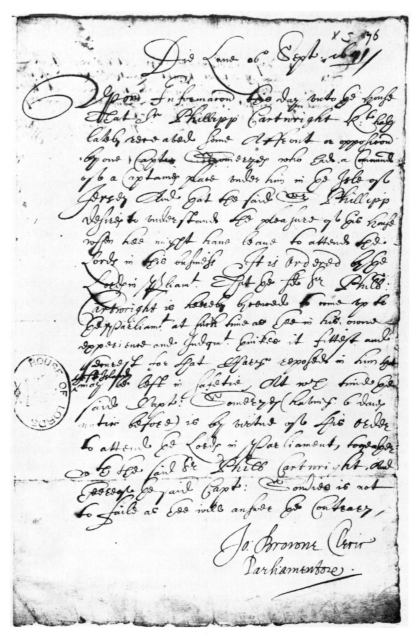

Plate VIII Order of the House of Lords (relating to Sir Philip Carteret, Lieutenant-Governor of the Isle of Jersey) in John Browne's hand; dated 6 September 1641.
(*By permission of the Clerk of the Records, House of Lords.*)

books bear his signature, and of two pairs of initials on the contemporary
calf covers of the books, one, 'I.B.', presumably refers to him, while the
other, 'W.L.', doubtless refers to William Lawes, whose music they
contain. Browne's handwriting is particularly evident in manuscripts in
Christ Church, Oxford (*GB-Och* 367-70, 379-81, 423-8 and 473-8),
which all contain consort music of the early and middle years of the 17th
century; in two sets of books in the Rowe Music Library, King's College,
Cambridge (*GB-Ckc* 112-13, 113A, 114-17), which include a similar
repertory;[4] and in the so-called 'Braye Tablature Book', containing music
for bandora and lyra viol, now in the possession of Robert Spencer, of
Woodford Green, Essex.[5] In *Och* 430, the organ part to Lawes's two sets of
violin sonatas, Browne's hand appears in the headings and time signatures
and in a direction at the back to his brother-in-law, 'This for Robert Packer
Esq' at Shellingford [Berkshire]'. A copy of Robert Tailour's *Sacred Hymns*
(London, 1615), now in the Music Library of the University of Illinois at
Urbana, was bound in the 17th century to include 11 pages of manuscript
music at the front and 18 at the back, embracing psalm tunes by Alison,
Bennet, John Farmer, Kirbye, the elder John Milton, Morley, Ravenscroft
and John Tomkins and also the superius part of Byrd's *Lullaby—be still*
and the medius (in fact the highest) part of Hooper's *Behold it is Christ*.
The title-page of the printed book is signed 'Geo. Iliffe 1656', and
although the manuscript additions are not in Browne's hand he did add
the clarification '5 voc.' at the head of the single parts by Byrd and
Hooper. Another source that may have passed through Browne's hands
(*GB-Lbm* Add.29366-8) is a compilation of sacred, secular and instrumental music assembled early in the 17th century. There are later
additions in a hand bearing a superficial resemblance to Browne's literary
hand and also to what, as will be seen, may be suggested as his musical hand, while the vellum cover of each volume bears the name 'IO:
BROWNE': with so common a name this cannot in itself be regarded as
grounds for positive identification, and we are inclined to accept Monson's
suggestion that this Browne could well be a Cambridge University wait of
that name, especially as the source seems to have strong East Anglian, and
in particular Cambridge, connections[6].

The view that all of the above-mentioned manuscripts may have a
common provenance is reinforced by scribal concordances—that is, the
appearance of a particular copyist's hand in two or more of them. Probably
the earliest and certainly the most professional, a beautifully formed
calligraphic hand (Hand *A*) which often used red ink for the headings
and the frequently elaborate terminations, copied the opening layers of

Och 367–70 and 379–81 and *Ckc* 112–13 and 114–17 and a little of *Och* 423–8.[7] It disposed the music so that different textures and forms were copied into different sets of books: thus two-part music belongs to *Ckc* 112–13, three-, four- and five-part fantasias in *Ckc* 114–17, dances in *Och* 367–70 and 379–81 and six-part music in the appropriate section of *Och* 423–8, which had already been begun by a scribe who divided it into sections for pieces in three, four, five and six parts respectively and whose hand appears nowhere else in these sources. A second major musical hand (*B*) is common to the same five sets of partbooks and to *Ckc* 113A and the 'Braye Tablature Book' too. To a great extent it appears to be consciously modelled on *A*, both in its calligraphy and in its presentation of the music, but it is obviously amateur. It usually contributed the second layer to a manuscript, starting where *A* stopped, though the two hands sometimes overlap. This is the hand that may have made later additions to *Lbm* Add.29366–8 (see above). A third hand (*C*) occurs as copyist of nos. 40–66 of *Och* 379–81, the Coprario pieces occupying pp. 10–12 at the reverse end of *Ckc* 113A, and portions of *Och* 423–8. A fourth hand (*D*) was principally responsible for nos. 4–82 in *Ckc* 112–13 and 113A and the second layer of four- and five-part pieces in *Ckc* 114–17 but also copied nos. 40–44 of the five-part pieces and nos. 34–41 of the six-part pieces in *Och* 423–8. The four hands, *A–D*, are here placed in the order in which they contributed to the various manuscripts. *B* is of crucial significance, not only because it is frequently found in conjunction with Browne's literary hand but because three of a group of four pieces in it, nos. 21–4 of the five-part section of *Och* 473–8 (whose contents are arranged in a similar way to those of *Och* 423–8), are signed in at least one partbook with the initials 'J.B.' in what is obviously Browne's hand.[8] Nos. 21 and 22 are complete and are signed in two and three partbooks respectively. Nos. 23 and 24 appear only in the cantus book; only no. 24 is signed (see Plate IX), but no. 23 is presumably by 'J.B.' too, especially as the four pieces together form a Lawes-like consort suite. Thus it seems to us extremely probable that Browne was not only a collector who, as mentioned above, added headings and other directions to the manuscripts that he acquired, but also a musical scribe and a composer; no doubt he played the viol too.

The foregoing account isolates a number of now largely dispersed manuscripts as once belonging to Browne because they contain his handwriting or musical hand or both. At this point it is relevant to refer to three other manuscript sources which, although they do not contain his hand, are closely connected with some that do and thus may have belonged to

Plate IX *GB-Och* Mus. 473, f.72: the cantus part of a pavan signed 'J.B.', presumably
by John Browne.
(*By permission of Christ Church, Oxford.*)

him too. Of these it is likeliest that he owned *Och* 1004. This is a companion organ book to what are called in it the 'ruffe' and the 'white'
books, which from many specific references can readily be identified as
Och 423–8 and *Ckc* 114–17 respectively; it is, moreover, entirely in the
same hand as pp.1–8 of the reverse end of *Ckc* 113A (Hand *E*, also found,
incidentally, in *Och* 744–6 and the first part of *Lbm* 11608). It is less likely
but still possible that Browne owned *Och* 716–20, another set of viol
books, which includes not only four pieces in Hand *C* but also the two six-

part fantasias by William White found in *Och* 1004, one of which occurs in *Och* 423–8 too, thus encouraging the belief that these three sources may be interdependent. Finally—and this is a very tenuous connection— a violin book containing music by Coprario and Lawes, now in the possession of Layton Ring, of Hexham, Northumberland, may also have belonged to Browne. This single part of what was once a set of four, for two violins, bass viol and organ, has two connections with Browne manuscripts: repertorial in that Coprario and especially Lawes are pro- minent among the composers represented in them, scribal in that the Coprario pieces are in the hand (*F*) that copied no. 39 of the five-part pieces in *Och* 423–8, while the Lawes pieces were copied by a scribe of *Och* 430, a manuscript that, as mentioned above, was titled by Browne. The book was given to the present owner about 1954 by Nathalie Dolmetsch, who recalls that it was bought about 1930 from the now defunct London booksellers Davis & Orioli; nothing further is known of its provenance.

Although little is known about the previous history of the various manuscripts that, as has been suggested above, Browne almost certainly owned, that little makes it seem even likelier that he did so. The most direct evidence is afforded by the 'Braye Tablature Book' and *Ckc* 113A. The first of these is so called because it carries the bookplate of the 5th Lord Braye, who succeeded to the title in 1879 and died in 1935. Robert Spencer bought it in 1966 from the London bookseller Otto Haas, who had obtained it through private negotiation. It consists of two layers, the first of bandora music dating from about 1600, the second of lyra viol pieces from about 1635–40. The back flyleaf bears the name 'Thomas Turner of London', and the full-calf binding is stamped with the initials 'T.B.', which may well denote John Browne's father, Thomas Browne (1567–1621), and is decorated by a central gold-tooled ornament on the upper cover that is similar, but not identical, to that appearing on *Ckc* 113A, the Zimmerman books and the Illinois volume. *Ckc* 113A has a similar recent history in that it was acquired by King's College from Haas in 1967 and carries the same bookplate. Thus two of the manuscripts with which we are concerned definitely belonged to the library of the Lords Braye. Their seat is Stanford Hall, with which several of the other manuscripts under discussion can also be connected by circumstantial or inferential evidence. *Ckc* 113A is an organ book whose contents correspond very closely to *Ckc* 112–13, though the four five-part pavans by Alfonso Ferrabosco (ii) occur not in *Ckc* 113A but in *Och* 423–8. Nevertheless, *Ckc* 113A clearly belongs to and completes *Ckc* 112–13, which were presented to King's College together with *Ckc* 114–17 by Lord

Keynes in March 1939. Circumstantial evidence strongly suggests that all of these King's College manuscripts were once at Stanford Hall, a suggestion perhaps supported by a receipt dated 1936 among Keynes's papers at King's College which, though not specific, suggests equally strongly that Keynes bought from the Birmingham booksellers Lowe Bros. all the manuscripts that he later presented to his college.[9] Stanford Hall is some 35 miles from Birmingham.

The Braye family, who still live at Stanford Hall, are the direct descendants of the Cave family who originated in Yorkshire in the 11th century and were politically influential in the 16th and 17th centuries; Sir Thomas Cave purchased the manor and advowson of Stanford in 1540, at the dissolution of the monasteries. The Cave baronetcy was created in 1641, and the Braye title reached the family through the marriage of the third baronet, Sir Thomas Cave, who succeeded his father in 1703. On 26 March 1676 the second baronet, Sir Roger Cave, married Martha, Browne's daughter and heir.[10] This marriage offers the most obvious clue as to how a number of the manuscripts that can definitely be shown to have passed through Browne's hands later came to be at Stanford Hall. They may, however, have gone there *via* James Callcott, for over 40 years steward to the Caves and previously in Browne's employ, who, to judge by his substantial memorial on the south wall of St Nicholas, Stanford-on-Avon, was a servant of some standing. The removal of Browne's music manuscripts to Stanford Hall and their dispersal during the present century are paralleled by the known movements of a large number of state papers originally in Browne's possession and many in his hand. They are mostly official records, but there are also some Parliament Office papers and a few family papers. About 1885 they were seen by Henry Maxwell-Lyte on behalf of the Historical Manuscripts Commission at Stanford Hall ('stowed away in no order in a lumber room') in the custody of the 5th Lord Braye, and many of them were then calendared.[11] Between 1947 and 1962 these manuscripts, together with others from StanfordHall, were sold in a series of auctions and private sales; either the originals or photocopies of all of Browne's other parliamentary papers were subsequently acquired by the House of Lords Record Office, where they are now kept as a separate collection.[12]

This background of dispersal is useful for an understanding of the seemingly haphazard way in which a number of Browne's music manuscripts, some of them traceable to Stanford Hall, have come to light in the present century. The dispersal of the music manuscripts, however, seems to have begun earlier. We have seen that Keynes bought his manuscripts, which very likely came from the hall, in 1936. Interestingly, both the Zimmerman partbooks and the Illinois volume were sold as 'the property of a nobleman' in the same public auction in 1929, thereby strengthening the possible association of the Illinois book with both Browne and Stanford Hall.[13] The Zimmerman books were acquired by a British collector, Richard Border, of Pulborough, Sussex, and were bought by Zimmerman at the sale of his collection after his death in 1962. Tailour's *Sacred Hymns* was bought by the London booksellers Bernard Quaritch, whence the University of Illinois obtained it in the late 1940s.

The connection of Browne with Stanford Hall raises the possibility that other manuscripts compiled before 1691 that definitely passed through Stanford Hall may also have formed part of Browne's collection. Three such manuscripts are known to have been housed there. The first consists of lute music and now belongs to the collection of the late James M. Osborn now at Yale University. It was described by Maxwell-Lyte in his account of the Stanford Hall manuscripts and was sold in 1952 with a number of Browne's personal and parliamentary papers ('The property of the Rt. Honble. Lord Braye') as

MUSIC. MS MUSIC OF THE SIXTEENTH CENTURY, BY OR IN THE STYLE OF JOHN DOWLAND: among the pieces may be found: The King's Pavane, A fancye of Francys Myclayne, O God that are my rygtuusness, The base of Spayne, Fantagia Francis de Mycayne, Mark Antonys Gallyarde . . . 38pp., at end of volume are MS verses of the 16th Century and some Cookery Receipts. 57 ll. in all, oblong 8vo, red morocco, gilt.[14]

John M. Ward has described the book, which dates from about 1570, as one of a number that were 'the product of amateurs . . . and of interest chiefly to the historian of popular song'.[15] Apart from the undisputed connection of this manuscript with Stanford Hall, there is no evidence indicating that Browne may have owned it, and his hand does not appear in it, but since the evidence of the 'Braye Tablature Book' suggests that earlier members of Browne's family may have had musical interests the Osborn manuscript may likewise have been handed down to him. On the other hand the inclusion of a piece called 'The Lady Caves Delight' in Tobias Hume's *Poeticall Musicke* (London, 1607), a volume of lyra viol music, suggests an interest in music on the part of at least one earlier member of the Cave family. The Osborn manuscript could presumably have reached Stanford Hall through either family. The second manuscript, which is now in private hands, was described by Maxwell-Lyte as consisting of 39 leaves in two layers copied by two scribes. The first layer was said to consist of music seemingly of the period *c*1590–1600, the second of pieces by Thomas Robinson, 'Captaine Winn' and William Lawes. The volume is signed 'Matthew Otley'.[16]

The third manuscript with Stanford Hall connections that may have passed through Browne's hands, though this seems rather unlikely, is a Barber manuscript at the University of Birmingham *(GB-Bu* 5001), which bought it at a sale at Hodgson & Co., of London, in 1949.[17] It consists essentially of 31 autograph works, mainly anthems and odes, in the copies that the five composers represented—Blow, Cooke, Humfrey, Purcell and Turner—must have provided for copying for performances at court. The latest of these works had been written by about 1685. Bound in between f.152 and f.153 is a design addressed 'To Sir Thomas Cave Bar! at Stanford' for 'Posts and Rail'; this clearly was intended for the bridge over the River Avon in the grounds of Stanford Hall, for the posts, recognisable from the design, still stand there today. John Barker, composer, organist and copyist, signed the back flyleaf in 1731. This would appear to indicate, as Watkins Shaw observed,[18] that the various autographs had been bound together by that date, but the fence design may have been slipped into the volume later and bound in only when the volume was rebound after reaching Birmingham University. The Sir Thomas Cave to whom the design was addressed could have been the third baronet, who succeeded to the title in 1703, or a later one; it is difficult to date the posts on grounds of style, and we have not been allowed access to any evidence there may be at Stanford Hall. It may well be significant that on 20 October 1731 Barker was appointed organist of Holy Trinity, Coventry, only some 15 miles from Stanford Hall. He may have brought *Bu* 5001 with him from the Chapel Royal and presented it to the Cave family, perhaps when he left Coventry (Capel Bond, who was presumably his successor as organist of Holy Trinity, was appointed on 26 May 1752, and Barker is known to have been living at Lichfield in 1755).[19] This seems more likely than that the Caves should have presented him with the manuscript shortly after his arrival in 1731. He was certainly connected with them; members of the family took nine copies of his *Twelve Songs* (Coventry, 1741), as the subscription list in it shows. It may be noted in passing that another notable ornament of royal music-making had already arrived at Stanford. This is the fine organ at the west end of St Nicholas's, which appears to have been moved from the Palace of Whitehall about 1663 through the intervention of the Cave family,[20] and it could have been one of them who likewise arranged for the volume of autographs to be taken to Stanford.[21]

It seems unlikely, then, that either the Osborn manuscript or *Bu* 5001 belonged to Browne's collection, despite their connections with Stanford Hall, and it is perhaps worth adding that our strong doubts expressed above as to whether *Lbm* Add.29366–8 belonged to him are, if anything, strengthened by their deviation from the standard pattern of dispersal. According to a note on the inside of the upper cover of Add.29366, the British Museum acquired them at the sale of Thomas Oliphant's collection on 24 April 1873, and indeed they must surely be those described in the sale catalogue[22] as

> Lot 536: A collection of Compositions, for 5 and 6 voices, chiefly sacred, by Rich Deering, Wilbye, Weekes, Ramsay, Wilkinson, Gibbons, Warwicke, etc. Cantus, Bassus, and Quintus parts, *fine old transcript*, 3 vols. *vellum* obl. folio.

At this date a number of Browne's music manuscripts were still housed, presumably unnoticed, at Stanford Hall, but Oliphant acquired most of his collection during the 1840s and 1850s, especially at the Latrobe, John Stafford Smith, Lady Mary Sykes and first Novello sales.[23] This does not, however, necessarily mean that they did not emanate from Browne's collection, since the Christ Church manuscripts discussed above, which certainly belonged to him because they contain his hand, must have become separated from the Stanford Hall manuscripts at an early stage. They were evidently at Oxford in 1718, when the elder Richard Goodson, Professor of Music there from 1682 to 1718, bequeathed his collection to Christ Church, since the manuscript catalogue made in 1787 by J. B. Malchair,[24] which distinguishes between Goodson's collection and that of Dean Aldrich (presented to Christ Church in 1710), includes a number of entries that refer quite explicitly to the manuscripts that we have associated in this paper with Browne. Since the Packer family, into which Browne married in 1636, had strong Oxford connections, it is possible that they found their way to Oxford through them; alternatively Browne may have worked on these manuscripts at Oxford during the Civil War, when his parliamentary duties were very light and when he may have met Lawes.

We have shown in the earlier part of this paper that Browne owned and added to—as both copyist and composer—a number of important sources of viol and lyra viol music: indeed, Tailour's *Sacred Hymns* is, with Hume's two volumes of 1605 and 1607, one of the three most important early printed sources of lyra viol music and the only printed book of sacred music calling for the lyra viol.[25] Browne's interest in this music strongly suggests that he was himself a performer. He seems almost certainly to have copied some of the music himself, and he may well have supervised the copying of later layers. Much of the repertory in the manuscripts is unified, suggests close court associations for them and may well indicate that Browne knew some of the composers, especially Lawes and Milton, who are represented in them.[26] A detailed study of the repertory contained in Browne's manuscripts could be of great importance for the dating and evaluation of the sources of English viol music.

JOHN BROWNE'S MUSIC MANUSCRIPTS

(i) *Definite*
    Och 367–70
           379–81
           423–8
           430
           473–8
    Ckc 112–13
           113A
           114–17
    Braye Tablature Book
    Us-U x783.9 T136s cop. 2
    Zimmerman partbooks

(ii) *Possible but likely*
    Och 716–20
           1004

(iii) *Possible but unlikely*
    Bu 5001
         5002
    Otley Ms
    Ring MS
    US-NH Osborn Box 22 no. 10

(iv) *Untraceable*
    '18th-century' Coprario MS (see note 17 below)

NOTES TO CHAPTER 5

1. We are not concerned here with the actual music of the various sources: for that see A. Ashbee: 'Instrumental Music from the Library of John Browne (1608–91), Clerk of the Parliaments', *ML*, lviii (1977), 43. Dr Ashbee, Robert Ford and David Pinto were generous in sharing information and ideas, and we are very grateful to them, as we also are to Layton Ring and Robert Spencer, for permission to consult manuscripts in their possession, to G. E. Aylmer, for helpful comments relating to Browne's public career, and to Peter Marr, for unpublished information about John Barker.

2. Two files of information about Browne, extracted by Mary Edmond from a wide range of sources, are kept in the House of Lords Record Office. Anyone working on Browne must be grateful to her for making the product of her researches so conveniently available. We are also grateful to Maurice F. Bond and his staff at the record office for their courteous help. Browne is also discussed in M. F. Bond: 'Clerks of the Parliaments, 1509–1953', *English Historical Review*, lxxiii (1958), 78, and in G. E. Aylmer: *The King's Servants: the Civil Service of Charles I, 1625–42* (London, rev. 2/1974), 1, 6.

3. There is a microfilm of them at the Pendlebury Library of Music, Faculty of Music, University of Cambridge, as there also is of the copy of Tailour's *Sacred Hymns* mentioned later.

4. The two-part pieces in *GB-Ckc* 112–13 are discussed in W. Coates: 'English Two-part Viol Music, 1590–1640', *ML*, xxxiii (1952), 141.

5. This source is briefly discussed in W. A. Edwards: *The Sources of Elizabethan Consort Music* (diss., U. of Cambridge, 1974), i, 308ff.

6. See C. Monson: *Voices and Viols in England, 1600–1650: the Sources and the Music* (diss., U. of California, Berkeley, 1974), 204ff.

7. Facs. in *John Jenkins: Consort Music of Four Parts*, ed. A. Ashbee, MB, xxvi (London, 1969), xxi.

8. Thurston Dart, without comment, identified 'J.B.' with John Banister (i); see T. Dart: 'Purcell's Chamber Music', *PRMA*, lxxxv (1958–9), 90.

9. The catalogues of Lowe Bros for 1936 in Birmingham Central Library are missing, and it has proved impossible to make contact with the firm. The invoice refers to Music MSS 4, 2 and 1, which presumably were to become *Ckc* 114–17, 112–13 and 2 ('Turpyn's Book of Lute Songs') respectively; these seven books are the only music manuscripts that Keynes is known to have owned.

10. John Browne's family must not be confused with the Brownes of Stretton-en-le-Field, Leicestershire, the family into which Sir Roger's second son, Roger, married. It was as a result of this connection that John Cave-Browne took the name Browne by Act of Parliament in 1752; the present form of this family's name is Cave-Browne-Cave.

11. *Historical Manuscripts Commission, tenth report*, appx, pt.vi (London, 1887), 104ff.

12. See M. F. Bond: *Guide to the Records of Parliament* (London, 1971), 269ff.

13. Sotheby & Co.: *Catalogue of Important Literary & Medieval Manuscripts, Autograph Letters, Valuable Printed Books, etc . . . 11–14 November 1929*, items 236 (Lawes part-books) and 240 (Tailour). It may be added that another item in this sale was the 1667 edition of Christopher Simpson's *Chelys . . . the Division-Viol, or The Art of Playing Ex tempore upon a Ground* (lot 246).

14.   Sotheby & Co.: *Catalogue of Valuable Printed Books, Autograph Letters, Historical Documents, etc . . . Monday, 23 June 1952*, item 131. For Maxwell-Lyte's description see the volume cited above, note 11, 108. See also B. Boito: 'Manuscript Music in the James Marshall and Marie-Louise Osborn Collection', *Notes*, xxvii (1970–71), 239.

15.   J. M. Ward: 'The Fourth Dublin Lute Book', *LSJ*, xi (1969), 28.

16.   This manuscript was untraceable when we were writing this paper, but a gittern manuscript matching Maxwell-Lyte's description exactly was sold as follows: Sotheby, Parke, Bernet & Co.: *Bibliotheca Phillippica. New Series: Nineteenth Part, Catalogue of English, French, Greek and Icelandic Manuscripts . . . 27 June 1977*, lot 4852. It was bought by the bookseller Richard Macnutt, of Tunbridge Wells, Kent, who sold it to its present owner.

17.   The sale catalogue reads: *A Catalogue of Fine and Rare Books Including a Further selection from the Castle Howard Library . . . 14 July 1949*, and the manuscript was lot 53, in the section headed 'A Selection from a Country Library mostly Bound in old Calf'. For descriptions of the manuscript see W. Shaw: 'A Collection of Musical Manuscripts in the Autographs of Henry Purcell and Other English Composers, *c*. 1665–85', *The Library*, xiv (1959), 126, and I. Fenlon: *Catalogue of the Printed Music and Music Manuscripts before 1801 in the Music Library of the University of Birmingham, Barber Institute of Fine Arts* (London, 1976), 113f. *Bu* 5002, which can be dated *c*1680, was bought at the same time from the same library, and if *Bu* 5001 belonged to Browne it may have done so too; it consists of sacred and secular songs, cantatas, etc, by, among others, Purcell and Carissimi. Another manuscript sold on the same occasion was described as containing 18th-century transcriptions of ayres and fantasias by Coprario, but it is possible that this was misdated and was in fact another manuscript that may have been owned by Browne. It is specially significant that the sale catalogue stated that the 'headings and ornaments [were] in red': cf p.157 above.

18.   *The Library*, xiv (1959), 129 (where 'Hanford' is of course a misreading of 'Stanford').

19.   There is no evidence that Barker was a vicar-choral of Lichfield Cathedral as stated in D. Franklin: 'Five Manuscripts of Church Music at Lichfield', *RMARC*, iii (1963/R1970), 55, and in Purcell Society, xxx (1965), p.xiv.

20.   See A. Freeman: 'Organs Built for the Royal Palace of Whitehall', *MT*, lii (1911), 720.

21.   This is perhaps the place to point out that the library at Stanford Hall still contains what look to be volumes of music that could affect the content of this paper, but questions about them to the present Lord Braye and his staff have not been answered.

22.   *Catalogue of the Rare and Interesting Musical Collections of the late Thomas Oliphant, Esq., . . . to be sold by Messrs. Puttick & Simpson.*

23.   Further on Oliphant's collecting habits see A. H. King: *Some British Collectors of Music* (Cambridge, 1963), 37, 42f, 45, 49, 98.

24.   *GB-Lcm* 2125; see King (1963), 14.

25.   See F. Traficante: 'Music for the Lyra Viol: the Printed Sources', *LSJ*, viii (1966), 7; also V. L. Moore: 'Psalmes, Teares, and Broken Music', *Bulletin of the John Rylands Library*, xlvi/2 (1964), 411.

26.   See D. Pinto: 'William Lawes' Consort Suites for the Viols, and the Autograph Sources', *Chelys*, iv (1972), 14, where some of Browne's manuscripts are mentioned as sources of Lawes's music. It is perhaps worth adding that, just as Thomas Myriell's *Tristitiae remedium* (1616; *Lbm* Add.29372–7) is almost the only manuscript source of Milton's vocal music, *Och* 423–8 is the sole source of his consort music; Myriell had been rector of St Stephen Walbrook, in the City of London, where Browne later married his second wife, and this church was also connected with the Merchant Taylors Company, to which Browne's grandfather belonged. Further on Myriell see P. J. Willetts: 'The Identity of Thomas Myriell', *ML*, liii (1972), 431, and C. Monson: 'Thomas Myriell's Manuscript Collection: One View of Musical Taste in Jacobean London', *JAMS*, xxx (1977), 418–65.

6

Gregorio Piva and Steffani's Principal Copyist

Colin Timms

Agostino Steffani (1654–1728) occupies an important position in the history of Italian secular vocal music in the late Baroque period. His reputation as a composer rests mainly on his operas and on his chamber duets for two voices and continuo. He has been described as 'the principal intermediary between the Italian opera of the late 17th century and the German operas of Keiser and Handel',[1] and his Hanover operas, in particular, 'set a standard as exemplary and binding in Germany as those of Lully did in France'.[2] His chamber duets also were models of their kind. 'In this form of composition', wrote Mattheson in 1739, 'the aforesaid Steffani surpassed every other composer known to me and deserves to be taken as a model to this day; for such things do not easily grow old'.[3] In fact, Steffani's duets had already been imitated by Handel nearly 30 years before these words were written,[4] and Steffani appears to have been the only major composer of the period whom Handel later acknowledged that he had taken as a model.[5]

As is well known, however, not all of Steffani's life was devoted to music. At Hanover, where he went as Kapellmeister in 1688, he became increasingly involved in diplomatic activities. He had a hand in the negotiations leading to the elevation of Hanover to the ninth Electorate in 1692,[6] and in the following year was appointed Hanoverian 'envoy extraordinary' to the Bavarian court at Brussels[7] (the Elector Maximilian II Emanuel had been made Imperial Lieutenant of the Spanish Netherlands in 1691 and had moved to Brussels in 1692). Steffani was continually away from Hanover on diplomatic missions from about 1696 and played an important part in the manoeuvres preceding the War of the Spanish Succession.[8] His main concern was to persuade Maximilian to support the Emperor rather than Louis XIV, and his failure to do so was one of the greatest disappointments of his career. He returned to Hanover in July 1702 and threw himself that autumn into revision of his chamber duets.[9]

The remainder of his life was spent largely in the service of the Church.

He had already been ordained a priest at Munich in 1680; three years later he was made Abbot of Lepsingen, a sinecure in the Protestant earldom of Öttingen-Wallerstein,[10] halfway between Augsburg and Nuremberg. He is described as an Apostolic Protonotary in the sub-title of his brief dissertation *Quanta certezza habbia da suoi principii la musica*, which was published at Amsterdam in 1695, but the date on which he was appointed does not appear to be known. When he moved from Hanover to Düsseldorf in the spring of 1703 he was installed as President of the Spiritual Council for the Palatinate and for the Duchies of Jülich and Berg, and later that year he was also made General President of the Palatine Government.[11] He was consecrated as Bishop of Spiga *in partibus infidelium* in Bamberg cathedral in January 1707[12] and appointed Apostolic Vicar of northern Germany in April 1709.[13] Like earlier incumbents of this onerous position, he made Hanover his base: he moved back there in November 1709, and apart from a three-year period in Italy (1722–5) remained there for more or less the rest of his life.

His activities as a diplomat and churchman appear to be the main reason why, as a composer, he adopted a pseudonym. This is the explanation given by Hawkins, and there seems little reason for doubting its veracity:[14]

> He was now considered in the light of a statesman, and was besides a dignitary of the church; and having a character to sustain, with which he imagined the public profession of his art not properly consistent, he forbore the setting his name to his future compositions, and adopted that of his secretary, or copyist, *Gregorio Piva*. Influenced, perhaps, by the same motives, in the year 1708, he resigned his employment as chapel-master [at Hanover], in favour of Mr *Handel* . . . .

Hawkins does not say when Steffani adopted his pseudonym, but seems to imply that it was before 1708. Since, however, his account of Steffani's resignation and Handel's appointment as Kapellmeister at Hanover is thoroughly unreliable, it would be unwise to accept this date before investigating the matter a little further.

Corroborative evidence is to be found in Steffani's correspondence with the singer and composer Ruggiero Fedeli. On 18 November 1713 Fedeli sent him an account of the musical life at the court of Kassel, where he was employed: ' . . . we have operas from Hanover, besides all those composed by you at Düsseldorf, and also your esteemed chamber duets'.[15] Ten days later Steffani replied:[16]

> Now we come to music. That was a sin of my youth. I confess to you that I still love it more than ever. But I can truthfully say that sometimes I have

gone many years without seeing a harpsichord. You speak to me of Düsseldorf operas: I do not know that I composed any, but there are operas by Signor Gregorio Piva. However that may be, it gave me the greatest pleasure to hear that those bagatelles amuse His Serene Lordship the Landgrave . . . .

The only pieces mentioned by Fedeli and attributed by Steffani to Piva are the Düsseldorf operas. Steffani is normally credited with three such works,[17] but the first of them, *Arminio* (1707), is a pasticcio assembled from some of his Munich and Hanover operas and containing only a small proportion of newly-composed items, while the second, *Amor vien dal destino* (1709), was almost certainly composed at Hanover: it may have been intended for performance in 1694, but no new opera was produced there that year, perhaps on account of the Königsmark affair.[18] The third of the Düsseldorf operas, *Il Tassilone* (1709), seems to have been an almost entirely new composition. It has been suggested that it is inferior to Steffani's operas and that it may have been composed by a lesser figure, possibly Gregorio Piva.[19] The title-page of the continuo book (*GB-Lbm* Royal 23.i.18) actually bears the words 'Musica/di Gregorio/Piva', but since Piva, as we shall see in a moment, does not appear to have been a composer, it seems reasonable to suppose that this is an example of his name being used as Steffani's pseudonym. The fact that part of the overture is taken from *La libertà contenta* (Hanover, 1693) means that some (at least) of the work is by Steffani, and the remainder is normally attributed confidently to him. The earliest of these 'Düsseldorf' operas, from the point of view of performance, dates from the year in which he was consecrated as Bishop of Spiga: by this time, at the latest, he seems to have found 'the public profession of his art' inconsistent with his ecclesiastical position.

It is significant that Steffani did not disown his Hanover operas or his chamber duets. Admittedly, Fedeli does not say that the Hanover operas known at Kassel were those of Steffani, but the heyday of opera at Hanover (1689–97) coincided almost exactly with Steffani's period as Kapellmeister there and the majority of the works performed during those years were composed by him. The opera house was closed down soon after the accession of Elector Georg Ludwig in 1698, so Fedeli could not have been thinking of any later works, and it seems extremely unlikely that he was referring to any of the (very few) operas performed at Hanover in the decades prior to Steffani's arrival.[20] It would appear, therefore, that Steffani adopted his pseudonym after 1695, the date of the last Hanover opera (*I trionfi del fato*) of which he was undoubtedly the composer.

Given these outer limits of 1695 and 1707, it would seem most likely that he did so after moving in 1703 to Düsseldorf, where, as we have seen, he was mainly concerned with affairs of church and state. Since the first work that he is known to have 'composed' there is in fact *Arminio*, he presumably had little need of a pseudonym until early 1707, when this opera was first performed. In view of this, it seems safe to conclude that the pseudonym was adopted for works composed, circulated or performed after Steffani had been made Bishop of Spiga.

This conclusion is supported by what little is known of the life of the real Gregorio Piva. He is first encountered as a singer and copyist at the court of Dresden; he was appointed in 1691 and, if he was still there, was presumably dismissed along with all the other Italian musicians of the Kapelle in 1694.[21] It is not certain where he spent the next few years, but from 1703, at the latest, to 1716 he was employed as an instrumentalist at Düsseldorf.[22] He was appointed as an instrumentalist and copyist at Bonn in December 1717;[23] on 8 January 1727 he also took on the post of court music librarian, and he died in 1740.[24]

The point to note is that he and Steffani were in Düsseldorf at the same time. This may have been what led Einstein to suggest that Steffani could have made Piva's acquaintance at Dresden in 1692 or 1693 and have invited him to Hanover,[25] and that he probably took him with him to Düsseldorf in 1703.[26] According to one authority, however, Piva had already moved to Düsseldorf by 1697.[27] Moreover, there is no evidence that he was employed prior to 1703 at Hanover, either as a musician or as a copyist—though it must be said that an account book which may have contained information on this point appears now to be lost.[28] He could perhaps have been Steffani's own secretary, a word used by Hawkins, but his name is not mentioned in the titles of any of the documents in the 'Registratur des Bischofs von Spiga'[29]—the collection of Steffani's papers left in Hanover at the time of his decease—or in the 'Fondo Spiga'—the collection deposited shortly afterwards in the archives of the Sacred Congregation of Propaganda, Rome. Furthermore, if Piva had been Steffani's secretary, one might expect him to have copied a substantial proportion of his master's music.

The Manuscripts

Before considering any copies he may have made, we must first establish the identity of his hand. It has been said that the principal sources of *Il Tassilone* (score: *E-Mn* M.2258/9; orchestral parts: *GB-Lbm* Royal

23.i.18–24) were copied by him,[30] but no evidence appears to have been published in support of this claim. One powerful piece of evidence is Piva's application for the post of music librarian at Bonn (Plate X(a)).[31] The fact that this document bears the words 'umilissima supplica di Gregorio Piva' does not necessarily mean that it was penned by him, but since he had already been court copyist for ten years it is hard to imagine why any other scribe should have been asked to write it out. The hand is identical to that found in the score and parts of *Il Tassilone* (cf. Plate X(b)), so there seems little reason for doubting that the latter were copied by Piva.

Apart from the principal sources of *Il Tassilone*, only two other manuscripts are known by the present writer to be in the same hand: *Lbm* Royal 23.f.15 (*Arminio*) and Royal 23.h.6 (*Henrico Leone*). The fact that *Il Tassilone* and *Arminio* both survive in copies made by Piva suggests rather strongly that his activity as Steffani's copyist may have been restricted, as one might expect, to those years when both men were at Düsseldorf. The absence of a copy by Piva of Steffani's other 'Düsseldorf' opera, *Amor vien dal destino*, does not vitiate this argument but lends further weight to the suggestion that the opera was composed elsewhere. Moreover, if Piva was Steffani's Düsseldorf copyist, this would presumably explain why there seem to be so few surviving copies of his music in his hand: *Arminio* and *Il Tassilone* are the only works that Steffani is known to have composed there. Why Piva also made a copy of *Henrico Leone*, his first Hanover opera (1689), cannot now be ascertained—there appears to be no evidence that it was ever performed at Düsseldorf, or at Heidelberg or Mannheim.[32]

Perhaps because Piva was described by Hawkins as Steffani's secretary or copyist, it has also been said he was his favourite copyist.[33] Whether or not this was the case, it is abundantly clear that another copyist, here to be known as scribe *A*, is of far greater importance as a transmitter of Steffani's music. His hand (cf Plate X(c)) appears in a larger number of Steffani manuscripts—and these represent a higher proportion of his output—than was copied by Piva or by any other copyist of the period:

D-Mbs	5321	chamber duets
GB-Lbm	Royal 23.k.12	chamber duets
	Royal 23.k.13	
	Royal 23.k.15–17	chamber duets
	Royal 23.k.19–20	
	Royal 23.h.10	*Henrico Leone*
	Royal 23.i.10	*Orlando generoso*

GB-Lbm	Royal 23.i.2	*I trionfi del fato*
	*Royal 23.h.2	*Amor vien dal destino*
	*Royal 23.h.12	arias from *Henrico Leone, La lotta d'Hercole con Acheloo* and *La superbia d'Alessandro*
	*Royal 23.i.16	arias from *Orlando generoso* and *Le rivali concordi*
	*Royal 23.i.6	arias and duets from *La libertà contenta* and *I trionfi del fato*
	*Royal 23.k.5	duets from *Henrico Leone, La lotta d'Hercole con Acheloo, La superbia d'Alessandro, Orlando generoso, Le rivali concordi, La libertà contenta, I trionfi del fato, Baccanali, Briseide* and *La costanza nelle selve*
GB-Lgc	G.Mus.418	six motets from *Sacer Ianus quadrifons*
I-Rc	2223	chamber duets

The significance of the asterisks in the list of scribe *A*'s copies will be explained in due course.

The works copied by scribe *A* provide a number of clues as to his

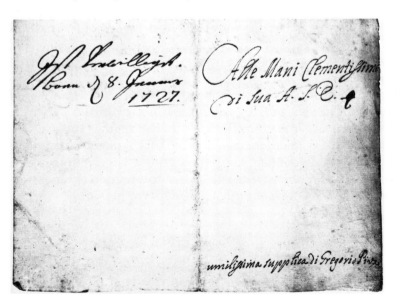

Plate X (a) Piva's application for the post of music librarian at Bonn.

Plate X (b) The opening of Scene I, *Il Tassilone*.

Plate X (c) The hand of scribe *A*.

identity. It seems very likely, first of all, that he was based primarily at Hanover. With the exception of *Amor vien dal destino*, which, as we have seen, was almost certainly composed there, all the operas that he copied, in whole or in part, were first performed there between 1689 and 1697. Most of them are by Steffani, but there is still some doubt about the authenticity of *La lotta d'Hercole con Acheloo* and *Baccanali*; *Briseide* was probably composed by Pietro Torri, and *La costanza nelle selve* (also known as 'La pastoralle') is by Luigi Mancia.[34] In addition to the manuscripts listed above, scribe *A* also made a copy of the whole of *Briseide* (*Lbm* Royal 23.g.22) and wrote out a volume of arias drawn from this work and from *La costanza nelle selve* (*Lbm* Royal 23.g.23).

The dating of scribe *A*'s activity is an intricate operation. The dates of the operas will provide some guidance, but these can only be taken as a *terminus non ante quem*. *Amor vien dal destino* is attributed by scribe *A* to Gregorio Piva and dated 1709; the fact that all the other works in the list except the six motets, which will be discussed below, are not ascribed to Piva could mean that they were copied before about 1707 when, as we have seen, this pseudonym appears to have been adopted, but it could also indicate that they were merely composed before then. The covers of *Lbm* Royal 23.k.5 are gold-stamped with the initials 'G.A.' and with a rearing horse, the emblem of Lower Saxony, so this volume was probably bound for the Electoral Prince Georg August some time after 1697, the date of the latest duets it contains, and before 1714, when he moved from Hanover to England. It may have had something to do with his marriage in 1705 to Princess Caroline of Ansbach, who was very interested in music: Leibniz records that she possessed 'la voix merveilleuse'[35] and Mainwaring says that she was particularly fond of chamber duets.[36]

The majority of these works are undated, but it is possible to show beyond any reasonable doubt that *Lbm* Royal 23.k.13–20 represent the remains of a new manuscript collection on which Steffani embarked when he began to revise his duets in the autumn of 1702. The circumstances that led him to undertake this project have already been mentioned. He received a great deal of support during this period from Queen Sophie Charlotte of Prussia, and his correspondence with her constitutes the most important source of information on his progress.[37]

Evidence that he worked on this project at this time is to be found in his letter to her of 9 November 1702:[38]

> . . . je me suis jetté à corps perdu dans la Musique . . . Je me divertis à bouleverser tous mes Duos, qui ne me plaise [sic] plus, et je les fay d'une maniere, qui me donne beaucoup de plaisir . . . Mais je ne sçaurois donner

à mon nouvel Ouvrage la forme que je luy destine, à moins, que V[otre] M[ajesté] n'aye la Benignité de m'assister, en faisant en sorte que le Sr Attilio [Ariosti] me renvoye la Musique, que Mr de Kielmanseck luy a laissée; et particulierement le livre n° 8. des Duos qui est encore entre ses mains, et les trois que j'ay eu l'honneur d'envoyer à V. M. de Bruxelles. . . .

It is clear from his reference to 'le livre n° 8. des Duos' that there was a collection of his duets in existence at the time this letter was written, but it is equally clear from the words 'mon nouvel Ouvrage' and 'la forme que je luy destine' that he was hoping to replace it. His desire to retrieve all the duets that he had composed up to that time indicates that he wanted his new collection to be as complete as possible.

The manuscripts *Lbm* Royal 23.k.13–20 do not bear the name of any composer, but their contents have long been recognised as the work of Steffani. They are included in Einstein's index of his duets[39] and are attributed to him in Hilda Andrews's catalogue of the miscellaneous manuscripts in the King's Music Library.[40] The attribution can be substantiated in several ways. Many of the duets in the collection are ascribed to Steffani in other early sources, such as *Lbm* Royal 23.k.7 and *I-Fc* D.331–2,[41] and six of them are mentioned, by implication, in his correspondence with Sophie Charlotte and with the former Bavarian princess Violanta Beatrice after her marriage to Grand Prince Ferdinando de' Medici.[42] Moreover, two of the volumes (*Lbm* Royal 23.k.14 and 18) were copied not by scribe *A* but by the composer himself;[43] these appear to be the only surviving autographs of his duets.

Although the collection is now clearly defective, there are signs that it was intended to be complete. Each of the eight surviving volumes has a Roman numeral stamped on the outside of the front cover, and it appears from these that at least five volumes have been lost:

Royal 23.k.13:	I	Royal 23.k.17:	IX
Royal 23.k.14:	II	Royal 23.k.18:	X
Royal 23.k.15:	V	Royal 23.k.19:	XII
Royal 23.k.16:	VI	Royal 23.k.20:	XIII

Since there is no contemporary index to the collection as a whole (or to individual volumes), it is not certain whether vol. XIII was the last of the set; but this volume contains Steffani's only six duets with instruments other than continuo, and these larger works may have been intended as the crown of the collection. If the missing five volumes contained six duets apiece, as do all the survivors, then the total number of duets in a set of 13 volumes would have been 78. Einstein credited Steffani with 85 duets, but I have suggested elsewhere that three of them are unreliable attributions,[44] and these may now be joined by a fourth.[45] Of the 81 reliable attributions that remain, two were almost certainly composed too late for inclusion in the collection planned in 1702,[46] and this could also be true of one other duet.[47] Even if the latter were composed by or shortly after the end of 1702, Steffani would not have had enough duets to fill 14 volumes at six duets per volume; it seems very likely, therefore, that *Lbm* Royal 23.k.13–20 did comprise exactly 13 volumes and that it was a more or less complete collection of the duets available at the time of compilation.

A further reason for associating these manuscripts with the collection planned in 1702 is that they do not include the earlier version of any duet that Steffani is known to have revised: they contain only the revised versions. At least 19 duets survive in two versions and seem therefore to have been revised. Sixteen of these appear in both forms in Einstein's index,[48] while the earlier versions of the other three have come to light in the course of more recent research.[49] Ten of the revised versions are to be found in what survives of the *Lbm* Royal 23.k.13–20 set, and all but one of these are included in one or other of the two autograph volumes (vols. II and X); the exception, *Torna a dar vita*, is the last duet in vol. IX.

The fact that *Lbm* Royal 23.k.13–20 contains revised versions in Steffani's hand is the main reason for thinking that this collection, not *D-Mbs* 5321, is the one on which he began work in the autumn of 1702. This Munich source also appears to have been a complete collection, although, again, only eight volumes now survive. The contents of five of the volumes are identical to those of five of the volumes in *Lbm* Royal 23.k.13–20,[50] but the other three consist entirely of duets no longer extant in that set and may correspond with three of the volumes now missing from it. The Munich manuscripts also include the later versions only of duets that Steffani revised, but none of these is in his hand: all the surviving volumes are in the hand of scribe *A*. The only other volumes of duets copied by this scribe, *Lbm* Royal 23.k.12 and *I-Rc* 2223, are similar in size and format to the London and Munich collections discussed above, but since they duplicate duets found in both they are unlikely to have belonged to either; and since they duplicate duets in each other they are unlikely to have belonged together in a further complete set.

Having established that *Lbm* Royal 23.k.13–20 is almost certainly the collection on which Steffani embarked in 1702, we may now consider the date of its completion. This must depend to some extent on when he stopped revising. There are signs that this was either in late 1702 or in early 1703. On 7 December 1702 he wrote to Sophie Charlotte:[51]

. . . lors qu'on aura le bonheur de servir V. M. icy, elle y trouvera une
bonne recreue de Duetti, puisqu'il y en a dejà un Couple de douzaines à son
très-humble service.

The duets in question are undoubtedly those in *Lbm* Royal 23.k.7-8, a
pair of manuscripts that was clearly intended for presentation to Sophie
Charlotte.[52] These manuscripts originally contained 26 duets,[53] of which
18 are known to be revised versions. Since only one other duet (*Torna a dar
vita*) survives in two versions, it seems unlikely that Steffani revised many
duets after these two volumes had been compiled—or after writing to
Sophie Charlotte on 7 December 1702.

Furthermore, this letter seems to have been one of the last that they
exchanged—any later correspondence appears to have been lost or
destroyed. Why their relations should have come to such an early end is
not entirely clear. Sophie became increasingly eccentric as she grew older,
and alarmingly unpredictable in her relations with other people:[54] Steffani
may simply have been a casualty of this. Alternatively, he may have
offended her, either in his letter of 7 December, which apart from the
paragraph on the duets is thoroughly unpleasant and partly sarcastic in
tone, or soon after, when he tried to arrange for the release from her
service of Attilio Ariosti.[55] Since she had been such a tower of strength in
the earlier stages of the revision project, it seems doubtful whether
Steffani would have continued with this work after their relations had
come, for whatever reason, to an end.

It also seems likely, in view of everything that has been said, that he
wrote out the two autograph volumes in late 1702 or before moving to
Düsseldorf in the spring of 1703. The volumes in the hand of scribe *A*,
however, could have been copied at a slightly later date. Steffani is said to
have been correcting his duets at Düsseldorf, with the aid of Joseph Paris
Feckler, in 1708–9,[56] and there are signs that scribe *A* was still active then.
His copy of *Amor vien dal destino* probably dates from this period, for on
the title-page he ascribes the work to Gregorio Piva and gives 1709 as the
year of its performance. If he was still active at this date, he could still have
been copying Steffani's duets, possibly after a break of several years
(1703–7), and it could have been his copies that Steffani is said to have
been correcting.

Further evidence that the autograph volumes and those copied by scribe
A may date from slightly different periods is provided by the bindings of
the manuscripts. For the autographs and the copies are not identically
bound. The covers of the autograph volumes are decorated in the centre
with an attractive, gold-stamped pinwheel design which also adorns the

autograph scores of three of Steffani's Hanover operas,[57] a collection of numbers from his *Rivali concordi*,[58] a copy of *Briseide* (*D-Mbs* 172) and a volume of chamber duets and trios by Handel (*Lbm* Royal 18.b.11). Since all of these manuscripts are decorated in the same distinctive manner, it seems clear that they were all bound by one and the same binder. The earliest work to bear the design, *Le rivali concordi*, was performed in 1692, but some of Handel's duets may date from his period as Kapellmeister at Hanover in 1710–11.[59] All of the manuscripts are connected with Hanover in one way or another, so it seems reasonable to suppose that they were bound there, apparently by Rosenhagen,[60] between 1692 and, at the earliest, 1710. The volumes of duets copied by scribe *A*, on the other hand, lack the pinwheel design, and the tooling round the edges of the covers also differs from that on the autograph volumes. It would appear, therefore, that the volumes copied by scribe *A* were bound at a different time from the autograph volumes, probably by a different binder and possibly in a different place.

It is not certain how the collection came to be in this condition, but one possible account of its genesis might run as follows. Steffani may have copied the autograph volumes at Hanover in 1702–3, shortly after revising the duets that they contain; he may also have copied some of the volumes now missing from the set, though it seems unlikely that he did much copying after moving to Düsseldorf in the spring of 1703. The volumes in his hand would then have been bound at Hanover and stamped with the elaborate pinwheel design in use there at around that date. Some time after he had stopped work, scribe *A* would have copied out all the duets that Steffani had rounded up and of which he had not made a fresh copy; at least one of these (*Torna a dar vita*) was a revised version, but the majority appear to have been unrevised, and the order in which scribe *A* copied them may reflect the order in which they appeared in the earlier collection that Steffani attempted to reassemble in the course of his revision project. When scribe *A* had finished his work, the volumes in his hand would have been given to a different binder, who was asked to emulate the binding of the two autograph volumes as closely as he could. He found a matching leather and imitated the earlier bindings using his own border and central device. It must also have been this binder, or possibly a later one still, who stamped the Roman numerals on the covers of all the volumes. There seems little reason why the autographs should have been numbered II and X, and this suggests that the numeration was added at a time when Steffani could have had little to do with the manuscripts.

Although the collection appears to have been begun by the composer, it seems to have been destined at a fairly early stage to become part of the electoral music library at Hanover. Hawkins, if he is referring to this set of manuscripts, says in the first edition of his *History* that it was made for 'the late Queen Caroline, while she was at Hanover':[61]

> The most complete collection of Steffani's duets now extant is one in nine or ten small volumes, in oblong quarto, made for the late Queen Caroline, while she was at Hanover, containing near a hundred duets; it was afterwards in the possession of Frederick Prince of Wales, and is now in that of his present majesty.

On the surface, this seems a sensible suggestion. After the death of her mother in 1696, Caroline was brought up in Berlin by Sophie Charlotte, who presumably introduced her to Steffani's duets. But even so, the manuscripts cannot have been originally intended for her 'while she was at Hanover', for she did not move there until her marriage to Georg August in 1705. Moreover, if the manuscripts had been completed specially for her, one would have expected them to appear in the inventory of her library that was drawn up in 1743.[62] She could, admittedly, have given the manuscripts to Frederick, her son, at almost any time before her death in 1737, or they could conceivably have been removed from her library between then and 1743; all the same, the fact that they do not appear in the inventory suggests that they may never have belonged to her at all.

The origin of the manuscripts is described rather differently in the 1853 edition of Hawkins' *History*, which includes his posthumous notes:[63]

> Frederick Prince of Wales had a collection of Steffani's duets in ten or twelve volumes in small oblong quarto, finely written, and the initial letters ornamented. It was probably made for the princess Sophia or the elector her son (George I) and contained about one hundred duets. This collection, excepting two volumes that were left behind by accident, the Prince gave to the lady of Signor Capello, ambassador from the Republic of Venice about the year 1744.

The suggestion that the manuscripts were made for the dowager Electress Sophie or for her son, the Elector Georg Ludwig, may be nearer the mark.

After the death of Elector Ernst August in 1698, Georg Ludwig, presumably encouraged by his mother, took steps to ensure the preservation of music that had been composed or performed at Hanover during his father's reign. He immediately ordered a list to be compiled of all the operas that had been produced there up to that time, and commissioned new copies of scores then in the electoral library. These copies are now in the Royal Music Library. They are in the hand of a single professional copyist (scribe *B*), who appears to have been called in specially for the purpose, and most of them (those marked with an asterisk) are uniformly bound in heavy leather bindings that were clearly meant to last:[64]

*Royal 23.k.23	*Paride in Ida*
*Royal 23.h.11	*Henrico Leone*
*Royal 23.h.15	*La lotta d'Hercole con Acheloo*
*Royal 23.h.13	*La superbia d'Alessandro*
Royal 23.i.11	*Orlando generoso*
*Royal 23.i.17	*Le rivali concordi*
*Royal 23.h.16	*La libertà contenta*
Royal 23.h.17	*La libertà contenta*
*Royal 23.f.16	*Baccanali*
*Royal 23.i.1	*I trionfi del fato*
*Royal 23.g.21	*Briseide*
*Royal 23.h.1	*La costanza nelle selve*

Four of these operas also survive in copies made by scribe *A*. There would appear to have been little point in his making copies of these works if this uniform set had already existed, so it seems likely that scribe *A*'s manuscripts are slightly earlier in date and that these and Steffani's autographs served as models for scribe *B*.

Despite this, there are signs that scribe *A* was also involved in the same undertaking as scribe *B*. Six of scribe *A*'s manuscripts—those marked with an asterisk in the list on page 174 and *Lbm* Royal 23.g.23 (arias from *Briseide* and *La costanza nelle selve*)—have bindings which are virtually identical to those of the new opera copies. One of these six manuscripts (*Lbm* Royal 23.h.2) contains the only 'Hanover' opera of the period not copied by scribe *B* (*Amor vien dal destino*), while the other five are collections of operatic arias and duets. Thus, whereas scribe *B* made complete copies of the opera scores, scribe *A* compiled collections of numbers from them. The work of the two scribes does not exactly overlap, and this suggests that they may both have been engaged in the same project.

The manuscripts *Lbm* Royal 23.k.13–20 also fit into this scheme. The set is mainly in the hand of scribe *A*, and there are no surviving copies of the duets in that of scribe *B*. Steffani may have had his own reasons for starting the collection in 1702, but its completion would appear to have been a result of the desire of Georg Ludwig and/or his mother to preserve the music of Hanover's recent past and to augment the holdings of the electoral library. Scribe *A* seems to have been one of the copyists involved in this work, and in this way he helped to lay the foundations of the Royal Music Library as it is known today.

He may also have been active in Hanover some 20 years later. On 1 June 1727 Steffani was elected President of the Academy of Vocal Music in London, the institution later and better known as the Academy of Ancient Music:[65]

> This Day it was agree'd Nemine Contradicente, that D. Agostino Steffani, Bishop of Spiga (commonly known by the name of Abbot Steffani) be President of the Academy of Vocal Musick establish'd in London; N:B His Compositions att present goe under the Name of Gregorio Piva.

The Academy already possessed copies of some of his works, and they soon acquired more: by 16 September one of its members was able to tell him that they had the Italian and German versions of his treatise, a substantial number of his chamber duets, two madrigals and 12 motets.[66] The motets had been published under the title *Sacer Ianus quadrifons* at Munich in 1685, but it is almost certain that what the Academy possessed is a manuscript copy now in the Royal College of Music (*GB-Lcm* 1023).

It would appear that Steffani later sent the Academy a further copy of six motets, for on 26 May 1731 it was moved 'That D[r] Pepusch be desired to demand of D[r] Green the Six Mottetts y[e] Bishop of Spiga sent the Academy'.[67] Although much of the music that belonged to the Academy cannot now be traced, these six motets appear to survive in the form of Gresham College music manuscript 418. A direct link between the composer and the manuscript is provided by the familiar hand of scribe *A*, who copied the entire volume. Since this manuscript does not seem to be included in the list given above, it probably arrived after 16 September 1727; and since it was apparently sent by Steffani himself, it was presumably dispatched before he died on 12 February 1728: if it had been sent afterwards by somebody acting on his behalf, the news of his death would not have taken over a year to reach the Academy.[68]

It is not certain, however, when the manuscript was actually copied. Scribe *A* attributes its contents to Gregorio Piva, so it was presumably copied after about 1707; but why Piva's name should have been used in connection with sacred music that had already been published as the work of Steffani is a question that calls for some kind of answer. It may be, of course, that after about 1707 scribe *A* invariably attached Piva's name to his copies of Steffani's music, irrespective of the nature or date of the composition(s) concerned—though this could not be said of every Steffani copyist[69] and if it were true of scribe *A* then the Gresham College manuscript would seem to be the only volume in his hand to survive from this period.

All the same, it is clear from the minute of 1 June 1727 that was cited above, that the members of the Academy to whom this manuscript appears to have been sent were fully aware of Steffani's pseudonym, and it is tempting to view this rather puzzling ascription as an acknowledgement of this fact—as a compliment to the Academy, or even as a kind of secret code or in-joke. If this interpretation is correct, in whole or in part, the manuscript could well have been copied specially for the Academy in 1727-8; and if this were the case, this might explain why the spaces left for decorated initial letters at the beginning of each motet are still vacant: Steffani may have been prompted by the decline in his health to dispatch the volume before it was completely ready.

The Identity of Scribe *A*

By looking in some detail at the manuscripts that scribe *A* copied, we have established that he worked at Hanover possibly from about 1698 and probably from around 1702-3; that he was almost certainly still active in 1708-9, possibly at Düsseldorf; and that he may also have been at Hanover as late as 1727-8.

Given this rather slender information, it seems impossible to ascertain the identity of scribe *A*. A number of names must, however, be considered. Feckler, although he apparently helped Steffani correct his duets, was clearly not the copyist in question. He seems to have been in Italy from 1690 to 1707 and then to have become court chaplain and Director of Chamber Music to the Elector Johann Wilhelm at Düsseldorf.[70] His hand does not appear to resemble that of scribe *A*,[71] and there is no evidence that he ever worked at Hanover.

One person who is reported to have been employed there as a copyist at around this period is a Frenchman by the name of Valoix: in a chapter entitled 'Theater in Hannover 1680' by the rather unreliable 19th-century historian, Carl Ernst von Malortie, Valoix is described as a violinist and orchestral copyist.[72] This statement is not supported by the results of more recent research: Valoix seems to have been appointed as a court musician in 1688, though he may have been one of a number of unnamed French musicians recorded at Hanover in 1681[73]—this possibility would appear to be strengthened by the fact that he composed the music for two ballets performed there in 1685.[74] It is not known what type of instrument he played, and there seems to be no evidence that he was ever appointed as a copyist.[75] Furthermore, there is no sign of any copyist among the staff of Elector Ernst August in 1696, a list of whom was published elsewhere by Malortie himself,[76] and Valoix's name disappears from the records at Hanover in 1698.[77] Thus, even if he were a copyist, he could hardly be associated with the work of scribe *A*.

A third possibility is Philippe La Vigne, Kapellmeister at the neighbouring court of Celle from 1666 until the dissolution of the musical establishment in 1705.[78] According to Heinrich Sievers, it appears from the Hanover treasury accounts (*Kammerrechnungen*) that in 1705 La Vigne received a sum of 40 Thalers for 'Copien musicalischer Sachen', but of these copies only a few insignificant pieces are said by Sievers to survive in Hanover today.[79] My attempts to find an example of La Vigne's hand in the Niedersächsisches Hauptstaatsarchiv, or in the Landesbibliothek, have so far proved unsuccessful. It is conceivable that he was scribe *A*, but rather unlikely. In order to have become Kapellmeister at Celle in 1666, he must have been born by about 1650 at the latest. This means that he would have been nearly 80 in 1727-8, when the Gresham manuscript may have been copied. The handwriting in this volume is virtually indistinguishable from that in the other manuscripts copied by scribe *A*; it does not look like the work of an octogenarian, and this may mean that La Vigne was not the copyist in question.

The *Kammerrechnungen* also record payments to other individuals for the copying of music, but they provide few clues as to the identity of scribe *A*. In 1697-8, for example, 'Maillard' was paid 30 Thalers 'for paper and completed copying work', and in 1699-1700 'Luca Totti' was granted 16 Thalers for a copy of an opera.[80] 'Maillart' was one of several French instrumentalists at Hanover in 1698, just after the accession of Elector Georg Ludwig, but he does not appear to have been in the orchestra when Handel was there in 1710-11.[81] I have not encountered 'Totti' in any other context, but among Maillard's colleagues in 1698 was a Friedrich or Federico Lotti[82] and from 1686 to 1702 Francesco Lotti was employed as a musician at Lucca.[83] Whatever the identity of these men, however, the sums they were given would not have paid for more than a fraction of the copying done by scribe *A*, and no similar payments to either of them are listed in the *Kammerrechnungen* for 1698-1714. Indeed, there seems to be no mention of any payment for music copying that would have been large enough to account for the number of manuscripts that scribe *A* produced. Thus if he was active in Hanover at around this time, as he appears to have been, he was presumably paid out of a different fund;[84] and if he was still there in 1727-8, he may well have been Steffani's personal secretary, for the level of musical activity at Hanover was somewhat reduced after the succession to the throne of England in 1714 and there would appear to have been little need to employ a full-time music copyist.

Apart from this, what can be said by way of conclusion is that scribe *A* seems to have been by far the most important copyist of Steffani's music; that he—and Steffani's music—played a prominent part in the expansion of the electoral library in the reign of Georg Ludwig; and that, whoever this principal copyist was, he was not Gregorio Piva.

NOTES TO CHAPTER 6

1.   D. J. Grout: *A Short History of Opera* (New York, 2/1965), 105.

2.   M. Bukofzer: *Music in the Baroque Era* (New York, 1947), 306. The standard works on Steffani's operas are H. Riemann: 'Agostino Steffani als Opernkomponist', DTB, xii/2 (Leipzig, 1912), VII-XXIII and G. Croll: *Agostino Steffani (1654-1728): Studien zur Biographie: Bibliographie der Opern und Turnierspiele* (diss., U. of Münster, 1960).

3.   'Besagter Steffani hat sich in dieser Gattung vor allen andern, die ich kenne, unvergleichlich hervorgetan, und verdienet bis diese Stunde ein Muster zu seyn. Denn solche Sachen veralten nicht leicht', J. Mattheson: *Der vollkommene Capellmeister* (Hamburg, 1739/R1954), 215. The only extended published survey of Steffani's duets is in F. Chrysander: *G. F. Händel* (Leipzig, 1858-67), i, 326-37; but see also C. R. Timms: *The Chamber Duets of Agostino Steffani (1654-1728), with Transcriptions and Catalogue* (diss., U. of London, 1976), from which most of the material for this essay is extracted.

4.   C. R. Timms: 'Handel and Steffani: a New Handel Signature', *MT*, cxiv (1973), 376f.

5.   Chrysander (1858-67), i, 312.

6.   R. Brockpähler: *Handbuch zur Geschichte der Barockoper in Deutschland* (Emsdetten, 1964), 214.

7.   L. Bittner and L. Gross: *Repertorium der diplomatischen Vertreter aller Länder seit dem Westfälischen Frieden, 1648*, i (Oldenburg and Berlin, 1936), 66.

8.   For an account of this war and its implications for some musicians, see U. Kirkendale: 'The War of the Spanish Succession reflected in the Works of Antonio Caldara', *AcM*, xxxvi (1964), 221-33.

9.   C. R. Timms: 'Revisions in Steffani's Chamber Duets', *PRMA*, xcvi (1969-70), 120. In addition to the works referred to there, see also F. W. Woker: *Aus den Papieren des kurpfälzischen Ministers Agostino Steffani . . . 1703-1709*, Erste Vereinsschrift der Görresgesellschaft (Cologne, 1885), 2.

10.   A. Einstein: 'Agostino Steffani', *Kirchenmusikalisches Jahrbuch*, xxiii (1910), 26.

11.   Woker (1885), 3-7.

12.   Woker (1885), 15. Steffani was actually nominated as Bishop of Spiga in Sept 1706 (G. Riccati: 'Notizie di Monsig. Agostino Steffani', *Nuova raccolta d'opuscoli scientifici e filologici*, xxxiii (Venice, 1779), 11-14).

13. F. W. Woker: *Agostino Steffani, Bischof von Spiga i.p.i., apostolischer Vikar von Norddeutschland 1709–1728*, Dritte Vereinsschrift der Görresgesellschaft (Cologne, 1886), 5.

14. J. Hawkins: *Memoirs of the Life of Agostino Steffani* [London, 1749–52], p.v. The reasons for the suggested date of publication are as follows. Hawkins submitted a manuscript of the *Memoirs* to Dr Johnson for his perusal, and he became associated with the Johnson circle in 1749 (P. A. Scholes: *The Life and Activities of Sir John Hawkins* (London, 1953), 27ff and 34f). In the course of the *Memoirs* Hawkins said that he was indebted for some of his information to 'the truly learned Dr Pepusch': if the work had been printed after the death of Pepusch in 1752, Hawkins would probably have made some reference to this event. The *Memoirs* were later published in *The Gentleman's Magazine*, xxxi (1761), 489–92.

15. '. . . habbiamo Opere d'Hannover, come tutte le di Lei composti [sic] in Düsseldorff, ancor li pregiati Duetti . . .', J. Loschelder: 'Aus Düsseldorfs italienischer Zeit: Römische Quellen zu Agostino Steffanis Leben', *Beiträge zur rheinischen Musikgeschichte*, i (Cologne and Krefeld, 1952), 49.

16. 'Veniamo alla Musica. Sono delicta Juventutis. Io le confesso che l'amo ancora più che mai. Ma con verità posso dire che alcune volte stò molti anni senza veder un cembalo. Lei mi parla di Opere di Düsseldorff; Io non so haverne fatte; ma sono Opere del Sig.r Gregorio Piva. Comunque siasi, Io hò Inteso con grand:mo compiacimento che quelle bagatelle divertiscano il Ser:mo Sig:r Landgravio . . .', Loschelder (1952), 52.

17. The information given about them, unless separately footnoted, comes from G. Croll: 'Zur Chronologie der "Düsseldorfer" Opern Agostino Steffanis', *Festschrift Karl Gustav Fellerer zum sechzigsten Geburtstag* (Regensburg, 1962), 82–7.

18. P. Keppler: 'Agostino Steffani's Hannover Operas and a rediscovered Catalogue', in *Studies in Music History: Essays for Oliver Strunk*, ed. H. S. Powers (Princeton, 1968), 351.

19. P. H. Lang: review of G. Croll, ed.: *Tassilone*, Denkmäler rheinischer Musik, viii (Düsseldorf, 1958) in *MQ*, xlv (1959), 412–17.

20. For a survey of opera at Hanover during this period, cf. Brockpähler (1964), 212–23.

21. M. Fürstenau: *Zur Geschichte der Musik und des Theaters am Hofe zu Dresden* (Dresden, 1861–2), i, 310; ii, 8.

22. Brockpähler (1964), 142.

23. D-DÜha Kurköln II, 468. The date 1719 given in Brockpähler (1964), 77, fn. 20 is evidently incorrect.

24. R. Eitner: *Biographisch-bibliographisches Quellen-Lexikon der Musiker und Musikgelehrten* (Leipzig, 1898–1904), vii, 465.

25. DTB, vi/2 (Leipzig, 1905), XII, fn. 2.

26. A. Einstein: 'Italienische Musiker am Hof der Neuburger Wittelsbacher 1614–1716', *Sammelbände der Internationalen Musikgesellschaft*, ix (1907–8), 409.

27. F. Lau: 'Die Regierungskollegien zu Düsseldorf und der Hofstaat zur Zeit Johann Wilhelms (1679–1716)', *Düsseldorfer Jahrbuch: Beiträge zur Geschichte des Niederrheins*, xl (1938), 271.

28. Keppler (1968), 342f.

29. For this information I am indebted to Dr Gieschen of the Niedersächsisches Hauptstaatsarchiv, Hanover.

30. Ed. Croll, 254.

31. *D-DÜha* Kurköln II, 475.

32. Cf. Brockpähler (1964), 145f, 228f, 262f; and F. Walter: *Geschichte des Theaters und der Musik am kurpfälzischen Hofe* (Leipzig, 1898), 362–8.

33. Ed. Croll, 254 and in *MGG*, xii (1965), col. 1211.

34. Keppler (1968), 348ff, 352.

35. R. L. Arkell: *Caroline of Ansbach, George the Second's Queen* (Oxford, 1939), 8.

36. J. Mainwaring: *Memoirs of the Life of the late George Frederic Handel* (London, 1760), 85.

37. Cf. R. Doebner, ed.: *Briefe der Königin Sophie Charlotte von Preussen und der Kurfürstin Sophie von Hannover an hannoversche Diplomaten*, Publicationen aus den Königlichen Preussischen Staatsarchiven, lxxix (Leipzig, 1905), 78ff; A. Ebert: 'Briefe Agostino Steffanis an die Königin Sophie Charlotte von Preussen', *Die Musik*, vi (1906–7), 158–71; A. Einstein: 'Die Briefe der Königin Sophie Charlotte und der Kurfürstin Sophie an Agostino Steffani', *Zeitschrift der Internationalen Musikgesellschaft*, viii (1906–7), 85–90.

38. A. Ebert (1906–7), 166. 'M^c de Kielmanseck' was presumably the wife of the Baron Kielmansegg familiar to students of Handel. The duets that Steffani sent Sophie Charlotte from Brussels appear to have been *Che volete, o crude pene*, *Inquieto mio cor* and *Placidissime catene* (A. Einstein (1906–7), 86).

39. DTB, vi/2, XIIf, XX-XXV.

40. W. B. Squire and H. Andrews: *Catalogue of the King's Music Library* (London, 1927–9), ii, 196f.

41. The date of *Lbm* Royal 23.k.7 will be discussed below. The title-pages of *I-Fc* D.331–2 bear the inscription 'DVETTI / Di M^gnor S^Tefani / Copiati in Dusseldorft l'anno / 1718'.

42. Five duets appear to have been composed specially for Sophie Charlotte—those listed in note 38 above, plus *Crudo Amor, morir mi sento* and *Io mi parto* (A. Einstein (1906–7), 86f). The aria 'Crede ogn'un che sia pazzia' mentioned in Violanta Beatrice's letter of 25 August 1693 (cf. Loschelder (1952), 38) is not a lost chamber duet, as listed in *MGG*, but the second stanza of the soprano solo in the extant duet *Oh! che voi direste bene*.

43. Though pp. 81–98 of *Lbm* Royal 23.k.18 were copied by a second, unidentified, scribe. For facs. of Steffani's hand, see *MGG*.

44. (1969–70), 121, fn. 12.

45. *Non voglio, non voglio, no, no*—no.48 in Einstein's index. The reasons for doubting its authenticity are discussed in Timms (1976), i, 339ff.

46. *Dolce labbro, amabil bocca* and *Quando ti stringo*. Cf. Timms (1976), i, 90ff.

47. *Dolce è per voi soffrire*. Cf. Timms (1976), i, 91 (and 81–4).

48. The earlier versions of *Lungi dal idol mio* and *M'hai da piangere* must, however, be considered as unreliable attributions: Timms (1976), i, 324–31.

49. *Ah! che l'hō sempre detto:* F-Pn Vm⁷ 54; *Ribellatevi, o pensieri:* I-Vnm Cod.It.IV. 952; *Saldi marmi,* the earlier version of which is entitled *Fredde ceneri* (the first stanza was discarded in revision): D-MÜs Santini 4074.

50. Not four, as stated in my (1969–70), 120, fn. 9. The first 96 pages are missing from one of these Munich volumes, but what remains of the manuscript indicates that it probably duplicated the contents of *Lbm* Royal 23.k.19.

51. Ebert (1906–7), 171.

52. Timms (1969–70), 121; and DTB, vi/2, XIII.

53. A twenty-seventh, *Quando un eroe,* is a later addition which cannot reliably be attributed to Steffani (DTB, vi/2, XIII).

54. A. Yorke-Long: *Music at Court: Four Eighteenth-Century Studies* (London, 1954), 98.

55. A. Ebert: *Attilio Ariosti in Berlin (1697–1703)* (Leipzig, 1905), 88–93.

56. A. Gottron: 'Joseph Paris Feckler, Kurmainzer Hofkapellmeister 1728–1735', *AMw,* xix–xx (1962–3), 189f.

57. Those listed in Keppler (1968), 342, except *Henrico Leone, La superbia d'Alessandro* and *Orlando generoso.*

58. I-MOe Mus.G.282, which includes a dedication in the composer's hand to the Duke of Modena.

59. Timms (1973), 376.

60. According to Keppler (1968), 349, Rosenhagen was the Hanover bookbinder and he bound this copy of *Briseide.*

61. J. Hawkins: *A General History of the Science and Practice of Music* (London, 1776), iv, 290, fn.

62. *A Catalogue of the Royal Library of her late Majesty Queen Caroline: Distributed into Faculties: 1743,* manuscript in the Royal Library at Windsor Castle.

63. Hawkins: *A General History* (London, 2/1853), ii, 666, fn. Pietro Andrea Capello presented his credentials on 31 March 1744 and took his leave in Aug 1748 (F. Hausmann: *Repertorium der diplomatischen Vertreter aller Länder seit dem Westfälischen Frieden, 1648,* ii (Zurich, 1950), 414). The manuscripts were presumably given to his wife as a token of goodwill and returned to Frederick before her departure. Frederick died in 1751, and the manuscripts were in the possession of 'his present majesty' (George III) by the time Hawkins published the first edition of his *History* in 1776.

64. Keppler (1968), 344ff, 353f. It is not known why scribe B made two copies of *La libertà contenta,* the second of which does not appear in Keppler's list. *Lbm* Royal 23.i.11 is surely the copy of *Orlando generoso* which Keppler thought was lost. Scribe B also copied *Lbm* Royal 18.b.11, the volume of chamber duets and trios by Handel, and added *Quando un eroe* to *Lbm* Royal 23.k.7 (cf. note 53).

65. Cited from the original minute-book, *Lbm* Add.11732, f.4. The name of the Academy was changed on 26 May 1731 (*Lbm* Add.11732, f.16); cf. C. R. Timms: 'Steffani and the Academy of Ancient Music', *MT,* cxix (1978), 127ff.

66. J. Loschelder (1952), 46ff. Steffani's *Quanta certezza* was translated by A. Werck-meister as *Sendschreiben, darinnen enthalten, wie grosse Gewissheit die Musik, aus ihren*

Principiis und Grundsätzen habe (Quedlinburg and Aschersleben, 1699). The two madrigals were *Gettano i rè dal soglio*, a copy of which in *GB-DRc* Mus.E.15 is headed 'Abbas Stephano—5 Voc: Sent to our Academy at yᶜ Crown Tavern 1726', and the three-part *Al rigor d'un bel semiante*.

67.   *Lbm* Add. 11732, f.16, paragraph 9. I am grateful to Dr H. Diack Johnstone for help in establishing that the manuscript about to be discussed, and that in the Royal College of Music, once belonged to the Academy.

68.   Steffani's name is entered as President for the Seventh Subscription, which began on 8 May 1729 (*Lbm* Add.11732, f.9).

69.   Cf. note 41.

70.   Gottron (1962–3), 187.

71.   The inscription in *A-Wn* 17641, mentioned by Gottron (1962–3), 191, is clearly not in the hand of scribe *A*.

72.   C. E. von Malortie: *Beiträge zur Geschichte des Braunschweig-Lüneburgischen Hauses und Hofes* (Hanover, 1860–72), iv, 128.

73.   H. Sievers: *Die Musik in Hannover* (Hanover, 1961), 162.

74.   F. Berend: *Nikolaus Adam Strungk (1640–1700)* (Hanover, 1915), 68.

75.   Sievers (1961), 162.

76.   *Der hannoversche Hof unter dem Kurfürsten Ernst August und der Kurfürstin Sophie* (Hanover, 1847), 37–41.

77.   Sievers (1961), 162. This 'Valoix' is presumably not to be confused with the 'Valoix' who, according to R. E. Wallbrecht: *Das Theater des Barockzeitalters an den welfischen Höfen Hannover und Celle*, Quellen und Darstellungen zur Geschichte Niedersachsens, lxxxiii (Hildesheim, 1974), 137ff, was employed at Hanover as an actor from March 1702 to Feb 1712.

78.   Brockpähler (1964), 108.

79.   Sievers (1961), 57f.

80.   'Dem Musicant Maillard vor Papier und verrichteter Copysten Arbeit uf befehl 30 rtlr.' (Hanover, Niedersächsisches Hauptstaatsarchiv: Hann. 76c A Nr. 117, p.405); 'Luca Totti einem Italiäner vor eine opera abzuschreiben 16 rtlr.' (Hann. 76c A Nr.119, p.405). For this and other information from the *Kammerrechnungen* I am again indebted to Dr Gieschen.

81.   G. Fischer: *Musik in Hannover* (Hanover, 1903), 27, 30.

82.   Ibid, 27 and Sievers (1961), 58.

83.   Eitner (1898–1904), vi, 228.

84.   Steffani's salary as Kapellmeister to Ernst August had been paid out of the so-called 'Osnabrückschen Geldern'—funds which the duke, as titular Bishop of Osnabrück, had at his personal disposal; cf. Keppler (1968), 342f and Fischer (1903), 13.

7

'Tang Music' and its Fate in Japan

Laurence Picken

The term 'Tang music' (Tôgaku) refers to that portion of the Court music repertory of Japan (Gagaku) which tradition asserts, and documentation confirms, was taken over by the Japanese (during the 8th and early 9th centuries) from the repertory of entertainment-music performed at the Chinese court during the Tang Dynasty. According to the most extensive Japanese lists of titles of Tang music, a total of about 140 items was borrowed. Of those items still available in score, eight are suites of up to six movements, several are items of two or three movements, and the rest are single movements—in all about 130 items of which between 55 and 65 are still at least occasionally performed. Many items were ballet scores, and some movements were songs. A number of items are still danced as part of the repertory of Bugaku ('dance music'); but though the texts of the songs survive in some instances, they are no longer sung. When performed as Bugaku (often in the open air) strings are omitted. In contrast, that portion of the repertory which is performed without dance is referred to as Kangen ('pipes and strings').

Twenty years ago, it became apparent to me that, in a manner analogous with the slowing of plainsong melodies and their use as a basis for composition with the addition of new, decorative melodic lines, the original melodies from the Tang repertory, in minimally decorated forms, have all undergone such an excessive retardation, that their original tempos of crotchet = 200 (let us say) have been reduced 16- to 32-fold, to crotchet = 12 and less. All items in the Tang music repertory are today played *accelerando*, the pace increasing from about crotchet = 7 to the higher speed of crotchet = 12 and faster. The crotchet value in these equations is that of the most frequent note duration in the original tune, as revealed in the mouth organ parts. In a recent study, Gamô[1] has assembled the results of precise measurements of change in tempo during the performance of 13 purely instrumental items and seven items with dance. Her crotchet values, however, are one quarter of the basic note value in the original tune. They correspond to metrical units equivalent to semiquavers in the decorative treatment of the original. Her initial speeds are therefore approximately four times faster than ours.

The precise measurement of the initial tempo is made difficult—if one attempts to measure the duration of individual beats—by the practice of lengthening the last beat in each measure. A precise measurement can be obtained, however, by measuring the time-interval between bass drum (*taiko*) beats and dividing by the number of beats intervening.

As a result of the massive retardation described above, the original melody cannot be grasped as such in modern performance, and Japanese musicians and musicologists (as well as foreign such) tend to view the complex texture of Tang music pieces as florid melody (from transverse flute and cylindrical double-reed pipe) accompanied by lute and zither (playing evanescent broken chords) and free-reed mouth organ (playing sustained, five- or six-note cluster-chords in high tessitura).

The crucial observation, made in 1953, was: that tablatures for mouth organ, lute, and zither present the same melody in versions appropriate to the mechanics of each instrument, while tablatures for flute and pipe present more conspicuously embellished versions of this same melody. At that time, a photograph of a single tune, in both mouth organ tablature and lute tablature, was the only source I had seen in quasi-facsimile. The only complete set of parts available were those of a single movement, the 'Quick' (*Kyû/Ji*), from a three-movement suite: 'Music of the Five [Confucian] Virtues' (*Goshôraku/Wuchangyue*) published in engraved facsimile by Dr Leopold Mueller,[2] who was Physician to the Emperor of Japan in the latter half of the 19th century, and the first European to give a fairly detailed account of the Court Music, its notations, its repertory, and its instrumentarium.

Thurston Dart's interest in my transcriptions from Chinese and Sino-Japanese notations doubtless owed something to propinquity—to our living in the same College; but the keenness of that interest sprang from a quite unusual width of musical vision. One aspect of the transformation of the Tang music repertory which we discussed was the Japanese practice of placing a cluster-chord, at times including semitones (and painfully dissonant by Chinese standards), on each note of the mouth organ tunes. In the Chinese tradition, the mouth organ tends to be played in parallels—5ths above or 4ths below the melody note, with occasional octaves to the melody note where the range of the instrument permits. It was, I suggested to him, as if the Japanese, having forgotten how to perform this Chinese diaphony, remembered only that another note (or notes) was added to the tune, and put their fingers over sizeable handfuls for good measure.

Somewhat to my surprise, Dart replied that such a change in the interpretation of a notation, and in the handling of an instrument, could occur quite quickly, if pupil were separated from teacher at an early stage in their association. I had myself envisaged a relatively slow pace of modification, consequent upon the decision of the Japanese to send no further mission to China for three centuries after the return of the mission of 834 in 841. By the 12th century, when contact was resumed, the Song Dynasty had replaced the Tang, and a nationalistic and strongly Confucian China, weakened by foreign aggression, had swept away the scandalous court musics and dances of the previous dynasty, in part musics of tributary nations.

In 1972, I was able to spend three months working in Japanese libraries, with the aim of assembling a series of microfilms and photocopies of dated manuscripts of Tang music, for all five melodic instruments, back to the earliest surviving sources. Since returning to Cambridge in September, 1972, a group[3] of young colleagues and I have explored the manuscript treasures accruing from that expedition.

This chapter offers a brief account of the documentary basis of the Tang music tradition, and of the metamorphosis of this tradition in Japan, in the light not of the performing tradition merely, but also of documentary sources and, in particular, of the notations themselves, from the early 9th century onwards.

Some of the titles of the Tang music repertory are those of items known to have been performed at the Chinese court, not merely in the Tang period, but also in the previous dynasty of the Sui (late 6th and early 7th centuries); and Chinese tradition, enshrined in texts not later than the 9th century, ascribes some of these items to yet earlier times. A majority of the basic tunes do not display the characteristics of Japanese melody, and some are clearly 'foreign' even by Chinese standards. A proportion are, for both Western and Eastern ears, distinctly 'Western' in character. On purely musical grounds, therefore, there is reason to accept that at least a proportion of these tunes are tunes from Tang China. A detailed analysis of the various musical languages of pieces in the repertory has yet to be made.

From the manner in which Japanese chronicles refer to items from the Chinese court repertory, it seems likely that the adoption of items by the Japanese began piecemeal. Japanese interest in Chinese court music is first implied by an edict of 701, in which year an Imperial Music Bureau was established by Emperor Mombu (reigned 683–707) in imitation of Tang precedent.[4] (The introduction of Korean music, on the other hand, occurred considerably earlier, in the latter half of the 5th century.) In this earliest period, performers were either Koreans or Chinese, not Japanese. Among the earliest traditions of importation or performance of Chinese items are: the importation of the piece, 'Liquid-Amber Incense' (*Sogôkô/Suhexiang*) by Wanibe no Shimatsugu in the time of Emperor Kwammu, who reigned from 736 to 805; the performance of 'The King of Luoling' (*Ryô-ô/Luoling Wang*) at least since the middle of the 8th century; and a performance of 'The Music of Peace' (*Taiheiraku/Taipingyue*) in 702[5] (second year of Taihô). Of this earliest period of importation, the only surviving notation (see later, however, pp.203–4) is a fragment of a modal prelude for lute,[6] written on the back of a receipt, dated 747/8.

In the light of our examination of the earliest surviving scores, there is now good reason to believe that the profusion of existing manuscripts of the Tang music tradition (documents of all periods, up to the 19th century, in five different tablatures for five different melodic instruments— three woodwinds, two strings) derives from a very small number of sources, perhaps no more than one per instrument. Examination of a series of dated manuscript scores in tablature, for each instrument, reveals that the musical identity of any one piece is essentially unchanged throughout the centuries. Descent from a single source is therefore highly probable. Already in the compendious 12th-century scores for lute and zither, for example, such variants as existed were set out in sequence (as 'like pieces'—*dô kyoku*), following a received, primary version. Such variants are usually more decorated in style than the primary version and, in the string parts, frequently employ a style of mensural notation characteristic of post-10th-century documents, suggesting that they are derivatives of, and indeed descendants from, the primary versions (observations by Wolpert and Picken).

A precisely determined moment in time at which the entire tradition might have been transmitted to Japan as a single manuscript was that when Fujiwara no Sadatoshi[7] returned to Japan in 841. In Yangchow (Kiangsu Province, China), Sadatoshi had studied with an 80-year-old master, Lian Chengwu; and one item brought back by him was a lute tutor, written in Yangchow in 838. Parts of it survive in a single copy, the *Fushiminomiya-bon biwa-fu* (FBBF) dated 920/21, and preserved in the Library of the Imperial Household (Kunaichô Shoryôbu). In the biography of Sadatoshi in *Sandai-jitsuroku*, chap. 14, it is stated that a Chinese, Liu

Erlang, 'gave ten scrolls of tablature as a present'. Conceivably, these included Tang music; but if the gift comprised the entire repertory, ten scrolls could not have contained a complete set of scores for more than a single instrument. In the Palace lute manuscript, *Sango-yôroku* (*SGYR*— see later), Tang music alone occupies seven out of a total of 12 scrolls.

Since Sadatoshi studied the lute in China, the ten scrolls might well have included a complete lute version of the court repertory. There is no direct evidence for this, however. Though flute scores are mentioned by titles and/or authors in marginal notes in *SGYR* (as also in the zither manuscript, *Jinchi-yôroku* (*JCYR*); see later), no specific reference to a lute score associated with Sadatoshi occurs. References to lute sources are in the form: 'the old score [or scores, since the plural is not indicated] states'.[8] The absence of a specific reference might perhaps be taken to mean that only one lute score, known to all, was available; whereas the existence of several different flute sources made specification essential.

Marginalia in *SGYR* and *JCYR* make frequent mention of 'The score for transverse flute by Nangû' (*Nangû ôteki-fu*), compiled by a pupil of Sadatoshi, Prince Sadayasu, and 'The score for transverse flute by the Ministerial Chief Long-Autumn' (*Chôshû-kyô ôteki-fu*), compiled by Minamoto no Hiromasa (whose title was Chôshû-kyô; also known as Hakuga). This latter score was probably identical with the collection in part preserved to this day, commonly referred to as 'The flute scores of Hakuga' (*Hakuga no fue-fu*) (*HFF*), but correctly entitled 'Scores newly selected and edited' (*Shinsen gaku-fu*).[9] Of Hakuga's collection, a portion only survives, corresponding to the fourth and last scroll of the original score.

It is certain, therefore, that the editor of *SGYR* and *JCYR* consulted pre-existing scores, both for lute and flute, in the course of his editorial work. Of *SGYR* the Palace Library preserves a copy, largely written in 1328, and stated in colophons to be a copy of a copy made in 1208. If indeed Sadatoshi returned with ten scrolls that included a definitive set of lute scores of the Tang music, it may be assumed that *SGYR* preserves his legacy, albeit in modified form. The work was compiled and edited by the Prime Minister (Dajôdaijin), Fujiwara no Moronaga, between 1171 and his death in 1192. The difference in bulk (if the figure of ten scrolls is correct for the original) is due in part to the inclusion in the Palace copy of two other repertories from the court music, namely, those of Komagaku and Saibara.

Even though *SGYR* may ultimately derive in part from a manuscript brought to Japan by Sadatoshi, it is certain, however, that Moronaga's text reflects not Tang lute practice but Japanese practice after three centuries of isolation from contact with China.

By the date of completion of the 920/21 copy of *FBBF*, a distinction was being drawn between what a Tang score indicated, and what 'the Teacher' played. This 'teacher' was presumably Sadatoshi himself.[10] The modal preludes in the tutor are followed by a statement: 'Details for oral transmission only . . . Now it is my opinion that in all these scores you either pluck, pressing down at a single fret, as in Tang scores, or you pluck striking several strings, as in the teaching handed down by the Teacher' (*FBBF*, trans. Picken). A feature of the tutor-scroll is: that it contains no explicit reference to the use of a plectrum (*bachi*)—used today on all Japanese lutes. The scroll defines a system by which finger-plucking of the strings, by thumb, first, or second finger, can be notated. The system also provides for the notation of chords that can only be played with the fingers, since courses may be skipped. The notations of two preludes show throughout which finger plucks the string, for each note. In the latter half of the 8th century, it was indeed Chinese practice to use the fingers of the right hand, rather than a plectrum, to pluck the strings; at an earlier date the Chinese had used a large plectrum. The technique displayed in *FBBF* is therefore that which the date of the original manuscript (838) would lead one to expect in an account of Chinese lute technique at that time.

This finger-plucking technique was first introduced into China on the five-stringed lute (according to the *Wenxian tongkao*) and by a foreign musician, Pei Loer, between 627 and 650.[11] The use of plectrum by some, and fingers by other, Chinese lutenists in the latter half of the 8th century is attested,[12] and technical terms for the right-hand technique appear—in poems, for example—at the same time.[13] To strike 'striking several strings' describes what lute players do in the Court Orchestra of Japan at the present time, and striking is done with a very large plectrum. In modern practice, every crotchet note of the original Tang tune is sounded together with all the open strings lower in pitch than the string stopped by a finger of the left hand. Two observations are to be made about this practice: first, the use of the plectrum represents the early Tang (and indeed pre-Tang) usage, and there is no indication that the late Tang finger-plucking technique ever became current in Japan; secondly, the sounding of the lower, open strings is a means of augmenting sonority, of increasing loudness. This occurs not merely because by striking more than one string more energy is dissipated as sound, but also because the arc of swing of the plectrum, and hence its momentum, can be increased if the player need not concentrate attention on striking a single course. Furthermore, if the instrument is in tune, energy may be transferred from strings of lower pitch—with a longer reverberation time—to the highest string that carries the melody note, thus delaying sound-decay.

In playing a tune on a lute, it quickly becomes desirable to increase sonority, by one means or another, if the pace of the tune becomes so slow that the decay of the individual notes threatens to abolish continuity of sound from one excitation to the next. If, as the passage cited above in translation suggests, Sadatoshi struck several strings, it is possible that he was already playing pieces more slowly than his teacher had played them in Yangchow. Whether he used a plectrum does not emerge from the text.

A second, highly significant technical difference between Tang practice and that of 'the Teacher' is stated immediately following the statement made about 'adding many strings': 'Again, in Tang scores, there are few glossing notes; in the Teacher's teaching there are many glossing notes' (*FBBF*, trans. Picken). The text describes such ornamental additions as 'commentary notes' (literally), because they are written, in small tablature signs, to the right of the main column of tune notes, in the place where, in a literary text, a marginal comment might be placed—also in small characters. If Sadatoshi was adding musical glosses in the second half of the 9th century, this again suggests perhaps that his tempos were slower than those of Tang performance.

That this relative freedom of Tang scores from ornaments was not a peculiarity of *FBBF* is suggested by another manuscript, *Gogen kin-fu* (literally, 'The five-stringed zither-score'—*GKF*), for five-stringed lute, preserved in the Yômei-Bunko Library in Kyoto. The date at the end of this scroll is 842. It contains six modal preludes (not, however, identical with any of those in *FBBF*), and 22 Tang music pieces. Ornaments are rare in most pieces, but finger-plucking dots (perhaps indicating use of the thumb), and occasional chords that skip courses, suggest that the five-stringed lute also was finger-plucked at this date. This linear, largely monophonic, finger-plucked technique of four- and five-stringed lutes, revealed by *FBBF* and *GKF*,[14] implies a relatively rapid pace of performance, such that the musical line, largely consisting of individually plucked notes, coheres.

In contrast to the Tang music pieces in *GKF*, the Tang music in *SGYR* is conspicuously decorated and, as already mentioned, the sequences of primary version and 'like pieces' suggest that the degree of decoration increases in later versions.

So far, the case for believing that 'in Tang scores, there are few glossing notes', has rested on the statement in the lute tutor of 920/21, and on the evidence of the notations for five-stringed lute in the manuscript of 842. Further evidence of the truth of this contention comes from the earliest surviving flute manuscript, already mentioned (*HFF*), compiled in 966.[15] No early copy of this work is known. All recorded copies are ultimately copies of a lost copy dedicated in 1098; and the oldest dated copy at present known to us was written in 1732. The fact that the several mensural systems employed in this manuscript may have become unintelligible to Japanese musicians by Moronaga's time speaks volumes for the faithfulness of Japanese traditional scholarship in preserving, because of its great historical importance, a document that could no longer be read. The analytical studies of Marett have recently disclosed the principles on which the various mensural systems of the Hakuga manuscript operate, and the contents can now be transcribed with certainty.

The total of items in *HFF* as it survives amounts to about one third of the entire Tang music repertory of Hakuga's time. The colophon to this manuscript furnishes a valuable account of its compilation. In particular, it makes plain that *HFF* originally incorporated Prince Sadayasu's three flute-score scrolls and a scroll of modal preludes. The colophon places the first assembling of materials in the lifetime of the Prince (870–924) and in the Engi Period, between 901 and 923; but the list of flute teachers whose scores contributed to the Prince's compilation, carries the Tang flute tradition back into the 8th century.

Marett[16] has observed variation between different pieces in *HFF* in the method of mensural notation adopted, and in one instance this variation can be correlated with a particular named flute teacher whose dates are not known, but who was active between 820 and 835. Within the body of pieces preserved in the substantial fragment of *HFF* which survives, it is now plain that the pieces in the oldest mensural notation are also those with least notated ornamentation (in the form of quasi-mordents—*yu*). Again, the evidence suggests that the tunes were freer from ornamentation in Tang practice, and this was perhaps correlated with a faster pace in the earlier period.

It is always possible, of course, to argue that any notation is an imperfect reflection of performance, and that sparsity or absence of ornaments from a score does not imply that contemporary performance was equally austere. Nevertheless, until textual evidence for the view that the score does not mean what it says is produced, we have no choice but to accept it at face value; and we must not forget the inverse correlation that exists necessarily between the pace of a tune and practicable degrees of ornamentation.

From marginalia in *SGYR* and *JCYR*, it seems probable (as made clear by Marett) that, in the case of at least one piece, Moronaga no longer understood the mode of operation of the system of mensural notation; indeed, it now seems probable that even Hakuga himself did not fully understand the various older systems.

While manuscripts of late Tang date, or (like *HFF*) with explicit Tang connections, are available for lute and flute, no Heian score for the cylindrical double-reed pipe, hichiriki, is known; quotations in hichiriki tablature occur, however, in marginalia in *JCYR* (observations by Marett and Condit). A set of hichiriki notations for pieces in the Banshiki mode derive perhaps from an original of the 11th century,[17] and a manuscript of the 14th century has recently come to light in Japan (Marett, 1977).

Turning to the parts for 13-stringed zither (gaku-sô—a kind of koto), the oldest substantial manuscript is from the Heian Period (782–1184) about 1000. It contains pieces in the mode Hyôjô/Pingdiao, and is preserved in Tenri University Library. This is the 'Old zither score' (*Kosô-fu*) (*KSF*), recently published in facsimile.[18] In 1974 I drew attention to the musical importance of this manuscript, and Jonathan Condit transcribed versions of the piece *Etenraku/Yuedianyue* both from *KSF* and from *JCYR*.

From the notes on the tablature signs at the beginning of the latter manuscript, as well as from comments on zither-technique in Lady Murasaki Shikibu's 'Tale of Genji' (*Genji monogatari*), completed about 1000, it is known that the zither was then played using the left hand to sharpen notes, or to grace notes—by pressing on the strings beyond the bridge before plucking, releasing, and then re-applying pressure; or by pulling the string towards the bridge after plucking and then releasing. Unpublished observations by my colleague Dr Mitani Yôko and myself show that while some reduction in the use of signs relating to left-hand techniques (and to certain right-hand techniques) occurs in a series of five manuscripts of zither scores, with dates ranging from the 10th to the early 19th centuries, the left-hand signs do not disappear completely until the compilation of the standard Meiji scores (*Sentei-fu*—post-1867). At a certain stage (the precise date has not been determined) the tuning of the instrument in certain modes was changed, so that notes at one time obtained by raising the tension of the string by pressing could be obtained as open-string sounds.

Another feature of modern gaku-sô practice[19] is the elaboration of what were originally simultaneous or broken octaves into extended standard formulae, each of five plucking movements.

The cause of both these changes in technique, it may be assumed, was progressive retardation. At less than a certain pace, no trace of the notes of the melody as played in Tang and early Heian times would have persisted from one note to the next. Hence the compelling need for the development of the type of figuration that became standard, and which Garfias[20] accepts as Heian practice. The change to a technique in which all notes were open-string notes will have decreased the rate of decay of individual notes; but with increasing retardation the interpolation of standard figurations restored continuity of sound between the original notes of the melody while concealing that melody.

A further change to be observed in the notations of Tang music over the centuries is the progressive multiplication in the numbers and kinds of mensural signs. The five-stringed-lute score (*GKF*) exhibits no mensural sign other than a stop. *KSF* regulates the flow of the melodic line by duration signs and a stop. In *HFF*, *SGYR*, and *JCYR*, however, that beat in the measure on which the bass drum beat falls (the third in a measure of four, the fifth in a measure of six, the fifth in a measure of eight, etc) is marked (with rare exceptions) by a lexigraph (read as *hyaku*). The measure is subdivided into binary segments either by the Sino-Japanese lexigraph for 'one', placed to the right of, and below, the tablature signs (as in *HFF*), or by dots within the column of tablature signs (as in *SGYR* and *JCYR*). In the late Heian and Kamakura Periods (1185–1331), a more explicit system of mensural notation appears. Each beat is marked by a small dot placed to the right of the tablature sign, save the drumbeat, which is marked either by *hyaku* (as before) or by a large dot. In *SGYR* and *JCYR*, this system is frequently used in the secondary variants (the 'like pieces'). This new system of mensural notation is superimposed on the old, or on a vestige of the old. The 'ones' of *HFF* tend to disappear from later manuscripts; but the dots (usually hollow dots), interrupting the columns of notes and marking off binary segments, persist.

The oldest precisely dated manuscript (as opposed to a copy) that incorporates the new type of mensural notation is the 'Newly edited and selected mouth organ score' (*Shinsen shô-teki-fu*) (*SSSTF*) of 1302 (Yômei Bunko Library, Kyoto). This is the oldest and the most complete collection of Tang music pieces in mouth organ tablature, though late copies of earlier and less complete manuscripts exist (Marett, 1977). At times the beat dots are not in register with the notes to which in modern scores they correspond. The reason for this lack of alignment is not that the Chinese scribe, Pure Wisdom (Jingzhi, a Buddhist priest) was careless (here and there he perhaps was), but that the dots were accessory. The earlier mensural system retains its full force in displaying the phrasing of the melodic line as a chain of cells, each commonly composed of two basic duration units, but also consisting, occasionally, of three, four, or more such units. The simplest function of the dot is: to display the total number of beats within the measure.

The oldest complete collection of scores in flute tablature to which access is permitted, the *Chû Ôga ryûteki yôroku-fu* (*COTF*) (Tenri University Library), exhibits the use of both small and large dots and is perhaps a quarter of a century later than *SSSTF* (between 1321 and 1330).[21] (An older collection—*Kaichû-fu*—with a colophon dated 1095, but known only from late copies, contains only 35 items, as compared with more than 100 in *COTF*.)

It seems possible that the new system of mensural notation was introduced so as to offset uncertainty that had arisen in the interpretation of the earlier system or systems, and/or to bring precision to the execution of certain standard metrical variants, e.g. *tadabyôshi* and *gakubyôshi*. In the late Heian period, the decline of the court music, associated with the passage of political power from the aristocracy to the provincial military in the late 12th century, may have reduced the number of those competent to interpret the earlier system(s).[22]

As compared with their equivalents in *HFF*, decorated only with quasi-mordents, the tunes in *COTF* are elaborately glossed. The quasi-mordent sign occurs frequently and the melodic line is notated in detail, save that the two rhythmic patterns ♩♫ and ♫♩ are occasionally not distinguished by the system of mensural notation adopted. The increased decoration of the flute parts suggests that the speed of performance in the Kamakura period had been reduced, as compared with that of the same tunes in Hakuga's day.

From the standpoint of melodic interest, increasing decoration of the flute parts (as also of those for reed pipe) will have helped to compensate for the disappearance of melodic significance from the plucked-string parts, as a consequence of retardation. Under these conditions, the glossed melodies of flute and hichiriki will have become *the* tunes of the Tang music repertory in the Kamakura period, as they are at the present time.

Although the notes of the mouth organ melodies did not suffer from decay as a consequence of retardation, they too lost all significance as elements in a melody. They became so many changing pedal points that formed a melodically meaningless background to the glossed melodies of flute and reed pipe. It was perhaps in an attempt to regain satisfaction as performers, as well as to regain attention, that the mouth organ players began to apply cluster-chords above the notes of the original tune. At what point in time such chords came to be added and acquired their now fixed constitutions is not known. As noted by Marett, as late as the turn of the 13th century, a Gagaku-handbook by Koma no Asakuzu, *Zoku-Kyôkunshô* lists pairs of mouth organ notes a 5th apart, as if only parallel 5ths (or 4ths) were played by the mouth organ. It is possible, however, that diagrams (of which *Zoku-Kyôkunshô* offers examples) in which zigzag lines link notes in the cycle of 5ths within the circle of pipes of the mouth organ, led to the development of the Japanese style of playing the mouth organ—so profoundly different from the Chinese style and at times so dissonant by Chinese standards.

A number of factors contribute to the dissonance of modern Tang music performance. One is that the modal characteristics of Tang music pieces have not remained unchanged since they were transferred to Japan. Whereas in *FBBF*, Sadatoshi provides 27 lute-tunings in approximate numerical correspondence with the 28 mode-keys of the Tang (equivalent to four diatonic modes in each of seven keys), the number is reduced to nine in *SGYR*. The original cause of this reduction may have been a reduction in the number of different flutes available for performance. At the present time, a single size of transverse flute is in use for the performance of all Tang music in the current repertory. As the number of flutes available was reduced, pieces will of necessity have been transposed to other keys, and at times to other modes. In the latter case, as Marett has shown,[23] the quasi-mordents (*yu*) in *HFF* afford clues to the original mode of the piece, in some instances. Perhaps as a consequence of this transfer from key to key and from mode to mode, versions of the same piece for different instruments may show discrepancies, particularly in the treatment of modally sensitive notes; in Banshiki, for example, G may appear as G♯ or G♮, although in the equivalent Tang Banshe (equivalent to Sanskrit *pañcama*) mode, G was sharpened. In a quarter of the pieces in the modern repertory, the 3rd may occasionally be both minor and major in the mouth organ part of a single piece, while other instruments show no such variation. It is not known whether this reflects an originally modally ambiguous structure, or a conflation of two modally different versions ('major' and 'minor'). Again, in pieces in the Ichikotsu mode, deriving from the Tang Yiyue mode (Mixolydian; final D), the lute parts regularly show G♯ and C♯, where the winds have G♮ and C♮. Indeed, as the full scores of modern performance published by Sukehiro Shiba[24] show, lute (and zither) consistently play sharps against the naturals of the winds in Banshiki.

Yet another factor leading to chromatic dissonance in modern performance is the slowing down of the slurred passage from one note to the next. Even though the original melodies are almost without exception diatonic, slowed slurs confer a highly chromatic surface on the effect in ensemble. This is further coloured by slowed, slurred attack at certain points, on the part of the hichiriki (most conspicuously) and of the flute.

Since the flute and reed pipe parts provide the whole of the melodic interest in the performance of Tang music today, and since so much fine detail is cultivated today in pitch variation, attack and dynamics, it is understandably difficult for the present generation of court musicians, or for those performing at other centres of Gagaku performance, to imagine a pace of performance at which *all* parts would have melodic interest. At such a speed all the fine detail of current flute and reed pipe performance would be impossible of execution.

How little it occurs to a Japanese musicologist to think that a zither part, for example, could ever have been a piece of music of equal melodic standing with a flute or reed pipe part, is revealed by Tanabe's comment, as reported by Adriaansz, 'that it is senseless to try and play a gagaku composition on the koto alone'.[25] In fact, even 19th-century koto parts, played 'straight'—reading merely what is written—and at a pace of about crotchet = .90, are recognisably tunes. When the 12th century parts in *JCYR* are played according to the instructions in the score, they emerge as complete musical works, requiring support from no other instrument.[26]

If I and my group of collaborators read all five instrumental parts as tunes, it is because, in the first place we follow strictly the instructions of the manuscripts and ignore current interpretations; secondly, we read the scores as if they were Chinese (instead of Sino-Japanese) musical documents, to be read so as to make *musical* sense as they stand; thirdly, we bear in mind the milieu whence this music came to Japan, and its function as Court *entertainment* music in China. At the Chinese court, this repertory had none of the associations of the old Confucian 'banquet music', and still less those of court dynastic rites. Because of its association with the prestigious Chinese court, however, the Japanese assumed towards it an attitude of reverence more appropriate to a religious music.

In our view, the Tang music repertory can be restored by reading the earliest surviving manuscripts (*GKF* and *HFF*) as they stand, as if they were Chinese scores, and by stripping off ornamentation even from the least ornamented versions of the tunes in later manuscripts, so that flute, reed pipe, mouth organ, lute and zither parts approach the condition of the melodic line in *GKF* and *HFF*.

The conception of the texture of Tang music as a species of monody, of wind-melody accompanied by plucked strings and mouth organ—a view accepted by Japanese musicians under the influence of Western observers—implies a method of composition for which there is no evidence. It is retardation alone that has led to the parts for mouth organ, zither, and lute now appearing as accompaniment. As we hear the music today, the texture is a mechanical consequence of the operation of time, in producing retardation, and of practical steps taken to compensate for sound-decay, consequent upon retardation. The cause (or causes) of retardation remains a topic for investigation. Dart and I saw no reason to suppose that the reasons for the slowing of Tang music were different from those that led to the slowing of plainsong melodies, or to the slowing of chorale melodies to the pace of performance that characterised pre-war congregational singing in Germany, for example. In these different environments, a major common factor is likely to be the attitude of respect.

Summarising then, we have the remarkable situation that the tunes enshrined in the written parts of Tang music have (with certain exceptions) remained essentially unchanged since the time of production of the earliest surviving scores in the 9th and 10th centuries. How soon perceptible retardation of Japanese, as compared with Tang, performance occurred, we cannot say. If we are justified in accepting that a movement known as the 'Quick' (the last in a suite) was executed according to our notions of what constitutes 'quick', retardation must already have been quite considerable by the end of the 12th century, three centuries after the break with Tang. The ornamental detail in Moronaga's lute scores could not be played by a Chinese lutenist today at a speed very much in excess of crotchet = 92.

Returning to my discussions with Thurston Dart: from where we are today in our study of the Tang music repertory, it looks not so much as if the Japanese forgot any part of their inheritance, but rather as if they changed performance practice so as to preserve a musically cogent surface, notwithstanding the inescapable consequences of this retardation. The creativity of the musicians could not be denied. As Dart said: 'The utterly inflexible repetition of a received text is more than musicianly flesh-and-blood can stand, in the long run'. The surprising thing is not that Tang music has changed in Japan, but that it has changed (as regards the written parts) so little.

NOTES TO CHAPTER 7

1. Mitsuko Gamô: 'The *tempo* in *Tôgaku*', in *Nihon ongaku to sono shûhen*, ed. Koizumi Fumio, Hoshi Akira and Yamaguchi Osamu, and dedicated to Kikkawa Eishi, Ongaku no tomosha (Tokyo, 1973), 143-55.

2. L. Mueller: 'Einige Notizen über die japanische Musik', in *Mittheilungen der ostasiatischen Gesellschaft* (Tokyo, 1874-6), vi, 13-19; viii, 41-7, ix, 19-29. See last instalment, Tafel XIX, fig.5; Tafel XX, figs 1-4.

3. Dr R. F. Wolpert, Dr A. J. Marett, Dr J. Condit. As a 'Tang Music Project', sponsored by the American Council for Learned Societies, our collective activities have been variously financed by the Andrew W. Mellon Foundation, by the University Grants Committee of New Zealand, and by the Bavarian Ministry of Culture, to all of whom our gratitude is expressed. We are particularly grateful for the warm personal interest in our work manifested by Prof. Denis C. Twitchett (U. of Cambridge), Prof. Dr Herbert Franke (U. of Munich) and the late Prof. Arthur F. Wright (Yale U.).

4. 'Gagaku, Kangen and Bugaku', *KBS Bulletin on Japanese Culture*, xcix (Oct-Nov 1969), 2. Such a Music Bureau was required to supervise music and dance in court ceremony, to maintain standards, and to see that traditions were faithfully preserved. An account of music in Japan before the introduction of Buddhism, and of the first appearance of foreign music in Japan, will be found in R. Garfias: *Music of a Thousand Autumns* (Berkeley and Los Angeles, 1975), 5-15.

5. H. Eckardt: *Das Kokonchomonshû des Tachibana Narisue als musikgeschichtliche Quelle* (Wiesbaden, 1956), 181, 199, 247.

6. This identification was made by R. F. Wolpert and is discussed in his study, 'A Ninth-century Sino-Japanese Lute-Tutor', *Musica asiatica*, i (1977), 111-65, see pp.151, 162.

7. Wolpert (1977), 111.

8. Information from R. F. Wolpert.

9. Kenzô Hayashi: 'Hakuga fue-fu kô', in *Gagaku*, Tôyô ongaku senshô, x (Tokyo, 1969), 283-308.

10. Wolpert (1977), 111.

11. M. Gimm: *Das Yüeh-fu Tsa-lu des Tuan An-Chieh* (Wiesbaden, 1966), 306, 333, 380f.

12. Gimm (1966), 309.

13. Gimm (1966), 346ff.

14. See note 6 above. A Study of *GKF* by R. F. Wolpert is in course of preparation for publication. The observations here recorded are his.

15. A. J. Marett: 'Tunes Notated in Flute-tablatures from a Japanese Source of the Tenth Century', *Musica asiatica*, i (1977), 1-60.

16. A. J. Marett: unpublished observations.

17. L. E. R. Picken: 'Tenri Toshokan shozô no jûyô na Tôgaku-fu ni kansuru oboegaki', *Biblia*, vii (1974), 2-12, esp.3ff.

18. Tenri Toshokan: *Kogakusho ishu*, Zenpon sôsho, xvi (Tokyo, 1974), 4-54.

19. W. Adriaansz: *The Kumiuta and Danmono Traditions of Japanese Koto Music*

(Berkeley and Los Angeles, 1975): R. Garfias: 'Koto Ornamentation Technique in 11th Century Japanese Gagaku', in *Studia instrumentorum musicae popularis*, iii (Stockholm, 1974), 44–50.

20. (1974), 44–50.

21. Picken (1974), 5.

22. Garfias (1974), 23ff.

23. Marett, unpublished observations (1977).

24. *Gosen-fu ni yoru gagaku sôfu* (Tokyo, 1968–72).

25. Adriaansz (1975), 4.

26. J. Condit: 'Differing Transcriptions from the Twelfth-century Japanese Koto Manuscript *Jinchi yôroku*', *Ethnomusicology*, xx (1976), 87–95.

Part II

INTERPRETATION
AND PERFORMANCE

8

English Music for the Scottish Progress of 1617

Philip Brett

To contemplate the musical institutions of any society is to reach some understanding of its attitude to the art.[1] More imaginatively, it is to gain some sense of the composer's environment, and particularly of such elusive matters as musical traditions and shared artistic assumptions—a sense that leads inevitably to a finer perception of the music itself. The pre-eminence of the Chapel Royal and of the King's Musick in Tudor and Stuart England has long been recognised. The archival researches of this century have demonstrated how sporadic and uneven, by comparison, were the maintenance and achievements of other establishments both sacred and secular. Yet the musical implications of this state of affairs have never been fully explored. Continuity of both composers and repertory creates a special situation, particularly within the Chapel Royal: Byrd absorbed the work of Tallis, Purcell the music of Gibbons. Indeed, it is arguable that it was the Chapel in particular, giving a lead to the English church in general, that helped most to preserve and foster an indigenous musical idiom that endured in spite of the influx of French airs and dances, Italian madrigals and motets and so on, and shaped the musical thinking of each successive generation.

In roughly the same way that an ecclesiastical style had remained little altered from the death of Dunstable to the advent of the Reformation, so the Anglican style initiated by Tallis and Tye was hallowed by Byrd, and lived on to be revitalised by Orlando Gibbons and transformed by Henry Purcell. Its characteristics—thick texture, close imitation, shortwinded points, and a liberal and gratuitous display of false relations—can be heard in the church works of a host of composers, minor and major, Elizabethan and Jacobean, many of whom donned quite different musical garb when they hung up their cassocks and surplices. It is as difficult to recognise the hand of *April is in my Mistress' Face* behind *Nolo mortem peccatoris* (difficult enough, indeed, to cast doubt on Thomas Myriell's ascription of the latter to Morley)[2] as it is sad to contemplate the adventurous spirit of

O Care, thou Wilt Despatch me reduced to the tired clichés of *Alleluia! I Heard a Voice*. Yet these are only extreme instances of a general and readily perceptible phenomenon.

To all but the most partial critic, achievements in the secular sphere appear to shine rather bright against this dim religious light. Yet instrumental music aside, no vocal idiom other than that patronised by the Chapel composers survived or flourished so long. The English madrigal enjoyed and lost its vitality in less than 20 years. Its initiator, Thomas Morley, did hold a Chapel post, but its two brightest stars, Wilbye and Weelkes, were respectively a successful estate agent and the bibulous organist of a low-grade provincial cathedral. The high ideals of the Dowland lute-song had scarcely been displayed in print before they were first undermined by an intelligent dilettante, Thomas Campion, and later sacrificed for charm and a new set of Italianate notions by a number of lesser lights. Yet Thomas Tudway could report with some accuracy at the end of the 17th century: 'the Standard of Church Music begun by Mr. Tallis & Mr. Bird, &c. was continued for some years after the Restauration, & all Composers conform'd themselves to the Pattern which was set by them'.[3]

Owing, moreover, to the inclusive use of the terms 'madrigal' and 'air', and the desire of E. H. Fellowes (most notably) to create a national school out of an odd assortment of classmates, it was not until recently appreciated that certain composers, and leading Chapel composers at that, pursued in secular music a vein as indigenous as that of their church composition and in many respects related to it. To fall back on critical terms like 'old-fashioned', 'conservative' and 'unliterary' to describe this phenomenon, as more recent scholars have done, is eventually to invite misunderstanding. If a style can regenerate itself from time to time in music of such quality as that of Byrd and Gibbons, if it can take from outside what it needs and still remain true to its own character and ideals, then it is 'adventurous' and 'progressive' enough to be judged without the prejudice such labels are bound to suggest. But I have argued this at length elsewhere, attempting to show, in the case of Byrd, how his means of setting poetry, so very appropriate and intelligent, demonstrates a 'literary' consciousness as highly developed as, but different in nature from, that of the madrigalists.[4] In this essay I aim merely to propose one instance of the musical vitality of the Chapel, an example of a composer's responding to the demands of a particular occasion with some brilliance by weaving a new and fresh musical tapestry out of diverse threads spun inevitably in the recesses of his own creative imagination, but coloured through and through by the assumptions and traditions of the institution to which he belonged.

★   ★   ★

The primary duty of the Chapel Royal was to provide daily religious services for the monarch and his court in any of the palaces in the London area, and occasionally (as we shall see) on progresses further afield. It was not a fixed body like the royal chapel at Windsor, but part and parcel of the sovereign's retinue. Its sphere, however, extended beyond the daily religious office into the ceremony and entertainment which constantly surrounded and supported the crown. Besides the great occasions such as coronations, and the more domestic ones such as christenings, weddings and funerals, there were the masques which in their own way celebrated the ideals of kingship and the role of the court; and music also had its function in political events such as the occasion in 1611 when the King and the French ambassador swore to the maintenance of a league between the two nations, taking the oath in Chapel where the organs played and anthems were sung to solemnise the event.[5]

On one occasion in the reign of James I, however, the Chapel Royal rose above a generally supporting role to become a veritable instrument of royal policy. This happened in 1617, during the King's first and last return to his native land after ascending the English throne in 1603. Clarifying his intentions to the Scottish Privy Council, James wrote of 'a salmonlyke instinct . . .a great and naturall longing to see our native soyle and place of our birth and breeding'.[6] He went on in the same letter to deny rumours that he desired to reform Scottish government civil or ecclesiastical, but his protestations cannot have cut much ice with the Scots, who had good reason to fear for the continued independence of their Presbyterian church.

To James, who embraced the Anglican faith as a natural adjunct to his elevated notion of kingship, the Scottish Kirk was not merely a thorn in the royal flesh but a threat to his sovereignty, as he made clear at the famous Hampton Court Conference of 1604 to the unfortunate Puritan Dean who had dropped the word 'presbyteri'. If his party aimed at a Scottish Presbytery, the King exclaimed, it 'as wel agreeth with a Monarchy, as God and the Devill. Then *Iack* & *Tom*, & *Will*, & *Dick* shall mete, and at their pleasures censure me and my Councell and all our proceedinges'. And after more of this kind, he turned to the bishops and said, 'if once you were out and they in place, I know what would become of my *Supremacy. No Bishop, no King*, as before I said'.[7] And so, having established firm political control over Scotland through the Duke of Lennox and a body of trusted councillors, James began from England to reduce the power of the Kirk. By 1605 he had virtually overthrown the General Assembly, and the year following summoned eight of its most vociferous troublemakers to England from whence only two returned. The notorious Andrew Melville, who caused a notable stir by plucking at the sleeves of the Archbishop of Canterbury's white lawn surplice and calling them 'popish rags', was incarcerated in the Tower and later banished abroad. Meanwhile the King completed his domination over the Kirk by forcing bishops upon it, and by gradually increasing their status and powers over the years.

Had it ended there all would have been well, for the Presbyterian system was far from destroyed, the Scottish bishops were moderate men of good sense, and above all, ordinary church-goers detected no change in the accustomed pattern of their worship. But whether out of growing zeal, or owing to that schoolmasterly temperament that would never leave well alone, James determined in his fiftieth year to teach the Scots to imitate better English customs (as he remarked) than drinking healths, wearing gay clothes, and taking tobacco. To bring the churches of the two nations into line upon matters of ceremony and ritual was, then, to be the major and scarcely concealed purpose of the Scottish Progress. And towards this end James ordained, in a characteristically didactic stroke of policy which exercised the traditional function of music and the other arts to persuade through delight, that throughout his stay the Anglican rite should be celebrated in all its glory at Holyrood by the English Chapel Royal.

It should be pointed out at this juncture that summer progresses were held annually throughout the reigns of Elizabeth and James. They took the court away from town when plague was apt to flare up, and they gave Elizabeth in particular a chance to inspect local government and also to beggar any families rising above their station by giving them the expensive pleasure of entertaining her royal majesty and retinue. James's interest ran more to the country pleasures of hunting and hawking; and there was plenty of that on the way up to Scotland in 1617. Indeed, the journey took over two months to the exasperation of the nobility commanded to attend; so many of them defected on the way that at one point, according to the Earl of Dorset, there was only a single lord left.

It is a tribute to the King's enormous tenacity of purpose that the Scottish journey was ever undertaken. It called forth a storm of protest, including an earnest plea for postponement from the reigning favourite, young George Villiers, newly created Earl of Buckingham, whom James turned on so roundly that it is said he was glad to get away. The major difficulty was finance, with the Crown, as usual, heavily in debt. Finally the London merchants were prevailed upon to lend £100,000 on security of the crown jewels, and the tax farmers £50,000. Those who arranged the loan had the consolation of a knighthood on the day of departure; one who refused to pay was made to follow on foot until he complied.

Meanwhile the Scots had been busy for a whole year sprucing up the streets of Edinburgh, ridding the city of vagabonds, and providing lodging for an estimated 5,000 men and horse. Some Englishmen reported well on arrival: 'the entertainment very honourable, very general, and very full', wrote John Chamberlain to Sir Dudley Carleton, 'every day feasts and invitations. I know not who paid for it'.[8] But the sophisticated English attitude is perhaps better reflected in the scurrilous prose of Sir Anthony Weldon, who took the occasion to write what must be one of the classics of racial invective. Peppered with remarks such as 'there is great store of fowle, as Fowle houses, fowle sheets and shirts, fowle lynnen, fowle dishes and potts, fowle trenchermen and napkins', it concludes with the scandalous opinion that 'the men of olde did no more wonder that the great Messias should be borne in so poore a Towne as Bethlem in Judea, as I do wonder that so brave a Prince as King James should be borne in so stinking a Towne as Edenborough in lousy Scotland'.[9]

Such schoolboyish petulance pales into insignificance, however, beside the anger of the Scots at the doings in Holyroodhouse. 'The Kings palice was reformit with all expiditoun of maissons and wrycht wark, his chappell royall was decorit with organis, and uthir temporall policie', reports an anonymous Scottish historian somewhat tersely.[10] A considerable instrument costing above £400, the organ arrived by sea from London accompanied by its builder, Thomas Dallam, who on returning confessed he had been better used among the Turks (whom he had visited with an organ for the Sultan in 1599). Worse was to follow. The refurbished chapel designed by none other than Inigo Jones included gilded images of the patriarchs and apostles. On the arrival of these statues the workmen at Holyrood simply downed tools, and people murmured, it is said, 'that the Organs came first, now the Images, and ere long they should have the Mass'. The Scottish bishops negotiated the removal of the offending statues, but only at the expense of a theological lecture on the nature of pictures and images from his majesty, who made the telling remark that no one would have minded had the figures been of 'lyones, dragones and divells'.[11]

The day after the King arrived in Edinburgh many months later, as one Presbyterian historian reports, 'the English service was begunne in the Chappell Royal, with singing of quiristours, surplices and playing on organes'.[12] The Scots commanded to attend, more than annoyed at having to kneel for Communion, considered it 'staining and polluting the house of religion by the dregs of popery'.[13] Indeed, the general perturbation was so great that it led Anthony Weldon to remark, 'I am persuaded that yf God & his angells should come downe in their whitest garments they would run away and cry, "The Children of the Chappell are come agayne to torment us; let us fly from the abomination of these boys, & hide ourselves in the mountaynes"'.[14]

Major incidents seem somehow to have been avoided, and the King pursued his aims by presenting to an informal gathering of clergy at St Andrews five proposals: that Communion should be received kneeling not sitting (which to many Scots involved the doctrine of the Real Presence); that private Communion might be administered in cases of necessity (which smacked of the last rites); that private Baptism might be administered; that the great church feasts should be observed (which contravened the self-sufficiency of the Sabbath); and that the bishops should conduct confirmations (which increased their limited powers). Nothing was decided on these scores during the visit, but the following year a General Assembly of the Kirk, summoned at Perth and subjected to outrageous pressures, accepted the Five Articles, as they came to be known. It was a Pyrrhic victory, though, for James realised that they could not be enforced. Indeed, they were generally unobserved until Charles and his stiff-necked Archbishop Laud adopted a less conciliatory approach to the same issues and thereby precipitated the so-called Bishops' War, the first open hostilities in a civil war that rent the nation and led eventually to the temporary eclipse of the monarchy.

A remaining question about the royal visit is why it was not the Scottish Chapel Royal that provided the services at Holyrood. Charles Rogers, author of *A History of the Chapel Royal of Scotland* (Edinburgh, 1882), assumed it did, without quite showing how. The native establishment had once flourished, of course, but since 1603 its revenues had gone to line the pockets of royal favourites, in particular a faithful Scots servant named John Gib; and it had declined in spite of the efforts of the Dean and the Scottish Parliament to preserve it as a national institution. It is true that a few sung services appear to have been held in the wake of the King's visit, but the organ soon broke down (Dean Galloway wrote that it had been 'too commonlie visited'[15]), and all fell once more into decay. Indeed, the situation that Rogers and other Scottish historians outline makes it extremely unlikely that a choir could be found in the whole of Scotland to do justice to the English choral service. The actual evidence that the English Chapel was present comes, first, from a petition addressed by the Gentlemen to King Charles in 1633 before they embarked on a similar journey: 'when they attended the late King into Scotland there was delivered to the Dean of the Chapel towards their charge £400 and there was also allowed them a good ship well victualled'.[16] And Sir Anthony Weldon corroborated their method of transport in his own manner:[17]

> the skipper that brought the Singing-men with their papisticall vestments complaines that he hath beene much troubled with a strange singing in his head ever since they came aborde his ship, for remedy whereof the Parson of the parish hath perswaded him to sell that prophane vessell, and distribute the mony amongst the faythfull brethren.

By far the most rewarding evidences of the visit, however, are two works specially written for the occasion by Orlando Gibbons, chief organist of the Chapel, who must himself have been in attendance. One of these pieces, designated 'for the King's being in Scotland' in its sole source (*GB-Occ* 21), has long been known from the *Tudor Church Music* edition.[18] Its opening lines confirm the designation:

> Great King of gods, whose gracious hand hath led
> Our sacred sovereign head
> Unto the place where all our bliss was bred,
> O send thine angels to his blessed side
> And bid them there abide,
> To be at once his guardian and his guide.

These words may seem at first sight more pagan than Christian, until we recall the manner in which James was accustomed to refer to the monarchy: 'For kings are not only God's lieutenants upon earth and sit upon God's throne, but even by God Himself they are called gods'.[19]

The other Gibbons piece was brought to my attention some 20 years ago by Thurston Dart who on a visit to the United States found it in the manuscript collection of the New York Public Library. It occurs in Drexel manuscripts 4180–5, a set of early 17th-century partbooks which came from the library of Edward Rimbault according to whom they had once belonged to the diarist, John Evelyn; it is also conceivable that they were among the books Rimbault removed from Christ Church Library.[20] I was myself subsequently able to identify the original scribe, John Merro, by comparing this set with another (*GB-Lbm* Add.17792–6),[21] which shares the same hand and some of the same repertory, and which had been included by Pamela Willetts among the group of manuscripts, many of them associated with Oxford, that she had shown to be the work of this copyist, whose name she uncovered.[22] Arnold Ashbee has since pointed out that Merro was a singing man at Gloucester Cathedral mentioned in a visitation of 1609 and in subsequent years; he died on 23 March 1636 and was buried in the Lady Chapel.[23] Craig Monson in his recent study of the secular manuscripts of the period argues convincingly that the partbooks were begun around 1615 and probably completed in the years shortly after 1625; they constitute one of the largest and most interesting collections of the time, even exceeding in size and scope of repertory Thomas Myriell's *Tristitiae Remedium* (*Lbm* Add.29372–7, begun in 1616), with which they are roughly contemporary.[24]

How the only extant copy of one of these occasional pieces comes to be found in a set of manuscripts inscribed by a Gloucester lay clerk (and otherwise including Gibbons only as the composer of the *Cries of London* and the three-part fantasias) is a mystery. One tentative clue, however, arises from the career of the author of the poem. Since publishing an edition of the piece, it has come to my attention that the words also occur in another manuscript (*Lbm* Harl.1423, f.102) attributed to a certain Dr Hall, who may safely be identified with the English divine, Joseph Hall (1574–1656).[25] Having been chaplain to the ill-fated Henry, Prince of Wales, Hall was pressed into service on the Scottish Progress as a moderate Puritan who might help to win over the Scots to the King's point of view. Something of a Vicar of Wakefield, it seems, he was suitably rewarded by preferment. On return from Scotland he went to the Deanery of Worcester (where Merro might perhaps have had access to a copy of Gibbons's setting?), in 1627 to the Bishopric of Exeter (having turned down Gloucester in the meantime), and finally to the illustrious See of Norwich. In his earlier days up at Cambridge round the turn of the century he had gained some attention as a poet, being mentioned by Francis Meres as one of the foremost English satirists on account of his *Virgidemiae*. There are three poems for the Scottish visit, the first two of which Gibbons set with great resource as a continuous whole. The third, addressing James as Phoebus, begs him to return to England ('Turne the[e] agayne o Phebus Fayre'), no doubt indicating the mind of the poet, who petitioned to leave at the earliest moment. The poems Gibbons set are reproduced below as they appear in the Harleian manuscript. Though perhaps fulsome to our ears, the verse is in the best Jonsonian manner, and the invocation of the spirits of the plain and the music of the spheres is genuinely delightful.

Cearten veerses written by Doctor Hall upon
the kings coming into Scotland.

Doe not repyine fayre sun to see these eyne
   welcomer far then thyne
To see the beames of a moore glorius face
   Shine one his native place
And overrun the to his Northerne lyne
   fayre sonn doe not repyine
And yea thrise blessed bowers wch longe agone
   His cradle rocked one
W^{ch} at the first that vitall breath did geve
   whereby our worlde doth live
Doe not invie the spheres of heaven above
   In his deare lyght and love
whose presens under Arthures seate can frame
   An Eden both indeede and name

finis
Dr Hall

2

Ioye that Alone wth better bayes
and mirtle bowes and highest dayes
   Crownest thy kinglie browes
Come come alonge to day wth me
welcome the flower of Royaltie
   Home to his native howse
Now doe thy best and more then all
To make a merry festivall
   Oh now or never doot
All the day longe feast dance play and singe
And Spend upon this revalinge
   Thy nimblest handes and feete
Call to thee all thy lightheeld trayne
Nimphes and phares of the playne
   And bid them trip it round
And cause the cirkles of the Skyes
Answare the cherminge melodyes
   In there consorted sounde

Still may the burden be welcome
welcome greate king to thy first home
   Then add unto the rest
Good speede home to thy other home
That count the hower whilest thou art gone
   And use to love the best.

                                    finis Docter Hall

    Gibbons's setting of this and of the other text, *Great King of Gods*, both call for countertenor and bass soloists, a vocal chorus, and a quintet of instruments, presumably viols which as usual are not specified. *Great King of Gods* appears in the recent edition of Gibbons's verse anthems presumably because it refers to the Deity;[26] *Do not Repine* is excluded, presumably because it does not: but they obviously both belong to the same genre of composition. It was most generally known, then as now, by the term 'verse anthem'; but a designation less ecclesiastical in implication might help to make the secular origins of the form, and its inclusive nature, more widely appreciated. Its distant forerunners, to be sure, are the medieval English carol and motet, the one with its alternation of verse, refrain and burden, the other with its insistence upon changes of texture. But the immediate ancestor is the solo song for voice and viols, always secular in context and function if not in sentiment, which arose out of 16th-century court entertainment, particularly the Elizabethan choirboy theatre, and which reached its artistic peak in the works of William Byrd. Consort songs with spiritual texts could be—and were—adapted for church (where viols were not allowed) by the substitution of the organ for the obbligato consort part; and the increasing number of such arrangements in Jacobean times was matched by a growing tendency to bypass the consort version and write for organ from the very start.

    It is becoming increasingly clear that the verse anthem or consort song form occupied a leading position in Jacobean vocal music, not only by a mere head count—it has a considerable edge numerically over both full anthem and madrigal—but also as regards composers' attitudes towards it. Evidently Jacobean composers of differing outlooks and persuasions all found in this medium a challenge to their ingenuity and a stimulus to their originality. It was above all a flexible form, less dependent than the madrigal or full anthem on the musical portrayal of verbal imagery, and less restricted than the lute-song to strophic arrangement. It could be written along the established lines worked out by Byrd; on the other hand it could absorb a good deal of madrigalian technique such as pictorial word-setting, expressive harmony or even contrasts of scoring. At the same time it presented some intriguing problems of overall design and of the relationship of chorus and solo passages which prompted an enormous variety of solutions. And it could span the whole range of taste and decorum from the flimsy trifles of Ravenscroft's publications to the most ambitious and serious compositions of the period, among which are Gibbons's own works.

Gibbons, of course, was no less alive to the possibilities of the form than Weelkes, Tomkins, Ward, Peerson or a host of others. David Brown in his monograph on Weelkes sees Gibbons's work as conservative by comparison,[27] but in fact his sense of expressive nuance and of formal design is a good deal more subtle than that of the Chichester composer, who favoured the dramatic gesture and the schematic plan. Gibbons's works in this idiom, indeed, stand second only to the songs of Byrd as monuments to the sturdiness and vitality of the native tradition. It is true, however, that one of the two Scottish pieces, *Great King of Gods*, represents the Gibbons who is most restrained and ecclesiastical in style and simple in organisation. The most notable event in this sober piece is the repeat of the last seven bars of the first chorus in the final chorus, serving to tie the piece together musically, and perhaps to make a flattering connexion between 'the place where all our bliss was bred' and 'Thy celestial state'. *Do not Repine, fair Sun*, though it belongs to the same genre, projects a rather different atmosphere or 'decorum', which is reflected most immediately in the notation in smaller values—the point is obscured of course by the wanton halving of note values in modern editions of church music of the period. The piece relates to *Great King of Gods* in much the same way as Purcell's court odes relate to his verse anthems, the difference being that Gibbons, so far as I can discover, had no really established tradition to fall back on in composing this extended work which, because it refers personally (not allegorically) and directly (not ambiguously) to the monarch, anticipates in a remarkable manner the Restoration welcome song.

Some of the purely musical aspects are also interestingly prophetic. Instead of the customarily more immediate entrance of the solo voice or voices after a short, often imitative, introductory passage that flows right into the vocal passage, there is here a seven-bar instrumental 'Preludium' (as it is labelled in the manuscripts), separated both by its musical material and by a cadence and rest from the ensuing vocal duet (see ex.1).

The musical material is different, to be sure, but in emphasising stepwise movement in parallel 3rds and 10ths, quasi-canonic writing with overlapping figures at the unison, and in introducing the rhythmic figure *x* that plays so important a part later on, the composer clearly establishes the whole mood and texture of what follows. This embryonic ritornello, moreover, prefaces both parts of the first poem, which Gibbons treats as two stanzas, each being first enunciated by a pair of soloists and then repeated in different but related musical terms by the chorus—the one literal repeat consists merely of the last two bars of the second 'stanza' (bb.90–3, 113–6),[28] which are the same in both solo and chorus versions.

Ex. 1

On the other hand, in setting the poetry strictly in couplets, which in the first chorus, for instance, take precedence (judging by the main cadences) over the syntactical reading that would seem to demand a break after the fifth line, Gibbons follows the age-old tradition of embodying poetic form rather than searching for prosaic sense, a principle he undoubtedly learnt from his master Byrd.

There is a novel feature about the music for the second poem that also forecasts a later development in the verse anthem. To set the first eight lines Gibbons adopts a rhythmic, chordal style that might even vaguely invoke the Restoration to some ears. The composer takes his cue, however, from later lines of the poem and here refers to the dance—not merely in spirit, moreover, but specifically to a type of branle, which the English called 'brawls'. In order to have his dance, though, Gibbons is obliged to alter the metre and structure of Dr Hall's poem (turning three lines into a quatrain and repeating a two-syllable word in each third and fourth line) in a way that Byrd might not have countenanced. The whole of this second section of the work is full, with no verse passages, but Gibbons aims for a different kind of textural contrast in this predominantly homophonic style by isolating high or low trios from time to time. After a repeated strain and an extra half-strain of the brawls (bb.125–36), the music breaks into galliard rhythm, which lasts up to exactly half way through the second poem. Here the original time signature is resumed, together with a fully polyphonic manner reminiscent of the very opening of the piece; there also appears the rhythmic figure that is one of the elements which bind the work together, and in this appearance it also recalls the opening melodically (see ex.2). This figure occurs for the last time just before the climax of the work at the actual word, 'Welcome!', where again the verse form is disrupted, and the music breaks into an extremely fast *tripla*—an unusually dramatic gesture for Gibbons (see ex.3 over).

Ex. 2a

Ex. 2b

To cap this and to create an even greater sense of musical unity without resorting to the oppressively schematic or mechanical, Gibbons takes up all the threads in the last section in an interesting and masterly way. After plain chords for 'Then add unto the rest', there is first a setting of 'Good speed home' that in its falling stepwise progressions in 3rds and 10ths suggests an inversion of the initial idea of the 'Preludium'. 'To thy other own' wittily rearranges the rhythmic pattern of 'Do not repine', which has figured so largely in the piece. Then, at 'that count the hours whilst thou art gone', we are momentarily back in the world of the branle before the literal repetition of the music of 'Oh now or never do't' (bb.137–40) for 'And vie to love thee best' (bb.198–201), a repetition which gives the ear a nudge, so to speak, towards hearing this last section as an imaginative recalling of various strands of the composition to satisfy the claims of overall coherence which Gibbons, as a pupil of Byrd, always acknowledges

Ex. 3

even when he does not quite do justice to them. The final peroration, preceded by a dramatic rest in all the voices, is a bar shorter than the 'Preludium' (ex.4). It does not of course employ the same material. But it does move in a similar manner, if a little more grandly across a larger tessitura; in focussing attention on the chords on E, C and A, with G and D as subsidiary, it covers in miniature the main harmonic gestures of the piece; and in falling away from a melodic peak of G, to which the 'Preludium' had first aspired (an octave lower of course), it makes a very satisfactory closing melodic gesture. In short, it concludes the business of the work in every possible way; more important, it does so with verve and artistry.

Ex. 4

The piece, then, is a remarkable and novel attempt, firmly rooted in the verse anthem tradition established by Byrd, but stretching the conventions of the form in a way the older master would perhaps not have countenanced. More than anything else, it testifies to the vigour and flexibility of the native idiom in the hands of one of its greatest proponents. A decade or so earlier, at the beginning of the reign, the Italian vein would have been considered more appropriate for such a composition. Indeed, both Gibbons and Weelkes wrote madrigalian settings of the text *Hosanna to the Son of David* presumably to welcome the King on some occasion, if not his entry to London in 1603. And in 1613 nearly everyone wrote elaborate Italianate settings of David's lament for Absolom when the nation mourned young Prince Henry. By 1617, however, the long-lived and enduring form of the consort song or verse anthem was coming back into its own, and was asserting an independence that would support it throughout the musical and political vicissitudes of the next half-century.

★ ★ ★

The more mundane question of when the piece was actually performed still remains. The most appropriate occasion seems to be at some point during the first great event of the Progress which is graphically recounted by an anonymous Scot in the records of the High Court of the Justiciary[29]—see Plate XI for a view of Edinburgh which, though 18th-century, is based on a view of about 1650:

> The saxtene day of May 1617, the Kingis Majestie enterit at the Wast Poirt of Edinburgh, quhair the Provest, the four Bailyeis, the haill Counsell of the Toun, with ane hundreth honest men and mae, war all assemblit in blak gownes all lynit with plane velvet, and their haill apparrell was plane black velvet. At quhilk tyme first the Proveist, William Nisbet maid ane Harrand, welcoming his Majestie to his awin Citie; thareafter ane Harand was maid be Mr John Hay in name of the haill Citizens; ane purse contening five hundreth double angellis laid in a silver basing double overgilt, was propynit to his Majestie, quha with ane myld and gracious countenance resavit thayme with thair propyne, come tharefor throw the Citie to the Kirk, quhair ane Sermone was maid be the Archbishope of St Androis, Spottiswood; tharefter come directlie doun the streit towardis his awin Palice in Halyrudhous, being conveyit be the honest men of the Toun to the Corse callit St Johne's Croce, quhair be the drawing of ane sword his Majestie knychtit the Proveist.

At the gate of the Inner Court of Holyrood, the King was presented with a

A General View of the City, Castle of EDINBURGH, *the Capital of Scotland.*

Plate XI Print by Morris and Hogg (c1765) based on a print by Van Hoyen (c1650)

book of verses by the College of Edinburgh, one of whose members made a speech, in Latin. After this, James presumably entered the Palace— pleased with his 'five hundreth double angellis' no doubt, but fatigued by the 'harrands' that might have reminded him uncomfortably of his youth. *Do not Repine* must surely have been designed for performance during this latter part of the day. Its musical style is suited to the chamber not the open air; its verse refers to Arthur's Seat, the hill that broods over the palace; and the choir itself would scarcely have been welcome outside Holyrood. Whatever the truth of the matter, musical history would be a dull affair if we could not linger for a moment to imagine the King's pleasure at seeing the familiar faces of his own Chapel, and his delight on hearing the music of its distinguished organist and composer. And imagination may perhaps extend so far as the hope that he took upon himself the part of Maecenas, and matched both pleasure and delight with an accustomed liberality.

NOTES TO CHAPTER 8

1. Based on a paper delivered to the National Conference of the American Musicological Society at Toronto in 1970.

2. *GB-Lbm* Add.29372–7, f.8*v*.

3. *GB-Lbm* Harl.7338, f.2*v*; quoted in J. A. Westrup: *Purcell* (London, 5/1965), 199.

4. 'Word-setting in the Songs of Byrd', *PRMA*, xcviii (1971–2), 47–64.

5. See W. R. Woodfill: *Musicians in English Society from Elizabeth to Charles I* (Princeton, 1953), 174.

6. J. Nichols: *The Progresses, Processions, and Magnificent Festivities of King James the First* (London, 1828), iii, 309.

7. From an account of the Conference by William Barlow, Dean of Chester, printed in *James I by his Contemporaries*, ed. and introduced by R. Ashton (London, 1969), 183f.

8. Nichols (1828), iii, 347.

9. *GB-Lbm* Harl.5191, printed in Nichols (1828), iii, 338–43.

10. *The Historie and Life of King James the Sext*, Bannantyne Club Publications, xiii (Edinburgh, 1825), 395.

11. John Spottiswoode: *The History of the Church of Scotland* (1655), ed. M. Russell and M. Napier (Edinburgh, 1847–51), iii, 239.

12. David Calderwood: *The True History of the Church of Scotland from the beginning, unto the end of the reign of James VI* (Rotterdam, 1678), ed. T. Thomson (Edinburgh, 1842–9), vii, 246.

13. Robert Johnston: *Historia rerum Britannicam* (Amsterdam, 1655), 518, trans. in Robert Chambers: *The Domestic Annals of Scotland* (Edinburgh, 1842), i, 476.

14. Nichols (1828), iii, 340.

15. Rogers (1882), 127.

16. *State Papers Domestic 1633–34*, 38.

17. Nichols (1828), iii, 340.

18. iv (Oxford, 1925), 197–202.

19. From a speech to the House of Commons, quoted by D. Harris Wilson in *King James VI and I* (London, 1956), 243.

20. See W. G. Hiscock: *Christ Church Miscellany* (Oxford, 1946), 127–33.

21. See *Consort Songs*, MB, xxii (London, 1967), 173.

22. 'Music from the Circle of Anthony Wood at Oxford', *British Museum Quarterly*, xxiv (1961), 71–5.

23. *ML*, xlviii (1967), 310f.

24. *Voices and Viols in England, 1600–1650: The Sources and the Music* (diss., U. of California, Berkeley, 1974), 226–49.

25. They are included in *The Collected Poems of Joseph Hall*, ed. A. Davenport (Liverpool, 1949), 150ff.

26. Ed. D. Wulstan, EECM, iii (London, 1964), where it appears with words written by Bramley for Ouseley's edition of 1893. Granted the original words are unsuited to modern use in church, there are several 17th-century adaptations, involving changes merely in the first three lines, that will serve. Two of them are as follows:

> Great King of Gods, whose gratious hand hath led
>   our Sacred Soverain Head
> out of their hands, our ruine that would have bred (etc.)
>   (*GB-Ob* Rawl. poet. 23, p.168)

> Great God of Kings whose gracious hand hath led
>   our sacred Sovereign Head
> Unto the Throne from whence our bliss is bred: (etc.)
>   (*A Collection of Private Devotions . . . published by Autoritie of Queen ELISA,*
>   *1560* (London, 1655), 210).

27. *Thomas Weelkes* (London, 1969), 170, 174.

28. The bar numbers refer to my edition (London, 1961).

29. Nichols (1828), iii, 317f.

9

English Keyboard Fingering in the 16th and early 17th Centuries

Peter Le Huray

It was in 1955 that Thurston Dart began his exciting series of recordings of English keyboard music for Oiseau-Lyre. These attracted glowing reviews, for he had an instinctive feel for articulation and phrasing, and an impeccable sense of timing that made each performance an occasion to remember. I always felt that he and John Bull would have found much in common with each other: virtuosity certainly, tremendous vitality and a uniqueness that is the hallmark of the great interpreter. One of the problems that particularly fascinated him at the time was the degree to which English keyboard techniques, as revealed in fingering, ornamentation and the musical textures themselves, could suggest solutions to deeper problems of interpretation. As he himself wrote in 1954 of keyboard sources: 'Many problems of phrasing and of musica ficta may be conclusively solved by a study of contemporary fingering techniques'.[1] In those days, however, a systematic examination of the evidence was hardly practicable, for the Musica Britannica critical editions of the music of Tomkins, Bull, Gibbons, Farnaby, and Byrd were yet to come, as were also the smaller yet important editions of the keyboard music of Cosyn, Lugge, Morley, Tallis and Tisdale, and the editions of the Bunbury, Cromwell, Matchett, Rogers and Tisdale 'virginal books',[2] nearly all of which were inspired, if not actually undertaken, by Dart himself. Now that these have been completed the time is perhaps ripe for a closer survey of the evidence, in the hope that a pattern may emerge for some more systematic and detailed research into problems of technique and interpretation.

Sources

Where should one begin?—conveniently (since the entire field could not possibly be covered in a short essay of this kind) by limiting the enquiry to those sources in which fingerings are to be found, and to those pieces that have by chance been provided with fingerings. Out of a total of some 60 sources, close on 30 have fingerings in them. Ten of the 30 are of considerable importance:

1. *GB-Cfm* 32.G.29 (Fitzwilliam Virginal Book).
   Ed. J. A. Fuller Maitland and W. Barclay Squire (Leipzig, 1899/*R*1963).

2. *GB-Lbm* Add.30485. Probably compiled by one of Byrd's pupils (?John Holmes, of Winchester and Salisbury); contents mostly by Byrd, copied *c*1590–*c*1610.

3. *GB-Lbm* Add.31403. Contents include elaborately fingered preludes and a table of ornaments; unlikely to be in the hand of Bristol musician Elway Bevin (see below and Plate XII).

4. *GB-Lbm* Add.36661. Compiled in 1630s by Thomas Tunstall; opening section of some dozen pieces by Frescobaldi and Bernardo Pasquini, and substantial collection of Orlando Gibbons and English contemporaries.

5. *GB-Lbm* Royal 24.d.3. Important source, extensively fingered; contents mostly by Byrd; index, dated 31 Jan 1624, signed 'Will Forster'.
   Ed. E. H. Fellowes (London, 1950).

6. *F-Pc* Rés 1185. Two principal layers, the first for some time thought to be in the hand of Bull, the second (completed by 1652) added by Benjamin Cosyn; contents mostly by Bull; fingerings scattered through source and associated almost entirely with Bull's music.
   Ed. M. Maas: *English Pastime Music, 1630–1660* (Madison, 1974) [selection and discussion of source].

7. *F-Pc* Rés 1186*bis* (I and II). Contents by Bull, Gibbons and others, mostly anon.; fewer fingerings than source 6.
   Ed. M. Maas (Madison, 1974) [selection and discussion of source].

8. Private collection (Priscilla Bunbury's Virginal Book). Extensively fingered collection of pieces for an amateur player, similar in scope to 7 and q, ideal for performer who wishes to get to grips with English techniques.
   Ed. J. L. Boston (London, 1962) [selection of 16 pieces]; contents listed ibid: *ML*, xxxvi (1955), 366.

9. Private collection of Earl of Dalhousie (Clement Matchett's Virginal Book) [on loan as *GB-En* Panmure 9]. Copied between 1612 and 1614, important source for an advanced player; contents 'professional' music, much of it elaborately fingered.
   Ed. T. Dart (London, 1957); see ibid: *ML*, xxxv (1954), 93–106.

10. Private collection of Marquess of Abergavenny (My Ladye Nevells Book). Copied by John Baldwin, member of choir of St George's Chapel, Windsor (completed 11 Sept 1591); contents entirely by Byrd; Brown (xxvii, p. 170) points to elegance of format and reliability of text and suggests that Byrd may have been responsible for corrections and additions; fingerings, not profuse but informative, could be by Byrd.
Ed. H. Andrews (London, 1962/R1969).

To these should be added one printed source:

A. *Parthenia In-Violata* (London, *c*1625).
Ed. T. Dart (New York, 1961); facs. (New York, 1961).

A further 18 sources contain isolated fingerings, and merit at least some brief description:

a. *D-Bds* Lynar A1–2. Comprises German, Italian, Dutch and English keyboard works.
See A. Curtis: *TVNM*, xx (1964–5), 45; ibid: *Sweelinck's Keyboard Music* (Leyden and London, 1969, 1972).

b. *GB-Cu* Dd.4.22. Small lutebook dated *c*1600; contains two keyboard pieces, of which one, Bull's Prelude (xix:121) is fingered.

c. *GB-Lbm* Add.23623. Compiled by Gulielmus à Messaus, succentor at St Walburga's, Antwerp, from loose papers formerly in Bull's possession; contents predominantly by Bull.

d. *GB-Lbm* Add.29485 (Susanne Soldt's Virginal Book). *c*1599; opening prelude fingered.

e. *GB-Lbm* Add.29996. Contents date from between the mid-16th and mid-17th centuries; owned in 1647 by Thomas Tomkins.

f. *GB-Lbm* Add.30486. A small collection of pieces by Byrd and anon., *c*1600, three of which have some fingerings.

g. *GB-Lcm* 2093. Second half of 17th century; contents anon. (early Restoration style), three pieces by Byrd, Bull and Gibbons.

h. *US-NYp* Drexel 5612. Compiled *c*1620, possibly in Salisbury area; contains 'Ayre' by Gibbons (xx:35) fingered.

i. *GB-Ob* Mus.Sch.c.93. Composite volume of separate gatherings; includes two fingered pieces by Tomkins.

j. *GB-Och* 89. Continental; liturgical, catholic organ music, mainly anon., but ascriptions to P. Cornet, Philips, Bruno and Gibbons, whose Prelude (xx:2) is fully fingered.

k. *GB-Och* 92. Composite volume of mid-17th century; contents mainly anon. (one, 'Hyde Park', fingered), but pieces by 'Holmes'.

l. *GB-Och* 378. Contents, from mid-17th century, wholly anon., three opening pieces fingered.

m.   *GB-Och* 1142. Mid- to late 17th century; the first, untitled and incomplete piece fingered.

n.   *GB-Och* 1179. Restoration manuscript; contents include pieces by
Blow, Bull and Purcell; one anon. 'Ground' fingered.

o.   *GB-Och* 1207. Early 17th century; contains only two pieces, an anon.
'Voluntary' and a fully fingered 'Miserere' by Bull (xiv:34) which is
of considerable importance.

p.   *F-Pc* Rés 1122. Holograph and major source of Thomas Tomkins's
music; a Prelude, 'Miserere' and Galliard fingered.

q.   *F-Pc* Rés 1186. See sources 6 and 7 above.
Ed. M. Maas (Madison, 1974) [selection and discussion].

r.   Private collection. Oxford MS, *c*1630, possibly in hand of Oxford
organist Edward Lowe. See xx, p. 92 (source IB).

A glance down this secondary list will show that in many cases important
manuscripts contain no more than fragmentary evidence of fingering
patterns: *GB-Lbm* Add.23623 (c), Add.29996 (e) and *F-Pc* Rés 1122 (p)
are particularly disappointing in this respect. There are, moreover, other
important books that contain no single trace of fingering, notably the
Tisdale book with bindings that show it to have been owned by Bull (*GB-
Cfm* Marlay Additions 15), two Oxford manuscripts (*GB-Och* 49 and
1113) compiled by John Lugge and William Ellis, the John Cosyn Virginal
Book (*GB-Lbm* Royal 23.1.4), and especially the most famous of all
virginalist sources, *Parthenia*, which according to Antony à Wood 'was the
prime Book for many years that was used by Novices and others that
exercised their hand on that instrument', and which was reprinted as late
as 1646, 1651 and 1655.[3]

The very earliest fingered source of English keyboard music is My Ladye
Nevells Book. Its importance, as has been suggested, lies not so much in
the quantity of fingering that it contains as in the close connection that
this source evidently had with the 'father' of English music, William Byrd.
English sources that pre-date Nevell are of course few: two early 16th-
century manuscripts in the British Library (Royal App.56 and 58), three
mid-16th-century books, again in the British Library (Add.15233, the
early layers of Add.29996, and the Mulliner Book, Add.30513)[4] and two
others, dating from the early years of Elizabeth's reign (*GB-Och* 371,
which has close connections with the Mulliner Book, and the so-called
Dublin Virginal Manuscript which is bound up with the Dallas Lute-
book).[5] None of these contains fingering, nor is there much ornamentation in any but the Dublin manuscript. Nevell, its direct successor, is a
whole 20 years younger.

As might be expected, our list of fingered compositions is dominated by the names of Byrd and Bull. Gibbons, a less prolific composer, is also well represented. It is perhaps surprising that so few other composers are included, and especially Thomas Tomkins, whose work for the most part is only known in holograph, and not in the working copies of his contemporaries.

COMPOSER/SOURCE INDEX OF FINGERED PIECES

In the following list, letters and Arabic numerals refer to sources as set out above, Roman numerals in parentheses to volume numbers of Musica Britannica; 'Maas' and 'Boston' to editions by those editors (source 8 is unfoliated, hence numbers are those given by Boston in *ML*, xxxvi (1955), 365–73); * denotes an important source;[6] + denotes a source in which there is little fingering of significance.

Anon.

Alma redemptoris mater, vers 2	(xix, p.222), c:33
Alma redemptoris mater, vers 3	c:34
Almain	5:416
Almain	A:10
Almain	A:16
Almain	7/2:2—wrongly attrib. Gibbons (*see* xx:53)
Swinnerton's Almain	(Boston:10), 8:10*v*
Birch and Green Holly	(Boston:9), 8:9*v*
The Buildings	(Boston:11), 8:12*v*
The Canaries	g:10
Captain Owen's Delight	(Boston:14), 8:15
Chacone: French Lesson	7/1: 27
Colebran: *see* Saraband	
Coranto	f: 22*v*
Coranto	8:12
French Coranto	(Maas:12), q:33
Another French Coranto	(Maas:13), q:34
An easy one for a new beginner	4:51*v*
Fantasia: *see* Orlando Gibbons	(xx:1), 7/2:44
The first Mask: *see* Mask	
The first part of the Old Year	A:7
A French Lesson	8:9*v*
French Lesson: *see* Chacone	
The Friend's Goodnight	(Boston:2), 8:2
Galliard	2:84*v*

Anon (continued)

Galliard	(Maas:85), 7/2:32
Piper's Galliard	5:442
Gaudent in coelis	7/2:26
George	(Boston:7), 8:7*v*
Gray's Inn Mask	(*see* 'The Fairest Nymph', Orlando Gibbons, xx:43)
Ground	7/1:27
Ground	7/1:11—the following piece (untitled) is on the same Ground, and is by Price
Ground	9:11
Mr. Ffaranella's Ground	7/1:33
Hyde Park	k:12
Irish Dance	A:3
The Princes Jegg	(Maas:79), 7/2:4
Jigg	8:3
Rappak's Jigg	8:4*v*
The King's Morisck	A:1
Lachrymae	2:71
A Lesson of Voluntarie: *see* Voluntary	
Mask	8:9
Mask	8:11*v*
The first Mask	4:52*v*
The Maukin	(Boston:6), 8:7
Miserere	A:9
Money is a gallant thing	(Boston:5), 8:4
Muscadin	1:xix
The Neatherland	(Maas:49), q:68
The New Rant	8:14
New Noddy	A:5
Old Noddy	8:14*v*
The Parson of the Parish	8:14*v*
Spanish Pavan	7/2:6
Prelude	5:137
Prelude	5:458
Prelude	g:2*v*
Prelude	g:3*v*
Prelude	g:4*v*
Prelude	g:5*v*
Prelude	g:8*v*
Prelude	7/1:1
Mrs. Priscilla Bunbury, her Delight	(Boston:8), 8:8

Anon (continued)

Put up thy dagger, Jimmy	(Boston:4), 8:3v
Saraband	(Boston:3), 8:2v
Tell me Susan	(Maas:7), q:23
Trenchmore	(Maas:11), q:32
Voluntary	g rev:45
Voluntary	g rev:44
Voluntary	g rev:41v
Voluntary	g rev:40
Voluntary	g rev:36v
Voluntary	g rev:34v
The White Ribbon	(Boston:1), 8:1v
Why ask you [probably by Bull]	(see xix:63 and Textual Commentary on p.227), 7/2:1

Anon without title:

1.	2:115
2.	4:52
3.	4:59v
4.	5:141
5.	5:352
6.	5:360
7.	j:307
8.	1:1
9.	m:1
10.	q:87

Bull, John

Alman	(xix:135), 6
Alman Fantazia	(xix:134), 6
Duke of Brunswick's Alman	(xix:93), 6
French Alman	(xix:95), 6
German's Alman	(xix:94), 6
Ionic Almain	(xix:110), 6
A Battle, no Battle	(xix:108), 6 +
Bonny Peg of Ramsey	(xix:75), 6 +
Bonny Sweet Robin [probably rev. Farnaby]	(xix:65), 1, 6
Bull's Goodnight	(xix:143), 6
French Coranto	(xix:105), 6
Duchess of Brunswick's Toy	(xix:97), A +
Dutch Dance	(xix:99), 6

Bull, John (continued)

English Toy	(xix:96), 6 +
Fantasia	(xiv:11), 4*
Galliard	(xix:66 B), 5, 6
Galliard	(xix:78), 6 +
Galliard	(xix:88 B), 6
Galliard	(xix:130 B) 6 +
Battle Galliard	(xix:109 B) 6 +
Chromatic Galliard	(xix:87 B), 6 +
Fantastic Galliard	(xix:86 B), 1, 5
Lady Lucy's Galliard	(xix:72), 6
Lord Hunsdon's Galliard	(xix:133), 6
Lord Lumley's Galliard	(xix:129 B) 6
Melancholy Galliard	(xix:67 B), 6
Regina Galliard	(xix:132 B), 6
Regina Galliard	(xix:132 C), 6
Trumpet Galliard	(xix:128 B), 6 +
Vaulting Galliard	(xix:90), 1, 4, 6
Go from my window	(xix:123), 7
Goodnight: *see* Bull's Goodnight	
Ground	(xix:102 A), g +
Ground	(xix:102 B), g +
In nomine	(xiv:24), 6, p
Irish Toy	(xix:112), 6 +
The King's Hunt	(xix:125), 6
Miserere	(xiv:34), 7, o
My Jewel	(xix:141), 6 +
My Self	(xix:138), 6
Pavan	(xix:66 A), 5, 6 +
Pavan	(xix:88 A), 6
Pavan	(xix:130 A), 6
Battle Pavan	(xix:109 A), 6 +
Fantastic Pavan	(xix:86 A), 1*, 6*
Lord Lumley's Pavan	(xix:129 A), 6
Quadran Pavan	(xix:127 B), 5*, 6*
Quadran Pavan	(xix:127 C), 6
Prelude	(xix:117), 3*
Prelude	(xix:121), 3*, b*, g*
Salvator mundi	(xiv:37), 6 +
Salvator mundi	(xiv:38), 3 +
Walsingham	(xix:85), 6
What care you	(xix:116), 6 +
Why ask you: *see* Anon.	

Byrd, William

Alman	(xxviii:89), 5 +
Mounsiers Alman	(xxviii:87), 9 +
Mounsiers Alman	(xxviii:88), 1, 2, 5 +
The Barley Break	(xxviii:92), 10 +
The Battle: March before the Battle, or the Earl of Oxford's March	(xxviii:93), 10
The Battle: The Irish March	(xxviii:94), 10 +
The Battle: The Soldiers Summons	(xxviii:94), 10 +
The Battle: The Trumpets	(xxviii:94), 10 +
The Battle: The Galliard for the Victory	(xxviii:95), 10 +
The Carman's Whistle	(xxvii:36), 1, 5, 9, 10, f*
First French Coranto	(xxvii:21 A), 5 +
Second French Coranto	(xxvii:21 B), 5 +
Third French Coranto	(xxvii:21 C), 5 +
The Earl of Oxford's March: *see* The Battle	
Fantasia	(xxvii:13), 1 +
Fantasia	(xxvii:25), 10
Fantasia	(xxviii:63), 1 +
Fortune	(xxvii:6), 5, 9*
Galliard	(xxvii:5 B), 5 +
Galliard	(xxvii:33 B), 5 +
Galliard	(xxviii:55), 5 +
Galliard	(xxviii:71 B), 5 +
Galliard	(xxviii:73 B), 2 +
Galliard	(xxviii:77), 5 +
Galliard Jig	(xxvii:18), 10 +
Passamezzo Galliard	(xxvii:2 B), 5, 10
Quadran Galliard	(xxviii:70 B), A 5
Galliard, Sir William Petre	(xxvii:3 B), 10 +
The Ghost	(xxvii:78), 9
Go from my window	(xxviii:79), 5 +
Ground	(xxvii:9), 5 +
Ground	(xxvii:43), 5 +
Ground	(xxviii:86), 5
Hugh Aston's Ground	(xxvii:20), 5
My Lady Nevell's Ground	(xxviii:57), 10
Tregian's Ground: *see* Hugh Aston's Ground	
Hornpipe	(xxvii:39), 5
The Irish March: *see* The Battle	
Kapasse: *see* Qui Passe	

Byrd, William (continued)

Lavolta	(xxviii:91), 5 +
Pavan	(xxvii:17), 10 +
Pavan	(xxvii:30 A), 2 +
Pavan	(xxvii:33 A), 5
Pavan	(xxviii:71 A), 2, 5, 10
Pavan	(xxviii:73 A), 2 +
Pavan, Johnson's Delight	(xxvii:5 A), 5 +
Lachrymae Pavan	(xxviii:54), 5
Passamezzo Pavan	(xxvii:2 A), 1, 5, 10 +
Quadran Pavan	(xxviii:70 A), 5
Pavan, Sir William Petre	(xxvii:3 A), 5, 10
Prelude	(xxvii:24), 1 +
Prelude	(xxviii:96), 5: Anon? +
Qui Passe, for My Lady Nevell	(xxvii:19), 5, 10*
Rowland	(xxvii:7), 5
Salvator mundi	(xxviii:68), 2
The Trumpets: *see* The Battle	
Voluntarie, for My Lady Nevell	(xxviii:61), 10 +
Walsingham	(xxvii:8), 5
The woods so wild	(xxviii:85), 2, 5, 10

Coprario, John

The Lord's Masque	(A:2)

Farnaby, Giles

Bonny, Sweet Robin	(xxiv:35)—also attrib. Bull: *see* Bull
Daphne	(xxiv:36), 1 +
The King's Hunt	(xxiv:49), 1
Tower Hill	(xxiv:26), 8

Farnaby, Giles and Richard

Meridian Alman	(xxiv:24)—also attrib. Bull (*see* Bull, Alman Fantazia)

Gibbons, Orlando

Alman ['Ayre' in h]	(xx:35), h +
Alman, The King's Jewel	(xx:36), 4
Fantasia	(xx:5), 4
The Fairest Nymph	(xx:43), 8
Plainsong Fantasia	(xx:48), also attrib. Bull, 4
Galliard	(xx:24), 4*

Gibbons, Orlando (continued)

Galliard	(xx:25), a
The Italian Ground	(xx:27), 4
Mask, Welcome Home	(xx:42), 8*
Prelude	(xx:1), 7
Prelude	(xx:2), 3, 7, j*
Whoop, do me no harm good man	(xx:31), 7, 8*
The woods so wild	(xx:29), 4*

Hooper, Edmund

Almain	A +

Jewett, R.

Almon	(Boston: 13), 8:13 +
Churton's Farewell	(Boston: 12), 8:13 +
Untitled piece	8:8*v* +

Kiderminster, El

Prelude	1

Lever

Coranto	(Maas:45), q:65*v* +

Loosemore, [Henry]

Coranto	(Maas:21), q:38 +

Morley, Thomas

Go from my window: also attrib. John Mundy	1 +

Mundy, John

Fantasia	1, no.2 +
Fantasia: Fair Weather	1, no.3 +

Price

Untitled—a Ground	7/1:12

Tallis, Thomas

Felix namque	ed. D. Stevens (London, 1953, no.9), 5*

Tomkins, John

John come kiss me now	e +

Tomkins, Thomas

Bits or morcels	(v:73), p
For Edward	(unpublished), i
Galliard	(v:44), p
In nomine	(v:6), p
Offertory	(v:21), i +
Pavan	(v:43), p
Piece of a Prelude	(v:2), p
Prelude	(v:3), p
Robin Hood	(v:63), 5
Ut, mi, re	(v:38), i
Ut, re, mi, fa	(v:35), i, p

Techniques

These extant fingerings may be most conveniently considered under the three main headings: techniques, interpretation and ornamentation. Scalic figurations are of fundamental importance in English virginal music, and the manner in which these were played is best observed in the various fingered preludes that have survived. These, for the most part, take the form of finger-warming exercises or elementary teaching pieces, and it is no accident that so many of them are profusely fingered. Bull's Prelude (xix:121) and Gibbons's second Prelude (xx:2) are of special interest, for each is fingered in a number of separate (and apparently independent) sources. All of them conform to the English norm, the right hand playing upward scales with 343434 . . .[7] and downward ones with 323232 . . ., the left hand going upwards with 121212 . . . (less commonly 323232 . . .) and downwards with 343434. . . . The thumb and third fingers were considered to be the relatively strong fingers, and were placed wherever possible (that is to say, almost invariably) on the comparatively strong beats. There is a parallel here with the principle of the down-bow that was observed by baroque string players, namely that the strongest physical actions should occur on the strongest accented beats. By far the most common types of keyboard fingering are those reminding the player that he must synchronise fingers and accents in this way.

The paired fingering system now seems strange to us, since we use black notes as freely as white notes, and since the distance between the edge of the black note and the edge of the white note has been so greatly extended. Some scholars have even argued that paired fingerings resulted in paired phrasings and rhythmic inequalities.[8] Yet paired fingerings are not quite as odd as they might seem when comparatively few black notes are called for. (I was reminded of this when my four-year old son started playing downward scales with his right hand using 323232 . . . ., quite evenly!)

The marked exceptions to this general rule are extraordinarily few. There are no more than a couple of dozen, all told, and nearly all are explicable within the broader context of what was to come. They either ensure the articulation of a note, or avoid a possibly awkward sequence of fingers, or achieve a legato phrasing, or place a strong finger on an ornamented note, or prepare for the 'correct' fingers in a subsequent passage (as in Byrd's Passamezzo Pavan (xxvii:2a, 45–6)), or simply occur because the passage in question can be played 'unconventionally' with less effort: see notably Byrd's 'Ground' (xxviii:86, 69), his 'Ghost' (Matchett:5, 43), his 'Hugh Aston's Ground' (xxvii:20, 5) and his Pavan (xxvii:30A, 28–30). In the case of his 'Ghost' (ex.1), by placing 2 on g', rather than the 'correct' 3, the subsequent b', $c\sharp''$, d'' may be taken with 2, 3, 4, the third being then placed for the ornamented $c\sharp''$. With the one exception of Bull's 'Fantastic Galliard' all the odd fingerings relate to pieces by Byrd.

Ex. 1

Although paired fingerings were the basis of conjunct passage work (even Bach made his son Wilhelm Friedemann practise paired scales, although by that time his own technique had progressed far beyond this) they were certainly not the only fingerings that were then used, a fact that has by no means received sufficient emphasis. The left hand was in this respect treated with greater freedom than the right. Upward pairs of 121212 . . . were commonly substituted for the more correct 323232 . . ., and both the thumb and the little finger were used with considerable freedom, a tendency that arose perhaps out of the left-hand function of chordal accompaniment for which both thumb and little finger were often required. The most common use of 1 and 5 was at the top or bottom of a scale passage, as in Bull's 'Go from my window' (xix:123, 30–31):

Ex. 2

Whether or not a player used 1 and 5 in this way was entirely a matter of choice, as is shown in the variant fingering from Byrd's 'Fortune' (xxvii:6, 23–4):

Ex. 3

In placing right hand 2 on the last *d‴* of the first bar Matchett implied the use of 3, 4, and 5 on the first note of the next bar. Forster on the other hand preferred to avoid the stretch from *g′* to *d‴* in the right hand, and 'incorrectly' placed 3 on *d‴*; *e″*, *f″* and *g″* are then played by 4,3,4.

Thumbs and little fingers are most commonly used in left-hand scales, such as is the case in ex.4, from 'My Lady Nevell's Ground' (xxviii:57, 113–4), and those in which after the 5 to 1 sequence has been completed the scale continues upwards with 121212 . . .

Ex. 4

Similar situations exist also in xxvii:5a, 79 and in Tallis's 'Felix namque', Fitzwilliam Virginal Book, cx, 16–17, 20–21 *et passim*, fingering from source 5. In such a case as xix:88a, 62:

Ex. 5

the 1 obviously implies a downward run to 5: and as with other similar examples, the strong fingers are always correctly placed on strong accents, since the firmest control is needed at such speeds.

Quite a few fingerings do seem to have been arrived at for no other reason than the avoidance of a thumb or a little finger, as in bb.29–30 of

Byrd's 'Galliard for the Victory' (xxviii:95), in which thumbs would be
more correct than second fingers:

Ex. 6

On closer analysis, however, most of these arise from other causes, and
principally from the need to place a strong finger on a strong beat. By far
the most common situation involves a large leap, often of an octave or
more, in which the modern player would naturally use his maximum
stretch, from 5 to 1. Tomkins's 'Ut, mi, re', (v:38, 1–3) provides one of
many such instances:

Ex. 7

Other similar leaps are to be found in xx:29, 40, v:63, 5 & 139, xx:29, 35,
xxviii:57, 64 and xxviii:57, 100. These show beyond doubt that disjunct
movements were well articulated. It would be wrong to argue, however,
that the use of 5 to 1 to cover an octave leap is an indication of legato:
a comparison of b.38 and b.40 of xx:29, Gibbons's 'The woods so wild':

Ex. 8

shows that the 2 is used in b.40 to ensure a strong 3 on the adjacent
(stepwise) note. A pronounced articulation is of course unavoidable in
b.40: by analogy, the articulation should be similarly pronounced in b.38.
Some further examples that illustrate methods of disjunct fingering include xx:2, 5 & 22, xiv:34, 35, 40, 55 & 71, xix:85, 63 & 71, xxviii:95, 41
and xxvii:33a, 89.

Far from the thumb being systematically avoided, it is at times used in a surprisingly modern manner, being placed under the palm of the hand, or the fingers being passed over it. The commonest situation of the kind involves a change of direction in a left-hand upward scale, as in b.26 of Gibbons's Prelude (xx:2, 25–6) (see ex.9): this is of course merely a form of the left-hand 121212 . . . upward fingering:

Ex. 9

Much less common is the introduction of a thumb into a run, as in b.26 of xix:132c, Bull's 'Regina Galliard':

Ex. 10

and into more complex figurations such as those of xix:125, 68, Bull's 'The King's Hunt':

Ex. 11

Quite a few leaps are taken, too, by placing the thumb under the second finger, to align a strong finger with a strong note, as in xix:125, 73:

Ex. 12

Other cases are xxviii:73a, 13 & 26, xix:66a, 17, xiv:34, 41, xix:127c, 57–8 and xix:85, 63–4. The placing of fingers over thumbs is rather less common, and all examples that have been noted occur in the left hand, very much in the manner of xix:143, 32:

Ex. 13

Far from thumbs being disallowed they are placed, here and there, on black notes, especially in the left hand, as in b.27 of v:38, Tomkins's 'Ut, mi, re':

Ex. 14

The thumb is even used as a changing finger on a repeated note, as for instance in the opening imitative point of xiv:11, 7, Bull's 'Fantasia':

Ex. 15

The comparatively few right-hand black-note thumbs include b.11 of Bull's 'Irish Toy' (xix:112, 11), his 'Miserere' (xiv:34, 30 & 46–7) and Byrd's 'My Lady Nevell's Ground' (xxviii:57, 102–3).

The thumbs-under technique was also applied to passages in two or more parts, a point which deserves to be stressed, in view of François Couperin's well-known statement that passages of consecutive 3rds were before his day often played as $\frac{4}{2}$, $\frac{4}{2}$, $\frac{4}{2}$. Ex.16 shows how Miss Priscilla Bunbury was taught to play 3rds: ex.16*a* comes from the anonymous 'Swinnerton's Alman' (Boston:10, 17–18), ex.16*b* from the anonymous 'The Buildings' (Boston:11, 11–12):

Ex. 16a

Ex. 16b

The implications of the isolated fingering shown in ex.17, from Byrd's 'Walsingham' variations (xxvii:8, 105 6), are that the passage should be played with a sequence of left-hand $\frac{1}{3}$, $\frac{2}{4}$ fingers, and that at the beginning of b.106 all five fingers should be brought into play:

Ex. 17

Presumably, too, much the same has to be attempted in b.31 of Gibbons's 'The woods so wild' (xx:29), though here the upper fingers of the paired notes are not given. Where, however, the parts move slowly enough, and the movement is staggered, as in Gibbons's Prelude (xx:5, 10–12), one finger was transferred from note to note. The fingerings in sources 7 and o of Bull's first 'Miserere' (xiv:34) are a mine of information on all aspects of technique (sadly, the editors chose not to include them in xiv). Thumbs-under and fingers-over situations abound, as for instance in bb.11–13 (ex.18). Parallel situations arise in xxviii:54, 30 and xix:21, line 4, bb.5–6.

Ex. 18

The extant fingerings suggest that players generally strove to maintain a natural hand position, with adjacent fingers lying over adjacent notes of the keyboard and a minimum of hand extension and contraction. The most striking exceptions are to be found in Bull's 'Miserere' (xiv:34), which seems to have had the function of a Chopin study. Here we find thumb and third finger in the left-hand spanning an octave (b.65, first beat), and right-hand 3 and 5 covering the melodic interval of a 6th in a swiftly moving semiquaver passage (b.57). Less extreme hand extensions are more commonly found, and especially the one in which the interval of a 3rd is taken by adjacent fingers (v:38, 30, xix:132b, 14–15, xiv:34, 4, 35 *et passim*, xxviii:57, 69 and xxviii:89, 16). Situations involving hand contraction are few: one or two leaps of a 3rd are fingered 5–2, and 1–4, and here and there conjunct movement is taken by 3–5 and 2–4 as, for instance, in xiv:34, 69:

Ex. 19

Fingering as Interpretation

So far we have been dealing primarily with technical matters, although even here the boundaries between technique and interpretation overlap. In the following section we shall be examining the extent to which technique, in the form of fingering, offers unequivocal evidence of interpretation.

The articulation of leaps and repeated notes has already been touched upon. There is no conceivable way in which such a figuration as that on the first beat of b.37 of Bull's 'Regina Galliard' (xix:132c, 37–8) (ex.20*a*) could be made legato: by analogy the unfingered leaps that develop the same pattern should also be well articulated:

Ex. 20a

Similarly, the phrasing patterns that unavoidably result from the fingerings of b.51 (beat 4) and b.52 (beat 1) must be consistently applied to that figuration in its development elsewhere (xix:86a, 51–2) (ex.20*b*).

Ex. 20b

There are well over a dozen fingerings of repeated notes, all calling for finger change on each repetition, of which easily the most intricate and challenging one is in xiv:24, 52–3 of the Bull 'In nomine':

Ex. 21

Bull's 'Miserere' (xiv:34), that mine of information, also yields much of interest, notably in the closing 15 bars in which the motif in b.64 is developed extensively:

Ex. 22

Similar patterns occur in xx:29, 21, xix:75, 14, xxvii:6, 33–4, xxvii:33a, 89–91 & 95–6, xxvii:19, 89 & 93, xxviii:77, 21 and xiv:11, 7. In some half a dozen cases, too, fingerings indicate the phrasing of imitative motives, in which there are repeated notes. The pattern set at the beginning of Byrd's 'Carman's Whistle', (Matchett:3,1) (ex.23), for instance, is maintained throughout the variations. Comparable cases occur in xxviii:86, 1, xxviii:79, 1, xxvii:20, 1 and in Boston:1,1. Only a handful of fingerings call for the repetition of a note by the same finger, and all are dictated by the need to place a strong finger on the following (strong) note (xiv:11, 16 and xx:36, 45).[9]

Ex. 23

Closely allied to the problem of repetition is the situation in which a swiftly moving line passes through a sustained note. Two unequivocal fingerings suggest that the sustained note should be repeated: the first is from Gibbons's 'The woods so wild' (xx:29, 44), the second (ex.24) from Bull's 'The King's Hunt' (xix:125, 70):

Ex. 24

In complex textures that involve the coverage of two or more notes simultaneously in one hand, long notes do often seem to have been shortened somewhat. The premature release, for instance, of the left-hand semibreve in xix:88b, 14 is imperative:

Ex. 25

Other impossible stretches include xix:127b, 47, xix:85, 208, xxvii:3, 122 and Matchett:3, 25. Many shorter notes, too, have to be cut, such as those in b.6 and b.72 of Bull's 'Fantastic Pavan' (xix:86a). A particularly common pattern, to be found in almost every keyboard composition of the time, is represented by ex.26, bb.9–10 from Matchett:5, Byrd's 'Ghost':

Ex. 26

The fingering is Matchett's: the notation of the left-hand minims at the beginning of b.10 is in this case an instruction to sustain the notes as long as possible (and even perhaps to linger on the first beat).

The shortening of ties, too, may well have been a common practice. This fingered passage (ex.27a) from Tallis's second 'Felix namque', for instance, occurs unfingered in another source (ex.27b) in a rather different form (Fitzwilliam Virginal Book: cx, 5th and 6th bars from the end):

Ex. 27a

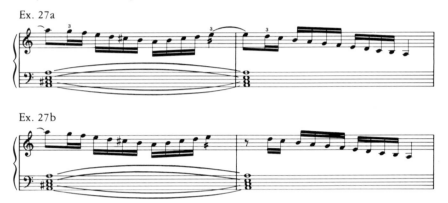

Ex. 27b

Similarly, many syncopated notes have articulated fingerings, for example those in Bull's 'Miserere' (xiv:34, 20).

Further evidence of articulation is provided by some dozen or so passages in which successive and adjacent notes are played by the same finger. These stem for the most part from the rule of the strong finger, as in this figuration from xx:24, 57, which might be found in almost any piece of virginals music. Some light articulation is suggested by the transfer of right-hand 3 from c' to d'.

Ex. 28

The articulation occurs equally in the downward direction, as in xx:24, 65. In swiftly moving passages such as that in ex.29 the separation between notes is inevitably more marked, and, as might be expected, the transfer of a finger is in nearly every case from a weaker to a stronger note (xx:43, 3–4):

Ex. 29

Similar cases are found in xx:36, 23, xx:29, 69, v:63, 47, xx:24, 65 and xix:102b, 4. In one or two places disjunct notes are played by the same finger. In such a stock situation as ex.30, for instance, Priscilla Bunbury was not expected to produce a legato left hand (Boston:10, 6–7):

Ex. 30

Whereas however the solution here was dictated as much by technical convenience as interpretative intention, there can be no doubt that the fingering in b.1 of ex.31 was wholly motivated by the desire to give the imitative entry the maximum emphasis (xiv:11, 1–4):

Ex. 31

There are many instances, too, other than those involving the transfer of a finger from note to note, that inevitably result in heavy articulation. If the left-hand fingerings at the end of b.46 of Gibbons's 'The woods so wild' are indicative of general practice, the player should lighten the third beat of triplet rhythms such as those in xx:29, 44:

Ex. 32

As has already been mentioned, the resultant articulation almost always moves from a weaker to a stronger beat. Possibly the most common, and the most extreme, situation in which this occurs is at an emphatic cadence point. To reach the final chord in ex.33 a rapid change of hand position is needed, and Miss Bunbury's teacher, for one, made no attempt to mitigate the gap that inevitably must have preceded it (Boston 10:7–8):

Ex. 33

Comparable situations occur in xxviii:57, 73, A:4, 19–20, Boston:10, 21, xiv:34, 2–3 & 15–16, xix:90, 28–end (fingers in sources 1 and 4 not printed), xix:123, 17, xxvii:5b, 21, xix:85, 120, Matchett:5, 7, Boston:1, 1, Boston:9, 9 and Boston:11, 10. Nothing, however, quite reaches the eccentricity of Tregian's fingering of Kiderminster's Prelude (Fitzwilliam Virginal Book; xxiii:17–19):

Ex. 34

Whilst most of the fingerings imply an articulated rather than a legato style of performance there are a dozen or so fingerings that seem to have been selected to ensure a continuous line. Throughout the whole of Bull's 64-bar 'Chromatic Galliard' for instance there is but a single finger (xix:87b, 17). In this case it is obviously an indication of departure from a norm, in which the first note, being strong and also ornamented (see below) would automatically have been taken by right-hand 3 as also the second note:

Ex. 35

Was the aim here, perhaps, to avoid a break between *b'* and *a'* ? Such cases arise also in xxvii:2a, 54–5, and xxvii:3a, 25–7 & 59). To these possible indications of legato may be added those, mentioned above in the discussion of technique, in which thumbs are passed under fingers, and fingers over thumbs.

Ornaments and Fingerings

A study of fingerings as they relate to ornaments, while producing no hard and fast conclusions, does something at least to clarify the possible interpretations of single- and double-stroke signs. Unfortunately there are practically no source parallels where a passage ornamented in one is fully written out in another. The kind of alternative found, for instance, in two independent sources of Byrd's 'Pavan' (xxvii:30a, 10) comes closest to this:

Ex. 36

It is plain enough however that the written-out ornament here could not be applied to the right-hand *g'* of the following bar, and that the version marked 'Wr' (from source 2 in the list above) is an alternative to, and not a realisation of the ornamental sign. A similar case is xxvii:24, 20. Some hint as to the fingers that were preferred in the performance of ornaments is to be got from a number of fingered passages that approximate closely to written-out trills and turns, as in Byrd's 'Ground' (xxviii:86, 45160):

Ex. 37

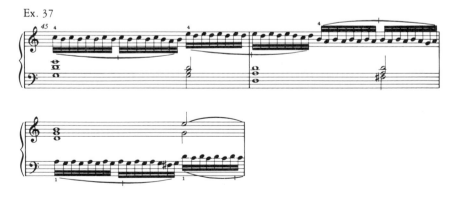

This provides the most extensive illustration of its kind, continuing very much as it begins in ex.37. Comparable illustrations occur in xx:31, 3, xix:121, line 5, b.1, and v:3, 1. These show that Elizabethan fourth and little fingers were certainly agile enough to play quite quickly.

As is well known, only one source translates ornaments into exact notation: this is *GB-Lbm* Add.31403, the first 30 folios of which—it has been suggested (xiv:p.159)—may be in the hand of the Bristol musician Elway Bevin who was organist of the cathedral there from 1585 to 1638 and Gentleman Extraordinary of the Chapel Royal. Certain pieces known to be by Elway are however ascribed in the source to 'Edward', Elway's third son (*b* 15 May 1595).[10] The likelihood that the source is at all closely connected with the Bevins is therefore remote. The table of ornaments is found amongst the opening Preludes, which may have been copied out during the 1620s (see Plate XII). There are good reasons, however, for arguing a much later date (in addition to the British Library dating of the paper at 'c.1700'), not least being the fact that two of the four ornaments in the table are to be found in no Elizabethan or early Jacobean source of keyboard music. The two in question—the second and third—are indeed of a pattern not far removed from those that were in use during the early Restoration period. Be this as it may, their relevance to earlier conventions has yet to be established. For this reason, the interpretation of the first and fourth ornaments, which are found in such profusion in late 16th- and early 17th-century sources, must be treated with considerable caution. By far the more common of the two is the double-stroke ornament; here it is fingered 3 and played as a slow trill with a turn at the end. The snag, of course, is that it is rarely found in such leisured surroundings: there is no time for lingering in such a typical situation as ex.38*a* (Matchett:5, 21). Nor would Edward Bevin's cadential turn be quite right in less hectic situations, such as ex.38*b* from Bull's 'Miserere' (xiv:34, final bar):

Ex. 38a   Ex. 38b

Even so, it is perhaps worth noting that Bevin fingers the ornamented note 3, that this finger is on balance more commonly used than any other for the double stroke (see below), and that the ornament is attacked from the upper note, the trill being started by the fourth finger.

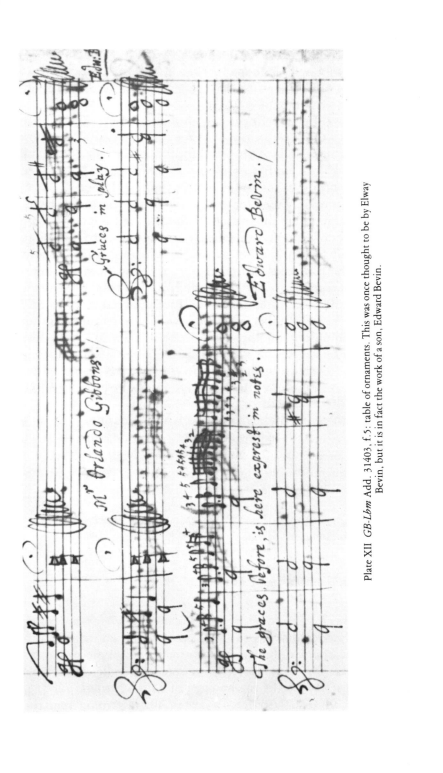

Plate XII *GB-Lbm* Add. 31403, f. 5: table of ornaments. This was once thought to be by Elway Bevin, but it is in fact the work of a son, Edward Bevin.

The rarer single-stroke ornament is approached, according to Bevin, from the 3rd below in a deliberate manner: in his example this results in quite a lengthy open 5th on the first beat. The fingering is 5, and it applies as before, to the written note.

To what extent are Bevin's fingerings corroborated by Elizabethan fingerings? The single-stroke figure occurs in the fingered examples almost invariably at the top of a phrase. Out of a recorded total of 33 right-hand fingered ornaments of this kind, 13 give the fourth finger, 17 the fifth, and only three the third. Not one single-stroke figure is fingered 1 or 2, although 2 is quite commonly used for the double stroke. In the left hand, six single-stroke ornaments are fingered 1, 13 are fingered 2, and four are fingered 3. Again, not one single-stroke figure is fingered 4 or 5, although 4 is occasionally used for the double stroke. In all cases, therefore, the single stroke could be played as Bevin suggests, starting from the lower 3rd, though there is rarely time for the measured dotted quaver-semiquaver figure. The more or less equal balance between right-hand 4 and 5 is not without interest: either fingering would have had its snags for the performer (assuming our interpretation to be correct); 5 meant that the ornament could be started on a strong finger, i.e. 3—appropriately enough since all the fingered ornaments begin on relatively strong notes. On the other hand 5 was less used than 2, 3, or 4, all of which would be brought into play with the fingering 4.

There yet remain three imponderables, all relating to harmony. Bevin's example conveniently enough begins on a harmonic note, though as we have seen it results in a bare 5th. Many of the single-stroke situations however necessitate a start on a non-harmonic note, and produce a marked harmonic scrunch, as does that in xix: 130a, 14:

Ex. 39

But this may have been considered a virtue at a time when, as Morley pointed out, the false relation was so much in fashion! The second imponderable relates to the simultaneous performance of single-stroke ornaments in two parts. The one fingered example of parallel ornaments that has so far been noted occurs in the copy of Bull's Fantasia (xiv:11, 25–7) in *GB-Lbm* Add.36661 (source 4): see ex.40. Assuming that the

Ex. 40

right- and left-hand ornaments were played at the same speed, parallel 6ths would result between the last notes of b.25 and the first notes of b.26. This would fit well with the harmonic context and be perfectly acceptable. A spot check of the simultaneous single-stroke ornaments in Gibbons's keyboard music, however, reveals quite a number that would result in parallel octaves, 4ths and 5ths: see for instance xx:10, 55, xx:30, 43, xx:40, 4 and xx:41, 7. The third imponderable is perhaps the least explicable of the three. It concerns a number of three-note chords in which the middle note has a single stroke through it, and which is quite unplayable as an upward 3rd: one such example comes from the Galliard (by Tomkins, Cosyn or Gibbons) printed in xx:50, 49. Can it perhaps be that the upward 3rd was modified where necessary to a one-note ornament either below or above the written note?

Ex. 41

Attempts to crack the double-stroke code produce even more difficulties. It may be well to begin by reminding ourselves that on occasions at least the ornament can have been of no great complexity (xix:94, 30):

Ex. 42

Were the right-hand part of this passage to consist only of the lower line, second finger on c'' would be an instruction to place the third finger on the ornamented b' following it. It is doubtful whether such can have been intended in b.30 as it stands, for this would leave the ornamented d'' and *b'* to be played by the fifth and third finger, a downward mordent being the only practicable ornament. There is no reason to suppose, either, that an early 17th-century performer would have found the passage any easier to play than we would today. An alternative solution would be to place third finger and thumb on the ornamented *d''* and *b'*, treating the ornament as an upward mordent. This would certainly be more comfortable. Other similar examples that well repay study are to be found in xix:133, 28, xix:138, 46, xxvii:19, 21, xix:66a, 58 and xx:24, 27 (the fingering in source 4).

It does seem, nonetheless, that the double-stroke ornament was played beneath the written note, under certain circumstances. There is a handful of such ornaments fingered right-hand 5, and left-hand 1, and all must be played under the note, if, that is, Bevin's fingering principles are applicable here. There are incidentally no left-hand fifth fingers or right-hand thumbs on the double stroke—fingerings that would demand an upward ornament (see xx:24, 6–7 in source 4, xx:31, 24, xx:36, 9, 34 & 45, xix:97, 4, xix:102b, 6, xix:138, 2 & 9, xix:117, 5, xxvii:19, 59 and xx-vii:2a, 60 (fingering in *GB-Lbm* Royal 24.d.3 (source 5)).

Whilst the most commonly used fingers for the double-stroke ornament are right-hand 2 and 3 (there being comparatively few left-hand ornaments, and still fewer that are fingered) a comparison of sources—and thus to a large extent of composers—reveals significant variations in practice. There are no fewer than 100 fingered double-stroke ornaments in the source-6 versions (*F-Pc* Rés 1185) of Bull's music: the source is a particularly important one, and at one time its earlier leaves were thought to be in Bull's hand (xix:p.159). Only one in ten of these is fingered with 3; right-hand 4 and 5 are used no more than half a dozen times, and the majority are fingered 2. *GB-Lbm* Royal 24.d.3 (source 5), on the other hand, is the most liberally fingered of the major sources of Byrd's music. Here the proportions are very different. Of a total of just under 100 right-hand double-stroke fingerings in Byrd's music just over 50% are 3, the remainder being 2, apart that is from a few instances of 4 and one of 5. These proportions are reflected in My Lady Nevells Book, a source that was particularly close to the composer (the figures being a dozen or so right-hand 3 and an equal number of right-hand 2). Matchett's Byrd fingerings, on the other hand, give substantially more right-hand cases of 3 than 2, a difference that arises at least in part from Matchett's tendency to put down a great deal of 'normal' fingering, whereas in source 5 there was a more pronounced tendency to note only important departures from the norm. It would be rash therefore to attempt conclusions from such figures until a thorough survey has been undertaken of each source and composer. At least we can say that right-hand 2 and 3 predominate, that they relate to notes that range in duration from a semiquaver to a semibreve, that they cannot therefore conform to one set pattern (such as that suggested by Bevin) and that the most likely interpretations are, for long notes an extended mordent or trill, and for shorter notes a simple mordent, upper or lower. It may well be too, as Bevin suggests, that ornaments should be started on the ornamental note whenever the context allows; and it could be, moreover, that the character of the ornament depended on whether it was placed above or below the note head, as Thurston Dart suggested in his preface to *Parthenia* (source A).

NOTES TO CHAPTER 9

1.   'New Sources of Virginal Music', *ML*, xxxv (1954), 93–106.

2.   Benjamin Cosyn: *Three Voluntaries for Organ,* ed. J. Steele (London, 1959); John Lugge: *Three Voluntaries for Double Organ*, and *Two Toys and a Jigg*, eds. Susi Jeans and J. Steele (London, 1959, 1958); Thomas Morley: *Keyboard Works*, ed. T. Dart (London, 1959); Thomas Tallis: *Complete Keyboard Works*, ed. D. Stevens (London, 1953); William Tisdall: *Complete Keyboard Works*, ed. H. Ferguson (London, 1958, 2/1970); for Bunbury and Matchett, see sources 8 & 9 in the list of sources; for *Parthenia In-Violata*, see source A.

3.   Ed. T. Dart (London, 1960).

4.   For further discussion of these sources see J. Caldwell, ed.: *Early Tudor Organ Music I*, EECM, vi (London, 1966) and D. Stevens, ed.: *The Mulliner Book: a Commentary* (London, 1952).

5.   John Ward, ed.: *The Dublin Virginal Manuscript*, Wellesley Edition, iii (Wellesley College, 1954).

6.   A practical anthology of the most instructively fingered pieces, ed. P. G. Le Huray, is published as a companion to this article: *The Fingering of Virginal Music* (Stainer & Bell, 1981).

7.   The system of reference used throughout this essay is thumb = 1, little finger = 5, for both left and right hands.

8.   The literature is extensive: see F. Neumann: 'The French Inégales, Quantz, and Bach' in *JAMS*, xviii (1965), 313. *Anne Cromwell, A Manuscript Music Book* (facs.ed.1900); ed. H. Ferguson, as *Anne Cromwell's Virginal Book, Parthenia*, ed. T. Dart (Stainer & Bell, 1960), *Tisdale's Virginal Book*, ed. Alan Brown (Stainer & Bell, 1966), p.18.

9.   There is perhaps a danger of overstressing the articulating function of alternating fingers. C. P. E. Bach remarked that alternation was better than repeated fingers, since repeated fingers 'cause an excessive detaching of the notes', *Essay on the True Art of Playing Keyboard Instruments*, trans. W. J. Mitchell (London, 1949), p.60.

10.   J. G. Hooper: *The Life and Work of Elway Bevin* (Bristol, 1971), 3.

10

The Musical Aims of J. S. Bach's
Clavierübung III

Peter Williams

Third Part of the Keyboard Practice consisting of various Preludes on the Catechism and other Hymns for the Organ. Prepared for Music Lovers and particularly for Connoisseurs of such Work, towards the Recreation of the Spirit, by Johann Sebastian Bach, Royal Polish and Electoral Saxon Court Composer, Capellmeister and Director of the *chori musici*, Leipzig. Published by the Author [Michaelmas? 1739][1]

Even including the *Orgelbüchlein*, there is no volume of organ music by J. S. Bach or any other composer to have been so often written about, either as a collection *in toto* or as several groups of pieces. No doubt this reflects the great feeling of respect-rather-than-affection which the volume commonly inspires; organists may well feel that the patent mastery of piece after piece not only is forbidding in itself but also makes it peculiarly difficult to grasp what the composer is doing. That he is assumed to be 'doing' something in the collection is clear from the recent publications that survey its organization or symmetry,[2] various aspects of its styles,[3] its theology,[4] its individual 'symbolisms'[5] and collective 'meanings',[6] the implications of the Catechism itself[7] and so on.

At least certain more prosaic aspects of the volume have recently become clearer. It is now certain that the first of the two engravers working on the volume simply copied the composer's handwriting and cannot be shown to have been J. S. Bach himself.[8] The volume seems to have appeared around Michaelmas 1739 (see *Dokumente*, ii, p.335)[9] in a year with no less than three Reformation festivals in Leipzig itself.[10] Also, apart from what may possibly be an earlier version of the trio on 'Allein Gott' BWV676a, all the pieces appear to have been specially composed for the publication. Despite a few pointers, the volume is unique and no approach to it can be fairly rejected, for its complexity is undeniable and its several layers of meaning or significance can only gradually be unfolded. Each approach to it will yield a vital clue. Thus although it may not arouse agreement amongst Bach scholars that the celebrated Four Duets

BWV802–5 in some way represent four prayers, or the Elements, or the Gospels, or the Church Fathers—each of which has been suggested—it is certainly true that with the Catechism chorales Bach is offering the third of the great gifts that the early reformers also claimed to offer, and that were most suitably commemorated in the year 1739. These gifts were the Bible, the hymnbook and the Catechism. In the Passions and elsewhere Bach had already offered many major settings of biblical texts; he had recently collaborated on a hymnbook (Schemelli, 1736); and with *Clavierübung III* he was now supplying the Catechism in musical terms. There is thus a clear background for a theological interpretation.

Yet the music itself may become only obscurer as a result of such reasoning, for each chorale has a technical and conceptual difficulty not made any easier by such backgrounds, however well drawn. The very first major reference to the volume seems to express respect rather than affection (Lorenz Mizler, review of 1740, in *Dokumente*, ii, p.387):

> The author has given here new proof that in this kind of composition he excels many others in experience and fortune. No one will improve on him in this sphere and indeed very few will be able to imitate him. This work is a powerful argument against those who have ventured to criticise the music of the Court Composer.[11]

Since the last remark is almost certainly aimed at J. A. Scheibe, it is probably fair to conjecture that Scheibe found little in the new volume to make him change his opinion (1737, in *Dokumente*, ii.p.286) that:

> This great man would be the admiration of whole nations . . . if he did not through a stifling and confused essence deprive his pieces of what is natural, and obscure their beauty through all too great an art . . . All voices must work with each other and with equal difficulty.[12]

Scheibe's characteristic distinction between Nature and Art is weighted and was very likely uninteresting to cantors, organists and any other practical musician who (in Mizler's words at the end of the composer's Obituary in 1754) 'did not involve himself in deep theoretical speculation, but was all the stronger in practical music' (*Dokumente*, iii, pp.88f).[13] But the distinction is important since for centuries it has been drawn by writers and performers alike. In the case of *Clavierübung III*, the Art or artifice is a stylistic matter and deserves to be understood as such, for the composer's consciousness of style is without doubt. Quite apart from the evidence in the music itself, documents and biography verify it. One of Birnbaum's counter-arguments to Scheibe's attack was that the composer understood the 'Italian taste' of Palestrina and others 'so highly treasured these days' (*Dokumente*, ii, p.305); in 1739 Mizler pointed out that in his cantatas Bach could write both (a) full inner parts as in the music 'of 20 or 25 years ago' and also (b) 'entirely in accordance with the latest taste' (*Dokumente*, ii, p. 336). Music which Bach extemporised or composed for musicians abroad followed various local styles: the old fantasia style for Reincken at Hamburg in 1720, the chromatic Sighing Melody of *Das musikalische Opfer* for Frederick II at Berlin in 1747. The Mass in B Minor and *Das wohltemperirte Clavier II*, to name only two of the collections that were assembled by the composer in his last decade or so, are a veritable catalogue of musical styles then familiar to a musician who was well versed in practice and theory, in performance and pedagogy, in Variety and Art.

Clavierübung III is no exception to the composer's preoccupation with assembling—and in this case publicly presenting—collections of music in different styles. Moreover, 'style' is not to be understood in the narrow sense of *stile antico* or *Galantstil* etc, but more as a term which covers compositional techniques, devices or approaches. Each movement in *Clavierübung III* is an *exemplum* of motivic creation, i.e. it can and perhaps did serve a composer as a practical demonstration of how to develop this or that motif. A key word in Mizler's last sentence above is *Ausübung* ('practical music'), for while it has long been known that '*Clavierübung*' was used by several contemporaries for collections of keyboard music (Kuhnau, Krieger, Lübeck, Sperontes, Sorge, J. L. Krebs) and was thus somewhat 'anonymous', Bach's use of the term has not yet been compared with the then crucial distinction between practical and theoretical study. If by '*Clavierübung*' Bach means not so much 'music for practising', or 'practical music for performance', but *musica prattica* as distinct from *musica teorica*, the organist/composer of the period could have found in the volume a putting into written or realised form of many techniques otherwise widely scattered, inadequately described in books and certainly nowhere demonstrated with such solid skill. Such an interpretation shifts the whole emphasis of the volume into a firm, musical framework. The performer's duty becomes one of understanding the musical techniques against a background of orthodox Lutheran music-making. Nevertheless any musical emphasis should not be taken to be a denial of the theological or symbolic. That the presentation of such an organist/composer's repertory of styles was for J. S. Bach no idle, abstract musical activity is certain from the custom and nature of the man; *soli deo gloria* was no idle, abstract formula.

Plan of *Clavierübung III*

The plan of *Clavierübung III* can be summarised as follows:

(1) Overall plans in which volumes were arranged take various forms and were not uncommon. They may reflect practical needs in the mass (e.g. Couperin's 21 pieces in *Messe pour les Paroisses, c*1690) or Office (e.g. Kerll's Magnificat versets in *Modulatio organica,* 1686). They may reflect a composer's interest in variety of chorale-treatment (e.g. J. L. Krebs's *Clavierübung, c*1742) or in complex counterpoint (e.g. Buxtehude's *Fried- und Freudenreiche Hinfarth,* 1674). The common title 'German Organ Mass' for Bach's *Clavierübung III* is incorrect, since (a) more is involved than the Lutheran *Missa brevis,* (b) it is not an organ mass in the sense of *messe pour l'orgue,* (c) the only way then to explain the *Vier Duette* would be to take them as Communion pieces, for which there is no objective evidence despite confident claims to the contrary. That there are 21 chorales—like the 21 movements of a French mass—is in this respect insignificant.

(2) The associations of the volume with the Holy Trinity are undeniable. In the Leipzig hymnbook of G. Vopelius (1682 etc) the *Missa* is contained in the section of hymns for or 'Of the Holy Trinity'; that the first nine preludes contain three groups of three strengthens this association, as do the three parts of the three Trinity trios (see below), the three themes of the Eb Prelude (with three flats) and the three themes or sections of the Eb Fugue. Even the total number of pieces seems to refer to three (27 = 3 x 3 x 3).[14] The composer's own information—that the preludes are based 'on Catechism and other hymns'—does not explain why the collection is framed by the Eb Prelude and Fugue nor why an organist needed such hymns, since the Leipzig Catechism Examination seems not to have used organ.[15]

Luther's Greater and Lesser Catechisms consisted of a series of questions and answers outlining the principles of faith; from them could be drawn six particular headings introduced by the German Kyrie and Gloria. Thus the arrangement can be seen to be as shown on p. 263. Five of the hymn melodies (1,2,3,4,6) can even be combined in a quodlibet if the notes are juggled somewhat, as a catechism tradition still known in the 19th century shows.[16] All six hymns are in Luther's hymnbooks and signify the six headings in the Smaller or Lesser Catechism; there is no mystery in Bach's inclusion of no.5 ('Aus tiefer Not') despite conjectures sometimes considered necessary. Moreover the six hymns present a front of pure classical Lutheranism: six pillars of orthodoxy, important in the jubilee year 1739

		BWV	Praeludium	pro organo pleno
		552i	Praeludium	pro organo pleno
Luther's reformed liturgy	Kyrie	669	Kyrie, Gott Vater	CF in soprano
	Christe	670	Christe, aller Welt Trost	CF in tenor
	Kyrie	671	Kyrie, Gott heiliger Geist	CF in pedal con organo pleno
		672	Kyrie, Gott Vater	3/4 manualiter
		673	Christe, aller Welt Trost	6/8 manualiter
		674	Kyrie, Gott heiliger Geist	9/8 manualiter
	Gloria	675	Allein Gott in der Höh'	Trio in F (manualiter)
		676	Allein Gott in der Höh'	Trio in G
		677	Allein Gott in der Höh'	Trio in A (manualiter)
Luther's reformed doctrine	Ten Commandments	678	Diess sind die heilgen zehn Gebot	CF in canon
		679	Diess sind die heilgen zehn Gebot	manualiter
	Credo	680	Wir glauben all' an einen Gott	in organo pleno
		681	Wir glauben all' an einen Gott	manualiter
	Prayer	682	Vater unser im Himmelreich	CF in canon
		683	Vater unser im Himmelreich	manualiter
	Baptism	684	Christ, unser Herr, zum Jordan kam	CF in pedal
		685	Christ, unser Herr, zum Jordan kam	manualiter
	Penitence	686	Aus tiefer Not schrei' ich zu dir	CF in pedal organo pleno
		687	Aus tiefer Not schrei' ich zu dir	manualiter
	Eucharist	688	Jesus Christus, unser Heiland	CF in pedal
		689	Jesus Christus, unser Heiland	manualiter
		802	Duetto I	3/8 E minor
		803	Duetto II	2/4 F major
		804	Duetto III	12/8 G major
		805	Duetto IV	2/2 A minor
		552ii	Fuga	pro organo pleno

and a kind of answer not only to the concept of hymn-songs in Schemelli's hymnbook[17] but also to the directive of the Saxon Consistory in 1730 that 'new hymns . . . shall not be used in public divine service' without permission.[18]

(3) Despite appearances, there is nothing to connect the Greater and Lesser Catechism with the bigger and smaller chorale-settings. The manual or 'lesser' preludes are mostly—though not all—shorter; they are not necessarily simpler in any sense. Moreover, they present a more unified group than the greater settings, being all in very varied ways fugal. Only the last (BWV689) is a fugue fully comparable to those of *Das wohltemperirte Clavier II*; the others are shorter, offering *exempla* of fugal treatment or fugal devices beyond those described in even the new fugue theory books (e.g. Marpurg).[19] In addition, the volume supplies a catalogue of cantus firmus treatment, not complete—there are e.g. no coloratura settings—but on one hand encompassing treatments known since at least the time of Scheidt (e.g. BWV669) and on the other so blending contrapuntal skill and *galant* harmony (e.g. BWV682) as to be beyond the abilities of any other known composer.

(4) That the cyclic or rather organizing elements in the volume are more striking to the eye than the ear—the Table on p. 263 allows many patterns to be discerned—may be readily acknowledged but does not lessen their significance or, alas, always clarify it. For example, the central movement (no.14 of 27) is a setting of 'Wir glauben' (BWV681) in the jerky rhythm of a French *Ouverture* as understood by Bach, though in this case applied to a fughetta not its prelude. Is this rhythm expressing the regal splendour of the God of the Credo? In Cantata 61, the *Ouverture* elements signify the 'opening' of the Church Year on Advent I. Perhaps the French elements of BWV681 are there for variety? Yet any performer in *c*1745 who owned all four volumes of *Clavierübung* might have noticed a curious coincidence: the central or near-central movement in all of them has the same French rhythms: *Clavierübung I* at the opening of the fourth Partita of six, in D major; *Clavierübung II* at the opening of the second of two works, the B minor *Ouverture*; *Clavierübung III*, no.14 of 27 pieces, BWV681, in E minor; *Clavierübung IV*, Goldberg Variation no.16 of 30, in G major. There are even two pairs of relative keys involved (D/B minor, E minor/G). Few readers of these remarks would deny themselves conjecture as to what is coincidence and what not; yet even were the composer himself to admit to coincidence, that would not be the end of the search for 'significances'. Similarly, that the *stile antico* of certain movements is at least partly a question of notation does not invalidate it, since much of

the pattern-making in Bach's late works is indeed notational—conceptual rather than perceptual.

★   ★   ★

The composer's intention of presenting a collection of pieces written in various styles can also be understood under various headings. It is possible that any prolonged experience of *Clavierübung III* will yield further symmetries or further varieties of technique, but the following are some of the most crucial.

Modality

(5) The question of modality needs careful definition. There is an unconventional, even at times strange, quality about the counterpoint of much of *Clavierübung III* that has very likely always puzzled thinking organists. Already in the 1770s Kirnberger pointed out that only the Trinity Trios (BWV675–7) were put firmly in major keys (*Dokumente*, iii, p.221), but in practice the trio BWV677 in A major no more has an easy diatonicism than does e.g. BWV674 in E-Phrygian. Both have an ambiguity of 'key' in their first bar. Kirnberger's modal labels were again partly notational: he judged from the key-signatures.[20] In the A major chorale BWV677 neither key signature nor cadences are ambiguous in any obvious way; yet despite the anchoring half-cadences (bb.7, 16) there is still an uneasy tonality occasioned by the subject itself (ex.1). It is instructive to compare the fugue subject of BWV547 which contains the same motif but in a much clearer diatonic context (ex.2). The A major diatonicism of

Ex. 1   Ex. 2

BWV677 leaves an 'uneasy tonality' by such details as the mediant harmony in b.3, the mediant entries in bb.7–8 and the slow settling down of key between b.10 and b.14. That its two fugal themes are both derived from lines in the chorale (see ex.3) is (though rarely observed) less a part of its strangeness than is the nature of that derivation and what it leads to.

On the other hand, the implications of a latter-day modality cannot be dismissed, since the composer is often at pains to refer to some specific modal element, notably cadences (ex.4). Such references are not unique

Ex. 3

Ex. 4

and can be found in some of the Advent/Christmas fughettas,[21] e.g. 'Lob sei' BWV704. Nor would it be surprising to find 'modality' in the sense of 'unrigid diatonic tonality' at work in the three great Kyrie–Christe–Kyrie preludes (BWV669–71), since obviously it can be regarded as a factor of the *stile antico*. Even then, however, *stile antico* in the St Anne Fugue does not lead to such tonal ambiguity. In short, while such labels as 'modal' and 'diatonic' can be used only with caution, different movements of *Clavierübung III* do have different characteristics in this direction, and it may be that the variety could be shown to cover several carefully marked degrees of diatonicism.

The *stile antico*

(6) The *stile antico* has been described in a recent book by Wolff, and its stylistic elements are clearly enough defined for it to be certain that no less than five of Bach's strictest pieces in the style are contained in *Clavierübung III*: BWV669 monothematic, ricercar-like, vocal polyphony; BWV670 cantus firmus *en taille*, freer treatment; BWV671 several subjects combining in turn with cantus firmus; BWV686 six parts, periodic exposition; BWV552ii (first fugue). However, that the *stile antico* is worked to varied ends is clear from the formal details: the monothematic BWV669 is

in concept contrasted with the sectional BWV686. Similarly, as remarks above show, the diatonic implications of e.g. BWV686 and BWV552ii vary.

Bach seems to have acquired his own copy of Fux's *Gradus* soon after it was published in 1725,[22] and others in his circle admired it. Mizler translated and annotated the treatise in 1742 ('very well', according to Schering),[23] and lectured on it in the University of Leipzig. While the clearest signs of *stile antico* are the note values (4/2 for 4/4),[24] the style as a whole probably meant to Bach (a) a stricter polyphony than was usual in keyboard *alla breve* music, (b) a style less dependent on the text and more dependent on the harmonic demands of the contrapuntal 'style', (c) despite this, a vocal character to the lines, ideally within a narrow compass (BWV669 traverses *D-eb"* only), (d) a style for which the tonal ambiguities of so-called modes were particularly suitable, and (e) in the case of chorale-preludes, movements in which the cantus firmus could remain truer to its Gregorian origin (if it had one) than was usually the case. Even in *Clavierübung III* however it would be a mistake to see J. S. Bach's pieces in *stile antico* as strict textbook demonstrations, as an example can show.

While the great 'Aus tiefer Noth' BWV686 may well be the composer's strictest organ-motet,[25] a 'model for *contrapunctus floridus*',[26] the detail of the lines suggests a very lively musical imagination relying on *stile antico* formulae only for a framework in which to compose. Certainly the careful variety in texture and in spacing matches the attention paid to producing good lines (e.g. the top part in the last 11 bars), but it is characteristic of Bach rather of Fux or Palestrina that the texture is strategically planned: the opening single notes gradually widen in texture until the chord of widest extent is reached exactly halfway (the 27th bar of 54, excluding repeat). The lines themselves are constantly allusive: a sample passage such as that in ex.5 may contain a motet subject from the cantus firmus (a), the same in answer (b), a counter-subject like a previous motif *inversus* (c), but also like the same cantus firmus line in diminution (d). Similarly, the movement has more parts, its polyphony is more continuous, there are more counter-subjects, the expositions are less

Ex. 5

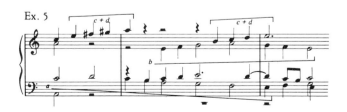

stereotyped and the final section more keyboard-like than the choral motet movements that the style seems at first to be imitating, such as the opening chorus of BWV38, Cantata 38 'Aus tiefer Not' (subject is marked 'x', counter-subject 'y'):

Ex. 6

The three sections of the E♭ Fugue have naturally led writers to find parallels in the work of Frescobaldi, Froberger, Buxtehude, Böhm and others, but usually the use of different versions of one and the same subject for different fugal sections applies mostly to canzona or capriccio types, not ricercare. Such fugue subjects as the following from G. Muffat's *72 Versets* (1726) have in common with BWV552 a 'quiet' 4/2 character, rising 4ths, suspensions, narrow compass and Italianate invertibility:

Ex. 7

But it is only a fughetta and it offers no more than a hint of the *stile antico* development of BWV552. Moreover, the formal intention behind BWV552 is the combining of fugue subjects rather than the varying of the themes themselves. It is strange even then that for a fugue supposedly full of thematic combination, the second fugal subject (b.37) has to be altered in order to fit the first (bb.59–60)—a detail rarely noticed. While the practical composer would soon have seen that such subjects lead naturally to easy harmony (e.g. bb.21-5), the Fuxian scholar would also have appreciated that such a subject would occasion 'proportional' counter-subjects: 4/2 crotchets in the first section (cf the 'species' counter-subject in the E major fugue of *Das wohltemperirte Clavier II*), 6/4 quavers in the second, 12/8 quavers in the third. In turn, the organist should infer a proportional tempo change: 4/2 crotchet equals 6/4 crotchet, and 6/4 minim equals 12/8 dotted crotchet.

This would accord with the didactic elements in the work, towards which the player of the fugue is helped at each juncture by details in the organ writing. Both BWV552 and the E major fugue of *Das wohltemperirte Clavier II* demonstrate the *fuga grave* as it is listed by such writers as J. G. Walther,[27] down to such details in common as the stretto beginning after the end of the first full exposition and the parallel 3rds and 6ths, known in some books as *canon sine pausa*.

Development of Motifs

(7) The development of motifs is unique neither to *Clavierübung III* nor to J. S. Bach. That the *Orgelbüchlein* chorales, for example, exploit motif to better musical ends than the collections of J. G. Walther or Pachelbel is easier to claim than to explain; comparison may well lead to a conclusion that at least in some cases the genius of Bach turns on caprice, on under-use. Walther's chorale attributed to Bach by Kirnberger, BWV693, shows a doctrinaire constancy of motif unknown in genuine Bach chorales using the same motif, e.g. 'Erstanden ist der heil'ge Christ' BWV628. In other words, J. S. Bach does not exploit a motif in all possible ways, on all possible occasions; on the other hand, its appearance or use is more fully planned than in the work of, for example, Böhm.

If, as would be possible, a graduated list were to be prepared showing the degrees of motivic involvement of each movement in *Clavierübung III*, the composer could be shown to be supplying a kind of catalogue, from those such as BWV687 in which motifs constantly change to those such as BWV688 in which motifs are constantly and repetitiously extended. The finished product implies a quite different bar-by-bar creative process in the composer's mind. Particularly interesting in this respect is the larger Ten Commandments prelude, BWV678. A great deal of wonderful symbol-searching has coloured interpretations of this piece, and like others in *Clavierübung III* the subject of the hymn is itself an amalgam of the narrative and the symbolic such as to inspire musical imagery-seekers. But the real fibre of the movement is its unusual array of motifs. These motifs are contrasted, and it is scarcely an exaggeration to see the piece from beginning to end as a kind of fantasia on them. About a dozen motifs can be shown to pervade the whole piece, in varying order and with differing melodic/harmonic implications. A pair of extracts can illustrate the technique involved (see ex.8a and 8b). As these show, however, there is again no prolix use of motif beyond what real musical impetus demands; the Rincks and Albrechtsbergers of a later generation could have used motifs even more cleverly.

Ex. 8a

Ex. 8b

(8) Obviously related to the development of motifs is the careful use of conventional *figurae* as listed or discussed by such writers as J. G. Walther (1708) and revised more recently.[28] Whatever the exact nature of the professional regard between Bach and Walther, certain aspects of the doctrine of rhetorical figures—the *Figurenlehre*—must be assumed to have been common knowledge or property. This does not mean that in, say, 'Das alte Jahr vergangen ist' BWV614 the composer was merely supplying textbook *exempla* of the ascending/descending chromatic 4th described by earlier theorists as *passus duriusculus*; the good composer did not work in this way, nor did the textbooks expect him to. But it does mean that a stylistic distinction ought to be seen between motif composition in the Credo prelude BWV680 and motif composition in the Ten Commandments prelude BWV678.

(9) Both movements involve highly concentrated use of motif, but the Credo has a clearer Italianate quality. The general suspension style is at times reminiscent of Italian trios; but the details of figuration also recall the textbook repertory of *figurae*, unlike the more original, almost *galant* motifs of BWV678. Thus all the figures shown in ex.9 are used in the course of the Credo prelude, as a sample few bars demonstrate. In addition to these *figurae*, the Italian allusions in BWV680 are unmistakable: a striding ostinato bass line was found in the opening Credo section added by J. S. Bach to G. B. Bassani's Mass in F,[29] and in Frescobaldi's *Fiori musicali* (known to Bach) is a fugue with a five-note ostinato bass theme, *recercar con obligo del Basso*.

Ex. 9

bb. 9–14

Thus BWV680 contributes to the volume not only a distinct counterpoint based on *figurae* and given an impetus unknown in a *stile antico* fugue, but also a distinct Italian flavour throughout. It is probably this factor which 'explains' the *alla francese* setting of the same chorale melody to follow, and to which reference was made above. As BWV680 is a long fugue incorporating Italian elements and general fluency, so BWV681 is a 'tight' fugue decorating the opening lines of the chorale melody with French rhythms. Luther's German Creed is thus glossed with French and Italian elements.

Ritornello Structure

(10) Naturally, the ritornello structure of an organ chorale would be in one way or another affected by such details as these; a result is that *Clavierübung III* also presents an array of ritornello possibilities. The term 'ritornello' is analogous and suggests no drawn-out, well-spaced concerto

movement. In the case of 'Jesus Christus, unser Heiland', for example, the form may be expressed as: fugal through-composed monothematic trio on two manuals, with pedal cantus firmus in long notes, line by line. However, the main theme itself includes motif-repetition (see ex.10). This motif is treated to inversion (bb.63, 112), mirror image (bb.47, 83), mirror image inversion (bb.51, 87, 104) as well as syncopation (bb.20–) and mirror image syncopation (b.112). In its various forms the motif appears some 72 times—providing an open invitation to numerological 'interpretations'—but the fugal codetta (the semiquavers in ex.10) also contains an important motif which is treated in several ways or combined apparently at random with others. Not the least important detail is that the main motif, and hence its *inversus* form also, is essentially a one-bar phrase. The particular shape of the theme can be seen to suggest a cross[30]:

Ex. 10

or even with its *inversus* the monogram 'jota-chi', that is 'J.C.', meaning 'Jesus Christus'.[31] By comparison, seeing it as an expression of the 'life-strengthening beliefs' of verse 5 of the text,[32] the separation and coming together of God and Man,[33] the 'lively exertions' implied in verse 6,[34] or the 'treading of the wine press',[35] is relatively modest. Either way, the originality of detail—i.e. the one-bar phrases, the leaping subject, the inversions, the constant reference to the theme—fuses any ritornello elements and produces a new kind of form.

Similar conclusions may be drawn about the larger Lord's Prayer setting, BWV682, though for different reasons. Its main theme is more clearly based on the chorale melody than is the case in BWV688, but more importantly its three/five parts are organised to different ends: it is a ritornello trio-sonata movement incorporating several thematic figures of different kinds (bass quavers, coloratura elements, detached triplets, legato appoggiaturas) through which the cantus firmus is played in slow octave canon by means of two further voices. The motifs of the 'trio-sonata melody' are adapted for the cantus firmus and in every way 'allow' for it. Despite the length of the opening ritornello section, there is little actual repetition of it later in the movement; rather each of the later sections introduces motifs from it in order. Through the motivic lines an important musical style is hinted at: the *Seufzermelodik* or *galant* chromatic sequences such as that shown in ex.11. The luxuriousness of motif and part-writing, however, is

Ex. 11

countered by a simplicity of ritornello key plan; despite the dominant passage in the middle, the work repeatedly returns to the tonic, using the motifs with a variety of uncompleted cadences so as to avoid over-strong tonics.

Paraphrase Techniques

(11) Related to motif and form are the various paraphrase techniques. That J. S. Bach was already, in his middle-to-late Weimar years, master of intricate melodic paraphrase treatment is clear from Cantata 161 (1715) and the organ chorale 'Komm, heiliger Geist' BWV651a, in which the chorale melody is spun around with little figures so as to create new melodic lines not always of any fixed period but able to expand as required. A natural extension of the idea is that the 'little figures' become material usable both to introduce and to accompany the cantus firmus in its simpler form in another voice. *Clavierübung III* has many such very finely wrought examples, e.g. in BWV675:

Ex. 12

A further development might be that, were there to be more than one such paraphrase subject, they can be combined, as in BWV677, b.17 (ex.13), where 'a' marks the original counter-subject to both subjects, I and II.

Ex. 13

Partly due to their Gregorian quality, some *Clavierübung III* melodic paraphrases are complex. It is possible, for example, to find the chorale melody working twice, at different phases, in the new theme in BWV684:

Ex. 14

In at least one other instance, subject, counter-subject and answer can all be traced to the chorale melody itself (see ex.15, BWV680 plus chorale BWV437). Also characteristic is the double subject, both parts of which are derived, as in ex.16. There are even moments when a chorale melody is implied rather than stated (see ex.17a, pedal of BWV678 and 17b, end of BWV681). As for the little Kyrie–Christe–Kyrie settings, it is impossible to exhaust the thematic allusion.

Ex. 15

Ex. 16

Ex. 17a

Ex. 17b

CF

Moreover, the derived lines are often treated to a contrapuntal ingenuity that might be thought more typical of subjects specially written for the purpose. Thus the derived fugue subject of the last chorale, BWV689, is given in no less than six different kinds of stretto: bb.1–2 in the middle voices, after six beats, b.10 in the upper voices, after one beat, b.16 in the middle voices, after two beats, bb.23–4 in the lower voices, after four beats, bb.26–7 in the upper voices, after five beats, and b.57 in the middle voices in stretto-augmentation, simultaneous.

Fugal Variety

(12) Fugal variety has already been hinted at in the case of chorale-settings in *Clavierübung III*, but further types of remarkable counterpoint will be found reserved for the most puzzling pieces of the volume, the *Vier Duette*. As Forkel has said, they are 'models of duets admitting of no third part',[36] but they are also varied and patterned in such a way as to suggest that they are again models for a 'repertory of possibilities' in the special category of duo-writing. It would be totally misleading to see them as at all similar to the two-part inventions, for example. Considered as a quartet, they include important techniques succinctly demonstrated: regular fugue, double fugue, *ABA* fugue, strict invertibility, canon, inversion, fugue-with-bass ('invention fugue'), motif derivation and motif imitation, all against a background of variety in mode (major/minor), rhythm and metre (duple, triple, compound, *alla breve*). It is even possible that they have a common pulse, though this would presumably mean a fast no.3. The invertibility of counterpoint itself becomes a further facet of Bach's continuing, even increasing, interest in canon and genuine melodic counterpoint void of Italianate formulae. Also, the techniques result in several elements well outside Fuxian counterpoint. The falling augmented octaves of the chromatic bass in Duetto I, the augmented triad effect of the canonic stretto in Duetto II, the bouncing *Stützbassfuge* of Duetto III, the *galant* episodes of Duetto IV: the contrast between these elements and the St Anne Fugue that 'follows' the *Vier Duette* is only too

evident. Even the key change from A minor to E♭ major is as extreme as possible. Quite apart from that, however, the patent variety of duo technique presented in the course of a handful of pieces more than suggests that that is the purpose as well as result of the *Vier Duette*.

★   ★   ★

It must indeed have been 'Music Lovers and particularly Connoisseurs of such Work' who had their spirits recreated by *Clavierübung III*. The term *Ergötzung* though familiar from title-pages implied a pious concept of 'recreation' in a theological sense, a refreshment of the spirit from which faith can operate always anew.[37] The organist, the instrument and his 'refreshed spirit' correspond to the attributes 'knowledge, power and love' given as belonging to the Trinity itself.[38] *Clavier-übung* thus becomes an organist's corollary to his own *Catechismus-übung*. But if the musician works *ad majorem gloriam dei* he can only do so fully if he applies his musical science as exactly and skilfully as possible to the matter in hand, which in this case is composing 'preludes on the Catechism and other hymns' and thus assembling a repertory of *musica prattica*.

NOTES TO CHAPTER 10

1. 'Dritter Theil der Clavier Übung bestehend in verschiedenen Vorspielen über die Catechismus- und andere Gesaenge, vor die Orgel: Denen Liebhabern, und besonders denen Kennern von dergleichen Arbeit, zur Gemüths Ergezung verfertiget von Johann Sebastian Bach, Koenigl. Pohlnischen, und Churfüstl. Saechs. Hoff-Compositeur, Capellmeister und Directore Chori Musici in Leipzig. In Verlegung des Authoris'.

2. E.g. C. Wolff: 'Ordnungsprinzipien in den Originaldrucken Bachscher Werke', *Bach-Interpretationen*, ed. M. Geck (Göttingen, 1969), 144–67.

3. E.g. C. Wolff: *Der Stile antico in der Musik Johann Sebastian Bachs* (Wiesbaden, 1968).

4. E.g. R. A. Leaver: 'Bach's "Clavierübung III": Some Historical and Theological Considerations', *Organ Yearbook*, vi (1975), 17–32.

5. E.g. J. Krause: 'Die grosse Bearbeitung von Jesus Christus unser Heiland aus Clavierübung III von J. S. Bach', *Musik und Kirche*, xxv (1965), 117–26.

6. E.g. C. Albrecht: 'J. S. Bachs "Clavierübung Dritter Theil": Versuch einer Deutung', *Bach-Jahrbuch*, lv (1969), 46–66.

7. K. Ehricht: 'Die zyklische Gestalt und die Aufführungsmöglichkeit des III. Teiles der Klavierübung von Joh. Seb. Bach', *Bach-Jahrbuch*, xxviii (1949–50), 40–56.

8. M. Tessmer, ed.: *Dritter Teil der Klavierübung*, Neue Bach-Ausgabe, iv/4, Notenband (Kassel, 1969).

9. *Bach-Dokumente*, ii, ed. W. Neumann and H.-J. Schulze (Leipzig and Kassel, 1969); iii, ed. H.-J. Schulze (Leipzig and Kassel, 1972).

10. The bicentenary of Luther's sermon in St Thomas (25 May 1739), the bicentenary of the Augsburg Confession (12 Aug 1739) and the regular Reformationsfest (31 Oct 1739).

11. 'Der Herr Verfasser hat hier ein neues Exempel gegeben, dass er in dieser Gattung der Composition vor vielen andern vortrefflich geübet und glücklich sey. Niemand wird es ihm hierin zuvor thun, und gar wenige werden es ihm nachmachen können. Dieses Werk ist eine kräfftige Widerlegung derer, die sich unterstanden des Herrn Hof Compositeurs Composition zu critisiren'.

12. 'Dieser grosse Mann würde die Bewunderung gantzer Nationen seyn . . . wenn er nicht seinen Stücken durch ein schwülstiges und verworrenes Wesen das Natürliche entzöge, und ihre Schönheit durch allzugrosse Kunst verdunkelte . . . Alle Stimmen sollen mit einander, und mit gleicher Schwierigkeit arbeiten'.

13. 'liess sich zwar nicht in tiefe theoretische Betrachtungen der Musik ein, war aber desto stärcker in der Ausübung'.

14. The number and arrangement of gatherings in the engraved volume make it unlikely that the *Vier Duette* were added simply to fill empty pages.

15. G. Stiller: *Johann Sebastian Bach und das Leipziger Gottesdienstliche Leben seiner Zeit* (Berlin, 1970), 242.

16. C. L. Hilgenfeldt: *Johann Sebastian Bachs Leben, Wirken und Werke* (Leipzig, 1850), Table 1.

17. There is a case to be made for Bach's contribution to such a hymnbook being not a salute to pietism but an attempt to 'control' its musical manifestation and keep it relatively conservative.

18. H. T. David and A. Mendel: *The Bach Reader* (New York, 1945; rev. with suppl., 1966).

19. F. W. Marpurg: *Abhandlung von der Fuge*, ii (Berlin, 1754).

20. It is not simply a question of having a sharp or flat too few in the key signature, as had once been common.

21. One of several reasons for regarding these curiously underrated fughettas as late works.

22. Wolff (1968), 28.

23. A. Schering: *J. S. Bach und das Musikleben Leipzigs im 18.Jahrhundert* (Leipzig, 1941).

24. Fux's *tempo binarium* as distinct from *presto* (2/2) or *allegro* (4/4); see *Gradus ad Parnassum* (Vienna, 1725), 238.

25. Most of the 'motet-style' organ chorales have livelier textures than their vocal equivalents and ought to be called something else in the general histories of keyboard music.

26. Wolff (1968), 69.

27. J. G. Walther: *Praecepta der musicalischen Composition* [1708], ed. P. Benary (Leipzig, 1955).

28.   A. Schmitz: 'Die Figurenlehre in den theoretischen Werken Johann Gottfried Walthers', *AMw*, ix (1952), 79–100.

29.   Wolff (1968), 203ff.

30.   Leaver (1975).

31.   Krause (1965).

32.   P. Spitta: *Johann Sebastian Bach*, ii (Leipzig, 1879), 694.

33.   F. Dietrich: 'J. S. Bachs Orgelchoral und seine geschichtlichen Wurzeln', *Bach-Jahrbuch*, xxvi (1929), 1–89.

34.   R. Steglich: *Johann Sebastian Bach* (Potsdam, 1935), 123.

35.   Leaver (1975).

36.   J. N. Forkel: *Ueber Johann Sebastian Bachs Leben, Kunst und Kunstwerke* (Leipzig, 1802), chap.9.

37.   Stiller (1970), 96, 209.

38.   Leaver (1975).

11

The *Erotokritos*:
Variation in a Cretan Folksong

Lucy Durán

The *Erotokritos* is a long narrative poem written by the Cretan Vitzentzos Kornaros sometime between the late 16th century and 1669, while Crete was still under Venetian rule.[1] First published in 1713 in Venice, it went through many subsequent editions and achieved a wide circulation throughout Greece, reaching as far as Romania and Asia Minor.[2] Modelled on the French courtly romance *Paris et Vienne* (1432), the *Erotokritos* is written in Cretan dialect, in the verse form of 15-syllable rhymed couplets. It represents the most conspicuous achievement of the literary movement that developed in Crete after the fall of Constantinople, when Crete became a refuge for scholars from that city.

The *Erotokritos* plays an important role in present-day Cretan life, not only for its literary interest or as a symbol of regional identity, but also for its widespread occurrence in folksong. It would not be an exaggeration to say that most Cretans know by heart at least a few lines of the *Erotokritos*. In rural Crete it is common to hear fragments of 150 lines or more; there are also occasional accounts of performances from memory of the entire poem (which in its printed version is 10,052 lines long).[3] The medium of performance is spoken recitation or, more usually, unaccompanied or accompanied song, to a melody that is known throughout the island as 'Rotokritos' melody' (*Tou Rotokritou o skopos*).

In an earlier study of this melody, versions of which have been found throughout the Aegean and Dodecanese islands as well as among Asia Minor Greeks, Professor Baud-Bovy provides strong evidence that it is French in origin and was introduced into Cyprus in the 15th century, during Frankish rule.[4] From Cyprus, where it was known as 'Sousas' song', (*Tis Sousas to tragoudi*), the melody was brought to Crete by refugees from the Turks and was then adopted by Cretans for the recitation of the *Erotokritos*.[5]

At what point the *Erotokritos* began to be sung to this melody, or whether or not it was ever sung to any other melody is not known. Its 'folklike' verse form, imagery and use of dialect, and possibly its many references to music[6] (Erotokritos himself is a skilled lute player) may have encouraged sung performances, even if it was not written with this in mind.[7] As might be expected it is omitted from collections of Cretan folksong texts. Though the 19th-century travellers to Crete, Pashley and Spratt, mention the text as being widely known, they do not specify whether it was sung.[8] The melody is likewise omitted from most collections and studies of Cretan folksong,[9] an omission explained partly by their emphasis on the *rizitika*, an unaccompanied song repertory from the White Mountains of western Crete. Yet the *Erotokritos* probably has a higher incidence of performance than any other song in the island.

The present study is based on some 50 versions, of which more than half were selected for detailed analysis, recorded during three successive field trips to Crete (1969–73). Cretan versions in printed sources have also been considered.[10] As can be seen from ex.1(i), this melody (in its simplest form) is a couplet-tune, that is, it repeats itself with each rhymed couplet; it has four sections, each section corresponding to a hemistich, with the main caesura at the end of line 1; lines 1 and 2 of each couplet are isorhythmic; the text is syllabic, with the duration of even-numbered syllables prolonged to twice or more the value of other syllables.[11] Melodic movement is mainly conjunct. Versions are mostly diatonic with a flat 3rd, though 'chromatic' versions (that is, with an interval of an augmented 2nd between the 2nd and 3rd degrees) have been found in the east of the island and outside Crete.[12]

The Text: Some Observations

The *Erotokritos*, in the form of dialogue, with commentary by the 'poet', relates the story of Princess Aretousa (daughter of a mythical King of Athens), who falls in love with Erotokritos, son of the King's attendant. When the king hears of their love he banishes Erotokritos from the kingdom in order to prevent Aretousa from marrying beneath her rank. Erotokritos returns in disguise, however, and successfully defending the kingdom in battle from the enemy, wins the hand of Aretousa. But before revealing himself to her he first tests her fidelity by pretending that Erotokritos has been killed by wild beasts. The poem ends with their marriage.

The *Erotokritos* very quickly captured the popular imagination. That it was already in wide circulation, in either oral or manuscript form, before it was published, is shown by the editor's preface to the first edition:[13]

I decided on the advice of many people to publish the *Erotokritos*, an old poem, which is greatly praised and honoured in the Adriatic islands, in the Peloponnese, and . . . Zakynthos where as elsewhere are still to be found the descendants of the unfortunate Cretans . . . who took refuge there after the fall of their country. It was they who popularized the poem, composed in the native Cretan tongue, and made it known throughout the island and in other places, where it seems to have been enjoyed by all who read it.

The subsequent history of the *Erotokritos* through its many different editions, has been the subject of much scholarly research. Suffice it here to say that the *Erotokritos* is one of the few non-religious books to be found in villages today in Crete. Although many informants—some of whom, over 70, were illiterate—stated that they had learnt parts of it through oral tradition, divergences from the written text are surprisingly few, consisting mostly of modernizing archaic Cretan dialect, or omitting lines. Thus although epic in content and length it cannot be described as an 'oral epic',[14] since the performer seems to be consciously tied to a written model, his aim being accuracy of memory rather than recomposition.

Although it is not uncommon for Cretans to claim to know large sections and even the whole of the *Erotokritos* by heart, in practice only a few fragments (*apospasmata*) of 50 to 100 lines are regularly performed. Of these the most popular are: the 'Farewell' (*o apocheretismos*) from Book G, lines 1355–1400, where Erotokritos takes his leave of Aretousa; and the 'Tale' (*to paramythi*) from Book E, lines 883–958, where Erotokritos tests Aretousa's fidelity.[15] The popularity of these two fragments may be attributed to the fact that they represent the two moments of highest dramatic tension in the poem, and that in style; content and language they are strikingly close to Greek folksong texts. Stylistically, the parallel to folksong texts is displayed in the absence of enjambement from line to line; in the role of the second line of each couplet as a semantic echo of the first rather than its introducing new material, and in the frequent use of textual formulaic phrases common to Cretan folksong.

Parallels in content are particularly clear in the 'Tale', which, in common with a Cretan wedding song known as 'The Recognition', has the basic elements of a 'return' song as defined by Lord: 'the focal point of the song is the return itself, and this is always surrounded by a) disguise, b) deceptive story, and c) recognition'.[16]

Erotokritos and Aretousa are often depicted in folklore, not only in Crete but in other parts of Greece;[17] Aretousa is held up as a model of constancy in love, while Erotokritos stands as a symbol of courage and strength, side by side with modern national heroes such as Venizelos and

Prince George, High Commissioner of Crete after liberation from the Turks in 1898 (Plate XIII). The closeness of the poem to folksong, its embodiment of traditional moral values, and its Cretan origin, account for the special place the *Erotokritos*, and by association its melody, occupies in Cretan folklore.

The Performance Context

Like other Cretan narrative songs, the *Erotokritos* may be performed by both men and women and is not attached to any particular occasion. Unlike other narrative songs, which are unaccompanied, however, it may be accompanied by the traditional Cretan duet of *lyra* (three-string fiddle) and *laouto* (long-necked fretted lute with five courses), which also provide instrumental interludes based on the vocal melody. It is also performed as an instrumental solo on *lyra* accompanied on either *laouto* or, in eastern Crete, *daouli* (small bass drum), as in ex. 1 (viii) (see Plate XIV); as well as on *askomaṇdoura* (bagpipe) or *thiamboli* (duct flute), as in ex.4(ii).[18] It is thus one of the few vocal melodies not connected with dance to have entered the instrumental repertory. Nevertheless, as instruments are played in most cases only by semi-professional or professional musicians, it is more usual to hear the *Erotokritos* sung unaccompanied as in most of the examples here.

Throughout the island, most singers will spontaneously perform the *Erotokritos* in the process of singing through their repertory. Rotokritos' melody may also be sung to other narrative texts in 15-syllable rhymed couplets (and even sometimes to unrhymed texts, e.g. ex.3(i)), though this is more common in central and eastern than in western Crete, where another melody[19] is used for narrative texts, Rotokritos' melody being reserved mainly for the *Erotokritos* and *St George and the Dragon* (ex.2(i)). If, as Politi states (p.40), the poem was more widely circulated in the east, then its melody would also have been more widely known there than in the west. According to local tradition, the 'true' version of the melody is that performed in the Sitia district, where Kornaros was born. Only one variant from Sitia, ex.1(v), (viii), however, differed significantly from variants in other parts of the island, and that difference is purely rhythmic.

In all its variants, whether sung to the *Erotokritos*, to another text, or performed instrumentally, informants without exception referred to the tune as 'Rotokritos' melody'. This identification of a melody by a title based on a text is otherwise rare in Crete, most melodies, if identified at

Plate XIII Cretan blanket showing Erotokritos and Aretousa at their wedding (left), Erotokritos on his horse (centre) and Prince George and the royal family (right).

all, being identified according to the context in which they are usually performed (e.g. *tsi nifis o skopos*, 'the bridal tune').

An interesting aspect of the *Erotokritos* is the role it seems to play in women's repertory. Except in certain ritual contexts such as weddings and funerals, public singing by women in rural communities is considered a severe moral lapse and is strongly censured. Even privately, women are sometimes reluctant to sing.[20] In spite of this, some women willingly performed the *Erotokritos* in public, though refusing to sing any other melody. The usual reason given was that it was the only song they could remember. Afterwards, however, they explained that they had felt free to sing *Erotokritos* because 'everyone knows it', unlike other women's songs which were 'improvised' and 'personal'.

The implications of this are: first, that the singer is aware of a fixed text to which he must adhere, an attitude which possibly extends also to the melody; and second, that it is the improvisatory element in women's singing which is censured, while, paradoxically, it is precisely this element that is most highly valued in men's singing.[21]

How Many Rotokritos Melodies Are There?

The initial description of Rotokritos' melody shows that all the Cretan versions share basic metrical, sectional and cadential features which in most classification systems would be treated as constituting a single melodic family. Furthermore, it has been seen that the versions collected were always identified by both performers and listeners with one title ('Rotokritos' melody'). Thus it seems reasonable to treat differences in rhythm and melodic contour as variants of a single melody.

The versions presented by Baud-Bovy (1956) from Cyprus and elsewhere correspond in length to one couplet. At least two other authors, however, in reference to Cretan versions, describe the melody as corresponding to *two* couplets. Politi (1968) states: 'They sing [the *Erotokritos*] to a type of recitative, which varies slightly in different regions, with, however, roughly the same melodic line that extends across two couplets . . .' (p.40). (Politi's version of this melody as performed in Irakleion province is shown in ex. 3(iii).) Morgan (1960), in the course of discussing the text, states: 'there are two melodies, the second line of both being the same, and the first considerably different'. Like Baud-Bovy he believes the first melody to be of French origin, while the second 'seems to be a particular invention of Crete' and serves to heighten the tension (p.57). (He does not, however, provide a transcription.)

Examination of Cretan versions shows that: (1) there are three basic variants differentiated mainly by the melodic contour of the first line of each couplet; these will be labelled here Variant A, B and C in order of predominance; and that (2) these variants are performed not only on their own as single-couplet tunes; they are also sung in different (but regular) combinations of two together, becoming two-couplet tunes, and three together, becoming three-couplet tunes. More rarely, and in instrumental versions only, Variants A, B and C may be combined in a pattern that is repeated every four or more couplets.[22]

Out of 33 Cretan variants examined in detail, 16 are single-couplet tunes, nine are two-couplet tunes, four are three-couplet tunes and two are four-couplet tunes.[23] Before discussing the combinations of A, B and C melodies in two or more couplet tunes, the three basic variants will be described.

Variant A (ex. 1)

Variant A predominates among single-couplet tunes and is found throughout the island. It falls mostly within a range of a 5th or 6th, from the seventh degree to either the fourth (ex. 1(ii), (iv)) or the fifth (ex. 1(iii), (v)–(viii)). The first hemistich of line 1 starts on the seventh or first degree, often with a three-fold repetition of the first note (ex. 1(ii), (iv)). This section ends either on the first degree (ex. 1(i), (ii), (iv)), in which case the second hemistich begins on the seventh; or on the third degree with the second hemistich beginning on the second (ex. 1(iii), (v)–(viii)), as in most of the eastern Cretan versions. The second hemistich of line 1, though more subject to variation than the first, almost invariably starts with a four-note motive ascending by step.

The majority of the non-Cretan versions belong to this type, as do all Cretan single-couplet instrumental versions.

Variant B (ex. 2)

Variant B is less frequent than A as a single-couplet tune, versions being mostly from central and eastern Crete. It occurs, however, in two- and three-couplet tunes throughout the island. It has a range of an octave or more (usually seventh degree to seventh above or seventh degree to octave above). This is clearly the melody which Morgan (1960, p.57) believes to be 'a particular invention of Crete', introduced by the singer to 'tense and emphasise the narration'. The first hemistich ascends from either the first or fourth degree and ends on the fifth (in single-couplet B melodies the singer may alternate between initial first and fourth degrees, as in ex. 2(i) and (ii)). The second hemistich ascends from fourth degree to seventh, cadencing on fourth or third (ex.2). This phrase is however necessarily modified when played on the duct flute or bagpipe, which only have a range of a 6th; cf ex.4(ii).

Variant C

Variant C melodies are rarely performed as single-couplet tunes, the only example considered here being from West Crete; but occur in two- and three-couplet tunes (exx.3 and 4). Thus it appears that C melodies originated, and are used primarily as a means of variation in two- and three-couplet tunes, where the variant often occurs as the first tune (ex.3(ii); ex.4(i), (ii)).

The first hemistich is descending in form (unlike the first hemistichs of Variants A and B). It starts on the fifth degree and cadences on the third. The second hemistich has a 'U' shape, starting on the second degree descending to the seventh, and invariably cadencing on the fourth (ex.3(i)).

The greatest degree of consistency and stability within each variant thus occurs in line 1 of each couplet. The situation with regard to line 2 is quite different. It is here that most individual variation occurs, in particular within the first hemistich of line 2 (whereas it can be seen from the examples that the cadential phrase of the final hemistich is basically the same for all three variants, A, B and C). Apart from examples of in-dividual variation, three main types of melodic line emerge for the first hemistich of line 2, also differentiated by melodic contour. Within certain limits, they occur interchangeably in A, B and C variants:

Type a: descending (usually stepwise) from third degree to seventh, followed by a leap to third or fourth. This occurs mainly in A variants, ex.1(ii)–(viii); but it is also to be found in B, ex.2(iv) and C, ex.3(ii), (iii);

Type b: an arch form, starting on second degree, rising to fifth and ending on third (cf the second hemistich of A variants). It is found in all variants: e.g. A, ex.1(i); B, ex.2(iii); C, ex.4(i), (ii);

Type c: an arch form, ascending from fourth degree to seventh or eighth, ending on third (cf the second hemistich of B variants). It is not found in any A variants, but occurs in both B, ex.2(i), (ii) and C, ex.3(v).

These relationships can be summarized as: (1) A + a, or less often b,

(2) B + a or b or c, (3) C + a or b or c. In single-couplet tunes, the performer may stick to one combination (e.g. B + c, as in ex.2(i), (ii)) or he may freely alter it, though without any pattern of regularity, e.g. B + c, B + a, B + b.

In two- and three-couplet tunes, variation is mainly achieved through the alternation of A, B and C, the second half of the melody remaining the same. In only a few examples, two different halves were regularly alternated (e.g. ex.3(ii): C + a, A + individual variant of b), or irregularly alternated.

Incidence and Combinations of Variants
in Single-, Two- and Three-couplet Melodies

The relative incidence of variants A, B and C as single-couplet tunes is shown in fig.1(a), and their combinations as two-couplet melodies in fig.1(b). It can be seen that A, B and C variants occur about equally in two-couplet melodies, types beginning with C being predominant. No instrumental two-couplet melodies were found.

Fig. 1a Single-couplet tunes

Variant:	A	B	C	Total
Number of examples:	10	5	1	16

Fig. 1b Two-couplet tunes

Variant:	AB	BA	AC	CA	BC	CB	Total
Number of examples:	1	2	1	2	2	3	11

Alternation between the two variants is usually, though not always, regular. In some AB and CB examples, there is a tendency roughly halfway through the song to use only the B phrase, so that in effect these performances change from two-couplet to single-couplet structure. The fact that it is the B variant which is thus used suggests that this melody is felt to create greater dramatic tension.

Of the melodies considered here using all three variants, three combine A, B and C in irregular patterns, with two variants predominating. One example consists of a regular alternation of A, B and C, as in ex.4; and two consist of ABCB, thereby comprising four-couplet strophes (e.g. as in Nikos Xylouris, the 'Tale', on EMIAL Regal XREG 2015, II/8).[24] The significant feature of three-couplet melodies is that most of them are instrumental; and even in vocal three-couplet melodies the tendency to melismata suggests influence from an instrumental idiom, e.g. ex.4(i).

Formulaic Phrases

Further study of variants A, B and C reveals that the entire body of couplet-tunes draws heavily on a few motifs, the chief of these being a four-note phrase ascending stepwise, from either the seventh, second or fourth degree (e.g. ex.1, and all second hemistichs of ex.2); its inversion, i.e. a four-note phrase *descending* stepwise, as in the second hemistich of ex.2 and third hemistich of ex.3(iii); and the threefold repetition of one note at the beginning or the end of a hemistich, as in the first hemistich of ex.1(ii) and (iv), the third hemistich of ex.1(v) and ex.2(i); and the final hemistich of all examples.

Summary and Conclusions

Individual variation in Rotokritos' melody consists mainly of the performer's selection of one of three stabilized variants which are subject to minimal individual variation, and the performance of one of these variants on its own or in regular alternation of two or more. A further means of variation lies in the choice of different combinations of two halves of a couplet tune. Rotokritos' melody thus differs from other Cretan melodies sung to rhymed narrative texts, these melodies being subject to considerable individual and regional rhythmic and melodic variation within each line.

The three variants, A, B and C, are not regional but can be found throughout the island. The only regional variant (ex.1(v), (viii)) differs from other examples in its rhythmic structure, being in regular duple time.

The A variants predominate in both Cretan and non-Cretan versions as well as in Cretan single-couplet tunes. This suggests that it was the first tune to which the *Erotokritos* was sung. Since, however, both B and C variants are found in non-Cretan two-couplet versions,[25] a Cretan origin cannot necessarily be ascribed to them.

Rotokritos' melody is the only Cretan melody which may correspond in length to more than one couplet. Even in those genres which involve single-couplet tunes—the narrative songs, lullabies, *mantinades* and laments—lines 1 and 2 are differentiated primarily by their incipit, both lines cadencing on the first degree (except one melody, unpublished, used in Anogia for recent historical texts such as the burning of Anogia during World War II—ex.5).

The difference between Rotokritos' melody and other Cretan melodies can be ascribed at least in part to its association with a widely-known text which, though oral in circulation, was literary in origin.

The lack of marked regional variations in Rotokritos' melody may be the result of the wide circulation of the text, and the awareness of a fixed model, both textual and melodic. Commercial recordings of the *Erotokritos* may also have contributed to this.

The strong sense of identity attached to Rotokritos' melody may be because of its couplet structure, which as has been shown is significantly different from other Cretan melodies; and because all variants make use of a small number of rhythmic and melodic motives.

Plate XIV Cretan *lyra* accompanied by *daouli*.

TRANSCRIPTIONS (page 292–297)

Layout: (1) bar-lines reflect text structure only: the half bar-line marks the end of a hemistich, the whole bar-line the end of a complete line of text, the double bar-line the end of a couplet; (2) each whole couplet is laid out as a single line across two pages so that melodic sections of all four hemistichs may be compared; (3) the versions are given in order of their provenance from West to East, thus showing regional variation.

Tempo, rhythm: (1) rate of narration is highly consistent at crotchet = 200–220 for all examples; (2) most of the examples do not fall into any regular time division, the rhythmic values being determined by the syllabic rendition of the text with durations in a relationship of 1:2 (cf Baud-Bovy (1956), p.380). In the few examples that do have a regular rhythmic structure going across the text structure, a time signature in parentheses has been used.

Pitch (1) to facilitate comparison, all melodies have been transcribed to final pitch *d'*: the original pitches of all vocal melodies fall between finals *g* and *d'*, reflecting the proximity of male and female ranges in Crete: (2) an upward or downward arrow above a note indicates a pitch slightly sharper or flatter than written.

COMMENTARY

Information under each item is given as follows: source (printed or otherwise; 'LD' denotes number in the author's tape collection); place of recording; first line or title of text; modern edition (*EDT* denotes *Ellinika Dimotika Tragoudia (Eklogi . . . ton Kimenon)*); name of performer.

Ex. 1: Single-couplet melodies: Variant A

(i)   Source: Notopoulos (1959) 29, from Sfakia; text: the 'Tale', sung by D. Skordiles.

(ii)   Source: LD33/14, from Moni Dioskouron (near Axos); text: *Tou Manoura* (cf St George and the Dragon), in M. I. Kalokyri: *Anogia— Mylopotamou Rethymnis (Laografia Syllogi)* (Irakleion, 1970), 23–6; sung by Chrisi Jmali.

(iii)   Source: LD65/4, from Tzermiadon, Lasithi; text: *Apo mia moanta*; sung by Maria Chalkiadaki.

(iv)   Source: LD29/17, from Lakonia, Mirambellou; text: *O Xopateras*, in Kriaris (1969), 100; sung by Eleni Kounenou.

(v)   Source: LD73/5, from Malles, Lasithi; text: *O kynigos eperase se perdika kynigi*; sung by Chrisi Papadaki.

(vi)   Source:LD69/13, from Stavrochori, Sitia; text: *Mia kori roda mazeve*, in Kriaris (1969), 372; sung by Christina Pevkianaki.

(vii)   Source: LD69/16, from Stavrochori, Sitia; text: *I kaki pethera*, in *EDT*, i, 348; sung by Maria Papachatzaki.

(viii)   Source: LD72/7, from Armeni, Sitia; played by Mathios Garifalakis (*lyra*) and Lefteris Pathiakis (*daouli*).

Ex. 2: Single-couplet melodies: Variant B

(i)   Source: LD46/12, from Alones, Rethymnon; text: *Ai Giorgi*, in Kriaris (1969), 7–10; sung by Evangelia Petraki.

(ii)   the second couplet of ex.2(i).

(iii)   Source: LD52/11, from Anogia, Rethymnon; text: *Tragoudi tou Makraki*; sung by Irini Kefaloyianni.

(iv)   Source: LD65/6, from Tzermiadon, Lasithi; text: *Ai Giorgi* (cf ex.2(i)); sung by Maria Michail Antriani.

Ex.3: Two-couplet melodies

(i)   Source: LD40/1, from Kali Sikia, Rethymnon; text: *Erodis' i anatoli*, in *EDT*, i, 361 (see also note 16 below); sung by Efsevia Alevizaki.

(ii)   Source: LD62/1, from Dories, Mirambellou; text: *O Laretzakis ke o Papadakis*; sung by Petros Xenos.

(iii)   Source: Politi (1968), 54, from Irakleion province; text: Opening lines of the *Erotokritos;* singer not specified.

(iv)   Source: LD78/7, from Zoforous, Iraklion; text: *Tou Koraka to tragoudi*, in Kriaris (1969), 156; sung by Michalis Starakis.

(v)   Source: LD52/19, from Anogia, Rethymnon; text: the 'Tale'; sung by Eleni Soultatou.

Ex.4: Three-couplet melodies

(i)   Source: LD39/5, from Alones, Rethymnon; text: *Tou Kastana to tragoudi*, in G. I. Peraki: *Rantologia* (Athens, 1972), 93–7; sung by Irini Alevizaki.

(ii)   Source: LD32/11, from Kroustas, Mirambellou; played by Michalis Lathiotakis, (*thiamboli*—duct flute).

Ex. 5:   Source LD57/3, from Anogia; text: 'The Burning of Anogia', in Kalokyri (1970), 58f; sung by Evridiki Manoura.

Ex. 1 Single-couplet melodies Variant A (each line extends across two pages)

Ex. 2 Single-couplet melodies Variant B

Ex. 3 Two-couplet melodies

(i)

AC

Βρίχ - νω   μία   κό - ρη   πού 'πλη - νε   σέ   μαρ - μα - ρέ - νια   γούρ - να

Κό - ρη   γιά   βγά - λε   μοῦ   νε - ρό   τήν   κα - λη - μοί - ρα   νά - 'χεις

(ii)

CA

καί   πόρ - ι - σεν'   εἰς   τά   Χα - νιά   δια - βά - ζει   τά   φερ - μά - νια

Μιά   πα - ρεσ - κήν   ἠ - μέρ'   ἠ - τό   τσῆ   δέ - κα   'πά - νω   κά - τω

(iii)

AB

τοῦ   κύκ - λου   τά   γυ - ρίσ - μα - τα,   π'ἀ - νε - βο - κα - τε - βαί - νου

μέ   τοῦ   και - ροῦ   τ'ἀ - λλά - μα - τα   π'α - να - παη - μό   δέν   ἔ - χου,

(iv)

BA

Στά   χί - λια   ὀχ - τα - κό - σι - α   δύ - ο   καί   ὀγ - δο - ην - τα

εἰς   τά   ὀχ - τώ   τοῦ   Σεπ - τεμ - βριοῦ   εἶ - ναι   γιορ - τή   με - γά - λη

(v)

CB

Τ'ἄ - κου - σες   Ἀ - ρε - τού - σα   μου   νά   σοῦ   τό   πῶ   καί   γροί - κα

εἶ - ναι   δύο   μῆ - νες   σή - με - ρα   πού   'λαχ'   σέ   κά - ποια   δά - ση

Ex. 4 Three-couplet melodies

Ex. 5

κρυ - φέ - ως τὴν ἐ - λά - τρε - νε ὡ - σὰν τὴν Πα - να - γί - α

« Ἀ - λεκ' αὐ - τό δέν θά γί - νη ν' αὐ - το - κτο - νή - ζω θέ - λει»

κι' ἡ Μα - ρι - ῶ ὥς τ' ἄ - κου - σε κα - κό στό νοῦ τζη βά - ζει

ρουγ - κασ - τῆ - τε νά σᾶς πῶ λυ - πη - τε - ρό τρα - γού - δι

NOTES TO CHAPTER 11

1. Detailed information on the origins, sources and style of the *Erotokritos* can be found in L. Politi: Introduction to *V. Kornaros: Erotokritos*, ed. S. Xanthoudidis (Athens, 1968). A prose translation can be found by J. Mavrogordato (London, 1929). The only extant manuscript is *GB-Lbm* Harl.5644. Line numbers cited here are those of the edition by S. Xanthoudidis (Irakleion, 1915).

2. Xanthoudidis (1915), 165; Mavrogordato (1929), 1f; G. Morgan: 'Cretan Poetry: Sources and Inspiration', *Kritika Chronika*, xiv (1960), 7–68, 204–70, 379–425, see p.406; Politi (1968), 40.

3. E.g. R. Bryans: *Crete* (London, 1969), 88; J. A. Notopoulos: 'Modern Greek Heroic Oral Poetry', Ethnic Folkways FE 4468, disc notes (New York, 1959), p.29; D. A. Petropoulou: 'Tou Daskaloyianni ta tragoudia', *Kritika Chronika*, viii (1954), 230; P. Leigh Fermor: Introduction to trans. of *G. Psychoundakis: The Cretan Runner* (London, 1955/R1968), 13. Though during my field work many informants described having heard such performances, the longest fragment of the *Erotokritos* I recorded was 220 lines. I recorded the anon. *Voskopoula* ('The Fair Shepherdess'), a 16th-century Cretan play, sung in its entirety; see S. Alexiou, ed.: *Voskopoula: Kritiko Idyllio tou 1600* (Irakleion, 1963).

4. S. Baud-Bovy: 'La strophe de distiques rimés dans la chanson grecque', *Studia memoriae Belae Bartok sacra* (Budapest, 1956), *passim* and 368f.

5. S. Baud-Bovy: 'Tis sousas to tragoudi', *Mnimosynon Sofias Antoniadi* (Venice, 1974), 286f.

6. E.g. Book A, lines 391ff, 515, 522, 607, 643, 741, 752, 879, 931 etc.

7. Cf Baudy-Bovy's remark (1956), 379 fn.

8. R. Pashley: *Travels in Crete* (Cambridge, 1837/R1970), i, 11; T. A. B. Spratt: *Travels and Researches in Crete* (London, 1867), i, 357f (appx by Viscount Strangford). For references to mentions of the *Erotokritos* by travellers in other parts of Greece see Xanthoudidis (1915), pp.cxxxvff.

9. But it is quoted by G. I. Chatzidakis: *Kritiki Mousiki* (Athens, 1958), 165. Baud-Bovy omits Rotokritos' melody from his *Chansons populaires de Crète occidentale* (Geneva, 1972), stating (p.4) that he will include it in a subsequent volume on eastern Crete, where the melody occurs in 'nombreuses' variants.

10. Chadzidakis (1958), 165, from Irakleion; Baud-Bovy (1956), ex.21, from Kritsa; Politi (see my ex.3(iii)); Notopoulos (see my ex.1(i)). Also an example recorded by Julie du Boulay in Kallikrati, Sfakia, in BBC Archives, disc LP 29438.

11. See Baud-Bovy (1956), 380–83 for a discussion of rhythms.

12. Eastern Cretan versions: e.g. Chadzidakis (1958), 165; Athens Academy Folklore Archives no.17829 (recorded by G. Amaryiannakis in Sitia region). Non-Cretan versions: e.g. S. Baud-Bovy: *Tragoudia ton Dodekanison (Chansons populaires du Dodecanese)* (Athens, 1935–8), i, 354f; K. Artemidou: 'Apo ta Kypriaka dimotika tragoudia', *Kypriakai Spoudai*, xvi (1953), ex.10; D. W. Holton: ' "The Leprous Queen": a Ballad from Lesbos', *Byzantine and Modern Greek Studies*, i (1975), 101.

13. Quoted in Xanthoudidis (1915), p.xxiii.

14. E.g. Notopoulos (1959), 29.

15. The 'Farewell': Chatzidakis (1958), 165; it can be heard on EMIAL Regal XREG

2015, sung by the Cretan *lyra* player Nikos Xyloukis (side II band 7). On the same disc (II/8) he sings the 'Tale'. Another recording of the 'Tale', from Sfakia, can be heard on Folkways FE 4468 (recorded in 1952–3 by Notopoulos). His transcription is quoted here as ex.1(i); the text of ex.3 is also the 'Tale'.

16.   A. B. Lord: *The Singer of Tales* (Cambridge, Mass., 1960), 121; the 'Recognition', quoted in A. Kriaris: *Kritika Dimotika Tragoudia* (Athens, 1920, 3/1969), 296, as a *rizitikotis stratas* ('road song'). It is quoted in another version by G. S. Amaryiannakis: *Symboli is tin meletin tis dimodous kritikis mousikis (melodiai tou gamou)* (Irakleion, 1967), 10, as a wedding song. See also ex.3(i).

17.   See Politi (1968), 40; Xanthoudidis (1915), pp.cxxxv–clxv. Baud-Bovy, in *La chanson populaire Grecque du Dodecanese I: Les textes* (Paris, 1936), 350, quotes a wedding song from Karpathos mentioning Erotokritos and Aretousa. They also appear frequently in Cretan *mantinades* (improvised rhymed couplets) and wedding songs.

18.   For a description of all these instruments see F. Anoyianakis: *Instruments de musiques populaires grecs* (Athens, 1965). The *lyra* and lute duet may be replaced in the West (Kissamos) by violin and lute, and in the East (Mirambellou and Sitia) by violin and guitar or *lyra* and guitar.

19.   See Notopoulos (1959), p.27, transcr. of the 'Song of Daskaloyiannes'. This melody is often referred to as *Lypiteros skopos* ('sad melody') since the narrative texts to which it is sung are so often about tragic historical events.

20.   Noticeably more in the West than in the East; cf Pashley's remark: 'it must be observed that no woman of the island ever sings: and the Sfakian women, whose seclusion and reserve is even greater than that of other female Cretans, never even dance' (i, 255).

21.   As in *mantinades*, improvised rhymed couplets.

22.   Cf Lomax's method of coding phrases which are variants of each other, but which are repeated in a consistent pattern: 'Then each phrase in each segment is considered different from the others and the form is considered to be ABC ABC': A. Lomax: *Folk Song Style and Culture* (Washington, D.C., 1968), 57.

23.   These figures are representative of the occurrence of single-, two- and three-couplet melodies in my whole collection of Rotokritos' melodies.

24.   Xylouris' version of the 'Farewell', on the same disc, II/7, is in a slightly different pattern: Introduction: C — Song: ABC — Interlude: C — Song: C⁴ACB — Interlude: C — Song: ACB — Interlude: C — Song: C⁴ACB. C, however, is still used as the pillar melody.

25.   Two-couplet melodies in non-Cretan versions may be more common than indicated in printed transcriptions, since these usually give the melody for one couplet only. Examples of two-couplet non-Cretan melodies are in Baud-Bovy (1935–8), i, 354, 355 (from Castellorizo); *Ellinika Dimotika Tragoudia (Eklogi . . . ton Kimenon)*, iii, ed. G. K. Spyridaki and S. D. Peristeri (Athens, 1968), 15, 110 (from Cyprus).

Part III

THE USE OF ARCHIVES

12

Archival Material relating to Music in England, 1660–1720

Margaret Laurie

The exploration of contemporary documents for information is an essential, if occasionally frustrating, task. Each source may only supply one or two facts, yet these gradually add up to a fuller picture, and clues pursued often lead in unexpected directions.[1]

In this chapter I shall discuss the main types of material likely to be useful with some indication of the sort of information which they contain, what indexes there are to help one find both the originals and modern transcripts where they exist, and some other related problems. In order to cover the main areas of importance, I have included a section concerning theatres, concerts etc, although many of the documents discussed there are printed and therefore strictly speaking not archives. I make no claim, however, to be entirely comprehensive.

Many record offices publish guides to their collections, and some have detailed indexes to various classes of documents in their care. Librarians and archivists in charge are usually extremely helpful in advising one how to make best use of their collections, though naturally one must not expect them to do one's work for one. It is generally advisable to write before one's first visit, giving as precise a definition of one's field of enquiry as possible. Some repositories, such as the Public Record Office, require one to obtain a reader's ticket beforehand.

When searching records for a particular name, the possibility must be borne in mind that several people may have had that name—especially at this period, when children were rarely given more than one Christian name. For example, Zimmerman points out that there were at least three other Henry Purcells living in London at the same time as the composer.[2] Moreover, spelling was wholly unstandardised, and may be inconsistent even within a single document. Hence a name must be searched for under all its possible variant forms.

Until the reform of the calendar in 1752, the year in Britain officially began on 25 March, though many people thought of it as beginning on 1 January. Often both years are given for dates between the two—e.g. 2 February 168$\frac{1}{2}$, but this date can equally correctly be indicated by either '2 February 1681' or '2 February 1682'. When dealing with dates in the first three months of the year, great care must therefore be taken to establish from context which year is intended. Moreover, most continental countries already followed the Gregorian calendar while Britain retained the Julian calendar until 1752; as a result, continental dates before 1700 were ten days, after 1700 11 days, in advance of British ones, e.g. 12 October 1682 in Holland corresponded to 2 October 1682 in Britain. Some foreign correspondence bears both dates.

Local Records and Private Papers

In seeking biographical material, it is usually advisable first to establish the main outlines of a man's professional career and then to search for his will (and those of close relatives if known) before tackling parish registers, for wills in general are somewhat easier to find. They are indexed (if sometimes imperfectly), and they give a lead at least to the burial notice since they usually mention the testator's parish of residence at the time the will was made (often shortly before death). They also provide limits for the date of death, since this must have occurred between the date on which the will was made and the date on which probate was granted—the latter being always noted at the end (or endorsed on the back of an original). The time taken to obtain probate varied considerably; it could be granted on the day after death, but more often took anything between two weeks and two months, and occasionally longer. A will also generally names close relatives, such as wife and children, and may provide other useful information.

Although the wills of many people living in the southern half of England were proven in the Prerogative Court of Canterbury, and are now in the Public Record Office, others were submitted to archdeaconry, consistory or other local courts whose records are preserved in a number of repositories. There are, for instance, at least seven places where wills of Londoners alone may be found. Two books exist to clarify the situation: A. J. Camp: *Wills and their Whereabouts* (London, 4/1974), and J. S. W. Gibson: *Wills and Where to Find Them* (Chichester, 1974). These indicate where wills for different districts are now located, stating what type of documents are available and what indexes have been printed.

Normally wills were copied into large volumes called registers, for which indexes were made, usually year by year. These indexes are cumbersome to use and have a number of omissions, but nonetheless considerably lessen the labour of searching. The Index Library series (1881–) contains modern indexes to wills and administrations for the Prerogative Court of Canterbury up to 1700, for Chelmsford, Essex (covering some parts of East London) and for some six other provincial courts for our period so far; others are in progress.

Several repositories still have some original wills; these usually bear at least the signature of the testator, and may be entirely in his hand, though it was common to employ a scribe, especially if the testator were on his deathbed. An inventory was generally drawn up of the man's goods; and this was filed sometimes with the original will, but more often separately. Not many have survived, but they may be worth investigating.

Unfortunately, many people did not make wills; when a man died intestate, the next-of-kin could (but did not always) apply for letters of administration appointing him administrator. Such administrations are indicated in the indexes to wills; the entries in the court act-books (usually in Latin) give only the date of probate, the administrator's name and sometimes the deceased's parish.

Since there were no certificates of birth, marriage or death at this period, parish (or similar non-conformist) registers of baptisms, marriages and burials are often the only official records of these events, and they vary widely in comprehensiveness from place to place. Baptisms generally took place within a fortnight of birth but were sometimes saved up for feast days or other special dates. The registers give the father's (and usually mother's) name and sometimes the father's occupation, but only a few give the actual date of birth. Marriage registers often give the marital status and parish of residence of both parties. They only occasionally give their occupations or their parents' names. Allegations for marriage licences (then, as now, the alternative to having banns declared) often give rather more details. These licences were issued by the bishop; the allegations for them are therefore among the cathedral records discussed below. Burial registers generally note 'child' where appropriate and sometimes enter occupation, but rarely much else. Where the church in which a man was buried still stands, it may be worth looking there for a tombstone or other memorial, for these can supply biographical details, such as age at death, unrecorded elsewhere.

Parishes were supposed to submit transcripts of their registers to their bishop each year; in some areas these 'bishop's transcripts' are fuller than the actual registers, but in others the regulation seems to have been ignored—there are, for instance, virtually no bishop's transcripts for

London, Middlesex or Essex. The surviving transcripts are again among cathedral records.

Some parish registers are still held by the original church; increasingly, however, those that survive are being deposited in the appropriate town or county record office. A *National Index of Parish Registers,* giving details, county by county, of original registers and bishop's transcripts, and of modern copies where available, is now in progress, though not yet complete. Meanwhile the Local Population Studies' *Original Parish Registers in Record Offices and Libraries* (Matlock, 1974) covers those in public custody. Some county record offices have published lists of locations of parish registers in their counties; Inner London ones, for example, are covered by two surveys of parish registers in the Dioceses of London and Southwark respectively (published by The Greater London Record Office, London, 1969, rev. 2/1972; 1970), with further details of those held by the Guildhall Library being supplied by the latter's *Parish Registers: a Handlist* (London, 1967–72). Many parish registers have now been microfilmed by the Latter-Day Saints. Copies of these films are available in the relevant county record offices. Microfiches of the Latter-Day Saints' *Computer File Index* of names are held by their genealogical branch libraries, the Society of Genealogists in London and the Institute of Heraldic and Genealogical Studies in Canterbury.

Transcripts of a fair number of parish registers have been published, notably by the Harleian Society in its Register Series, the Parish Register Society, the Phillimore Parish Register Society (marriages only), religious bodies such as the Catholic and Huguenot Societies, and various local record societies. Guides to the 19th-century ones can be found in G. W. Marshall, *Parish Registers* (London, 1900–04) and G. F. Matthews, *Contemporary Index to Printed Parish (and Non-Parochial) Registers* (London, 1908); the former, arranged by parish, covers rather more ground; the latter, arranged by county, gives a few more details. Later ones are listed under place in the British Museum subject indexes, 1881–1960. Further aids to finding works in series will be discussed later.

The Society of Genealogists has produced lists of unpublished transcripts in existence, many of which are in its own library.[4] This also contains various useful card indexes, such as those to marriage and burial registers and apprenticeship and inhabitants of London lists. It also has a good collection of relevant books. It is open to non-members upon payment of a fee. Many non-conformist registers were deposited with the Registrar General after the 1840 Non-Parochial Registers Act. These are now in the Public Record Office, and are listed in the General Register

Office, *Lists of Non-Parochial Registers and Records in the Custody of the Registrar-General* (London, 1859).

Records of church affairs, including the maintenance of the organ and dealings with employees such as the choir and organist, were usually kept in such documents as churchwardens' accounts and vestry minutes. The Guildhall Library publishes handlists of its holdings of such books; others, if preserved, are probably with the parish registers.

Cathedral records are naturally more complex than those of parish churches. Those documents most likely to interest musicologists are: accounts (sometimes in several sequences) and chapter act-books, giving information concerning employees and lessees; the cathedral's own registers and the bishop's transcripts; allegations for marriage licences, and possibly deeds and other material relating to church property. Some cathedral records, for example those of Chichester, are deposited in local record offices, but most cathedrals have their own libraries. The Pilgrim Trust's two-volume typescript *Survey of Ecclesiastical Archives* (1952), of which copies are kept in the British Library, Bodleian Library, Oxford, and University Library, Cambridge, provides a comprehensive guide to cathedral records (but does not deal with parish material). A shorter but more readily available account of this material is given in D. M. Owen, *The Records of the Established Church in England, Excluding Parochial Records,* Archives and the User, i (London, 1970), with supplement in *Archives*, x (1971–2), 53–6.

Rates were levied mainly through the parish and were recorded either in the general overseer's accounts or in special rate-books. Such records are usually arranged street by street, giving the names of the occupiers. Thus they can be used to establish people's residences, and also to give some idea of their financial standing since the rate charged was related to the tenant's property. Records of other taxes, such as hearth-tax (levied 1662–88) and poll-tax (levied 1660–1700) may also yield information; assessments for poll-tax should list every member of each household over the age of 16; sometimes, however, they give status only—e.g. 'wife', 'maidservant', with no names—and unfortunately not very many such lists seem to have survived. A central record of these taxes was kept until 1689; the documents are now in the Public Record Office.[5] Thereafter such lists were only kept locally; surviving records will probably be in the local record office. The Guildhall Library's *London Rates Assessments and Inhabitants Lists* (London, 1961) details their holdings of such records, mostly from the City of London, and the Westminster Public Library possesses a number of rate-books etc from its own area.

Many towns still employed waits, who combined a watchman's with a musician's duties. Information concerning them is to be found in municipal records, both accounts and (usually more fruitful) corporation minutes. Apprenticeship lists may also contain matter of interest.[6] Such documents are also now usually in the local record office, and some have been published, often by local record societies.

University and school records may also be worth examining. Zimmerman, for instance, found entries in Eton's accounts for payments made to Purcell for teaching John Weldon.[7] Lists of pupils have been published for Oxford and Cambridge Universities and several schools, including Eton, Harrow and Westminster. A bibliography of these can be found in P. M. Jacobs, *Registers of the Universities, Colleges and Schools in Great Britain and Ireland: a List* (London, 1964).

Many families have preserved a wide range of family papers, including estate and household accounts, invoices, deeds, diaries and letters. Financial documents range from those of major landowners such as the Duke of Bedford who employed musicians and sponsored performances and publications[8] to those of ordinary people, like Daniel Fleming,[9] whose interest in music did not stretch much beyond providing harpsichord lessons for their daughters and perhaps paying a piper at Christmas time.

Many family collections are still kept in the family home. The library at Chatsworth House, Derbyshire, for instance, still contains papers not only of the Duke of Devonshire's own family, but also of several others connected to it.[10] Other collections, like the Ashtead Manor accounts,[11] have been deposited in county record offices or other libraries. Both the Bodleian Library, Oxford and the Reference Division of the British Library have sizeable collections of such material. The British Library holdings are indexed in the second volume of *Public Revenue, State Establishments, Private Accounts*, apart from the single letters for which there is a separate index.[12] Yet other family collections have been acquired by American libraries.[13]

The location, examination and publication of some of this vast range of material has been the principal concern of the Historical Manuscripts Commission over the last 100 years. Its work has been supplemented by national historical societies such as the Camden and Harleian Societies and local record societies at both county and town level. The appendices to the Historical Manuscripts Commission reports vary in presentation from little more than a list of documents—not always covering the whole collection— to almost verbatim transcriptions. Many of the collections covered were at the time in private hands and some have since changed location; a list of the present locations is maintained by the Historical Manuscripts Commission's Office. Name and place indexes to the Reports are provided by two sets of *Guides to the Reports*, for 1870–1911 (London, 1914–38) and 1911–57 (London, 1966–73) respectively. These name indexes, however, are not entirely comprehensive. Although the Historical Manuscripts Commission, through its offshoot the National Register of Archives, still publishes some reports, most of those compiled since 1945 exist only in typescript, for the Commission has felt it more important to concentrate limited resources on locating and examining manuscripts than to do so on the time-consuming and costly procedure of preparing copy for publication. Both the original reports and name, place and subject indexes to them are kept in the Historical Manuscripts Commission's Office,[14] which is open to *bona fide* students without formalities.[15] A list of the reports added each year was published in the *Bulletin of the National Register of Archives* from 1948 to 1967, then in *The Report of the Secretary to the Commissioners* for 1968/69–1970/71 and since 1972 in the appropriate *List of Accessions to Repositories*. The latter list manuscripts added to British record offices and other libraries each year, though since 1972 they have not included deposits of parish registers. The first two such lists, those for 1954 and 1955, were published as volumes vi and viii of the *Bulletin of the National Register of Archives*: subsequent ones have been published separately. An index to the *Lists for 1954–58* has also been published. Accessions and migrations of historical manuscripts had in fact been included in the *Bulletin of the Institute of Historical Research* from its inception in 1923, but these lists had grown so large by 1951 that they were then drastically curtailed—a policy which prompted the Historical Manuscripts Commission to start publishing its own fuller lists.

Finding out what local records, private papers etc have actually been published can be quite a formidable task. M. J. Kaminkow's *A New Bibliography of British Genealogy with Notes* (Baltimore, 1965) is a helpful starting-point, listing books by topic, with a section organised on a county basis which includes guides to county record offices. It also notes, but does not give detailed lists of, local record society publications. For these, E. L. C. Mullins, *A Guide to the Historical and Archaeological Publications of Societies in England and Wales, 1901–1933* (London, 1968) is the best approach, for its index includes not only names and places but also extensive subject references. Unfortunately its date-limits exclude much useful material. The same author's *Texts and Calendars: an Analytical Guide to Serial Publications* (London, 1960) gives complete lists of all the series (except some parish register series) likely to be of use, but has no index to subjects.

In addition there are a few manuscripts devoted specifically to music. Most of Roger North's writings on music (*GB-Lbm* Add.32531–7) have been published[16] but only extracts from Wood's biographical notes (*GB-Ob* Wood D.19(4)) have been printed[17] while the anonymous *Collections for a History of Musicians,* dating from about 1700 (*Ob* Mus.e.17), seem little known although they contain some scraps of information not recorded elsewhere.

Oxford University Music Faculty and the Royal Society of Musicians both possess collections of portraits of musicians, though the Royal Society has not many 17th-century ones.[18]

State Papers

I have already mentioned several types of record of a mainly local character which are preserved among central government papers at the Public Record Office. The state papers containing most information of musical interest, however, are those relating to the royal household, which included several groups of musicians. In Charles II's time these consisted of trumpeters, fife-and-drummers; violins (including three or four composers), wind music and private music; and gentlemen and children of the Chapel Royal. The core of the private music were 'lutes, viols and voices' but some of the violinists belonged to it as well. In fact, there was considerable overlap between these different groups (apart from the trumpeters), for most of the 'voices' came from the Chapel Royal, and many of the instrumentalists played both string and wind instruments. Additional groups of French and Italian musicians are occasionally mentioned but these were probably short-lived. The Queen and Queen Mother had their own Chapels, but references to their staff are rare. By the time of James II, the distinction between violins, wind and private music seems to have disappeared, the last term being applied to all. In 1687, James established a Catholic Chapel, served by a separate choir of 16 men (ten called Gregorians) and seven boys.[19] William and Mary reduced the number of musicians in their employ, not only discontinuing this Catholic Chapel but also reducing the number of instrumentalists (apart from the trumpeters etc) to 25.[20]

The royal musicians came mainly under the jurisdiction of the Lord Chamberlain, but references to them occur not only in his records but also in the Domestic Papers, various Treasury Books and Papers including the

Declared Accounts, and sometimes in other sequences such as Patent Rolls and Secret Service Accounts as well.

The instrumentalists' appointments, disciplinary orders, livery payments and issues of clothing, travelling charges for accompanying the king out of London, and payments for various other special tasks undertaken, including the purchase and repair of instruments and the copying of music, are recorded mainly in the Lord Chamberlain's records with some duplication and supplementation in the other main sequences. Payments of ordinary salaries were recorded only in the Treasury Books and Declared Accounts. Both the Lord Chamberlain's books and the Treasury Books occasionally note dates of death, and the former contain transcripts of a few wills, but the usual intimation of a man's withdrawal from service was the appointment of his successor. Occasionally payments were made to other musicians drafted in for special purposes, for example for the masque of *Calisto* in 1675 or to accompany William III to Holland in 1691.

The situation concerning the members of the Chapel is more complicated. Appointments of the Gentlemen (normally mentioning date of resignation or death of predecessor) and most regulations are recorded in *The Old Cheque-Book of the Chapel Royal from 1561 to 1744*,[21] apart from the appointments of James II's Catholic Chapel which were noted in the Treasury Books. Special payments, including travelling charges, fees for copying (rare until 1718), payments to the Master of the Children and other musicians for the education and upkeep of the boys, the allowances of money and clothing made to each boy when he left the Chapel after his voice broke, and some regulations, are recorded in either the Lord Chamberlain's books or the Treasury Books, sometimes in both; but the actual salaries for Chapel personnel were paid by the Cofferer and are therefore rarely mentioned in the Treasury Books since that official normally received a block grant.[22] His Declared Accounts are not helpful since they are always presented in block form. In 1676 a list of anthems and services performed by the Chapel Royal was entered in the Lord Chamberlain's books. This was an isolated phenomenon, though in 1712 the Chapel Royal issued a word-book[23] which gives a more extensive picture of their repertoire.

Traditionally, cavalry regiments included trumpeters (and occasionally, as a mark of distinction, kettledrummers), while infantry regiments had fife-and-drum bands. Oboes were first introduced into infantry regiments in 1678[24] and by 1700 several had one oboe and one side drum per company. The trumpeters and kettledrummers attached to the King's and

Queen's regiments were at least sometimes supplied with instruments and livery by the royal Wardrobe and are therefore mentioned from time to time in the Lord Chamberlain's books. There are also occasional references to the oboists and drummers of the Grenadiers of the Horse Guards. Otherwise, although the number of instrumentalists employed can be found in the Army Establishment Lists (Public Record Office W.O.24), it does not seem to be possible to discover their names, for the Army Lists only name officers, and the Muster Books, naming all ranks, do not go back far enough.

The Domestic Papers and Lord Chamberlain's books also record the efforts of the Corporation of Musicians (dominated by the King's Musick)[25] to maintain their right to impose a 'closed-shop' situation on musicians in general. A draft edict of April 1664 decreed that no-one in England and Wales should 'exercise or teach musique for reward or advantage (except such as take degrees in the universities . . .) but such as are free of or have the approbation of the s[ai]d Corporation'.[26] All trumpeters etc wishing to play publicly were similarly expected to obtain a licence from the Sergeant Trumpeter. The Lord Chamberlain's books record the names of musicians arrested on several occasions for defying these regulations[27] though efforts to enforce them seem to have ceased after 1673.

Calendars have been published for the Domestic Papers (to 1704), Treasury Books (to 1718) and Treasury Papers. The Treasury Books series include the Declared Accounts (in their Introductions) from volume xi (1698–1702) only; by then salary payments were usually presented in block form; some 'special' payments are still itemised in the actual Treasurer of the Chamber's Accounts, but these are summarised in the Calendars.

Calendars reckon to convey the essential information contained in the documents concerned as briefly as possible. For many purposes they are sufficient, but inevitably points of interest are sometimes lost. For example, in about May 1661 William Saunders applied for a post in the King's Musick, his application being supported by a certificate from Nicholas Lanier and four others, not named in the Calendar.[28] The original documents[29] not only bear the signatures of all five referees, but also tell us (a) that Saunders played both sackbut and bass violin, (b) that the King's Musick were short of bass violinists at this point, and (c) that the sackbut was required specifically for the Chapel Royal. Nonetheless, the Calendars are the best starting point for consulting the original documents for they are copiously, if not entirely consistently, indexed. Entries for musicians can be found under such headings as 'Charles II, household', 'Royal household', 'King's Musicians', 'Chapel Royal', 'St James's—Chapel Royal', or only under their individual names. In general, references to musicians in the Domestic series are frequent in the 1660s but subsequently much rarer. The Treasury Books give a fair amount of detail until about 1690, after which entries are few, with salaries being paid *en bloc* through the Master of the King's Musick.

The references to musicians up to 1700 in the Lord Chamberlain's documents in Public Record Office classes L.C.2, 3, 5 and 9 were abstracted and published by Lafontaine in *The King's Musick*. This is also a calendar, with some entries given verbatim, but others, such as appointments, payments and claims for arrears given in compressed form, with parallel information from several sources conflated. Inevitably there are mistakes and omissions, and not all the relevant documents were consulted; nevertheless the book is an invaluable tool. Unfortunately since it was published the Lord Chamberlain's collection has been entirely renumbered, and, as far as I can discover, the Public Record Office has kept no collation of old and new numbers, so that checking Lafontaine references can be a time-consuming business. Such a collation is supplied at the end of this chapter.

Most of the original Lord Chamberlain's books have some kind of index; the alphabetical ones, however, are often very sketchy; relevant references in them are more likely to be under 'Chapel Royal' and 'Musicians' than under individual names. Other books have a running index, often under several different headings; these are usually more comprehensive.

The numbers of the main classes of documents are given in the published *Guide to the Contents of the Public Record Office* (London, 1963-8); from a combination of this and the information given in the Calendars it is sometimes, but not always, possible to deduce the order number of the original document, but to be sure of ordering the correct document one needs to consult the Public Record Office's various Lists and Indexes. Some of these are published but many are available only in the Public Record Office itself. In the Round Room there is also a name-index to some of the documents in L.C.5 and the Cairncross index to theatre references in the Lord Chamberlain's books. The Treasury, Inland Revenue and War Office documents have recently been moved to the new Public Record Office building in Kew. Most of the other material mentioned is still at Chancery Lane.

Not all state papers are still preserved in the Public Record Office. Some of the original lists, bills, petitions etc seem to have been kept by the officials concerned; for instance, Susi Jeans discovered some notes about musicians among the papers of the Duke of Dorset, Lord Chamberlain 1689–97,[30] while a collection of theatre documents originally submitted to Thomas Coke (Vice-Chamberlain, 1706–26) was in W. H. Cummings's possession in 1914[31] and is now in the Theatre Collection in Harvard University Library.[32] The Secret Service Accounts for 1679–88 were in 1851 in the possession of the family of a Secretary of the Treasury in Queen Anne's time.[33] Thus a search through the family papers of other high officials of the period might prove fruitful. The British Library has a number of state papers among its manuscripts; those concerning the royal household are indexed in the first volume of *Public Revenue, State Establishments, Private Accounts*. Various other state papers are in the Rawlinson Collection in the Bodleian Library.

A secondary, but convenient, source of information about state officials at this period are the various editions of E. Chamberlayne's *Angliae notitia*, i–xxii (1669–1707), which were continued as *Magnae Britanniae notitia*, xxii–xxv (1708–18); these must be treated with some caution, however, as they are not always completely up to date.

Theatres, Concerts etc

The London theatres were carefully controlled by the Crown. The players of both permitted theatres were technically members of the royal household (without pay) and the Lord Chamberlain, at first through his subordinate the Master of Revels but increasingly directly, censored their plays, settled their disputes and punished misdemeanours. At first, the king's violinists were expected to play in the theatres as needed, but both must soon have acquired orchestras of their own. Quite probably these were still augmented by royal musicians for more elaborate productions— at least two royal trumpeters, for instance, performed in the Purcell semi-operas.

Some references to the theatres, including lists of 'comedians', occur in the Lord Chamberlain's books considered above, but most of the theatre documents are classed in Public Record Office L.C.7.

These include licences, complaints, judgments on them and other orders, payments for royal visits to the theatres and provision of equipment for the court theatre. Many of them are reproduced in A. Nicoll, *A History of English Drama, 1660–1900*, i–ii (Cambridge, rev.1961) and E. Boswell, *The Restoration Court Stage, 1660–1702* (Cambridge, 1932). Instrumentalists, dancers and even singers (with some exceptions) were minor members of the theatrical companies and are rarely named in the earlier documents; with the development of opera, particularly from 1690 onwards, however, they became more prominent.

Only a few other theatre documents for this period are known to have survived. The most extensive collection is the Coke papers mentioned above; A. M. Broadley's manuscript *The Annals of the Haymarket* contains a number of documents, some of which may be strays from the same source.[34] Some Drury Lane bills from the years 1714–17, including several for copying music, are preserved in *Lbm* Egerton 2159, while a Haymarket account book for the 1716–17 season is now in Hampshire Record Office.[35] The Duke of Bedford's papers include two bills from Weldon relating to a performance of his *Judgment of Paris* in 1702, which list five soloists and 25 chorus singers, presumably from Drury Lane.[36]

A useful source of information for theatre performances and almost the only source for concerts, apart from those held at the Stationers' Hall mentioned in the Stationers' Company accounts, are contemporary newspapers.[37] Until the licensing laws lapsed in 1695 all publications were strictly controlled. An official newspaper, *The London Gazette*, was published twice weekly, but there were few others. Several new ones, including *The Post Boy* and *The Post Man*, appeared in 1695 or shortly afterwards but the first daily paper, *The Daily Courant*, was not established until 1702. Publications and, to some extent, concerts were advertised in *The London Gazette* (and occasionally other papers) throughout the Restoration period, and a few notices of Drury Lane performances appeared in *The Post Boy* and *The Post Man*; but such advertising increased greatly with the inauguration of *The Daily Courant*, and the Drury Lane theatre soon began to announce its performances fairly regularly, though Little Lincoln's Inn Fields was much slower to do so. *The London Stage, 1660–1800*, parts 1–2, ed. W. B. van Lennep and E. L. Avery (Carbondale, Ill., 1960–65) and Tilmouth's 'Calendar' are key sources of reference to this material, though both understandably give the information in a compressed form. The former, in attempting to reconstruct a day-by-day list of stage performances and concerts, draws on all available sources (including the Lord Chamberlain's documents mentioned above) not just newspapers. Most of the original London papers are in the Burney Newspaper Collection in the British Library; their press-marks are not entered in the general catalogues and to obtain them one has to ask for the photocopy of Burney's own catalogue at the enquiry desk in the Reading Room. A convenient compendium of the original notices is provided by F. Latreille's manuscript *Play-Bills of London*

Theatres, 1702–46, i–ii (*Lbm* Add.32249–50). Provincial newspapers are listed in G. A. Cranfield, *A Hand-List of English Provincial Newspapers and Periodicals, 1700–1760* (Cambridge, 1952).

There was no musical criticism as we know it, but there were a number of cultural magazines (generally short-lived) containing a certain amount of musical comment, including *The Gentleman's Journal* (1692–4), *Muses Mercury* (1707), *The Tatler* (1709–11) and *The Spectator* (1711–14).[38] A certain amount of comment can also be gleaned from contemporary diaries and letters. The diaries of Pepys and Evelyn are the most informative—and best known—but are not the only relevant ones. Others can be found through W. Matthews, *British Diaries: an Annotated Bibliography . . . between 1442 and 1942* (London, 1950), for the entries are arranged chronologically and the annotations give some indication of the scope of each document. Letters of musicians, such as Tudway to Humphrey Wanley (*Lbm* Harl.3782), and of playwrights, such as Dryden, Congreve and Steele, and of members of the audience, such as the Bertie family,[39] are also worth investigating.

The remaining major type of source of information about music at this period are the actual publications. From 1690, both play-texts and songbooks increasingly gave information about singers, and before the advertising of performances became widespread the publication date of the text or a songbook, or both, containing some of the music was often the only clue to the date of the first production of a play and therefore the music written for it.

Most music published before 1700, and virtually all books, bear the date of publication; but Walsh stopped putting this on his title-pages shortly after he started business in 1695, and other music publishers soon followed suit. Even when the year of publication is given, more precise dating can often be desirable; this can sometimes be deduced from a licence date, entry in the Stationers' Registers or Term Catalogues, or a newspaper advertisement. Although until 1695 all publications were supposed to be officially licensed, not very many carry the licence date on their title-pages. When they do, it precedes publication (as indicated by newspaper advertisement) on average by about two weeks, though sometimes by as little as five days or as much as three months, very occasionally more. Entry of a publication in the Stationers' Registers provided some protection in the days before copyright laws; but by no means all publications were so entered, and by the end of the 17th century such entries were very few. The registers, stretching from 1554 to 1842 (with a few early gaps), are still kept at the Stationers' Hall and those up to 1708 have been printed.[40]

Volumes seem usually to have been entered in the registers just before they became available to the public, though occasionally a whole series of books was entered together—for example, all five books of Playford's *Choice Ayres* were entered in the Stationers' Registers on 5 June 1683, a date corresponding to the publication of Book IV, Book I having appeared ten years earlier.

From 1668 to 1709 an enterprising bookseller, Robert Clavell (with some assistance) published a catalogue of new and reprinted books in the middle of virtually every law term, the Hilary list appearing in February, the Easter one in May, the Trinity one in late June or early July and the Michaelmas one in November.[41] After 1702 what music they include is usually bunched together in the Trinity catalogue, but earlier catalogues, though never entirely comprehensive, are much more informative. Entry in them usually occurred shortly after publication.

Curiously, about a fifth of the pre-1702 songbooks for which more or less precise dating can be ascertained are post-dated: i.e. they appeared before the year given on their title-pages. This phenomenon is quite common in printed books also. Such books are generally listed in the Michaelmas Term Catalogue of the previous year; Arber interpreted this to mean that books were sometimes entered in the Term Catalogues from proof copies before publication; this may occasionally have been the case, but where newspaper advertisements exist they generally confirm November or December publication. This can have important results; for instance, Purcell's *Dido and Aeneas* could be definitely dated to 1689 when it was realised that D'Urfey's *New Poems* (containing its epilogue) though dated 1690 appeared in the Term Catalogue for Michaelmas 1689.

C. L. Day and E. B. Murrie, *English Song-Books, 1651–1702* (London, 1940) is a mine of information for this material; not only does it contain first-line, composer and author indexes for each song, but it also lists the known dates for each book. The coverage of newspaper advertisements, however, is not entirely comprehensive; some supplementary dates can be gleaned from Tilmouth. W. C. Smith, *A Bibliography of the Musical Works Published by John Walsh, 1695–1720* (London, 1948) is useful for the early 18th century, increasingly dominated by this publisher. The lists of plays at the ends of the first and second volumes of Nicoll give dates of publication for play-texts.

Opera (including 'semi-opera') texts seem often to have been available for perusal in the theatre at the first performance. Ordinary play-texts, however, do not usually seem to have been available so soon, for their prefaces quite often refer to the reception afforded the play on its first appearance, and must therefore have been written after it. Nicoll thus usually allows a month between performance and publication, but does not always take into account the fact that the principal actors, at least from the 1680s, acted very little during the summer months (from mid-July to the end of September) and that therefore new works were unlikely to have been produced then.[42]

A rather longer time usually elapsed between first performance of a play and publication of any music from it, though this varied considerably and evidence is scant. The average songbook seems to have taken anything from seven months to a year to produce, judging by the gaps between successive books in the same series; but smaller collections, such as songs from a particular work, could have taken far less. In general, however, when music was written for the first production of a play, the date of publication of the play-text is likely to be a better indicator of the production date than that of the music. When, however, music was written for a revival, not for the first performance, as was frequently the case, dating can be more difficult. A reprint of the text usually indicates a revival, but revivals took place without reprints, and publication of the music is often the only guide to its date. The same is, of course, true of non-dramatic music, for even if this appears in manuscript sources as well, these are rarely dateable. Judging by those theatre songs which can be dated, the songbooks were on the whole fairly well up to date, though obviously composers may from time to time have submitted older songs for publication.

CONCORDANCE OF OLD AND NEW L.C. NUMBERS (1660–1700)

55–6	= 9/104–5		440	= 9/43
57	= 9/376, pt.1		458	= 9/376, pt.3
58–85	= 9/106–32		460–8	= 9/195–203
152–7	= 9/375		477	= 3/2
167	= 9/255		478	= 3/26
168	= 9/262		479	= 3/73
180–1	= 3/33		480	= 3/28
183–4	= 3/61–2		481	= 3/30
185–6	= 3/56–7		482	= 3/25
195–8	= 9/258		483	= 3/27
199	= 9/342		484	= 3/29 (lost)
201–10	= 9/271–8, 280–1		485–6	= 3/31–2
407	= 2/10(1)		487	= 3/3
429	= 2/13		488	= Lost?

545	= 5/223		724	= 3/53
547	= 5/193		734	= 5/86
560	= 2/9		741-56	= 5/137-152
561	= 2/11(1)		757	= 5/166
601-2	= 5/107-8		771-6	= 5/12-17
603	= 5/112		802-6	= 5/39-43
618	= 5/81		814-15	= 5/52-3
649-57	= 5/184-92		817	= 5/60
709	= 3/85		836	= 5/63
711-13	= 3/37-39		837	= 5/165
715	= 3/40			

Some of the bundles have been amalgamated and possibly rearranged. Most of the relevant material in them is probably now in L.C.5/115, 118-25, 131 & 9/347, though some may be in L.C.9/377-390.

NOTES TO CHAPTER 12

1. Useful general introductions to the field of archives are: A. J. Camp: *Tracing Your Ancestors* (London, 1964); D. E. Gardner and F. A. Smith: *Genealogical Research in England and Wales* (Salt Lake City, 1956-65); D. Iredale: *Enjoying Archives* (Newton Abbot, 1973); E. D. Mackerness: 'Sources of Local Musical History', *Local Historian*, xi (1975), 315-20; and the 24 'Short Guides to Records', in *History*, xlvii-lvi (1962-71). Valuable for chronology are C. R. Cheney: *Handbook of Dates for Students of English History*, Royal Historical Society Guides and Handbooks, iv (London, 1961); S. H. Steinberg: *Historical Tables, 58 B.C.-1972* (London, 9/1973).

2. F. B. Zimmerman: *Henry Purcell, 1659-1695: his Life and Times* (London, 1967), 81, 281.

3. This section is indebted to this.

4. Located at 37, Harrington Gardens, London, S.W.7; see the Society's brochure *A Simple Guide to the Library of the Society of Genealogists* (1960), and also its two-volume *Parish Register Copies* (1963-71).

5. Lay Subsidy Rolls (E.179).

6. Lists of apprenticeships from 1710 were submitted for tax purposes to the Inland Revenue. They are now at the Public Record Office (I.R.1).

7. Zimmerman (1967), 237.

8. G. S. Thomson: *The Russells in Bloomsbury, 1669-1771* (London, 1940), chap.6.

9. J. F. Macgrath: *The Flemings in Oxford*, Oxford Historical Society, xliv (1904), appx E, *passim*.

10. G. R. Potter: 'A Note on the Devonshire Papers at Chatsworth House, Derbyshire', *Journal of the Society of Archivists*, iv (1970-73), 124-9.

11. Zimmerman (1967), 238.

12. These indexes are in the Manuscripts Room.

13. See, for instance, J. Preston: 'Collections of English Historical Manuscripts in the Huntington Library', *Archives*, vi (1963–4), 95–107.

14. Quality House, Quality Court, Chancery Lane, London, W.C.2.

15. Further information is given in F. Ranger: 'The National Register of Archives, 1945–69', *Journal of the Society of Archivists*, iii (1965–9), 452–62; H. M. G. Baillie: 'The Use of the Resources of the Historical Manuscripts Commission', ibid, 462–6, to which this paragraph is much indebted.

16. R. North: *Memoirs of Musick*, ed. E. F. Rimbault (London, 1846); *The Musicall Grammarian*, ed. H. Andrews (London, 1925); *Roger North on Music*, ed. J. Wilson (London, 1959).

17. H. W. Shaw: 'Extracts from Anthony à Wood's "Notes on the Lives of Musicians"', Hitherto Unpublished', *ML*, xv (1934), 157–62.

18. R. L. Poole: 'The Oxford Music School and the Collection of Portraits Formerly Preserved there', *The Musical Antiquary*, iv (1912–13), 143–599.

19. *Calendar of Treasury Books, 1685–89* (London, 1923), 1326, 1441–2.

20. *Calendar of Treasury Books, 1689–92* (London, 1931), 609.

21. Transcript ed. E. F. Rimbault, Camden Society, new ser., iii (London, 1872).

22. The grant made to the Cofferer on 9 Nov 1664 specifically to meet Chapel Royal salaries (*Calendar of Treasury Books. 1660–1667* (London, 1904), 623) is a rare exception. The '400 *l.* per an. for 20 musicians [i.e. £20 each] attending the Chapel Royal' (*Calendar of Treasury Books, 1676–1679* (London, 1911), 399 etc) refers to payments to those instrumentalists who played for Chapel Royal services, not to the choirmen's salaries (cf Lafontaine: *The King's Musick* (London, 1909), 176).

23. *Divine Harmony: or a New Collection of Select Anthems Us'd at Her Majesty's Chapells Royal* (London, 1712).

24. H. G. Farmer: *Military Music* (London, 1950), 20f.

25. See their Minute Book: *GB-Lbm* Harl.1911.

26. S.P. 29/96.

27. Lafontaine (1909), 162–257 *passim*.

28. *Calendar of State Papers, Domestic, 1660–1661* (London, 1860), 598.

29. S.P. 29/36.

30. 'Seventeenth-Century Musicians in the Sackville Papers', *Monthly Musical Record*, lxxxviii (1958), 182–7.

31. 'The Lord Chamberlain and Opera in London, 1700–1740', *PRMA*, xl (1913–14), 37–72.

32. Thr 464.4.15*. I am grateful to Martha R. Mahard, Assistant to the Curator, for supplying this information. A partial transcript, dating from *c*1823, is in *Lbm* Add.38607.

33. [H. Guy]: *Moneys Received and Paid for Secret Services of Charles II and James II . . . 1679 to . . . 1688*, ed. J. Y. Akerman, Camden Society, lii (London, 1851).

34. Westminster Public Library, Archives Department; see R. C. Kern: 'Documents Relating to Company Management, 1705–11', *Theatre Notebook*, xiv (1959–60), 60–65.

35.   MS 15 M 50/127; see S. Rosenfeld: 'An Opera House Account Book', *Theatre Notebook*, xvi (1961–2), 83–8.

36.   I am much indebted to Philip Olleson for bringing these documents to my notice. They are mentioned in Thomson (1940), 132, but the chorus's names are not reproduced.

37.   M. Tilmouth: 'A Calendar of References to Music in Newspapers published in London and the Provinces (1660–1719)', *RMARC*, i (1961), ii (1962), see i,p.iii.

38.   For present locations, see the *British Union Catalogue of Periodicals*.

39.   *The Manuscripts of His Grace the Duke of Rutland, K.G., Preserved at Belvoir Castle*, HMC, 12th report (1888–1905), appx iv/2.

40.   G. E. B. Eyre, ed.: *A Transcript of the Registers of the Worshipful Company of Stationers, from 1640–1708 A.D.* (London, 1913–14).

41.   E. Arber, ed.: *The Term Catalogues, 1668–1709 A.D.* (London, 1903–6).

42.   Cf E. A. Langhans: 'New Restoration Theatre Accounts, 1682–92', *Theatre Notebook*, xvii (1962–3), 118–34; J. L. Hotson: *The Commonwealth and Restoration Stage* (Cambridge, Mass., 1928), 308.

13

Musical Information in the Archives of the Church of S. Maria Maggiore, Bergamo, 1649–1720

Robin Bowman

Bergamo lies at the junction of the Lombardy Plain and the Alps. Its historic centre is situated on an easily defensible knoll which, as a premonition of the Alps, rises abruptly several hundred feet above the plain. Some 30 miles east-north-east of Milan, it lay on the trade route between Milan and Venice; transport and postal organisation were directed from Bergamo and this made interchange possible with the other main towns on the route—Brescia, Verona and Padua. In the mid-17th century Bergamo was for all intents and purposes a frontier town, its businessmen fluent in the economies and currencies of the Venetian Republic, whose outpost it was, and those of the Spanish duchy of Milan to the west. With the rise of Austrian domination after the confusion of the first decade of the 18th century, Bergamo's importance declined.[1]

The church of S. Maria Maggiore occupies the south side of the central piazza, of which part of the eastern side is taken up by the cathedral. The whole of the town is liberally supplied with parish churches. S. Maria, however, had no parish function: it was run by a body called the *Misericordia Maggiore*,[2] a charitable foundation active since 1265 whose considerable income was spent primarily on relieving the needs of the town's poor. Treasure was amassed in times of plenty, and sold whenever the struggle for survival became hard, in order to supplement the *Misericordia*'s other income in providing gifts of flour and wine to keep the citizens alive. Any remaining monies were used to provide elaborate patterns of worship in S. Maria, with many priests and musicians; and to provide education for boys of the town, some of whom were admitted free of charge (see discussion below), and many of whom formed a fleet of part-time vergers to look after the fabric of the church under the guidance of a *custode*. Thus the *Misericordia*, which is still loosely in existence today as an insurance company, undertook to sustain the bodies, minds and spirits of the citizens of the town.[3] It was a progressive organisation, perhaps the most powerful single social force in the town. The commercial and religious activities were united under the authority of one council, a 14-member body elected annually in February. The big annual holiday, when the wealthy lived off the fat of the land, generally lasted from September through to November. In 1649 there were no council meetings between 13 September and 29 November (1649 I ff.21*v*–23*v*). Council members who happened to be in town during this period were empowered to make urgent minor decisions in the name of the council (e.g. 1695 I f.295*v*). The head of the legal staff of the *Misericordia*, the chancellor, guided discussion at the meetings, and the notary kept the minutes. He did this in a simple and sometimes colourful vernacular, with marginal identifying tags in heavily abbreviated Latin, which nonetheless sometimes include details omitted from the main record. The hand is mostly a graceful italic, and the volumes of minutes were obviously compiled with pomp and pride. In 1716 the council decided to produce, within five years, a printed history of its activities over the previous 100 years (1716 I f.234). I have found no evidence that the publication ever appeared, but it was clearly timed to mark 100 years of government according to the precepts of its *Institutioni e ordini*,[4] which had been printed and published in 1620, and which formed its code of contemporary conduct. The council would meet up to 30 times a year, depending on the amount of business to be handled, and these meetings, as they are preserved in the *Terminationes*, seem like the nerve-centre of growth and development for the *Misericordia*. Each volume of these *Terminationes* covers from six to 14 years in some 400 folios during the period under discussion. They are the most unified, consistent and organised part of the whole network of archives at S. Maria.

References in this chapter to these *Terminationes* bear the code-number 'I', preceded by the date and followed by the folio number (or in some cases the day and month). References to the *Giornali*, catalogues of the day-to-day business dealings, including actual salary payments made, usually quarterly, to musicians, bear the code-number 'II'; and those to the *Spese della Chiesa*, volumes preserving payments made by the *Misericordia* for services rendered, items purchased or work accomplished, bear the code-number 'III'. Most of the items here are in the form of invoices, sometimes of astonishing detail, as ratified by the council. References to the *Scritture presentate al consiglio*, letters written to the council which required some action on its part, bear the number 'IV'. Unfortunately, by the latter half of the 17th century, the council no longer found it necessary to preserve copies of its own outgoing letters on musical matters.[5] Further, for reasons to be intimated below, the compiling of inventories of music books became markedly less regular; it did not stop altogether, but was relegated from the volume marked *Inventarium* to a rag-bag of miscellaneous papers called *Scritti*, here designated 'V'. These latter consist mostly of material which the council felt worthy of preservation, but which required no immediate action.

The Archival Task

The proper evaluation of such a body of archives is a task for a team of scholars trained in a variety of disciplines. It would take many years. Only teamwork such as this could, for example, assess the irrigation schemes at Fara d'Adda, or the labour troubles at Comun Nuovo, or the influence of the office of mayor of Bergamo (1705 V 26 Sept), or the economic and social force of peacetime military activity in the town (e.g. 1651 I f.93, 1697 IV f.109—this latter when the church's viola player asked to leave its service in order to join a troop of soldiers passing through the town). Only then could information about musicians take its rightful place as part of the total system of life.

By contrast, my initial purpose in first visiting the Bergamo archives, in 1971, was (as the last student that Thurston Dart set on the road towards PhD) to discover what they revealed of the life and work of Carlo Marino, active in the music-making of S. Maria at various periods between 1680 and 1707. I had, like so many users, little inkling of the archives in their own terms.

Such parallel searches as I had hoped to make in the civic, cathedral and parochial archives of the town proved impracticable: lacking a family of notaries such as the Basso family at S. Maria to keep their affairs in strictly recorded order during the 17th and early 18th centuries, or the orderly efficiency of the Biblioteca Civica Angelo Mai where the S. Maria archive is housed, these archives were devoid of organisation. So it was purely by chance that I stumbled upon a volume in the town's parochial archive (now centralised at S. Pancrazio) giving census returns for the parish of S. Michele, one of the most central parishes of the old town. This showed that a number of S. Maria's musicians lived thus close to their employer, and also indicated what they claimed to be their ages and how many children they had. The same volume[6] brought me up against one of the problems referred to in chapter 12 above, a problem which Dart encountered with his work on John Bull: the occurrence of a given name in profusion, and in a variety of occupations.[7] The priest in charge of the parish of S. Pancrazio in 1673[8] was one Giuseppe Marino, on the occasion when Giuseppe Marino, the father of the composer Carlo, presented one of his other sons for baptism. In 1683 there lived in the parish a 70-year-old Carlo Marino, when the musician of the same name cannot have been more than 12 or 13.

As will become apparent, most of the comings and goings mentioned in the archives concern locations outside the centre of Bergamo. Information about musical life outside S. Maria but inside the town is scarce indeed. Musicians from the cathedral were sometimes employed as visiting soloists (e.g. 1649 III f.205, 1652 III f.352) and musicians from S. Maria were often required for celebrations at the cathedral (e.g. 1650 I f.28v, 1711 IV f.411, 1716 I f.231). Giovanni Battista Quaglia, *maestro di capella* at S. Maria, wrote an oratorio for the cathedral;[9] an oratorio, here described as *sacra operetta* was on at least one occasion performed in a suburban church;[10] an *accademia* was performed in S. Maria (1702 III f.69), and on one occasion, the church used the *contrabasso della Comedia* for the celebrations of the Assumption of the Virgin (1716 III f.386). The *accademia*, by analogy with a local secular example,[11] was presumably an oratorio formed of spoken dialogue, and incidental music with or without verbal text.

However, when I revisited the S. Maria archive at Easter 1975 for the 16 seven-hour days of work on which the present chapter is based, my intention was, by examination of archival materials on a much broader basis, to cover in detail the whole 72-year period from 1649 to 1720. This broader examination greatly altered my view of Marino's part in the church music. It soon became clear, though, that to investigate so large a period in such depth was not a practical proposition, and I decided to resort to the procedure of sampling. I selected two periods within the 72-year span, 1649–58 and 1711–20, starting and finishing in February, at the point where the resident musicians' contracts were confirmed, shortly after the election of the new council. For the intervening years, I enlarged upon the work I had done vis-à-vis Marino, and picked out what seemed to be points of especial interest.

The Church and its College

By 1650 the area was well recovered from the disastrous plagues of the late 1620s,[12] the church was extremely wealthy, and setting about modernising its interior. In 1648 the two organs, high up, one on the east wall of each transept, were removed. One was sold and the other enlarged and set in a new case some ten feet up on the Gospel side of the chancel (1648 I f.395, 1648 V ff. 175–177, 1649 I f.9). The 1650s saw discussion on the stuccoing of the church (e.g. 1651 I f.80*v*), a process carried out piecemeal during the rest of the century. Likewise in 1656 the cupola was started (1656 V 6 July). By 1695 all available space in the interior was either stuccoed or covered with a painting (1693 I ff.225*v*-226¹ʲ), thus changing the acoustic from a resonant one suitable for Palestrina and *prima prattica* in general to its present absolutely non-resonant one of exceptional clarity. This would have been ideal for balancing the thick intricate melodic textures of the *sonate da chiesa* that Marino wrote for the church.

There were incidental misfortunes and hard times: references to 'la povertà nelle presenti calamità' (1649 I f.24), and to further poverty of unspecified cause (1676 I f.57*v*). Perhaps this was a more general slump, for there were many salary cuts around 1670 (1669 I f.33*v*), the musicians receiving theirs, of about 7%, on 7 February 1671 (1671 II p.278). A careful eye was kept on the amount of money expended on musicians. One document (1657 I f.7) contains a tirade against reckless expenditure on the hiring of outside musicians for the feast of the Assumption. It is perhaps significant that for 21 years after the departure of Cazzati in that year (see page 345), the church was without a long-serving *maestro*. A number were elected, but apart from Felice Maria Arconati, who stayed from 1662 to 1664 (1662 I f.140, 1664 I f.184), they only put in a token appearance, or could not be persuaded to take up the post at all. Indeed, in 1678, at the annual confirmation of contracts, appears the first reference I have been able to trace to Giovanni Battista Quaglia as *maestro* (1678 I f.86*v*). This was internal promotion after long service, for Quaglia was appointed *organista solo* on 23 July 1649 (1649 I f.14) and is later mentioned as *vicemaestro*, from 1675 (1675 I f.6*v*). Earlier, the penning of the realisations that neither Pietro Paolo Pelli (1650 I ff.44*v*-45) nor Giovanni Battista Menigoni (1653 I f.140*v*) were in fact going to come to Bergamo to take up the post of *maestro* to which they had been elected, is followed in each case by the recording of the release of money for charity. Thus the sums paid to musicians and the amounts available for charity may be seen sometimes to have been direct alternatives.

At the beginning of the 1680s the lapsed custom of giving musical tuition in the school was renewed, and this tuition underwent elaborate expansion. A dozen boys were daily to receive one and a half hours of instruction in *canto figurato* (1681 IV ff.162-165). The church's wealth reached a high-point around the turn of the century, with expensive provision being made for visiting virtuoso instrumentalists as well as the customary singers. From August 1701 (1701 I f.199*v*) to March 1702 (1702

I f.222) music was suspended in the church, and abandoned again, for reasons of military interference in everyday life, from September 1705 (1705 I f.60*v*) to March 1708 (1708 I f.155*v*). For each of these two periods, only an organist was retained. Music then progressed fairly smoothly from 1708 until the end of the period under discussion, but the aftermath of war and a series of summer droughts prevented any great prosperity, the accounts remaining full of huge lists of donations to the poor, the same names appearing in list after list. Some of these names— e.g. Bonomino (1712 I f.63*v*), Violino (1713 I f.83), Ecord (1714 I f.113*v*, 1719 I f.46*v*)—were those of church musicians or their widows. It was not until 1719 (1719 I f.64*v*) that steps could be taken to reopen the college, which must have ceased to function in the panic of late 1705.

The college appears to have had two divisions: the residence (*accademia*) and the instruction (*scuole*). The *accademia* had grown to contain 50 boys by 1655 (1655 I f.225) and had to be kept at that number for lack of lodging space—brothers had already been requested to share the same bed (1649 I f.11*v*). In the *scuole* the boys learned specific subjects in greater detail. The term *scuola* seems to have denoted any particular discipline being taught, for after 1681 music is included as one of the *scuole*. Boy sopranos might be admitted free to the *scuole*, or even on occasion to the *accademia* (1649 I f.13). Indeed the sons of musicians, often very poor (1651 I f.93*v*[14]), and of other church officers, perhaps not so poor (1650 I f.35[15]), were often admitted free to the whole educational system on account of services rendered by their parents. The *Institutioni* claim that poverty should be the sole criterion for free admission to the school.[16] From the boys of the college were chosen the *chierici servienti*, the fleet of part-time vergerial staff mentioned earlier, 24 in number prior to 1656,[17] but despite an annual salary of 40 scudi they did not take their tasks seriously. Some of the council thought the office should be abolished, and it appears that for a time it was, with even more disastrous results. When reinstated the number was limited to ten, with a salary of only 32 scudi per annum, and the proviso that they might be recruited from outside the college (1656 I f.231*v*–232). They were tested by the *maestro del canto fermo* before being admitted to perform any musical tasks (1658 I f.16), and it was from their numbers, which had risen to 18 by 1684 (1684 I f.31*v*), that in 1681 Quaglia was to choose a dozen for instruction in *canto figurato*. It is perhaps not surprising that this vigorous upgrading in the status of music as an educational subject brought its backlash in the form of complaints that the other subjects were being neglected, boys over-pressurised, and unsuitable people included in the dozen to make up the number and then lapsing into absenteeism (1681 IV ff.162–165, 1682 IV f.223). However, this same tuition must be held at least partly responsible for the renewal of native excellence in the music of S. Maria during the late 1680s and the 1690s.

The teaching of plainsong was handled by two of the resident priests,[18] both graced with the title of *chorista*, at least one of whom had to be present every time plainsong was sung in the church, an arduous encumbrance cited in their demands for more pay (1650 IV f.461). In 1650, the fourth and least paid master of the school was designated *maestro del canto fermo* (1650 I f.36v). Sometimes this post was held by one of the two *choristi* (1654 I ff.167, 176). Some clue as to the nature of this training is provided by the fact that one Hercole Olmo was rewarded in 1652 for having made six *tavolette di canto fermo* which were placed on display on the wall of the *accademia* (1652 I f.125v). Shortly afterwards he became one of the *choristi* (1653 I f.130).

The Musicians: Confirmations, Wages

The really outstanding musicians who graduated through the college could be taken on to the soloist musical staff. Santino Bettoni began receiving a salary when he left the college (1650 I ff.37,63), though he had been singing as a soloist for some time (1649 I f.6), and a previous attempt by his father to gain payment on his behalf had been rejected (1649 IV f.418). The case of Carlo Baratta is an interesting one. Described on his arrival as a Bolognese soprano (1649 I f.13), he was granted free accommodation and education in lieu of salary. During 1650 his voice began to break, and in December of the same year Lazzaro Norsino, who appears as a ripieno string player for the great feasts around this time (e.g. 1652 III f.376, 1654 III f.479), was paid the sizeable sum of 22 scudi (154 lire) for having had Baratta castrated (1650 I f.63v). Baratta duly appears in the list of contracts confirmed in 1651 with the description *musico soprano* (1651 I f.71). He was, however, an unsound investment, for in the summer of 1652 he fled Bergamo (1652 IV f.60), never to return to the service of S. Maria. Having received his castration at the expense of the church, he doubtless went away to seek his fortune in the opera house. The cathedral had a castrato too, for one described as *il castratino del Duomo* sang in S. Maria five times during 1649 (1649 III f.205). Faustino Marchesi, who was employed from 1693 until after 1726 (1693 I f.242, 1726 I f.267), is described on his appointment as *musico soprano castrato*. The report makes it clear that he is returning to his native town. If the church was instrumental in his castration, it got better value for its money than with Baratta. Maybe Marchesi's return to Bergamo marked his operatic retirement. Certainly he stayed at Bergamo long enough for his voice to fall from soprano to contralto as he aged (see below). He became a priest in 1702 (1702 I f.243), immediately following the first period of suspension of church music. His new status must have proved a useful insurance policy against the hardships to come!

It was not only as singers that boys from the college graduated to become musicians on the church payroll. Some were never able to gather to themselves the name of *musico*, i.e. 'singer', and had to be content with the lesser rank of *suonatore*, 'instrumentalist'. Giovanni Battista Scolari first appeared as soprano (1671 I f.95), then as basso (1672 I f.122). In 1676 he was listed as *basso e violino* (1676 I f.35v) and by 1679 his vocal activities were no longer deemed worthy of mention (1679 I f.107). Carlo Marino first appears in the church records as a soprano (1681 III f.175), but it was as a prodigy teenage violinist that he joined the payroll (1686 I f.86). Indeed, there are a number of instances of apprenticeship-type training, when boys petitioned to go and sit beside the organist (1692 IV f.700) or to play in the church band purely for the experience (1698 I f.85v). In the 1710s the young Alessandro Rota played the oboe in lieu of his master Giovanni Ecord, when the latter went to other towns to play for opera (1712 IV f.434, 1716 IV f.37).

The following table presents the lists of musicians' confirmations at 22-year intervals (chosen to yield an unbroken sequence of years, and particularly full lists) from 1650 to 1716 (1650 I f.37v, 1672 I f.122, 1694 I ff.252v–253, 1716 I f.212v):

Year	Name	Position	Number of Objectors
1650	D. Ottavio Mazza	V. Maestro di Capella	—
	D. Giovanni Legrenzi	Organista	—
	D. Gio Batta. Quaglia	Organista	3
	D. Astolfo Bressani	Soprano	—
	D. Giacomo Antonio Gallinoni	Basso	—
	D. Gio Batta. Pescara	Tenore	—
	D. Carlo Valcarengo	Tenore	—
	D. Gio Batta. Marchese	[Contralto]	2
	D. Franco. e Gio Batta Moreschi	[Suonatori]	—

Year	Name	Position	Number of Objectors
1650 (continued)	D. Achille Morari	[Tenore]	—
	D. Lodovico Vavassore	Basso	—
	Carlo Baratta	Soprano	—
1672	Dno. Ottavio Mazza	V. M.	—
	Dno. Gio. Batta. Quaglia	Orga.	—
	Dno. Livio Anda. Todeschino	Contralto	—
	Dno. Gio. Batta. Marchesi	Tenore	—
	Dno. Gio. Batta. Scolari	Basso	1
	Dno. Bio. Batta. Pinelli	Soprano	3
	Dno. Franco. Celidone	Baritone	1
	R. D. Franco. e Ventura Moreschi	Suonatori	—
	Dno. Gio. Parenti	Suonatore [di violone]	—
1694	Franco. Balarotti	Mº di Capella	1
	D. Giaco. Quaglia	Organista	—
	Dno. Gio. Batta. Marchesi	Tenore	—
	Faustino Marchesi	Soprano	—
	Bernadino Cauda	Contralto	—
	Giorgio Violino	Basso	—
	Girolo. Marini	Tenore	—
	Gio. Parenti	Sonator di Violone	—
	Gio. Batta. Scolari	pmo. Violino	—
	Carlo Marino	2do. Violino	—
	Pietro Marino	Sonator di Viola	—
	Girolo. Mazza	Sonator di Tiorba	—
	Anda. Laxigner	Sonator di Tiorba	—
1716	Gio. Batta. Bassani	Mº di Capella	—
	Franco. Quaglia	Organista et V. Mº di Capella	—
	Michele Stella	Soprano	—
	D. Faustino Marchesi	Contralto	—
	Giaco. Marchesi	Tenore	—
	Giuseppe Strada	Basso	2
	Giorgio Violino	Baritone	—
	Ludo. Ferronato	pmo. Violino	—
	Franco. Marchesi	2do. Violino	—
	Marc'Ant. Bernardi	Contrabasso	1
	Vincenzo Paganelli	Violoncello	—
	Gio. Ecord	Oboe	—

Objectors were members of the council who voted against the confirmation. Giovanni Battista Moreschi was the father of Francesco and Ventura—all were violinists (1651 I f.93*v*, 1652 I f.123*v*, 1675 I f.6*v*). Girolamo and Ottavio Mazza were adept at both violin and theorbo (1689 I f.128). The abandonment of a second regular organist, the decrease in the number of singers and a corresponding increase in number of instrumentalists, and the arrival of wind can all be seen from the above table. While the term *suonatori* was regarded as sufficient for the instrumentalists in the first two lists, later the instruments came to be specified. The first list to distinguish between first and second violin occurs in 1687 (1687 I f.97*v*). Here now are annotated salary lists for years as close to the above years as I have preserved (1650 II p.165, 1671 II p.278, 1695 II p.375, 1715 II p.389). Items of information in diamond brackets are supplied from the surrounding pages of the documents:

Year	Name	Lire	
1650	Ottavio Mazza	455	
	Astolfo Bressani	840	
	Gio. Batt. et R. Francesco		
	Moreschi	840	[together]
	Pescara	800	
	Legrenzi	560	
	Gallinoni	560	
	Vavassori	168	
	G. B. Marchesi	210	
	Carlo Valcarengo	350	
	Santino Bettoni <tenore>	168	
	Pietro Paolo Vassalli <contralto>	840	
	Quaglia	210	
	Francesco Guerrieri <musico>		
	[voice not specified]	350	

By comparison, the headmaster and the three other schoolmasters received L.1,400, L.560, L.280 and L.350 respectively; the last of these included a sum for being *maestro del canto fermo*. L.1,400 was Cazzati's salary as *maestro di capella* between 1653 and 1657 (e.g. 1654 II p.349, 1656 II p.157).

1671	D. Ottavio Mazza	490	plus a small amount in grain
	G. Quaglia Organista	525	
	Fr. Celidone	980	

Year	Name	Lire	
1671	Liviand Todeschini	630	
(con-	G. B. Marchesi Tenore	630	
tinued)	G. Parenti Violone	266	
	G. B. Scolari Soprano	280	p.a. to 4 April, 140 p.a. thereafter [presumably as his voice broke]
	G. B. Pinelli	350	
	R. Franc. e Ventura Moreschi	665	plus a small amount in grain

This was the year in which all but Mazza, Marchesi and the Moreschis received an across-the-board pay-cut of about 7%. Marchesi had a rise from L.515 to L.630 on the same date (7 February), whilst, significantly, the three instrumentalists remained unchanged.

Year	Name	Lire	
1695	Girolamo Mazza Violino e Tiorba	280	
	B. A. Cauda Contralto	980	
	G. B. Marchesi Tenore .	450	
	G. B. Scolari Violino	385	
	G. Parenti Violone	504	
	Carlo Marino 2do violino	315	
		350	for Girolamo his brother, tenor
		70	for Pietro his brother, viola
	F. Balarotti Maestro di Capella	700	
	A. Laxigner Tiorba	186	
	F. Marchesi Musico Soprano	1,050	
	Francesco Quaglia Organisto	553	plus 2 *brente* of wine, but paid as an extra L.28 in cash
	G. Violino Musico Basso	252	plus 6 *brente* of wine, paid as L.84 cash
1715	Gio. Ba[ssani]	1,050	
	R. Faustino Marchesi Musico Contralto	1,050	
	Giaco. Marchesi Musico Tenore	455	
	Marc'Anto. Bernardi Sonatore di Contrabasso	630	

Year	Name	Lire	
1715 (con- tinued)	Lodo Ferronato Sonator di primo violino	630	
	Franco. Marchesi 2do violino	280	
	Giuseppe Strada Musico Baritone	910	
	Michele Stella Musico Soprano	1,120	
	Gio. Ecord Suonatore	280	
	Franco Quaglia Organista	700	of which L.140 was for the post *of vice-maestro*, and plus 2 *some* of flour and 2 *brente* of wine
	Giorgio Violino Musico Basso	168	plus 2 *some* of flour and 6 *brente* of wine
	Vinco. Paganello Suonatore di Violoncello	490	
	R. M'Anto. Rassi Suonatore di Violoncello	157	up to his departure on 12 April

This last list is almost identical with that for 1713 (1713 II p.112) when the four members of the legal staff received L.1,400, L.840, L.700 and L.350 respectively, in each case augmented by 2 *some* of flour and 6 *brente* of wine. The *maestro del canto fermo* received L.140. For musicians not represented on the relevant confirmation list I have added the instrument or voice type in the salary table. In some cases the confirmation list conceals versatility or gives something different from the relevant salary list. These annotations I have added too. Giovanni Ecord demands a special word. He describes himself (1711 IV f.432) as 'il Contrabasso, L'oboé, Violino, ó Violetta, secondo la necessita ché sarà nel Orchestra ó l'ordine ché mi sarà imposte'. Though the church thought of him primarily as an oboist, its first on the regular payroll, it was as a ripieno violinist that he made his earliest appearance in the church band (1708 III f.441).

The presence in the last two lists of singers better paid than the *maestro* is interesting—there was never a singer paid anywhere near the L.1,400 received by Cazzati. However, the absence of a long-serving *maestro* thereafter, and the relatively low salaries of Ottavio Mazza and Giovanni Battista Quaglia,[19] served permanently to depress the remuneration S. Maria gave to its *maestro*. Giovanni Battista Marchesi's falling worth is apparent, as is the considerable difference between the two organists in the first list, though Quaglia was to rise near Legrenzi's level, and Francesco his son to surpass it, by which time of course there was only one organist, though Balarotti himself was a capable player. By 1715, the first violin, cello and double bass were commanding quite high wages, entirely fair in view of the increasing intricacy and brilliance of what was required of them.

Inventories, Repertory

Roche presents a 1628 inventory of the music at S. Maria.[20] Another was made in 1643 under the surveillance of Crivelli (1643 V sheet no.411). Cazzati could not trouble himself to engage similarly on his arrival, so a 1654 inventory was made by Ottavio Mazza the *vicemaestro* (1654 V ff.1,110–1,111). Buying had obviously proceeded apace and kept abreast of changing musical fashion. The latter two lists are given below. New items not represented in the previous inventory are in each list marked with a plus sign. Items discarded between 1643 and 1654 are marked with a minus sign in the former list. All the *stile antico* music must have been retained in an almost antiquarian spirit by the middle of the century. The 1643 inventory reads as follows:

Inventario de libri di Musica di ragione del V^do Consortio della MIA. Maggior di Bergamo consegnati in mano del S.r Gio Batta. Crivelli M^ro di capella de quali promette renderme buon conto ad ogni richiesta de S.r Deputati.

+ Due copie de Motetti del Colombini a 2. 3. e 4
   Messe e + motetti a 8 del Gastoldi
+ Moteti di Aless^ro Grandi a 2. 3. e 4
+ Hinni del Lassi a 4 voci
– Messe a nove voci del Mortara
– Salmi a cinq di Orfeo Vecchi
   Salmi a otto del Bernardi
   Messe a quattro di Giulio Belli
   Salmi a cinq del Colombi
– Motetti di Orfeo Vecchi a cinq
   Motetti del Palestrina a cinq e sei voci
– Offertorii del Palestrina a cinq voci
   Introiti a otto di Valerio Bona
   Salmi e Messe a cinq del Galerano
– Compiete a otto di Giulio Belle manca una parte
+ Compieta a cinq del Righi
+ Messe e moteti a cinq del Bazini

+ − Motetti a sette del Palestrina

− Messe a otto del Mortara

+ − Lamentat[ni] del Palestrina a cinq

Motetti a 2. 3. 4. e 5 di Gio. B[a] Crivelli L° p?

− Salmi a sette del Negri

Passii dell' Asola a quattro

+ − Messa de morti a quattro del Bernardi

Magnificat a 4 del Morales

Messe del Palestrina a quattro

Messe a quattro di Arcangelo Crivello   Libri

Messe a quattro di Orlandi Lassi   grandi

+ Hinni del Palestrina a quattro   per

+ Magnificat a quattro del Vittoria   Capella

+ Messe a quattro del Vittoria

+ − Responsorii a quattro del Florio

In fede di che esso S[r] Crivelli sottoscrivera le pnte. di propria mano alla
pnza.

Io Gio. Batta. Crivelli maestro di Capella di S[a] Maria Maggior di Berg[mo]
confirmo haver in Consegna li soprascritti libri di musica quali si trovano in
capella di detta chiesa.

The 1654 inventory reads as follows:

Inventario delli libri di musica di raggione del V? Consortio della mia.
Maggiore di Bergamo: che si ritrovano nell' Armario essistente sopra l' organo
Custodite da D. Ottavio Mazza V[c] M? di Capella.

Himni del Lassi a 4

Motetti di Alessandro Grandi a 2. 3. 4

Messe a 4 di Giulio Belli

Salmi a 5 del Colombo

Introiti a 8 di Valerio Bona

Salmi e messe a 5 del Galerano sono rotti

Compietta a 5 del Righi

Messe e motetti a 5 del basilio

Motetti a 2. 3. 4. 5 di Gio. Batta. Crivelli

Li Passi del Asola a 4

Mag[cat] a 4 del Morales in librazzi grandi

Messe a 4 del Palestrina in librazzo

Messe a 4 del Cribelli in librazzo

Messe a 4. 5. 6. di Orlando Lasso in librazzo

Himni a 4 del Palestrina in librazzo

Mag[cat] a 4 del Vittoria in librazzo

Messe a 4 del Vittoria in librazzo

+ Motetti del Rigati a voce sola senza il partito lib° p?

+ Motetti del detto libro 2º
+ Motetti a 2. 3. con una messa del medemo
+ Motetti a 2. 3. del Rovetta libro 3º
+ Motetti del medemo a 2. 3. 4. 5. con letanie
+ Motetti del medemo a 2. 3. con letanie a 4
+ Salmi del detto a 8
+ Motetti del Porta a 2. 3. 4.
+ Salmi a 8 del Sanses
+ Salmi a 4 del istesso
+ Motetti a 2. 3. 4. 5 del sudº
+ Salmi a 4 del Moro
+ Salmi et motetti del Tarditi
+ Salmi a 8 con Istromenti del Fontei
+ Sonate del Uccellini
+ Motetti a 2. 3. 4. del Sebaldini
+ Motetti a 2. 3. 4. del Casati con messa libº Pº
+ Motetti del istesso a 2. 3. 4. libro 3º
+ Motetti del istesso a 1. 2. 3. 4. scielta
+ Messa e salmi del detto a 4. 5.
  Motetti del Palestrina a 5. 6.
  Motetti a 2. 3. 4. 5. del Colombino libro 3º
+ Motetti del medemo a 2. 3. 4. 5. libro 4º
+ Compiette a 8 di Biaggio Ghirardi conletanie
+ Motetti a 8 del sudetto.
+ Motetti a 5 del sudetto.
+ Compiette a 3. 4. 5. 6. con Instromenti et senza del sudº
+ Responsorii per la Setimana Santa scritti a 4
+ Messe a 8 del Bernardi
  Messe a 8 del Gastoldi
  Salmi a 8 del Bernardi
+ Messa e salmi a 8 del Brusso con un Tedeum
+ Salmi a 8 del Givelli
+ Salmi a 9 del Ganassa
  Introiti a 5 del Asola [in 1628 inventory]
+ Motetti del Chiozzotto a 8
+ Messe a 8 del Alberghetti
+ Messe a 5 del Tarditi con violini et senza
+ Compietta a 5 del Ghizzolo
+ Salmi a 5 del Gastoldi
+ Salmi a 5. 6. 7. 8. con Istromenti di D. Natal Monferato
+ Salmi a 8 del Tarditi

Io Ottavio Massa vᵉ mº di Capella della Chiesa di Sª Maria Maggiore di
Bergamo, mi chiamo in Custodia et in deposito tutti li sudᵗⁱ libri, et mi

obligo ad ogni richiesta delli Sig.[ri] Presidenti renderli distinto conto delle medesimi libri, et bona restit.[ne] in fede ho sotto scritto la presente di propria mano ottavio massa sud.º

The items in the above inventory from the Bernardi *Messe a 8* to the Ghizzolo *Compietta a 5* inclusive arrived at S. Maria on 3 May 1654 (1654 III f.459). The inventory is dated 18 May.

Cazzati, therefore, was not idle in matters of repertory. Further, in June 1656 the following arrived from Venice and were immediately despatched to the binders. I give below the two lists, one for the expenses of the purchase, and one for the binding (1656 III ff.140, 143). The binder shows the trait exhibited by many library cataloguers of including a part-name as the start of the title. The repertory is almost entirely concertato vocal church music for the resident soloists, as yet very little music *a voce sola*, and few volumes exclusively devoted to instrumental music. The Monferrato solo motets appear disproportionately expensive, and certainly cost little enough to bind. The list of purchases reads:

	Lire
Messe, e salmi a 3 del Rigati	8
Salmi, e messa del Matioli	7
Himni del detto.	5:10
Concerti di Gasparo Casati	3:10
Compositioni di Giuseppe Allevi	7
Salmi del Tarditi a 3.	5:0
Motetti del d.º opera 35.	4:0
Motetti a voce sola di Natal Monferato	10:0
Salmi di Marco Ucelini con Violini	12
Motetti di D. Nadal monferato a 2 3	5
Racolta de diversi Autori	3
Salmi del Filipini	4
Salmi del d.[to] con Violini	4
Salmi di Simon Resi con violi	12
Messa, e Salmi del Sarti	4
Sonate a 3 di Tarquinio Merula	5:10
Sonate a 2, 3, e 4 Marto Ant.º Ferro	5:0
	104:10

The music was delivered from Venice, and the cost of carriage etc. meant a grand total to the *Misericordia* of 118:15 lire.

The list of binding costs reads as follows:

	Lire
Basso Continuo Messe et Salme a 3.4.5. Voce del Mattheolo libri 6	1:4
Salme a 3 et 5 Voce del Bacellieri libri 6	1:4
Sonati a 2. a 3. et 4 voce di Marc'Ant? Ferro libro 5	1
Basso Continuo Motetti a 2. 3. d'Horatio Tarditi libro 4	0:18
Basso Continuo, Messe, et Salmi a 3. Voci con duoi violini ripiena del rigati libri 8	1:12
Motetti a 2. 3. 4. di Gioseppe Alievi libro 5	1
Raccolto de Motetti a 1. 2. 3. di Gasparo Casati libro 4	0:16
Himni a 1. 2. 3. 5. 6. del Matteoli libri 7	1:8
Salmi a 3. 4. del Sarti libri 5	1
Motetti del Casati Opera terza a 2. 3. 4. libro 5	1
Motetti del Casati libro P^{mo} a 1. 2. 3. 4 libri 5	1
Salmi di Stefano Filoppina libri 6	1:4
Sonate di Violino di Tarquinio libri 4	-:16
Motetti a 2 voci di Gasparo Casati libri 3	-:12
Salmi a 3 di Horatio Tarditi libri 4	-:16
Motetti a voce sola di D. Natale Monferrato libri 2	-:8
Salmi di Marco ucellini libri 9	1:16
Motetti di D. Nadal Monferrato libri 4	-:16
Salmi di Simon Rezzi libri 11	2:4
	20:16

The assessment of this large body of music and its detailed suitability for the resources of S. Maria must be left for a later study. After the departure of Cazzati, the evidence becomes scantier. The home-grown Ottavio Mazza provided continuity in running the church music in the absence of a *maestro*. Perhaps the repertory became more homespun and Bergamo ran rather ahead of the rest of Italy in turning away from printed materials towards dissemination of parts in manuscript. Certainly, Mazza's son Girolamo is described by the council as a composer (1689 I f.128) though there is no evidence that he ever had anything published, and Balarotti (1693 IV f.13) claims part-copying as a major expense and consumer of time. With individual singers demanding higher and higher salaries, it would seem unlikely that Quaglia's two books of solo motets, the second actually published in Bergamo,[21] were not intended for use in S. Maria, and that much similar music was not bought for performance there as music once again assumed a position of high importance in the life of the church. Girolamo Marino (1694 IV f.37) claimed 'nelle solennità maggiori, accompanar con il Violoncello in publico motetti, e sonate'. That Quaglia was regarded very highly outside Bergamo as a composer of solo motets is shown by the fact that his contributions to two *raccolte* of such motets, form, in each case, the first item in the volume.[22]

Further evidence of an increase in homespun music and of material to keep well-occupied those prestigious instrumentalists who by then had gathered in the employ of S. Maria is given in a letter from Carlo Marino (1702 IV f.272). Presumably he had not been idle in the church's cause during the suspension of church music the previous winter. Here is the relevant passage:

> Ma sempre di continuo, et specialmente nelle principali fontioni faccio sentire in Chiesa sonate da me con studiosa fatica comporre, nel che non si essende al debito del Maestro di Capella. Oltre il picciol merito del studio nel componere vi entra la spesa della carta, et delle coppie per distribuire le parti delli accompagnarsi a tutti li Virtuosi della Sacra orchestra.

If these were the sonatas later to be published as Op.6 (the date fits[23]), then the presence in the printed edition of solo and tutti designations should not surprise, for the 'Sacra orchestra' was swelled for the principal feasts of Easter and the Assumption, with a lesser acknowledgement for Christmas and sometimes certain other high days, to well beyond one player per part. Indeed the presence of a third violinist on the payroll in the 1680s (e.g. 1684 I f.29, 1685 I f.50*v*, 1687 II p.456) and requests from 'students' to be allowed to join the band or group of singers, without salary (see p. 345, and e.g. 1687 I f.92*v*, 1714 I f.141*v*) suggest that doubling of parts may have been very much the rule.

For the Assumption of 1707, when the church had no resident musicians save the organist, and had spent no money other than his salary on music for two years, the following group was assembled (1707 III f.317–317*v*):

	Lire
A Franc.º Grandi Soprano doppie 18 di Spagna	621
A Pro. Ant.º Stroppa Sop.º Filippi 18 et una doppia Spagna	214:10
A Grassino Contralto Filippi n.º 17	170
Ad Ant.º Bigoni Basso filippi dieci	100
A Carlo Marini Violino filippi 18	180
A Copelotti Violino di Lodi filippi dieci	100
A Paghetti Violino di Crema filippi cinque	50
A Bart.º Zoccoletti Violino di Brescia filippi otto	80
Ad Appiarino Violoncello filippi quindeci	150

	Lire
A Girol? Bonomini Violoncello filippi sette	70
A Faustino Marchesi Contralto	30
A Pegonari Soprano	30
A Giac? Marchesi Tenore	18
A Gio. Batta. Marchesi Tenore	12
A Georgio Violino Bariton e fig?	27
A Recaldini Tromba	30
A Gio. Batta. Scolari Violino	18
A Marchesi Violino	18
A Prandino Viola	12
A Balarotti Viola	12
A Marc' Antonio Bernardi Contrabasso	18
A Girol? Mazza Contrabasso	18
A Gio. Bª Marino Violoncello	9
Ad Andª Marchesi 2d? Organista	12
A D. Lorenzo Marchesi sonator di Basso	12
A Franc? Balarotti Mʳᵒ di Capella	100
in tutto	2117:10

As Marino was paid L.180 for the one weekend, nearly twice as much as the next most expensive violinist, he may have performed one or more of his violin concertos, three of which survive in manuscript.[24] It is unlikely that the more modest technical demands of the extant concertos by Lodovico Ferronato,[25] his successor as first violin at S. Maria, were not conceived with this church in mind, since by far the greater part of Ferronato's working life was spent there.[26]

The following undated sheet appears in the volume of *Spese* commencing in 1711. It forms f.2, and a 20th-century hand has added the date 1722, which seems reasonable, and would represent the considered desires of Giacomo Gozzini, the Bolognese *maestro* appointed at the end of 1717 (1717 I f.302*v*). It is a modest list of purchases and refurbishments. Much less newish music was available in print in 1722, but two of the items for refurbishment can be found in the 1643 inventory, just as that inventory itself contained some music about a century old:

Nota de libri di musica proveduti da me Giacomo Gozzini, per servitio della Chiesa di S. Mª Maggiore

	Lire
Responsorii della Settimana santa, libri dieci	8:16
Moteti del Silvani a duo o tre, Libri sette	6:12
Moteti del Caldara a tre voci, Libri cinque	6:12

		Lire
Salmi di Vespro pieni del Bellinzani libri dodici		14:6
sono in tutto libri trenta quatro		
per legatura de detti		10:10
		46:16

Altri libri vecchi restaurati

Salmi del Cazzati a 8. pieni	libri dieci	
Li motetti dell'Aldrovandini	libri sette	
Li salmi pieni del Gastoldi	libri sei	
Le messe del Galerano	libri sei	
Li salmi pieni del Colombo	libri sei	
sono in tutto	libri trenta cinque	10
		56:16

Leave of Absence, Dismissals

The contracts of the resident instrumentalists and singers empowered them to take leave once a year to go to other towns to perform in opera. The annual holiday of the *Misericordia* formed the most popular time for such leave. Some took this leave regularly, and were often asked to provide substitutes at their own expense. Marc'Antonio Bernardi, the Bolognese double bass player, was one such, for whom the priest Diego Cesareni consistently substituted (e.g. 1713 IV f.484, 1714 IV ff.5, 25). The church had its regular standby violinist Antonio Fontana, who frequently received a gift of flour from the council for his trouble (e.g. 1698 I f.64*v*, 1704 I f.9). In 1698 he claimed 20 years in this capacity, in 1704, 32! Certainly his name can be traced back to 1681 (1698 IV f.119, 1704 IV f.318, 1681 IV f.158).

As far as more local visits went, an edict of 1635 forbade S. Maria musicians to accept special invitations to perform in other churches of the town and neighbourhood without taking the *maestro* with them (1635 I f.39*v*). Three of the singers, who pleaded in 1657 to be allowed to go to Ferrara for a few days on such a trip, were not given permission (1657 I f.299*v*). Not only did this help to stabilise and build up the pattern of music at S. Maria, but, at least in theory, it gave opportunities to the *maestro* to supplement his income. In 1687, at the request of G. B. Brevi, then *maestro* at Bergamo cathedral, this rule was relaxed (1687 IV f.496, I f.95*v*). Thereafter, until 1719 when it was reinforced (1719 I f.46), the minutes of council meetings are full of requests for brief absences, usually granted, enabling little groups of S. Maria musicians to go and perform at other churches within reach. Carlo Marino and his viola-playing father were often granted such leave for a weekend or a day—e.g. with Laxigner the theorbist (1691 I f.185*v*), with two singers (1687 I f.100), with another violinist (1687 I f.106*v*). The first of these groups could have been self-supporting, but it is often clear that the host church would have had to provide at least a harmony-instrumentalist. Perhaps the S. Maria musicians went to spearhead a group of local amateurs. Sometimes the whole company of musicians went to perform elsewhere—e.g. at the cathedral (1650 I f.28*v*, 1716 I f.231), or at the suburban church of S. Alessandro in Colonna (1686 I f.84, 1689 I f.140*v*).[27] Occasionally groups absented themselves without permission. For the Assumption of 1696, of all the days in the year, everyone except the viola player and one of the theorbists went to perform at an unspecified suburban church, to the deprivation and chagrin of all at S. Maria, where 'the solemn music was unable to be performed' (1696 I f.23*v*). (The ire of the notary indicates that the council considered this a major scandal.)

Musicians were fined for such absences without leave, and also for late arrival at celebrations. Sometimes the priest acting as prefect (*pontatore*) delivered a very detailed list of such misdemeanours, which, preserved as if a letter, gives considerable insight into the days and ways of church music-making. Here is the very full list for 1714 (1714 IV f.1):

1714 Mancanze de Sig.ri Musici

L1:10	Il Sig. Bassani Maestro di Capella manco al Oratione dopo il Vespro alli 3 d'aprile 3.ª Festa di Pasqua
	Il Sig. Don Faustino Marchesi manco al Oratione dopo il Vespro della 3.ª festa di Pasqua alli 3 aprile
L3	alli 15 magio manco alla Messa solenne de morti
L3	alli 12 lulio manco alla Messa solenne de morti

L1:10	Il Sig. Stella manco al Oratione dopo il Vespro della 3.ª festa di Pasqua 3 aprile
L3	alli 15 magio alla Messa de morti
L6	alli 22 lulio manco tutto il giorno

L1:10	Il Sig. Giacomo Marchesi manco alli 3 aprile al Orat.e dopo il
L3	Vespro, et alli 15 magio alla messa de morti

L1:10	Il Sig. Strada manco al Orat.e dopo il vespro della 3.ª festa di
L3	Pasqua, alli 15 magio alla messa de morti, et alli 5 Settembre alla Messa de morti; disse per non esser stato avisato.

L2	Il Sig. Giorgio Violini manco alla compietta alli 26 marzo
L1	alli 3 aprile 3ª festa di Pasqua al Oratᵉ dopo il Vespro
L2	alli 6 magio gⁿᵒ di S. Gioanni ante Porta Latina al Vespro
L2	alli 15 magio alla Messa de morti
L5	alli 22 magio 3ª festa di Pentecoste al Vespro, et Oratᵉ
L5	alli 27 magio gⁿᵒ della Sᵐª Trinita al Vespro, et Oratᵉ
L17	

	Il Sig. Lodovico Feronati pᵒ Violino manco
L1:10	alli 3 aprile 3ª festa di Pasqua al Oratᵉ dopo il Vespro
L3	alli 22 magio 3ª festa di Pentecoste arrivo al quarto salmo del Vespro
L6	alli 26 lulio manco tutto il giorno
L6	alli 29 lulio tutto il giorno
L3	alli 8 decembre arrivo in fine del Gloria in excelsis
L19:10	

L1	Il Sig. Francesco Marchesi 2ᵒ Violino e mancato solo al Oratᵉ dopo il Vespro della 3ª festa di Pasqua

L1	Il Sig. Gioanni Ecorti Sonatore del Aboe manco alli 3 aprile 3ª festa di Pasqua al Oratᵉ dopo il Vespro
L4	alli 22 lulio tutto il giorno
L2	alli 10 agosto al Vespro
L1	alli 25 9ᵇʳᵉ arrivo al quarto salmo del Vespro

L1:10	Il Sig. Vincenzo Paganelli Violoncello manco alli 3 aprile al Oratᵉ
[del.]	dopo il Vespro—et alli 29 lulio alla Messa
L3	

L1:10	Il Sig. Marc'Antᵒ Bernardi manco alli 3 aprile 3ª festa di Pasqua al Oratᵉ dopo il Vespro
L1:10	alli 29 aprile arrivo dopo la Chirie della Messa
L3	alli 6 magio al Vespro
L3	alli 17 giugno al Vespro
L3	alli 6 agosto alla Messa
L6	alli 16 agosto al Vespro
L3	alli 18 9ᵇʳᵉ al Vespro
L21	

Compassionate leave was often granted (e.g. 1700 I f.147*v* when Francesco Quaglia is given leave to attend to his late father's estate; whilst he was asked to provide a substitute, the leave was willingly given). After much travel to and fro (e g. 1700 I f.145*v* 12 May, 1701 I f.164*v* 10 Jan, f.175v 1 March), Antonio Pelandini was at last (1701 I f.188 4 June) put on half pay on account of spending so much time in Milan with his sick wife. The council was extremely patient with what appears to have been the tenor Giovanni Battista Pescara's slow journey into insanity during the 1650s (1651 I f.80v, 1654 I f.184v, 1655 I f.218v, 1656 I f.233, 1656 IV f.223). It was also content to let its *maestro* Teodoro Reggiani remain in Rome for months during 1691 (1691 I f.184, 1692 I f.210v). However, both Marc'Antonio Bernardi and Carlo Marino nearly lost their jobs for outstaying the agreed length of operatic leave (1704 I f.11v).

Dismissals could be dramatic. Two of the longest single items in the council minutes concern those accorded to Crivelli and Filippo Vitali (1648 I f.393v, 1649 I ff.25–26). One of the problems in the latter case was that the already dilatory and unpopular *maestro* expected the church to refund part of his expenses in going to Venice to have a volume of his music printed. He suggests that such financial aid had been the council's custom in the past, and, as he draws attention to the expense of the work's running to 70 printed sheets, he must have been hoping for aid towards production costs (1649 IV f.433). The seeming boom in 17th-century Italian music publishing makes more sense in the knowledge that much of it may not have been financed by the publisher.

The real motives for dismissal are often undisclosed. Great feeling was aroused over Giovanni Battista Legrenzi, the council dividing equally about whether or not he was to be dismissed (1654 I ff.191, 195, 1655 I ff.197, 227v). All in all it was over a year before the issue was finally settled and Legrenzi departed for Ferrara.[28] The exact nature of the contention is not known. Equally frustrating are reports in the council minutes that a request was presented in person (e.g. 1692 I f.211v, 1694 I f.265), for there is no corresponding letter to elucidate the substance of the request.

The departure of Cazzati is also rather mysterious. The minutes record (1656 I f.278) that in December 1656 he was to be granted 'an adjusted status, so that there be no scandals or disorderliness such as we deem very likely to occur'. On 12 March 1657, he submitted a request to be relieved of his priest's office (1657 I f.295) and a fortnight later he was asked to leave altogether (1657 I f.297v). Maybe he transgressed his vow of chastity or of obedience; certainly his industry and acumen as *maestro* had been exemplary for he was frequently awarded gifts of money, or flour and wine, for his strenuous efforts in providing music for the major feasts (1654 I f.164v, f.190v, 1656 f.236). Thus even with archives as full and well-ordered as these, there are omissions; the pride that engendered the commissioning in 1716 of a book detailing the previous century of the

Misericordia's existence, as mentioned earlier, is unlikely to have arisen overnight. Some scandals were best not recorded.

Visiting Musicians

The process of leave-taking was a two-way one, and the church often benefitted from the services of visitors. These may have been singers briefly in the employ of a local nobleman (1650 I f.61) or people like Biaggio Ghirardi, *maestro di capella* at Verona (presumably at the cathedral) who wrote asking that he be permitted to perform and direct compositions of his own at the feast of the Assumption in 1651 (1651 I ff.65, 89*v*). He duly came, was thanked and given L.350 rather than offered the job of *maestro* at S. Maria, for which doubtless he was angling (1651 I f.91*v*). Giovanni Battista Menegoni could have been luckier. He came from Genoa for the Assumption of 1652, presumably at the invitation of the two members of the church council who were usually detailed to research into such possibilities (e.g. 1651 I f.121). He was offered the job of *maestro* there and then at the full salary of L.1,400 and his entourage given salaried posts (1652 I ff.121, 126, 126*v*). However, they all returned south-westwards, and the church was no better than before (1653 I ff.140*v*, 141*v*). Nonetheless it was following employment as a visitor in 1699 (1699 III f.546) that in 1700 Carlo Marino returned to the service of the church after a gap of just over three years (1700 I f.138, 1696 I f.28). Michele Stella, a soprano who lived up the Val Seriana at Albino had on occasion served the church as a distinguished visitor (e.g. 1697 III f.425, 1699 III f.546). Indeed, the church once gave its blessing to his employment so late that a runner had to be sent to apprise him of the engagement (1699 III f.532). Perhaps he was growing too old for opera by 1710, or was merely worn by the hard times, but in that year he joined the salaried staff (1711 I f.27). It is true that one document (1713 II p.112) shows him to have been the most highly paid church musician. The visiting virtuoso was sometimes paid a fabulous sum (see the list of musicians, p.334). For Easter 1716 the Perone brothers, violin and cello, received L.412 between them (1716 III f.292). Such sums for a pair of visiting instrumentalists would have been unthinkable in 1650. Among other instrumentalists to find their way into the church on such occasions were a Neapolitan theorbo virtuoso (1705 III f.227) and a military trumpeter from Brescia (1712 III f.113); but when Luigi Taglietti came from Brescia on the same occasion, it was his cello, not his tromba marina that he brought with him.[29]

Two documents (1698 III f.482 and 1700 III f.561) indicate that a cornett was used for Easter Day. In 1700 the same instrument returned for the Assumption (1700 III f.578). A salaried cornettist was appointed in 1654 (1654 I f.179) but seems never to have taken up his post. This was probably an attempt to stem the tide of musical progress, since appointment is recorded as long ago as 1587 of a salaried cornettist to play 'every time there is music in the church' (1587 I f.91). By 1700 his duties were reduced to one or two days a year. The decline in importance of the lute is apparent from the fact that when Andrea Laxigner left (1698 I f.63) the church was content to remain with only one on the salaried staff, and consistently to employ Francesco Napoli *cetra*—presumably chittarone—for the great feasts as an extra (e.g. 1697 III ff.427, 445, 1703 III f.131; the 1698 reference to Laxigner occurs at the annual confirmation of musicians, when, it is remarked, he has been absent from the church for many months). The first hiring of an oboist is recorded in 1703 (1703 III f.131). If one suspects that Giovanni Ecord was a Frenchman, there is no doubt about Monsù Noiè in 1703!

There are some interesting comments concerning the local players brought in as ripienists: 'l'organista del duomo con la viola, ma si paga come organista L.15'. This sum, for the Assumption (1654 III f.475), was rather more than those paid for other viola players on the same or comparable occasions (e.g. 1653 III f.413). The same 1654 expense account makes mention of 'D. Maffioletto Basso, et per far la battuta alli organi di ripieno L.15'. By comparison, a contrabasso string cost L.3:12 for this occasion. The expenses for Assumption in 1652 mention a special sum for porterage of the second organ for the rehearsal, which did not take place in the church (1652 III f.376). Later in the century, although Balarotti the then *maestro* used to play the organ (1692 IV f.700), and although the church also had a regular organist, another was hired for the great occasions (e.g. 1697 III f.445, 1698 III f.482). This is evidence either of three organs—though I have never come across references to porterage for a third organ, nor was there a third organ always in the church (1694 II f.266)—or of shift work on the part of the organists, or that Balarotti was acting as a non-playing conductor of his large forces. Fifty years earlier, as already mentioned, the need for a beat was recognised.

Among ripienists for these special occasions are to be found past or future members of the regular musicians' payroll (1694 III 16 April includes Gioseppe Balarotti as an extra, 1684 I f.29, 1685 I f.50v, 1686 I f.75v etc, up to 1690 I f.155 when he was dismissed, report him as salaried; see page 334 concerning the employment of Giovanni Ecord).

Exactly what was involved in taking part in the biggest annual celebration—
Holy Week and Easter—can be seen from the table set out below. Drawn
up by the painstaking Reggiani (1690 III ff.54, 54*v*, 55), it shows for
which services the visitors were used and how much they received.

Suonatori, e Cantori che sono intervenuti nelle fontioni della
Domenica delle palme, e Settimana Santa.

Domenica delle Palme
Alla distributione delle Palme, e Passio
Sig. D. Maritato Basso	1
Sig. Alessandrino Alto	1
Sig. Corno Tenore	1

All'Espositione del Sant^{mo} Sagramento

All'Espositione del Sant^mo Sagramento
Sig. Alessandrino Alto	1
Sig. Fontana Violino	1

Lunedi mattina, e restante del giorno sino alla sera
Sig. Fontana col violino	2
Sig. Alessandrino Alto	2
Sig. D. Gio. del Violoncello	2

Martedi mattina, alla repositione
Sig. Fontana col Violino	1
Sig. Alessandrino Alto	1
Sig. D. Gioanni col Violoncello	1

Mercoredi al Mattutino Benedictus, e Miserere.
Sig. Alessandrino Alto	1
Sig. Corno Tenore	1
Sig. D. Maritato Basso	1
Sig. D. Gioanni col Violoncello	1
Sig. Fontana col Violino	1
Sig. Curti con la Viola	1

Giovedi mattina alla Messa
Sig. Alessandrino Alto	1
Sig. Corno Tenore	1
Sig. D. Maritato Basso	1

Giovedi al mattutino e sue sequenze
Sig. Alessandrino Alto	1
Sig. Corno Tenore	1
Sig. D. Maritato Basso	1
Sig. Fontana col Violino	1
Sig. Curti con la Viola	1
Sig. D. Gioanni col Violoncello	1

Venerdi Mattina al Passio ed altro concernente all Messa processione

Sig. Alessandrino Alto	1
Sig. Corno Tenore	1
Sig. D. Maritato Basso	1

Venerdi sera al mattutino

Sig. Alessandrino Alto	1
Sig. Corno Tenore	1
Sig. Fontana col Violino	1
Sig. Curti con la Viola	1

Venerdi alla processione di notte

Sig. Alessandrino Alto	1
Sig. Corno Tenore	1

Sabbato Santo alla Messa e Vespro

Sig. Alessandrino Alto	1
Sig. Corno Tenore	1
Sig. Curti Viola	1

Alla compieta solenne

Sig. Alessandrino Alto	1
Sig. Corno Tenore	1
Sig. Curti Viola	1
Sig. Fontana col Violino	1

Giorno di Pasqua alla Messa, e Vespro

Sig. Alessandrino Alto	2
Sig. Corno Tenore	2
Sig. Fontana col Violino	2
Sig. Curti con la Viola	2

Sig. Alessandrino, Alto	fontioni n?	15
Sig. Corno, Tenore	fontioni n?	11
Sig. Fontana	fontioni n?	10
Sig. Curti	fontioni n?	7
Sig. D. Gioanni	fontioni n?	5
Sig. D. Maritato	fontioni n?	5

	n? 53 a L.3	L.159
Portatura del Organo, ed Organo		L. 20
		L.179

The archives contain references to musicians coming from, or going to, most of the large towns bounded by a line joining Venice (e.g. 1691 I f.194), Ferrara (e.g. 1657 I f.299*v*, 1712 I f.56*v*; recording that Bassani came to Bergamo therefrom; also see p. 345), Bologna (e.g. 1700 I f.150),

Modena (e.g. 1714 I f.113*v*), Reggio (e.g. 1655 I f.197*v*), Parma (e.g. 1655 I f.194*v*), Genoa (see p 346), and Turin (e.g. 1690 I f.148*v*), and returning to Venice by way of the southern edge of the Alps. There is surprisingly little contact with Rome (however see p. 345), though the council realised it was to Corelli at Rome that they must send the young Pietro Antonio Locatelli for the furthering of his prowess as a violinist.[10] There is more contact with Naples (e.g. 1653 III f.420, 1718 I f.27, 1719 I f.56)—indeed there were strong trading links between the *Misericordia* and the southern city. Filippo Vitali came to Bergamo from Florence (1648 I f.398), and in 1717 Paolo Benedetto Bellinzani of Udine was an applicant for the post of *maestro* (1717 I f.302*v*). The contralto Todeschino (e.g. 1678 IV f.32) was presumably of German extraction—on one occasion a *soprano tedesco* is specifically mentioned (1700 III f.561). The first S. Maria oboists were French (see p. 347).

Milan (e.g. 1695 I f.297, 1713 IV f.484), Genoa (e.g. 1714 IV f.5, 1715 IV f.25) and Turin (e.g. 1690 I f.148*v*) were the chief centres which invited S. Maria musicians to participate in opera, though some of Balarotti's operas were put on in Cremona (1700 I f.162*v*), Piacenza (1692 IV f.709) and Reggio (1692 I f.211*v*) as part of each city's carnival festivities. Balarotti sometimes wished to take S. Maria musicians with him on such occasions (e.g. 1696 I f.28).

When a visiting virtuoso came from as far afield as Ferrara, the expenses of fetching and returning him with due style and ceremony often exceeded the cost of his fee (1648 III f.168, 1657 III f.205). Many such virtuosi travelled with a servant-companion (1648 III f.173) thus increasing the expense still further. On a few occasions there survive accounts for the expenses of travel, changing horses, buying meals etc (e.g. 1650 III f.282). The two accounts for feeding the visiting musicians for one of the two great annual festivals sometimes specify the cost of the various items of food at every meal, and the cost of replacing a broken cup or two (e.g. 1653 III ff.415–416*v*, 1663 III ff.19–20). An expert in 17th-century Italian diet could probably tell at exactly what social level these people were treated.

The small towns in the immediate vicinity of Bergamo, e.g. Crema (e.g. 1648 III f.173), Caravaggio (e.g. 1656 III f.151), Clusone (e.g. 1645 I f.279*v*—the appointment of Giovanni Legrenzi from this town to be the organist of S. Maria) and Salo (e.g. 1649 I f.14—the similar appointment of Quaglia) all produced noteworthy musicians who were in occasional or regular employ at S. Maria. Indeed, one of these men, G. B. Pederzoli of Chiari (1645 I f.288) so impressed the church that he was invited to serve as *maestro* (1664 I f.189*v*), a post he only retained for a year (1665 I f.209*v*).

Violone and Double Bass

In these archives, even in the 1650s, the two terms *violone* and *contrabasso* are found in circumstances which indicate a complete interchangeability (1657 III f.30, 1653 III ff.425, 431, 1656 III f.24). *Violoncino* (1653 III f.413) occasionally appears for a man who elsewhere plays the violone (1653 III f.432 etc). The term *violone* remains frequently to be found in the council minutes until *c*1700. Even as late as 1716 (1716 III f.288) the aged Bassani was using the term. Every year the church of S. Grata used to petition to borrow 'il violone grande' for the feast of S. Croce (e.g. 1692 IV f.691). Another reference (1696 I f.22*v*) records a similar loan to a different suburban church. Yet a further such occasion (1697 I f.47*v*) mentions *il violone novo*. In 1702 (1702 I f.238) the wording is *uno delli contrabassi*, and Marc'Antonio Bernardi is referred to in his appointment (1700 I f.150) and always thereafter as *sonator di contrabasso*. Around the same years the function of the 16-foot bass instrument must have changed too. Prior to the appointment in 1697 of Bartolomeo Bernardi as first violin (1697 I f.51*v*)—the most expensive violinist ever in S. Maria's employ, and yet always heavily in debt (1699 V 6 April, 10 Oct)—the *sonator di violone* is always placed immediately under the names of the singers and before those of the instrumentalists in the annual list of confirmation of employment (e.g. 1696 I f.9). However, after that appointment, the *sonator di violone* and latterly *di contrabasso* is placed under the confirmation of the instrumentalists (e.g. 1699 I f.94, and see p. 333), the last singer being followed by the first violin. It was still true that the double bass was the inseparable companion of the organ. When all the instrumentalists got leave from attendance at the *compiette* of Quadragesima (1720 I f.81), the double bass player was specifically refused this exemption, thus clarifying Giovanni Parenti's claim, as part of a bid for increased salary (1687 IV f.480), that it was his duty to accompany the organ at all times. Nonetheless, after 1699 the double bass player was also accorded status and salary as a virtuoso instrumentalist comparable with the players of first violin and cello. Certainly he is needed for the athletic bass parts of Marino's *sonate da chiesa* if they are not to be undercut by the cello line, with unstylish second inversion chords as a result.[31] The following document, which I can no more translate in full than fully understand, may record the physical conversion of a violone into a double bass, if such a conversion there was. Evidently the resulting instrument had only four strings (1701 III f.10).

> Fattura per haver aggiustato il contrabasso di S.ᵗᵃ M.ᵃ
>
> Primieramente per haverlo d'intorno aggiustato et incolato, perche era mezzo rovinato, et posia fatto il seagnello, et messa l'anima, et ponolo nel fondo.
>
> Per haver fatto li biroli piu grandi, et rifatto il capotasto, et haver aggiustata la coperta del manico, et con diligenza messo della colla anco ci centro. Questa fattura importa per il manco ducatti tre

L. 18:12

Lista delle Corde per il Violone di Sᵗᵃ Maria	
il Canto	2
la Seconda	3
la Terza	5
la quarta coperta d'argento di Bologna	8
	18

The church always paid for repairs to this large expensive instrument. Obviously it was communally, rather than personally owned. The same appears to have been true of Laxigner's theorbo (1692 II f.166). The council's expense in maintaining the organ was lessened by the fact that various members of the Quaglia family were used for this task (e.g. 1686 I f.88*v*, 1692 III f.156, 1701 III f.50). They were presumably cheaper than outside contractors. The organ seems to have had a 16-foot rank (*li contrabassi del organo*) which had not functioned for many years prior to 1701, when it appears to have been put in order (1701 III f.50). Presumably the welcome presence of a 16-foot string bass was one of the reasons why Italian organs were slow to grow pedalboards. Before leaving the subject of the bass line, it is interesting to note that Giovanni Parenti, the *sonator di violone*, was also regarded as custodian of the bass line, for it was to him that the council entrusted two trombones for safe keeping until they might be in fashion again (1691 V 26 Feb).

Social Status

Comments in musicians' letters suggest that even the players and singers on the regular payroll were paid nothing like a living wage, with the possible exception of the *maestro di capella*. Letters petitioning for salary increases mention the falling off in the number of jobs obtainable outside the service of the church (e.g. 1678 IV f.28, 1699 IV f.153). Many players were obviously amateurs with quite another main occupation. Giuseppe

Marino gained admission to the church band on the understanding that he wanted to advance himself as a viola player, an activity he had not long taken up. He also deemed it worth mentioning that he could read music (1680 IV f.110), as did Laxigner the theorbist when submitting a very similar request about the same time (1680 IV f.118). By 1683 (1683 I f.3) Giuseppe Marino was receiving a pittance of a salary, but one that was never increased above L.70, not even when he handed over the position of *sonator di viola* to one of his sons (1692 IV f.685, 1695 II p.395). There must have been other musical employment in Bergamo—it would appear for instance that the cathedral had some sort of regular musical staff. For as distinguished a player and composer as Carlo Marino is unlikely to have given up music altogether after his guest appearance as violinist in 1707 (see p. 341). He played no more for the church, yet he was resident in Bergamo in 1712 and in 1717, on both occasions applying unsuccessfully for the vacant post of *maestro* (1712 I f.56*v*, 1717 I f.302*v*). Despite Balarotti's secular and instrumental leanings,[32] the church preferred *maestri* whose reputations were more specifically ecclesiastical.

One document (1696 I f.28) records the ordination of one of the resident musicians as a priest; Legrenzi and Cazzati were both priests (1654 I f.167)—*cappelani semplice*, licensed to celebrate. So too were Marchesi and Cesareni, as mentioned on pp. 330, 342. More complex were the cases of *cappelani residenti*, resident priests who sang regularly in the plainsong choir, to one of whose number Lodovico Vavassore the bass singer was elected, whilst retaining his right to sing as a soloist with a soloist's salary (1649 I ff.11*v*–12, 1650 I f.28). Some of the more local visiting musicians were also priests (e.g. 1647 III f.129). Young musicians asking to join the church band for the experience claim to be pupils of one of the instrumentalists already playing there (see p. 330), and teaching must have provided a useful extra income for the better players, quite apart from that carried out by the *maestro* at the instigation of the authorities.

★   ★   ★

Short of an expert and thorough-going review of the economy of Bergamo during this period, it is impossible to assess the value of the church's payments to its recipients, and only relative observations can be made. Certainly, commodity prices seem to have undergone little long-term change or inflation, so that alterations in the pattern of church music financing are real, and not just 'paper'.[33] Much remains to be done. I have not touched on the geography of the music inside the church. Did the

soloists perform from the organ lofts? Did they mount the ten feet or so
'sopra la cantoria'?—There would have been room for all the regulars if
both sides were used, but there would have been some striking spatial
antiphony. There is, in addition to what has been included here, a wealth
of further documentation about the organs of the church, their alteration
and maintenance. What is really needed is some kind of *catalogue
raisonné* of the musical material in the archive during these years, but that
would be a sizeable book.

   Working in archives such as this is a potent and far-reaching source of
personal education, and the insights gained into the life of a musical
community and the performance practice of the music on which it fed are
useful and provocative, though time-consuming to gather and sift.[34] The
whole exercise forms a living example and a sound vindication of the
technique of the education authorities in Hermann Hesse's *The Glass
Bead Game*, where each student, during the course of his training, has to
construct and write up three imaginary lives researched from times and
places other than his own.[35]

NOTES ON CHAPTER 13

1.   B. Belotti: *Storia di Bergamo e dei Bergamaschi*, iv (Bergamo, 1959), esp. 247–53.

2.   C. Scotti: *Il pio instituto musicale Donizetti in Bergamo* (Bergamo, 1901) contains
accounts of the early history of the *Misericordia*. The present chapter should also be read as
something of a sequel to J. Roche: 'Music at S. Maria Maggiore in Bergamo, 1614–1643',
ML, xlvii (1966), 296–312. Roche's article has greatly assisted the preparation of the
present chapter.

3.   Belotti, 183.

4.   Marc'Antonio Benaglio: *Istitutioni e ordini della Misericordia Maggiore di Bergamo*
(Bergamo, 1620).

5.   Roche (1966), 297, fn. 4, 301, fn. 14, 306, fn. 29.

6.   *Status animarum S. Michaelis ab arcu 1683*.

7.   T. Dart: ' "The Name's the Same" or: a Warning to Searchers', *RMARC*, ii (1962),
16f.

8.   Contemporary baptismal register of the parish of S. Pancrazio, f.61*v*. The son was
Pietro, the viola-player, see above p. 325 (1697 IV f.109), and p. 353 (1692 IV f.685, 1695
II p.395).

9.   Giovanni Battista Quaglia: [Libretto] *La vittoria di David contro Golia* (Bergamo,
1680).

10.   Francesco Quaglia: [Libretto] *Le lagrime della penitenza* (Brescia, 1697); this bears a
statement that it was written for the church of S. Defendente in Borgo S. Leonardo,
Bergamo.

11. [Libretto] *Accademia detta in lode dell'ill^mo et ecc^mo Signor Francesco Donado, capitano grande, nella sua partenza dalla citta di Bergamo* (Milan, 1709), music by Carlo Marino. See also *Li splendori della croce sotto li simboli del crociero e di venere, Accademia recitata in Bergamo, li 23 december, 1685* [no imprint].

12.   Roche (1966), 308f.

13.   S. Angelini: *Santa Maria Maggiore in Bergamo* (Bergamo, [?1968]), esp.p.84.

14.   'Si accettino alle scole . . . Ventura di M. Gio. Batta. Moresco attesa la sua povertà gratis'.

15.   'Si accettino alle scole di questo Collegio Paolo Emilio e Girolamo figliuoli di me notario . . . gratis'.

16.   Benaglio (1620), 17.

17.   Benaglio (1620), 71ff.

18.   Benaglio (1620), 65.

19.   See the 1671 wage list above. 1679 II p.153 records that Quaglia, in the year after he first appears to have gained the title of *maestro*, received a salary rise from L.700 to L.875 p.a.. 1687 II p.456 shows that he received L.1,260, but this was after agreements concerning a strenuous teaching commitment in the college, and the maintenance of the organs. 1693 II p.376 shows Ballarotti on only L.700, though this was up to L.980 by 1703 (1703 II p.428).

20.   J. Roche: 'An Inventory of Choirbooks at S. Maria Maggiore, Bergamo, January 1628', *RMARC*, v (1965), 47–50.

21.   Giovanni Battista Quaglia: *Motetti sacri a voce sola, libro primo* (Bologna, 1668); *libro II* (Bergamo, 1675).

22.   Ed. Marino Silvani: *Nuova raccolta di motetti sacri a voce sola* (Bologna, 1670); *Motetti sagri a voce sola con instrumenti* (Bologna, 1695).

23.   Carlo Marino: *Sonata a tre e a quattro, Op.6* (Amsterdam, [1706]). As Op.5 appeared in 1699 and Op.7 in 1704, both in Venice, it seems likely that Op.6 appeared in the same place *c*1702–3.

24.   *GB-Mp* Newman Flower Collection.

25.   *A-Wn*.

26.   Scotti (1901), 198. Having remained as first violin until 1745, he rose to the post of *maestro*, and died in office in 1767 (!) having since 1760 had his duties discharged by a deputy.

27.   1700 I f.150*v* records that the council forbade leave for a large group of musicians to go and perform at the distant village of Ardesio. Matters were complicated by the fact that some had already started on the journey.

28.   E. Selfridge-Field: *Venetian Instrumental Music from Gabrieli to Vivaldi* (Oxford, 1975), 164.

29.   'Taglietti, Giulio', *MGG*.

30.   A. Meli: *Pietro Antonio Locatelli: Quaderno no. 2* (Bergamo, 1970), 18f.

31.   Numerous examples can be found in Op.3: e.g. 2 iv 18; 3 iv 5, 11, 29.

32. See p. 350 above, also his publication *Balletti. arie. gighe. corrente. alemande. sarabande, capricci da camera a tre istromenti, due violini e violone overo spinetta*, Op.1 (Milan, 1681).

33. Nicolo Malinconico in 1693 received the enormous sum of L.24,800 for painting 13 paintings in S. Maria. He was permitted to work some of them in his native Naples, and from the above sum he was to find all his travelling expenses, board and lodging in Bergamo, technical assistance etc. A year later he received L.1,240 more for two further paintings whilst he was resident in Bergamo (1693 I ff.225v–226, 1694 I f.247).

34. Even more engrossing in some ways are the innumerable comments about the non-musical activities of the musicians: e.g. 1683 V 26 March—Giuseppe Ballarotti witnesses the signing of a contract; 1696 V 6 Feb, Giorgio Violino is behind with the rent, etc, etc.

35. Hermann Hesse: *The Glass Bead Game* (Zurich, 1943; Eng. trans. R. and C. Winston, 1972), 107–10, 416–519.

14

Music and British Travellers Abroad, 1600–1730

Michael Tilmouth

Charles I, the dedicatee of William Lithgow's *Totall Discourse of the Rare Adventures and Painfull Peregrinations of Long Nineteene Yeares Travayles* (London, 1614), would not necessarily have agreed with its author that 'thrice happy and blest was the Kingdome, when old men bore sway and ruled the State, and young men travelled abroad' to widen their experience and improve their judgment. Over the next ten years he could well have spared some of the older and the younger men. Be that as it may, the number of Britishers travelling abroad increased rapidly over the ensuing 100 years with hardy adventurers like Lithgow, a sort of late survivor of the questing spirit of the Elizabethan age, giving place to the young gentlemen of leisure and means intent (or not so intent) on completing the 'grand tour' with its quota of enlightenment to be derived from the circuit of Europe and, in particular, the edification offered by what was to become the almost obligatory giro of Italy.

Not all, however, were merely seeking a genteel finishing touch to their education or making good the deficiencies of Oxford and Cambridge. For long enough Leyden had opened its doors to Scottish students of law and medicine, and scholars had undertaken the kind of fact-finding research tours that were later exemplified in Dr Burney's travels. Peterhouse, Cambridge, instituted, quite early, two travelling Fellowships: Fynes Morison's *Itinerary*[1] was the outcome of one, embodying the fruits of its author's experiences begun in 1591, and providing a useful handbook for travellers well into the 17th century. Some were forced out of the country by religious persecution or political circumstance at home; others on embassies or trading missions sought the political or commercial advantage of their country or themselves abroad.

The pattern of travels changed with changing times: inevitably the attraction of Spain had scarcely exceeded the period of Mary's reign and the Elizabethan took himself to France. During the Civil Wars France provided a haven and catholics were well received in Italy too, though it

357

was not until late in the 17th century that travel there for protestants was
without the possible danger of religious persecution. In German-speaking
countries the devastation of the Thirty Years War was hardly repaired until
the 18th century. Only then, particularly with the period of respite offered
by the more general peace in Europe after 1713, did they begin to appear
regularly among the places visited or considered worth visiting by those
bent on social and cultural enlightenment, though merchants, whose net
was cast wider and often as far as the Baltic states and the Middle East,
might visit them.

This motley collection of travellers—students, scholars, ambassadors,
traders and adventurers, grand tourists and their tutors, the persecuted
and exiled—left a massive record of their experiences in letters and reports
and in diaries or journals kept by themselves or for them by servants or
tutors. Much has been published but much remains in manuscript or is
relatively unknown. Observations on music in them are numerous, for as
the Baroque art blossomed in church and theatre and chamber only the
most jaundiced of British eyes or ears could fail to be struck by its
manifestations in Italy and France in particular, and few altogether resisted
the attempt to capture their impressions even if that attempt was limited
to the most well-worn encomiums of the Italian Opera.

Whatever the reasons for their journey—whether it was to be conceived,
as Howell would have it, as 'a peripatetic school'[2] with a broad curriculum,
or more narrowly as a means of learning a language, gaining some understanding of the classics or perhaps acquiring the technical education
necessary to an architect, or even if it was the result of the kind of mind-
lessness expressed by Sir Philip Sydney, 'a certain tickling humour to do as
other men had done'—a musical ear undoubtedly increased the pleasures
of travel, and musical occasions are often described with more relish than
the properer pursuits of study. The antiquities of Rome, the paintings at
Florence, the churches of Venice had all been described a thousand times
before and too often accounts of them were merely transcribed or translated from some convenient source into a journal designed to convey the
impression that the appointed itinerary had been kept. Musical occasions
were on the whole less obligatory and perhaps as a result when they were
described at all they were recounted with that much greater zest.

Italy

Of all countries Italy had most to offer to the musically inclined, and Sir
John Clerk of Penicuik probably wrote for many of them when, after

travelling there against his father's wishes, he recorded that it had been his greatest desire to see a country 'so much excelling all other countries in painting and musick'. 'I am sure', he added, that 'nothing in life had ever made me happy if I had denied myself this great pleasure and satisfaction'.[3]

Church music in Italy, particularly in the great centres of Rome and Venice, almost invariably struck the British visitor by its flamboyance. Thomas Raymond, secretary to Lord Fielding who was ambassador extraordinary to Venice in 1634, confesses that he repaired to the churches simply 'for the musick sake, which was very excellent'.[4] Lady Catherine Whetenall, who travelled to Rome for the Jubilee celebrations of 1650, presumably attended for more devout purposes but Richard Lascells, who travelled with her to record her activities, seems sometimes to have been as much preoccupied with the music they heard, in particular the voice of a nun on St Benedict's Day which, he writes, 'to my thinking was the onely thing, next unto the Jubily which made my Journey up to Rome a saveing Journey'.[5]

Among the churches Lady Catherine visited in Rome was that of S. Apollinaro. Nine years later Francis Mortoft was there and he noted that Carissimi had '3 thousand Crownes a yeare . . . to maintaine Musicke every Sunday' there.[6] He too heard Bonnaventure at the Chiesa Nova where the music seems to have ravished him much as it had done John Evelyn[7] in 1644:[8]

9 March 1659: to the Chiesa Nova, where wee heard that never enough to be praised and delightful Musicke. The subject was made by A Prince of Rome and composed by Charissima, who for that is accounted the best in the world, and sung by Bonnaventure, Sinesia [L. C. Sanese] and the two Vuulpies [Vulpios], all which made so sweete a harmonye, that never the like must be againe expected, unlesse in heaven and in Rome.

Like the ear-witnesses mentioned later by Roger North who, during the clangour of the grander sort of Italian church music, 'could not conceive any one nerve or vein in their whole bodys to be at rest',[9] Mortoft appears to have been a young man of extreme sensibility. At any rate he was bowled over by the music practically every time he entered a church, whether it was the '3 or 4 Eunuchs and singing Masters, with the Organs, Base Viols and Trumpets' at the Jesuit Church at Genoa, 'at least 20 Eunuchs' at St Peter's in Rome, or the 'some dozen voyces, a Lute, Violin and Organs' who performed music in praise of St Thomas Aquinas at the auditory of S. Marcello.[10] The warmth of Mortoft's response is perhaps rendered a little suspect by the similarity of some of his sentiments to those expressed by a traveller from the Low Countries a few years earlier,[11] but they were nevertheless shared by many others. Robert Moody, who had been in Rome before, persuaded his master Banister Maynard to visit S. Apollinaro for its 'rare Musick' on Christmas Eve 1660 (*GB-Ob* Rawl. D.84, f.13) and precisely three years later Philip Skippon and his party attended the sane midnight service after 'excellent vocal and instrumental musick' and a supper at the Pope's palace to which all strangers were freely admitted.[12]

Few travellers could make the kind of detailed technical comments that are to be found in the journal of such an informed amateur as Robert Bargrave,[13] but until the close of the 17th century the sound of eunuchs' voices rarely failed to elicit notice. John Raymond's reaction in 1646 was a typically English one when he observed that the Italians were so addicted to music, vocal music in particular, that 'great Persons keep their *Castrati*, viz. *Eunuch's* whose throates and complexions scandalise their breeches' (f.8). But later this offence to masculinity and nature gave rise to less heated comment as when John Ray, visiting Rome in 1664, found the vocal music of eunuchs and nuns 'doubtless the best in the world'[14] or when William Acton visited the churches in Turin.[15] Nor did the scale of musical celebrations on feast days go unmentioned: William Bromley noted that four organs took part in a 'noble Consort of Instrumental and Vocal Musick' which marked the feast of St Anthony at the church of that saint in Padua. When he heard Vespers at St Peter's on St Peter's Day in Rome the music was performed polychorally by four choirs.[16]

Prompted by his uncle, Pepys's nephew John Jackson naturally made the most of the opportunities to hear music when he was in Italy. In December 1699 he attended midnight devotions at the church of S. Lorenzo where he heard 'most ravishing musick suited to the occasion; Paluccio, an admired young eunuch, singing, and Corelli, the famous violin, playing, in concert with at least 30 more; all at the charge of Cardinal Ottoboni'.[17] With the beginning of the sacred Jubilee Year the next month operas and comedies were forbidden in Rome, 'to the great grief of most of our young gentlemen here, who, impatient of so insipid an amusement as the bare study of antiquitys only, are hastening away as fast as they can for the Carnevals of Naples and Venice'. Jackson joined the exodus, but was back in Rome by March enjoying music almost every night of the week at Cardinal Ottoboni's, Cardinal Sacrapanti's, Don Livio's or at some church or fraternity, the best of it, he thought 'worthy of any that ever was heard in Italy, or perhaps will be again till the next 100th year'.

Jackson himself excitedly anticipated the music to be heard in Holy Week, particularly that 'at the Pope's Chappel, much celebrated for the voices unassisted by instruments' which Uncle Pepys insisted he must hear at all costs. When he did he was obviously disappointed in it, but as he tactfully observed to his uncle when reporting the occasion, 'I fear the want of judgment on my part' (pp.263, 299f).

Only rarely are any very exact details given about the music performed. Sir John Clerk was present in 1698 at the Pope's celebration of mass on the Festival of St Peter when 'the musick was exceedingly divine, being the compositions of the famous Palestrina' (p.29, note 3), but we do not learn precisely which of his masses was given. Richard Pococke wrote to his mother from Rome in April 1734 and mentioned that he had heard the *Miserere*—obviously Allegri's ('’tis said they cannot divulge the notes under pain of excommunication')—but he was more intrigued by the ceremony of the distribution of palm branches at the Pope's chapel at Monte Cavallo when the Passion was sung or chanted in dialogue (which he found 'a very uncouth performance') and by solemn high mass celebrated by the Maronites (*GB-Lbm* Add.22978, f.68-68*v*). Edward Wright too, visiting Bologna, tells us something about the nature of the oratorio, a species of composition which must have been new to him at the time of his travels in the early 1720s, though he does not identify the music he heard.[18]

The churches of Italy provided much that was delightful or impressive to the eye and the ear of the traveller, but for those who would use the niceties of manners and customs supposed to belong to those without our realm to polish and refine the deficiencies of those within, meetings of the academies and assemblies at private houses were presumably felt to be more fruitful. When Milton visited Italy in the 1630s he was actually made a member of the Academy of the Svogliati in Florence and probably met Giovanni Battista Doni there. In Rome Cardinal Francesco Barberini invited him to a musical entertainment and it seems likely that the three Latin epigrams on Leonora Baroni were the result of his having heard her sing there accompanied by her mother and sister on the theorbo and lute.[19]

Others, less distinguished perhaps but socially as acceptable, enjoyed similar entertainment. In 1645 John Evelyn was invited to 'the Prince Galicanos, who himselfe compos'd the Musique to a magnificent Opera' (3 May 1645)—his *Proserpina rapita* was performed that year. Not all such entertainments, however, were perfectly innocent in their intentions as Thomas Raymond perceived. At Ferrara in 1646 his party were invited to dinner by the Prefect of the English Jesuits but as they left there was some controversy over religion (*GB-Ob* Tanner 93, f.53):

> that we should depart from his Colledge sweetned, the old man invited us to the Musick of a Concord of Violyns, performed by some of the younge students and soone after very kindly dismissed us. These Invitations are done to our Nation certaynely to gayne what they can upon those of our Religion, and soften us as to theirs, and at that tyme our Nation was very kindly used in that place and all lawfull liberty given them. I remember desiring one day to be admitted unto an Enterlude in *Stilo recitativo* acted before some Cardinals and persons of quallitie being demanded what Country we were of, to which was replyed *Inglesi*; we were presently bid goe in and had given us very comodious seats.

In Rome the evening concerts given by the abdicated Queen Christina were among the regular resorts of English travellers. On 7 January 1659, for instance, Francis Mortoft 'went to the Queene of Sweedland's Pallace . . . it being her custome every Wensday night to have the best Muscitianers at her Pallace, she being much delighted in Musicke' (p.97). Philip Skippon was there on 28 December 1665 for a two-hour entertainment of vocal and instrumental music, though part of the time the Queen spent talking to Cardinal Azzolino and the other guests (p.676).

Skippon (who became a Fellow of the Royal Society and was knighted in 1674) and his three inquisitive colleagues—the celebrated naturalist John Ray, Francis Willoughby and Nathaniel Bacon—must have formed a fascinating group. Ray has been called the father of natural history in England and was the first to attempt a true systematic account of the animal kingdom. He was a member of Trinity College, Cambridge where he taught the humanities and was noted as a good Hebrew scholar as well as being a distinguished naturalist. The other three were in fact his pupils and in 1662 the four of them decided to attempt a systematic description of the whole organic world. This in fact was the main purpose of their journey commenced in 1663, though on it they also recorded details of antiquities, local customs and institutions. Willoughby left them at Montpellier so that he could visit Spain, but the others proceeded to Holland, Germany, Switzerland, Italy, Sicily and Malta. Their joint observations were originally published in 1673 though Ray, as has been seen, also published his own travel journal independently. Skippon's account was several times reprinted.

On the way to Rome they had visited Padua where they minutely observed the process of making viol strings which Skippon describes in detail with illustrations (pp.532f). They also visited the palace at Verona where the celebrated Academici Filarmonici met. The prime concern of the Academy was to promote music and the palace contained a music room with a small organ and other rooms accommodating instruments and a music library. Skippon listed the officers and members of the Academy and recorded its rules and the subjects of 14 portraits of members hanging in the hall as well as transcribing the ancient inscriptions in the courtyard (pp.544–7).

Few detailed descriptions of the meetings of the Italian academies have survived, but there is one in the commonplace book (*GB-Lbm* Egerton 1632) kept by Robert Southwell (later Sir Robert and Secretary of State for Ireland) between November 1660 and April 1661 when he travelled as a young man to Rome. The volume itself is rather a jumble of oddments— Italian song-texts, titles of books and jottings such as the following tantalising glimpse of a certain member of the Steffkins family who had presumably travelled to Rome from Leghorn: 'Speaking of Mr Stefkins yᵉ violest one said he was almost mad at Ligorne, then judges say he was recovered; (for here he was quite mad)' (f.29v).

Southwell himself was entertained on various occasions by Cardinal Pallavicini and other cardinals. On 17 January 1661 he notes (ff.27–28v):

> At the Spanish Embassadors we had this pleasant entertainement.

> In a noble large Sale carpeted in the middle and railed in with Seates on three sides, with 3 table[s] within and at the other side or rather upper end passed a wicker partition while like lettuss [lattice?] behind wᶜʰ was the Embass: his wife &c, unseene. at yᵉ 1ˢᵗ table opposite sate the 3 Italian Musitians. on yᵉ left side a table of yᵉ Academists, and opposite an Italian Harpsecalls, and a treble and tenor Euenuch with a bass all Spanish voyces.

> The bell being rung on yᵉ table, yᵉ Popes Musick played.

> Next an Academist read some halfe a Score papers of very witty Subject with a little Prose and ending with a Stanza of verses burliske [burlesque?] thereon.

> Then Sang yᵉ Spanish Musick.

> The[n] An Academist at yᵉ table Secretary to yᵉ Embass: read a noble long Panegerick in verse of the Embass: and his Ancesters glory agˢᵗ the turkes.

> Then yᵉ Italians changed to yᵉ base violl, and a halfe lute &c.

> Then yᵉ 1ˢᵗ Academick read agen that such An Academist by name had made verses or Sonet on such a Subjecte & was desired to read it to yᵉ Company. So he sitting on the Inner bench, and all yᵉ rest alsoe a Servant with a Suttocup[?] of Silver with yᵉ Paper thereon and a Candle in his hand finds yᵗ academist out, and he reades to yᵉ whole company. And in like

manner did some 20 their verses after ye recital of the subject carryed to them, & then they reciting all agen.

Onely some were recited at ye table ye persons being Absent.

This done ye Theorbo man Lelio Colista played rare volenteryes. and then begun a physitian to Conclude the Act making in Prose a most ingenious S[c]hool Caracter of each Poets performance, cencuring all, and Still ending with a Stanza which was Sung plainely by ye base Spaniard and gave very great Gusto.

After this came in 2. dancers with a Harpe ye one ended with 45. Capers. and Luca with ye Saraband and after 30. Soe all ended.

The forme of this entertainement was very delightfull for the variety sake, and all thing and ye candlesticks, seates &c ranged in very good Order.

A few years earlier William Dobbyus had described Robert Southwell in glowing terms: 'as well a fashioned and handsome young gentleman, and of a mild good disposition and very modest and civil, as I have seen'.[20] But even this youthful paragon was apparently sufficiently a creature of his age to enjoy the earthy humour of the academists, which seems not always to have been much above the level of a men's catch club if we may judge by Southwell's next page (f.29):

Some of their Subjects were:

If Love or Interest prevailes most in female addresses.
On an old woman who being blind with one eye, who have painted her face and by mistake used lime and soe putt out ye other.

On an Academist who on halfe an houres warning came from Madrid by ye vertue of a wind he brought in his belly &c.

On an old woman who lamented of her paine of ye toothach, when she had none but what were putt into her head.

Perhaps our notion of what went on at some of these academies is too refined. At least on this occasion the ambassador's latticed wife could blush unseen.

At the turn of the century the pre-eminence which had belonged to Queen Christina's musical gatherings attached itself to those of the poet-Cardinal Pietro Ottoboni whose glittering assemblies drew in all the fashionable world of Rome. In a letter of 2 November 1695 to his sister, the Countess of Erroll, James Drummond, Earl of Perth, tells how Ottoboni had invited him and his wife:[21]

to partake of the pleasure of musique and opera when we pleased; he has one who is known by the severall names of le Bollognese Archangelo (for his name is Michael or Corelli), a fidler, but who waits on him as a gentleman here; the best player on the fidle that ever was, and the greatest master for composeing; he with one he has bred, who plays little worse than he, and three eunuchs with the others to compleat the company, sing and play every night at the Cardinall's, and certainly nothing can be finer . . . .

We have already seen how John Jackson enjoyed Ottoboni's hospitality in 1700, and many others shared this privilege for a number of years. The sometimes lavish nature of it may be deduced from Edward Wright's report that 150 performers took part in a vocal and instrumental entertainment given by Ottoboni to celebrate the installation of a new Pope (p.281).

Sir John Clerk, as a pupil of Corelli, would almost certainly have visited Ottoboni's palace though he seems not to have recorded any such occasion. However, he was certainly befriended by Monsignor Chaprigni at whose house in 1697 he attended 'Weekly Assemblies of Virtuosos'. Chaprigni also conducted a learned academy whose tone may have been more elevated than that described by Southwell. Clerk writes that 'we had likeways at his house privat Assemblies thrice a week, and in these we discoursed of all new discoveries in Literature and Antiquities. Some made orations in Latine, and some read verses in Greek, Latine and Italian, of their own compositions' (p.27). When he was making his way home in 1699 he stayed a week in Genoa and 'was entertained with great Civility at one of the Assemblies, where there was Musick and Gameing'. But Clerk had no taste for the latter and observed that Genoa 'was not the best place in Italy for Musick' (p.31). As with so many travellers, Rome had spoiled his appetite for anything that was not of absolute excellence.

Occasionally Rome even managed to capture some of the gaiety and spectacle in its music-making that was more commonly the preserve of carnival time in Venice. Wriothesley Russell (later the second Duke of Bedford) described his musical experiences in Rome in 1698 in letters to his mother, remarking that there were always fine serenades to be heard.[22] Charles Talbot, Duke of Shrewsbury, gave this account of one such on 24 August 1704:[23]

> . . . went to Piazza di Spagna where Prince Senestina gave a noble Serenade upon the birth of the d[uke] of Britany. it was before the Sp[anish] Amb[assador's] Palace. about 2 at night the musicians came in three sumptuous open Coaches like triumphant Chars all gilt; and 12 lighted by about 32 torches, each footman a rich Livery and white feathers. the Musicians all handsomely drest (in their own Cloaths) with white feathers and 3 woemen who sung finely drest. The Serenade lasted about an hour:

the woemens voices could not well be heard in so wide a Place. the three Coaches were driven, that which carry'd the woemen and near 20 other musicians, by Prince Prestini, an other by Cavalier Buongionanni and the 3[d] by an other Roman Gentm[n]; the Postillions also were Gentlemen, all well drest, & the Coachmen sat upon one of the wheele horses. As soon as the Coaches arived, the Prince lighted and went to make a compliment to the Ambassadress and Amb[r] and then returning, the Serenade began. I saw it from a chamber hired over against the Amb[rs] . . . many heard it from other windows, and many in open coaches planted there from the morning without horses and ranged by the Gentlemen of the horse some of P[rince] Prestini; when the serenade began the torches were put out, and a few candles lighted, that the musick might see their notes.

Of all the Italian cities, Venice equalled, if indeed it did not exceed, the attractions of Rome for British visitors in the 17th century—as it still does, though now in a rather melancholy, valetudinarian way. The fantastic, watery unreality of the place exerted a spell which all but silenced criticism and left only astonishment and admiration for at least nine-tenths of its vanities. To William Lithgow, who quickly forgot the stone set in the silver sea he had left, Venice was 'a Garden of riches, and worldly pleasures, the chiefe flowre of Commonweales, and the perfect mirrour of civill and politicke Governement'.[24] When Thomas Coryat heard the music pro-moted by one of the city companies in their hall on St Roche's Day (16 August) 1608 he found it 'so good, so delectable, so rare, so admirable, so super excellent, that it did even ravish and stupifie all those strangers that never heard the like', and he himself was 'for the time even rapt up with Saint *Paul* into the third heaven'.[25] The key phrase is 'that never heard the like', for the elaborate *cori spezzati* piece which Coryat goes on to describe was obviously an example of that Venetian flamboyance calculated to bowl over the uninitiated.

The musical novelties of the recitative style and the opera with its elaborate stage machinery coupled with their Venetian setting continued to work their magic for much of the 17th century. To John Evelyn, Rovetta's *Ercole in Lidia* which he saw in June 1645, with its 13 changes of scene, was 'one of the most magnificent & expensfull diversions the Wit of Men can invent'. No wonder it held him and his companion, Lord Bruce, 'by the Eyes and Eares til two in the Morning'. The English merchant Robert Bargrave was thrown into a similar state of ecstasy by Cavalli's *Artemisia* in 1656 which he saw 16 times and was still so far from being wearied by it that he would have ridden 'hundreds of miles' to see it again.[26]

Philip Skippon and his party were in Venice for the carnival season of 1664-5. They saw three operas: *La Rosilena* of G. B. Volpe and *Scipione Africano* of Cavalli at the Teatro Grimano (SS Giovanni e Paolo) and Cavalli's *La Deidamia* at the Teatro S. Salvatore, though characteristically Skippon, like other writers, does not mention the composers' names in his lengthy account of them (pp.506ff). The singing, costumes and dancing seem to have satisfied him but what really intrigued him (perhaps recalling that his prime purpose was to produce an account of the whole organic world) was the elaborate stage machinery, and he gives a detailed description illustrated with diagrams of the engines which were used to change the scenery and to fly down a god.

In 1675 John Clenche apparently saw Legrenzi's *Eteocle e Polinice* at the Teatro S. Salvatore. He writes of the 'incomparable Opera's' of Venice though he adds that 'the Scenes and Voices so far excel the *French*, that they have scarce resemblance'[27]—a comparison hinting at the French-Italian controversy that was soon to envelop the operatic world.

From the third quarter of the 17th century travel diaries and letters make frequent reference to the Venetian opera though few contain much significant information about it. Peregrine Bertie was in Venice for the carnival of 1686-7; though there was 'very good musicke every day' in the four weeks before the opera officially began a letter to the Countess of Rutland suggests that time dragged heavily until the opportunity presented itself for him to attend 'the proofe of an opera'—presumably a rehearsal. When the operas were over he seems to have found church music a poor substitute.[28] Some years later opera was a substitute for more vigorous action when James III was in Italy and his supporters were desperately trying to keep him amused: their letters are full of references to operas he had enjoyed for want of better things to do and thankfulness on the Duke of Mar's part that music was 'one of the best remedies against the spleen'.[29]

In fact the 18th century brought from Englishmen an altogether more critical attitude to opera, heralded by the rationalistic views of writers like Addison, who toured Italy in 1701-3. He went to the opera in Florence on 6 November 1701 in the company of the Duke of Shrewsbury and Sir Thomas Derham,[30] and saw several carnival operas at Venice. His account of these[31] is less well known than the later articles on opera in London which were to appear in *The Spectator*. He already shared the prejudice of every true-bred Englishman against the voice of the castrato particularly in heroic roles, and though he found the music good and the language beautiful and apt he deplored the ridiculous plots with their lack of observance of the unities and the ignorance that in one case allowed Cato to withdraw to a study furnished with volumes of Plutarch and Tasso.

Some later writers, like Thomas Nugent, their minds primed with Addison, did little more than echo his comments on and criticism of the Venetian opera.[32] Others, as the important operatic developments shifted to different centres and the mere novelty of the form wore off, were less inclined to respond to what Venice offered them with the starry-eyed astonishment of the 17th-century British travellers. Edward Wright found the new *Intermezzi* 'very comical in their way, which is somewhat low' but thought that they disrupted the unity of the main piece too much and would have been better at the close (p.83). He thought the audience ill-mannered too, with things being thrown from the upper boxes into the pit, though in this respect he confessed that the opera at Reggio, 'generally esteem'd the best in *Italy* . . . was the most noisy one I ever heard; the Company went from Box to Box to visit one another; others were playing at cards; and minded the Opera no more (though Faustina sung) than if it had been . . . a Sermon' (p.30).

Although operas in towns such as Milan and Siena[33] are occasionally mentioned, other than in Rome and Venice it is only music in Florence that receives much attention from British 17th-century travellers. Tuscany had early been singled out as the subject of a tourist's guide in Sir Robert Dallington's *Survey of the Great Dukes State of Tuscany. In the Year . . . 1596* (London, 1605). Sir Toby Mathew, the erring son of the Archbishop of York and a catholic convert, not only found good food and drink there in 1608 but was able to 'looke upon excellent devout pictures, and hear choyce musique'.[34] The Yorkshire royalist Sir John Reresby apparently made 'large mention' of the city in one of the volumes of his travel journals (1654–8) which has not survived.[35] He was present, however, at the obsequies of the Emperor Ferdinand III solemnised in the church of the Ss Annunziata. The ceremony lasted three hours and was 'set off with the best voices and other music in Italy'. Reresby was a good practical musician and acute enough to note in particular 'a trumpeter, who played an upper part in concert with violins and hautboys, so exactly both as to flats, sharps, and measure, that it was impossible for any instrument to have been more just and harmonious, as he governed it'.[36] But perhaps the instrument was a cornett.

Shortly after their arrival in Florence on 17 June 1661. Banister and William Maynard saw 'an Opera which was play'd severall nights one after another, and the famous Commedian Scaramuccio did sing and act in that Opera',[37] but Robert Moody, their servant, who was recording the events

of their travels is sparing of any further details. Forty years later Charles
Talbot, Duke of Shrewsbury, was there, his head still full of the opera at
Paris and Montpellier. On 30 October 1701 he took a box with Sir Thomas
Derham (p.113):

> The scenes were poor, the theatre little, no dancing, and not above two or
> three good voices, but the music pleased me much better than the French. It
> is always set to express the meaning of the words. They sing the dialogue
> much faster than the French; almost as fast as if it were spoke, which makes
> it less tedious. Their songs have many repetitions, but many of them ex-
> treme fine.

He visited the opera again on 6 and 9 November but seems to have been
disappointed by the orchestra at Florence. 'It is a great want in these
operas', he writes, 'that they have no flutes nor hautbois'.

France

Until the close of the 17th century France was visited by British travellers
more frequently than Italy, but perhaps because it was never regarded to
anything like the same extent as a source of musical enlightenment,
musical events there received scant attention in the travel journals and
diaries. One of the Elizabethan guides to the country was Sir Robert
Dallington's *The View of France* (London, 1604) also issued as *A Method
for Trauell, Shewed by Taking the View of France, as it Stoode in 1598*.
Dallington commends French dancing—a universal pastime there, for all
could perform 'your *Quarantes, Leualties, Bransles*, & other Dances
whatsoever . . . and rather than faile, the old women themselves, both
Gentle & base, who have moe toes then teeth, and these that are left,
leaping in their heads, like jacks in Virginals, will beare their part'
(sig.V2). The musical imagery is characteristically Elizabethan, but musical
matters are little noticed though Dallington does go on to censure,
probably without much justification, the French preference for the 'ef-
feminate' Ionic and Lydian modes and to quote, with more reason, the
Italian proverb that 'the French neither pronounce as they write, nor sing
as they pricke, nor thinke as they speake'.

In 1642 James Howell considered that Paris was where the student
should acquire the social graces—'Riding, Dancing, Fencing &c', but that
for 'Policy, Learning, Musique, Architecture and Limning' he should
repair to Italy.[38] Although, as we shall see, plenty of Englishmen learnt the
French lute and theorbo when they studied in France, in other respects

that country might well have looked up to England musically. It is perhaps not surprising that Sir John Finch in Paris in March 1652 recorded that 'the English Nunnery' (an institution whose foundation was forced upon the Archbishop of Paris by Richelieu) 'thrives well, their choice musick drawing all the nobility of France thither'.[39] However, the source of admiration may well have been the choice nuns rather than their music, for each of the inmates paid £400 for admittance to this select establishment.

In 1660 Charles Bertie, the youngest son of the Earl of Lindsey, was gratified by the organs and 'constantly excellent voices' at the Jesuits' Church in the rue St Antoin in Paris; a little later he saw a masque at the College of Navarre, but it was the dancing and the acting of the furies and other 'antique postures' that drew his praise.[40] In 1661 the Maynard brothers saw 'several Operas and Commedies' in Paris but unfortunately their servant and scribe Robert Moody found them 'too long to particularise' (f.3) and passed on to the more important matter of the Maynards' audience with the Queen Mother.

Later in the century the opera naturally received more attention. In 1698 Martin Lister, the zoologist and physician, accompanied the new ambassador, the Earl of Portland, to Paris as his medical adviser. 'I did not see many Opera's', Lister writes:[41]

> not being so good a French-Man, as to understand them, when Sung. The opera called *l'Europe Gallante* [by André Campra], I was at several times, and it is lookt upon, as one of the very best. It is extreamly fine, and the Musick and Singing admirable: The Stage large and magnificent, and well filled with Actors: The Scenes well suited to the thing, and as quick in the removal of them, as can be thought: The Dancing exquisite, as being performed by the best *Masters* of that Profession in Town: The Cloathing rich, proper, and with great variety.
>
> It is to be wondered, that these Opera's are so frequented. There are great numbers of the Nobility that come daily to them, and some that can Sing them all. And it was one thing, that was troublesome to us Strangers, to disturb the Box by these voluntary Songs of some parts of the Opera or other; That the Spectators may be said to be here as much Actors, as those imployed upon the very Stage.

Lister was no courtier but his book, which contains interesting information about Paris and the manners of the city, became quite a well-known guide. Thomas Nugent obviously purloined his material on the French opera from Lister just as he copied that on the Italian opera from Addison (iv,14).

Sir Dudley Ryder, whose distinguished legal career was to reach its zenith in 1754 with his appointment as Chief Justice, had been debarred from Oxford and Cambridge as a nonconformist and spent his student years at Edinburgh, Leyden and Paris before entering the Middle Temple. When he went to see the 1716 revival of *Dioclesian* in London he could not help comparing Purcell's opera with those he had seen in Paris: 'There are a great many very good dances in *Dioclesian* and singing, but as for the drama I think that is but very indifferent. The decorations are some of them very fine, but I think the Paris Opera is much finer. There were choruses of singing just like the French Operas'.[42]

His memories of the Paris opera were revived again on 27 March 1716 when, during an evening's chamber music (Ryder was a good flautist and bass viol player):

a Frenchman came in who sang some of the French Opera songs in concert with our two flutes and the bass. He sung particularly that part of the opera *Psyche* [by Lully] which we saw at Paris, in which the Vulcans come in and sing Frappons, etc. It pleased me very much as it revived in me the ideas I had when I was at Paris and filled me with that same kind of pleasure which I had when I was in the opera there. The French music has a very different air and manner from ours; it is extremely simple and easy, but there is a peculiar kind of harmony which touches me very sensibly.

But the Italophiles among the tourists reacted quite differently. Sir John Clerk returned from Rome via Paris in 1699 and summed up his dislike of things French, unusual in a Scot, in one sentence: 'Operas and comedies here, Musick, and all entertainments except Dancing, displeased me exceedingly' (p.34). The Duke of Shrewsbury approached Italy by way of Paris and perhaps initially had fewer prejudices against French music, but he reacted coolly to an opera (the name of which he could not even remember) which he heard at Paris on 21 November 1700: 'I thought the music and voices of the Opera very indifferent: it was called ------. The scenes are fine, and the dancing, especially Bullon, and one woman, is incomparable. Their action when they sing in such a piece is more graceful than the method of our people, who stand upon the stage like statues'.

A month later, in Montpellier on 21 December 1700, he dined at the Comte de Roure's who ordered his own box for the Duke at the opera and had him escorted thither and back again by four of his guards. However, Shrewsbury was disappointed: 'The Opera was Amadis de Grece [by Destouches], indifferent, and worse executed' (p.22). Even when Richard Pococke saw Rameau's latest opera in October 1733 he had nothing to say about the music, and precious little about the scenery and dances: 'We saw Hyppolitus & Aricia an opera last night, the scenes & Dancing extraordinary, especially one Madam Camargo, & a man dances most incomparably' (*GB-Lbm* Add.22978, ff.22–22*v*).

Other Countries

If we except already well-known writings such as those of Bulstrode Whitelocke, accounts by British travellers of musical events outside France and Italy are comparatively rare in the 17th century. The reception of Queen Christina of Sweden into the Roman Catholic church at Innsbruck in November 1655 excited a good deal of attention in England: perhaps it was felt that her circumstances might easily be paralleled in this country. A letter by an unnamed eye-witness[43] gives a long description of the ten days' entertainment given by Archduke Ferdinand Charles to mark the occasion: The Queen was met about a mile-and-a-half from the city and entered it:

'with Trumpets, Drums, and other loud Musick very fine . . . . The next day . . . all the time of dinner, was the sweetest harmony of Voices, Lutes, Harpsicals, and other Musick, that ever I heard, the Duke having caused many Eunuchs, that are esteemed the prime of Italy, to be at Court. When the Fruit and Banqueting-stuff came to the Table, the D[uke] caused a Treble and Base-Viol to play together, which was in my Judgement most excellent: He that plaid upon the Base-Viol was an Englishman, esteemed the best in Europe, named Mr You[n]g . . .

After her profession of the Roman Catholic faith the Te Deum was sung 'with most excellent Voices, and Instruments of all sorts, and Drums, which I never saw before in a Church'. The ex-Queen 'dined with her former company publickly in the great Hall, with the former Music and Magnificence. At night the Archduke entertained her with a very fine Masque and Dance, where the Scenes were changed often, and very finely contrived, so that the Queen said often, *O Che Bella!* But that was not so good as the Masque, with which he entertained her the last night, esteemed by those Italians that understand them, and have seen others, to be the rarest that ever they saw: For my part, I could not but infinitely admire at all things, for I never saw the like in my life; it was all in Musick; the Scenes changed eight times, and were very richly painted'. This second 'masque' for which all the audience had printed librettos lasted until four in the morning and was said to have cost £15,000 sterling.

This rather naive account by a newcomer to opera is corroborated by that of John Bargrave,[44] though since part of the latter's purposes was to expose the extravagance of the Roman Church it is not altogether unbiassed. Bargrave rightly describes the second 'masque' as an opera—it was Cesti's *L'Argia*—and adds that all the 'actors' were Italians, and, 'as some of themselves told me, they were 7 *castrati* or eunuchs; the rest were whoores, monks, fryers, and priests'. The performance lasted about six or seven hours and clearly Bargrave enjoyed its 'most strangely excellent scenes and ravishing musick'. He was told 'by an Englishman of the Archduke's musick', presumably William Young, that the ten days cost the Archduke '30,000.*l* English'.

Almost equally extravagant were the musical tastes of Leopold I as Sir John Clerk discovered when he visited Vienna in 1697 on the way to Italy, his studies at Leyden concluded and a paltry £100 in his pocket from his father who would have preferred to have his son at home, rather than gallivanting about Europe. But Sir John made excellent use of the opportunity. In Vienna he stayed with Lord Lexington, William III's envoy to the Emperor. 'I was always with him', Clerk writes (pp.21ff):

> at the Emperor's Leves and Drawing-Rooms. He introduced me to him, and when the Emperor understood from him that I was a great lover of Music, he invited me to his private opera, kept in the Imperial Garden of the Favretti, where the Emperor always resided, about 3 quarters of a mile from Vienna. The Assembly there was very great, and I believe no Court in Europe cou'd afford a Traveller a more magnificent appearance. The Emperor and Empress [Eleonora Theresa, whose sense of secular duty bade her attend the court opera though her religious scruples made her go with a copy of the Psalms in her hand, bound to look like the libretto], two sones, Ignatius and Charles, and 3 daughters, with his sisters, the Queen of Poland, sat in the fore part af an amphitheater dressed up with boughs of Trees, Green Leafs, and flowers. The Ladies sat behind in 8 or 10 Artificial Benches, and, to the best of my observation, about 4 or 500 without any admixture of men amongst them. The schenes were little real palaces of Timber, and finely painted with all the ornaments of Architectory, the Musick was very grand, viz. two Herpsecords, one on each side, 4 Great Bass violins, as many Lutes and Theorbs, and above 30 violins and other instruments. The actors or singers were mostly Italians, for as his Imperial Majesty was himself not only fond of Musick to distraction, but a performer himself on the Herpsecord, he took care to entertain all the best Musitians that Italy cou'd produce, and they were all provided with the best salaries and offices at his court that any way suited their occupations. His Capelmasters were Italian, and all his operas and comedies were in this Language; there was indeed very little else spocken at Court, and in Vienna there seem'd to me more Hungarians and Italians than Germans.

Clerk greatly esteemed Leopold's knowledge of music and abilities as a composer but deplored the way in which he would 'sit down and entertain the company with his Musick', even though he sang and played 'very finely'. He thought that 'nothing coul'd be more rediculouse than the odd figure the poor old Emperor made on such occasions', a sentiment with which Lord Chesterfield, who was to insist absolutely on no piping or fiddling on the part of his son, would have heartily agreed.

Lord Chesterfield would probably also have disapproved of women of quality undertaking travels, but Lady Mary Wortley Montague risked such disesteem and, with Mr Wortley, went further afield than most men did into the bargain. On 14 September 1716 she attended the court opera at Vienna, now the plaything of Charles VI, Leopold's second son. 'Nothing of that kind ever was more magnificent', she writes, 'and I can easily believe, what I am told, that the decorations and habits cost the emperor thirty thousand pounds sterling'. The stage was built over a canal to facilitate the representation of a naval battle and the opera, which concerned the enchantment of Alcina, gave 'opportunities for great variety of machines and changes of the scenes, which are performed with a surprizing swiftness . . . the habits, in the utmost magnificence, [were] to the number of one hundred and eight'. The operas, she notes, commonly marked some particular occasion at court.[45]

Lady Mary was back in Vienna in January 1717 for the carnival there. She attended some balls which were 'very magnificently furnished, and the musick good, if they had not that detestable custom of mixing hunting-horns with it, that almost deafen the company. But that noise is so agreable here, they never make a concert without them'. She noted too that it was the fashion to conclude balls with out-of-date English country dances, wrongly danced (p.55).

She must have been one of the first Western Europeans to take notice of Middle Eastern folk music. Writing to Pope from Adrianople on 1 April 1718 she describes rural music-making and the use of the *fistula*, 'or an instrument perfectly resembling it'. It is clear that she had prepared for her journey by reading Addison's *Remarks* in which he suggests that inconographic evidence ought to be considered in studying the music of classical antiquity; she notes that 'all the instruments depicted in Greek and Roman statues are to be found in use here'.[46]

Accounts of musical events at the other end of the Mediterranean, in Spain, are not much easier to find than those concerned with the eastern end. When the Earl of Nottingham, Lord High Admiral of England, went to Madrid in March 1605 as ambassador extraordinary to conclude the peace between Spain and England, the event, as befitted a great state occasion, was duly recorded by the Somerset Herald, Robert Treswell.[47] Both sides made the most of it, the English retainers numbering over five hundred, all magnificently accoutred. They were lavishly entertained at court with a masque—the kind of political musical display which was to become such a feature of the early Stuart court. 'After two or three several songs, sung by divers voices in parts, placed severally in the same hall for that purpose', 30 musicians entered, followed by the masquers who 'descended by four and four at a time, on a stage made in the fashion of a cloud'. In the concluding grand dance the King and Queen of Spain took part, as did the Earl of Perth, Lord Willoughby and the Ambassador himself (pp.91f).

The spaced choirs at this early date in Spain are worth noting. The effect was to ravish the ears of Robert Bargrave when he visited the king's private chapel at the Escurial in 1655.[48] When practically another half-century had passed, however, John Jackson hurried to Madrid to hear Spanish church music on Christmas Eve 1700 only to be bitterly disappointed: 'it proved insufferable, and the whole solemnity more comedy-like than any thing else: the mobb mocked the musick aloud, the priests themselves not only bearing with it, but seeming as well pleased as the best of them' (Pepys, ii, 150).

British Travellers and Musical Skills

By no means all of those who travelled in Europe were mere passive observers of the musical scene. Many took advantage of the opportunity to improve their own musical skills even if to some writers the perfecting of accomplishments like music and dancing was the least important activity to be indulged and to others, particularly towards the close of the 17th century, such practical participation was to be actively discouraged as not proper to the conduct of a gentleman.

Before he went abroad, Lord Herbert of Cherbury was already competent at singing and lute playing, two activities he cultivated to refresh his mind after study and, as he rather priggishly remarked, that he 'might not need the company of young men, in whom I observed in those times much ill example and debauchery'. In France in 1608 he applied himself to learning 'the rules of the French masters', something which is evident in his lutebook in the change from English to French techniques and tuning.[49] In 1609 Henry Lord Clifford, Salisbury's son-in-law, learned the lute and other accomplishments at M. de Pluvinel's Academy, a new school for the sons of the French nobility next door to which he took his lodgings in Paris.[50]

In 1633 we find Thomas Abdy at Blois hiring a viol for his recreation 'at quart d'escu p. mois',[51] and in 1644 John Evelyn, bored with sight-seeing in Rome, stayed at home for a week in November taking lessons on the theorbo with an Italian music master. In 1650 an account book, probably Richard Symonds', records 'Hyring a Theorbo for one month . . . 3s–4d' in Paris (*GB-Lbm* Harl.943, f.47), whilst Sir John Reresby, at Blois and Saumur in 1654 and 1655, learnt the guitar and the lute, the latter 'of the famous du But' (pp.7–11).

In October 1676 it was thought that the 19-year-old Sir Philip Perceval should travel to France to study geography, law, and languages and learn dancing and fencing. His chief inclination, however, was towards music and he spent much of his time practising on the flute, guitar, flageolet and virginals. His expenses at Angers included 'a guitar and case. . . . 40 *l.*', and two crowns a month to the guitar master who visited him in his chambers. His tutor, John Gailhard, confessed that Sir Philip made great progress in music if not in things 'more substantial'. A young man of spirit, he 'committed some excesses' with young Lord Kingston who shared the same *pension*, and eventually quarrelled with Gailhard who perhaps reported back too minutely on his activities to old Sir Robert Southwell, Sir Philip's guardian[52] (and, incidentally, father of the Robert Southwell we have already met travelling in Rome).

No doubt instances of such musical studies could be greatly multiplied but one further example will suffice. Sir John Clerk was an able harpsichord player and violinist at an early age if we may accept his own testimony. At Leyden he devoted many of his leisure hours to the harpsichord and the 'speculative part' of musical theory, making, 'perhaps, more advance than became a Gentleman'. In Rome, Bernardo Pasquini was his harpsichord teacher: 'I continued with him all the time I lived in Rome for an hour or two every day, and had many things composed for me by him'. Although he devoted himself to the harpsichord and composition rather than the violin, his violin teacher was none other than Corelli of whom Clerk wrote, 'He seldom teaches any body; yet, because he was pleased to observe me so much taken with him, he allowed me 3 lessons a week during all the time I stay'd at Rome . . . . He was a good, well-natured man, and on many accounts deserved the Epithet which all the Italians gave him of the divine Arc Angelo' (pp.14f, 28).

Many travellers took hold of the opportunity to collect musical scores in Italy just as they were prone to trundle home paintings, sculptures and books. In 1607 we find George Rooke, who accompanied Sir Henry Wotton on his embassy to Venice, buying song books in Venice and Padua for a friend in England,[53] and it is well known that Milton shipped home 'a Chest or two of Choice Musick-books' including works by Marenzio, Monteverdi, Vecchi, Gesualdo and others.[54] Music sent home from Italy by Lord North and Grey was acknowledged by Roger North in a letter of 13 January 1698;[55] Wriothesley Russell's many purchases of musical scores in Rome in that year were mentioned in letters to his mother from his tutor, Sir John Chardin,[56] whilst James Sherard, in the preface to his Op.1 trio sonatas, confesses that it was his brother William's returning home with sonatas that first gave him a true idea of that sort of music in Italy. In 1700 John Jackson remembered to get hold of a copy of an opera for a friend of his uncle's (Pepys, i, 299), and in 1718 William Drummond wrote to the Duke of Mar from Bologna to confirm the despatch of fifty sheets of airs from some of the latest operas, which he had had specially copied.[57]

The activities of our tourists were not by any means wholly acquisitive. Not content merely to observe the musical life of other nations, some made their own entertainments abroad too and others made a very real contribution to the musical life of the places they visited. Sir John Clerk found in Leyden (pp.15, 28):

> that there was no keeping of good and verteous company in either Holand, France, or Italy, and far less in Germany, without as much of the practise of musick as to enable one to bear a part in a Concert, I bestowed a great deal of pains on the Harpsecord, and in a year after was as well qualified to perform my part on that instrument as any Gentleman in Holand. I found that this piece of skill was indeed of very great use to me afterwards in the course of my Travels through Germany, Italy and France.

In Rome he confesses that his practical ability in music, in which he 'excelled to a fault', gave him 'easier access to the best company than other strangers had'. The same was true at Leyden and Amsterdam which Clerk revisited on his return journey to Scotland. As a student at Leyden his chief companion had been Hermann Boerhaave, who was to become one of the most celebrated physicians of the 18th century. Boerhaave was an excellent lutenist and the two of them together assiduously attended and performed at concerts.

On 2 February 1704 the Duke of Shrewsbury attended 'a musick and a great supper' which Lord Cardigan gave in Rome for the English community there. And when Gouge, the portrait painter, was in Rome in

1707 making copies for Sir John Perceval, he wrote to Sir John telling him how:[58]

> our gentlemen . . . have every Friday a concert very fine at Mr Brown's. The performers are Pauluci, Nicolino, Pipo, that famous bas violist and two other violins; Mr Blathwayt and Mr Cope likewise, one with the harpsichord, the other the violin, make no small figure in this concert. I wish, with all my heart, we had the honour of your performance amongst them.

'Pipo' later turned up in England, and these little musical gatherings seem to be very similar to the ones that were later to characterise the activities of the Perceval family.

In dispensing musical hospitality even the navy was not to be found lacking. In 1699 Admiral Aylmer, on a goodwill cruise to Italy, gave entertainments for four nights successively at Leghorn, each concluding with a ball and 'a fine Consort of Musick'.[59] More significant, since Cardinal Ottoboni must have entertained countless British guests, was the spectacle and entertainment given as a compliment to the Cardinal and the Pope by John Talman in Rome. In a letter to his father dated 6 June 1711 he writes: 'I had the best musick in Rome composed on purpose, and a poem of above four hundred verses composed for this occasion in praise of arts and commending several persons there present, who were all the top virtuosi in Rome both for learning and arts'. After seeing a spectacle of flowers the guests heard 'fine musick' and a feast was followed by a 'symphony of musick and singing'. Talman promised his father that he would make another such entertainment which would be 'ten times finer' when he left Rome the following April.[60]

A nice north country touch was added to a masquerade in the Piazza S. Marco in 1655. The Cavalier Yorkshireman Sir John Reresby travelled in Europe, not with a trumpeter as Robert Bargrave did, but with a boy who played the bagpipes. In Venice he smothered the boy with voluminous petticoats so that no sight but only the sound of the instrument could be perceived. This so excited the curiosity of the crowd that the pair were hotly pursued and the boy nearly stripped to discover the source of the unfamiliar music (p.14). Since to be followed by a large crowd was the esteemed goal in a Venetian masquerade, Reresby felt he had achieved his object in no uncertain manner.

★   ★   ★

Many British travellers, of course, who perhaps did not include music in their interests, made no reference to it in the accounts they left of their travels, and it must be admitted that many of the references we do find are trivial or naive and only rarely give us full details of the kind we would like to have.[61] Obviously they can be amplified from other writings such as those of André Maugars or the Uffenbach brothers, or from the memoirs and travels of foreigners like the Baron de Pöllnitz or M. de Blainville (which appeared in English translations and were perhaps to influence the journeys and attitudes of the next generation of British travellers). But this article restricts itself to writers from this country who braved the Channel and faced journeys whose often considerable hazards and discomforts would deter the packaged hordes of our jet and motorway age. Their leisurely progress gave them time to stand and stare and to write about what they saw and heard, and from these writings we can reconstruct a small but significant element in the social musical history of the period.

For the 17th century we lack the professional musician's view of Europe such as Burney grandly and sweepingly provides for the 18th, but from their jottings—and those of men like Sir John Clerk, that 'Burlington of Scotland', are by no means negligible—we can piece together a view of the kind of things they saw and the sort of music that impressed them and influenced them when they returned home. That an amateur like Clerk should return able to handle by no means incompetently the Corellian style of composition, or that Wriothesley Russell should bring back to Southampton House Haym and Cosimi, the two musicians who were to provide the basis of his own domestic chamber music, show how their 'new view of Europe' fashioned their tastes and helped to lessen the musical insularity of their country. The shift towards the French manner in lute playing in the first half of the 17th century, the introduction of the recitative style, the development of machinery on the musical stage, the participation in the French/Italian operatic controversy, and eventually the 'possession of our Pernassus' (as Roger North put it) by Italian instrumental music[62]—all of these owed not a little to the enthusiasms generated by that 'numerous traine of yong travellers of the best quallity and estates' who between them traversed the length and breadth of Europe at this time.[63]

NOTES TO CHAPTER 14

1. Fynes Moryson: *An Itinerary . . . containing his Ten Yeeres Travell* (London, 1617/*R* Glasgow, 1971).

2. James Howell: *Instructions . . . for Forraine Travell* (London, 1642), 5. Howell's and Lithgow's books with John Raymond's *An Itinerary Contayning a Voyage made through Italy in the yeare 1646 and 1647* (London, 1648), Edmund Warcup's *Italy, in its Original Glory, Ruine and Revival* (London, 1660)—a translation of a work by Franciscus Schotus— and Richard Lassels' (or Lascells') *The Voyage of Italy* (Paris, 1670) reprinted as *An Italian Voyage, or, a Compleat Journey through Italy* (London, 1698) were among the most used guidebooks of the 17th century as Addison's *Remarks on Several Parts of Italy &c In the Years 1701, 1702, 1703* (London, 1705) was to become in the 18th.

3. *Memoirs of the Life of Sir John Clerk of Penicuik*, ed. J. M. Gray, Publications of the Scottish Historical Society, xiii (Edinburgh, 1892), 1.

4. *Raymond and Guise Memoirs, 1622–1737*, ed. G. Davies, Camden Society, 3rd ser., xxviii (London, 1917), 54.

5. R. Lascells: *The Voyage of the Lady Catherine Whetenall from Brussells into Italy in the Holy Yeare*, GB-Lbm Sloane 4217, ff.28v–29.

6. *Francis Mortoft, his Book: Being his Travels through France and Italy, 1658–1659*, ed. M. Letts, Hakluyt Society, 2nd ser., lvii (London, 1925), 143.

7. John Evelyn: *Kalendarium*, ed. de Beer (Oxford, 1955), 8 Nov 1644.

8. Ed. Letts, 146.

9. *Roger North on Music*, ed. J. Wilson (London, 1959), 125.

10. Ed. Letts, 43f, 47, 104f, 118f, 136, 140, 144f.

11. See Aerssen de Sommelsdyck's account of music at S. Marcello in his *Voyage d'Italie* [1654], in *Congresso internazionale di scienze storiche: Roma 1903*, iii, 184.

12. Sir Philip Skippon: *A Journey through Part of the Low-Countries, Germany, Italy and France* [1663] in A. and J. Churchill: *A Collection of Voyages & Travels* (London, 1732), 671.

13. See M. Tilmouth: 'Music on the Travels of an English Merchant: Robert Bargrave (1628–61)', *ML*, liii (1972), 143.

14. John Ray: *Travels through the Low Countries, Germany, Italy and France* (London, 2/1738), 312.

15. William Acton: *A New Journal of Italy* (London, 1691), 5.

16. [William Bromley]: *Remarks in the Grande Tour of France & Italy: Lately Performed By a Person of Quality* (London, 1692), 76, 222.

17. Samuel Pepys: *Private Correspondence and Miscellaneous Papers 1679–1703*, ed. J. R. Tanner (London, 1926), i, 257.

18. Edward Wright: *Some Observations Made in Travelling through France, Italy . . . in 1720–22* (London, 1730), i, 449.

19. S. G. Spaeth: *Milton's Knowledge of Music* (Princeton, 1913/*R*1963), 21f.

20. *Report on the Manuscripts of the Earl of Egmont*, HMC, 63rd ser. (1905–9), ii, p.x.

21. *Correspondence of James [Drummond], Earl of Perth*, Camden Society, old ser., xxxiii (London, 1845), 86.

22. G. S. Thomson: *The Russells in Bloomsbury 1669–1771* (London, 1940), 87.

23. *Journal of his Grace Charles, Duke of Shrewsbury, 1700–1706*, Shrewsbury Papers (Northamptonshire Record Office), xxi, 1–493, see p.87.

24. William Lithgow: *The totall discourse of the rare adventures . . .* (London, 1614, 2/1632/R Glasgow, 1906), 35.

25. Thomas Coryat: *Coryats Crudities, hastily gobbled up in five moneths travells in France, Savoy, Italie* (London, 1611), 249–53. A short extract is reprinted in T. Dart: *The Interpretation of Music* (London, 1954, 4/1967), 104f.

26. See Tilmouth (1972), 156.

27. [John Clenche]: *A Tour in France and Italy made by an English Gent., 1675* (London, 1676), 105.

28. *The Manuscripts of His Grace The Duke of Rutland, K.G., preserved at Belvoir Castle*, HMC, 24th ser. (1888–1905), ii, 111f.

29. *Calendar of the Stuart Papers belonging to His Majesty the King, preserved at Windsor Castle*, HMC, 56th ser. (1902–23), vi, vii.

30. Duke of Shrewsbury (see above, note 23), 114.

31. Joseph Addison: *Remarks on Severall Parts of Italy &c In the Years 1701, 1702, 1703* (2/The Hague, 1718), 64–7.

32. [Thomas] Nugent: *The Grand Tour, or, A Journey through the Netherlands, Germany, Italy and France* (London, 2/1756), iii, 89.

33. Evelyn, May 1646, Oct 1644; Raymond, 174.

34. *CSP*, Tuscany, ii, 210.

35. See *The Memoirs of Sir John Reresby*, ed. A. Browning (Glasgow, 1936), 16.

36. *Memoirs and Travels of Sir John Reresby*, ed. A. Ivatt (London, 1904), 75.

37. Robert Moody: *The Travels of the Honourable Banister Maynard . . . through the Chief Countreys of Europe . . . 1661 & 1662*, GB-Ob Rawl. D.84, f.20. See also Lascells (1670), 140.

38. James Howell: *Instructions for Forraine Travell*, ed. E. Arber (London, 1869), 27, 42.

39. *Report on the Manuscripts of Allen George Finch, Esq., of Burley-on-the-Hill, Rutland*, HMC, 71st ser. (1913–22), i, 63.

40. *Supplementary Report on the Manuscripts of The Late Montague Bertie, Twelfth Earl of Lindsey, Formerly Preserved at Uffington House, Stamford, Lincolnshire, A.D. 1600–1702*, HMC, 79th ser. (1942), 285, 289.

41. Dr Martin Lister: *A Journey to Paris In the Year 1698* (London, 2/1699), 170f.

42. *The Diary of Dudley Ryder 1715–16*, ed. W. Matthews (London, 1939), 17 Jan 1716.

43. *Mercurius Politicus*, GB-Lbm, Burney Collection of Newspapers, xlviiia for 1655, 29 Nov 1655.

44. John Bargrave: *Alexander VII and his Cardinals*, ed. J. C. Robertson, Camden Society, old ser., xcii (London, 1866), 70.

45. *Letters of Lady Mary Wortley Montague Written during her Travels* (Paris, 1800), 20, 35.

46. P.100, and see Addison, 213f.

47. Robert Tresswell: *A relation of Such Things as were Observed to happen in the Journey of the Earle of Nottingham* . . . (London, 1605), in *Somer's Tracts*, 4th ser. ii, (London, 2/1809–15), ed. Sir W. Scott, ii, 70ff.

48. See Tilmouth (1972), 155.

49. *The Life of Edward Lord Herbert of Cherbury Written by Himself*, ed. S. Lee (London, 1886), 43, 72; and see T. Dart: 'Lord Herbert of Cherbury's Lute-Book', *ML*, xxxviii, (1957), 138.

50. J. W. Stoye: *English Travellers Abroad* (London, 1952), 49.

51. Stoye (1952), 402.

52. HMC, 63rd ser., ii, pp. vii–viii, 52–63.

53. Stoye (1952), 151.

54. H. Darbishire: *The Early Lives of Milton* (London, 1932), 59.

55. *Autobiography of Roger North*, ed. A. Jessop (London, 1887), 243.

56. Thomson (1940), 87.

57. HMC, 56th ser., vii, 26.

58. HMC, 63rd ser., ii, 217.

59. *The London Post*, 18 Aug 1699.

60. *Calendar of the Manuscripts of The Marquis of Bath, preserved at Longleat, Wiltshire*, HMC, 58th ser. (1904–8), ii, 179.

61. Mechanical instruments, not necessarily a trivial preoccupation, seem to have fascinated some travellers. See, for example, *GB-Lbm* Add.22978, f.74, for Richard Pococke's account of a multiple keyboard instrument at the Verospi palace. Lascells (1670), p.199, describes the water organ at Frescati; Acton (1691), pp.30f, and Raymond (1648), pp.117ff, 171, describe others at Aldobrandina and Rome.

62. Ed. J. Wilson, 310, 358f.

63. I wish to express my gratitude to his Grace, The Duke of Buccleuch for permission to reproduce extracts from The Shrewsbury Papers.

15

Music in Auctions:
Dissemination as a Factor of Taste

Lenore Coral

Book auction records have been preserved as documents of historical interest almost from the inception of the phenomenon of the sales themselves.[1] And yet their potential as tools for the scholar has only recently begun to enjoy a vogue.

The mode of selling by auction—that is, by competitive bids taken publicly—has a long history. Auctions are known to have taken place of the weapons of slain Roman legionnaires by their own comrades. And the booty captured in war was disposed of in this manner in Spain as early as 1142. In the 16th century, auctions were frequently used for disposing of inheritances about which heirs were unable to agree; they were also used as a method of settling a deceased person's debts.[2]

The Dutch were the first to hold book auctions which resemble in detail those we know today. The earliest such sales were conducted by the founder of the famous Dutch firm of printers and publishers, Louis Elzevier, in Leyden in the last decade of the 16th century. Lot-numbered catalogues were printed and distributed to prospective purchasers prior to the sale. The Elzeviers quickly opened another sale room in The Hague, and regular book auctions seem to have been conducted in both cities as well as in other Dutch locales in the earliest decades of the 17th century. The practice soon spread to other countries, so that by the time of the first English book sale in 1676 similar auctions were occurring in Belgium, Denmark, Sweden and northern Germany.

English auctions of chattels began earlier than book sales. Pepys reports on such an event in 1662.[3] Some Englishmen were alive to the possibility of selling their books by auction on the Continent early in the 17th century. Henry Savile of Banke (*d* 1617) proposed to dispose of his manuscripts in this way.[4] There is fairly clear evidence that the idea for the first English book auction came from a Presbyterian minister, Dr Joseph Hill. He had lived for some years in Leyden and Zeeland where he had doubtless witnessed some of the Elzevier sales.[5]

In the preface to the catalogue of the first English book auction, that of the collection of Dr Lazarus Seaman sold on 31 October 1676, William Cooper, the auctioneer wrote:[6]

It hath not been usual here in England to make sale of books by way of Auction, or who will give most for them; but it having been practised in other countreys to the advantage both of buyers and sellers; it was therefore conceived (for the encouragement of learning) to publish the sale of these books in this manner of way; and it is hoped that this will not be unacceptable to schollers.

Musical items first appeared in an English sale only two years after the Seaman auction.[7] It must be understood that this and most other sales containing musical items were sales of mixed contents. It was rare then and remains so today to find a single sale devoted exclusively to items of musical interest. The Voet sale contained just four items out of 9,000 of interest to us:

756	Simpson's Compendium of Practical Musick. Lond. 1668
881	Wilson's (John) Cheerful Airs or Ballads. 1666
259	Morley's (Tho.) Introduction to Musick. 1597
287	Playford's Select Ayres. Lond. 1659

These are given in the order in which they appear in the catalogue. The apparent discrepancy in the numbering results from items in these early sales being arranged according to size, with each size category numbered separately. Before 1750 only three English sales were devoted exclusively to music (one of these although originally advertised as an auction was actually sold in a retail manner).[8] These three do not begin to account for the over 10,000 musical items which were auctioned during this same period.

Bibliographical Tools

A brief review of the bibliographic apparatus available to the person who seeks information about book auction sales is appropriate. Auction sale catalogues are by their very nature ephemeral. They are created to sell a collection. Once the collection is sold their original raison d'être has ended. Afterwards they may serve as the permanent record of a now dispersed library, reflecting a collector's tastes, interests, or even skill in amassing his collection. Or the catalogues may serve only as a record of the existence and dispersal of an important, rare printed book or a manuscript. For less scarce items the catalogues may serve as a guide to value or price. And a collection of catalogues can provide an overview of taste in a given period.

The list of catalogues which William Cooper printed in 1682 was the first attempt at a bibliography of sales. In the catalogue for the sale of 14 February 1687 Cooper reprinted his list with an appendix bringing it up to date. These lists contained not only sales held by Cooper but almost all of the sales conducted in England. And amazingly enough, all but one of the catalogues in the list survive.[9]

In 1898 John Lawler produced a 'Chronological list of book auctions in England in the seventeenth century as far as known to the author',[10] but this list is quite incomplete even for the limited period which it covers. Lists of sale catalogues are often found as lots in 18th- and 19th-century sale catalogues; and while these cannot be considered as attempts at bibliography they do sometimes help us to discover sales for which catalogues are no longer extant.

The most comprehensive list of English book auction catalogues is the *List of Catalogues of English Book Sales, 1676–1900, now in the British Museum*, which was published by the Museum in 1915. This list, arranged chronologically with an alphabetical index of consignors at the end, provides an inventory of most of the holdings of this material in the Museum's Department of Printed Books plus a 'Supplementary List' of some of the catalogues in the Department of Manuscripts. The latter are catalogues amassed for the use of the staff in carrying out their acquisitions and cataloguing work; they are sometimes made available to the public on request.

The British Museum collection of sale catalogues is an especially rich one, due in large measure to their good fortune in receiving the archival runs of catalogues from a number of English auctioneers. These include Evans, Southgate, Lewis, Wheatley, Puttick, Phillips,[11] Hodgson and those of the firm which began as S. Baker and today is known as Sotheby and Co. Of the list above Sotheby's is the only firm which dates back to the 18th century. Christie's, the other major firm still in existence which traces its history back to the 18th century—it was founded 32 years later than Sotheby's, in 1766—still retains its archives on the firm's premises.

None of the runs of catalogues in the British Museum collection is absolutely complete. Some of the sets mentioned above were acquired after the 1915 *List* was compiled. Lack of funds has prevented the Museum from keeping their records up to date.

Sotheby's has recently begun publishing a complete set of all of their catalogues, not just of book sales. Until the 20th century, books and manuscript sales comprised about 60% of the firm's activities. With the completion of this project there will be, for the first time, a virtually complete bibliography of Sotheby sales. Unfortunately, Christie's has not yet seen fit to do likewise.

The document that is perhaps the most important resource for finding English book auction sale catalogues is not as yet generally available to the public. It is an annotated copy of the *British Museum List* compiled by the late Dr A. N. L. Munby.[12] The Munby copy almost doubles the number of catalogues known to survive. It includes items in the libraries at Oxford and Cambridge as well as most of the important American collections, including those of the Grolier Club, Harvard College, Yale University and the Huntington Library, and the Bibliothèque nationale in Paris. A copy of the Munby list current to 1972 is available in the North Library of the British Museum. Other copies, with annotations up to 1965, can be seen in the Bodleian Library, Harvard College and the Grolier Club libraries.

Art sales are on the whole better documented. It would be well to remember that besides their obvious interest to the music iconographer such sales often contained musical instruments. The standard bibliography of art auctions is Fritz Lugt's *Répertoire des catalogues de ventes publiques, intéressant d'art ou la curiosité* (The Hague, 1938–) whose three published volumes cover the period 1600–1900. The next volume, which will contain catalogues up to 1925, is now being edited. This bibliography which aims to be universal in coverage already contains information on approximately 58,700 separate sales. The value of Lugt's *Répertoire* lies in the fact that it is a union list; that is, it gives locations of copies of catalogues in many libraries. Its chief weakness results from the method used in compiling it. Each of the contributing libraries sent in data which the editors did not then verify. Because, particularly in the 19th century, subsections of catalogues were frequently issued separately, only actual examination of the catalogues can clarify this relationship.

English auction sales have received some attention from music historians. Hawkins noted a few sales in his *General History* and thus preserved some information which might otherwise have been lost.[13] Several of the auctions mentioned by him have no extant catalogues. Presumably these formed a part of Hawkins's own library, some of which was destroyed by fire in 1785. But Hawkins was not thorough in his accounts. He certainly did not mention all of the sales which pertain to the many persons whose biographies make up the major portion of his *History*.

Apparently no writer on music took further notice of auction sales until 1880, when Barclay Squire's article on musical libraries for the first edition of Grove's *A Dictionary of Music and Musicians* reminded scholars of this resource.[14] During the 1940s two refugees from the continent, Otto Erich Deutsch and Paul Hirsch, who had settled in Cambridge, inspired further work in this area. Their many musico-bibliographical discussions led one Cambridge librarian, D. R. Wakeling, to cull from the *British Museum List* all of the items which had indications of musical content. The very nature of the *List* itself precludes Wakeling's compilation from being very thorough.

It must be realised that the *British Museum List* is really a handlist. Since its compilation was interrupted by World War I, the entries are at best inconsistent. Sometimes special collections contained in a single catalogue are noted, although this never occurs unless the information is found on the title-page of the catalogue in question. Thus Wakeling's list contains only catalogues whose musical contents, shown on their title-pages, had been transcribed into the *British Museum List*.

More recently A. Hyatt King utilised sale catalogues in the preparation of his Sandars Lectures, given at Cambridge in 1961. These lectures, subsequently published under the title *Some British Collectors of Music* (Cambridge, 1963), drew extensively on a copy of Wakeling's typescript list. That King dealt with only a limited number of 18th-century sales can be attributed in part to this source of his information. Further, King was concerned only with the avowed music collector, the person with 'a real personal interest in music'.[15] Such commitment is difficult to discern from the 18th-century documents. Therefore it is hardly surprising that his discussion centres on 19th- and 20th-century collectors.

Other musicologists have used auction catalogues in attempts to trace provenance. For instance, Denis Stevens in his biography of Thomas Tomkins bemoans the loss of certain auction records which might have clarified the disappearance of some of his subject's manuscripts.[16] And H. Colin Slim tried to discover the peregrinations of the Newberry partbooks through clippings from unidentified sale catalogues pasted in the cover of one volume.[17] At best such a search is a haphazard affair because no index to the items sold in auctions was compiled for sales before the beginning of the 20th century.[18]

While published resources for locating English book auction sales records are incomplete, those for the book auctions of other nations are virtually non-existent.[19]

With this brief resumé of the history of the phenomenon and the resources for approaching its bibliographical remnants let us now turn to the English sales of the late 17th and 18th centuries as material for musicological inquiry.

Catalogues as Source Materials

In the preceding pages I have mentioned two ways in which auction sales records may now be utilised in historical research: for tracing the provenance of a manuscript or printed volume, and for the study of the library of a noted collector. Material culled from sale catalogues may also, if certain caveats are observed, provide data for the study of taste. To examine how this might be done we will use evidence from English sales between 1676 and 1750.[20]

Let us work backwards. What causes a library to come to the auction block? Auctions are often used in the settling of estates. Whether the heirs do not share the interests of the deceased, cannot figure out an equitable way to divide the material, or are in financial need is relatively un- important, though indeed all of the above have been and continue to be viable explanations. Sometimes a person will sell all or a portion of his collection during his lifetime. Reasons for this are also numerous. A collector may lose interest in a topic and wish to free his capital for new pursuits. Thomas Britton, the 17th-century smallcoal-man, is known to have disposed of his Rosicrucian collection in 1694 for this reason.[21] Alternatively a person may fall upon hard times, run out of space in his library, or dispose of duplicate copies. Needless to say the reason for disposition will in some way influence what is disposed of. But this last statement is irrevocably connected to the earlier process of collecting or amassing a library.

It is by no means clear that having a library makes one a book collector, at least not if one defines collecting as having an underlying rationale. Nor is it particularly necessary that a study of taste should seek out the avowed collector of a particular thing. In fact it might be better to avoid such people or to approach their collections with caution, for the development of a complete collection may cause the acquisition of items which a less catholic appetite might avoid.[22]

Taste, that is the manifestation of the collective preference of a definable group or class of society in a given period, is a difficult thing to identify let alone define. Many factors both external and internal may act on an individual or on a larger group of persons. To use as our example the books in a man's library presumes that he has control over every item present there. But supposing he receives a gift from a person whose perception of his tastes is not accurate and yet the recipient does not discard the item but allows it to lie on the shelf, perhaps unread. Or another book which purchased in haste turns out to have been a mistake also remains on the shelf. But the observer has no way of judging which books fall into categories such as the above and which are genuine important items in the collection.

What reaches the auction room then is coloured by the vagaries of what reaches the collection. However, several other factors enter in. Favoured material may be withheld from a sale by heirs or owners. Items may be put into a sale which had nothing to do with the putative consignor—this was an especially prevalent practice in the 18th century, but it continues today. Nor did all collections reach the auction room. In fact it is quite impossible to say what proportion did get sold in any particular manner. It has been suggested that the book auction is merely a symptom of the strength of book-collecting. To a certain extent this is true, for without an interested market, namely collectors or booksellers acting for them, materials would not move through the auction room.

Auctions have long been regarded by the book trade as the place where values are set.[23] If the associational factors are taken into account this statement becomes an explanation of how the prices of used books are determined. Sometimes, of course, a book will fetch a high price because it is believed to be rare. Notice of the value brings additional copies out of the box in the attic and prices may fall. But this is more the exception than the rule.

Some of the items regarded as of antiquarian interest by us today were similarly valued in the 18th century. A copy of Glareanus's treatise, *Dodecachordon*, for example, was offered for sale in 1711 with the note, 'lib. rariss.'.[24] In fact this was by no means the rarest treatise sold. Eight copies were offered in English auctions between 1688 and 1750, perhaps eight of the 65 copies known in the United Kingdom today.[25]

But musical scores offered for sale in England between 1676 and 1750 do not reveal any substantial antiquarian musical interest. And nothing exists to corroborate the renaissance revival postulated by others.[26] For example no Palestrina or Stradella works were offered for sale; the most minimal offerings of Byrd and Tallis, most coming from one sale noted for its large collection of antiquarian material,[27] can hardly be construed as exhibiting any great interest. The few items of any antiquity which did appear did not command unusual prices, that factor which is generally considered in assessing their collecting value. Prices (as far as can be determined) for both old and current material were about the same. At least out-of-style music was not considered worthless.

The programmes of concerts do not appear to have played an overwhelming role in influencing the selection of those who purchased music for their libraries either. Remarkably few of the pieces advertised as to be

performed in concert ever appear in auction sale.[28] And few of the items in
the Britton sale, presumably composed largely of the performing parts
from his concert series, occur in any other.[29] This is partly, but not entirely, because many of the items in the Britton collection were manuscript
copies.

It is often said that manuscripts were the most frequent means for the
dissemination of music in the early 18th century.[30] This is not borne out by
the evidence from English auctions of this period. The proportion of
manuscript to printed titles in the sales is about 1:6. Of actual volumes of
manuscripts the proportion is even smaller. We do of course know that
Handel allowed virtually none of his operas and oratorios to be published
during his lifetime. All that appeared in print were the hit tunes. Instead,
he employed a team of copyists to provide the desired scores and performance parts. This must in part have reflected his realisation that a
controlled method of distribution would be more remunerative. Vivaldi
also came to this conclusion. And more interestingly his decision pertained
to precisely the sort of music which was commonly available in print in
England. A recently discovered letter states that he has 'resolu'd not to
publish any more Concertos, because he says it prevents his selling his
Compositions in Mss wch He thinks will run more to account'.[31]

If manuscript copies were a common method of distribution in
England, one would expect advertisements offering the services of
copyists. From the Restoration on, newspaper-publishing flourished. The
advertisements contained in the tabloids offered editions of published
music as well as announcements of concerts, music instruction and musical
instruments, but not the services of copyists. Nor is there evidence that
music dealers handled this kind of material in England. Unlike Breitkopf
who clearly lists items available in manuscript as well as printed copies[32]
neither John Playford nor John Walsh ever offered manuscripts for sale. A
few manuscript items can be found in Henry Playford's 1698 catalogue,[33]
but there is nothing to indicate that he was prepared to offer anything
other than a copy that had come to hand.

Most of what was published was music for the home. The larger works
such as operas and oratorios were generally not published. Only excerpts of
these appeared in print. There would be no reason to publish parts for
orchestras since large works were rarely performed.

The Thomas Britton sale (12 December 1714), preserved only in
Hawkins, superficially appears to contradict our notion that manuscript
copies were relatively rare in England. The catalogue contains what appears to be approximately 80% manuscript material. Virtually all of it is

chamber music. This is clearly the music used by performers at the concerts sponsored by Britton. Perhaps, then, music for public performance was generally in manuscript while pieces for home use would normally be printed?

One explanation of the relative scarcity of manuscripts is the higher cost of acquiring manuscript copy. If the evidence of prices in Henry Playford's 1698 advertisement can be considered normal, manuscripts cost about three times as much as prints.[34] The compensating features are that manuscripts are more attractive and also easier to read. This latter consideration prevailed at least until engraved editions superseded those produced from movable type.

Another factor to be considered in contemplating the relationship of manuscripts to prints in private collections in England is that manuscript copies are only superseded by printed editions as a means of dissemination when there is a market large enough to support the sale of sufficient copies for printing costs to be recouped. The interest in chamber music in England at this time was apparently sufficiently large.

Composers and music publishers apparently came to recognise that a public whose taste was whetted by the growing number of public concerts would require the more readily obtainable printed editions. This increased the dissemination of their work, which in turn enlarged their audience. The additional exposure offset the greater monetary rewards to be realised from the more controlled sale of manuscript copies. Composers always had the option of attempting to raise money for publication by public subscription. The newspaper advertisements calendared by Tilmouth reveal many such efforts. Not all of them succeeded of course.[35]

But manuscript copies were not completely superseded. And most of the manuscripts offered for sale do not appear to have been in the collector's class. They were intended to facilitate performance.[36] Thus it is not surprising that no special fuss was made over them in the sale room. Perhaps the other sort of manuscript was withheld from a sale when a library was dispersed, although this is not characteristic of sales in general. Of course, the sale of 18th-century playing copies would arouse considerably more response today; and, by the same token, manuscripts regarded as valuable in the 18th century could have diminished in value in the eyes of the modern collector. A. N. L. Munby has recently shown how taste for medieval miniatures in 1850 was 'diametrically opposed' to that of a century earlier.[37]

In the period between 1676 and 1750 approximately 1,200 music titles were sold in English book auctions in about 10,000 lots. Approximately

450 sales of the period contained at least one music item, only about 25 contained more than that. Of these, eight sales are either the collections of unidentifiable consignors or from a group of persons whose libraries cannot be disentangled.

Who were these people whose libraries were consigned to the sale room? The largest group were clergy. This is hardly surprising since the clergy were the largest professional class educated at university during the period. The next largest group were those holding the title of doctor. These might be either physicians or academics or others who appended this learned title to their names for reasons unknown.[38] This composite group of 'doctors' was only half as numerous as the men of the cloth. Two other identifiable groups had members whose libraries were sold in some measurable quantity: lawyers and booksellers. These are found represented in about equal numbers. For the booksellers it might be the disposal of their personal libraries or of their stock in trade.

Generally speaking music found in sales of this period represented perhaps a diversion for a man whose main interests lay elsewhere. Very few persons known to have a direct connection with music are represented, with Thomas Britton, John Playford and Nicola Haym as the three exceptions.

Chamber Music

The largest body of musical material in these early sales consisted of chamber music. This is undoubtedly the result of the well-developed tradition of home music which had been strengthened by the restrictions imposed on public musical activity during the Commonwealth. Home music activities continued even after the Restoration and the rapid rise of public performance. As far as one can tell the repertories of public and private musical gatherings were essentially the same. Unfortunately the newspaper advertisements are so vague that we can determine in only a few instances exactly what piece was to be performed.[39] A comparison of the catalogue of the library of Thomas Britton, the founder of one of the earliest and most important concert series, with the contents of private libraries contemporary with it confirms the near identity of the repertories.

Chamber music provides the most vivid example of the transition in musical taste. The change from collections filled with predominantly English works, mostly vocal in character, to those with largely Italian instrumental music occurred in the 75 years between 1676 and 1750.

Charles II returned to England with a taste for French music acquired while he was in exile. For various reasons this affinity was not to be shared with his subjects. For one thing the violin had not yet achieved the popularity required for the rapid assimilation of French chamber music. For another the large number of Italians employed in various noble households overwhelmed the French court musicians.[40]

The unemployed professional musicians of the Commonwealth who had found music in the privacy of the home were now able to turn to the hastily opened public concert halls, theatres and the coffee houses. Here they joined Italian soloists for weekly performance. But these same professionals seem to have continued to play privately as well. Pepys often recounts evenings spent with such musicians.[41]

All of these developments provided incentive for English music publishers. After a publishing hiatus of almost 50 years they responded with vigour. The music which was issued under the aegis of Playford and his successors, especially Walsh, was, if not overwhelmingly profound, lively. The publications, at first solely the compositions of English composers,[42] expanded in the days of Walsh to include the works of many Italians, especially Corelli and Vivaldi.

Two points need remarking on here. Both pertain to what might have been expected in collections at the beginning of the period, $c1676$. The first is a notable lack of volumes from the 'Glorious Age of English Music Publishing'—the late 16th and early 17th centuries. With the special exception of the John Playford sales virtually no music of that period is to be found in the auction room. Bruce Pattison has suggested that these works were, 'quickly printed and as quickly forgotten',[43] a claim that is hard to accept today.

In spite of Pepys's oft-cited observation that pairs of virginals were to be seen in one boat out of three fleeing the 1666 fire of London,[44] very little solo keyboard music is to be found in 17th-century sales. A few copies of works by Babell, Handel, Jones, Loeillet and Mattheson did appear in sales from 1720 on.

Catches

Playford's knack for providing music appropriate to the public he served was uncanny. He, for instance, was one of the active promoters of the singing of catches and rounds, one of the most popular musical activities in taverns where men gathered. Their often bawdy texts would have been unsuitable for the parlour, but their frequency in the sale room confirms the diarists' reports about their many rousing coffee house renditions.[45]

Actual evidence about catch books from the sales is interesting. Two items appeared in the Playford 1691 sale. The first was catalogued as 'Three old Catch Books'.[46] This is probably identical with an item in the 1690 sale also linked with Playford. The earlier item was described as 'Three old Catch-Books Palmelia'.[47] Doubtless both of these represent copies of the earliest published collection of catches: *Pammelia, Deuteromelia* and *Melismata*. At least two of these volumes appeared in the important 1653 John Playford broadside advertisement mentioned above. Neither appears in any other sale in the period.

The second catch-related item in the 1691 sale was 'a book of catches and tunes for the violin'.[48] The use of the word 'Catches' in the description must imply either that the tunes were borrowed from catch books or something about the contrapuntal nature of the music. Unfortunately this volume is not identifiable today.

The most commonly found catch book in sales was the popular *Musical Companion* published by Playford in 1673. Interestingly, only a few copies of John Hilton's compilation, *Catch that catch can*, appeared in any sales in spite of its numerous editions. This can probably be explained by the custom of catch societies developing their own libraries. Thus, although numerous copies were required they rarely found their way into private collections. Only one manuscript known to contain catches was sold and this in the 1691 Playford sale.[49]

Although many, many volumes of partsongs were offered, few reappeared in enough sales to merit special mention here. Among the most popular volumes in the earlier sales were Purcell's *Orpheus Britannicus* and Blow's *Amphion Anglicus*. Later Bickham's *The Musical Entertainer* quickly rose to popularity. All of these publications with their artful songs and flexible instrumentation were ideally suited to the private and public concert life of the late 17th and early 18th centuries.

The growth in popularity of Corelli's music in England can be amply demonstrated from the auction room. Although no single work or edition appeared with any abundance at sale, a great number of his sonatas and concertos were offered from the late 1720s onward. This is about 30 years after their first appearance, in pirated editions, in the music shops. About the time of its first appearance in sales North observed,[50]

> Then came over Corelly's first consort that cleared the ground of all other sorts of musick whatsoever. By degrees the rest of his consorts, and at last the conciertos came, all which are to the musitians like the bread of life.

Corelli's music was certainly some of the most frequent but it was by no means the only instrumental music, Italian or English, which appeared. The works of other Italian composers begin to appear in numbers in the late 1720s[51] and during this period a few collectors are responsible for the vast majority of items. These collections amassed on tours are in marked contrast to the widespread ownership of Playford's publications.

Some lacunae occur which are hard to explain. One such is the lack of Vivaldi editions in any sales except one of 1729,[52] noted for its large Italian collection. This is in spite of the fact that by then Walsh had issued about 20 Vivaldi editions, not to mention those imported from Amsterdam. Perhaps North's opinion that Vivaldi composed only light programme music explains his neglect.[53]

Psalms and Hymns

Settings of the metrical psalms formed a substantial body of musical material sold by auction. Approximately 100 different editions are to be found, including some with texts in Latin, French, Dutch and German as well as the more frequent English versions. Most of these editions make only a single appearance during the sales of this period.

Although publication of complete collections of psalms was controlled by strictly enforced licensing laws, the number of editions was great. This stems from two factors: (1) the number of copies which could be pulled from one type setting was regulated;[54] for such a popular work this meant vast numbers of re-editions; (2) collections not containing the entire set of psalms were issued without licensing restrictions.

The singing of psalms and hymns formed an integral part of English devotional services from the Reformation on. Though attitudes differed somewhat, both the state church and those of the non-conformists all allowed some musical settings of these sacred texts to be included in their services.

Furthermore, the singing of metrical psalms was one of the most praised forms of entertainment in the Puritan home. The practice was by no means restricted to the non-conformists; Pepys, for example, is known to have enjoyed this pastime.[55] Most of the editions of psalms contained unharmonised settings of the traditional tunes. But although not as numerous, there were always multi-voiced editions available and some of these, for instance Ravenscroft's four-voice settings, enjoyed a continuous vogue.

John Playford went to some considerable length to reform the singing of psalms in England. His mission was to publish current versions of tunes by replacing outdated editions and ultimately to introduce harmony into the singing of psalms in the parish church. The first of his editions of psalms was issued in 1658. Prior to this he had reprinted William Child's three-voice settings first issued in 1639.

Playford's 1658 publication was a monophonic setting with a bass which he suggests may be played on the 'Organ, Virginals, Theorbo-Lute, or Bass-Viol'.[56] His preface indicates the didactic nature of his endeavours. It was not until 1671 that he published a version to be sung in parts.[57]

If one looks at the evidence of extant earlier editions it becomes quite apparent how rare multi-voiced editions were prior to Playford. It is also clear that the few that were issued were intended for the home rather than for parish use. Notes on the title-pages and the actual formats themselves reveal the publisher's expectation of their purpose.[58]

In a recent study Nicholas Temperley discussed the experimental quality of the 1671 settings.[59] Temperley regards Playford's failure to reissue this edition as a tacit admission that it was not a success. And yet the 1671 volume turns up in more auction sales than any other—though many others do appear.

The tradition of psalm singing in the home continued unabated after the Restoration, a fact reinforced by the numerous copies of psalm books in private collections in the years after Charles II's return to the throne and by the number of editions of harmonised settings which Playford and others published.[60]

Inevitably we are faced with the question 'What does its frequent sale prove?' That it was not valued by its owners? That in fact very few copies were changing hands? Or that its immense popularity is exhibited by the frequency with which the psalms turn up in sales? The publishing statistics help to reinforce this last hypothesis. They are more reliable, too, than for other sorts of publishing, for the licensing laws which gave the Stationers' Company a monopoly on complete editions also ensured their zealous enforcement.

It is clear that multi-voiced editions of the psalms must have been intended for places other than the church even in the period after the Commonwealth. Most churches were without organs, choirs did not exist and the congregation required the psalm to be lined out—that is, the line of music to be chanted by the parish clerk before it was repeated by the congregation—because they were not able to read music. This practice, disruptive of continuity, is not generally useful where part-singing is expected.[61] Thus these editions must have been used for chamber music. It comes as no surprise that Thomas Britton owned five copies of the 1671

Playford four-voice edition. The cataloguer of his library characterised these as 'proper for a Shopkeeper'.[62]

Many of the editions of psalms offered for sale by auction were monophonic. Unlike the polyphonic settings these were often offered long after their publication dates. Even as much as 60 to 100 years was not an unusual time lag. This prolonged delay before a first appearance in the sale room, peculiar to this class of material, is doubtless indicative of the continuous use by a family. Psalm tunes did not change very rapidly, and these books, like Bibles, often had associational values.

The only commonly found French publications to be offered in English auctions were editions of the psalms set to music with French texts. This occurrence is readily enough explained by the influx of Huguenot refugees from France which began even before the revocation of the Edict of Nantes in 1685.[63] One of the most curious editions offered is a French psalm book published in Berlin in 1701.[64] A copy of this edition is preserved in the British Museum.[65]

Interest in the continuing controversy regarding the appropriate performance of music in the church was high throughout the period of this study. Besides the variety of different editions of the psalms published to meet the varying needs, a number of discussions of the topic appeared in print. Arthur Bedford's *The great abuse of Musick* (1711) and Henry Dodwell's *A Treatise concerning the Lawfulness of Instrumental Musick in Holy Offices* (1706) are the titles most frequently found. But the remarks of earlier writers continued to be read and books such as John Case's *The Praise of Musick in Churches* (1586) appeared in several sales.[66]

Conclusion

All of the preceding illustrations show that analyses of items offered in the sale room can support, confirm or even deny ideas about musical taste postulated by studying publishing and concert performance data. They lend evidence on the elusive question of what went on in the home, just as what people play at home on the piano today may or may not have a great deal to do with the concert life and recording industry whose products are more easily observed.

NOTES TO CHAPTER 15

(Numbers in square brackets refer to the page and lot number within the catalogue under discussion.)

1. William Cooper, the first English book auctioneer, printed a notice at the end of his 19 June 1682 sale catalogue: 'To gratifie the Curious whose genius may lead them to make perfect their collection, I have caused to be printed the names of those person whose Libraries have been sold by Auction, and the Series of the time when' (*GB-Lbm* 821.i.3(2)).

2. For a summary of the historical development of the auction sale see A. Hobson: 'A Sale by Candle in 1608', *The Library*, 5th ser., xxvi (1971), 230f.

3. H. B. Wheatley, ed.: *The Diary of Samuel Pepys, M.A., F.R.A.* (London, 1893), ii, 305f (3 Sept 1662).

4. A. G. Watson: *The Manuscripts of Henry Savile of Banke* (London, 1969), 6.

5. Letter from Edward Millington to Joseph Hill, 25 June 1697; *GB-Lbm* Stowe 747, f.6: 'For your great Service done to Learning and Learned Men in your advising and effectually setting on foot that admirable and universally approved of way of selling Librarys by Auction amongst us'.

6. Lazarus Seaman catalogue, 31 Oct 1676, W. Cooper, Auctioneer (*GB-Lbm* 11906.e.l).

7. Gisbert Voetius: *Catalogus variorum librorum instructissimae bibliothecae . . .* (Moses Pitt: the White Hart, St Bartholomew's Close, 25 Nov 1678). Copies of this catalogue are preserved at *Gb-Lbm, Lv, Ob, US-NH.*

8. The sales involved are the two Playford sales, 11 June 1690 and 17 Dec 1691, and the Thomas Britton sale, 6 Dec 1714.

9. *Catalogus librorum bibliothecae viri cujusdam literati* (14 Feb 1687). Copies of the catalogue are preserved at *GB-Cjc, Cu, Lbm, Ob* and The Grolier Club.

10. J. Lawler: *Book Auctions in England in the Seventeenth Century (1676–1700)* (London, 1898/R1968), 215–24.

11. Part of the Phillips archive went to the Wallace Collection in London. The British Museum set begins with the 15 Jan 1850 sale.

12. See A. N. L. Munby and L. Coral: *British Book Sale Catalogues, 1676–1800: A Union List* (London, 1977), which has been published since this was written.

13. Sir John Hawkins: *A General History of the Science and Practice of Music* (London, 1776; 2/1853/R1963).

14. W. Barclay Squire: 'Music Libraries: Great Britain and Ireland: Private Collections'. In later editions this article was updated by C. B. Oldman. In the 5th edition (1954) it was superseded by O. E. Deutsch: 'Collections, Private'.

15. King (1963), 7.

16. D. Stevens: *Thomas Tomkins, 1572–1656* (London, 1957), 125ff.

17. H. C. Slim: *A Gift of Madrigals and Motets* (Chicago, 1972), i, 11ff.

18. See the list of book auction records in C. Winchell: *Guide to Reference Books* (Chicago, 8/1967), 20.

19. For an analysis of the bibliographic tools which do exist for sale catalogues of other countries see A. Taylor: *Book Catalogues: Their Varieties and Uses* (Chicago, 1957), particularly chap.3.

20. A complete index to the musical items sold at auction in this period can be found in the author's unpublished *Music in English Auction Sales, 1676–1750* (diss., U. of London, 1974).

21. 1 Nov 1694. This catalogue is preserved in *GB-Lbm*, *Ob* (John Johnson Collection), *US-CA*.

22. For a more elegant discussion see J. Carter: *Taste and Technique in Book Collecting* (London, 1970), Introduction, 1–10.

23. M. Plant: *The English Book Trade* (London, 1965), 247.

24. *Catalogue of Greek, Latin, Italian, Spanish . . . Books* (14 March 1711) [2:56]. Catalogue: *GB-Lbm* S.C. 246 (10), *Owc*.

25. *RISM*, B VI/2, 365f.

26. See T. Day: 'A Renaissance Revival in Eighteenth-Century England', *MQ*, lix, (1971), 575–92.

27. *A catalogue of ancient and modern musick books* (17 Dec 1691) [10:39]. Catalogue: *GB-Lbm* 821.i.9 (27).

28. M. Tilmouth: 'A Calendar of References to Music in Newspapers published in London and the Provinces (1660–1719)', *RMARC*, i, (1961). It is often remarkably difficult to identify exactly what was to be performed from the newspaper advertisements—so the correlation may indeed be somewhat greater than it appears.

29. 6 Dec 1714. The catalogue for this sale survives only in a transcription in Sir John Hawkins: *A General History*, ii, 792f.

30. B. S. Brook: *The Breitkopf Thematic Catalogue* (New York, 1966), p.x: 'In the earlier eighteenth century, the principal method of music dissemination was the manuscript copy prepared on direct order by the professional copyist'. M. Bukofzer: *Music in the Baroque Era* (New York, 1947), 409: 'The composer had no other way of assuring that nobody but he himself reaped the fruits of his labors except to keep the composition in manuscript form, or to acquire a monopoly of printed music'.

31. In a quotation from a letter of Edward Holdsworth to Charles Jennens. Christie's sale catalogue, 4 July 1973, p.20. The quotation is undated but comes from the period 1729–41.

32. Brook (1966), 1–28.

33. *A General Catalogue of all the Choicest Musick-Books*, *GB-Lbm* Bagford Collection, Harl.5936/422–428.

34. *A General Catalogue.* Playford offered 'Bassani's Sonata's printed' for 10s., 'And fairly prick'd', for £1 10s.; Corelli's Op.1–4 printed for £2 and in manuscript for £6 (f.425).

35. For a list of music successfully published by subscription see F. J. G. Robinson and P. J. Wallis: *Book Subscription Lists: a Revised Guide* (Newcastle upon Tyne, 1975).

36. All of the manuscripts offered between 1676 and 1750 were volumes of music. Manuscript copies of treatises were not sold by auction in England during this period with the exception of a few tutors or books of lessons.

37. A. N. L. Munby: *Connoisseurs and Medieval Miniatures, 1750–1850* (Oxford, 1972), 160.

38. Many persons appear to have used the title 'dr.' without any cause. In this survey all those who were listed on the title pages of the catalogues with this designation were lumped together unless some other information about their profession could be found.

39. See the advertisements in *The Daily Courant*, 30 Jan 1705, and *The Post Man*, 13 April 1706, as cited in Tilmouth for examples.

40. The Dukes of Chandos and Bedford were particularly noted for their musical entourages. See G. S. Thomson: *The Russells in Bloomsbury, 1669–1771* (London, 1940), particularly chap.7, and C. H. Collins Baker and M. I. Baker: *The Life and Circumstances of James Brydges, First Duke of Chandos* (Oxford, 1949), especially pp.129–40.

41. Pepys, i, 60f (21 Feb 1660) and i, 18f (16 Jan 1660) for instance.

42. If one examines the 1653 Playford catalogue of 'All the Musick Bookes that have been printed in England' (*GB-Lbm* Bagford Collection, Harl.5936/421) one discovers that no music of foreign origin had been published.

43. 'Notes on Early Music Printing', *The Library*, 4th ser., xix (1939), 46f.

44. Pepys, v, 395 (2 Sept 1666).

45. Pepys, i, 190f (21 July 1660), and J. Wilson, ed.: *Roger North on Music* (London, 1959), for instance p.352.

46. A *Catalogue of ancient and modern Musick Books* (17 Dec 1691) [10:39]. Catalogue: *GB-Lbm* 821.i.9(27).

47. A *curious collection of musick-books* (11 June 1690) [3:93–94]. Catalogue: *GB-Lbm* Bagford Collection, Harl. 5936/419–20, *Ob, US-NH* Medical Library.

48. (17 Dec 1691) [10:43].

49. (17 Dec 1691) [10:61].

50. North (1959), 310f.

51. Albinoni, Geminiani and Taglietti are probably the most frequently found names.

52. Frederick Ashfield, 24 March 1729. Catalogue: *GB-Lbm* S.C. 450.

53. North (1959), 293.

54. A Stationers' Company document calendared by W. W. Greg in his *A Companion to Arber* (Oxford, 1967), 94f, dated 16 Nov 1635, limits the number of impressions of privilege books (of which the psalter was one) to 6,000 and states that although standing formes are allowed for these privilege books the type must be distributed at least once a year.

55. Pepys, iv, 284 (11 Dec 1664) and iv, 276 (27 Nov 1664).

56. These settings occur as an appendix to his *Introduction to the Skill of Musick* (London, 1658).

57. *Psalms & Hymns in Solemn Musick of Foure Parts* (London, 1671).

58. N. Temperley: 'John Playford and the Metrical Psalms', *JAMS*, xxv (1972), 333.

59. Temperley (1972), 355–60.

60. While the number of editions of unharmonised settings was at its peak in the decade 1631–40 at 57, the harmonised versions reached their heyday between 1691 and 1720. See Temperley (1972), 334.

61. Exactly such a mnemonic device is still in use in the performance of four-part Black Sacred Harp singing in South-eastern Alabama today, so it can be used in multi-part singing. I am indebted to Doris Dyen Root for this information.

62. Hawkins, ii, 793 [Vocal musick: 37].

63. G. N. Clark: *The Later Stuarts, 1660–1714* (Oxford, 1955), 109.

64. *Bibliotheca Ledettiana* (18 March 1734) [2:54]. Catalogue: *GB-Lbm* S.C.532(4).

65. *GB-Lbm* 3434.a.40.

66. (5 April 1731) [63:1529], *GB-Lbm* S.C. 335(2) and *Librorum in omnibus ferè linguis* . . . (2 Dec 1740) [119:2104]; *Cu.*

16

Daniel Defoe's Plan for an Academy of Music at Christ's Hospital, with some Notes on his Attitude to Music

Brian Trowell

In 1728, just three years before his death, Daniel Defoe published a short book of 63 pages entitled *Augusta Triumphans: or, the Way to make London the most flourishing City in the Universe.*[1] It is a compendium of seven suggestions for improving the quality of life in 'Augusta', as London had come to be called during the reign of Queen Anne. And the fifth of these is a proposal to establish an Academy of Music at Christ's Hospital, the famous charity-school founded in 1552 and principally supported by the merchants of the City of London: Defoe refers to the main boys' school, which was then situated on Newgate Street in the City[2] (there were institutions for girls and infants elsewhere).

Defoe's plan occupies eight pages (pp.16–23). I reproduce it verbatim below. Like the other reforms he proposes, it is a sane and on the whole very practicable scheme, couched in his usual plain and conversational style. Music, he writes, is an innocent and commendable diversion which in an age of debauchery deserves support. The honourable title of 'Academy' has been wrongfully usurped by the Royal Academy of Music (that curious attempt at establishing Italian opera in London on the lines of a joint-stock company, which was tottering to its premature end even while Defoe was writing). English instrumentalists have already proved their worth, and the example of Purcell shows that our native musicians need only to be encouraged in order to thrive. Foreign opera-singers are extremely expensive, and we should seek ways to train our own. Thirty boys, and perhaps a few girls, should be selected as students in a music-school attached to Christ's Hospital; six are to study woodwind instruments with an excellent teacher, 16 to study string instruments with another, and eight to study singing and keyboard instruments with a third. All are to learn to read and write as well. After seven or eight years they are to be apprenticed to the Hospital.

In a few years, he goes on, there will be an orchestra of 40 and a body of 20 singers, including a handful of excellent soloists. By mounting their own concerts, operas and oratorios in the Hospital's own hall, and by hiring out apprentice performers to other organisations, the school could maintain 60 young musicians for an outlay of only £300 in 10 years, whereas an Italian singer costs £1,500 for a single year's engagement. [3] The musical academy would not merely support itself, but would eventually bring in a good income for the Hospital's other charitable purposes. What is more, if the bishops would allow Sunday performance of solemn music, sacred verse and 'Rhetorick' (i.e. sermons: see note 35 below), the proposed academy would provide devotional recreation and help to keep idle people out of mischief on the Lord's day.

It is on the face of it rather surprising that Defoe's imaginative scheme has managed to escape the attention of historians of English for over 250 years. (The one possible exception is Charles Burney, as I shall later suggest.) There are, I think, three reasons for this, two general and one particular.

First, Defoe was a Puritan, and traditional prejudice tells us that all Puritans dislike music. [4] We have been slow to learn the lesson to the contrary that Percy Scholes read us in his monograph on *The Puritans and Music*. [5] Otherwise some musical researcher would have hunted through Defoe's works by now. In the one book of his that everyone has read, of course—*The Life, and Strange Surprising Adventures of Robinson Crusoe*—there is no mention of music at all. Crusoe, fighting for mere survival, does not have time to twang a bowstring, let alone sing a metrical psalm. And it is only fair to point out that Defoe himself expected his readers to be surprised when he set up as an authority on music: the first sentence of his scheme runs: 'It will no doubt be asked, what have I to do with Musick?' No wonder we have neglected him.

The second reason is the forbiddingly huge number of works that Defoe published—at least 545 at the last count [6]—and the fact that the greater part of them have never been reprinted. Apart from the famous novels and the pseudo-histories of the period 1719-25, much of his output was topical, journalistic and ephemeral. His writings on trade and commerce are now of interest only to the economic historian, and his political tracts have an equally restricted readership. The literary value of the dialogue in his didactic books on morals still goes unrecognised. A search through the more accessible modern reprints of his works, and some early editions, has nevertheless thrown up many references to music to place beside the two which have already found their way into musicological literature, a short advertisement from his *Review*, [7] and the well-known account of the Duke of Chandos's musical establishment at Cannons. [8]

The third and more particular reason for the long neglect of *Augusta Triumphans* is the extreme rarity of the first edition of 1728. The work was in fact reprinted in 1841, but the editor clearly did not have access to the first edition and therefore used the second edition of 1729 instead." Otherwise, the eye of a musical researcher would undoubtedly by now have lighted on the list of contents displayed on the title-page of the 1728 edition, where the scheme in question is described thus: 'V. To avoid the expensive Importation of Foreign Musicians, by forming an Academy of our own'—almost the same wording as the less obvious title introducing the scheme itself later on. This entry vanishes from the title-page of the second edition. The scheme has been promoted to third place, but the heading in the list of contents has been changed, puzzlingly, to: 'III. By forming an Academy of Sciences at *Christ*'s-*Hospital*'. Any reference to music has here disappeared—though the old caption is kept in the body of the book—and this was the misleading form of the title-page used for the only modern edition.

For an explanation of the change to 'An Academy of Sciences' we have to turn to Defoe's *The Generous Projector* of 1731. This pamphlet, dedicated to the Lord Mayor of London, reprints selected passages from *Augusta Triumphans*, including the musical scheme. Referring to the latter, Defoe prefixes an 'After-Thought' which plainly accounts for the change of title and must have been omitted by accident from the second edition of 1729: 'The Scheme . . . may be so improv'd to extend to Painting, Sculpture and other curious arts: Under good Masters the Youths may so improve to make *England* emulate *Greece* and *Rome*, not to mention the Profits that will accrue from their Labours'. His suggestion anticipates the foundation of the Royal Academy of Arts nearly 40 years later. In the unusual linking of music and fine arts in one institution it also recalls the strange and understandably abortive scheme of the Royal Academies of 1695, first discovered and ably discussed by Michael Tilmouth[10] (funds were to be raised by a lottery, and the students selected in the same way!). Defoe was 35 years of age at that time, and at the end of his life he may well have remembered the outline of this earlier plan.

For *Augusta Triumphans*, even more than the other works he published during his last period from 1725 onwards, returns to the matter and manner of his first important books of the 1690s. Though much shorter, it very much resembles *An Essay upon Projects* (1697). This too was a compendium of good ideas for social improvement, all of which, except the first, have now been realised in one form or another: an English equivalent of the Académie Française; coinage reform; a register of seamen; local county banks and factories; commissioners in bankruptcy; pensions for poor-relief; a central policy for road-building; properly run lunatic asylums; and improved public education, especially for women. Defoe had continued to press for these and similar ideas in other books and in his journalistic writings, most notably in the 'Scandal Club' section of his *Review of the Affairs of France* (1704–13), a weekly and later three-weekly journal which formed the model for Steele's famous *Tatler*. During the period 1719–25, however, when Defoe was pouring out the torrent of novels and quasi-biographical fiction which earned him immortality, he ceased to campaign so diligently for social reform.

From 1725 onwards, though, his creative powers of imagination seem to have been exhausted. He went back to writing on critical, moral and economic subjects, and his damped-down passion for social improvement flared up again in several works. *Augusta Triumphans*, comparatively short though it is, was actually his last published volume of any size at all. Ageing, tired, sick and hounded by creditors, he seems to have known that the end was not far off. 'I have but a short Time to live', he began:

> nor would I waste my remaining Thread of Life in Vain, but having often
> lamented sundry Publick Abuses, and many Schemes having occur'd to my
> Fancy, which to me carried an Air of Benefit; I was resolv'd to commit them
> to Paper before my Departure, and leave, at least, a Testimony of my good
> Will to my Fellow Creatures.

It is worth setting his musical proposals in context by listing all the seven schemes as advertised on the title-page of *Augusta Triumphans*. London is to be made 'the most flourishing City in the Universe':

> FIRST, By establishing an University where Gentlemen may have
> Academical Education under the Eye of their Friends.

It was over a century before the first colleges of what is now London University were founded. 'What Benefits', Defoe added further on, 'may we not in time expect from so glorious a Design? Will not London become the Scene of Science?'

> II. To prevent Murder, &c. by an Hospital for Foundlings.

He later notes with satisfaction that a subscription for this purpose has already been opened; but Thomas Coram's Foundling Hospital was not properly launched until 1740. Had such an institution already existed in 1728, Defoe would very likely have chosen it in preference to Christ's Hospital, as Burney did in his scheme of 1774, to house his academy of music.

III. By suppressing pretended Mad-houses, where the Fair Sex are unjustly confin'd . . . and many Widows are lock'd up for the Sake of their Jointure.

This was a malpractice that he had complained of earlier, in his *Review*. The technique is still in use, but has now become a means of restraining unwelcome political views.

IV. To save our Youth from Destruction, by clearing the Streets of impudent Strumpets, suppressing Gaming-Tables and Sunday Debauches.

The latter two points were gained quite quickly. It took well over two centuries to achieve the first, whereupon the others were again relaxed.

V. To avoid the expensive Importation of Foreign Musicians, by forming an Academy of our own.

As befits the author of *The Complete English Tradesman*, Defoe naturally presents it as a matter of import controls.

VI. To save our low Class of People from utter Ruin . . . by preventing the immoderate use of Geneva . . . .

This was effected by raising the price through taxation, so that the Demon Gin is now predominantly a middle-class vice.

And concluding with An effectual Method to prevent STREET ROBBERIES.

Defoe's suggestions include proper street lighting and a well-regulated police force, both of which took a century to come into effect.

The Plan

Defoe's fifth proposal runs to just under 2,000 words. It is here reproduced entire, in its original spelling and punctuation. The paragraphs have been numbered for ease of reference.

A Proposal to prevent the expensive Importation of Foreign Musicians, &c. *by forming an Academy of our own.*

1. IT will no doubt be asked, what have I to do with Musick? to which I answer, I have been a Lover of the Science from my Infancy, and in my younger days was accounted no despicable Performer on the Viol and Lute, then much in Vogue. I esteem it the most innocent Amusement in Life; it gently relaxes, after too great a hurry of Spirits, and composes the Mind into a Sedateness, prone to every thing that's generous and good; and when the more necessary parts of Education are finish'd, 'tis a most

genteel and commendable Accomplishment; it saves a great deal of Drinking and Debauchery in our Sex, and helps the Ladies off with many an idle Hour, which sometimes might probably be worse employ'd otherwise.

2. Our Quality, Gentry, and better sort of Traders must have Diversions; and if those that are commendable be denied, they will take to worse; Now what can be more commendable than Musick, one of the seven liberal Sciences, and no mean Branch of the Mathematicks?

3. Were it for no other Reason I should esteem it, because it was the favourite Diversion of his late Majesty, of glorious Memory;[11] who was as wise a Prince as ever fill'd the *British* Throne. Nor is it less esteem'd by their present Majesties,[12] whose Souls are form'd for Harmony, and who have not disdain'd to make it a part in the Education of their sacred Race.

4. Our Nobility and Gentry have shown their Love to the Science, by supporting at such prodigious Expence, the *Italian Opera* improperly call'd an Academy;[13] but they have at the same time shown no small Partiality in discouraging any thing *English*, and over-loading the Town with such heaps of Foreign *Musicians*.

5. An Academy, rightly understood, is a Place for the Propagation of Science, by training up Persons thereto from younger to riper Years, under the Instruction and Inspection of proper Artists: How then can the *Italian Opera* properly be call'd an Academy, when none are admitted but such as are, at least are thought, or ought to be, adepts in Musick? If that be an Academy, so are the Theatres of *Drury-Lane*, and *Lincolns-Inn-Fields*: nay, *Punch*'s *Opera* may pass for a lower kind of Academy. Would it not be a glorious thing to have a *Opera* of our own, in our own most noble Tongue, in which the Composer, Singers, and Orchestre, should be of our own Growth? Not that we ought to disclaim all Obligations to *Italy*, the Mother of Musick, the Nurse of *Corelli, Handel, Bononcini,* and *Geminiani*; but then we ought not to be so stupidly partial, to imagine our Selves too Brutal a part of Mankind, to make any Progress in the Science: By the same reason that we love it, we may excel in it; Love begets Application, and Application Perfection. We have already had a *Purcel*, and no doubt, there are now many latent Genius's, who want only proper Instruction, Application, and ENCOURAGEMENT, to become great Ornaments of the Science, and make *England* emulate even *Rome* it self.

6. What a number of excellent Performers on all Instruments, have sprung up in *England* within these few Years? that this is owing to the *Opera*, I will not deny, and so far the *Opera* is an Academy, as it refines the Taste, and inspires Emulation.

7.   But tho' we are happy in Instrumental Performers, we frequently send to *Italy* for Singers, and that at no small Expence: To remedy which, I humbly propose, that the Governours of *Christ's-Hospital* will show their publick Spirit, by forming an Academy of Musick on their Foundation, after this or the like manner.

8.   That out of their great number of Children, thirty Boys be selected, of good Ears and Propensity to Musick.

9.   That these Boys be divided into three Classes, *viz.* Six for Wind-Instruments, such as the Hautboy, Bassoon, and German-Flute.

10.   That sixteen others be selected for String-Instruments, or at least the most useful, *viz.* the Violin and Bass-Violin.

11.   That the remaining eight be particularly chosen for Voice, and Organ, or Harpsichord. That all in due time, be taught Composition. The Boys thus chosen, three Masters should be elected, each most excellent in his Way; that is to say, one for the Wind-Instrument, another for the String'd, and a third for the Voice and Organ, &c.

12.   Handsome Salaries should be allowed these Masters, to engage their constant Attendance every Day, from eight till twelve in the Morning; and I think a 100*l. per Annum* for each, would be sufficient, which will be a Trifle to so wealthy a Body.[14] The multiplicity of Holidays should be abridg'd, and only a few kept; there cannot be too few, considering what a hinderance they are to juvenile Studies. It is a vulgar Error that has too long prevail'd all over *England*, to the great Detriment of Learning, and many Boys have been made Blockheads, in Complaisance to Kings and Saints, dead for many Ages past.

13.   The Morning employ'd in Musick, the Boys should go in the Afternoon, for so many Hours, to the Reading and Writing-School, and in the Evening should practice, at least two Hours before Bed-time, and two before the Master comes in the Morning. This Course held for seven or eight Years, will make them fine Proficients; but that they should not go too raw, or young, out of the Academy, 'tis proper, that at the stated Age of Apprenticeship, they be bound to the Hospital to engage their greater Application, and make them thorough Masters, before they launch out into the World: for one great hinderance to many Performers is, that they begin to teach too soon, and obstruct their Genius.

14.   What will not such a Design produce in a few Years? will they not be able to perform a Consort, Choir, or Opera, or all three among themselves, and over-pay the Charge, as shall hereafter be specify'd?

15.   For Example, we will suppose such a Design to be continued for ten

Years, we shall find an Orchestre of forty Hands, and a Choir or Opera of twenty Voices, or admitting that of those twenty, only five prove Capital Singers, 'twill answer the Intent.

16. For the greater Variety they may, if they think fit, take in two or more of their Girls where they find a promising Genius, but this may be further consider'd of.

17. Now, when they are enabled to exhibit an Opera, Will they not gain considerably, when their Voices and Hands, cost them only a College Subsistance? And 'tis but reasonable the Profits accruing from Operas, Consorts, or otherwise, should go to the Hospital to make good all former and future Expences, and enable them to extend the Design to a greater Length and Grandeur; so that instead of 1500*l. per Ann.* the price of one *Italian* Singer, we shall for 300*l.* once in ten Years, have sixty *English* Musicians regularly educated, and enabled to live by their Science.

18. There ought moreover to be annual Probations, and proper Prizes or Premiums alloted, to excite Emulation in the Youths, and give Life to their Studies.

19. They have already a Musick-School, as they call it, but the Allowance is too poor for this Design, and the Attendance too small; it must be every Day, or not at all.

20. This will be an Academy indeed, and in Process of Time, they will have even their Masters among themselves; and what is the Charge, compar'd with the Profits or their Abilities?

21. One thing I had like to have forgot, which is, that with Permission of the Right Reverend the Lords Spiritual, some Performance in Musick, suitable to the Solemnity of the Day, be exhibited every Sunday after Divine Service: Sacred Poesy and Rhetorick, may be likewise introduc'd to make it an Entertainment suitable to a Christian and Polite Audience; and indeed, we seem to want some such commendable Employment for the better Sort: For we see the publick Walks and Taverns crowded, and rather than be idle, they will go to *Newport-Market.* [15]

22. That such an Entertainment would be much preferable to Drinking, Gaming, or profane Discourse, none can deny, and till it is proved to be prejudicial, I shall always imagine it necessary. The Hall at the *Hospital*, will contain few less than seven hundred People, conveniently seated, which at so small a Price as one Shilling per Head, will amount to 35*l.* per Week; and if the Performance deserve it, as no doubt it will in time, they may make it half a Crown or more, which must considerably encrease the Income of the *Hospital.*

23.   When they are able to make an Opera, the Profits will be yet more considerable, nor will they reap much less from what the Youths bring in during their Apprenticeship, when employ'd at Consorts, Theatres, or other publick Entertainments.

24.   Having advanc'd what I think proper on this Head, or at least enough for a Hint, I proceed to offer . . . .

One or two matters arising from Defoe's plan call for comment. First, why did he choose Christ's Hospital? The answer must be that it was the only large institution in London that was in the least like the *conservatori* or *ospedali* in Naples and Venice where music was taught to poor children. Though he does not allude to them here, Defoe's previous scheme, for a Foundling Hospital, refers to 'the Venetians, the *Hamburgers*, and other foreign *States, &c*, who have for Ages past prosecuted this glorious Design' (p.16). Christ's Hospital, however, was not a refuge for foundlings, but a residential school for the children of the deserving poor. While the less academically gifted boys left early for an apprenticeship with little more than the ability to read and write, a more able lad might study the classics, in which case the Hospital would support him on his way through Oxford or Cambridge; or mathematics, which would open up for him a career as an officer in the Royal Navy. There was also a drawing school. In the Hospital's early days, the trade of music had been thought a poor career for a boy: it had been agreed in 1569 'that from henceforthe none of the children harbored and kept in this Hospitall be put apprentis to any Musissioner othere than suche as be blinde or Lame and not able to be put to other Trades'.[16] Still, the school had always had a master capable of teaching music, and the gift of two endowments at the beginning of the 17th century led to the foundation of a small Music School in which a dozen children received instruction. Among the early music-masters were the composers Richard Farrant and Thomas Ravenscroft. Little is known of their pupils, though the boys in the Music School appear to have studied no other subjects except music.

By and large, though, this early promise was not fulfilled, and by 1728 Defoe was doubtless right to suggest that the Music School was an under-nourished affair (§19). He must however have seen some potential for development. Perhaps he had heard the united voices of the charity children singing their famous Easter psalms during the annual civic ceremonies at Paul's Cross or the Spital Cross. From §22 it is plain that he had been inside the Great Hall of Christ's Hospital, where there was a fine Dallam organ that was played at the 'Public Suppers', to which visitors were admitted. At the Public Supper on Easter Sunday one of the specially-composed Easter psalms was repeated in the Hall. This occasion was no doubt an annual pleasure for many of the inhabitants of London. Defoe, a Freeman of the City, must surely have attended. On 10 March 1687, John Evelyn went to a Public Supper: the children 'sung a psalm before they sat down to supper in the Great Hall to an organ which played all the time with such a cheerful harmony that it seemed to me a vision of angels'.[17]

Since much of the material in *Augusta Triumphans*, including the scheme for a music-school, was reprinted twice in four years, some of it must have provoked discussion leading to renewed demand. I therefore searched the minute books of the Court of Governors and the Council of Almoners of Christ's Hospital to see whether they ever debated the plan for a musical academy. If they did, the comments were of that deliciously indiscreet kind that the speaker prefaces with the phrase 'not for minuting'. There is not a word on the subject. The only thing out of the ordinary is in the Almoners' minutes for 9 August 1728, when it was 'Ordered that the Singing Master do from henceforwards present the Names of Such Boys as he shall make Choice of for his School to the Committee with their Ages for their Approval' (*GB-Lgc* 12,827/2). This perhaps suggests some uneasiness at Defoe's comments; but if the order was ever carried out the names were never recorded. The music-teaching at the school continued on its slow decline until in 1901 the Hospital's official historian could write: 'In modern times the barrenness of the music teaching . . . is excusable enough; for specialism is crowded out by much else and the music is a mere *parergon*'.[18] Nowadays, however, music is flourishing at the school as never before.

Other Schemes

In 1972, Jamie Croy Kassler published Charles Burney's 'Sketch of a Plan for a Public Music-School', drawn up in 1774 for consideration by the governors of the Foundling Hospital, together with a similar scheme, at once more pretentious and less precise, which she had discovered in a book by John Potter published in 1762.[19] Potter's plan, for an independent music-school 'establish'd by the authority of legislative power', does not appear to relate to Defoe's. He makes almost no detailed suggestions, saying that it would be 'too tedious to consider the more trifling particulars to be observ'd in the establishing such an academy'. He does however wish to 'excite emulation' by conferring 'degrees of honour on those that excel' (p.99; cf Defoe, §18): he also suggests apprenticeships (p.99) and laments the high cost of Italian opera (p.104). Potter envisages his academy as a state monopoly regulating entrance to the musical profession, rather as the Musicians' Company, a craft guild, had licensed musical performers in London. Defoe would probably have disliked this. As one who had thrice been pilloried for publishing opinions unwelcome to the authorities, he would certainly have opposed Potter's fantastic notion that his academy should not only dictate standards of taste and correctness, like a musical Académie Française, but also enforce them through censorship:

> An authority should be granted by the legislative power to the masters of this academy, to have a right to command the sight of all musical compositions intended to be made public, by all, even [those] out of the academy; and to make such alterations and corrections as they should think necessary, without which, and a licence from the academy, no music should be suffered to be printed. By this means, nothing would hereafter be made public, but what is correct and compleat, and fit to be left for the use of posterity.

Burney's scheme, unlike Potter's, has many ideas in common with Defoe's; and although there is not one that could not have occurred to Burney quite independently, it seems to me unlikely that Burney, who prided himself on his knowledge of literature, had not read *Augusta Triumphans*.[20] Both Burney and Defoe attach their musical academies to charitable institutions, Burney to the Foundling Hospital, whose establishment Defoe had suggested in the pages immediately preceding his musical scheme. Defoe draws attention to the Great Hall of Christ's Hospital as a suitable venue for musical performances (a hall which was already in occasional use for this purpose): Burney draws attention to the Chapel of the Foundling Hospital, which was already the venue for an annual Musical Performance [of *Messiah*] for the benefit of the Charity' (Defoe, §22; Burney, p.227). Both men complain about the fashionable preference for foreign music and musicians, and the great expense of Italian opera-singers (Defoe, §§4, 7, 17; Burney, p.229). Both contrast this with the very practical commercial advantages to be gained from mounting public performances by the young scholars, and from hiring out apprentice professionals to other institutions (Defoe, §§13–15, 17, 21–23; Burney, pp.228, 231, 233). While Defoe, a Puritan, does not suggest hiring apprentices to churches, he and Burney both recommend sacred concerts on Sundays (Defoe, §21; Burney, p.233). Both suggest that

female students should be recruited (Defoe, §16; Burney, p.230). Both
envisage the abler scholars undertaking some of the teaching (Defoe, §20;
Burney, pp.233f). There is one slight verbal echo, between the following
sentences: 'Our Quality, Gentry and better sort of Traders must have
Diversions; and if those that are commendable be denied, they will take to
worse' (Defoe, §2); and 'Music we *must* have, in our Churches, our Ar-
mies, our Theatres, & our private Amusements; and since its encouragement is inevitable, why should it not be good . . . . (Burney,
p.229, note 36).

The other feature that the two schemes have in common is that neither
got off the ground, though Burney's very nearly did. But if Burney did
borrow ideas from Defoe he is hardly to be blamed for failing to
acknowledge the fact in a private manuscript memorandum which was
destined to be read by the governors of the Foundling Hospital and not by
musical historians. It would in fact have been highly unwise to refer to a
scheme so similar to his own, which had earlier been thought impractical
and come to nothing.

Defoe and Music

Some of Defoe's other works refer to music in the context of education
and morals. In hunting out these passages I have come across many other
comments on music from his pen which I shall discuss later on. They make
it clear that Defoe liked and understood music, as he said himself in §1
above; though a Puritan, he was an intelligent and humane one, and
disliked music only when it was associated with frivolity, sensuality or the
wrong sort of politics, or when it distracted the attention from thoughts of
God during divine service.

On the other hand, he did not consider that the art was of primary
importance in the education of a gentleman, except 'when the more
necessary parts of Education are finish'd' (§1, above). His manuscript *The
Compleat English Gentleman* (1728-9) does not list music as one of those
'parts of needfull knowledge as are peculiar beauties in the life of a
gentleman'.[21] Still, the philistine 'Gentleman' in Defoe's dialogue appears to have liked music:

> *Gent:* I have no books! What should I do with them?
> *Friend:* But your Father S.[r] Anthony had a library, I don't doubt.
> *Gent:* Yes. I'll giv you a catalogue of them. There was a g.[t] Bible . . .; and
> not to leav out the most valuable things: there was an old ballad of
> Chevy Chace set to very good music, with Robin Hood and some

more of the antient heroes of that kind; a[n] old base viol, two fiddles, and a music book . . . . (p.135)

For the Compleat Gentleman and his lady:

conjugal life was all harmony and musick, peace and joy; tenderness and affeccion are the sum of their united enjoyment . . . . From this conjugal harmony all the beauty of a Heaven upon earth is to be seen. (p.240)

Defoe never completed his manuscript tract *Of Royall Educacion*, which seems to date from the mid-1720s. If he had, he would doubtless have expanded his remarks about William III, George II and his consort Caroline of Ansbach, whose love of music he mentions in §3 above. The latter pair had indeed 'not disdain'd to make it a part in the Education of their sacred Race', since they had engaged Handel to teach the young princesses. Defoe notes in his tract that Henry VIII, 'also skill'd in ornamentall learning, was a good astronomer, a curious musitian and poet, a good orator . . .'.[22]

For the ladies, music was a rather more necessary accomplishment, and 'helps them off with many an idle Hour, which sometimes might probably be worse employ'd otherwise' (§1 above). In the Academy for Women that Defoe advocated in *An Essay upon Projects* (1697):

The Persons who Enter, shou'd be taught all sorts of Breeding suitable to both their Genius and their Quality; and in particular, *Musick* and *Dancing*, which it wou'd be cruelty to bar the Sex of, because they are their Darlings.

Moll Flanders, as yet a mere girl and accordingly well-behaved, learned these arts in the genteel family that took her in, poor relation though she was:[23]

I had all the advantages for my education, that could be imagined; the lady had masters home to teach her daughters to dance, and to speak French, and to write, and others to teach them music; . . . and though the masters were not appointed to teach me, yet I learned by imitation and enquiry, all that they [the daughters] learned by instruction and direction. So that in short, I learned to dance and speak French as well as any of them, and to sing much better, for I had a better voice than any of them; I could not so readily come at playing the harpsichord or spinnet, because I had no instrument of my own to practise on, and could only come at theirs in the intervals when they left it; but yet I learned tolerably well, and the young ladies at length got two instruments, that is to say, a harpsichord and a spinnet too, and then they taught me themselves; but as to dancing, they could hardly help my learning country dances, because they always wanted me to make up even number . . . .

Musical ability is also a mark of genteel breeding in the estimation of Defoe's Colonel Jack.[24] On first seeing his future wife he takes her for a lady of good family 'who made an extraordinary figure indeed; she went very well-dressed, and was a most beautiful person. She was well-bred, sung admirably fine', and later he watches her through a window, though he cannot hear: 'She sung very often in her parlour, as well by herself as with two young ladies who came often to see her; I could see by their books, and her guitar in her hand, that she was singing' (pp. 201, 206). Marriage proves him wrong. Defoe's anonymous 'Cavalier'[25] has a similar experience when a high-class Italian courtesan, whom he also takes for a fine lady, invites him into her apartments (vi, p. 31):

> Her conversation exceeded, if possible, the best of quality, and was, I must own, exceeding agreeable; she sung to her lute, and danced as fine as ever I saw, and thus diverted me for two hours before anything else was discoursed of; when the vicious part came on the stage, I blush to relate the confusion I was in.

Defoe is aware of the ambiguous nature of music. It can attract us through its prettiness even when there is no meaning behind it. Discussing whether animals have souls or not, he uses the unthinking musician as an example of mechanisms without purpose:[26]

> we our selves can habituate our own Fingers, to make an Excellent Harmony . . . without any Direction of the Soul, for who has not seen a Musician Play an admirable Tune, while he has been thinking or speaking of another Matter?

At the same time, Defoe was a novelist. Though didactic, he was rarely one-sided. He knew how to use music, frivolous, sensuous or not, both as an image in its own right and as an element in characterisation. Roxana, though she is a demi-mondaine and no mere whore, is a good singer and a most accomplished dancer. The band from one of the London playhouses comes to perform at a dance in her apartments. We read of a masked dance 'à la Comique', an 'antic', a courant and other French dances to French tunes, including 'a very fine figure, invented by a famous master at Paris, for a lady or gentleman to dance single'. Roxana has also learned some Turkish songs and dances from a slave-girl, and astonishes even Charles II (who comes incognito) by dancing 'à la Moresque' in a sensational Turkish costume. (It is this that gains her the sobriquet 'Roxana': by birth, she was Huguenot French.) She later repeats her party piece at a court ball, where two other ladies, who have been in Persia, and who are clad in Georgian and Armenian costume respectively, perform 'such a dance as indeed nobody there had ever seen, and to an instrument like a guitar with a small low-sounding trumpet, which, indeed, was very fine'.[27] One would have wished for more precise information about this Eastern music. Defoe was expert at working genuine details into his fictional narratives and was probably using some contemporary source. He may however have invented the 'little country opera house' near Bury St Edmunds, where Moll Flanders filches a lady's gold watch (p.262).

In general Defoe mistrusts opera just as he dislikes the playhouse. In *Religious Courtship*, two young beaux start to sneer at a discussion of 'dull, religious stuff' in a chocolate-house. One of them starts to haul the other away to the opera, and an old nobleman banters him: 'Pray sir, says the lord, is it below a man of quality to be a Christian? O, my lord, says the other beau, . . . we are mighty good Christians at the opera' (xiv, p.51).[28] In *The Family Instructor*, a mother who rediscovers her lost faith gets into difficulties when she uses strong-arm methods to re-educate her irreligious children, as her daughter recounts (xv, pp.146,98):

> I was only humming to myself the tune of the last opera, and she flung to me and struck me, because it was sabbath-day, forsooth; for my part, I know no harm in it, not I, I did not sing the song out, as I told you, I only hummed softly, it might be a psalm tune for aught she knew.

It is surprising that Defoe's 'Cavalier' does not mention opera in his account of life in Italy, where he visited Milan, Genoa, Leghorn, Naples, Rome and Venice, 'but saw nothing in Italy that gave me any diversion . . . I saw nothing but lewdness . . . all the diversions here ended in whoring, gaming, and sodomy' (vi, pp.29f). It is to the opera that a vicious and criminal husband takes his mistress in *Augusta Triumphans* (xviii, p.25: he 'keeps his Mistress in black Velvet, and is seen with her every Night at the Opera or Play'). In a passage from the same book which Defoe expanded in *Second Thoughts are Best* (1729), he condemns *The Beggar's Opera* (first performed 29 January 1728) and Thomas Walker's *The Quaker's Opera* (24 September 1728) for romanticising crime and hence causing an increase in house-breaking and robbery with violence (xviii,p.34):[29]

> Vice in all kinds is so much winked at, that robbery is accounted a petty crime. We take pains to puff them up in their villainy, and thieves are set out in so amiable a light in the Beggar's Opera, it has taught them to value themselves on their profession rather than to be ashamed of it.
>
> There was some cessation of street robberies . . . until the introduction of this pious opera . . . London, that used to be the most safe and peaceful city

in the universe, is now become a scene of rapine and danger . . .

Not content with the mischief done by the Beggar's Opera, we must have a Quaker's Opera, forsooth, of much more evil tendency than the former; for in this Jack Shepherd is made the hero of the drama, and runs through such a scene of riot and excess, that but too many weak minds have been drawn away, and many unwary persons so charmed with his appearance on stage, dressed in that elegant manner, and his pockets so well lined, they have henceforth commenced street-robbers or house-breakers; so that every idle fellow, weary of honest labour, need but fancy himself a Macheath or a Shepherd, and there is a rogue made at once. Since, therefore, example, has such force, the stage ought to be reformed, and nothing exhibited but what might be represented before a bishop. They may be merry and wise: let them take the Provoked Husband for a pattern.

In another journal which Defoe edited, the *Mercurius Politicus* (1717–20), he kept a wary eye on the foundation of the Royal Academy of Music. The issue of March 1720 advertises on p.67 'A Letter from Signior *Benedette Baldeysaria*, of the Hay-Market, to Sir *Richard Steel* of *Drury-Lane*'. I have been unable to discover a copy of this publication, but it was doubtless a reply, probably burlesque, to Steele's fun at the castrato Benedetti's expense in *The Theatre*, nos.20–21 (March 1720).[30] The *Mercurius Politicus* for April 1720 (pp.50f) quotes an essay allegedly taken from *The Theatre*, no.29, where however it is not to be found, though it certainly reads like genuine Steele. Speaking humorously of the governors of the Royal Academy of Music, the passage informs us that:

no Man shall sit among them that has not taken the Oaths to the Government, and the Sacrament in the Church as by Law establish'd; for, as this Author tells us, otherwise we might have Treason convey'd to us in a Song, and *Popish* Sounds introduc'd to affront *Protestant Ears*. . . .

Although Defoe's scheme for a musical academy itself suggests that the apprentices might play in 'Consorts, Theatres, or other publick Entertainments', Defoe was uneasy about the vices that these normally frivolous assemblies encouraged. In *The History of the Plague in London* he noted with glee that in 1665 the new Frenchified 'Plays and interludes were forbid to act; the gaming-tables, public dancing rooms, and music-houses, which multiplied and began to debauch the manners of the people, were shut up and suppressed'; and he printed the Lord Mayor of London's order 'That all plays, bear-baitings, games, singing of ballads, buckler-play, or such like causes of assemblies of people be utterly prohibited' (ix, pp.30,47). A venture which aroused his special anger in the *Review* (III, pp.293ff, 301–4, 377–80) was a proposal to perform

Hamlet at Drury Lane Theatre with music and dancing, in order to raise money for the building of a:

> Chappel in Russel-Court . . . with singing by Mr. *Hughes, &c.* and Entertainment of Dancing by Monsieur *Cherrier*, Miss *Santlow* his Scholar, and Mr *Evans*. [He quotes the advertisement from the *Daily Courant*, and falls upon the performers:] *Peggy Hughes* [*sic*] sings, Monsieur *Ramandon* playes, Miss *Santlow* dances, Monsieur *Cherrier* teaches, and all for the Church; Here's heavenly Doings! Here's Harmony! Your singing of Psalms is *Hurdy Gurdy* to this *Musick* . . .

It is not theatre music or plays as such that he objects to, but the exercise of mindless frivolity when there are so many more serious matters to think about. At one point he suggests a 'virtuous' theatrical troupe performing for charity: 'Let us see a grave Opera, a sober Play, let us see the Triumph of Vertue upon the Stage' (III, p.129). In the summer of 1709, he says, Queen Anne was right to close the theatres at a time of 'earnest Prayers' for success in war at a time of crisis (VI, p.255):

> her Majesty . . . does not think, that Plays, Comedies, Opera's, and such like Divertisements, make any Harmony with Prayers, Confession of National Crimes, and Actions of general Humiliation joyn'd with earnest Petition, such as those Prayers so appointed really import.

Music, in other words, the most direct and 'sincere' of the arts, lost its special status for him when it was allied with mere 'Divertisements' or amusements. It must make harmony with the serious purposes of the nation, which led the Protestant alliance against the Catholic French. It must serve the Anglican church, the instrument of Protestant reconciliation, which in its turn must steer a middle course between the non-conformist sects and the 'High-flyers' or high-church party, who were suspected of Jacobite and therefore Roman sympathies. The bicentenary of the Reformation fell in 1717, and Defoe's *Mercurius Politicus* proudly noted the role of music in this Protestant jubilee, which in London was held on 17 November. The occasion (pp.814f):

> had been celebrated in Foreign Protestant Countries, with all possible Ceremony and Magnificence, particularly at the Courts of *Denmark* and *Prussia*; and in proportion it was the same here, especially at the *Danish* Church in *Well-Close Square*, and at the *Swedish* Church in *Trinity-lane*. The former had four sermons on the Sunday, and next day Te Deum sung to extraordinary fine Musick: But at the Swedish Church, if possible, they were resolv'd to out-do all the World; they had the best Musicians, and the best Voices that could be had, both Men and Women, and had an Anthem

finely sung in the Swedish Tongue, the Trumpets, Kettle Drums, and all manner of Musick that could be had, playing their Parts, and by the best Masters in Town; the whole was closed with a Sermon and a Benediction also pronounc'd with Musick.

The practitioners of church music must be sincere in their lives as well as in their art: one wonders who the 'poor Organist of *Cambridge*' was— evidently far too high-church for Defoe's liking (III, p.393; 17 August 1706)—

who could not forbear in his High-Flying Zeal to affront the QUEEN *for a Presbyterian*; though at the same time he made the Musick, sung to in the *Church* of *England*, supported by Her Majesty's particular Zeal.

But not only the composer, the listener too needed to be in harmony with music's purposes (VIII, p.254):

What is all the Charms of Musick; that Harmony of Sounds and Fineness of Stroke, that at another Time, or in another Person, would raise the Spirits from the deepest Melancholy; that Harp itself, that drove the Devil out of King *Saul* to a Man that has no Ear, it is all discour'd, scream, and meer emptyness.

In the little-read *Serious Reflections during the Life and Surprising Adventures of Robinson Crusoe* (1720), Defoe sent his now ageing hero to St Paul's Cathedral on 27 June 1706 (old style), to take part in the General Thanksgiving for the victory of Ramillies. Crusoe was surprised to find that people were paying three guineas to get in, and that nine-tenths of the congregation were simply there to see the Queen and enjoy the show. Even the musicians and the men of God let their attention wander.[31] Amongst the music that Crusoe would have heard on this occasion was Jeremiah Clarke's anthem, *The Lord is my strength*, specially composed for the service.[32]

Defoe appears to have had a hand in the composition of another piece of occasional music celebrating the same events, though perhaps he merely acted as broker between the unknown composer and his poet, who was expected to provide words for music already written: 'The Gentleman that sent the Author of this a Composition of Musick, on the subject of the late Victories, and desir'd some Words to it, is requested to leave Word at Mr *Matthews* in *Little-Britain*, how he may be sent to', runs an advertisement in the *Review* for 25 June 1706 (III, p.304). In 1711 we find Defoe well aware of the political uses of music. The Jacobites have made new verses to the old Cavalier song 'And the King shall enjoy his own again', and 'the

Hautboys of the City Train'd-Bands' dared to play it on the Pretender's birthday: 'that Tune, which . . . is the *Allegory*, the *Shiboleth*, the *Lilly-burlero* of the Jacobites'. Three months later he prints the offending words:

> *Now the Tories Reign,*
> *Our Hopes revive again,*
> *And the Revolution Rogueries*
> *shall come down.* (etc.)

and mentions another seditious song, 'Ye Round-Headed Cuckolds march on march on': he would have preferred '*Lilla-burlero, Greensleeves*', or some other tune (VIII, pp.314–19).

By August 1717 the authorities had learned that such demonstrations must be repressed. Defoe showed sympathy when his *Mercurius Politicus* reported (pp.521f) that:

> at *Hertford* Assizes, . . . two Men had the Misfortune to be liable to the Law for a Thing, which, on other Occasions, and more moderately managed, would have been allowed as a piece of Country Merriment, *viz.* a *Riding*, as they call it, at *Wotton*, near *Hertford.* It seems there was some Intemperance in the manner, and it was taken to have some Seditious design; so that when it came to be Try'd at the Assizes, the two principle [*sic*] Persons *viz.* A Carpenter, being the Person who Rode with a pair of Horns on his Head, and a Fiddler, who it seems made Musick to him, were Sentenc'd to be Whipp'd, the Fiddler once round the Market-place, and the Carpenter twice; the Fiddler to lie in Prison half a Year, and the Carpenter a whole Year; so they have Time to consider how to behave themselves for the future.

All the same, Defoe hated it when illegal and obscene street-ballads poisoned the imagination of the common people: 'Our Youth are corrupted by filthy, lewd Ballads, sung and sold publickly in our Streets: Nay, unlicens'd and unstamp'd, notwithstanding Acts of Parliament to the contrary' (xviii, p.25). The ballads and songbooks owned by the young sisters in *The Family Instructor* were surely not of this noxious kind, but they are nevertheless thrown in the fire along with their 'plays, novels, romances, and such like stuff'—in one case voluntarily, in the other forcibly. For such a household, the proper domestic music is psalm-singing.[33] An irreverent young husband in another family, teasing his pious wife for what he thought was excessive religiosity, 'got the ballad of Chevy Chace bound into her Psalm-book'.[34] Yet Defoe the artist understood how a good ballad could encapsulate strong, simple emotion, even though he despised the genre in principle. Moll Flanders meets an unnamed young woman in prison who knows she is soon to die (p.274):

> If I am hanged there's an end of me, and away she turned dancing, and sings as she goes, the following piece of Newgate wit:
>> If I swing by the string,
>> I shall hear the bell ring,
>> And then there's an end of poor Jenny.

(The bell is that of St Sepulchre's, which tolled for execution days.)

When the much-bedded Moll Flanders does eventually make a legal marriage, she too has music under her window, on her honeymoon this time: 'we had the bells set a-ringing the next morning early, and the music, such as the town ['Brickill'—?Bucks] would afford, under our window' (p.184). Those visiting the spa of Epsom, Defoe tells us in *A Tour Through the Whole Island of Great Britain* (1724), to take the waters, also had to run the gauntlet of the Town Waits on the first morning after their arrival, and had to stand the racket in both senses (i, letter ii, pp.112ff):

> The next Morning you are welcom'd with the Musick under your Chamber Window; but for a Shilling or two you get rid of them, and prepare for going to the Wells . . . . Then you Drink the Waters, or walk about as if you did; Dance with the Ladies, though it be in your Gown and Slippers; have Musick and Company of what kind you like . . . .
>
> . . . towards Evening . . . the Musick strikes up in the Great Room, and Company draws together a-pace: . . . the Ladies Dance . . . by Eleven a Clock the Dancing generally ends, and the Day closes with good wishes.

Music caught Defoe's eye several times when he was gathering materials for this work. At one moment it is the musical establishment at Cannons (ii, letter iii, pp.8ff), or the 'Four Choirs for Musick-Worship' to be found in the City of London (ii, letter ii, p.56), or a choral foundation in Aberdeen (iii, letter iii, p.184). At the next it is an ancient manuscript in Exeter Cathedral Library, 'an old Missal, or Mass-Book, the Leaves of Velum, and famous for its most exquisite Writing' (i, letter iii, p.85). It may be the balls held in the pleasure-gardens of 'Bell-size' (ii, letter ii, pp.180f), or a piece of *trompe-l'oeuil* painting in Bugden House, in Huntingdonshire, at that time a seat of the Bishops of Lincoln (ii, letter iv, p.167):

> the Chappel very pretty, although small; there is an Organ painted against the Wall, but in a seeming Organ-loft, and so properly placed and well painted that we at first believed it really to be an organ.

Defoe had also travelled widely on the Continent of Europe as a young merchant, like his fictional Captain Carleton, whose remarks about Spanish music and theatres do not read as though they had been culled from other men's accounts (viii, pp. 79, 183f, 205).

Perhaps Defoe's interest in exotic music led him to include in the *Mercurius Politicus* for March 1717 this account of Welsh junketings in London on the previous St David's Day, 1 March, which happened also to be the birthday of the Princess of Wales (pp. 159f):

> The *Welsh* Gentry vallued themselves mightily on this incident, and bestirred themselves annually to make a brighter Day than Ordinary at Court . . . . The Society, as it seems they now are, made a long Cavalcade, and adjourn'd from St. *James*'s Church to St. *James*'s Palace, to pay their Compliment to the Prince and Princess; and from thence into the City, and had a great Feast at Drapers Hall, where was some *Welsh* Musick, and a great deal of *British* Mirth. After Dinner they chose their Stuarts [Stewards] for the next Year, who are as follows . . . .

How Welsh the music really was we cannot tell: Pepusch is known to have composed an ode for this society in 1716.[35] A year later, however, they had set up something approaching an Eisteddfod: though the prize poems were in Latin and English, the Society presented the Princess with one in Welsh.[36]

Finally, and still in London, a paragraph in the *Review* for 11 November 1704 suggests that Defoe had attended, and enjoyed, the 1703 St Cecilia's Day performance (the last of the regular annual series) and one of Cavendish Weedon's sacred concerts. The context is a complaint that the Worshipful Company of Stationers had held a banquet without the usual entertainment of music. The St Cecilia Odes and Weedon's concerts had all been performed in their Hall, and Defoe fancifully supposes that the reverberations of the music are still echoing around the rafters:[37]

> And as to Musick, they [the Master and Wardens] thought it needless; but imagin'd, that being to eat their Dinner in the same Individual Room where all the Charming Performance of St. *Cecilia*'s Feast, and Esq; *Weedon*'s Divine Consort was heard: they made no Question, but the Harmony had inspir'd the House; which join'd to their own Nonsense, would be Musick enough.

Defoe's joke actually sums up his own attitude to the serious uses of music. Harmony must inspire the House. For Defoe, musical harmony was a symbol of the harmony of life itself, whether in moral, political, artistic, religious or political terms. In *An Essay upon Literature* he writes of

'Harmony, and the Beauties of Sound, which are the foundation of music, these are the Daughters of God' (p.30). When asked by Benjamin Jackson and 'Francisco' to settle a bet as to whether the term Harmony 'derived from musick or not' he referred half jestingly to the harmony of the British Constitution ('What Musick is this to the *English* Subject'); and then went on to a serious discussion of Dr Bates's *The Harmony of the Divine Attributes*, concluding (III, pp.414ff):

> thus there is music in every beautiful building, every delicious prospect, every fair object; all the regulated life of a just and pious man is music to the eye of the observer; the eloquence of the orator, the lines of the poet, make music in his soul. Who can read Virgil, Horace, Milton, Waller, and Rochester, without touching the strings of his soul, and finding a unison of the most charming influence there?

★   ★   ★

I cannot claim that this brief attempt to establish the background of Defoe's feelings about music, in order to set his plan for a musical academy in wider perspective, has done much more than scratch the surface of his enormous output of words. But from the sample I have taken, which represents a reasonable cross-section of his principal writings, it is plain that he loved Cecilia well, even if he did not worship her blindly as a saint. Although in the course of his career he sometimes dealt out hard knocks against what he considered to be wrong uses of music, he more than made amends for this with the imaginative suggestions of *Augusta Triumphans*. In them, as in many other matters, he was over a century ahead of his time.

NOTES ON CHAPTER 16

1.   Printed for J. Roberts in Warwick-Lane. No author's name appears on the title-page of the first edition; but appended to the volume is an open letter to Lieutenant-Colonel Samuel Robinson on the subject of the Orphans' Tax, dated 28 Feb 1728 and signed with the name 'Andrew Moreton, Esq.'. This was one of Defoe's many pseudonyms. He used it for a number of publications between 1725 and 1731; all of them contained proposals for social reform of one kind or another. Subsequent editions of *Augusta Triumphans* advance the name 'Andrew Moreton' to the title-page as author of the whole.

2.   I am myself an 'Old Blue', as alumni of the 'Bluecoat School' call themselves. The standard history of the school is E. H. Pearce's *Annals of Christ's Hospital* (London, 1901, rev. and enlarged 2/1908). The school moved to Horsham, Sussex, in 1902.

3.   See O. E. Deutsch: *Handel: a Documentary Biography* (London, 1955), 94: Senesino started at £2,000, later receiving £1,470; pp.99, 139, showing Faustina and Cuzzoni at £2,000 each.

4.   John Milton, of course, was the exception who proved the rule, but then his father was a composer.

5.   (London, 1934): had Scholes pursued his researches further into the 18th century, he would doubtless have had something to say about Defoe and his scheme.

6.   The most recent authority is J. R. Moore's *Daniel Defoe: Citizen of the Modern World* (Chicago, 1958); see also J. Sutherland's *Defoe* (London, 1937, rev. 1950).

7.   See M. Tilmouth: 'A Calendar of References to Music in Newspapers published in London and the Provinces (1660-1719)', *RMARC*, i (1961), 56. To this one might add the advertisement in Defoe's *Mercurius Politicus* of March 1720, p.67, which lists among recent publications 'The Monthly Mask of Vocal Musick: or, The newest Songs made for the Theatres, and other Occasions, for the Month of February [1720]'.

8.   See Deutsch (1955), 190f.

9.   *The novels and miscellaneous works of Daniel De Foe*, ed. Sir G. S. Lewis (Oxford and London, 1840-41); *Augusta Triumphans* is in vol. xviii. In the second edition the date of the concluding letter has been altered to 23 Sept 1728.

10.   *ML*, xxxviii (1957), 327-34; for a yet earlier operatic 'Royall Academy of Musick' founded by Robert Cambert on his arrival in London in 1673—a failure—see A. Tessier: 'Robert Cambert à Londres', *ReM* (1927-8), no.2, 101 and W. H. Grattan Flood: 'Quelques précisions nouvelles sur Cambert et Grabu à Londres', *ReM* (1927-8), no.10, 351.

11.   William III of Orange, Defoe's first patron, whom he never lost an opportunity of praising.

12.   George II and Queen Caroline of Ansbach.

13.   The Royal Academy of Music, then nearing the end of its final season.

14.   In *A Tour through the whole Island of Great Britain* (1724), Defoe noted of Christ's Hospital that 'near Five thousand Pounds a Year are expended on this Charity' (ii, letter ii, p.180f).

15.   Off Charing Cross Road, in an area which is still a haunt of vice.

16.   Pearce (1901, 2/1908), 135; for music in general, see the whole of chap.7. A more recent paper on music at Christ's Hospital, based on much valuable fundamental research, is S. Jeans: 'The Easter Psalms of Christ's Hospital', *PRMA*, lxxxviii (1961-2), 45. *The Christ's Hospital Book*, ed. E. Blunden and others (London, 1953), a quatercentenary publication, actually includes *Augusta Triumphans* in 'A Christ's Hospital Bibliography' on p.386; but since the editors quote only the 'Academy of Sciences' heading from the second edition, neither they nor Percy Young, who contributes a note on the school's music on pp.302ff, can have realised what was really involved.

17.   Quoted from Jeans (1961-2), 54f.

18.   Pearce (1901, 2/1908), 144.

19.   *MQ*, lviii (1972), 210 (my page references are to this). Potter's book, the first part of which is interesting for its aesthetics and general observations on contemporary music (he was a Gresham Professor), is called *Observations on the present State of Music and Musicians . . . To which is added, a Scheme for erecting and supporting a Musical*

Academy in this Kingdom (London, 1762). The survival of Burney's manuscript plan in the Osborn Collection was first noted by R. Lonsdale: see *Dr Charles Burney, a Literary Biography* (Oxford, 1965), 150ff and 495.

20.   I have not been able to check the catalogues of the sale of Burney's library in order to establish whether he owned the volume.

21.   Ed. K. D. Bülbring (London, 1890), 243. Kassler (1972), 212, observes that John Locke 'had noted that music should occupy last place in any curriculum proposed for study, for music, he wrote, was both a waste of a young man's time and associated with "odd" company' (*Some Thoughts concerning Education*, London, 1693). Bülbring (p.195) also makes the parallel, but notes that Locke at least thought dancing useful.

22.   Ed. K. D. Bülbring (London, 1895), 49.

23.   *Daniel Defoe: Moll Flanders and The Fortunate Mistress, in one volume* (London, 1929), 24f; see also pp.16, 50, 53f, 193. I regret that I have not had time to verify all the quotations in this article from the originals: some of them, like the present one, therefore appear in modern spelling.

24.   Lewis (1840–41), v, *The History and remarkable Life of . . . Colonel Jack.*

25.   Lewis (1840–41), vi, *Memoirs of a Cavalier.*

26.   *A Review of the Affairs of France*, facs. ed. A. W. Secord (1938), I, 24[*bis*] (Jan 1705 suppl.). (Large Roman numerals refer to Defoe's annual volumes, not Secord's smaller fascicles.)

27.   *Moll Flanders*, 7f, 105, 178f, 184f, 254ff, 293f, 299f. See also p.153 for song 'of Mr. ---'s: "Oh! 'tis pleasant to be free, / The sweetest Miss is liberty." '.

28.   Defoe's views on opera in general were probably very like those of another great Puritan, Thomas Carlyle, whose blistering essay on *The Barber of Seville* and Victorian opera deserves to be better known: see 'The Opera', in *Critical and Miscellaneous Essays*, iii, 507–514 (*Thomas Carlyle's Works: the Standard Edition*, vii, London, 1904).

29.   I quote the expanded version, which adds the third paragraph, from *Second Thoughts are Best*, 9f. *The Provok'd Husband* was a play by Vanbrugh and Colley Cibber, a comedy unusual for its lack of smuttiness.

30.   Quoted in part in Deutsch (1955), 101.

31.   See chap. 4, 'An Essay on the present state of Religion in the World'.

32.   See E. H. Fellowes: *English Cathedral Music* (London, rev. 5/1969), 185.

33.   xv, 74f, 77, 87, 99, 104f; for family psalms, see xv, 109; xvi, 65.

34.   xiv (*Religious Courtship*), 38, 82; 'Cheviot Case' [*sic*] is also mentioned in *Review*, VIII, 714.

35.   Mr Don Cook drew my attention to Pepusch's *Ode for the Birthday of the Princess of Wales*.

36.   *Mercurius Politicus* for Feb 1717/8.

37.   I, p.303. I at first imagined that 'Weedon' must be a misprint for 'Weldon', but Paul Hubbard has pointed out to me that there was indeed an 'Esquire' named Cavendish Weedon who, he writes, 'promoted concerts of sacred music at Stationers' Hall on January 31st 1701 and in May 1702, the texts of which were published: they consisted of anthems by Blow and Turner, poems by Nahum Tate and "orations" on the subject of sacred music.

The proceeds went to "The Relief of Poor Decay'd Gentlefolk", and "Erecting and Maintenance of a School for the Educating of Youth in Religion, Music, and Accounts"'. The information came too late for incorporation in the main text of this article, but Weedon's plans for yet another music school, apparently for parish clerks or singing-men/vergers, plainly served as a model for Defoe's scheme in at least one respect: Defoe's suggestion in his §21 for 'some Performance in Musick, suitable for the Solemnity of . . . Sunday', and including 'Sacred Poesy and Rhetorick', is so close to Weedon's 'Divine Consort' that Defoe must have lifted the idea from that quarter. Nothing more is yet known about Weedon's school. If Defoe mentions Weedon's sacred concerts in November 1704, it seems likely that there had been fairly recent performances later than May 1702. Tilmouth (1961), 40ff, lists further information about Weedon's activities, including several other concerts; from the end of April to August 1702 they were apparently mounted weekly on Thursdays.

Part IV

ROBERT THURSTON DART:
BIBLIOGRAPHY OF PUBLICATIONS

Editions of Music

Revisions of Other Editors' Editions

Gramophone Records

Broadcast Talks

Periodical Articles

Reviews

Other Writings

Robert Thurston Dart:
Bibliography of Publications

Davitt Moroney and William Oxenbury

Certain items are excluded from these lists: minor (editorial) entries in the *Galpin Society Journal*; unimportant offprints from revisions of other editors' editions; gramophone records on which it is not certain that Dart performed; some impromptu radio broadcasts; and numerous unimportant reviews in various periodicals. The majority of his published letters are also excluded, unless they contain scholarly information. Letters included have been listed under articles or reviews, according to their nature. The attempt to include new reissues of gramophone records is doomed to be out-of-date by the time of publication, but a current issue of *The Gramophone Catalogue* will include further reissues. We are aware that Dart published many articles in unexpected places, and will be pleased to receive any additions to these lists.

We are grateful to all the publishing houses, gramophone record companies, and librarians of private and public libraries, who have assisted in the compilation of this bibliography.

ABBREVIATIONS FOR BIBLIOGRAPHY

AcM	*Acta Musicologica*
arr.	arranged by
ASM	Academy of St Martin-in-the-Fields
BN	Boyd Neel Orchestra
CLP	His Master's Voice label
clvd	clavichord
CNRS	Centre National de la Recherche Scientifique
EAF	Argo label, 7-inch extended play
ECM	Eclipse label, mono
ed. (eds.)	edited by; editor(s)
edn.	edition
facs.	facsimile (edition)

FS	French Service of the BBC
GOS	(1) Ace of Diamonds label [in section C]; (2) General Overseas Service of the BBC [in section D]
GSJ	*The Galpin Society Journal*
GTP	German Third Programme
HLPS	His Master's Voice label, stereo
hpd	harpsichord
HS	Home Service of the BBC
IMSCR	*International Musicological Society Congress Report* [followed by number and year of conference]
JAMS	*Journal of the American Musicological Society*
JE	Jacobean Ensemble
L	*The Listener*
LD	Argo label, 78 rpm
LX	Decca label, mono
LXT	Decca label, mono
M	*Music*
MB	Musica Britannica
MEEKM	Masters of Early English Keyboard Music
ML	*Music & Letters*
MR	*Music Review*
MT	*The Musical Times*
N	Novello (London)
n.d.	no date
NOHM	The New Oxford History of Music (London, 1954–)
NT	Network Three of the BBC
OL	(1) Editions de l'Oiseau-Lyre (Monaco); (2) (Decca) L'Oiseau-Lyre (Monaco); (2) (Decca) L'Oiseau-Lyre label, mono
OLS	(Decca) L'Oiseau-Lyre label, stereo [often reprocessed]
org	organ
OUP	Oxford University Press (London)
PL	Philomusica of London
PRMA	*Proceedings of the Royal Musical Association*
PS	Purcell Society Edition
RBM	*Revue Belge de Musicologie*
rev.	revised (by)
RG	Argo label, mono
RMA	Royal Musical Association
RMARC	*R.M.A. Research Chronicle*
RN	*Renaissance News*
S	Schott (London)

SB	Stainer & Bell (London)
SDDB	Decca label, boxed set
ser.	series
SFL	Fontana, special label, stereo
SOL	(Decca) L'Oiseau-Lyre label, stereo
SRPN	*Society of Recorder Players Newsletter*
SXL	Decca label, stereo
TCBS	*Transactions of the Cambridge Bibliographical Society*
TP	Third Programme of the BBC
transcr.	transcribed by
UP	University Press
vol. (vols.)	volume(s)
X	His Master's Voice label, 78 rpm
XLΓ	His Master's Voice label
ZRG	Argo label, stereo
7 EP	His Master's Voice label, 7-inch extended play
33 CX	Columbia label
*	indicates reissue number

EDITIONS OF MUSIC
(i) Editions

1948

(1)   Handel, G. F.: *Duo in F major* (S)

(2)   —— : *Fitzwilliam Sonatas* (S)

(3)   —— : *Sonata in B* for oboe and piano, ed. with W. Bergmann (S)

(4)   Holborne, A.: *Two Fantasias* (S)

1949

(1)   Dart, R. T.: *Menuet* for recorder trio (S) [only published composition]

1950

(1)   Handel, G. F.: *Sonata in G minor* (S)

(2)   —— : *Suite for Two Keyboards* [second part reconstructed] (OUP)

1951

(1)   Handel, G. F.: *Grave and Allegro* for two recorders and continuo (S)

1953

(1)   Dowland, J.: *Ayres for Four Voices*, MB, vi, transcr. E. H. Fellowes, ed. with N. Fortune (SB for RMA), rev.2/1970

(2)   Purcell, H.: *Fantasia, Three Parts upon a Ground*, ed. with D. Stevens (Peters and Hinrichsen)

1955

(1)   ?Byrd, W.: *Salve Regina* (SB)

(2)   *Jacobean Consort Music*, MB, ix, ed. with W. Coates (SB for RMA), rev.2/1962

1956

(1)   Byrd, W.: *Fifteen* [Virginal] *Pieces* (SB), rev.2/1969

(2)   Lawes, H.: *Ten Ayres* (SB)

1957

(1)   *Clement Matchett's Virginal Book (1612)* (SB), rev.2/1969

(2)   Farnaby, G.: *Seventeen* [Virginal] *Pieces* (SB), rev.2/1968

(3)   Locke, M.: *Organ Voluntaries* (SB), rev.2/1968

(4)   Morley, T.: *Two Consort Lessons* [by R. Alison] (SB)

(5)   Purcell, H.: *Great Parent, Hail (1694)*, part of PS, xxvii (N)

(6)   —— : *Sonata no.I of III Parts* (SB)

(7)   —— : *Sonata no.X of III Parts* (SB), rev.2/1966

1958

(1)   Byrd, W.: *Fantasy Quartet no.4* (SB)

(2)   —— : *Fantasy Quartet no.5* (SB)

(3)   Purcell, H.: *March and Canzona for the Funeral of Queen Mary (1695)* (SB)

(4)   —— : *The Second Part of Musick's Hand-Maid* (SB), rev.2/1962, 1969

1959

(1)   Derosier, N.: *La Fuite du Roy d'Angleterre* (OUP)

(2)   Locke, M.: *Keyboard Suites* (SB), rev.2/1964

(3)   Lotti, A.: *Weeping a Lover Languished* (SB)

(4)   Morley, T.: *Collected Motets*, ed. with H. K. Andrews (SB)

(5)   —— : *Keyboard Works*, 2 vols (SB), rev.2/1964

(6)   Pepusch, J. C.: *Quintet in F* (S)

(7)   Purcell, H.: *Fantazias and other Instrumental Music*, PS, xxxi (N)

(8)   *Suite from the Royal Brass Music of King James I* (OUP)

(9)   Williams, W.: *Sonata in Imitation of Birds* (OUP)

1960

(1)   Bull, J.: *In the Departure of the Lord* (SB)

(2)   Byrd, W.: *Out of the Orient Crystal Skies* (SB)

(3)   *Clavichord Music of the Seventeenth Century* (SB), rev. 2/1964

(4)   Marchand, L.: *Pièces de clavecin* (OL)

(5)   Parcham, A.: *Solo* for treble recorder (OUP)

(6)   *Parthenia* (SB), rev.2/1962, 1969

1961

(1) Facy, H.: *Magnificat* (SB)

(2) Handel, G. F.: *Concerto for Descant Recorder and Orchestra* [arr. from op.3 no.3] (OUP)

(3) *Invitation to Madrigals 1* (SB)

(4) *Parthenia In-Violata or Mayden-Musicke* (New York, Peters)

(5) Purcell, H.: *Dido and Aeneas*, ed. with M. Laurie (N)

(6) ——: *Man that is Born of Woman* (SB)

1962

(1) Anon.: *Two Coventry Carols* (SB)

(2) King Henry VIII: *Quam pulchra es* (SB)

(3) Holborne, A.: *Suite*, transcr. and ed. Dart, arr. E. Siebert (OUP)

(4) *Invitation to Madrigals 2* and *Invitation to Madrigals 3* (SB)

(5) ?Kendall, J.: *The Dartmouth Magnificat* (SB)

1963

(1) Bull, J.: *Attend unto my Tears* and *O Lord, Turn Not Away* (SB)

(2) ——: *Keyboard Music II*, MB, xix (SB for RMA), rev.2/1970

(3) Ferrabosco, A.(ii): *In Thee, O Lord* (SB)

1964

(1) *Twenty-four Pieces from the Fitzwilliam Virginal Book* (SB)

1965

(1) *Intabolatura nova di balli (Venice, 1551)*, ed. with W. J. Oxenbury (SB), rev.2/1968

1967

(1) *Invitation to Madrigals 4* (SB)

(2) *Invitation to Medieval Music 1* (SB)

(3) Lassus, R de: *Super Flumina Babylonis* (SB)

1969

(1) Chambonnières, J. C. de: *Les deux livres de clavecin* (OL)

(2) *Invitation to Medieval Music 2* (SB)

(3) Playford, J.: *The First Part of Musick's Hand-Maid* (SB)

1971

(1) *Invitation to Madrigals 5* (SB) [posthumous]

1978

(1) *John Blow's Anthology*, rev., with intro., D. Moroney (SB)

(ii) Offprints from Editions

Each item in this list is cross-referenced to list (i) above: e.g. '1955:2' indicates that the item is extracted from the second publication listed above for 1955.

Coperario, G.: *Fantasia à3* (1955:2)
—— : *Fantasia à5* (1955:2)
—— : *Two Suites* (1955:2)
Dowland, J.: *Away with these Self-Loving Lads* (1953:1)
—— : *In This Trembling Shadow Cast* (1953:1)
—— : *Love, Those Beams That Breed* (1953:1)
—— : *O Sweet Woods* (1953:1)
—— : *Pavan* (1955:2)
—— : *Praise Blindness, Eyes* (1953:1)
—— : *Shall I See* (1953:1)
—— : *Thou Mighty God* (1953:1)
—— : *Were Every Thought an Eye* (1953:1)
—— : *What Poor Astronomers* (1953:1)
—— : *When Phoebus First* (1953:1)
—— : *Where Sin Sore Wounding* (1953:1)
Farrant, D.: *Four-Note Pavan à5* (1955:2)
Ferrabosco, A.(ii): *Fantasia à4* (1955:2)
—— : *Four-Note Pavan à5* (1955:2)
Gibbons, O.: *In Nomine à5* (1955:2)
Lupo, T.: *Fantasia à4* (1955:2)
Morley, T.: *Agnus Dei* (1959:4)
—— : *Eheu, sustulerunt Dominum* (1959:4)
—— : *Nolo mortem peccatoris* (1959:4)
—— : *O amica mea* (1959:4)
Phillips, P.: *Passamezzo Pavan* (1955:2)
Purcell, H.: *Fantazias and In Nomines* (1959:7), rev.2/1968
—— : *Music for Strings and Keyboard* (1959:7)
—— : *Trio Sonata for violin, bass viol and continuo* (1959:7)
Simpson, T.: *Bonny Sweet Robin* (1955:2)
—— : *Two Dances* (1955:2)
Tomkins, T.: *Alman à4* (1955:2)
Ward, J.: *Fantasia à4* (1955:2)
—— : *Fantasia à4* (1955:2)

REVISIONS
OF OTHER EDITORS' EDITIONS

The English Madrigalists in 36 vols (SB 1956–70), rev. of *The English Madrigal School*, ed. E. H. Fellowes (SB 1913–24): vols xiv, xv, xvii, xxx, xxxia, xxxib, xxxvb, xxxvi with associate revisers; iii, viii, xxiii left unrev. at his death.

The Collected Works of William Byrd (SB 1962–6), rev. of *The Collected Vocal Works of William Byrd*, ed. E. H. Fellowes (SB 1937–50): only vols ii, iii, xiv rev. Dart; vols xii, xiii rev. P. Brett under the direction of Dart.

The English Lute Songs, 1st ser. (SB 1959–69), rev. of *The English School of Lutenist Song Writers*, 2nd ser., ed. E. H. Fellowes (SB 1920–32): vols vii, x, xi, xv with associate revisers; an additional vol., xvii, was incorporated into the series.

Coprario, J.: *Funeral Teares (1600) / Songs of Mourning (1613) / The Masque of Squires (1614)*, ed. with G. Hendrie (SB 1959).

The English Lute Songs, 2nd ser., rev. of *The English School of Lutenist Song Writers*, 2nd ser., ed. E. H. Fellowes: only vols iv (SB 1925, rev.2/1959) and x (SB 1926, rev.2/1969) rev. Dart.

1955
Tomkins, T.: *Keyboard Music*, MB, v, ed. S. D. Tuttle (SB for RMA), rev.2/1964
—— : *Fifteen Dances*, from MB, v. ed. S. D. Tuttle (SB)
—— : *Nine Organ Pieces*, from MB, v, ed. S. D. Tuttle (SB)

1958
Byrd, W.: *The St John Passion*, ed. E. H. Fellowes (SB n.d.)

1959
Couperin, L.: *Pièces de clavecin*, ed. P. Brunold (OL 1936)

1960
Gibbons, O.: *A Selection of Short Dances*, ed. M. Glyn (SB n.d.)

1964
Clérambault, L.-N.: *Pièces de clavecin*, ed. P. Brunold (OL 1938)

1965
La Guerre, E. J. de: *Pièces de clavecin*, ed. P. Brunold (OL 1938)

1968
Couperin, F.: *Pièces de clavecin I-III*, ed. M. Cauchie (OL 1932)

1972
Couperin, F.: *Pièces de clavecin IV*, ed. M. Cauchie (OL 1933) [posthumous]

GRAMOPHONE RECORDS

(i) Solo Keyboard Recitals

(1)	MEEKM 1 Four centuries of music for organ, harpsichord and clavichord [Anon., Arne, Blitheman, Blow, Bull, Clarke, Croft, Farnaby, Gibbons, Hooper, Johnson, Newman, Roseingrave, Tallis, White]	OL 50075; *OLS 114
(2)	MEEKM 2 Byrd and Tomkins [hpd]	OL 50076; *OLS 115
(3)	MEEKM 3 Bull and Locke [org]	OL 50130; *OLS 116
(4)	MEEKM 4 Gibbons and Farnaby [hpd]	OL 50131; *OLS 117
(5)	MEEKM 5 Bull [hpd]	OL 255/SOL 255; *OLS 118
(6)	Two centuries of English organ music [Blow, Boyce, Bull, Byrd, Gibbons, Greene, Handel, Locke, Nares, Purcell, Stanley, Tomkins]	CLP 1212
(7)	Bach J. S.: French Suites [clvd]	OL 50208/SOL 60039
(8)	Bull, J.: Walsingham Variations [hpd]	X 541 (78rpm); *LXT 2796
(9)	—— : Salvator Mundi [org] *with* Tomkins: Fancy [org] [incidental music for *The Makers of History: Oliver Cromwell*]	CLP 1709; *XLP 40003
(10)	Byrd, W.: The Carman's Whistle	X 540 (78rpm); *LXT 2796
(11)	Clérambault, L.-N.: Complete Harpsichord Works *with* E. J. de la Guerre: Complete Harpsichord Works	OL 50183
(12)	Frescobaldi, G.: Capriccio [org]	HLPS 10
(13)	Froberger, J. J.: Clavichord Music	OL 50207/SOL 60038
	Guerre, E. J. de la: *see* (11)	
(14)	Handel, G. F.: Organ Pieces *with* Purcell: 2 Voluntaries and Fancy [org]	7EP 7051
(15)	—— : Harpsichord Suites 1–4	OL 50184; *OLS 152
(16)	Johnson, R.: Almain [with three anon. pieces]	X 543 (78rpm); *LXT 2795
(17)	Philips, P.: Pavana and Galliarda Dolorosa	X 542 (78rpm); *LXT 2796
(18)	Purcell, H.: Harpsichord Suites	RG 82–3
	Tomkins, T.: *see* (2), (6), (9)	

(ii) All Other Discs

(19)	Bach, J. S.: Brandenburg Concertos (ASM) [Dart died during the recordings]	Philips 6500 186–7 (6700 045)

(20)	—— : Brandenburg Concertos (PL)	SOL 60005–6
(21)	—— : Brandenburg Concertos 1, 2 and 4 (PL)	OL 50167
(22)	—— : Brandenburg Concertos 3 and 5 *with* Concerto for 2 violins (PL)	OL 50160
(23)	—— : Four Orchestral Suites *with* Brandenburg Concerto 6 (PL)	OL 50158–9; *OLS 104–5
(24)	—— : Four Orchestral Suites (ASM)	ZRG 687–8
(25)	—— : Harpsichord Concerto 5 *with* Concertos for 2 harpsichords (PL)	OL 50165
(26)	—— : Harpsichord Concerto 4 *with* Concerto for flute, violin and harpsichord, Sonata in C (from BWV 1037)	OL 50168/SOL 600067; *OLS 171
(27)	—— : Concerto for 3 harpsichords *with* Vivaldi-Bach: Concerto for 4 harpsichords; Vivaldi-Dart: Concerto for 4 harpsichords; G. Malcolm: Variations for 4 harpsichords	CLP 1120
(28)	—— : 3 Sonatas for gamba and harpsichord	OL 50161; *OLS 157
(29)	—— : St John Passion	RG 270-2/ZRG 5270-2; *GOS 628–30
(30)	—— : excerpts from St John Passion	ZRG 5422
(31)	—— : Magnificat in D *with* Purcell: Music for Funeral of Queen Mary	CLP 1128; *Seraphim 60001
(32)	—— : Cantata 54 *with* Cantata 53, Cantata 202 and *Erbarme Dich, mein Gott*	OL 50169
(33)	Bach, J. C.: 'Mr Bach at Vauxhall Gardens'	OL 50132; *OLS 103
(34)	Couperin, F.: Les nations, ordres 1–4	OL 251/SOL 251; *OLS 137 and OL 50182/SOL 60014; *OLS 138
(35)	—— : Pièces de violes	OL 50164; *OLS 148
(36)	Couperin, L.: Fantasies and Simfonies pour violes (JE)	OL 50145
(37)	Dowland, J.: Lachrymae (PL)	OL 50163; *OLS 164
(38)	Gibbons, O.: Tudor Church Music (dir. B. Ord) [Dart plays treble viol]	RG 151/ZRG 50151
(39)	Handel, G. F.: 6 Concertos op.3 (BN)	LXT 5020; *ECM 509/*ECS 509
(40)	—— : 12 Concertos op.6 (BN)	LX 3024, LX 3027, LX 3055, LX 3081, LX 3099, LX 3124; *LXT 5041–3; *ECM 550–2/*ECS 550–2

(41)   —— : 12 Concertos op.6 (ASM)   LXT 6369–71/ SXL
                                                    6369–71 *SDDB 295–7
(42)   —— : Water Music Suites 1–3 (PL)   OL 50178/SOL 60010
(43)   —— : Concerto for harpsichord
        with Concerto for lute, and Alexander's Feast   OL 50181/SOL 60013
(44)   —— : 4 Coronation Anthems   RG 369/ZRG 5369
(45)   —— : L'Allegro ed il Penseroso (PL)   OL 50195–6/SOL
                                                    60025–6
(46)   —— : Acis and Galatea   OL 50179–80/SOL
                                                    60011–12
(47)   —— : Semele   OL 50098–100; *OLS
                                                    111–3
(48)   —— : Sosarme   OL 50091–3; *OLS
                                                    125–6
(49)   —— : Selected Operatic Music (J. Sutherland)   OL 50170/SOL 60001
(50)   Lalande, M. R. de: Te Deum and Confitemini
        (BN)   OL 50153; *OLS 147
(51)   Lawes, W.: Consort Music   RG 555/ZRG 555
        Malcolm, G.: *see* (27)
(52)   Mozart, W. A.: Serenades and Epistle Sonatas (PL)   OL 50162; *OLS 101
(53)   Purcell, H.: 12 Trio Sonatas (1683) (JE)   LD 038–9/RG 84–5
(54)   —— : 10 Trio Sonatas (1697) (JE)   RG 112–3
(55)   —— : Golden Sonata with Fantasia (JE)   EAF 16
(56)   —— : Dido and Aeneas   OL 50216/SOL 60047
(57)   —— : The Fairy Queen   OL 50139–41; *OLS
                                                    121–3
(58)   —— : King Arthur   OL 50176–7/SOL
                                                    600068–9
(59)   —— : Songs from The Tempest   OL 50171/SOL 60002
        —— : *see also* (14), (31), (63)
(60)   Rameau, J. P.: Hippolyte et Aricie   OL 286–8/SOL 286–8
(61)   —— : Highlights from Hippolyte et Aricie   SOL 321
(62)   Scarlatti, A.: 2 Duet Cantatas   OL 50154; *OLS 154
(63)   —— : 2 Cantatas
        with Purcell: Songs   OL 50173
(64)   Vivaldi, A.: The Four Seasons   33 CX 1365
(65)   —— : The Four Seasons   XLP 30058
        —— : *see also* (27)
(66)   Dances of Shakespeare's Time   OL 50127
(67)   Songs for Courtiers and Cavaliers   OL 50128; *OLS 142
(68)   Concertos in Contrast [Corelli, Geminiani,
        A. Scarlatti]   OL 50129; *OLS 158
(69)   Jacobean Consort Music (JE)   OL 50133; *OLS 155

(70)	French String Music from Louis XIII to Louis XV (PL)	OL 50174
(71)	German 17th-century String Music (PL)	OL 50175
(72)	The Royal Brass Music of King James I	OL 50189/SOL 60019
(73)	Notre Dame de Paris in the 13th Century	SFL 14133/839 306 EGY/SXOL 20510
(74)	Music for 2 Keyboards (with I. Kipnis) [Byrd, Couperin, Farnaby, Handel, Mozart, Le Roux, Tomkins] [posthumous]	CBS 61300
(75)	Incidental music to Malory: Le Morte d'Arthur	ZRG 5227–9
(76)	Incidental music to complete Shakespeare plays	Argo

*indicates reissue number.

BROADCAST TALKS

1949

23 June   'Passymeasures, Quadro and Boogie' (TP)

1950

24 Sept   'Josquin des Prés' (TP)
5 Oct   'Bach and the Keyboard' (TP)

1951

11 March   'Francesco Landini' (TP)
15 June   'The Piano and its Predecessors' (HS Schools)
27 Sept   'English Composers Abroad' (TP)
6 Nov   '[Music in our Time:] New Lamps for Old' (HS)

1952

4 June   'Monteverdi's Orfeo' (TP)

1953

6 April   'English Lute Music: The Lute's Apology for her Excellence' (TP)
7 Aug   'C.P.E. Bach' (TP)
12 Oct   'Francesco Geminiani: The Art of Playing the Violin' (TP)
17 Oct   'The Lost Tradition' (TP) [unscripted discussion: Dart, A. Goldsborough, B. Lam and F. Rothschild]

1954

3 Jan   'John Dowland' (TP)
24 Feb   'Telemann' (TP)
20 Sept   'The Discovery of Mediaeval Music (3): John of the Sea' [on John Lloyd's mass and motet *O quam suavis*] (TP)

1955

7 May	'Henry Purcell' (TP)
8 June	'Early Scottish Music' (TP)
3 Nov	'Les rapports entre la musique française et écossaise pendant la renaissance' (FS)
2 Dec	'New Music by Byrd' (TP)

1956

5 Feb	'The early Bassoon' (TP)
1 March	'English and Netherlands Music' [in French] (FS)
1 April	'Purcell's Instrumental Music' (HS)
17 May	'L'influence française sur la musique anglaise du 17e siècle' (FS)
23 Aug	'Les origines de la musique de chambre en Angleterre' (FS)
8 Nov	'Les bouleversements de monde sonore' (FS)

1957

17 Jan	'Les Sonates en Trio d'Henry Purcell' (FS)
10 March	'Umwälzung in der Welt der Musik' (GTP)
2 May	'Thomas Morley' (FS)
30 July	'Thomas Morley' (TP)
13 Nov	'Thomas Morley' (GOS)

1958

24 Feb	'Arnold Dolmetsch' (TP)

1959

1 Jan	'Mr Haydn in London' (GOS)
8 Jan	'Mr Purcell's Band' (GOS)
15 Jan	'Mr Mozart in London' (GOS)
9 March	'John Coperario' (TP)
7 Sept	'Purcell's Chamber Music' (TP)
28 Nov	'Interpretations on Record: Bach's 2nd Brandenburg Concerto' [discussion: Dart, J. Westrup, B. Goldschmidt and J. Noble]

1960

12 Jan	'Background to Music; Musical Fashions (2): The Polyphonic Period (i)' (NT)
19 Jan	'Background to Music; Musical Fashions (3): The Polyphonic Period (ii)' (NT)
19 April	'Background to Music; Studies in Style (3): Bach's Brandenburg Concerto No. 4' (NT)
13, 15 & 18 June	'Portrait of an Orchestra' [Philomusica of London] (GOS)
22 Sept	'Miles Davis' [3rd item in 'Comment'] (TP)

| 8 Nov | 'Background to Music; The Symphony (6): Brahms' Symphony no.4 (i)' (NT) |
| 15 Nov | 'Background to Music; The Symphony (7): Brahms' Symphony no.4 (ii)' (NT) |

1961

24 June	'John Bull' (TP)
31 Oct	'Background to Music; The Concerto (5): Corelli and Handel' (NT)
7 Nov	'Background to Music; The Concerto (6): Bach's Concerto for 2 violins and Brandenburg Concerto no.2' (NT)
16 Dec	'Froberger' (NT)

1962

1 May	'Background to Music; The Concerto (29): Berg's Violin Concerto' (NT)
22 May	'Background to Music; The Concerto (32): Handel's Organ Concertos' (NT)
19 Aug	'Music Question no.6' [answered by R. Irwin, Dart, T. Harvey and R. North] (HS)

1963

| 9 Feb | 'Carl Philipp Emanuel Bach' (TP) |

PERIODICAL ARTICLES

1947

'Simone Molinaro's Lute Book of 1599', *ML*, xxvii, 258–61

1948

'Antony Holborne', *SRPN*, ii, May
'The Cittern and its English Music', *GSJ*, i, 46–63 [see also *GSJ*, ii, 31; v, 43; vi, 112]
'L'enseignement musicale aujourd'hui à Cambridge', *RBM*, ii, 143–6
'Morley's Consort Lessons of 1599', *PRMA*, lxxiv, 1–9
'The Story of Music (1): The Early Middle Ages', *M*, Summer, 45–51
'The Story of Music (2): The Late Middle Ages', *M*, Autumn, 19–25

1949

'An Eighteenth-Century Directory of London Musicians', *GSJ*, ii, 27–31
'The Music of J. H. Schein', *L*, xli, no.1045, 200
with R. Donington: 'The Origin of the In Nomine', *ML*, xxx, 101–6
'Samuel Scheidt and his Music', *L*, xli, no.1060, 864

1950

'A Background to Byrd's Chamber Music', *L*, xliii, no.1098, 264
'Josquin des Prés, Prince of Musicians', *L*, xliv, no.1129, 396

1951

'The Earliest Collections of Clarinet Music', *GSJ*, iv, 39ff
'The Greatest Figure in Fifteenth-Century Music' [Guillaume Dufay], *L*, xlv, no.1144, 196
with B. Schofield: 'Tregian's Anthology', *ML*, xxxii, 205–16

1952

'A Background for Musica Britannica', *Music 1952*, ed. A. Robertson (Harmondsworth: Penguin), 18–28
'The Cibell', *RBM*, vi, 24–30
'Four Dutch Recorder Books', *GSJ*, v, 57–60

1953

'Derosier's Guitar Tutor', *GSJ*, vi, 107
'English Music and Musicians in 17th-century Holland', *IMSCR*, v *Utrecht 1952*, 139–45
'The Ghent Chime Book', *GSJ*, vi, 70–74
'John Dowland and his Music', *L*, xlix, no.1264, 858
'The Mock Trumpet', *GSJ*, vi, 35–40
'Musical Instruments in Diderot's Encyclopaedia', *GSJ*, vi, 109ff
with J. Page-Phillips: 'The Peacock Feast', *GSJ*, vi, 95ff

1954

'Une contribution anglaise au manuscrit de Strasbourg?', *Hommage à Charles van den Borren*, *RBM*, viii, 122ff
'A Footnote for Morley's "Plain and Easy Introduction"', *ML*, xxxv, 183
'The Instruments in the Ashmolean Museum', *GSJ*, vii, 7–10
'A New Source of Virginal Music' [*GB-Ob* Douce 381], *ML*, xxxv, 201–4
'New Sources of Virginal Music', *ML*, xxxv, 93–106
'Rôle de la danse dans l'"ayre" anglais', *Musique et poésie au XVIᵉ siècle* (Paris: Colloques internationaux du CNRS), 203–9
'Renaissance Music: Some Urgent Tasks for Scholars', *RN*, vii, 84–91
Letter: 'Smith's Titian Canon', *RN*, vii, 17 [see *RN*, vi, 52–6]

1955

'Cambrian Eupompus' [John Lloyd], *L*, liii, no.1359, 497
'Cavazzoni and Cabezón', *ML*, xxxvi, 2–6 [see also *ML*, xxxvi, 203f]
Letter: 'Cavazzoni-Cabezón', *JAMS*, viii, 148
'A Hand-List of English Instrumental Music Printed before 1681', *GSJ*, viii, 13–26
'Jacobean Consort Music', *PRMA*, lxxxi, 63–75
'Le manuscrit pour le virginal de Trinity College Dublin', *La musique instrumentale de la renaissance* (Paris: CNRS), 237ff
'Origines et sources de la musique de chambre en Angleterre (1500–1530)', *La musique instrumentale de la renaissance* (Paris: CNRS), 77–84

1956

'Maurice Greene and the National Anthem', *ML*, xxxvii, 136–48

'The Printed Fantasies of Orlando Gibbons', *ML*, xxxvii, 342–9

1957

'Bressan and Schickhardt', *GSJ*, x, 85f

'Lord Herbert of Cherbury's Lute-Book', *ML*, xxxviii, 136–48

'Some Sixteenth-Century French Drawings', *GSJ*, x, 88f

1958

'The Achievement of Arnold Dolmetsch', *L*, lxix, no.1510, 400

'The Dartmouth Magnificat', *ML*, xxxix, 209–17

'Note: An Early Organ at Saffron Walden', *GSJ*, xi, 88f

with H. K. Andrews: 'Fourteenth-Century Polyphony in a Fountains Abbey MS Book', *ML*, xxxix, 1–12 [see also *ML*, xxxix, 148–53]

'Miss Mary Burwell's Instruction Book for the Lute', *GSJ*, xi, 3–62 [pp. 8–62 comprise a transcription into modern English of the text]

'La méthode de luth de Miss Mary Burwell', *Le luth et sa musique* (Paris: Colloques internationaux du CNRS), 121–6

'La Pandore', *Le luth et sa musique* (Paris: Colloques internationaux du CNRS), 225–9

'The Repertory of the Royal Wind Music', *GSJ*, xi, 70–77

with C. Vlam: 'Rosseters in Holland', *GSJ*, xi, 63–9

1959

'John Bull's "Chapel"', *ML*, xl, 279–82

'Morley and the Catholics: Some Further Speculations', *Monthly Musical Record*, lxxxix, 89–92

'Purcell's Chamber Music', *PRMA*, lxxxv, 81–93

'Purcell's Harpsichord Music', *MT*, c, 324f

'Recorder "Gracings" in 1700', *GSJ*, xii, 93f

'Search for the Real John Bull', *New York Times*, cix, section 2 (1 Nov) [repubd *Music and Dance*, li (1960), 20]

'Sweelinck's "Fantazia on a Theme Used by John Bull"', *Tijdschrift voor Musiekwetenschap*, xviii, 167ff

1960

'Bach's "Fiauti d'echo"', *ML*, xli, 331–41 [see also *ML*, xliii, 192f]

'Henry Loosemore's Organ-Book', *TCBS*, iii, 143–51

'Search for the Real John Bull', *Music and Dance*, li, 20 [repubd from *New York Times* (1 Nov 1959)]

with P. Brett: 'Songs by William Byrd in Manuscripts at Harvard', *Harvard Library Bulletin*, xiv, 343–65

'An Unknown Letter from Dr. John Bull', *AcM*, xxxii, 175ff

1961

'Handel and the Continuo', *Bulletin of the American Choral Foundation*, Jan, 1ff

'Early English Organ Pedals', *MT*, cii, 107f

'The History of "Mayden-Musicke"', *Bulletin of the New York Public Library*, lxv, 209–28 [abridgement of intro. to facs.]

'Music and Musicians at Chichester Cathedral, 1545–1642', *ML*, xlii, 221–6 [see also *ML*, xliii, 92–5, 193f]

'Ornament Signs in Jacobean Music for Lute and Viol', *GSJ*, xiv, 30–33

'Performance Practice in the 17th and 18th Centuries: Six Problems in Instrumental Music', *IMSCR*, viii *New York 1961*, i, 231–5

1962

'City Song', *Recorded Sound*, i, 262–5

'Elizabeth Eysbock's Keyboard Book', *Hans Albrecht In Memoriam* (Kassel: Bärenreiter), 84–7 [repubd with small changes, *Svensk Tidskrift för Musikforskning*, xliv (1962), 5–12]

'Francesco Geminiani and the Rule of Taste', *The Consort*, xix, 122–7

with B. Fagan: '"The Name's the Same" or, A Warning to Searchers', *RMARC*, ii, 16f

Letter: 'The Triumphs of Oriana', *MT*, ciii, 406

1963

'John Bull', *Canon* [The Australian Music Journal], xvi, March/April, 21ff

'John Bull 1563–1628', *MT*, civ, 252f

'A Letter of Recommendation Written for John Bull in 1617', *RBM*, xvii, 121–4

Letter: 'Musica Britannica', *MT*, civ, 419

'The Organ-Book of the Crutched Friars of Liège', *RBM*, xvii, 21–8

'Purcell and Bull', *MT*, civ, 30f

'A Suppressed Dedication for Morley's Four-Part Madrigals of 1594', *TCBS*, iii, 401–5

1964

'A Note on the Music [in a Bible of Evesham Abbey]', *English Historical Review*, lxxix, 777f

'The Origins of Music Degrees', *MT*, cv, 190f

Letter about Pierre de Manchicourt's death, *ML*, xlv, 310f

'Richard Motley, Dancing Master', *MR*, xxv, 96–9

'Two New Documents Relating to the Royal Music 1584–1605', *ML*, xlv, 16–21

1965

'Handel and the Continuo', *MT*, cvi, 348ff [see also *MT*, cvi, 523, 606]

'Musical Dinosaurs and Operational Research; Some Notes on the Goodman Report', *MT*, cvi, 591ff

1966

'Technical Means in Music Education', *Congress Report: 5th Triennial Congress, Association Européenne des Académies, Conservatoires et Musikhochschulen*, 19f

1967

'How They Sang in Jena in 1598', *MT*, cviii, 316f

1968

'Current Musicology's Project on Musicological Method: some Comments', *Current Musicology*, vii, 81–5

Letter: 'Handel's op.6', *MT*, cix, 918f

'Music and Musical Instruments in Cotgrave's Dictionarie (1611)', *GSJ*, xxi, 70–80

'Robert ap Huw's Manuscript of Welsh Harp Music (*c* 1613)', *GSJ*, xxi, 52–65

1969

'Elizabeth Edgeworth's Keyboard Book', *ML*, l, 470–74

'On Couperin's Harpsichord Music', *MT*, cx, 590–94 [see also *MT*, cx, 934]

1970

'Bach's Early Keyboard Music: A Neglected Source (Brussels BR Fétis 2960)', *AcM*, xlii, 236ff

'Two English Musicians at Heidelberg in 1613', *MT*, cxi, 29–32

1971

'An Early Seventeenth-Century Book of English Organ Music for the Roman Rite', *ML*, lii, 27–38

'Bononcini Sets Handel a Test', *MT*, cxii, 324ff [posthumous]

REVIEWS

Minor reviews are excluded from this list.

1948

E. Closson: *History of the Piano* (London: Elek, 1947): *GSJ*, i, 66ff

V. Denis: *De Musiekinstrumenten in de Nederlanden en in Italie* (Antwerp: Standaard-Boekhandel, 1944): *GSJ*, i, 65f

K. Jeppesen: *Die Italienische Orgelmusik am Anfang der Cinquecento* (Copenhagen: Munksgaard, 1943): *GSJ*, i, 68f

1949

G. van Esbroeck and F. Montfort Jr.: *Qu'est-ce que jouer juste?* (Brussels: Editions Lumière, 1946): *GSJ*, ii, 60

H. Hickman: *La trompette dans l'Egypte ancienne* (Cairo: L'Institut Français d'Archéologie Orientale, 1946): *GSJ*, ii, 55f

J. Manifold: *The Amorous Flute* (London: Workers' Music Association, 1948): *SRPN*, iii, April

Mélanges Ernest Closson (Brussels: Société Belge de Musicologie, 1948): *GSJ*, ii, 54f

1950

S. Clercx: *Le baroque et la musique* (Brussels: Librairie Encyclopédique, 1948): *GSJ*, iii, 51f

1951

W. Apel, ed.: *French Secular Music of the late Fourteenth Century* (Cambridge, Mass.: Medieval Academy of America, 1950): *GSJ*, iv, 49

C. van den Borren: *Pièces polyphoniques profanes de provenance liégeoise* (Cambridge, Mass.: Medieval Academy of America, 1950): *GSJ*, iv, 49

M. Bukofzer: *Studies in Medieval and Renaissance Music* (New York: Norton, 1950): *ML*, xxxii, 271ff

E. N. Doring: *The Guadagnini Family of Violin Makers* (Chicago: Lewis, 1949): *GSJ*, iv, 48f

H. G. Farmer: *Music Making in the Olden Days* (London: Hinrichsen, 1950): *GSJ*, iv, 48

E. H. Fellowes, ed.: *The Collected Works of William Byrd*, xv–xx (London: SB, 1948–50): *ML*, xxxii, 181–4

H. Isaac: *Choralis Constantinus*, bk iii, ed. L. Cuyler (Ann Arbor: U. of Michigan Press, 1950): *ML*, xxxii, 82–5

1952

G. Coperario: *Rules How to Compose*, facs. (Los Angeles: Gottlieb, 1952): *RN*, v, 79f

A. T. Davison and W. Apel: *Historical Anthology of Music*, ii (London: OUP, 1950): *GSJ*, v, 63f

H. Redlich: *Claudio Monteverdi* [English edn.] (London: OUP, 1952): *ML*, xxxiii, 175–8 [see also *ML*, xxxiii, 281; xxxiv, 85]

L. Schrade: *Monteverdi: Creator of Modern Music* (London: Gollancz, 1951): *ML*, xxxiii, 64f

D. W. Stevens: *The Mulliner Book: A Commentary* (London: SB, 1952): *ML*, xxxiii, 357ff

1953

F. Rothschild: *The Lost Tradition in Music: Rhythm and Tempo in J. S. Bach's Time* (London: Black, 1953): letter to *ML*, xxxiv, 355f [see also *ML*, xxxv, 89]

J. Stevens, ed.: *Mediaeval Carols*, MB, iv (London: SB, 1952): *ML*, xxxiv, 78f

R. Stevenson: *Music in Mexico: An Historical Survey* (New York: Crowell, 1952): *GSJ*, vi, 115ff

1954

Annales musicologiques: moyen-age et renaissance, i (Paris: Société de *Musique d'Autrefois*, 1953): *ML*, xxxv, 241ff

R. Kirkpatrick: *Domenico Scarlatti* (Princeton: Princeton UP, 1953): *ML*, xxxv, 144–7

C. Sachs: *Rhythm and Tempo: A Study in Music History* (London: Dent, 1953): *ML*, xxxv, 45f

1955

W. G. Waite: *The Rhythm of Twelfth-Century Polyphony: Its Theory and Practice* (New Haven: Yale UP, 1954): *ML*, xxxvi, 394f

1956

Hallische Händel Ausgabe, 4th ser., i, iii, iv (Kassel: Bärenreiter, 1955–6): *ML*, xxxvii, 400–3

G. P. Telemann: *Musikalische Werke*, i–iii, ix, x (Kassel: Bärenreiter, 1950–55): *ML*, xxxvii, 302–5

1957

N. Dufourq: *Nicolas Lebègue: étude biographique* (Paris: Picard, 1954): *ML*, xxxviii, 90f

S. Mayes: *An Organ for the Sultan* (London: Putnam, 1956): *GSJ*, x, 90f

H. Spanke, ed.: G. *Raynauds Bibliographie des Altfranzösischen Liedes* (Leiden: Brill, 1955): *ML*, xxxviii, 93

1958

Documenta musicologica, xi [Bermudo: *Declaración*]; xii [Bovicelli: *Regole Passagi*]; xiii [Salinas: *De Musica*] (Kassel and Basel: Bärenreiter, 1958): *ML*, xxxix, 392ff

J. Cabanilles: *Tientos 55–70*, ed. H. Anglès (Barcelona: Biblioteca Central, 1956): *ML*, xxxix, 92

T. Morley: *Canzonets for Three Voices*, facs., ed. J. E. Uhler (Baton Rouge: Louisiana State UP, 1957): *ML*, xxxix, 298

J. Playford: *The English Dancing Master*, facs., ed. M. Dean-Smith (London: Schott, 1957): *ML*, xxxix, 164–9

1959

D. O'Sullivan: *Carolan: The Life, Times and Music of an Irish Harper* (London: Routledge and Kegan Paul, 1958): *ML*, xl, 179–82

G. Morlaye: *Psaulmes de Pierre Certon*, ed. R. de Morcourt (Paris: CNRS, 1957); T. Mace: *Musick's Monument*, facs. (Paris: CNRS, 1958); R. Dowland: *Varietie of Lute Lessons*, facs. (London: Schott, 1958); F. Bossinensis: *20 Recercari da sonar nel lauto*, ed. B. Disertori (Milan: Zerboni, 1954): *GSJ*, xii, 105ff

C. Parrish: *The Notation of Medieval Music* (New York: Norton, 1957): *ML*, xl, 79f

1960

M. R. Coelho: *Flores de musica pera o instrumento de tecla & harpa*, ed. S. Kastner (Lisbon: Gulbenkian, 1959): *ML*, xli, 287f

M. Lefkowitz: *William Lawes* (London: Routledge and Kegan Paul, 1960): *ML*, xli, 256–9

A. Lehr: *De Klokkengeiters François en Pieter Hemony* (Asten, Holland: Eijsbouts, 1959): *GSJ*, xiii, 112

G. Le Roux: *Pieces for Harpsichord*, ed. A. Fuller (New York: Alpeg, 1959): *ML*, xli, 399f

P. Nuten: *De 'Madrigali Spirituali' van Filip de Monte (1521–1603)*, Verhandelingen van de Koninklijke Vlaamse Academie voor Wetenschappen, Letteren en Schone Kunsten van Belgie, Klasse der Schone Kunsten, Verhandeling no.14 (Brussels, 1958): *ML*, xli, 285f

T. Morley: *The First Book of Consort Lessons*, ed. S. Beck (New York: Peters, for New York Public Library, 1959): *GSJ*, xiii, 98–102

R. Russell: *The Harpsichord and Clavichord* (London: Faber, 1959): *ML*, xli, 57f

1961

H. Glahn: 'Tysk Barok-Cembalo og Fransk Rokoko-Harfe', offprinted from *Year Book 1950–1958* of the Oslo Kunstinductrimuseet (Oslo: Kirstes Boktrykkeri, 1960): *GSJ*, xiv, 83

A. Hughes and G. Abraham, eds.: *Ars Nova and the Renaissance, 1300–1540*, NOHM, iii (London: OUP, 1960): *ML*, xlii, 57–60

H. Neupert: *Harpsichord Manual* (Kassel: Bärenreiter, 1960); F. Ernst: *Der Flügel Johann Sebastian Bachs* (Frankfurt: Peters, 1955): *ML*, xlii, 163f

1962

E. T. Ferand, ed.: *Improvisation in Nine Centuries of Western Music*, Anthology of Music, xii (London: OUP, 1961; Ger. orig., Cologne: Arno Volk, 1956): *ML*, xliii, 174ff

L. Schrade: *La Représentation d'Edipo Tiranno au Teatro Olimpico* (Paris: CNRS, 1960): *ML*, xliii, 76f

1963

A. G. H. Bachrachs: *Sir Constantine Huygens and Britain, 1596–1687*, i *1596–1619* (London: OUP, 1962): *ML*, xliv, 82

H. M. Brown: *Music in the French Secular Theater, 1400–1550* and *Chansons of the 15th and Early 16th Centuries* (Cambridge, Mass.: Harvard UP, 1963): *RN*, xvi, 211ff

Recherches sur la musique française classique II (Paris: Picard, 1962): *ML*, xliv, 291f

A. Robertson and D. Stevens, eds.: *A History of Music, I Ancient Forms to Polyphony* (London: Cassell, 1962): *ML*, xliv, 55f [see also *ML*, xliv, 314]

1965

N. Carrell: *Bach's Brandenburg Concertos* (London: Allen and Unwin, 1963): *MT*, cvi, 193f

F. Harrison and J. Rimmer: *European Musical Instruments* (London: Studio Vista, 1964): *ML*, xlvi, 348ff

1967

W. W. Newcomb, ed.: *Lute Music of Shakespeare's Time: William Barley: A New Booke of Tabliture, 1596* (Pennsylvania and London: Pennsylvania State UP, 1966): *JAMS*, xx, 493ff

1969

A. Curtis: *Sweelinck's Keyboard Music* (Leiden and London: Leiden UP and OUP, 1969): *ML*, l, 513ff

OTHER WRITINGS

1949–54

Die Musik in Geschichte und Gegenwart (Kassel: Bärenreiter) [heavy type indicates longer articles]: *i*: 'Aston, Hugh'; 'Baldwin, John'; *ii*: 'Bull, John'; 'Campion, Thomas'; 'Catch'; 'Cebell'; 'Chapel Royal'; 'Chekker'; **'Consort'**; 'Coperario, John'; 'Cornyshe, William'; 'Cosyn, Benjamin'; 'Cowper, Robert'; *iii*: 'Dart, (Robert) Thurston'; 'Davy, Richard'; **'Dowland, John'**; 'Dump'; 'East, Thomas'; **'England *Von der Reformation bis zum Commonwealth*'**

1952

Foreword to T. Morley: *A Plain and Easy Introduction to Practical Music*, ed. A. Harman (London: Dent), pp. xvi–xxv

1954

Foreword to *English Lute Music*, ed. D. Lumsden (London: Schott)

The Interpretation of Music (London: Hutchinson), rev.4/1967; Ger. trans. as *Practica Musica: vom Umgang mit alter Musik* (Berne and Munich: 1959); Swed. trans. as *Musikalisk Praxis* (Stockholm: Natur och Kultur, 1964); Span. trans. as *Interpretacion de la Musica* (Buenos Aires: Leru, 1978)

Grove's Dictionary of Music and Musicians (5th edn., London: Macmillan) [heavy type indicates longer articles; *indicates that there is additional information, or corrections, in the Supplementary Vol.]: 'Acourt'*; 'Adriani (Adrianus), Francesco'; 'Adson, John'; 'Allegri, Domenico'*; 'Amener'; 'Anglia (Anglicanus), Gervasius de'; 'Antegnati'*; **'Ars Antiqua'**; **'Ars Nova'***; 'Bassano (basson, de Basson)'; 'Bassano, Giovanni'*; 'Basse-Danse'; 'Bataille, Gabriel'; 'Beldemandis, Prosdocimus de ⸱ (Prosdocimo de' Beldomandi)'; 'Bonaventura, Anterus Maria de S.'; 'Bonometti, Giovanni Battista'; 'Brade, William'; 'Bucenus (Bucaenus), Paulus'; 'Buttstett, Frans (Vollrath)'; 'Buttstett (Buttstädt), Johann Heinrich'*; 'Cebell'*; 'Ceretto, Scipione'; 'Chitarrone' [A. J. Hipkins, rev. Dart]; 'Cima, Giovanni Paolo'; 'Cima, Tullio'; 'Citole'*; 'Cittern'*; 'Cobb, John'; 'Consort'*; **'Cryptography, Musical'***; 'Cutting, Francis or Thomas'; 'Dalla Casa, Girolamo'; 'Dalla Casa, Nicolo'*; 'Dering (Deering), Richard'*; 'English Guitar'; **'English Musicians Abroad** *c*1575-1625'*; 'Eye Music'*; 'Forqueray'*; 'Ganassi, Sylvestro di'; 'Gervaise, Claude'*; 'Gittern' [F. W. Galpin, rev. Dart]; 'Giustiniana'; 'Gletle, Johann Melchior'*; 'Greghesca'; **'Ground Bass'**; 'Hely, Benjamin'; 'Hodsdon, (Wilfred) Alec'; 'Hole' [with W. C. Smith]; 'Hortus Musarum' [M. L. Pereyra, rev. Dart]; 'Howett (Huwett), Gregorio'; 'Ileborgh, Adam'; 'Intrada'*; 'Jaye, Henry'; 'Jigg'; 'Kapsberger, Johann Hieronymous'; 'Landini (Landino), Francesco'*; 'Lupo (Lupus, Luppo)'; 'Macque, Giovanni (de)'; 'Matachin (Matassins)'; 'Maynard, John'; 'Measure (1)'; 'Megli, Domenico Maria'; 'Melii, Pietro Paolo'; 'Morton, Robert'; 'Moss, John'*; 'Norcom(b)e'*; 'Notari (Notary, Notario), Angelo'*; **'Notation'***; 'Orpharion (Orpheoreon)'*; 'Partita'; 'Passamezzo'; 'Pearce, Edward'; **'Petrucci, Ottaviano dei'***; 'Price, John (i)'; 'Price, John (ii)'; 'Primrose' [addition to G. Hayes' article]; **'Proportions'**; 'Reusner, Esias'; 'Robinson, Thomas'; 'Rosseter, Philip' [addition to E. H. Fellowes' article]; 'Rowe'; 'Ruggiero (Rogero)'; **'Scheidt, Samuel'*** [J. H. Mee, rev. Dart]; **'Schein, Johann Hermann'*** [J. H. Mee, rev. Dart]; 'Simpson, Thomas'; 'Song 1500-1700'; 'Spinaccino, Francesco'; 'Steffkins'; 'Sturgeon, Nicolas'* [additions to J. Mark's article, with D. W. Stevens]; **'Tablature'**; 'Tregian, Francis'; 'Troiano, Massimo'; 'Vide, Jacques'; 'Vinci, Leonardo da'*; 'Voigtländer, Gabriel'; 'Weiss, Sylvius Leopold'; 'Williams, William'
See also 1961.

1958

Foreword to C. S. Terry: *Bach's Orchestra* (London: OUP, 1932, 2/1958)

1960

Introduction to John Bull: *Keyboard Music I*, ed. J. Steele and F. Cameron (London: SB for RMA, rev.2/1967)

'L'école anglaise', *Histoire de la musique: I Des origines à Jean-Sebastien Bach*, Encyclopédie de la Pléiade (Paris: Gallimard), 1337-54

1961

Historical Introduction to facs. of *Parthenia In-Violata* (New York: New York Public Library)

'The Clavichord' and 'The Viols' in *Musical Instruments Through the Ages*, ed. A. Baines (Harmondsworth: Penguin), 68–73, 184–90

1961

Grove's Dictionary of Music and Musicians: Supplementary Volume (5th edn., London: Macmillan): 'Aegidius (Egidio)'; 'Brandenburg Concertos'; 'Pandora (Bandora, Bandore)'; **'Plainsong Notation'**

1963

Editing Early Music: Notes on Preparation of Printer's Copy, with W. Emery and C. Morris (London: N, OUP and SB)

1965

Revision (with suppl. notes) of F. W. Galpin: *Old English Instruments of Music* (London: Methuen, 1910, 4/1965)

1968

'English Lute Music' in NOHM, iv (London: OUP)

Foreword to *Handbook for Music Teachers*, gen. ed. B. Rainbow (2nd edn., London: Novello)

Introductory note (with G. Beechey) to facs. of T. Arne: *VIII Sonatas or Lessons for the Harpsichord* (London: SB)

1972

Introduction to facs. of G. Animuccia: *Missarum liber primus* (Farnborough: Gregg) [posthumous]

INDEX

Index

Compiled by
David M. Baker
Sub-Librarian, Brynmor Jones Library,
University of Hull

(n. = footnote; *p* = *passim* for several pages; italic page references denote plates)

Abdy, Thomas, 376
Aberdeen, 422
Abergavenny, Marquess of, 229
Academici Filarmonici (Verona), 363f
Academy of Ancient Music, 183f, n.65, n.68
Academy of the Svogliati (Florence), 361
Academy of Vocal Music, 183f, n.65, n.68
accademia (oratorio): performances in Bergamo, 326
Acton, William, 360, n.15
actors, 17th–18th-century, 318
Adam de la Halle
  as trouvère, 30
  music
    sources: 30f, 49*p*; interpretation, 30, 32, 49*p*, 53; notation, 30*p*, 49f, 52f; *see also* individual sources
    editing: 30; by Coussemaker, 30, 36, 49; by Wilkins, 30ff, 36
    monophonic music: style, 53; chansons courtoises, 39*p*: texts ed. by J. H. Marshall, 30f, 36, 41; underlay, 46, 53; *D'amourous cuer*, 34; *Amours m'ont si doucement*, 39; *Au repairer*, 47; *Glorieuse virge Marie*, 34, 42; *Grant deduit*, 44; *Helas, il n'est mais nus ki n'aint*, 47; *Je nai autre retenance*, 49f; *Li jolis maus*, 34; *De tant con plus aproisme mon pais*, 31; *Tant me plest vivre*, 44
    jeu-partis: 30, 33, 36f, 41, 46f; *Assenes chi grievilier jugement*, 41
    Latin song *Adest dies*, 37f
    polyphonic music: motets, 37; rondeaux: 34f, 37, 39; *Dame or sui trais*, 34f, n.9
  plays, 30: *Robin et Marion*, 36, 52
Addison, Joseph, 367, n.30f, 370: *Remarks on Several Parts of Italy ...*, 374, n.2, n.46
administrations of estates, 305
Adriaansz, W., 203, n.19, n.25
Adrianople, 374, n.46
Aegean islands, 279
air: English, 210; French, 209
Alas, departyng is ground of woo (song), 115f
Aldrich, *Dean* Henry: musical MSS at *GB-Och*, 164
Alexander, J. J. G., 111
Alison, Richard: psalm tunes, 157
Allegri, Gregorio: *Miserere*, 361

Amadei, Filippo, 378
American libraries: acquisition of English family papers, 308, n.13
Amsterdam, 170, 377: music publishing, 395
Andrade, Drogo de Goes Lara de, 106
Andrews, Hilda, 177, n.40, 229
Angers, 376
Anglès, Higini, 51, n.16
Anne, *Queen of England*, 403, 408, 419
Anogia (Crete), 289
Anonymous IV, 66, n.1, 83
Anonymous VI, 100
Antico, Andrea, 129, n.2
Antwerp: St Walburga, 229
Aosta, 99
apprenticeships: music education, 330, 403f, 409f, n.14, 418; records of, 306, 308, n.6
Arber, Edward: *The Term Catalogues*, 317, n.41
Arconati, Felice Maria, 327
Aretousa, Princess, 279f, n.15, n.17
Ariosti, Attilio, 179, n.55
Army Establishment Lists: references to musicians, 312
Arpin, Gille, 113, n.33
Arras, Bibliothèque municipale, 657: *Chansonnier d'Arras*, 30, 33ff, 39, 47, 49, 50: facsimile, 33, n.6; notation, 34–7
art: auctions, 386
articulation: keyboard music, 245*p*
Asakuzu, Koma no, *see* Koma no Asakuzu
Ashtead Manor: accounts for, 308, n.11
askomandoura, 282, n.18
A solis ortus cardine (rondellus), 74f
auctions: bibliographical tools, 384*p*, n.19; catalogues, 384*p*: indexes, 387, n.18; history, 383*p*, n.1ff; prices, 389, n.23
Augsburg, 170
Avery, E. L., *see* Van Lennep, W. B.
à Wood, Anthony, *see* Wood, Anthony à
Aylmer, Admiral, 378, n.59
ayre: English, 210; French, 209
Azzolino, Cardinal, 362

Babell, William, 393
Bach, Johann Sebastian
  cantatas, 261: no.38, 268; no.61, 264; no.161, 273
  chorale preludes: 'Ach, Gott und Herr'

(sic–BWV 693), 269; 'Das alte Jahr vergangen ist' (BWV 614), 270f; 'Erstanden ist der heil'ge Christ' (BWV 628), 269; 'Komm, heiliger Geist' (BWV 651a), 273; *Lob sei* (BWV 704), 266
Clavierübung I, 264; *Clavierübung II*, 264; *Clavierübung III*, 259f, n.1–7, n.37f: cantus firmus in, 264, 267, 272f; and Catechisms, 262, 264, 276; definition of term, 261; fugue in, 264, 275f; and Holy Trinity, 262, n.14f; modality in, 265f, n.20, 274; motifs in, 269*p*; paraphrase in, 273ff; plan, 262–5; publication of, 259, n.8–9; reviews of, 260f, n.11–13; ritornello structure in, 271f; *stile antico* in, 266*p*; symbolism in, 269; title, 262; 'Allein Gott' (BWV 675), 273f, (BWV 676a) 259, 263, (BWV 677) 263, 265f, 273f; 'Aus tiefer Not' (BWV 686), 262f, 266*p*, n.26 (BWV 687) 269; 'Christ unser Herr' (BWV 684), 274; 'Dies sind die heil'gen zehn Gebot' (BWV 678), 269f, 274f; 'Jesus Christus, unser Heiland' (BWV 688), 263, 269, 272f, n.31–5, (BWV 689) 263, 275; 'Kyrie–Christie–Kyrie' (BWV 669–71), 263f, 266f, (BWV 672–4) 274f; Prelude and Fugue in E flat, 262f, (Fugue) 266f, 275; 'Vater unser' (BWV 682), 263f, 272f; 'Wir glauben all' (BWV 680), 271, 274f, (BWV 681) 262f, 271f
Clavierübung IV, 264
extemporisations, 261
fingerings, 239
and French *Ouverture*, 264
fugues, 264, 275f: in C (BWV 547), 265; in E flat, 266*p*, 275
Goldberg Variations, 264
hymnbook, 260, 264, n.17
Mass in B minor, 261
Musikalische Opfer, Das, 261
Orgelbüchlein, 259, 269
Passions, 260
    Prelude and (St Anne) Fugue in E flat, 262f: Fugue, 266*p*, 275
    styles, 260f, 266
    Wohltemperirte Clavier, Das, 261, 264, 269
Bach, Wilhelm Friedemann, 239
bachi (Japanese lute plectrum), 196f, n.12–13
bagpipe, 378: *askomandoura*, 282, n.18
Balarotti, Francesco, 353, n.32: confirmation in post, 331; as copyist, 339; as organist, 347; salary of, 341
Balarotti, Gioseppe, 347: operas, 350; salary, 337
Baldeysaria, Benedette, 418
Baldwin, John, 229
ballade, 115f
ballads: political, 421
ballet: in China, 191; in Hanover, 184, n.74
Baltic states, 358
Bancroft, Richard, *Archbishop of Canterbury*, 212
bandora: music, in 'Braye Tablature Book', 157
Banshe mode (Tang music), 202
Banshiki mode (Tang music), 199, n.17, 202f
baptisms: registration of, 305

Baratta, Carlo, 329f: confirmation in post, 331
Barber Institute, *see* Birmingham University
Barclay Squire, William: article on auction sales, 386f, n.14; and Fitzwilliam Virginal Book, 228
Bargrave, John, 372f, n.44
Bargrave, Robert: comments on music, 360, n.13; in Spain, 375, n.48; in Venice, 366, n.26
Barker, John, 163, n.1, n.19: *Twelve Songs*, 163
Baroni, Leonora, 361, n.19
Barrabas dimittitur (motet), 74
Bassani, Giovanni Battista, 349f: Mass in F, 271, n.29; salary of, 333
bass drum: *daouli*, 282, n.18, 289; in Tang music, 192, 200
Basso family, of Bergamo, 325
Bates, William: *The Harmony of the Divine Attributes*, 424
Baud-Bovy, Samuel, 279, n.4, 284
Bedford, Dukes of: household accounts, 308, n.8; reference to Weldon's opera *Judgement of Paris* in papers of, 315, n.36; visit to Rome of 2nd Duke, 365, n.22
Bedford, Arthur: *The great abuse of Musick*, 397
Bedyngham, Johannes, 99f: songs, 100, 114; ?*Durer ne puis*, 114, 120; ?*Mon seul plaisir*, 114f, n.36, 120; ?*O rosa bella*, 112, 114f, n.36, 120
Belgium: book auctions in, 383
Bellinzani, Paolo Benedetto, 350
Belsize Park, London, 422
Bennet, John: psalm tunes, 157
Berg, Duchy of, 170
Bergamo, 323f, n.1: Biblioteca Civica Angelo Mai, 130, 325; Cathedral, 326, 342f, 347 (castrati), 329 (music), 353; economy, 353f; holiday, 324, 342; mayor, 325; musicians, 325*p*, 352*p*; outtownships, 350f; parochial archives, 325*p*; plagues, 326, n.12; prosperity, 327; S. Defendente in Borgo S. Leonardo, 326, n.10; S. Grata, 351; S. Maria, 326; S. Pancrazio, 325f, n.8; trade, 323, 350
    Misericordia Maggiore, 323, n.2–3, 342, 346, 350: Council, 324, 343, 352; *Giornali*, 324; *Institutioni e ordini*, 324, n.4, 343, 345; *Inventarium*, 325; *Scritti*, 325, 352; *Scritture presentate al consiglio*, 324, n.5; *Spese della chiesa*, 324, 341; *Terminationes*, 324, 343, 345
    S. Maria Maggiore, 323*p*, n.2: acoustics, 327; archive, 325; *chierici servienti*, 323, 325, n.17; college of, 323, 327f (free education at), 323, 328, n.14–16; decoration of, 327, n.13; rebuilding of, 327; vergers, 323, 328, n.17
    instruments: chittarone, 347; cornett, 347; double bass, 334, 342, 347, 351*p*; lute, 347; oboe, 330, 334, 347, 350; organ, 326f, 347, 352; Sacra orchestra, 340; theorbo, 343, 347, 352; trombone, 352; violone, 351*p*

music, 325*p*: binding, 338f; education, 327ff, 353; inventories, 335ff; plainsong, 329, 353; purchase of, 341; repertory, 335ff
musicians, 325*p*: *choristi*, 329; instrumentalists, 330*p*, 340, 343, 346*p*; masters, 327, 332*p*; organists, 327f, 330, 340, 347; singers, 329*p*, 340, 343, 349*p*; absences, 342*p*, 350; apprenticeships, 330; confirmations in post, 330f; fines, 343; holidays, 342*p*, 350; salaries, 332*p*, 352*p*; status, 352*p*; visits by, 327f, 346*p*, 350; *see also* individual musicians
organs of, 326f, 347, 352
plainsong, 329, 353
Sacra orchestra, 340
Berlin, 181: French psalm book published in, 397, n.64; (East), Deutsche Staatsbibliothek, MS Lynar A1-2, 229; (West) Staatsbibliothek, MS theor. 1599, 107, n.19, 111, Kupferstichkabinett MS (78 C 28), 112, 124
Bernardi, Bartolomeo, 351
Bernardi, Marc 'Antonio, of Bergamo: absences, 342, 345; appointment, 351; confirmation in post, 331; fines on, 344; salary, 334, 341; *Messa di morti* à 4, 336; *Messe* à 8, 337f; *Salmi* à 8, 335, 337
Bertie family: letters, 316, n.39, 367; Charles, 370, n.40; Peregrine, 367
Besseler, Heinrich, 104, 114f, 118f, n.38, 124
Bettoni, Santino, 329, 332
Bevin, Edward, 252f, n.10, *253*
Bevin, Elway, 228, 252f, n.10, *253*
Bickham, George: *The Musical Entertainer*, 394
binariae, 47
Binchois, Gille de Bins dit, 101
binding of music, 338f
Birmingham University, Barber MSS, 5001-2, 163, n.17, 165
Birnbaum, J. A., 260f
births, registration of, 305
bishop's transcripts, 305f
black notation, 110, n.26-7, 113
Blainville, Charles Henri de, 379
Blois, 376
Blow, John: music in *GB-Bu* 5001, 163; *Amphion Anglicus*, 394; keyboard music, 229f
Bodel, Jehan: *Jeu de St Nicholas*, 36
Boerhaave, Hermann, 377
Böhm, Georg, 268f
Bologna, 101, 104, 113, n.31, 119, 349, 377, n.57: Civico Museo Bibliografico-Musicale, 99, 147: MS Q 70, 136f, 146, n.11, *137*, *139*; MS Q 73, 146; MS Q 74, *139*, 146; MS Q 75, 130, 142; S. Petronio, 101f, n.5, 119
Bond, Capel, 163
Bonetti, Ro., 102
Bonnaventure, ?: performing at Chiesa Nova, Rome, 359
Bonomino family, of Bergamo, 328
Bononcini, Giovanni Battista, 408
books: auctions, 383*p* (bibliographical tools), 384*p*; collecting, 388*p*, n.22

Border, Richard, 162
Bossinensis, Franciscus: lute volume of 1511, 136,*137*
Boston, J. L., 228, 231*p*, 243, 246, 249f
Boswell, Eleanore: *The Restoration Court Stage, 1660-1702*, 314
Bowers, Roger, 66, 86
branle, 220f
Braye, *Lords*, 160*p*: *5th Lord*, 160; Braye Tablature Book, 157*p*, n.5, 162, 165
Breitkopf family: sale of MSS, 390, n.32
Brescia, 323, 346
Brevi, Giovanni Battista, 342
Bristol, 228, 252
Britton, Thomas: music library, 390*p*; ownership of psalm-tune books, 396f, n.62; Rosicrucian collection, 384f, n.8, 390ff, n.21, n.29
Broadley, Alexander Meyrick: *The Annals of the Haymarket*, 315
Bromley, William, 360
Brown, Alan M., 229
Brown, David Clifford, 219, n.27
Browne, John, 155f, n.1-2: and Cambridge City Wait of same name, 157, n.6; appointment as Clerk of Parliaments, 155; as composer, 158, 164; daughter, 161, n.10; death, 155; documents of, 155, n.1, 161f, n.11; father, 160; friendship with Lawes and Milton, 164f; hand, 155, *156*, 157f, *159*, 161, 164; as law student, 155; as lyra-viol performer, 164; marriages (Temperance Crewe) 155, (Elizabeth Packer) 155, 164; member of Middle Temple, 155; music MSS, 155*p*, (dispersal) 161*p*, (at Stanford Hall) 161f, (Osborn lute MS) 162f, n.15, 165; ownership of Tailour's *Sacred Hymns*, 157, 164; Pavan by, *159*; signature, *159*
Bruce, *Lord*: visit to Venice, 366
Brunham, Robert de, 89
Bruno, Giovanni Battista Caletti di, 229
Brussels: Bavarian court, 169, n.7
Buckingham, Earl of, 213
Bugaku (dance music), 191
Bugden House, Huntingdonshire: *seat of the bishops of Lincoln*, 422
'Buildings, The' (keyboard piece), 231, 243
Bukofzer, Manfred Fritz, 66, n.2, 71, n.4
Bull, John: hand, 228, 256; ownership of *GB-Cfm* Marlay Add.15, 230
keyboard music: 227*p*, 234f; 'Chromatic Galliard', 234, 250; 'Fantasia', 234, 243, 254; 'Fantastic Galliard', 234, 239; 'Fantastic Pavan', 234, 247; 'Go from my window', 234, 246; 'The King's Hunt', 234, 242, 247; 'In nomine', 234, 246; 'Irish Toy', 234, 243; 'Meridian Alman', 236; 'Miserere', 230, 234, 243f, 252; 'Prelude', 229, 234, 238; 'Regina Galliard', 234, 242, 245f
Bulletin of the Institute of Historical Research, 309
Bulletin of the National Register of Archives, 309

Bunbury, Priscilla, 243, 249f: Virginal Book, 227f, n.2
Burgos, Monasterio de Las Huelgas, 51
Burgundy: ducal chapel, 100f, 119
burials: indexes to, 306; registration of, 305
Burney, Charles: and Defoe's *Augusta Triumphans*, 404; plan for an academy of music, 406, 413f; Newspaper Collection, 315; travels of, 357, 379
Bury St Edmunds, 155, 417: Benedictine Abbey, 66, 83
But, Du, 376
Buxtehude, Dietrich, 268: *Fried- und Freudenreiche Hinfarth*, 262
Byrd, William 209f, n.3: and My Ladye Nevells Book, 229; pupils, 228; as teacher of Orlando Gibbons, 221
music: sale of, 389, n.27; consort songs, 218f; *Lullaby-be still*, 157; verse anthems, 223; word-setting in, 220
keyboard music, 227p, 234f, 256: fingerings, 229; 'Carman's Whistle', 234, 246; 'Fortune', 234, 240; 'Galliard for the Victory', 234, 240; 'The Ghost', 234, 247; 'Ground', 234, 239, 251; 'Hugh Aston's Ground', 234, 239; 'My Lady Nevell's Ground', 234, 240, 243; 'Pavan', 235, 239, 251f; 'Walsingham Variations', 235, 244

Caelius Sedulius: hymn *A solis ortus*, 76
Cairncross index (Public Record Office), 313f
Calendar, reform of, 304
Caletti, Giovanni Battista, 229
Calisto (masque): payment of musicians for, 311
Callcott, James, 161
Cambrai, 113: Cathedral, 113
Cambridge
Fitzwilliam Museum: MS 32.G.29 (Fitzwilliam Virginal Book), 228, 240, 248, 250; MS Marlay Add.5 (William Tisdale's Virginal Book), 227, n.2, 230
Gonville and Caius College: MS 543/512, 74, 80
King's College, Rowe Music Library: MSS 112-13, 156p, n.4, n.9, 159f, 165; MS 113 A, 154p, 165; MSS 114-17, 156p, 159f, 165
Peterhouse: travelling scholarships, 357
Sandars Lectures, 387
Trinity College, 362
University, 216, 357, 371, 411: list of students, 308
University Library, 307: auction catalogues, 386, n.12; MS Dd. 4. 22, 229, Add.710, 67
Camden Society, 308
Camp, Anthony John: *Wills and their Whereabouts*, 304
Campion, Thomas, 210
Campra, André: *L'Europe Gallante*, 370
cancel sheets: Petrucci's editions, 129
Cannons, home of the Duke of Chandos, 404, n.8, 422
Canterbury: Institute of Heraldic and

Genealogical Studies, 306; Prerogative Court, 304f
canto figurato: instruction in, 327
cantus firmus: chorale preludes, 264
Caravaggio, 350
Cardigan, *Lord*, 377
Carissimi, Giacomo, 359, n.6
Carleton, *Sir* Dudley, 213, n.8
carol: medieval England, 218; in *GB-Lbm* Egerton 3307, 104
Caroline Wilhelmina of Ansbach, *Queen of England*, 176, n.35f, 181, n.61, 408, n.12, 415: library of, 181, n.62
Carteret, *Sir* Philip, *156*
Case, John: *The Praise of Musick in Churches*, 397, n.66
castrati, 360: in Cesti's *L'Argia*, 373; at Bergamo, 329; in Rome, 359
catalogues: auctions, 384p; *see also* individual catalogues
catch, 393f; catch-books, sale of, 394, n.46f; societies, 394
Catechism: Lutheran church, 260
cathedrals: accounts, 307; deeds, 307; records, 305, 307p
Catholic Chapel of James II, 310f, n.19
Catholic Society, 306
Cavalli, Pietro Francesco: *Artemisia*, 366; *La Deidamia*, 367; *Scipione Africano*, 367
cavalry regiments: instruments in, 311
Cave family, of Yorkshire, 161f
Cave, *Sir* Roger, *2nd Baronet*, 161
Cave, *Sir* Thomas, *3rd Baronet*, 161, 163
Cazzati, Maurizio, 327, 332, 339, 345, 351: choice of repertory at Bergamo, 338; salary, 332; *Salmi* à 8, 342
Ceccarelli, Giuseppe, 147
Celle, 185
Cesareni, Diego, 342, 353
Cesti, Antonio Pietro: *L'Argia*, 373
Chamberlain, John, 213, n.8
Chamberlayne, Edward: *Angliae notitia*, 314; *Magnae Britanniae notitia*, 314
chamber music: psalm tunes as, 396f; publication of, 17th-18th-century England, 391; sale of at auction, 392p
Chandos, Duke of, 404, n.8
Chansonnier Cangé, *see* Paris, Bibliothèque nationale, fonds fr.846
Chansonnier d'Arras, *see* Arras, Bibliothèque municipale, 657
Chansonnier de Noailles, *see* Paris, Bibliothèque nationale, fonds fr.12615
Chansonnier du Vatican, *see* Rome, Vatican City, Biblioteca Apostolica Vaticana, Reg.Cat.1490(a)
Chapel Royal, 209p, 310: choirboy plays, 218; Gentlemen, 215, n.16-17, 311, n.22; at Holyrood House, Edinburgh, 214, n.12-14; instruments in, 312, n.29; on James I's Scottish Progress, 212p, 224; list of anthems performed, 311; Master of the Children, 311; Old Cheque Book, 311, n.21; references in Lord Chamberlain's books,

313; of Scotland, 214f; word-book, 311, n.23
Chapman, Catherine, 129, n.2
Chaprigni, Monsieur, 365
chapter act-books, 307
Chardin, *Sir* John, 377, n.56
Charles, *Duke of Orleans*: *Mi verry joy*, 115, n.36
Charles VI, *Holy Roman Emperor*, 373–4
Charles I, *King of England*, 215, 357
Charles II, *King of England*: depicted in Defoe's *Roxana*, 416; musical taste, 392f; musicians of, 310
Chatsworth House, Derbyshire, 308, n.10
Chelmsford, Essex: wills for, 305
Chesterfield, *Lord*, 374
Chiari, 351
Chicago, Newberry Library: MS 54.1., 100; partbooks in, 387, n.17
Chichester Cathedral, 210: records, 307
Child, William: psalm-settings, 396
China: isolation from Japan, 193, 196; Japanese missions, 193; court music, 191, 193f, n.4, 203; lute technique in, 196f, n.11–13; mouth organ technique in, 202
chittarone, 347
choirboy plays, 218
choirs: church records, 307
chorales: preludes, 262, 264; retardation of, 204; singing, 204, 264, n.17
chord clusters: Tang music, 192f, 202
Chôshû-kyô, Japanese Ministerial Chief, 195
Chôshû-kyô ôteki-fu, 195
Christie's, *auctioneers*, 385
Christina, *Queen of Sweden*, 362, 364; conversion to Catholicism, 372
Christ's Hospital: Council of Almoners, 412; Court of Governors, 412; Great Hall, 404, 412, 413; income, 409, n.14, 411; music master, 411; Music School, 411f, n.16; opera at, 404, 411; organ at, 412, n.15; proposed academy of music, 403*p*, n.2, (salaries of masters) 409
Chû Ôga ryûteki yôroku-fu (flute MS), 201, n.21
Churchwardens' accounts, 307
circles, uses of in rondelli, 79f, 90f
Clarke, Jeremiah: anthem *The Lord is my strength*, 420, n.32
Clavell, Robert: catalogue of new and reprinted books by, 317
Clement Matchett's Virginal Book, 227f, n.2, 240, 247f, 250, 252, 256
Clenche, John, 367
clergy: 17th–18th-century England, as collectors of music, 392
Clerk, *Sir* John, of Penicuik: in Italy, 358f, n.3, 361, 379; in Leyden, 376; in Paris, 371; in Vienna, 373f; harpsichord tuition, 376f; pupil of Corelli, 365, 376
Clifford, *Lord* Henry, 375f
climacus, 34f, 39, 41, 45, 50f
clivis, 39, 50
Clusone, 350

coffee houses: music in, 393
Coimbra: Monastery of Santa Cruz, 106
Coke, Thomas: collection of theatre documents submitted to, 314f
Colista, Lelio, 364
Collections for a History of Musicians (*GB-Ob* Mus.e.17), 310
collectors of music, *see* music, collecting
Colombina chansonnier, 108
Colonna, S. Alessandro, 343, n.27
concert halls: 17th–18th-century England, 393
concerts: England, 389f, n.28–9, 393f, 404, 410f, 414, 417
Condit, Jonathan, 199
Confucius: 'Music of the Five Confucian Virtues', 192, n.2
Congreve, William: letters, 316
conjunctura, 34f, 39f, 41, 43, 45, 48
consort song, 218f, 223
Constantinople, fall of, 279
contrabasso, *see* double bass
Cooke, Henry ('Captain Cooke'): music in *GB-Bu* 5001, 163
Cooper, William, *auctioneer*, 384, n.6: list of catalogues compiled by, 385, n.9
Copenhagen, Det kongelige Bibliotek, MS 1848, 112, 124
Coprario, John, 158f: 'The Lord's Masque', 236
copyists, music, 390: at Düsseldorf, 180f, n.70–72, n.84; *see also* Steffani, Agostino
Coram, Thomas, 406
Cordiforme chansonnier, 112
Corelli, Arcangelo, 350, 365, 408: performance by, 360, n.17; publication of music in England, 393f; teacher of Sir John Clerk, 365, 376; concertos, 394; sonatas, 394
cori spezzati, 366
Cornet, Peeter, 229
cornett, 347, 368, n.36
corporation minutes, 308
Corporation of Musicians, 312, n.26
Coryat, Thomas, 366, n.25
Cosimi, 379
Cosyn, Benjamin: keyboard music, 227, n.2; as scribe, 228
Cosyn, John: virginal book, 230
Couperin, François *le Grand*, 243, 262; *Messe pour les Paroisses*, 262
court act-books: entries for administrations, 305
Coussemaker, Charles-Edmond-Henri de, 77, n.7: edition of Adam de la Halle's music, 30, 36, 49
Coventry, Holy Trinity, 163
Cranfield, G. A.: *A Hand-List ...*, 316
Crema, 350
Cremona, 350
Crete, 279*p*, n.1: Anogia, 288, n.26; dialect, 279, 281; folksong, 279f, n.9, 282, n.19, 288f, n.26, *see also Erotokritos*; Irakleion, 284; musical instruments, 282, 287, *see also* individual instruments; 'return' songs, 281, n.16; *rizitika*, 280; singing, 284, n.20f; Sitia, 282; under Turkish rule, 282; wedding song, 'The Recognition', 281

Crewe, Temperance, 155
Crewe, *Sir* Thomas, 155
Crivelli, Giovanni Battista: dismissal from S. Maria Maggiore, Bergamo, 345; inventory of music at Bergamo, 335f; *motetti* à 2–5, 336
Cromwell, Anne: virginal book, 227
Cummings, William Hayman, 314, n.31
Cyprus, 279, n.4, 284

Daily Courant, The, 315
Dajôdaijin (Prime Minister) of Japan, 195
Dalhousie, Earl of, 228
Dallam family: organ in Christ's Hospital (sic), 412, n.15; Thomas's organ for Holyrood House, Edinburgh, 213
Dallas Lutebook, 230, n.5
Dallington, *Sir* Robert: *Survey of the Great Dukes ...*, 368; *The View of France*, 369
dance: Bugaku repertoire, 191; in 17th-century France, 209, 369*p*, 376; in Defoe's *Roxana*, 416, n.25; in Purcell's *Dioclesian*, 371; *see also* individual dances
daouli, 282, n.18, *289*
Dart, Robert Thurston, 21f: as editor, 29, 227; interest in oriental notations, 192f, 204; and Musica Britannica, 29, 227; preface to *Parthenia*, 257; recordings of English keyboard music, 227; views on editing, 29; visit to USA, 215f
dates: problems of interpretation, 303f
David, Robert, 101, n.3
Davis and Orioli, *booksellers*, 160
Day, C. L. *and* Murrie, E. B.: *English Song-Books, 1651–1702*, 317
Declared Accounts (Treasury), 310f
Deering, Richard, *see* Dering, Richard
Defoe, Daniel: Academy for women, 415; and Charles Burney, 413f; and Duke of Chandos, 404, n.8; music, views on, 403f, 414f, 420; patrons, 408, 415; proposals for musical reform, 403f, n.4–5, 406*p*; and 'Scandal Club', 406
  works, 404, n.6: *Augusta Triumphans ...*, 403, n.1, 405f, n.9, 412ff, n.18, 417, 424; *Colonel Jack*, 416, n.24; *The Compleat English Gentleman*, 414, n.21; *The Complete English Tradesman*, 407; *An Essay upon Literature*, 423f; *An Essay upon Projects* 405, 415; *The Family Instructor*, 417, 421, n.31f; *The Generous Projector*, 405; *The History of the Plague in London*, 418; *Memoirs of a Cavalier*, 415f, n.23–4; *Memoirs of Captain Carleton*, 423; *Mercurius Politicus*, 418f, 423; *Moll Flanders*, 415ff, n.23, 422; *Religious Courtship*, 417, n.26; *Review of the Affairs of France*, 404, n.7, 406, 418, 420, 423; *Robinson Crusoe*, 404; *Roxana*, 416, n.25; *Of Royall Educacion*, 415; *Second Thoughts are Best*, 417; *Serious Reflections during the Life ... of Robinson Crusoe*, 420f, n.29–30; *A Tour Through the Whole Island of Great Britain*, 422
de la Halle, Adam, *see* Adam de la Halle
Denmark: book auctions, 383

Derby, Robert, 101, n.3
Derham, *Sir* Thomas, 367, n.30, 369
Dering, Richard, 164
d'Este, Isotta, 109, n.23f
d'Este, Rinaldo Maria, 102, 110ff
Destouches, André Cardinal: *Amadis de Grece*, 371
Deutsch, Otto Erich, 387, n.14
Devonshire, Dukes of: family papers, 308, n.10
diaries, 316, 358, 367, 393
Dijon, Bibliothèque municipale, MS 517 (Dijon chansonnier), 108, 124
dissonance: Tang music, 192f, 202f
Dittmer, Luther Albert, 77, n.9
Dobbyus, William, 364
Dodecanese islands, 279
Dodwell, Henry: *A Treatise concerning the Lawfulness of Instrumental Music in Holy Offices*, 397
dô kyoku (Tang music), 194
Dolmetsch, Nathalie, 160
Domestic Papers: Calendars, 312f; and the Corporation of Musicians, 312; references to musicians, 310, 312f
Doni, Giovanni Battista, 361
Dorset, *4th Earl*, 212; *6th Earl*, 314, n.30
dot: Tang notation, 200f
double bass, 334, 342, 347, 351*p*; *see also* violone
double-stroke ornaments: keyboard music, 251, 255f
Dowland, John: lute-songs, 210
drama, *see* theatre
Dresden, 172, n.21
drum, *see* bass drum
Drummond, James, *Earl of Perth*, 364f
Drummond, William, 377, n.57
Drury Lane Theatre, 408, 418f: accounts of, 315; advertisements of performances, 315; performance of Weldon's *Judgement of Paris*, 315, n.36
Dryden, John: letters, 316
Dublin: St Thomas', 66f; Troper, 67; Virginal MS, 230, n.5
Dubut, 376
Dufay, Guillaume, 101, 113, n.32–4: music, 109, 114; songs, 109, 113, 120f, (*Adieu m'amour*) 103f, 121, (*Entre les plus plaines*) 104, 121, (?*Mon seul plaisir*) 114f, n.36, 120, (*Le serviteur hault guerdonné*) 114f, 121; style, 114
Dunstable, John, 99, 114, 119, 209: death, 115; *Durer ne puis*, 114, 120; ?*O rosa bella*, 112, 114f, n.36, 120
D'Urfey, Thomas: *New Poems*, 317
Durham: Cathedral Library, MS C.I.20, 74
Düsseldorf, 170ff, n.11, n.15–17, n.22, n.26–7, 173f, n.32, 184f

Ecord family, of Bergamo, 328: Gioyanni, 330, 334, (confirmation in post) 331, 347, (fines on) 344, (salary) 334
Edinburgh, *224*: College, 225; High Court of the Justiciary, 223, n.29; Holyrood House, 212f, n.10, 223f, (Chapel) 213f, n.11–14,

225; King James I's Progress, 213f, 223f, n.29; University, 371
education, see music education
Einstein, Alfred, 172, n.25, 177f, n.39, n.44–5, n.48
Elizabeth I, *Queen of England*, 212
Ellis, William, 230
Elzevier, Louis, 383
Encarnação, D. Pedro da, 106, n.16–17
Engi period (Japanese history), 198
England: first book auction, 384, n.6; league with France, 211; musical influence abroad, 99; Reformation in, 209; Restoration, 219, 252; see also individual areas, composers, forms, institutions
enseignemens des philosophes, Les, 46
Epsom: town waits, 422
Ernst August, *Elector of Hanover*, 181, 185
Erotokritos, 279*p*, n.1–3, n.6: character in folklore, 281, n.17; accompaniment, 282, see also individual instruments; editions, 280f, n.10, n.13; 'Farewell', 281; fragments, 281, n.15; melodies, 279f, n.4–5, 282, see also Rotokritos melody; oral tradition of, 281, n.14, 289; performance, 280, n.7–8, 281, n.14, 282, 284; popularity, 281f; sources, 280f, n.10, n.13; story, 280; 'Tale', 281, n.15, 290, n.24; text, 280f, n.11
Erroll, Countess of, 364
Escorial, El, 375, n.48: chansonnier I, 112; II, 112, 123
Essex: bishop's transcripts for, 305f
Etenraku (Japanese zither piece), 199
Eton School: list of pupils, 308
eunuchs, see castrati
Evans, *auctioneers*, 385, n.11
Evelyn, John: diaries, 316; at Christ's Hospital, 412, n.17; in Rome, 359, n.7–8, 361; in Venice, 366; lessons on theorbo, 376; possible ownership of Drexel MSS 4180–5, 215
Exeter, 216: Cathedral Library, 422
Eydon, 155

false relations: English church music, 209; English keyboard music, 254
family accounts, 308
fantasia style, 261
Farmer, John: psalm tunes, 157
Farnaby, Giles: keyboard music, 227, ('Meridian Alman') 236
Farnaby, Richard: 'Meridian Alman', 236
Farrant, Richard, 411
Fayrfax, Robert, 101, 118: and *GB-Lbm* Add.5465, 110, n.28, 119
Feckler, Joseph Paris, 179, n.56, 184
Fedeli, Ruggiero, 170f, n.15
Fellowes, Edmund Horace, 210, 228
Ferdinand III, *Holy Roman Emperor*, 368
Ferdinand Charles, *Archduke*, 372
Ferrabosco, Alfonso II: pavans, 160
Ferrara, 99f, 105f, 109f, 113, 348: Bergamo musicians in, 342; cathedral, 101, n.4, 103, 105; court music at, 109f; English Jesuits

of, 361f; G. B. Legrenzi in, 345, n.28; and Oporto song collection, 99; school of illumination, 111
Ferronato, Lodovico, 341, n.25–6: confirmation in post, 331; fines on, 344; salary, 334
Févin, Antoine de, 140f, *141*, 149
Fielding, *Lord*, 359
Finch, *Sir* John, 370, n.39
fingering, English keyboard music, 227*p*: sources, 227*p*; index of pieces, 231*p*; leaps, 241, 245; repeated notes, 245*p*, n.9; spans, 245, 247; techniques, 238*p*, (change fingering) 243f, 249, (fingers-over) 242, 244, 251, (paired fingering) 238*p*; thumb, 238*p*, 256, (thumbs-under technique) 242f, 251; individual fingers, 238, 252, 254f
finger-plucking techniques: Tang music, 196*p*, n.11–14
fistula, 374, n.46
Fitzwilliam Virginal Book, 228, 240, 248, 250
Fleming, Daniel, 308, n.9
Florence, 113, 350: Academy of the Svogliati, 361; Biblioteca del Conservatorio di Musica 'L. Cherubini', MS D 331–2, 177, n.41; Biblioteca nazionale centrale, MS Magl.XIX 176, 124, MS Magl.XIX 178, 112; Biblioteca Riccardiana, MS 2356, 112, 120; opera in, 367f, n.35–6; paintings of, 358; S. Annunziata, 368
flute (Tang music), 192, 194, 198f, 201f; ornamentation, 201f, 204; Japanese sources, 196, 198, n.15, 201, n.21; tablature, 192, 201; Japanese teachers, 198
Folena, Gianfranco, 109, 113
folksong: Crete, 279*p*; Greece, 281; see also *Erotokritos*
Fontana, Antonio, 342, 348f
Forkel, Johann Nikolaus, 275, n.36
Forster, Will: virginal book, 228, 240, 256
Fossombrone, 129f, 136, 138, 142, 144: Biblioteca Passionei, 147
Foundling Hospital, 406, 412f: performances of *Messiah*, 413
Fountains Fragment, 66, 71, n.4, 74*p*, 79
Fournival, Richart de: Bestiary, 36
France: Ambassador to England, 211; British visitors to, 357f, 369*p*; league with England, 211; rule of Cyprus, 279; music, in Italy, 146; musicians, (in England) 393, n.40, (in Hanover) 185f; *Ouverture*, 264; psalm editions, 397, n.63; song tradition, 15th-century, 112
Franconian notation, 39, 43
Frederick Louis, *Prince of Wales*, 181
Frescobaldi, Girolamo, 228, 268: *Fiore musicali*, 271
Froberger, Johann Jacob, 268
Frye, Walter, 100
fugue, 264, 268, 271
Fujiwara no Moronaga, *Prime Minister of Japan*, 195, 198f, 204
Fujiwara no Sadatoshi, 194f, n.7, n.10, 202: biography in *Sandai-jitsuroku*, 194f; performances of, 196f, n.10
Fuller Maitland, John Alexander, 228

Fulsham, Robertus, 102
Fushiminomiya-bon biwa-fu (Tang MS), 194, 196, 202
Fux, Johann Joseph, 267f, 275: *Gradus ad Parnassum*, 267, n.22

Gagaku, 191, 203: handbook *Zoku-Kyôkunshô*, 202
Gaidifer d'Avion, 35
Gailhard, John, 376, n.52
gakubyôshi (Tang metrical variant), 201
gaku-sô, 199; *see also* zither
Galfridus de Anglia, 100, 109, 113, 115: songs, 113, 115f; *Io zemo*, 115f
Galicanos, Prince: *Proserpina rapita*, 361
Gallicus, Johannes: *De ritu canendi*, 110, n.26
Galloway, *Dean*, of Scottish Chapel Royal, 215
Gamô, Mitsuko, 191f, n.1
Garfias, Robert, 200, n.20
Gay, John: *Beggar's Opera*, 417
Gellius, Aulus, 111
Geminiani, Francesco Xaverio, 408
General Register Office: *Lists of Non-Parochial Registers ...*, 307
Genji monogatari ('Tale of Genji'), 199
Genoa, 346, 350, 417: Archbishop of, 87; Jesuit Church, 359; music in, 365; visit by Sir John Clerk, 365
Gentlemen's Journal, The, 316
Georg August, *Elector of Hanover, see* George II, *King of England*
Georg Ludwig, *Elector of Hanover*, 171, 181f, 185f
George I, *King of England*, 181
George II, *King of England*, 176, 181, 408, 413
George, *Prince of Greece, High Commissioner of Crete*, 281f, 283
Germany, 362: book auctions in, 383; chorale-singing in, 204; keyboard music, 229; influence of Italian music, 260f
Gervays [Gervasius de Anglia], 100
Gesualdo, Carlo, 377, n.54
Ghirardi, Biaggio, 346
Gib, John, 214
Gibbons, Orlando, 209f, 215, 224: music in *GB-Lbm* Add.29366–8, 164; *Cries of London*, 216; *Do not Repine, fair Sun*, 215p, n.28, (first performance) 223f; fantasias à 3, 216; *Great King of Gods*, 215, n.18, 218f, n.26; *Hosanna to the Son of David*, 223; verse anthems, 218f, n.27, (form) 220, 221; keyboard music, 227f, 231, 236f, 254; 'Ayre', 229, 236; Preludes, 229, 237f, 241, 244; 'The woods so wild', 237, 241, 244, 247, 250
Gibson, J. S. W.: *Wills and Where to Find Them*, 304
Giraldi, Guglielmo, 111f
Giunta family, 138, 147, n.20
Glarean, Heinrich: *Dodecachordon*, 389, n.24–5
Gloucester Cathedral, 216, n.23
Gogen kin-fu (zither MS), 197, 200, 203f
Golden Legend of St Katherine, 87f

Goodson, Richard, 164
Goshôraku ('Music of the Five Confucian Virtues'), 192, n.2
Gouge, E. (painter), 377f, n.58
Gozzini, Giacomo, 341
Greece, 279, 281: folksong, 281
Greene, Maurice, 183
Greensleeves, 421
Gresham College (Guildhall Library), MS G.mus.418, 174, 183f, n.67
Grolier Club, 386, n.12
Groombridge Place, Kent, 155
Grove, *Sir* George: *A Dictionary of Music and Musicians*, 386f, n.14
Guildhall Library: handlists of holdings, 307; *London Rates Assessments and Inhabitants Lists*, 307; *Parish Registers: a Handlist*, 306; *see also* Gresham College
Guild of Parish Clerks, London, 102, n.7: Leet Book, 102
Guillaume d'Amiens, Paignour, 35
guitar, 376

Haas, Otto, 160
Haberl, Franz Xaver, 102, n.8
Hakuga (Chôshû-kyô, Japanese ministerial chief), 195, 198f, 201
Hakuga no fue-fu (flute scores of Hakuga), 195, n.9, 198, n.15
Hall, Joseph, *Bishop of Norwich*, 216f, n.25: (poem) *Do not Repine*, 216, 220; *Virgidemiae*, 216
Halle, Adam de la, *see* Adam de la Halle
Hamburg, 261, 411
Hampshire Record Office: Haymarket account book, 315, n.35
Hampton Court Conference (1604), 211
Hanboys, John, 79f, 89
Handel, George Frideric, 408: Kapellmeister at Hanover, 170, 180, n.59; influence of A. Steffani, 169, n.4–5; tutor to the British royal family, 415; publication of music, 390; sale of keyboard music, 393; chamber duets and trios, 180; *Messiah*, 413; operas, 169, n.1
Handlo, Robert de: treatise, 76p, n.8, 83f, n.12, 87
Handschin, Jacques Samuel, 66, n.2, 80
Hanover, 169f, 172, n.29, 176, 180f, 184: 9th Electorate, 169, n.6; Electoral Music Library, 181, n.62; Landes-bibliothek, 185; Niedersächsisches Hauptstaatsarchiv, 185; treasury accounts, 185; ballets in, 184, n.74; music copyists, 184f, n.70–72, n.84; opera in, 169, n.2, 171, n.18, n.20, 173f, n.32, 180f, n.57, 184f; opera house closure, 171
Harleian Society, 308: Register Series, 306
harpsichord, 376f, 409, 415
Harrison, Frank Llewellyn, 74f, n.6, 85, n.13
Harrow School: lists of pupils, 308
Harvard University: auction catalogues, 386, n.12; Theatre Collection, 314, n.32
Hawkins, *Sir* John: *A General History ...*, 181, n.63, 386, n.13; *Memoirs of the Life of*

Agostino Steffani, 170, n.14, 172, 173, n.33
Haym, Nicola Francesco, 379, 392
Haymarket Theatre, 418: documents of, 315
hearth-tax, 307
Heian period (Japanese history), 199f
Heidelberg, 173, n.32
Henry VIII, *King of England*, 415
Henry, *Prince of Wales*, 216, 223
Herbert, Lord, of Cherbury, 375, n.49
Herculano, Alexandre, 106, n.18
Hermann, Hermann Julius, 111
Hertford: assizes, 421
hichiriki (double reed pipe), 192, 199, 201, 203: tablature, 192, 199, n.17
Hill, Joseph, 383, n.5
Hilton, John II: *Catch that catch can*, 394
Hiromasa, Minamoto no, *see* Minamoto no Hiromasa
Hirsch, Paul Adolf, 387
Historical Manuscripts Commission, 161: Office of, 309, n.14–15; reports, 308, (*Guides to the Reports*) 309; work, 308f; *see also* National Register of Archives
Hodgson & Co., *auctioneers*, 163, 385, n.11
Holland, 362, 383: keyboard music, 229
Holmes, John, 228f
Hooper, Edmund: 'Almain', 237; *Behold it is Christ*, 157
Horace, 423
Horse Guards, Grenadiers of the: musicians in, 312
Hostis Herodes impie (rondellus), 70, 76
House of Lords Record Office, 161
Howell, James: *Instructions ... for Forraine Travel*, 358, n.2; views on Paris, 369
Huguenot Society, 306
Hume, Tobias: *Poeticall Musicke*, 162
Humfrey, Pelham, 163
Huntington Library, San Marino, California, 386, n.12
hyaku (Tang notation), 200
Hyatt King, Alec: *Some British Collectors of Music*, 387, n.15
hymns: singing of, in England, 395f; *see also* chorales, metrical psalms
Hyôjô mode (Tang music), 199

Ichikotsu mode, 202
Iliffe, George, 157
Illinois University: Music Library, 157, 161f, n.13
illumination, 111: *see also* individual MSS
imitation: English church music, 209
incidental music, 17th–18th-century plays: publication date of, 318
Index Library series, 305
Innsbruck, 372
Institute of Heraldic and Genealogical Studies (Canterbury), 306
Institute of Historical Research: *Bulletin*, 309
instrumental music: 17th–18th-century England, 394f
Intermezzi, 368
inventories: in wills, 305
Ionic mode, 369

Irakleion (Crete), 284
Italy: academies, 362f, 365f; British visitors to, 357*p*; churches, 361; church music, 359, n.4; depicted in Defoe's *Memoirs of a Cavalier*, 416; French music in, 146; keyboard music, 229; madrigal, 209; motet, 209; music, in England, 209, 393, n.42, 395, n.51; musicians, in, 393, n.40; opera, 350, 358, (influence on English music) 403, 408, (German music) 260f; Spanish ambassadors to, 363f

Jackson, Benjamin, 424
Jackson, John, 377: in Italy, 360f, 366; in Spain, 375
Jacobi, Erwin Reuben, 130, n.5
Jacobites: music, 419f
Jacobs, P. M.: *Registers of the Universities ...*, 308
Jacopo de Voragine: *Legenda Sanctorum*, 87f
James I, *King of England*, 211, 215, n.19: entry into London, 223, (Edinburgh) 223f; government of Scotland, 212; Progresses, 212, (Scotland) 211*p*, n.6; religious aims, 214; speech, 'No Bishop, No King', 212, n.7
James II, *King of England*: Catholic Chapel of, 310f, n.19; musicians of, 310
James III, *King of England (the Old Pretender)*, 367
Japan: isolation from China, 193, 195f; missions to China, 193; court music, 191*p*, 201, 203; court orchestra, 196; Imperial Music Bureau, 193f, n.4; Library of the Imperial Household, 194f; musicians, 194, 203
Jean de Montchenu, 112
Jean de Renti, 42
Jeanroy, Alfred, 31, n.2, 33, n.6, 36, 41f, 43
Jehannot de l'Escurel, 45
Jehans des Murs [Johannes de Muris], 108: *Libellus cantus mensurabilis*, 105, n.14
Jeppesen, Knud Christian, 147
Jewett, Randolph, 237
Ji ('Quick'), from 'Music of the Five Confucian Virtues', 192, n.2
Jinchi-yôroku (zither MS), 195, 199f, 203, n.26
Jingzhi (Chinese scribe), 200
Johann Wilhelm, *Elector of Düsseldorf*, 184, n.70
Jones, Inigo, 213
Jones, Richard, 393
Jones, Robert I., 101, n.3
Josquin Desprez: masses printed by Petrucci, 131, 138, (facsimile) 145, n.17, (vol.I) 131, 140f *141*, 145f, (vol.II) 142, 149, (vol.III) 132, 138f *139*, 146, 148; *Preter rerum seriem*, 144
Joye, Gilles, 100
Jülich, Duchy of, 170

Kaichû-fu (flute MS), 201
Kamakura period (Japanese history), 200f
Kaminkow, M. J.: *A New Bibliography of British Genealogy ...*, 309

Kangen (Tang music: 'pipes and strings'), 191
Kassel: court music, 170f, n.15
Kassler, Jamie Croy, 413
Keiser, Reinhard: operas, 169, n.1
Kerll, Johann Kaspar: *Modulatio organica*, 262
keyboard music, England, 227*p*, n.1: sale of, at auction, 393; sources of, 227*p*; articulation, 245*p*; fingering, 227*p*; interpretation, 245*p*; leaps, 241, 245, 247; musica ficta, 227, n.1; phrasing, 227, n.1, 238*p*; techniques, 238*p*
Keynes, *Lord*, 160f, n.9
Kiderminster, El., 237, 250
'King of Luoling', The, 194
King's Musick, The, 209, 312, n.25
Kirbye, George: psalm tunes, 157
Kirnberger, Johann Philipp, 265, 269
Komagaku, 195
Koma no Asakuzu: *Zoku-Kyôkunshô* (Gagaku-handbook), 202
Korea: music of, 194
Kornaros, Vitzentzos, 279, 282
Kosô-fu (zither MS), 199f, n.18
koto, *see* zither
Krebs, Johann Ludwig, 261: *Clavierübung*, 262
Krieger, Johann Philipp, 261
Kuhnau, Johann, 261
Kwammu, *Emperor of Japan*, 194
Kyoto: Yômei-Bunko Library, 197, 200
Kyu ('Quick'), from 'Music of the Five Confucian Virtues', 202, n.2

Ladye Nevells Book, My, 229f, 256
Lafontaine, Henry Cart de: *The King's Musick*, 313, 319
Lanier, Nicholas, 312, n.28–9
laouto, 282, n.18
Lara de Andrade, Drogo de Goes, 106
Lascells, Richard, 359, n.5
Las Huelgas Codex, 51
Latini, Brunetto: *Li Livres dou Tresor*, 46
Latreille, F.: *Play-Bills of London Theatres, 1702–46*, 315f
Latter-Day Saints, Church of Jesus Christ of: *Computer File Index*, 306
Laud, William, *Archbishop of Canterbury*, 214
La Vigne, Philippe, 185, n.78
Lawes, William, 157, 160, 163, 165, n.26: meeting with John Browne, 164f, violin sonatas, 157
Lawler, John: 'Chronological list of book auctions ...', 385, n.10
Laxigner, Andrea, 343: confirmation in post, 331, 347; departure from Bergamo, 347; leave of absence, 343, 347; salary, 333, 353
leaps: English keyboard music, 241, 245, 247
Lebrung, Jean: *Recumbentibus undecim*, 144
Leghorn [Livorno], 363, 378, 417
Legrant, Johannes, 114, 121
Legrense, Johannes: *De ritu canendi*, 110, n.26
Legrenzi, Giovanni, 353: appointment as organist of S.Maria Maggiore, Bergamo, 350; confirmation in post, 330; departure from Bergamo, 345, 353, n.28; *Eteocle e Polinice*, 367; salary, 332, 335
Leibniz, Gottfried Wilhelm, 176, n.35

Leipzig, 259, n.10, 262; Catechism Examination, 262, n.5; Musikbibliothek der Stadt Leipzig, 126; University, 270
Lennox, Duke of, 212
Leopold I, *Holy Roman Emperor*, 373f
Lepsingen, 170, n.10
l'Escurel, Jehannot de, 45
letters: source of information, 358, (for concert and theatre performances) 316, 358, 367
Lever, ?, 237
Levy, Kenneth Jay, 67, n.3
Lewis & Co., *auctioneers*, 385, n.11
Lexington, *Lord*, 373
Leyden: auctions in, 383, n.5; University, 357, 371, 373, 376f
Lian Chengwu, 194
Lichfield, 163
ligature forms: *cum opposita proprietate*, 34f, 39, 40f, 45f, 48f, 52; *ligaturae plicatae*, 37, 50
Lignoquercu, Rob. de, 102
Lilla-burlero (song), 421
Lincoln, Bishop of, 422
Lincoln's Inn Fields, 315, 408
Lindsey, Earl of, 370; *see also* Bertie family
'Liquid-Amber Incense', 194
Lister, Martin, 370, n.41
Lithgow, William, 366, n.24: *Totall Discourse ...*, 357f, n.2
Livio, Don, 360
Local Population Studies: *Original Parish Registers ...*, 306
Locatelli, Pietro Antonio, 350, n.30
Loeillet, Jean Baptiste, 393
Loer, Pei, 196, n.11
L'Oiseau-Lyre, 227
London, 155, 403: bishop's transcripts for, 305f; church music in, 422; Drapers Hall, 422; entry of James I, 223; Fire of, 393, n.44; Greater London Record Office, 306; inhabitants, lists of, 306; merchants of, 213; opera in, 367, 371, n.42, 403; parish registers, surveys of, 306; plagues, 418; plays, 418; Protestant Jubilee, 419; rate records, 307; Royal Palaces, 211, (St James's Palace) 423; St James's Church, 423; St Paul's Cathedral, 420; St Sepulchre, 422; tax records of, 307; theatres, 314, *see also* individual theatres; Tower of, 212; wills of, 304f; *see also* particular areas, individual institutions
London, British Library, 307: auction catalogues, 385f, n.11; Burney Newspaper Collection, 315; family letters, 308; family papers, 308; King's Music Library Catalogue, 177, n.40; *List of Catalogues of English Book Sales ...*, 385f; North Library, 386; parish registers, 306; *Public Revenue, State Establishments, Private Accounts*, 314; State Papers, 314
manuscripts
Add.4909, 76*p*, n.7, n.9; 5465, 110, n.28; 5665, 118, n.37; 11608, 159; 15233, 230; 17792–6, 216, n.21; 22978, 361, 372; 23623, 229f; 24198, 66*p*, n.5,

69, 80f, 87f; 28550, 79; 29366–8, 157*p*, 163f, n.6; 29372–7, 216, n.24; 29996, 229f; 30485, 228, 250f; 30486, 229; 30513, 230, n.4; 31403, 228, 252, n.10, *253*; 32249–50, 315; 32531–7, 310, n.16; 36661, 228, 252; 38651 F, 79; 40011 B, 66, 71*p*, n.4, 79, 87*p*, *159*
Cotton Tiberius B IX, 76f, n.8, 83
Egerton 1632, 363*p*; 2159, 315; 3307, 104
Harleian 682, 115; 943, 376; 1423, 216f, n.25; 3782, 316
Royal 12.C.VI, 66; 18.b.11, 180; 23.f.15, 173; 23.f.16, 182; 23.g.21, 182; 23.g.22–23, 176, 182; 23.h.1, 182; 23.h.2, 174, 182; 23.h.6, 173; 23.h.10, 173; 23.h.11, 182; 23.h.12, 174; 23.h.13, 182; 23.h.15–17, 182; 23.i.1, 182; 23.i.2, 174; 23.i.6, 174; 23.i.10, 173; 23.i.11, 182; 23.i.16, 174; 23.i.17, 182; 23.i.18–24, 171, 174, n.30; 23.k.5, 174f; 23.k.7, 177, n.41, 179, n.52–3; 23.k.8, 179, n.52–3; 23.k.12, 173, 172f; 23.k.13, 173*p*, n.50, n.61, n.63; 23.k.14, 177*p*, n.43, n.50, n.61, n.63; 23.k.15–17, 173*p*, n.50, n.61, n.63; 23.k.18, 177*p*, n.43, n.50, n.61, n.63; 23.k.19–20, 173*p*, n.50, n.61, n.63; 23.k.23, 182; 23.l.4, 230; 24.d.3, 228, 239, 256; Royal App.56, 58, 230
printed music
   k.l.d.9, 146; k.l.d.10, 142; k.l.d.15, 143
London Gazette, The, 315
Loosemore, Henry, 237
Lord Chamberlain: censorship of theatres, 314; and Corporation of Musicians, 312; documents, collation of numbers, 313, 319, (references to musicians) 310f, (references to theatre) 313f
Lord, A. B., 281, n.16
Lotti, Federico, 185, n.82
Lotti, Francesco, 185, n.83
Louis XIV, *King of France*, 163
Lowe Bros, *booksellers*, 160, n.9
Lowe, Edward, 230
Lübeck, Vincent I, 261
Lucca, 185, n.83
Lugge, John: compiler of *GB-Och* 49, 230; keyboard music, 227, n.2
Lugt, Fritz: *Répertoire des catalogues ...*, 386
Lully, Jean-Baptiste: operas, 169, n.2, (*Psyche*) 371
Luoling Wang ('The King of Luoling'), 194
lute, 361: and *Erotokritos*, 280; *laouto*, 282; performance practice, (Bergamo) 347, (China and Japan) 196f, n.11–13; plectrum (Tang music) 196f, n.12; song, 210, 219; sources, (*GB-Cu* 4.22) 229, (Osborn MS) 162, (Japan) 195*p*, n.14; study of, (China) 194f, 197, (Japan), 194, (France) 369, 375f, n.41; Tang music, 192, 194f, n.6, 199, 201, (ornamentation) 197; tuning, 375, n.49, (Tang music) 202; tutor (China) 194, 197

Lutheran Church: Catechisms, 260, 262, n.14–15, 264; chorale singing, 204, 264, n.17; Creed, 263, 272; hymnbooks, 260, 262, 264, n.17–18; *Missa brevis*, 262; Reformation Festivals, 259f
Lydian mode, 369
lyra, 282, n.18, *289*
lyra viol, 160

Maas, M., ed.: *English Pastime Music*, 228, 230*p*
Madrid, 374f: Biblioteca nacional, M.2258/9, 172f, n.30, *175*
madrigal: England, 209f; Italy, 209; influence on verse anthem, 219
Maffioletto, D., 347
magazines: as a source of information for concert and theatre performances, 316
Magri, Gulielmo, 110f
Maillard, *instrumentalist*, 185f
Mainwaring, John, 176, n.36
Malchair, John Baptist: Catalogue of musical MSS at Christ Church, Oxford, 164
Malortie, Carl Ernst von, 184f, n.72, n.76
Malta, 362
Mancia, Luigi: *La costanza nelle selve* ('La Pastoralle'), 176, n.34, 182
Mannheim, 173, n.32
manuscripts: sale of, at auctions, 387, n.16–18, 390f, n.30, 394, n.49; *see also* individual MSS
Mar, Duke of, 367, n.29, 377, n.57
Marchesi, Faustino, 353: confirmation in post, 329f, 331; fines on, 343f; salary, 333, 341
Marenzio, Luca, 377, n.54
Marett, A. J., 198f, n.15–16, 202, n.23
Marino, Carlo Antonio: absences from Bergamo, 343, 345; in church records at Bergamo, 330; confirmation in post, 331, 346, (application for post of *Maestro*) 353; music-making at S. Maria Maggiore, 325f, 353; salary, 333, 340f, 353; concertos, 341, n.24; sonatas op.6, 340, n.23; *sonate da chiesa*, 351
Marino, Girolamo, 331, 339
Marino, Giuseppe, 326, 343, 353
Maronites: celebration of solemn high mass, 361
Marpurg, Friedrich Wilhelm: *Abhandlung von der Fuge*, 264, n.19
marriages: indexes, 306; licences, 305, 307; registration of, 305
Marshall, George William: *Parish Registers*, 306
Marshall, John H., 39: *The Chansons of Adam de la Halle*, 30f, 36, 41
Mary I, *Queen of England*, 357
masques: at College of Navarre, Paris, 370; at the English court, 211; at Innsbruck, 372f; at Madrid, 375
Master of the Revels: censorship of theatres, 314
Matchett, Clement: virginal book, 227f, n.2, 239f, 246f, 250, 252, 256
Mathew, *Sir*, Toby, 368, n.34
Mattheson, Johann, 169, n.3, 393

Matthews, G. F.: *Contemporary Index* ..., 306
Matthews, William: *British Diaries* ..., 316
Maugars, André, 379
Maximilian II, Emanuel, *Duke of Bavaria*, 169
Maxwell-Lyte, Henry, 161f, n.11, n.16–17
Maynard, Banister, 360, 368, n.37, 370
Maynard, William, 368, n.37, 370
Mazza, Girolamo, 332; confirmation in post, 331; salary, 333f, 341; as composer, 339
Mazza, Ottavio, 332: confirmation in post, 330f; salary, 332f; inventory of music at S. Maria Maggiore, Bergamo, 335f, (choice of repertory) 339
Medici, *Grand Prince* Ferdinando de', 177, n.42
Medici, Giovanni de', 113, n.32
Medici, Piero de', 113, n.32
Melville, Andrew, 212
Menigoni, Giovanni Battista, 327, 346
mensural notation, 65f, 77*p*, 83f, 87f, 110, n.26–8, 113: Tang music, 192*p*, n.16, 197*p*, n.22; trouvère chansonniers, 35, 52f
mensuration signs: Oporto song collection, 103f, 108; motet *Rota versatilis*, 80
Mercurius Politicus, 418, 419f, 423
Meres, Francis, 216
Merro, John, 216, n.21–3
Messaus, Guillaume (von), 229
metrical psalms: sale of, at auction, 395f, n.56–61
Middelburgo, Paulus de: *de recta Paschae*, 131, n.8–9, 148
Middle East, 358: in Defoe's *Roxana*, 416, n.25; folk music, 374
Middlesex: bishop's transcripts for, 305f
Milan, 323, 350, 368, 417: Biblioteca Ambrosiana, 111; Cathedral, 112
Milton, John, *the elder*, 424: epigrams on Leonora Baroni, 361, n.19; friendship with John Browne, 165; in Italy, 361, 377, n.54; music collecting, 377, n.54; psalm tunes, 157
Minamoto no Hiromasa, *Japanese Ministerial Chief*, 195
Mixolydian mode, 202
Mizler von Kolof, Lorenz Christoph, 260f, n.11, n.13, 267
modal rhythm, 32
Modena, 99, 350
modes: Bach's *Clavierübung III*, 265f, n.20; Tang music, 202; theory of, 108, n.20; *see also* individual modes
Modus componendi rotam versatilem (treatise), 66, 83
Mohamed III, *Sultan of Turkey*: organ for, 213
Mombu, *Emperor of Japan*, 194, n.9
Monferrato, Natal: motets, 338f
Monson, Craig, 157, n.6, 216, n.24
Montague, Lady Mary Wortley, 374, n.45f
Montchenu, Jean de, 112
Montecassino, Biblioteca dell' Abbazia: MS 871, 112, 124
Monteverdi, Claudio, 377, n.54
Montpellier, 362: opera, 369, 371

Moody, Robert, 360, 368, n.37, 370
mordent: Tang music, 198, 201f, n.23
Moreschi, Francesco, 331f
Moreschi, Giovanni Battista, 331f
Moreschi, Ventura, 331f
Morgan, G., 284f
Morley, Thomas: *April is in my Mistress' Face*, 209; at Chapel Royal, 210; on false relations, 254; keyboard music, 227, n.2 ('Go from my window') 237; *Nolo mortem peccatoris*, 209, n.2; *A Plaine and Easie Introduction to Practicall Musick*, 384, n.7; psalm tunes, 157
Mormon church, *see* Latter-Day Saints, Church of Jesus Christ of
Moronaga, Fujiwara no, *see* Fujiwara no Moronaga
Mortoft, Francis, 359f, n.6, n.10, 362
Morton, Robert, 100*p*, n.1–2: at Burgundian ducal chapel, 100ff, 104; songs, 100, n.2, (style) 101, 115, 119, n.39; *?O fallaze e ria Fortuna*, 101; *?Le serviteur hault guerdonné*, 114f, 121
Moryson, Fynes: *Itinerary*, 357, n.1
motet: isorhythm in, 84; Italy, 209; medieval England, 218; *see also* individual motets
mouth organ: Tang music, 192f, 201f, 204; source, 200; tablature, 192, 200
Mouton, Jean, 140, *141*, 149
Mueller, Leopold, 192, n.2
Muffat, Georg: *72 Versetl*, 268
Mulliner Book, 230, n.4
Mullins, Edward Lindsay Carson: *A Guide to the Historical and Archaeological Publications* ..., 309; *Texts and Calendars* ..., 309
Munby, Alan Noel Latimer, 386, n.12, 391, n.37
Mundy, John: keyboard music, 237f
Munich, 164f: Bayerische Staatsbibliothek, (MS 172) 180, n.60, (MS 5321) 173, 178, n.50, (mus. pr. 247) 136f, n.12, *137*, 146
municipal records, 308
Muris, Johannes de, 108: *Libellus cantus mensurabilis*, 105, n.14
Murrie, E. B., *see* Day, C. L.
Muses Mercury, 316
music: auctions, 384*p*, n.7, n.9, n.14, n.20, n.26, n.43; binding, 174, n.60, 338f; in church, 397, n.66, 404, 410f, 414; collecting, 376f, 387ff, 391f; copying, 390f; date of publication, 316; dealers, 390; domestic performance, 391*p*, n.41, 395*p*, n.58, n.60; editing, 29*p*; and politics, 420f; price, 389, 391, n.34; taste, 388*p*, n.22, 392*p*; title pages, 126, 316
education: at Bergamo, 327f, 353; of British travellers abroad 358f, 375f; and Charles Burney, 406*p*, 413; in China, 194f, 197; and Daniel Defoe, 403*p*; at Ferrara Cathedral, 101, n.4; in Japan, 198; and *Parthenia*, 230; in Paris, 375f; in plainsong, 329, n.18; and John Potter, 413
publishing, 316: 18th-century England,

390f, 393, n.41, 395f, n.54, (licensing laws) 395, (subscriptions) 391, n.35; Italy, 341, 345, 390, n.31
Musica Britannica, 29: keyboard music, 227, 231*p*
musica ficta: keyboard music, 227, n.1
Musicians' Company, London, 413
Mychelsen, Robert, 101, n.3
Myriell, Thomas, 168, 209, n.2: *Tristitiae Remedium*, 216, n.24

names, variants of, 303, 325f
Nangû, score for transverse flute by, 195
Nangû ôteki fu (score for transverse flute by Nangû), 195
Naples, 350, 417: carnivals, 360; *ospedale*, 411
Napoli, Francesco, 347
Nappi, Cesare, 103, n.9: (poem) *Iti caldi suspir'e mente afflitta*, 103f
National Index of Parish Registers, 306
National Library of Scotland, *see* Scotland: National Library
National Register of Archives, 309, n.15: Bulletin, 309; *List of Accessions to Repositories*, 309; *Report of the Secretary to the Commissioners*, 309
Nevell, Lady: virginal book, 229f, 256
newspapers: as sources of information for concert and theatre performances, 315f, n.37
New York, Public Library: Drexel MS 4180–5, 216, n.20; Drexel MS 5612, 229
Niccolo III, *Marchese*, 102
Nicoll, Allardyce: *A History of English Drama, 1660–1900*, 314, 317f
Nigrisoli, Girolamo, 109
Noble, (John) Jeremy, 130, n.6, 140, n.13, 142
non-conformist registers, 305
Non-Parochial Registers Act (1840), 306
Norsino, Lazzaro, 329
North, *Lord*, 377
North, *The Hon.* Roger, 377, n.55, 394, n.50: writings on music, 310, n.16, 379, n.62; on Italian church music, 359, n.8–9; on Antonio Vivaldi, 395, n.53
notation: Chinese music, 192*p*; Japanese music, 192*p*, 198*p*; of ornaments, 197*p*, 201; of plainsong, 32, 39f, 45f; transcription of, 29
Nottingham, Earl of, *Lord High Admiral of England*, 374f
Nugent, Thomas, 368, 370
Nuremberg, 170

Oakwood (?), Robert, 102
oboe, 330, 334, 347, 350: in infantry regiments, 311, n.24
occupations: listed in baptismal, marriage and burial registers, 305
Oiseau-Lyre, 227
Oliphant, Thomas, 164, n.22–3
Olmo, Hercole, 329
opera, 345: English proposals, 408, (views) 367f, 408; forbidding performance of, 360; *Intermezzi* in, 368; publication of, (scores)

390, (texts) 317f; singers' salaries 404, n.3, 410, 413f; stage machinery for, 366f, 374, n.45; Cremona, 350; Florence, 367; Genoa, 350; London, 367, 371, 410f, 413, (Christ's Hospital) 404, 411; Milan, 350, 368; Montpellier, 369, 371; Paris, 371*p*; Piacenza, 350; Reggio, 350; Rome, 360; Siena, 368, n.33; Turin, 350; Venice, 366*p*; Vienna, 371*p*
Oporto, Biblioteca pública municipal, 106, n.18:
    MS 714, 99*p*, n.12: collation, 105ff, 111; compilation, 104*p*, 113f; concordances, 111ff, 123f; date, 108*p*, n.22; dedication, 105; description, 104*p*; foliation, 105f; format, 105, 109; French texts, 113f; illumination, 106f, 111f, (payment for) 110f, n.29; ink, 107; inventory, 120f; mensuration signs, 103f; notation, 110, 113; provenance, 104*p*, n.16–18, n.31; repertory, 111f, 119; scribe, 105f, 114f; treatises in, 105f, n.21, 114; underlay, 105, n.15, 116f, 119
oral tradition: *Erotokritos*, 281, n.14
oratorio: at Christ's Hospital, 404; Italy, 18th-century, 361, (Bergamo) 326; publication of, 390
orchestral parts: publication of, 390; use of, 18th-century, 391, n.36
organ: accompaniment to psalms, 396, n.56; Leipzig Catechism Examination, 262, n.15; maintenance records, 307; mass, 262; pedals, 352; tuition, 409; in verse anthems, 218; Christ's Hospital, 412, n.15; Holyrood House, Edinburgh, 212f, n.10–11, n.15; Jesuit Church, Paris, 370, n.40; St Anthony, Padua, 360; S. Maria Maggiore, Bergamo, 326f, 347, 352; Sultan Mohamed III, 213; *see also* mouth organ
organists: records for, 307
ornaments: Tang music, 197f; English keyboard music, 238, 250f; table of, in *GB-Lbm* Add.31403, 228, 252, *253*
Orto sole serene (motet), 71
Orvieto, Ugolino of, 107f: *Declaratio musice discipline*, 105, n.13f, 110, n.27
Osborn, James M., 162f, 165, n.15
Otley, Matthew, 162, 165, n.16
Öttingen-Wallerstein, earldom of, 170, n.10
Ottoboni, *Cardinal* Pietro, 360, n.17: musical gatherings, 364f, 378
Ovet mundus (rondellus), 74f
Owen, Dorothy M.: *The Records of the Established Church …*, 307
Oxford
    Bodleian Library, 307: auction catalogues, 386, n.12; family papers, 308; Rawlinson Collection, 314
        manuscripts: Ashmole 191, 115f; Bodley 652, 65, 71*p*, 79f, 87f; can.misc.213, 112; E.Mus.7, 74; Hatton 81, 71, 74f, 80; Lat.lit.d.20, 80; Mus.Sch.C.93, 229; Mus.Sch.e.17, 310; Tanner 93, 362; Wood D.19(4), 310, n.17

Christ Church: removal of MSS from, 216, n.20
manuscripts: 49, 230; 89, 229; 92, 229; 367–70, 151*p*, 158f; 371, 230; 378, 229; 379–81, 157*p*, 164f; 423–8, 157*p*, 164f; 430, 157*p*; 473–8, 157*p*, 164f, n.7–8; 716–20, 159, 165; 744–6, 159; 1004, 159, 164f; 1113, 230; 1142, 230, 1179, 230; 1207, 230
Corpus Christi College: MS 21, 215, n.18
New College: MS 362, 67
University, 357, 371: lists of students, 308
Music Faculty list of students, 308

Pachelbel, Johann, 269
Packer family, 164: Elizabeth, 155, 164, n.26; John, 155; Robert, 157
Padua, 109, 323: making viol strings in, 362; sale of music in, 377, n.53; St Anthony's Church, 360
paired fingering: keyboard music, 238*p*
Palatinate: Spiritual Council, 170
Palestrina, Giovanni Pierluigi da, 261, 267: performance of mass by, 361; sale of music by, 389
Pallavicini, *Cardinal*, 363
Paluccio, *castrato*, 360, n.17
pañcama mode (Sanskrit), 202
paper: cost, 140, n.14, 146
paraphrase techniques: Bach's *Clavierübung III*, 273f
Pareia, Bartolomeo Ramos de: *Musica practica*, 103f, n.10–11, 108, 113
Parenti, Giovanni, 331, 351f
Paris: Académie Française, 413; British Ambassador to, 370; English Nunnery, 370, n.39; Jesuit Church, 370, n.40; musical education in, 375f; opera in, 369*p*; Pluvinel's Academy, 375f, n.50; visits to, 369*p*, 375*p*
Bibliothèque Nationale: auction catalogues, 386, n.12
manuscripts
Ancien fonds du Conservatoire National de Musique: Rés 1122, 230; Rés 1185, 228, 256; Rés 1186 *bis*, 228, 230
Fonds français: 146, 45; 846, 30f; 847, 30, 36, 39f, 50, (ink) 40, (notation) 41f, 56, (scribe) 39, 41f; 1109, 31, 46f, 50, (notation) 47f, 57; 1591, 31, 43f, 49f, 53, (gatherings) 44, n.12, (notation) 45f, 59, (scribe) 39, 45f, n.13–14, (underlay) 46; 12615, 31, 42f, (contents) 31, 42f, (notation) 43, 57, (scribe) 39, 43; 24406, 31, 48f, (notation)
Fonds français 25566: contents, 31; first section, 31, 36, n.10, 39, 43, (notation) 40f, 58; main MS, 31, 34, 36*p*, 42f, (illumination) 36f, (notation) 37f, 58, (scribe) 39f, 49, n.15, 52
Rothschild 2973, 112, 123
Paris et Vienne (courtly romance), 279
Parish Clerks, Guild of, London, 102, n.7; Leet Book, 102
parish of residence: marriage registers, 305

parish registers, 305*p*: deposit of, 309; guides to, 306; microfilming of, by Church of Latter-Day Saints, 306; records of church affairs in, 307; transcripts of, 306
Parish Register Society, 306
Parma, 350
Parthenia, 230, n.3, 257
Parthenia In-Violata, 229
partsongs: sale of, 394
Pashley, R., 280, n.8
Pasquini, Bernardo, 228
Patent Rolls: references to musicians, 311
Pattison, Bruce, 393, n.43
Paul's Cross, London, 411
Pavia, 100
Pederzuoli, Giovanni Battista, 350
Peerson, Martin: verse anthems, 219
Pelandi, Antonio, 345
Pelli, Pietro Paolo, 327
Pepusch, Johann Christoph, 183, 421, n.33: and *GB-Lbm* Add.4909, 77
Pepys, Samuel, 360f, 375, 377, 383, n.3, 393, n.41: diaries, 316; and psalm-singing, 392, n.55
Perceval, *Sir* John, 377
Perceval, *Sir* Philip, 376
performance practice: Chinese lute music, 196*p*; Japanese flute music, 203f; Japanese lute music, 196*p*, n.10–13
Perone brothers, of Bergamo, 346
Perth, 214: Earl of, 364
Pescara, Giovanni Battista, 345: confirmation in post, 330; insanity, 345; salary of, 332
Petrucci, Ottaviano dei: politics, 146, n.19; cancel sheets, 129f, 142f, 145; inking, 136, 138, 140, 143
letters: capitals, 130*p*, n.7, 145; distribution, 132*p*; replacement of, 131; styles, 131*p*, n.10; A4, 132; A6, 136; A11, 138, 140, *141*, 143; B6 128, 136, *139*; E4, 132; E10, 136; K4, 132; O10, 145; P4, 132, 145; S3, 131; S4, 132; V2, 132, 136f, *137*
multiple impression process, 131, 136; paper, 130, 135, 140, n.13, 142f, n.15, 146; partbooks, 130, 143, 145; proof corrections, 129, 131, 136; watermarks, 130, 140, 142, n.15
Bossinensis lute volume, 136, *137*; Févin edition, 140f, *143*, 146; *Frottole XI*, 138, *139*
Josquin masses, 130, 138, 148f, (facsimile) 145, n.17: I, 130, 140, *141*, 145f, 148; II, 142, 149; III, 132, 138, *139*, 146, 148
madrigal fragments, 147; Middelburgo, *de recta Paschae*, 131, n.8, 148, (gatherings) 131, n.9, 144f, n.16; *Misse Brumel*, 132
Motetti de la Corona, 129*p*, n.3–4: chronology, 130, 136f, 140, 142f, 146*p*; I, *137*, *139*, *141*, (title pages) 130, (variant editions) 129f; II, 130, 136, 138, *139*, *141*, 150; III, 138, *139*, *141*; IV, *137*; 138, 144f, n.16, 150
Mouton edition, 140f, 149; *Odhecaton*, 131, 147; *Odhecaton A*, 131; Pisano's

Musica, 140, *141*, 143, 146f, 150f; secular volumes, 146, n.18, 148f
Petrus le Viser, 83f, n.11–12
Philips, Peter, 229
Phillimore Parish Register Society, 306
Phillips & Co., *auctioneers*, 385, n.11
phrasing: keyboard music, 227, n.1, 238*p*, 245*p*
Piacenza, 350
Pilgrim Trust: *Survey of Ecclesiastical Archives*, 307
Pingdiao mode (Tang music), 199
Pipo (Filippo Amadei), 378
Pirrotta, Nino, 109f, n.22–5, 115
Pisano, Bernardo: *Musica*, 140, *141*, 143f, 146, 150
Piva, Gregorio: in Bonn, 172, n.23, 173, n.31, *174*; in Dresden, 172, n.21; in Düsseldorf, 172, n.22, n.26–8, 173f; in Hanover, 172, n.25, 28 as Steffani's secretary, 172, 173f, n.33; as copyist of Steffani's operas, 171, n.19, 173f, n.30, n.33; death, 172, n.24
plainsong, 329, n.18, 353: notation, 32, 39f, 45f; retardation of, 191, 204
Playford, Henry: sales, 390, n.33, 394, n.46, n.49
Playford, John, *the elder*: catches, 393; *Choice Ayres*, 317; *Musical Companion*, 394; and psalm-singing, 395f, n.56–60; publishing, 393; rounds, 393; *Select Ayres*, 384, n.7
plays: choirboys in, 218; forbidding of, 418; incidental music, 418, (publication) 318; texts, 316, (publication) 317f
plectrum: Tang lute music, 196f, n.12–13
plica forms, 34f, 37, 39f, 43, 45*p*
Pluvinel, de, 375f
Pococke, Richard, 361
podatus, 34f, n.7, 50
Politi, L., 282, 284
politics: and music, 211, 420f
Pöllnitz, Baron de, 379
poll-tax, 307
polychoral music: St Peter's, Rome, 360, n.16
Pomposa, Abbey of Santa Maria, 102, n.6
Pope, The: Capella Sistina, 102f, n.8, (music in) 361; celebration of mass, 361; concert for installation of, 365; delegations to, 141; Palace, 360
Pope, Alexander, 374
porrectus, 35
Portland, Earl of, 370
Post Boy, The, 315
Post Man, The, 315
Potter, John, 413, n.17
Power, Leonel, 99, 119
preludes: English keyboard music, 228, 252; Tang music, 196, 198
Presbyterian Church of Scotland, 211f: opposition to James I, 214
pressus, 43, 47
Price, John, 238
Princeton University Library: MS Garrett 119, 68, 80, n.10
Priscilla Bunbury's Virginal Book, 227f, n.2

Progresses, Royal, 212
psalms: singing of in England, 393f, n.56–61; at Christ's Hospital, 412, n.15; at Easter civic ceremonies, 412; *see also* metrical psalms
Public Record Office, 303f: Army Establishment Lists, 312; Cairncross Index, 313f; central government papers, 310; *Guide to the Contents of the Public Record Office*, 313; Lord Chamberlain's papers, 313, 319; non-conformist registers, 306; poll-tax records, 307
Purcell, Henry, 209, 403, 408; confusion with other composers, 303, n.2; payments for teaching, 308, n.7; music in *GB-Bu* 5001, 163; court odes, 219; keyboard music, 230; semi-operas, 314; *Dido and Aeneas*, 317; *Dioclesian*, 371, n.42; *Orpheus Britannicus*, 394
Pure Wisdom (Chinese scribe), 200
Puritans: attitudes to music, 404, n.4–5, 414f
Puttick & Co., *auctioneers*, 385, n.11

Quaglia, Francesco, 334f, n.10, 344f
Quaglia, Giovanni Battista, 325, 327f, 330, 350: confirmation in post, 330f; salary, 332f, n.19; as composer, 340; motets, 339f, n.22, (publication of vol.ii) 339, n.21; oratorio, 325, n.9
Quaritch, Bernard, *bookseller*, 162
'Quick' movement (Tang music), 192, n.2, 204

Rameau, Jean-Philippe: *Hippolyte et Aricie*, 371f
Ramos de Pareia, Bartolomeo: *Musica practica*, 103f, n.10–11, 108, 113
Ramsay, Robert, 164
rates: accounts for, 307
Ravenscroft, Thomas: at Christ's Hospital 411; *Deuteromelia*, 394; *Melismata*, 394; *Pammelia*, 394; psalm-settings, 157, 395
Rawlinson Collection (Bodleian Library), 314
Ray, John, 360, n.14, 362
Raymond, John, 360
Raymond, Thomas, 359, n.4, 361f
Raynaud, G.: *Bibliographie ...*, 30f, 36, 42f
Reaney, Gilbert, 36, 42
recita: uses of, in rondelli, 74f, 79, 89f
recitative: 17th-century Venice, 366
'Recognition, The' (Cretan wedding song), 281
record societies: publications, 309
red notation, 110, n.27
reed pipes: Tang music, 192, 199, 201, 203f; tablature, 192, 199, n.17
Reformation: England, 209; festivals, 259
Reggiani, Teodoro, 345, 348
Reggio, 350, 368
Regis aula (motet), 67f
Registrar General, 306
Reincken, Johann Adam, 261
Renart nouvel, 36, 39, 52
Renti, Jean de, 42
repeated notes: keyboard music, 245*p*, n.9
Reresby, *Sir* John, 368, n.35–6, 376, 378
residences: use of rate records to trace, 307

Review of the Affairs of France, 404, n.7, 406, 418, 420, 423
Richart de Fournival: Bestiary, 36
Rimbault, Edward Francis, 215, n.20
Ring, Layton, 159f, 165, n.1
ritornello structure: Bach's *Clavierübung III*, 271f
Ritson MS, 118, n.37
rizitika (Cretan folksong), 280
Robert de Handlo: treatise, 76*p*, n.8, 83f, n.12, 87
Robert, John, 101, n.3
Robertsbridge Codex, 79
Robertus de Anglia, 99*p*: identity, 100*p*, n.9; in Bologna, 101, n.5; in Ferrara, 101f, n.4, n.8, 109f, 113; at S. Maria di Pomposa, 102, n.4; at St Peter's, Rome, 102; at the Papal Chapel, 102; as compiler of Oporto song collection, 104, 108, 114, 119; and mensuration signs, 103f, 108; and Ramos de Pareia, 103f, 108; setting of poem by Cesare Nappi, 103f; *O fallaze e ria Fortuna*, 101, 116*p*; *?Le serviteur hault guerdonné*, 114f
Robinson, Thomas, 162
Roche, Jerome, 335, n.20
Rochester, *2nd Earl*, 424
Rochester University: Sibley Music Library, 141
Rogers: virginal book, 227, n.2
Rogers, Charles: *A History of the Chapel Royal of Scotland*, 214f
Roman de Fauvel, 45
Roman du Vergier et de l'arbre d'amour, 41
Romania, 279
Rome, 349, 375f, 417: antiquities, 358; Biblioteca Casanatense: (MS 2151), 110, n.27, (MS 2223) 174, 178; *castrati* of, 360; Chiesa Nova, 359; concerts in, 360*p*, 377f, n.60; music printing in, 147; opera in, 360; Sacred Congregation of Propaganda, 172; S. Apollinaro, 359f; S. Lorenzo, 360; S. Marcello, 359f, n.10; St Peter's, 102f, n.8, 359, (choral music in) 360*p*; Vatican, 360; Capella Sistina, 102f, n.8; choirbooks, 112; Biblioteca Apostolica Vaticana: MS C.G.XIII. 29, 112, 123; MS Reg.lat. 1490(a), 31, 33f, 39, 50, (notation) 34f, 55, (scribe), 34f; MS Urb.lat.1411, 112, 124
   visits to, 358*p*, 363, 365f, n.22–3, 371; vocal music in, 360
rondeaux, 34f
rondellus, 74f, 80, 86; *see also* individual compositions
Rooke, George, 377
Rosenhagen, *music binder*, 174, n.60
Rota, Alessandro, 333
Rota versatilis (rondellus), 65*p*, 69, 72, 73, 75: authorship, 82; date, 76, 86; edition, 66, 89f; form, 65, 68, 74*p*, 74, 80*p*, 85; layout, 68, 74*p*, 80*p*; notation, 65f, 77*p*, 89f, (circles) 79f, 80f, (*recita*) 74f, 79, 89f; performance, 68, 74f; reconstruction, 68, 78; rhythm, 84; sections, 66f, 68f, 71f, 78, 80,

90f; sources, 65*p*, *see also* individual sources; symmetry, 84f; text, 86f, (translation) 87; texture, 84; voices, 65f, 68, 71f, 79*p*
Rotokritos melody (Crete), 279f, n.4–5: form, 280, 284*p*; motifs, 285*p*; performance, 280, n.7–8; phrases, 288; sources, 280, n.10; texts, 282, n.19; versions, 280, n.10, n.12, 282, 284*p*, n.22–3, n.25, 290*p*; *see also Erotokritos*
round, 393f
Roure, Comte de, 371
Rovetta, Giovanni: *Ercole in Lidia*, 366
Royal Academies project (1695), 405, n.10
Royal Academy of Arts, 405
Royal Academy of Music (18th-century), 403, 408, n.11, 418f
Royal College of Music: MS 1023, 183; MS 2093, 229
Royal Navy, 411
Royal Society of Musicians: collection of portraits, 310, n.18
Russell, Wriothesley, *2nd Duke of Bedford*, 365, n.22, 379: music collecting, 377, n.56
Rutland, Countess of, 367
Ryder, *Sir Dudley, Lord Chief Justice*, 370f, n.42
Ryô-ô ('The King of Luoling'), 194

Sackville, Charles, *6th Earl of Dorset*, 314, n.30
Sackville, Edward, *4th Earl of Dorset*, 212
Sacrapanti, *Cardinal*, 360
Sadatoshi, Fujiwara no, *see* Fujiwara no Sadatoshi
Sadayasu, *Prince, of Japan*, 195, 198
Saibara, 195
St Cecilia's Day: 1703 concert, 423
St George and the Dragon (Cretan narrative song), 282
St Katherine of Alexandria: legend, 65, 87f
Salisbury, 228f
sales, *see* auctions
Salo, 350
Sandars Lectures, 387
Sanese, L. C., 359
Sango-yôroku (lute MS), 195, 200, 202
Sartori, Claudio, 129, n.3
Saumure, 376
Saunders, William, 312, n.28–9
Savile, Henry, 383, n.4
Savoy, Court of, 113
scandicus, 47, 50
Scheibe, Johann Adolph, 260, n.12
Scheidt, Samuel, 264
Schemelli, Georg Christian: hymnbook, 260, 264, n.17
Schering, Arnold, 267
Scholes, Percy Alfred: *The Puritans and Music*, 404, n.5
Scholze, Johann Sigismond (Sperontes), 261
school records, 308
Schubert, Johann, 43f, n.11
Schwan, E., 34, 36, 41, 43, 51, n.17
Scholari, Giovanni Battista, 330f, 333, 341

Scotland: Chapel Royal, 214f; James I's Progress, 211*p*, n.6, n.8, 223f; General Assembly, 212; government of, 212; Parliament, 215; Presbyterian Church, 211f; Privy Council, 211, n.6; National Library: MS Panmure, 227f, n.2, 240, 247f, 250, 252, 256

Seaman, Lazarus, 384, n.6

Secret Service Accounts: reference to musicians in, 311, 314, n.33

Sedulius, Caelius: hymn *A solis ortus*, 76

Segovia: Cathedral, 112

Sergeant Trumpeter, 312

Seville: Archivo capitular de la Catedral, 5-I-43, 108

Shakespeare, William: *Hamlet*, 419

Shaw, Watkins: views on *GB-Bu* 5001, 163, n.18

Sherard, James: Trio Sonatas, op.1, 377

Sherard, William, 377

Shiba, Sukehiro, 203, n.24

Shikibu, *Lady* Murasaki: 'Tale of Genji', 199

Shinsen gaku-fu (Tang flute scores), 195, n.9

Shinsen shô-teki-fu (Tang mouth-organ MS), 200f

Shrewsbury, Duke of, 365f, n.23, 367f, n.30, 371f, 377

Sicily, 362

Sidney, *Sir* Philip, 358

Siena, 368, n.33

Sievers, Heinrich, 185, n.73, n.75, n.79

Simpson, Christopher: *Compendium of Practical Musick*, 384, n.7

singing: tuition in, 329, n.18, 353, 409

single-stroke ornaments (keyboard music), 251, 254f

Sitia (Crete), 282

Skippon, *Sir* Philip, 360, 362, 366f

Slim, H. Colin, 387, n.17

Smith, William Charles: *A Bibliography of the Music Works Published by John Walsh, 1695–1720*, 317

Society of Genealogists, 306, n.4

Sogôkô ('Liquid-Amber Incense'), 194

Soldt, Susanne: virginal book, 229

songbooks, 316: collecting, 377, n.53; political, 421; publication dates, 317f

Song Dynasty, 193

Sophie Charlotte, *Queen of Prussia*, 176f, n.37–8, n.42, n.51–2, n.54, 181f

Sorge, Georg Andreas, 261

Sotheby's, *auctioneers*, 385f, n.11

Sousa's song, *see* Rotokritos melody

Southgate & Co., *auctioneers*, 385, n.11

Southwark, Diocese of: parish registers, 306

Southwell, *Sir* Robert, *the elder*, 376, n.52

Southwell, *Sir* Robert, *the younger*, 363*p*, 376, n.52: commonplace book, 363*p*

Spaccazocchi, Maurizio, 147

Spain, 375: ambassadors to Italy, 363f; church music in, 375; Defoe's views on music and theatre, 423; Spanish Netherlands, 169; visits to, 374f; War of the Spanish Succession, 169, n.8

Sparks, Edgar H., 144f, n.16

Spataro, Giovanni, 103

Spectator, The, 316: articles on opera by Addison, 367

Spencer, Robert, 157, 160, n.1

Sperontes (Scholze, Johann Sigismund), 261

Spiga, 170f, n.12, 183

Spital Cross, London, 411

Spratt, T. A. B., 280, n.8

Squarcialupi, Antonio, 113, n.34

stage machinery: 16th-century Vienna, 374, n.45; 17th-century Venice, 366f

Stanford Hall, Leicestershire, 144, 150*p*: Calendar of MSS, 161, n.11; fence design for, 163

Stanford-on-Avon, St Nicholas, 161: organ, 163, n.20

Stationers' Hall, London: references to concert and theatre performances, 315ff; Registers, 316f, n.40; Term Catalogues, 316f, n.40

Steele, *Sir* Richard, 406, 418: letters, 316

Steffani, Agostino: Abbott of Lepsingen, 170, n.10; Apostolic Vicar of Northern Germany, 170, n.13; Bishop of Spiga, 170f, n.12, n.29, 172f, 183; death, 183f, n.68; in Düsseldorf, 170*p*, n.11, n.15–17, 179f, n.56; envoy in Brussels, 169, n.7; in Italy, 170; Kapellmeister at Hanover, 169f, n.18, 173f, 180, n.57; musical hand, 177f, n.43; ordained priest, 170; President of the Academy of Vocal Music, 183, n.65; pseudonym, 170*p*, n.14, n.17, 183f. n.69; Scribes, (A) 173*p*, n.71, n.84, *175*, (B) 182*p*, n.64; treatise, *Quanta certezza*, 170, 183, n.66

chamber duets, 169f, n.3, n.9, n.15, 173*p*, n.38, n.40, n.46f, n.49, n.51–3, n.61, n.63, n.66; index, 177f, n.39, n.44–5, n.48; *Torna a dar vita*, 178f

madrigals, 183, n.66

motets, 174f, 183, n.66–7: *Sacer Ianus quadrifons*, 174, 183, n.66

operas, 169f, n.1–2, n.15–16, 173*p*: *Amor vien dal destino*, 171, n.18, 173f, 179, 182; *Arminio*, 171f, 173f; *Baccanali*, 174f, 182; *Briseide*, 174f, 180, 182f; *La costanza nelle selve*, 174f, n.34, 182f; *La libertà contenta*, 171, 174, 182; *Henrico Leone*, 173f, 182; *La lotta d'Hercole con Acheloo*, 174f, 182; *Orlando Generoso*, 173, 182; *Paride in Ida*, 182; *Le rivali concordi*, 174, 180, n.58, 182; *La superbia d'Alessandro*, 174. 182; *Il Tassilone*, 171, 172f, *175*; *I trionfi del fato*, 172, 174, 182

Steffkins family, 363

Stella, Michele, 346: absence, 343; confirmation in post, 331; salary of, 334

Stevens, Denis William, 238: *Thomas Tomkins, 1572–1656*, 387, n.16

Stevenson, Allen, 140, n.14

stile antico: in Bach's *Clavierübung III*, 266*p*

Stradella, Alessandro, 359

Suhexiang ('Liquid-Amber Incense'), 194

Sui Dynasty, 193

Susanne Soldt's Virginal Book, 229
Svogliati, Academy of the, 361
Sweden: book auctions, 383
Sweelinck, Jan Pieterszoon: keyboard music, 229
'Swinnerton's Alman' (keyboard piece), 231, 243
Switzerland, 362
Symonds, Richard, 376

tablature: Tang music, 192, 194f, 199f
tadabyôshi (Tang metrical variant), 201
Taglietti, Luigi, 346, n.29
Taiheiraku ('The Music of Peace'), 194, n.5
Taihô, second year of, 194, n.5
taiko (bass drum), 192, 200
Tailour, Robert: Sacred hymns, 157, 161f, n.2
Taipingyue, 194, n.5
Talbot, Charles, Duke of Shrewsbury, 365f, n.23, 367f, n.30
Tallis, Thomas, 209f, n.3: sale of music by, 389, n.27; keyboard music, 227, n.2, ('Felix namque') 238, 240, 248
Talman, John, 378, n.60
Tang Dyxasty, 191, 193, 200
Tang music (Tôgaku), 191p: chromaticism, 203; dissonance, 192f, 202f; Japanese imitation, 194, 198, n.4, n.7, 202f; melodies, 193, 196f, 200f, 203f; notation, 192p n.16, 197p, n.22; ornamentation, 194p; performance practice, 196p, n.10–13, 203f; retardation, 191f, 199f, 203f; rhythm, 201; sources, 193p, 203, see also individual sources; speed of, 191f, n.1, 197, n.14, 203f; tablature, 192, 194f, 199f; Zoku-kyôkunshô handbook, 202
Tatler, The, 316, 406
tax records, 307
Temperley, Nicholas, 396, n.59
Tenri University: Library, 199, n.18, 201
ternariae, 39f, 47
Theatre, The, 418, n.28
theatres: musicians in, 314p, 393, 417; in London, 406, (choirboy plays) 218; in Spain, 218; see also songbooks
theorbo, 343, 347, 352, 361, 364: accompaniment to psalms, 396; study of, 369, 375f
thiamboli, 282, n.18, 285f,
thirds: fingering of, keyboard music, 243f
Thirty Years War, The, 358
Thomas gemma/Thomas caesus (rondellus), 80
Tilmouth, Michael, 405, n.10: 'A Calendar of References …', 315, 317, n.37, 391, n.28, 404, n.7
Tinctoris, Johannes, 99
Tisdale, William: keyboard music, 227, n.2; virginal book, 227, n.2, 230
Todeschino, contralto at Bergamo, 350
Tôgaku, see Tang music
tombstones: biographical information, 305
Tomkins, John: 'John come kiss me now', 238; psalm tunes, 167
Tomkins, Thomas: Biography by Stevens, 387

n.16; MSS, 231. 387, n.16, (GB-Lbm 2999b), 229
keyboard music, 227, 229f, 238: 'Galliard', 230, 238; 'Miserere', 230; 'Prelude', 230, 238; 'Ut, mi, re', 238, 241, 243
verse anthems, 219
torculus, 34, n.7
Torri, Pietro: Briseide, 175f, 180, 182
Totti, Luca (sic), 185f, n.82–3
Treasurer of the Chamber: references to musicians in the accounts of, 312
Treasury, The: Calendars for books and papers of, 312; references to musicians in books and papers of, 310f
Tregian, Francis, 240: see also Fitzwilliam Virginal Book
Trent Codices, 99: Trent 87, 112
Treswell, Robert, 375, n.47
trill: English keyboard music, 251
triplets: English keyboard music, 250
Triumphat hodie (motet), 67
trombone, 352
Tudor Church Music, 215, n.18
Tudway, Thomas, 210, n.3: letters to Humphrey Wanley, 316
Tunstall, Thomas, 228
Turin, 350, 360, n.15
Turkey, 213, 279: rule of Crete, 282
turn: English keyboard music, 251
Turner, Thomas, 160
Turner, William II, 163
Tuscany, 368
Tye, Christopher, 209

Udine, 350
Uffenbach brothers, 379
Ugolino of Orvieto, 101f: Declaratio musice discipline, 105, n.13–14, 110, n.27
United States of America, 215: libraries, 308, n.13; see also individual libraries
University records, 308

Valoix, musician, 184f, n.72–7
Van der Werf, Hendrik, 32, n.5
Van Lennep, W. B. and Avery, E. L.: The London Stage, 1660–1800, 315
variant readings, 30, 32f; recording of, 30
Vatican Palace, see Rome, Vatican
Vavvasore, Lodovico, 331f, 353
Vecchi, Orazio, 377, n.54
Venice, 106, 136, 142, 181, 323, 338, 349f, 417: bagpipes in, 378; Biblioteca nazionale Marciana, 130, 142f; British Ambassador to, 359; carnivals, 360, 365, 367; churches of, 358, (music) 367; cori spezzati, 366; music publishing, 130, see also Petrucci, Ottaviano dei; opera in, 366p; ospedale, 409; rule of Crete, 279, n.1; sale of music in, 377, n.53; Teatro Grimono, 367; Teatro S. Salvatore, 367; visits to, 366p
Venizelos, Eleutherios, 281
Verdelot, Philippe, 147
Vernarecci, A., 146f, n.19
Verona, 323: Academici Filarmonici, 362f;

Biblioteca dell' Accademia filarmonica, 144; Cathedral, 346; palace of, 362f
verse anthem, 218f, 223: form, 220f
vestry minutes, 307
Vienna, 373f: Österreichische Nationalbibliothek, 140, 146
Villiers, George, *Earl of Buckingham*, 213
viol: strings, 362; bass-part to psalm-settings, 396; in consort songs, 218; in verse anthems, 218; *see also* lyra viol
Violanta Beatrice, wife of Ferdinando de' Medici, 177, n.42
violin: popularity of, in 17th-century England, 393: tuition, 409
Violino family, of Bergamo, 328
violone, 351*p*; *see also* double bass
Virgil, 424
virginals, 227*p*, 393: accompaniment to psalms, 396
Viser, Petrus le, 83f, n.11–12
Vitali, Filippo, 345, 350
Vivaldi, Antonio Lucio, 390, n.31, 393, 395, n.52–3
Voetius, Gilbert, 384, n.7
Volpe, Giovanni Battista: *La Rosilena*, 367
Vopelius, Gottfried, 262
Voragine, Jacopo de: *Legenda Sanctorum*, 87f
Vulpios, *singers*, 359

waits: at Epsom, 422; records of, 308
Wakeling, Donald R., 387
Wales: music of, 423, n.33–4; Princess of, 423, n.34
Walker, Thomas: *The Quaker's Opera*, 427
Waller, Edmund, 424
Walsh, John, *the elder*, 316f: publishing, 393, 395; sales, 390
Walther, Johann Gottfried, 269f, n.27–8: 'Ach Gott und Herr' (BWV 693 attrib. J. S. Bach), 269
Wanibe no Shimatsugu: *Sogôkô/Suhexiang* ('Liquid-Amber Incense'), 194
Wanley, Humphrey: letters from Thomas Tudway, 316
Ward, John: verse anthems, 219
Ward, John Milton, 162, n.15
Warwick, Thomas, 164
Weedon, Cavendish, 423f, n.37
Weelkes, Thomas: biography by Brown, 219, n.27; at Chichester Cathedral, 210; music in *GB-Lbm* Add.29366-8, 164; verse anthems, 219; *Alleluia! I Heard a Voice*, 210; *Hosanna to the Son of David*, 223; *O Care, Thou Wilt Despatch me*, 210
Weldon, *Sir* Anthony, 213ff, n.9, n.14, n.17
Weldon, John, 308: *Judgement of Paris*, 315, n.36
Wenxian tongkao, 196
Westminster Public Library: rate-books in, 307
Westminster School: list of pupils, 308
Wheatley & Co., *auctioneers*, 385, n.11

When David heard (various settings), 223
Whetenall, *Lady* Catherine, 359, n.5: visit to Rome, 359, n.5
White, William: fantasias à 6, 159f
Whitelocke, Bulstrode, 372
Wilbye, John, 164, 210
Wilkins, Nigel: *The Lyric Works of Adam de la Halle*, 30f, 36, 49
Wilkinson, ?: music in *GB-Lbm* Add.29366-8, 164
Willetts, Pamela Joan, 216, n.22
Will Forster's Virginal Book, 228, 240, 256
William III, *King of England*, 310f, 408, 415
Willoughby, Francis, 362
Wilmot, John, *2nd Earl of Rochester*, 424
Wilson, John: *Cheerful Airs or Ballads*, 384, n.7
Winchester, 228
wind instruments: tuition in, 409
Windsor, St George's Chapel, 211, 229
'Winn, Captaine', 162
Wolff, Christoph, 266
Wolpert, R. F., 194
Wood, Anthony (à), 230, 310, n.17
woodcuts: music printing, 130f, n.7
Worcester, 216
word-setting, 210, n.4: in the verse anthem, 219*p*
Worshipful Company of Stationers, London, 423
Wotton, near Hertford, 421
Wotton, *Sir* Henry, 377, n.53
Wright, Edward, 361, n.18, 365, 368: in Bologna, 361, n.18; in Rome, 365; in Venice 368
Wuchangyue ('Music of the Five Confucian Virtues'), 192, n.2
Wydow, Robert, 101, n.3

Xylouris, Nicos, 287, n.24

Yale University, 162f, 165, n.15: auction catalogues, 386, n.12
Yangchow, China, 194, 197
Yiyue mode (Tang music), 202
Yôkeo, Mitani, 199
Young, William, 372f
yu (mordent), 198, 201f, n.23
Yuedianyue (Japanese zither piece), 199

Zeeland, 383, n.5
Zimmermann, Franklin B., 155, 159, n.2, n.13, 161f; research on Purcell, 303, n.2, n.7, 308
zither: Tang music, 192, 199*p*, 203f, n.25; sources, 195, 197, n.14, 199, n.18; tablature, 192, 194, 199; tuning, 199
Zoku-Kyôkunshô (Gagaku handbook), 202
Zurich, Zentralbibliothek, 130, n.5